Pervasive Computing and Communications Design and Deployment:

Technologies, Trends and Applications

Apostolos Malatras
University of Fribourg, Switzerland

Information Science
REFERENCE

Senior Editorial Director:	Kristin Klinger
Director of Book Publications:	Julia Mosemann
Editorial Director:	Lindsay Johnston
Acquisitions Editor:	Erika Carter
Development Editor:	Hannah Abelbeck
Production Editor:	Sean Woznicki
Typesetters:	Jennifer Romanchak and Mike Brehm
Print Coordinator:	Jamie Snavely
Cover Design:	Nick Newcomer

Published in the United States of America by
Information Science Reference (an imprint of IGI Global)
701 E. Chocolate Avenue
Hershey PA 17033
Tel: 717-533-8845
Fax: 717-533-8661
E-mail: cust@igi-global.com
Web site: http://www.igi-global.com/reference

Library of Congress Cataloging-in-Publication Data
Pervasive computing and communications design and deployment: technologies, trends, and applications / Apostolos Malatras, editor.
p. cm.
Includes bibliographical references and index.
ISBN 978-1-60960-611-4 (hardcover) -- ISBN 978-1-60960-612-1 (ebook) 1. Ubiquitous computing. I. Malatras, Apostolos, 1979-
QA76.5915.P455 2011
004--dc22
2010040624

British Cataloguing in Publication Data
A Cataloguing in Publication record for this book is available from the British Library.

Table of Contents

Section 4
Security and Privacy

Section 5
Evaluation and Social Implications

Detailed Table of Contents

Section 1
Context Awareness

The cornerstone of enabling pervasive computing environments is the efficient and effective monitoring of the surrounding conditions and the discovery of the related generated information - called context information - that enables these environments to be adaptive. Context information comprises all aspects of the computing environment, e.g. device characteristics, available bandwidth, and of the users, e.g. user preferences, user history, mobility. As pervasive systems gain popularity, the notion of the context of the user becomes increasingly important.

The widely researched and of paramount important issue of accessing and retrieving data and context information in pervasive environments is the focus. This chapter is essentially a thorough state-of-the-art on querying issues in pervasive environments with a clear educational aim and can act as a reference for interested researchers. The authors propose a taxonomy that takes into account the mobility of the producers and the consumers of the data, its freshness and its pertinence, as well as whether the data has been produced in batch or it is a stream, and how often the queries are being executed. The chapter reviews a large number of related works and classifies them according to the proposed taxonomy, while other taxonomies are also compared to the proposed one. Furthermore, general guidelines to take into account when designing querying solutions for pervasive systems are highlighted, and suggestions on how to best satisfy the corresponding needs are also presented.

In this chapter, practical considerations on achieving context-awareness in real-world settings are examined and presented. This extremely interesting chapter follows a hands-on approach of describing practical examples of context aware service provisioning for smartphone appliances, with a special focus on digital signal processing techniques. The latter are utilized to support services such as audio processing (to identify the gender and the number of the speakers in a conversation and the matching of audio fragments), the location of a smartphone and the localization of its user (based on network signal strength), and user activity recognition (user movements recognition with the use of accelerometers). The authors illustrate the full extent of their experimental setup, from the prototypes/algorithms that have been used for evaluation are based on published work in the area, to the measured results based on their experiments.

Section 2
Frameworks and Applications

Pervasive computing environments have attracted significant research interest and have found increased applicability in commercial settings, attributed to the fact that they provide seamless, customized, and unobtrusive services over heterogeneous infrastructures and devices. Successful deployment of the pervasive computing paradigm is mainly based on the exploitation of the multitude of participating devices and associated data and their integrated presentation to the users in a usable and useful manner. The focal underlying principle of pervasive computing is user-centric provisioning of services and applications that are adaptive to user preferences and monitored conditions, namely the related context information, in order to consistently offer value-added and high-level services.

A software engineering framework to build adaptive, pervasive smart home applications is presented in this chapter; the case-study discussed in their work involves a personal medical appointment reminder service, which incorporates information from various context sources in a rather novel way of producing adaptable service-oriented applications for smart environments. The applicability of this approach is focused on service-oriented applications, and the adaptation occurs by means of dynamic service composition with the advanced feature of variation points, as far as the service bindings are concerned. The latter points allow for the runtime binding of services according to semantics that express specific architectural decisions. The software engineering theory that this approach is founded on is that of architecture-centric dynamic service product lines, and in this respect, this is a very motivating chapter, as it provides insight to dynamic software re-configuration approaches using the recently popular and widespread Web technologies, such as Web services. The merits of this approach are also presented, expressed by an evaluation study and a functional validation by means of several application scenarios.

This fundamental research work involves investigation on the composition of pervasive applications by means of the proposed CADEAU prototype system. The authors introduce the prototype, which allows to dynamically compose Web services based applications in ubiquitous environments using 3 modes of user control, namely manual composition, semi-autonomic, and fully autonomic. The architecture of CADEAU and its interaction design are clearly elaborated, and a discussion on its usability, and generally on end-user control in ubiquitous environments based on experiments over 30 participants, is pre sented. This chapter can serve as a major contribution towards better user acceptance of future systems for the composition of ubiquitous applications.

This chapter presents the design, development, and deployment of a realistically applicable pervasive system targeted at providing user-centered, localized tourist-related information and associated multimedia and augmented reality contents. The aim of this system is to provide location-aware services to visitors of archaeological sites or other sorts of museums, namely location-based multimedia contents related to specific locations inside the visited area. A key aspect of the proposed system is user localization, which takes place by means of an advanced and powerful mechanism that relies on a combination of Wi-Fi, GPS, and visual localization techniques. An assessment of the accuracy of the proposed integrated localization mechanism is presented, as well as details on the real-world evaluation of the overall system. The work presented here is an indicative representative of typical pervasive systems development research.

Concepts and results from a currently active research project are reported in this chapter. It reviews specific outputs of the EU funded project SOFIA on a model and ontology-based development of smart space applications. The main contribution here is the proposal of a novel software engineering approach for the development of smart spaces applications, which takes into account ontologies and semantic models in order to facilitate the implementation of the latter applications. The use of ontologies in modern pervasive applications is considered by many researchers as essential, in order to be able to capture the wealth of knowledge regarding a particular domain and effectively express it in ways that computing systems can utilize it to become context-aware. The authors present a tool called Smart Modeler that enables the graphical composition of smart space applications and the subsequent automatic generation of the actual code. This is very useful when end-user programming is considered, an aspect of special importance in pervasive computing, since promoting the involvement of end-users is always desirable. This is an ongoing research and future directions are given, illustrating attractive contemporary areas of interest.

Section 3
Pervasive Communications

Pervasive environments built on principles of ubiquitous communications will soon, therefore, form the basis of next generation networks. Due to the increasing availability of wireless technologies and the demand for mobility, pervasive networks that will be increasingly built on top of heterogeneous devices and networking standards will progressively face the need to mitigate the drawbacks that accordingly arise regarding scalability, volatility, and topology instability. Novel trends in pervasive communications research address such concerns include autonomic network management, re-configurable radio and networks, cognitive networks, use of utility-based functions, and policies to manage networks autonomously and in a flexible and context-driven manner, to mention a few.

Targeting the plethora of researchers striving to ameliorate pervasive communications, in terms of re-configuration and autonomic management, this chapter presents a state-of-the-art survey of self-addressing approaches for autonomous networking systems. This work is extremely useful from an educational point of view, with a target audience of researchers and students who wish to commence research on the specific domain. After briefly introducing background information on the need for auto-configuration, and hence self-addressing and discussing relevant design issues, the authors propose a classification of existing technologies. Based on the latter, specific systems are explained in detail, as indicative representatives of the various classes in the classification scheme, i.e. stateful, stateless, and hybrid approaches. The chapter concludes by discussing open issues and latest trends in the area of addressing, such as the support for IPv6, and exposes possible future research directions.

In this chapter, the implementation and deployment of an architectural framework that enables the integration of wireless sensor networks in an overall enterprise building architecture are presented. The overall aim for this service oriented architecture is to create an appropriate building services environment that can maximize benefits, reduce the costs, be reliable and provide continuous availability, and be scalable, stable, and usable. Wireless sensor networks play an important role in this architecture, and the particular considerations for this networking technology are taken into account in the description of this work. Of particular interest are the actual experiments in real buildings, where issues such as positioning of sensors, interference, and accuracy are emerging. Scalability, extensibility, and reliability are extremely important in the wireless domain and have been taken into account, and parallel security issues are also reviewed. The author has thoroughly discussed the functionality tests, experimentations,and system-level evaluations and provided some environmental monitoring results to determine whether the overall objectives of the proposed architecture have been realized.

The work presented here constitutes an interesting chapter with clearly a significant amount of research efforts behind it. The topic is focused on energy conservation in wireless sensor networks, and in particular, how this can be achieved by means of a signal processing technique called level crossing sampling. Emphasis on this chapter is placed on the latter technique, which is analyzed in detail from a theoretical perspective, while additionally, simulation analysis and practical experiments of the energy gains are presented. This work is extremely interesting in terms of pervasive computing deployments, since the energy constraints of the participating devices are usually neglected. Approaches such as the one presented in this chapter could greatly benefit the wider adoption and long-term deployment of practical pervasive computing applications.

Section 4
Security and Privacy

Pervasive computing incorporates a significant number of security concerns, since amongst all else, it implies the sharing of data and information amongst users of possibly different administrative domains and of no prior awareness of each other. Secure information management becomes, therefore, an absolute necessity in pervasive environments. Another security concern involves the adaptability of pervasive systems and their functionality in terms of dynamic and context-driven re-configuration, since both these aspects can be easily exploited by malicious users to adversely affect the operation of the system. Additionally, for any pervasive application to provide services customized to user needs and preferences, users should share personal information to that application to make it context-aware, thus raising privacy concerns.

The chapter discusses issues of dependability in the context of pervasive computing. An overall presentation of issues, such as functional correctness, safety, reliability, security and user trust, and possible ways to address them are given, with emphasis on the specific characteristics of pervasive computing systems. Of notable significance is a set of guidelines proposed by the author, on which system designers should target according to the nature of their systems. The notion of dependability is quite generic and encompasses many security and privacy aspects of pervasive systems, albeit at a higher level of abstraction. It is therefore more targeted at ICT practitioners delving into this particular field.

In this chapter, the challenges hindering the efforts to disseminate medical information over wireless infrastructures in an accurate and secure manner are discussed. The authors report on their findings from international research projects and elaborate on an architecture that allows secure dissemination of electronic healthcare records. Security threats and their respective counter-measures are detailed, using an approach that is based on software agent technologies and enables query and authentication mechanisms in a user-transparent manner, in order to be consistent with the principles of pervasive computing. This chapter has a dual role in exposing the open issues in the extremely active research area of electronic health services, as well as in illustrating the security considerations that should be thoroughly addressed in every pervasive computing system.

The chapter discusses privacy issues and the corresponding regulations (with a clear emphasis on EU legislation). Moreover, the related challenges in the context of pervasive systems are described, providing input to further research efforts. Human-related aspects of pervasive computing are as important - if not more - as their technological counterparts, since one of the main challenges of pervasive systems is that of user adoption. Taking this into account, privacy is a very interesting and very much open issue in the domain of pervasive computing, due to the need for users to share an abundance of personal information. As such, this chapter makes a great contribution to the interdisciplinary study of pervasive computing and communications, since it assists in covering all related aspects of pervasive computing, ranging from design, implementation, and deployment to social acceptance, security, and privacy issues with these technologies.

Section 5
Evaluation and Social Implications

A key theme of the book is evaluation of pervasive computing systems and the study of factors that enable its adoption and acceptance by users. Despite being of paramount importance for the success of the pervasive computing paradigm, this aspect is by and large neglected in most current research work, and the work presented in this book aims at partially filling this gap and also instigating further research in this direction.

In this chapter, a methodological approach to analyzing user satisfaction with mobile portals is presented. The authors study the issue of user satisfaction with information systems in general and define their notion of what a mobile portal is and what user satisfaction reflects in that context. Based on the latter definitions, specific properties of mobile portals are presented, which are later used to derive user satisfaction factors, also utilizing existing literature in the area. The authors validate their findings by means of a method that includes focus group discussions, which in this case established the validity of some of the findings and provided input for further user satisfaction factors. This particular case-study exposes the methodology used in consistently and accurately evaluating pervasive computing systems and can serve as a point of reference for researchers wishing to conduct similar evaluation studies.

A real-world deployment of a pervasive application is reported in this chapter. The focal point of the chapter justifies the high significance of this work, in that it presents a pervasive system from its design and implementation up until the actual deployment in a real environment. It is especially the latter part and the associated analysis, which forms the core of the work presented here, that distinguishes this work from the great number of existing research on pervasive systems, which usually is employed and tested in lab settings. Real-world evaluation and assessment of a pervasive system and explanations

Preface

INTRODUCTION

This IGI Global book, titled "Pervasive Computing and Communications Design and Deployment: Technologies, Trends, and Applications", has a broad scope since it is intended to provide an overview on the general and interdisciplinary topic of pervasive computing and communications. The book is intended to serve as a reference point and textbook to computer science practitioners, students and researchers, as far as the design principles and relevant implementation techniques and technologies regarding pervasive computing are concerned. Particular aspects studied in this book include enabling factors, key characteristics, future trends, user adoption, privacy issues and impact of pervasive computing on Information and Communications Technology (ICT) and its associated social aspects.

Pervasive computing environments have attracted significant research interest and have found increased applicability in commercial settings, attributed to the fact that they provide seamless, customized and unobtrusive services over heterogeneous infrastructures and devices. Successful deployment of the pervasive computing paradigm is mainly based on the exploitation of the multitude of participating devices and associated data and their integrated presentation to the users in a usable and useful manner. The focal underlying principle of pervasive computing is user-centric provisioning of services and applications that are adaptive to user preferences and monitored conditions, namely the related context information, in order to consistently offer value-added and high-level services. The concept of pervasive computing further denotes that services and applications are available to users anywhere and anytime. Pervasive behavior is guaranteed by adapting systems based on monitored context information and accordingly guiding their re-configuration. Pervasive computing solutions should also be unobtrusive and transparent to the users, thus satisfying the vision of seamless interaction with computing and communication resources, as first introduced by Weiser in his seminal article for Scientific American in 1991. Research on pervasive and ubiquitous computing has been prolific over the past years, leading to a large number of corresponding software infrastructures and frameworks and an active worldwide research interest, as expressed by the numerous related University B.Sc. and M.Sc. programs, doctoral dissertations, national and international research grants and projects, etc.

In terms of communications, the proliferation of ubiquitous networking solutions experienced in the last few years in the context of ever popular pervasive application scenarios and the high rates of user adoption of wireless technologies lead us to believe that there is an established paradigm shift from traditional, infrastructure-based networking towards wireless, mobile, operator-free, infrastructure-less networking. The latter constitutes the foundation of existing and prospective pervasive applications. Pervasive environments built on principles of ubiquitous communications will soon therefore form the basis of next generation networks. Due to the increasing availability of wireless technologies and the demand for mobility, pervasive networks that will be increasingly built on top of heterogeneous devices and networking standards will progressively face the need to mitigate the drawbacks that accordingly arise regarding scalability, volatility and topology instability. Novel trends in pervasive communications research to address such concerns include autonomic network management, re-configurable radio and networks, cognitive networks, use of utility-based functions and policies to manage networks autonomously and in a flexible and context-driven manner, to mention a few.

The cornerstone of enabling pervasive computing environments is the efficient and effective monitoring of the surrounding conditions and the discovery of the related generated information - called context information - that enables these environments to be adaptive. This monitoring is performed by means of sensors (or collections of them referred to as sensor networks) that can be either physical or virtual. The former interact with the actual environment and collect information about observed conditions, the status of users, etc., while the latter involve monitoring of computing systems and their properties. Context information comprises all aspects of the computing environment, e.g. device characteristics, available bandwidth, and of the users, e.g. user preferences, user history, mobility. As pervasive systems gain popularity the notion of the context of the user becomes increasingly important. Given the diversity of information sources, determining the context of a user is a complex issue that can be approached from different perspectives (technical, psychological, sociological, etc.). What needs to be clarified in relation to context is the fact that it cannot be strictly defined and bounded. It is the pervasive application or system and its use that actually defines what the corresponding context is. In other words, the intended usefulness and functionality of the pervasive application is tightly intertwined with its planned use. Nonetheless, most existing research frameworks and infrastructures for pervasive computing utilize context information in a rigid manner by tightly binding it with the prospective application use, limiting thus their potential extensibility. Therefore, the innovatory vision of pervasive computing, as seen within these infrastructures and platforms, will require users to acquire new applications and software, albeit the apparent contradiction with the promoted and anticipated notion of unobtrusiveness. Novel approaches to address this issue are thus required with the clear aim of making pervasive applications that will be used by users because they gain benefits from them and not merely as part of some research evaluation study.

Since the initial conception and introduction of the pervasive computing paradigm by Weiser in 1991 there has been a plethora of research work, both industrial and academic, with the aim of achieving the envisaged ubiquity, transparency, interoperability, usability, pervasiveness and user-friendliness of computing systems. While simplicity and seamless integration were the driving forces for this computing paradigm shift, the vast number of proposed related and enabling technologies, frameworks, models, standards, data formats, systems, etc. has significantly increased the perceived complexity and therefore acts as a hindering factor for its widespread deployment and adoption. Pervasive computing middleware approaches strive to alleviate these complexity issues, by building on principles of integration, abstraction, interoperability and cross-layer design. The publication of this book coincides with the 20 year anniversary of the pervasive computing realm, and in this respect it is important to examine existing approaches, in order to highlight the associated research problems and identify open issues and mainly look into future and innovative trends on middleware solutions for this domain.

From its inception, pervasive computing identified the need to make computing technologies easier, more useful and more productive for humans to use and to achieve this objective two enabling factors were pinpointed, namely transparency and unobtrusiveness. Users should not be tasked with the burden of explicitly interacting with computing facilities, an activity which can prove to be stressful and time-consuming and even act as a barrier to the adoption of technologies. Pervasive computing solutions were introduced with the goal of removing this hindering barrier and empowering the users by giving them the option of implicit interaction with more advanced and intelligent, context-aware systems. Unfortunately, the majority of solutions to enable pervasive computing proposed in the related research and academic literature involves specific platforms and rigid architectures that are tightly bound with their target applications and services. This approach suffers from a lack of interoperability and from having to introduce new context-aware applications, thus limiting deployment in existing configurations. Additionally, users are often asked to explicitly configure and parameterize the systems that they utilize. Nevertheless, the notion of pervasive computing calls for solutions to be tailored in accordance to user needs and not vice versa. For computing systems to become pervasive, being transparent and unobtrusive, handling context monitoring and ubiquitous communications issues behind the scenes, is a major requirement. A key theme of the book is evaluation of pervasive computing systems and the study of factors that enable its adoption and acceptance by users. Despite being of paramount importance for the success of the pervasive computing paradigm, this aspect is by and large neglected in most current research work and the work presented in this book aims at partially filling this gap and also instigating further research in this direction.

The mere notion of pervasive and ubiquitous computing adheres to the "anybody, anywhere, anytime" concept of user access to information and services around the network. This concept, albeit facilitating user interactions with technology, also incorporates a significant number of security concerns. The use of wireless networking solutions alone increases the level of security threats and risk and requires more advanced solutions to be fashioned compared to traditional wired networking. Furthermore, pervasive computing implies the sharing of data and information amongst users of possibly different administrative domains and of no prior awareness of each other. Secure information management becomes therefore an absolute necessity in pervasive environments. Another security concern involves the adaptability of pervasive systems and their functionality in terms of dynamic and context-driven re-configuration, since both these aspects can be easily exploited by malicious users to adversely affect the operation of the system. Additionally, for any pervasive application to provide services customized to user needs and preferences, users should share personal information to that application to make it context-aware. A major problem that arises in this respect is that of privacy; users are on one hand cautious about sharing sensitive personal information and on the other hand on allowing computing systems to take decisions on their behalf. To address this concern, the benefits of pervasive applications should be better clarified to their users, so that their value also becomes clear. Any proposed solutions should cater for the diversity of protocols, services, applications, user preferences and capabilities of devices and promote effective and efficient countermeasures for all possible security threats. In doing so, security mechanisms should ensure that they do not limit the underlying principles of operation of pervasive computing, chiefly that of adaptive re-configuration based on widely available information exchange, but instead promote this paradigm by instilling to the users high levels of safety and trust towards pervasive environments and hence increase their acceptance and wide adoption. Security and privacy are topics that are reviewed in this book and relevant open issues, potential solutions and specific security mechanisms are highlighted.

It becomes therefore evident that pervasive computing is a widely dispersed research field in computer science. This interdisciplinary field of research involves a broad range of topics, such as networking and telecommunications, human-computer interactions (multimodal, tactile or haptic interfaces), wearable computing, sensor technologies, machine learning, artificial intelligence, user-centered design, data interoperability, security, privacy, user evaluation, software engineering, service oriented architectures, etc. Researchers from all these fields strive to provide viable and usable solutions that reinforce the vision of pervasive computing and thus assist in reaching Weiser's innovative conceptualization of future computing that calmly integrates itself with human activities. Aside to traditional approaches in tackling the open issues in this area, it is worth mentioning the introduction of visionary and possibly imaginative use of innovative studies that draw inspiration from biology (e.g. autonomic management, swarm intelligence), sociology (e.g. data gossiping, social networks), and nanotechnology (e.g. implantable miniature devices and sensors). Pervasive computing research builds on top of all these fields of studies and it is for this reason that we argue that all these viewpoints need to be holistically addressed when delving into the domain of pervasive computing and communications.

This book on "Pervasive Computing and Communications Design and Deployment: Technologies, Trends, and Applications" serves as a reference for current, original related research efforts and will hopefully pave the way towards more ground-breaking and pioneering future research in the direction of providing users with advanced, useful, usable and well-received pervasive applications and systems.

ORGANIZATION AND STRUCTURE

This book comprises 15 chapters, which were selected through a highly competitive process. At the first stage more than 45 short chapter proposals were examined and reviewed by the Editorial Advisory Board, leading to the acceptance of 32 full chapter proposals that underwent a double-blinded reviewing phase. The latter involved at least two reviewers per chapter proposal; the reviewers are internationally renowned researchers and practitioners in fields closely related to the specific book. The completion of the reviewing process yielded 15 greatly appreciated accepted chapters for publication (overall acceptance rate lower than 33%), the authors of which span across 10 countries and 20 research centers and universities.

The book is organized in 5 sections, namely **Context Awareness**, **Frameworks and Applications**, **Pervasive Communications**, **Security and Privacy** and **Evaluation and Social Implications**. Each of these sections is comprised of chapters that illustrate key concepts and technologies related to the focus of the corresponding section, as well as provide pointers for future research directions.

Context Awareness

The widely researched and of paramount important issue of accessing and retrieving data and context information in pervasive environments is the focus of the chapter by *G. Vargas-Solar, N. Ibrahim, C. Collet, M. Adiba, J. M. Petit and T. Delot*. This chapter is essentially a thorough state-of-the-art on querying issues in pervasive environments with a clear educational aim and can act as a reference for interested researchers. The authors propose a taxonomy that takes into account the mobility of the producers and the consumers of the data, its freshness and its pertinence, as well as whether the data has been produced in batch or it is a stream and how often the queries are being executed. The chapter reviews a big number of related works and classifies them according to the proposed taxonomy, while other taxonomies are also compared to the proposed one. Furthermore, general guidelines to take into account when designing querying solutions for pervasive systems are highlighted and suggestions on how to best satisfy the corresponding needs are also presented.

In the chapter by *I. Bisio, F. Lavagetto and M. Marchese* practical considerations on achieving context-awareness in real-world settings are examined and presented. This extremely interesting chapter follows a hands-on approach of describing practical examples of context aware service provisioning for smartphone appliances, with a special focus on digital signal processing techniques. The latter are utilized to support services such as audio processing (to identify the gender and the number of the speakers in a conversation and the matching of audio fragments), the location of a smartphone and the localization of its user (based on network signal strength) and user activity recognition (user movements recognition with the use of accelerometers). These three use cases of context awareness can form the basis for advanced, user-centric service provisioning, as envisaged by the pervasive computing paradigm. The authors illustrate the full extent of their experimental setup, from the prototypes/algorithms that have been used for evaluation are based on published work in the area to the measured results based on their experiments.

Frameworks and Applications

A software engineering framework to build adaptive, pervasive smart home applications is presented in the chapter by *J. Yu, P. Bourret, P. Lalanda and J. Bourcier*; the case-study discussed in their work involves a personal medical appointment reminder service, which incorporates information from various context sources in a rather novel way of producing adaptable service-oriented applications for smart environments. The applicability of this approach is focused on service-oriented applications and

the adaptation occurs by means of dynamic service composition with the advanced feature of variation points as far as the service bindings are concerned. The latter points allow for the runtime binding of services according to semantics that express specific architectural decisions. The software engineering theory that this approach is founded on is that of architecture-centric dynamic service product lines and in this respect this is a very motivating chapter as it provides insight to dynamic software re-configuration approaches using the recently popular and widespread web technologies, such as Web Services. The merits of this approach are also presented, expressed by an evaluation study and a functional validation by means of several application scenarios.

The work by *O. Davidyuk, I. Sánchez Malara and J. Riekki* involves research on the composition of pervasive applications by means of the proposed CADEAU prototype system. The authors introduce the prototype, which allows to dynamically compose Web Services based applications in ubiquitous environments using 3 modes of user control, namely manual composition, semi-autonomic and fully autonomic. The architecture of CADEAU and its interaction design are clearly elaborated and a discussion on its usability and generally on end-user control in ubiquitous environments based on experiments over 30 participants is presented. This chapter is extremely interesting in that it can serve as a major contribution towards better user acceptance of future systems for the composition of ubiquitous applications.

The chapter by *P. Pace and G. Aloi* presents the design, development and deployment of a realistically applicable pervasive system targeted at providing user-centered, localized tourist-related information and associated multimedia and augmented reality contents. The aim of this system is to provide location-aware services to visitors of archaeological sites or other sorts of museums, namely location-based multimedia contents related to specific locations inside the visited area. A key aspect of the proposed system is user localization, which takes place by means of an advanced and powerful mechanism that relies on a combination of Wi-Fi, GPS and visual localization techniques. An assessment of the accuracy of the proposed integrated localization mechanism is presented, as well as details on the real-world evaluation of the overall system. This chapter is an indicative representative of typical pervasive systems development research.

Some very attention-grabbing ideas from a currently active research project are reported in the chapter by *M. Palviainen and A. Katasonov*. This is a highly interesting chapter, reviewing specific outputs of the EU funded project SOFIA on a model and ontology-based development of smart space applications. The main contribution here is the proposal of a novel software engineering approach for the development of smart spaces applications, which takes into account ontologies and semantic models in order to facilitate the implementation of the latter applications. The use of ontologies in modern pervasive applications is considered by many researchers as essential, in order to be able to capture the wealth of knowledge regarding a particular domain and effectively express it in ways that computing systems can utilize it to become context-aware. The authors present a tool called Smart Modeler that enables the graphical composition of smart space applications and the subsequent automatic generation of the actual code. This is very useful when end-user programming is considered, an aspect of special importance in pervasive computing, since promoting the involvement of end-users is always desirable. This is an ongoing research and future directions are given, illustrating attractive contemporary areas of interest.

Pervasive Communications

Targeting the plethora of researchers striving to ameliorate pervasive communications, in terms of reconfiguration and autonomic management, the chapter by *R. de O. Schmidt, R. Gomes, M. Johnsson, D. Sadok and J. Kelner* presents a state-of-the-art survey of self-addressing approaches for autonomous networking systems. This work is extremely useful from an educational point of view, with a target audience of researchers and students who wish to commence research on the specific domain. After briefly introducing background information on the need for auto-configuration, and hence self-addressing, and discussing relevant design issues, the authors propose a classification of existing technologies. Based on the latter, specific systems are explained in detail, as indicative representatives of the various classes in the classification scheme, i.e. stateful, stateless and hybrid approaches. The chapter concludes by discussing open issues and latest trends in the area of addressing, such as the support for IPv6, and exposes possible future research directions.

In the chapter by *A. Asgari* the implementation and deployment of an architectural framework that enables the integration of wireless sensor networks in an overall enterprise building architecture are presented. The overall aim for this service oriented architecture is to create an appropriate building services environment that can maximize benefits, reduce the costs, be reliable and provide continuous availability, be scalable, stable and usable. Wireless sensor networks play an important role in this architecture and the particular considerations for this networking technology are taken into account in the description of this work. Of particular interest are the actual experiments in real buildings, where issues such as positioning of sensors, interference and accuracy are emerging. Scalability, extensibility and reliability that are extremely important in the wireless domain have been taken into account, while in parallel security issues are also reviewed. The author has thoroughly discussed the functionality tests, experimentations, and system-level evaluations and provided some environmental monitoring results to determine whether the overall objectives of the proposed architecture have been realized.

The work by *H. Alasti* constitutes an interesting chapter with clearly a significant amount of research efforts behind it. The topic is focused on energy conservation in wireless sensor networks and in particular how this can be achieved by means of a signal processing technique called level crossing sampling. Emphasis on this chapter is placed on the latter technique, which is analyzed in detail from a theoretical perspective, while additionally simulation analysis and practical experiments of the energy gains are presented. This work is extremely interesting in terms of pervasive computing deployments, since the energy constraints of the participating devices are usually neglected. Approaches such as the one presented in this chapter could greatly benefit the wider adoption and long-term deployment of practical pervasive computing applications.

Security and Privacy

The chapter by *F. Ortmeier* discusses issues of dependability in the context of pervasive computing. An overall presentation of issues, such as functional correctness, safety, reliability, security and user trust, and possible ways to address them are given, with emphasis on the specific characteristics of pervasive computing systems. Of notable significance is a set of guidelines proposed by the author, on which system designers should target according to the nature of their systems. The notion of dependability is quite generic and encompasses many security and privacy aspects of pervasive systems, albeit at a higher level of abstraction. It is therefore more targeted at ICT practitioners delving into this particular field.

In the chapter by *P. Belsis, C. Skourlas and S. Gritzalis* the challenges hindering the efforts to disseminate medical information over wireless infrastructures in an accurate and secure manner are discussed. The authors report on their findings from international research projects and elaborate on an architecture that allows secure dissemination of electronic healthcare records. Security threats and their respective counter-measures are detailed, using an approach that is based on software agent technologies and enables query and authentication mechanisms in a user-transparent manner, in order to be consistent with the principles of pervasive computing. This chapter has a dual role in exposing the open issues in the extremely active research area of electronic health services, as well as in illustrating the security considerations that should be thoroughly addressed in every pervasive computing system.

Assuming a quite different stance compared to "traditional" IT papers that usually focus on research issues, experiments, description of systems, etc., the chapter by *Al. Liotta and An. Liotta* discusses privacy issues and the corresponding regulations (with a clear emphasis on EU legislation). Moreover, the related challenges in the context of pervasive systems are described providing input to further research efforts. Human-related aspects of pervasive computing are as important - if not more - as their technological counterparts, since one of the main challenges of pervasive systems is that of user adoption. Taking this into account, privacy is a very interesting and very much open issue in the domain of pervasive computing, due to the need for users to share an abundance of personal information. As such this chapter makes a great contribution to the book, since it assists in covering all related aspects of pervasive computing, ranging from design, implementation and deployment to social acceptance, security and privacy issues with these technologies.

Evaluation and Social Implications

In the chapter by *D. Seng, C. Wilkin and L. Sugianto* a methodological approach to analyzing user satisfaction with mobile portals is presented. The authors study the issue of user satisfaction with information systems in general and define their notion of what a mobile portal is and what user satisfaction reflects in that context. Based on the latter definitions, specific properties of mobile portals are presented, which are later used to derive user satisfaction factors, also utilizing existing literature in the area. The authors validate their findings by means of a method that includes focus group discussions, which in this case established the validity of some of the findings and provided input for further user satisfaction factors. This particular case-study exposes the methodology used in consistently and accurately evaluating pervasive computing systems and can serve as a point of reference for researchers wishing to conduct similar evaluation studies.

A real-world deployment of a pervasive application is reported in the chapter by *A. Komninos, B. MacDonald and P. Barrie*. The focal point of the chapter justifies the high significance of this work, in that it presents a pervasive system from its design and implementation up until the actual deployment in a real environment. It is especially the latter part and the associated analysis, which forms the core of the work presented here, that distinguishes this work from the great number of existing research on pervasive systems, which usually is employed and tested in lab settings. Real-world evaluation and assessment of a pervasive system and explanations on why in this case it did not work out as anticipated render this chapter as very useful in terms of pervasive computing research. It is worth noticing that the focus is not so much on the technological aspects, rather on the societal ones.

The evaluation of a typical pervasive application in the aged care services domain is presented in the chapter by *L. Sugianto, P. Smith, C. Wilkin and A. Ceglowski*. The proposed evaluation solution involves a modified version of the traditional balanced scorecard approach used in information systems research, which takes into account both business strategy optimization and the user related aspects of the adoption of the pervasive technologies in the considered domain. One of the most remarkable findings in this article is the excellent analysis of the considered application area, based on both the practical deployment of a pervasive system in a health care environment in Australia, but also based on the thorough review of related work in the area.

Prospective Audience

The prospective audience of the "Pervasive Computing and Communications Design and Deployment: Technologies, Trends, and Applications" publication is mainly students in informatics and computer science that engage themselves with pervasive computing and communications. The book will serve primarily as a point of reference handbook to related technologies, applications and techniques, as well as an indicator of future and emerging trends to stimulate the interested readers. On a secondary basis, researchers will benefit from having such a reference handbook on their field, indicating the main achievements in the interdisciplinary domain of pervasive computing and the future trends and directions that could be potentially pursued.

Impact and Contributions

The target of this book is to serve as an educational handbook for students, practitioners and researchers in the field of pervasive computing and communications, whilst giving an insight of the corresponding future trends. The overall objective of the proposed publication is to serve as a reference point for anyone engaging with pervasive computing and communications from a technological, sociological or user-oriented perspective. Since the research stream of pervasive computing has been extremely active and prolific in terms of results and projects over the last few years, this publication targets at collecting the aforementioned research output and encompassing and organizing it in a comprehensive handbook.

The field is quite vast and is dispersed in many disciplines, hence the necessity for a handbook to collect and uniformly present all related aspects of pervasive computing and communications.

As far as the potential contribution to the field of research in pervasive computing is concerned, this publication is intended to have a twofold effect, namely:

- Provide a collective reference to existing research in the domain of pervasive computing and communications, taking into account its enabling factors (context awareness, autonomic management, ubiquitous communications, etc.), its applications, its usability and the corresponding user adoption.
- Future and emerging aspects of pervasive computing are reported in this book, through extensive reference to existing and ongoing research work by renowned groups of researchers and scientists.

It becomes therefore evident that this book will have an impact as being a reference for scholars wishing to engage in pervasive computing and communications related studies or research, bringing together the much dispersed material from the diversity of disciplines that jointly constitute this computing paradigm.

Apostolos Malatras
University of Fribourg, Switzerland

Acknowledgment

The editor would like to thank all of the contributing authors for their invaluable efforts and work that allowed for the publication of this book. Additionally, the support of the reviewers and the Editorial Advisory Board is greatly appreciated, as well as that of the entire IGI Global production team. Throughout the production of this publication, the editor has been partially supported by the Bio-Inspired Monitoring of Pervasive Environments (BioMPE) research project funded by the Swiss National Foundation (Grant number: 200021_130132) and awarded to the Pervasive and Artificial Intelligence research group at the Department of Informatics of the University of Fribourg, Switzerland.

Apostolos Malatras
University of Fribourg, Switzerland

Section 1
Context Awareness

The cornerstone of enabling pervasive computing environments is the efficient and effective monitoring of the surrounding conditions and the discovery of the related generated information - called context information - that enables these environments to be adaptive. Context information comprises all aspects of the computing environment, e.g. device characteristics, available bandwidth, and of the users, e.g. user preferences, user history, mobility. As pervasive systems gain popularity, the notion of the context of the user becomes increasingly important.

Chapter 1
Querying Issues in Pervasive Environments[1]

Genoveva Vargas-Solar
CNRS, LIG-LAFMIA, France

Michel Adiba
UJF, LIG, France

Noha Ibrahim
LIG, France

Jean Marc Petit
INSA, LIRIS, France

Christine Collet
Grenoble INP, LIG, France

Thierry Delot
U. Valenciennes, LAMIH, France

ABSTRACT

Pervasive computing is all about making information, data, and services available everywhere and anytime. The explosion of huge amounts of data largely distributed and produced by different means (sensors, devices, networks, analysis processes, more generally data services) and the requirements to have queries processed on the right information, at the right place, at the right time has led to new research challenges for querying. For example, query processing can be done locally in the car, on PDA's or mobile phones, or it can be delegated to a distant server accessible through Internet. Data and services can therefore be queried and managed by stationary or nomadic devices, using different networks.

The main objective of this chapter is to present a general overview of existing approaches on query processing and the authors' vision on query evaluation in pervasive environments. It illustrates, with scenarios and practical examples, existing data and streams querying systems in pervasive environments. It describes the evaluation process of (i) mobile queries and queries on moving objects, (ii) continuous queries and (iii) stream queries. Finally, the chapter introduces the authors' vision of query processing as a service composition in pervasive environments.

INTRODUCTION

The market of data management is lead by the major Object-Relational Database Management Systems (ORDBMS) like Oracle (http://www.oracle.com), Universal DB2 (http://www-01.ibm.com/software/data/db2/) or SQLServer (http://www.microsoft.com/sqlserver/2008/en/us/). Dur-

DOI: 10.4018/978-1-60960-611-4.ch001

ing the last twenty years, in order to better match the evolution of user and application needs, many extensions have been proposed to enhance the expressive power of SQL and the DBMS functions. In this context, querying is one of the most important functions' (Wiederhold 1992; Domenig and Dittrich 1999) for accessing and sharing data among information sources. Several query-processing mechanisms have been proposed to efficiently and adaptively evaluate queries (Selinger 1979; Graefe and McKenna 1993; Graefe and Ward 1989; Kabra and DeWitt 1998; Haas and Hellerstein 1999; Bouganim 2000; Urhan and Franklin 2000; Avnur and Hellerstein 2000; Hellerstein et al. 2000; Raman and Hellerstein 2002). New classes of dynamic distributed environments (e.g., peer-to-peer where peers can connect or disconnect at any time) introduce new challenges for query processing. Some works add indexing structures to P2P architectures for efficiently locating interesting data and/or improving query languages expressivity (Abiteboul et al. 2004; Abdallah and Le 2005; Abdallah and Buyukkaya 2006; Labbe et al. 2004; Karnstedt 2006; Papadimos 2003). Such systems rely on a global schema and often pre-determined logical network organizations and are in general poorly adapted to query processing introduced in pervasive environments.

Pervasive computing is all about making information, data and services available everywhere and anytime thereby democratizing access to information and opening new research challenges for querying techniques. Today every activity (at home, for transportation and in industries) relies on the use of information provided by computing devices such as laptops, PDA's and mobile phones and other devices embedded in our environment (e.g. sensors, car computers). Given the explosion of amounts of information largely distributed and produced by different means (sensors, devices, networks, analysis processes) research on query processing is still promising for providing the right information, at the right place, at the right moment.

Motivating Example

Let us consider an application for guiding and assisting drivers on highways. We assume several devices and servers connected to various network infrastructures (satellite, Wifi, 3G) give access to services that provide different kinds of information about traffic or weather conditions, rest areas, gas stations, toll lines, accidents and available hotels or restaurants. Different providers can offer such services, but with different quality criteria and costs. Drivers can then ask "*Which are the rest areas that will be close to me in two hours and that propose a gas station, lodging facilities for two people and a restaurant and where hotel rooms can be booked on line*". Such a query includes classical aspects (*retrieve the list of hotels and their prices*) and continuous spatio-temporal aspects (*determine the position of the car in two hours with respect to traffic and average speed*). It may also use different kinds of technical services (look up, matching, data transmission, querying) and business services (hotel booking, parking places availability, routing).

In pervasive environments as the one shown in our example, query processing implies evaluating queries that address at the same time classical data providers (DBMS), nomadic services, and stream providers. Query processing must be guided by QoS (quality of service) criteria stemming from (i) user preferences (access cost to data and services); (ii) devices capabilities such as memory, computing power, network bandwidth and stability, battery consumption with respect to operations execution; (iii) data and service pertinence in dynamic contexts i.e., continuously locate providers to guide data and services access considering QoS criteria such as efficiency, results relevance and accuracy. Thus, querying in pervasive environments needs mechanisms that integrate business data providers, query evaluation and data management services, for optimally giving access to data according to different and often contradictory changing QoS criteria. In our example, query processing can be executed locally in the car, on a PDA or on a mobile phone or it can be delegated to a distant server accessible through Internet. In addition, when changes are produced in the execution environment (i.e., connection to a different network, user and services accessibility and mobility) alternative services must be matched and replaced. Therefore, getting the right information/function implies integrating fault tolerance (data and devices replacement), QoS, location, mobility and adaptability in query processing techniques.

Objective and Organization

The main objective of this chapter is to classify query processing issues considering the different dimensions that are present in pervasive environments. Accordingly, the chapter is organized as follows. First, it introduces a query taxonomy that classifies queries according to their execution frequency. It thereby introduces two general families: snapshot and recurrent queries. Then, it introduces successively the general principle of query evaluation for snapshot and recurrent queries that leads to other subcategories. The chapter compares, then, our taxonomy with existing query classifications. Finally, the chapter concludes sketching the perspectives of query processing in pervasive environments.

QUERY TAXONOMY

This chapter proposes (see Figure 1) a taxonomy of queries in pervasive environments, that takes into consideration the following important dimensions for query evaluation: mobility or not of the data producers and consumers, frequency of query execution (i.e., repeatedly or one-shot), data production rate (i.e., as a stream or in batch), validity interval of query results with respect to new data production (i.e., freshness), results pertinence with respect to the consumer location.

Data producers and consumers are classified according to whether they change their geographical position or not (i.e., static and mobile producer/consumer):

Figure 1. Query taxonomy

Mobility		Consumer: Static	Consumer: Mobile	Production Rate
Producer	Static	**Snapshot** • Give me the list of 3 stars hotels located along highway A48 (SPATIO TEMPORAL QUERY WITH STATIC SPATIAL RANGE) • Give me the list of hotels closest to my current position (SPATIO TEMPORAL QUERY, K-NN QUERY)	**Recurrent** Give me the list of 3 stars hotels located 100 KM around my future position in one hour (MOBILE LOCATION DEPENDENT ... MOBILE SPATIAL RANGE...)	*Batch*
		Recurrent Give me the traffic conditions in highway A48 between 10:00 and 14:00 (STREAM QUERY)	**Recurrent** (Stream mobile location dependent)	*Stream*
	Mobile	**Snapshot** Find the police patrols 100 KM around my current position (LOCATION AWARE QUERY)	**Recurrent** (Mobile location dependent and aware query with moving objects)	*Batch*
		Recurrent (stream location aware)	**Recurrent** (stream mobile location dependent and aware query –with moving objects producing streams--)	*Stream*

- **Static producer** does not change its geographical position or the pertinence and validity of the data it produces is independent of its geographical position (e.g., the Google maps web service, GPS service producing a position of a static entity).
- **Mobile producer** changes its geographical position or the pertinence and validity of the data it produces depends on its geographical position (e.g., a vehicle producing road data information).
- **Static consumer** does not change its geographical position and consumes data independently of its geographical position (e.g., a web service client on a stationary computer).
- **Mobile consumer** changes its geographical position and can consume location dependent data (e.g., person going around the city with an iPhone).

Consumers can ask for queries to be executed at different frequencies: repeatedly (e.g., *get the traffic conditions every hour*) and in a one shot manner (e.g., *get the gas stations located in highway A48*). This depends on the validity interval of the query results (i.e., freshness) and pertinence required by the consumer. Producers can produce data at different rates, namely, in batch (e.g., *the list of gas stations along a highway and the diesel price offered*) and in streams (e.g., *the traffic conditions in the French highways during the day*).

We propose a taxonomy of queries based on the above dimensions with two general families of queries according to frequency in which the query is executed, and then subgroups of queries in each family according to the mobility of data producers and consumers and data production rate (in stream or in batch): snapshot query and recurrent query. For each of these families existing approaches have specified data models extensions (representation of streams, spatial and temporal attributes), query languages (special operators for dealing with streams, and with spatial and temporal data) and query processing techniques. This chapter synthesizes these aspects for each of our query types, snapshot and recurrent.

SNAPSHOT QUERY

A snapshot or instantaneous query is executed once on one or several data producers and its results are transmitted immediately to the consumer. This type of query can be further distinguished as follows:

1. The validity and pertinence of the results are not determined by the consumer location. Instead, they are filtered with respect to spatial and temporal restrictions (spatio-temporal query). For example, *give the name and geographic position of gas stations located along the highway A48*; *which was the average number of cars traversing the border at 10:00 am.*
2. The validity and pertinence of the results are determined by the consumer location (location aware query). For example, *give the identifier and geographic position of the police patrols close to my current position.*

The following sections analyze the evaluation issues for each of static range and k-NN (k Nearest Neighbour) queries, for the spatio-temporal query family; and moving objects and probabilistic queries for the location aware family.

Spatio-Temporal Query

A spatio-temporal query[3] specifies location constraints that can refer to:

1. The range/region in which "objects" must be located (static range query (Xu and Wolfson 2003; Trajcevski et al 2004; Yu et al. 2006)). Note again that the classification assumes that the interesting region does not change along time. For example, *find hotels located*

within 5 KM depends on the location of the user issuing the query. The range itself can be explicit (e.g., *find the hotels located along highway A48*) on implicit (e.g., *find hotels located within 5 KM* denotes a region from the position of the consumer).

2. A nearest neighbour function retrieves the object that is the closest to a certain object or location (NN query Nearest Neighbour query (Tao et al. 2007)). For instance, *find the closest gas station to my current position*. When k objects satisfy the constraint then the query is a kNN query. For instance, *which are the closest gas stations from my current position*. (Chon et al. 2003) classifies NN and kNN queries as static when the target producer is not mobile and dynamic when the target producer is mobile.

Data Models

Queries with spatio-temporal constraints were introduced several years ago in spatial and temporal databases. Data models were proposed for representing and reasoning on spatial and temporal types (Allen, J.F 1983; Egenhofer, M. and Franzosa R. 1991; Papadias D. and Sellis, T. 1997; Adiba, M. and Zechinelli-Martini, J.L. 1999). Concerning space representation, the models proposed concepts for representing an "object" in the space as a rectangle (Minimum Bounding Rectangle) or as circular region (Minimum Bounding Circle). Such models represent also object types such as point, line, poly-line and polygon. According to the representation, the models define spatial relations semantics: directions, topological and metric. For representing time, existing data models can be instant or interval oriented. Duration is represented by a set of instants where each instant belongs to a time line where the origin is arbitrarily chosen. Other models adopt intervals for representing durations and for reasoning about time. The 13 Allen interval relations (Allen 1983) are often used for this purpose. Most models further enable the specification of other properties for representing objects in spatial and temporal spaces with predefined standards for specifying metadata like Dublincore (http://dublincore.org/) or FGDC (http://www.fgdc.gov/metadata). Constraints within queries can then be expressed with respect to the spatial and temporal attributes of the objects and also with respect to other attributes.

Spatio-Temporal Query Processing

According to the underlying spatial data model, the range of a query can denote (i) rectangular window, in which case the query is known by some authors as window query (Tao et al 2007); (ii) circular window, in which case the query is known as within-distance query by authors like (Trajcevski and Scheuermann 2003). Those queries return the set of objects that are within a certain distance of a specified object, for instance the consumer. Some works also classify as spatio-temporal queries, those that ask for the geographical position of an object explicitly (position query, *get my current position,* (Becker and Dürr 2005)) or implicitly (*give the geographical positions of the hotels of the 16ème arrondissement* (Ilarri et al. 2008)).

kNN queries can have further constraints that can filter the list of objects belonging to the result: (i) reverse kNN query (Benetis et al. 2006; Wu et al. 2008)) retrieves objects that have a specified location among the k nearest neighbours; (ii) constraint NN query specifies a range constraint for the list of retrieved objects (Ferhatosmanoglu et al. 2001). For example *which are the closest gas stations from my current position which are located around KM 120*; (iii) k closest pairs query (Corral et al. 2000) retrieves the pair of objects with the k smallest distances. For example, *retrieve the closest gas stations and hotels to my current position which are close from each other*; (iv) n-body constraint query (Xu and Jacobsen 2007) specifies a location constraint that must be satisfied by n objects that are closer than a certain distance from each other. For example *retrieve the closest gas stations and hotels to my current position, with 10 km of distance from each other.* A navigation query retrieves the best path for a consumer to get to a destination according to an underlying road network and other conditions such as the traffic (Hung et al. 2003; Li et al. 2005). For example, *how to get from my current position to the closest gas station?*

Existing Projects and Systems

The golden age of spatio-temporal data management systems around the 90's led to important data management systems, with data models, query languages, indexing and optimization techniques (Bertino et al. 1997). For example, (Tzouramanis et al. 1999) proposed (i) an access method based on overlapping linear quadtrees to store consecutive historical raster images; (ii) a database of evolving images for supporting query processing. Five spatio-temporal queries along with the respective algorithms take advantage of the properties of the quadtrees were also proposed. An important generation of geographical information systems also proposed important contributions for dealing with geospatial queries. The major commercial DBMS have cartridges for dealing with spatial data and queries.

The emergence of pervasive systems introduces the need of dealing (reasoning) with data spatial and temporal properties, its producers and consumers in different contexts like continuous queries and data flows, sensor networks, reactive systems among many others. For example, (Papadias et al. 2003) proposes a solution for sensor network databases based on generating a search region for the query point that expands from the query, which performs similar to Dijkstra's algorithm. The principle of this solution is to compute the distance between a query object and its candidate neighbours on-line. In our opinion, some important challenges of the current and future systems are dealing with data production rate, validity and pertinence of spatio-temporal query results, accuracy of location estimations, synchronization of data that can be timestamped by different clocks.

Location Aware Query

The location of the consumer is used to determine whether an "object" belongs to the result or not (location aware query (Seydim et al. 2001)). For example, *find the police patrols 100 KM around my current position*. In (Marsit et al. 2005) this query is described as moving object database query[4]. A moving object (mobile producer) is any entity whose location is interesting for some data consumers.

Data Models

Moving object databases (Theodoris 2003; Wolfson and Mena 2004; Güting et al. 2006) extend traditional database technology with models and index structures adapted for efficiently finding and tracking moving object locations. Modelling moving objects implies representing their continuous movements. The relational model enables the representation of sampled locations (Nascimento et al. 1999) but this approach implies continuous updates if all the locations need to be stored. One of the most popular model, MOST, was proposed in the DOMINO project (Sistla et al. 1997). It represents a moving object as a function of its location and velocity. It also introduces the notion of dynamic attributes whose values evolve according to the function definition even if no explicit updates are executed. In contrast, (Su et al. 2001; Vazirgiannis and Wolfson 2001; Ding and Güting 2004; Güting et al. 2006) define data types such as points, moving line, and moving region. They use constraints for representing a moving object in a road network and define functions for querying it. The constraint based query language TQ (Mokhtar and Su 2005) and Future Temporal Model –FTL for MOST- (Sistla et al. 1997) were also proposed.

Location Aware Query Processing

Location aware queries are classified according to the way moving objects interact among each other: whether objects are aware of the queries that are tracking them, whether they adopt an update policy, whether they follow a predefined trajectory. The update policy is the strategy adopted for locating moving objects either the moving object itself communicates its location or there is a mechanism for periodically locating it. Such strategies are out of the scope of this chapter, but the interested reader can refer to (Cheng et al. 2008) for more details.

Probabilistic query (Cheng et al. 2008; Wolfson et al. 1999b; Pfoser and Jensen 1999) implies estimating the location of moving objects (moving producers) using different techniques. For instance, (i) a threshold probabilistic query (Cheng et al. 2008) retrieves the objects and satisfies the query conditions with a probability higher than a threshold (Tao et al. 2007); (ii) a ranking probabilistic query orders the results according to the probability that an object satisfy a query predicate (Wolfson et al. 1999b; Cheng et al. 2008). (Tao et al. 2007) proposes static probabilistic range queries called probabilistic range search; other works define probabilistic range thresholding retrieval; probabilistic thresholding fuzzy range query; and probabilistic nearest neighbour query (Kriegel et al. 2007; Cheng et al. 2008) regarding a static query point.

In general, for evaluating location aware queries, location mechanisms are required for obtaining the location of a moving object, which require the object to be equipped with some connection. For example, moving objects can be hosted by mobile devices, for instance a PC in a car, a mobile phone with a GPS (*Global Positioning System*). Associated querying approaches depend on the model and on the types of queries.

Existing Projects and Systems

During the last decade, many research works have focused on modelling and querying moving objects (Güting et al. 2006). Mobi-Dic (Cao, Wolfson, Xu, and Yin 2005) or MobiEyes (Gedik et al. 2006) have focused on query processing issues in the context of mobile peer-to-peer databases (Luo et al. 2008). A mobile peer-to-peer (P2P) database is a database that is stored in the peers of a mobile P2P network (Luo et al. 2008). Such a network is composed of a finite set of mobile peers that communicate with each other via short-range wireless protocols, such as IEEE 802.11. A local database can then store and manage a collection of data items on each mobile peer. The Mobi-Dic project processes queries on vehicles searching available parking spaces (Xu, Ouksel and Wolfson, 2004). Reports are therefore generated by vehicles leaving a parking space and diffused to neighbouring vehicles to notify them about the resource. The mobile query processor receives streams of reports and processes them in order to compute the query result (e.g., *what are the five nearest parking spaces*?).

(Zhu, Xu and Wolfson, 2008) introduces a new type of query adapted to disconnected mobile networks. They indeed explain that processing kNN queries is too complex in such decentralized contexts. They claim that the most important for the user is not necessarily to get all possible results but rather to know if at least one data item exists. They therefore propose a strategy for disseminating queries in order to retrieve relevant information on remote peers. They also propose a solution to deliver obtained results to the data consumer (i.e., query issuer).

RECURRENT QUERY

A recurrent[5] query has to be re-evaluated repeatedly because:

1. The query is evaluated on streams. Since the production rate is continuous, the query is executed repeatedly as long as streams are flowing or the consumer is interested in receiving results (stream query). For example, *which are the traffic conditions of the highway A48;* or, *give me traffic conditions of highway A48 every hour from 9:00 to 17:00.*
2. The query is issued by a mobile consumer and thus, the validity and pertinence of its results changes according to the consumer location (mobile location dependent query). For example, *which are the nearest gas stations with respect to my current location?*
3. The query is executed repeatedly at specific points or intervals of time, as long as a condition is verified, or once an event is notified (continuous query). For example, *as long as I am driving in highway A48 inform me about the position of the police patrols which are 100 km from my position* (condition); *every hour send me the conditions of the traffic at the entrance of the nearest city* (at given points in time); *when there is an incident, give me its coordinates and possible deviations* (when an event is notified).

A recurrent query can be persistent (Sistla et al. 1997) if it considers current and past state of data (i.e., streams, moving objects). Furthermore, the notion of "complete" query result traditionally considered in classical (distributed) databases makes no sense in recurrent queries. Such queries rather produce partial results that have associated validity intervals and that have to be computed repeatedly for ensuring freshness. The data production rate, and consumer mobility that both have an impact on query results validity and pertinence can be used for identifying two recurrent query types: stream query and mobile location dependent query.

Stream Query

In contrast to traditional databases that store static data sets, data streams are continuously produced in large amounts that must be processed in real time (Babcock et al 2002; Golab and Özu 2003). Queries over data streams are continuous (e.g., every N minutes), persistent, long-running and return results as soon as the conditions of the queries are satisfied. For instance, *every hour report the number of free places available in the gas station located at KM 20 of the highway A48*. As for the other query types, dealing with stream queries depends on the data model used for representing streams. In the particular case of streams where the data production rate is continuous, timestamping and filtering strategies are required in order to correlate streams stemming from different producers.

Data Models

A data stream is an unbounded sequence of events ordered implicitly by arrival times or explicitly by timestamps. Most works use the notion of infinite sequence of tuples for representing a data stream. This model implies an implicit order of tuples (their position within the sequence), thus certain models assume that tuples are time-stamped by the stream provider (e.g., the production instant of the tuple). The explicit order of tuples given by the time-stamp, is used for modelling different transmission rates from different stream producers. This can lead to different production and arrival time-stamps. Global clock and distributed event detection strategies can be then used for solving the problem. Then, existing data models enable the definition of an infinite tuple sequence. Three major data models have been extended to deal with streams (Düntgen et al. 2009): the relational model (Arasu et al., 2003), the object-based model (Yao and Gehrke, 2003) and XML in StreamGlobe (Kuntschke et al. 2005).

(Arasu et al., 2003) defines a formal abstract semantics, using a "discrete, ordered time domain", where relations are time-varying bags (multisets) of tuples, and streams are unbounded bags of time-stamped tuples. Three categories of operators are clearly identified: relation-to-relation (standard operators: selection, projection, join), relation-to-stream (insert/delete/relation stream), and stream-to-relation (windows). SQL is extended to build CQL (Continuous Query Language) that enables the declarative definition of continuous queries[6]. (Kuntschke et al. 2005) defines an XML schema of tuples that represent sensor readings and that can include temporal and spatial attributes. XML data streams are then queried using XQuery expressions.

Stream Query Processing

In contrast to traditional query systems, where each query runs once against a snapshot of the database, stream query systems support queries that continuously generate new results (or changes to results) as new streams continue to arrive (Agarwal 2006). For stream query processing, infinite tuple streams potentially require unbounded memory space in order to be joined, as every tuple should be stored to be compared with every tuple from the other stream. Tuple sets should then be bounded: a window defines a bounded subset of tuples from a stream. New extensions of classical query languages have been proposed to take into account these new requirements, mainly with the notion of *windowed queries* and *aggregation*.

Sliding windows have a fixed size and continuously move forward (e.g., *the last 100 tuples, tuples within the last 5 minutes*). Hopping windows (Yao and Gehrke, 2003) have a fixed size and move by hop, defining a range of interval (e.g., *5-minute window every 5 minutes*). In (Chandrasekaran et al. 2003), windows can be defined in a flexible way: the window upper and lower bound are defined separately (fixed, sliding or hopping), allowing various window types. (Arasu et al., 2003) also defines a partitioned window as the union of windows over a partitioned stream based on attribute values (e.g., *the last 5 tuples for every different ID*). STREAM (Arasu, A., et al. 2003) defines the following window operators: binary, landmark, area-based, trajectory. PLACE (Xiong, X., et al. 2004) proposes spatial, temporal and predicate based windows. With windows, join operators handle bounded sets of tuples and traditional techniques can be applied for correlating streams. AURORA (Abadi, D. J., et al. 2005) also defines order sensible operators: bsort orders the tuples of a stream with the semantics of bubble sort; aggregate for defining spatial windows on a stream; join which is similar to equi-join[7]; and resample that implements interpolation on a stream.

For the time being there is no standard data model and query language proposed for streams. The different models and associated operators' semantics are still heterogeneous. The discussion on this issue is out of the scope of this paper but a complete discussion can be found in (Düntgen et al. 2009).

Existing Projects and Systems

Stream query processing attracts interest in the database community because of a wide range of traditional and emerging applications, e.g., trigger and production rules processing (Hanson et al. 1999), data monitoring (Carney et al. 2002), stream processing (Data Eng. 2009, Babu and Widom 2001), and publish/subscribe systems (Liu et al. 1999; Chen et al. 2000; Pereira et al. 2001; Dittrich et al. 2005). Several stream management systems have been proposed in the literature such as COUGAR, TINYDB, TELEGRAPHCQ, STREAM, AURORA/BOREALIS, NIAGARACQ, GLOBAL SENSOR NETWORK and CAYUGA.

COUGAR (Yao and Gehrke, 2003) and TINYDB (Gehrke and Madden, 2004) process continuous queries over sensor networks focusing on the optimization of energy consumption for sensors using in-network query processing. Each sensor has some query processing capabilities and distributed execution plans that can include online data aggregation to reduce the amount of raw data transmitted through the network. The TelegraphCQ system (Chandrasekaran et al. 2003) provides adaptive continuous query processing over streaming and historical data. Adaptive group query optimization is realized by dynamic routing of tuples among (commutative) query operators depending on operator load. Stream (Arasu et al., 2003) defines a homogeneous framework for continuous queries over relations and data streams. It focuses on computation sharing to optimize the parallel execution of several continuous queries.

Aurora/Borealis (Abadi et al. 2005; Hwang et al. 2007) proposes a Distributed Stream Processing System (DSPS) that enables distributed query processing by defining dataflow graphs of operators in a "box & arrows" fashion. Boxes are computation units that can be distributed, and arrows represent tuple flows between boxes. Adaptive query optimization is done through a load-balancing mechanism. Aurora defines operators for processing streams represented with a tuple oriented data model: (i) filter (similar to selection of the relational model), map (similar to projection) and union of streams with the same schema. These operators are not sensitive to the order of the tuples of the stream.

NiagaraCQ (Chen et al. 2000) introduces continuous queries over XML data streams. Queries, expressed using XML-QL, are implemented as triggers and produce event notifications in real-time; alternatively, they can be timer-based and produce their result periodically during a given time interval. Incremental evaluation is used to reduce the required amount of computation. Furthermore, queries are grouped by similarity in order to share a maximum of computation between them. Interestingly, they introduce the notion of "action" to handle query results. Although an action may be any user-defined function, it is used to specify how to send notification messages to users, e.g. "MailTo" action.

(Aberer et al. 2007) proposes the Global Sensor Network, a middleware for sensor networks that provides continuous query processing facilities over distributed data streams. Continuous queries are specified as virtual sensors whose processing is specified declaratively in SQL. Virtual sensors hide implementation details and homogeneously represent data streams either provided by physical sensors or produced by continuous queries over other virtual sensors.

Complex Event Processing (CEP) or Event Stream Processing (ESP) techniques express specialized continuous queries that detect complex events from input event streams. Cayuga (Demers et al., 2007) is a stateful publish/subscribe system for complex event monitoring where events are defined by SQL-like continuous queries over data streams. It is based on formally-defined algebra operators that are translated to Non-Finite Automatons for physical processing.

Mobile Location Dependent Query

Mobile location dependent queries are recurrent and their results must be refreshed repeatedly because their validity changes as the producers move. For example, *locate police patrols that are running close to me*. Location dependent queries are classified as moving range (Gedik et al. 2006; Ilarri et al. 2008), static range[8] (Prabhakar et al. 2002; Cai et al. 2006), nearest neighbour (Frentzos et al. 2007; Mouratidis and Papadias 2007), queries where data change location (i.e., queries on location aware data (Dunham and Kumar 1998; Lee 2007)).

Data Models

Data models proposed for this type of queries concern spatio-temporal data where spatial attributes are used for representing regions and temporal issues for representing timestamped locations and regions. Models adopt representation strategies of moving objects in the cases where producers are mobile. As described for spatio-temporal data models, spatial and temporal properties depend on the underlying models used for representing them. The challenge for data models for this type of queries is to associate temporal properties to regions and in general to spatial data in order to represent explicitly the moment or the interval in which they were valid. (Chen et al. 2003) distinguishes the continuous model that represents moving objects as moving points that start from a specific location with a constant speed vector and the discrete model where moving objects locations are timestamped. Indexing techniques are associated to these models in order to perform queries efficiently.

Processing Mobile Location Dependent Queries

Moving range query (mobile range query) is a query the results of which are made up of objects that satisfy the temporal restriction specified by the range and that must be executed repeatedly because the range moves. For instance, *retrieve the gas stations located within 5 KM of my position*. Assuming that *my position* changes as I am driving, then at different instants in time the query result will contain a different list of gas stations.

Existing techniques for handling continuous spatio-temporal queries in location-aware environments (Benetis et al. 2006; Lazaridis 2002; Song and Roussopoulos, 2001; Tao et al. 2007; Zhang 2003; Zheng and Lee 2001; Mokbel et al. 2004) focus on developing specific high-level algorithms that use traditional database servers for evaluating such queries. Most of the existing query processing techniques focus on solving special cases of continuous spatio-temporal queries: some are valid only for moving queries on stationary objects (Song and Roussopoulos 2001; Tao et al. 2007; Zhang 2003; Zheng and Lee 2001; Wolfson et al. 1999), others are valid only for stationary range queries (Carney et al. 2002; Hadjieleftheriou 2003; Paolucci 2002).

Existing Projects and Systems

The emergence of both handheld devices and wireless networks observed last years has strongly impacted query-processing techniques (Imielinski and Nath, 2002). Mobile devices are characterized by limited resources in terms of autonomy, memory and, storage capacity. They also provide an intermittent connectivity subject to frequent disconnections. There are two types of mobility according to (Ilarri et al. 2008): (i) Software mobility implies transferring passive data (e.g., files) or active data (mobile code, process migration) among computers. (ii) The physical mobility of devices while computing queries anytime anywhere. Mobile devices themselves change from a coverage area to another (handoff/handover) (Seshan 1995; Markopoulos et al. 2004), which introduces a location problem that requires a location infrastructure and a location update policy in order to be solved.

One of the important challenges in mobile contexts is to adapt data management and query processing. The concept of mobile databases highlights the differences with classic database systems (Imielinski and Nath 1993; Pitoura and Samaras 1998; Barbara 1999; Pitoura and Bhargava 1999): data fragmentation, replication among mobile units, consistency maintenance, approximate answers, query fragmentation and routing, location-dependent queries; optimization of query plans with respect to battery consumption, cost and wireless communication, bandwidth, throughput.

Most of existing mobile query processing techniques rely on a client/server architecture in the context of Location Based Services (LBS). Different algorithms have been proposed to compute continuous queries like SINA (Scalable INcremental hash-based Algorithm (Mokbel, M. F. et al. 2004)) and SOLE (Scalable On-Line Execution) (Mokbel, Xiong, and Aref, 2004; Mokbel and

Aref, 2008). Location dependent query processing has also been investigated on projects like DATAMAN (Imielinski and Nath 1992) and in (Seydim, Dunham, and Kumar, 2001). The ISLANDS project proposes evaluation strategies based on query dissemination (Thilliez and Delot, 2004). The LOQOMOTION project, studies the use of mobile agents to reach the same goal (Ilarri et al. 2008).

OTHER QUERY TAXONOMIES

This section refers to existing query taxonomies that have similar or different focus as the one we propose. To our knowledge there is no taxonomy with the ambition of classifying spatio-temporal, mobile, continuous, and stream queries according to query general processing dimensions in pervasive environments. Indeed, most taxonomies focus on data models associated operators and language extensions. Our objective was to analyze how different families of queries are processed and, when and how they have to be evaluated within a pervasive environment. It is nonetheless important to compare some relevant existing classifications.

(Huang and Jensen 2004) proposes a classification of spatio-temporal queries according to different types of predicates: one-to-many query (a predicate is applied to many objects, i.e., nearest neighbour query); many-to-many query (a predicate is verified for every object of a list in relation to every object of another, i.e., constraint spatio-temporal join (Tao et al. 2007; Sun et al. 2006); closest pair query where the predicate involves topological, directional or metric relationships (Corral et al. 2000). This classification focuses on the type of spatio-temporal constraints that can be expressed and processed within a query. In our classification these techniques are organized under the snapshot query family.

(Marsit et al. 2005) defines the following query types in mobile environments:

- Location Dependent Queries (LDQ) (Seydim et al. 2001) are evaluated with respect to a specific geographical point (e.g. "*Find the closest hotel of my current position*").
- Location Aware Queries (LAQ) are location-free with respect to the consumer location (e.g. "*How is the weather in Lille?*").
- Spatio-temporal Queries (STQ) (Sistla, et al. 1997) include all queries that combine space and time and generally deal with moving objects.
- Nearest Neighbours Queries (kNN) (Mokbel et al. 2004) address moving objects (e.g.. "*Find all cars within 100 meters of my car*").

This classification focuses on the mobility of data producers and consumers identified in our taxonomy. However, in our taxonomy we provide a finer grain classification of these types of queries identifying the cases where the consumer and the producer are not mobile combining also the notion of validity and pertinence of results, and execution frequency. This is important because the challenges of the evaluation strategies change when dealing with spatio-temporal restrictions alone or combined with mobility and different data production rates.

(Ilarri et al. 2008) identifies four types of queries depending on whether the producer and the consumer move: dynamic query and dynamic data (DD); dynamic query static data (DS); static query dynamic data (SD); static query and static data (SS). Note that this classification is equivalent in our taxonomy through the mobility dimension, i.e., static/dynamic data refer to producer mobility and static/dynamic query to consumer mobility. (Huang and Jensen 2004) proposes a classification considering the time instant at which a location dependent query is issued: predefined query, the query exists before the data it relies on are produced; ad-hoc query if it is defined after the data it relies on are produced. This dimension is partially considered by our taxonomy through the dimensions results validity interval and pertinence.

(Ilarri et al. 2008) discusses different classifications of location dependent queries according to criteria like mobile objects states, uncertain locations and time intervals. A query can be classified according to whether it refers to past, present and future states of mobile objects. This classification assumes that producers are aware of data states. Thus, a present query concerns the current state of mobile producers (i.e., objects). A past query filters data with respect to a time point or a temporal interval previous to a current instant. A future or predictive query encompasses some future time instant (e.g., *which will be the rest areas close to my position in two hours* (Xu and Wolfson 2003; Karimi and Liu 2003; Tao et al. 2007; Yavas et al. 2005; Civilis et al. 2005)). Other works also identify timestamp or time-slice queries (Saltenis et al. 2000) that are interval queries that refer to a time interval (Tao et al. 2007); and current/now queries that are interval queries where the starting point is the current time instant (Choi and Chung 2002; Tao et al. 2007).

A query can be also classified according to whether it handles uncertain locations ("may" semantics query) objects that may be in the result are considered; clear semantics ("must" semantics query) the result contains only objects that are for sure in the answer. Existing works have proposed modifiers for expressing such queries like *possibly* and *definitely* (Wolfson et al 2001; Trajcevski et al. 2004); and, *possibly*, *surely* and *probably* (Moreira et al. 2000). A query handles certain time intervals expressing *sometimes* semantics, where all the objects satisfying the query conditions during a period of time are included in the answer. A certain time interval query can also express an *always* semantics where the retrieved objects must satisfy conditions during the whole time interval; and at least semantics, a query that satisfies conditions during a percentage of a time interval.

QUERY PROCESSING PERSPECTIVES

This section sketches some interesting perspectives of query processing in pervasive environments. As far as we know, evaluating declarative queries in ambient environments in a flexible and efficient way has not been fully addressed yet. Existing techniques for handling continuous spatio-temporal queries in location-aware environments (e.g., see (Benetis et al. 2002, Lazaridis et al. 2002, Song et al. 2001, Tao et al. 2004, Zhang et al. 2003, Zheng et al. 2001)) focus on developing specific high-level algorithms that use traditional database servers (Mokbel et al. 2004). Most of the existing query processing techniques focus on solving special cases of continuous spatio-temporal queries: some like (Song et al. 2001, Tao et al. 2004, Zhang et al. 2003, Zheng et al. 2001, Wolfson et al. 1999) are valid only for moving queries on stationary objects, others like (Carney et al. 2002, Hadjieleftheriou et al. 2003, Prabhakar et al. 2002) are valid only for stationary range queries. A challenging perspective is to provide a complete approach that integrates flexibility into the existing continuous, stream, snapshot, spatio-temporal queries for accessing data in pervasive environments.

As service-oriented architectures (SOA) have been adopted as developing tools for applications in pervasive environments, we propose to base query evaluation on services and service composition. A query plan is therefore a service composition where services represent either data source access or operators on data (Cuevas et al. 2009). Techniques such as service composition, adaptation and substitution considering non-functional QoS properties of services have to be considered and adapted for query evaluation. Flexibility is highly desirable in ambient environments, especially when evaluating queries that are processed over mobile and dynamic data providers that can become unavailable during query processing. Our approach based on service coordination is geared towards flexibility. First, service coordination offers the capability to dynamically acquire resources by adopting a late binding approach where the best services available in the environment are bound at the query evaluation time. As evaluation may be continuous over a certain period of time, access to certain services that are subject to frequent disconnections is an important issue to handle. Our approach can be extended by enabling the replacement of services whenever such failures arise. In addition, when changes affect the execution environment (i.e., connection to a different network, user and services accessibility and mobility) alternative services must be matched and replaced in the service composition that implements the evaluation plan. Also, service composition must deal with service unavailability, overload and evolution. A failure occurring within a service often leads to a total failure of the application that uses it.

Current and future works concern two main aspects. Query coordination consistency and completeness to verify that the service based evaluation finds, in a limited time, all the possible solutions when evaluating a query at a given instant in a precise environment. Query optimization techniques for service coordination evaluation, including a formal definition of cost models dedicated to ambient environments. In these environments, unlike traditional query optimization, it is time-consuming to obtain on the fly statistics over data.

REFERENCES

Abadi, D. J., Ahmad, Y., Balazinska, M., Cetintemel, U., Cherniack, M., & Hwang, J.-H. … Zdonik, S. (2005). The design of the Borealis stream processing engine. In *Proceedings of Second Biennial Conference on Innovative Data Systems Research.*

Abdallah, M., & Buyukkaya, E. (2006). Efficient routing in non-uniform DHTs for range query support. In *Proceedings of the International Conference on Parallel and Distributed Computing and Systems (PDCS).*

Abdallah, M., & Le, H. C. (2005). Scalable range query processing for large-scale distributed database applications. In *Proceedings of the International Conference on Parallel and Distributed Computing and Systems (PDCS).*

Aberer, K., Hauswirth, M., & Salehi, A. (2007). Infrastructure for data processing in large-scale interconnected sensor networks. In *Proceedings of the 8th International Conference on Mobile Data Management.*

Abiteboul, S., Manolescu, I., Benjelloun, O., Milo, T., Cautis, B., & Preda, N. (2004). Lazy query evaluation for active XML. In *Proceedings of the ACM SIGMOD International Conference on Management of Data.*

Adiba, M., & Zechinelli-Martini, J. L. (1999). Spatio-temporal multimedia presentations as database objects. *In Proceedings of DEXA'99, 10th International Conference on Databases and Expert Systems Applications*, LNCS.

Agarwal, P. K., Xie, J., & Hai, Y. (2006). Scalable continuous query processing by tracking hotspots. In *Proceedings of the International Conference on Very Large Data Bases.*

Allen, J. F. (1983). Maintaining knowledge about temporal intervals. *Communications of the ACM, 26*(11). doi:10.1145/182.358434

Arasu, A., Babcock, B., Babu, S., Datar, M., Ito, K., & Motwani, R. (2003). STREAM: The Stanford stream data manager. *A Quarterly Bulletin of the Computer Society of the IEEE Technical Committee on Data Engineering, 26*, 19–26.

Avnur, R., & Hellerstein, J. M. (2000). Eddies: Continuously adaptive query processing. In *Proceedings of ACM SIGMOD International Conference on Management of Data.*

Babcock, B., Babu, S., Datar, M., Motwani, R., & Widom, J. (2000). Models and issues in data stream system. In *Proceedings of the 21st ACM SIGMOD-SIGACT-SIGART Symposium on Principles of Database Systems (PODS'02)*, (pp. 1–16).

Babu, S., & Widom, J. (2001). Continuous queries over data streams. *SIGMOD Record, 30*(3). doi:10.1145/603867.603884

Barbara, D. (1999). Mobile computing and databases – a survey. *IEEE Transactions on Knowledge and Data Engineering, 11*(1), 108–117. doi:10.1109/69.755619

Becker, C., & Dürr, F. (2005). On location models for ubiquitous computing. *Personal and Ubiquitous Computing, 9*(1), 20–31. doi:10.1007/s00779-004-0270-2

Benetis, R., Jensen, S., Karciauskas, G., & Saltenis, S. (2006). Nearest and reverse nearest neighbor queries for moving objects. *The VLDB Journal, 15*(3), 229–249. doi:10.1007/s00778-005-0166-4

Bertino, E., Ooi, B. C., Sacks-Davis, R., Tan, K., Zobel, J., Shidlovsky, J. B., & Catania, B. (1997). *Indexing techniques for advanced database systems*. Kluwer Academic Publishers.

Bidoit-Tollu, N., & Objois, M. (2008). Machines pour flux de données. Comparaison de langages de requêtes continues. *Ingénierie des Systèmes d'Information, 13*(5), 9–32. doi:10.3166/isi.13.5.9-32

Bouganim, L., Fabret, F., Mohan, C., & Valduriez, P. (2000). Dynamic query scheduling in data integration systems. In *Proceedings of International Conference on Data Engineering,* IEEE Computer Society.

Cai, Y., Hua, K. A., Cao, G., & Xu, T. (2006). Real-time processing of range-monitoring queries in heterogeneous mobile databases. *IEEE Transactions on Mobile Computing, 5*(7), 931–942. doi:10.1109/TMC.2006.105

Cao, H., Wolfson, O., Xu, B., & Yin, H. (2005). Mobi-dic: Mobile discovery of local resources in peer-to-peer wireless network. *A Quarterly Bulletin of the Computer Society of the IEEE Technical Committee on Data Engineering, 28*(3), 11–18.

Carney, D., Centintemel, U., Cherniack, M., Convey, C., Lee, S., Seidman, G., et al. Zdonik, S. B. (2002). Monitoring streams - a new class of data management applications. In *Proceedings of the International ACM Conference on Very Large Data Bases.*

Chandrasekaran, S., et al. (2003). TelegraphCQ: Continuous dataflow processing for an uncertain world. In *Proceedings of the First Biennial Conference on Innovative Data Systems Research.*

Chen, J., DeWitt, D. J., Tian, F., & Wang, Y. (2000). NiagaraCQ: A scalable continuous query system for Internet databases. In *Proceedings of ACM SIGMOD International Conference on Management of Data*, (pp. 379-390).

Cheng, R., Chen, J., Mokbel, M. F., & Chow, C.-Y. (2008). Probabilistic verifiers: Evaluating constrained nearest-neighbour queries over uncertain data. *International Conference on Data Engineering*, IEEE Computer Society, (pp. 973–982).

Choi, Y.-J., & Chung, C.-W. (2002). Selectivity estimation for spatio-temporal queries to moving objects. In *ACM SIGMOD International Conference on Management of Data* (SIGMOD'02), (pp. 440–451).

Chon, H. D., Agrawal, D., & Abbadi, A. E. (2003). Range and kNN query processing for moving objects in Grid model. *Mobile Networks and Applications, 8*(4), 401–412. doi:10.1023/A:1024535730539

Civilis, A., Jensen, C. S., & Pakalnis, S. (2005). Techniques for efficient road-network-based tracking of moving objects. *IEEE Transactions on Knowledge and Data Engineering, 17*(5), 698–712. doi:10.1109/TKDE.2005.80

Corral, A., Manolopoulos, Y., Theodoridis, Y., & Vassilakopoulos, M. (2000). Closest pair queries in spatial databases. In *ACM SIGMOD International Conference on Management of Data*, (pp. 189–200).

Cuevas-Vicenttin, V., Vargas-Solar, G., Collet, C., & Bucciol, P. (2009). Efficiently coordinating services for querying data in dynamic environments. In *Proceedings of the 10th Mexican International Conference in Computer Science*, IEEE Computer Society.

Delot, T., Cenerario, N., & Ilarri, S. (2010). Vehicular event sharing with a mobile peer-to-peer architecture. *Transportation Research - Part C (Emerging Technologies).*

Demers, A. J., Gehrke, J., Panda, B., Riedewald, M., Sharma, V., White, W. M., et al. (2007). Cayuga: A general purpose event monitoring system. *In Proceedings of CIDR*, (pp. 412-422).

Ding, Z., & Güting, R. H. (2004). Managing moving objects on dynamic transportation networks. In *16th International Conference on Scientific and Statistical Database Management*, IEEE Computer Society, (pp. 287–296).

Dittrich, J.-P., Fischer, P. M., & Kossmann, D. (2005). Agile: Adaptive indexing for context-aware information filters. In *Proceedings of the ACM SIGMOD International Conference on Management of Data.*

Domenig, R., & Dittrich, K. R. (1999). An overview and classification of mediated query systems. In *ACM SIGMOD Record.*

Dunham, M. H., & Kumar, V. (1998). Location dependent data and its management in mobile databases. In *1st International DEXA Workshop on Mobility in Databases and Distributed Systems*, IEEE Computer Society, (pp. 414–419).

Egenhofer, M., & Franzosa, R. (1991). Point-set topological spatial relations. *International Journal of Geographical Information Systems, 5*(2).

Ferhatosmanoglu, H., Stanoi, I., Agrawal, D., & Abbadi, A. E. (2001). *Constrained nearest neighbour queries*. In 7th International Symposium on Advances in Spatial and Temporal Databases (pp. 257–278). Springer Verlag.

Frentzos, E., Gratsias, K., Pelekis, N., & Theodoridis, Y. (2007). Algorithms for nearest neighbor search on moving object trajectories. *GeoInformatica, 11*(2), 159–193. doi:10.1007/s10707-006-0007-7

Gedik, B., & Liu, L. (2006). MobiEyes: A distributed location monitoring service using moving location queries. *IEEE Transactions on Mobile Computing, 5*(10), 1384–1402. doi:10.1109/TMC.2006.153

Gehrke, J., & Madden, S. (2004). Query processing in sensor networks. *Pervasive Computing, 3*, 46–55. doi:10.1109/MPRV.2004.1269131

Golab, L., & Özsu, M. T. (2003). Issues in data stream management. In *Proceedings of the ACM SIGMOD International Conference on Management of Data*, (pp. 5-14).

Graefe, G., & McKenna, W. J. (1993). The volcano optimizer generator: Extensibility and efficient search. In *Proceedings of International Conference on Data Engineering*, IEEE Computer Society.

Graefe, G., & Ward, K. (1989). Dynamic query evaluation plans. In *Proceedings of ACM SIGMOD International Conference on Management of Data.*

Güting, H., Almeida, V. T., & Ding, Z. (2006). Modelling and querying moving objects in networks. *The VLDB Journal*, *15*(2), 165–190. doi:10.1007/s00778-005-0152-x

Haas, P. J., & Hellerstein, J. M. (1999). Ripple joins for online aggregation. In *Proceedings of the ACM SIGMOD International Conference on Management of Data.*

Hadjieleftheriou, M., & Kollios, G. G., Gunopulos, D., & Tsotras, V. J. (2003). Online discovery of dense areas in spatio-temporal databases. In *Proceedings of International Symposium of Spatial Temporal Databases.*

Hanson, E. N., Carnes, C., Huang, L., Konyala, M., Noronha, L., Parthasarathy, S., et al. Vernon, A. (1999). Scalable trigger processing. In *Proceedings of the International Conference On Data Engineering*, IEEE Computer Society.

Hellerstein, J. M., Franklin, M. J., Chandrasekaran, S., Deshpande, A., Hildrum, K., Madden, S.,... Shah, M. A. (2000). Adaptive query processing: Technology in evolution. *IEEE Data Engineering Bulletin.*

Huang, X., & Jensen, C. S. (2004). Towards a streams-based framework for defining location based queries. In *Proceedings of the 2nd Workshop on Spatio-Temporal Database Management*, (pp. 73–80).

Hung, D., Lam, K., Chan, E., & Ramamritham, K. (2003). Processing of location-dependent continuous queries on real-time spatial data: The view from RETINA. In *Proceedings of the 6th International DEXA Workshop on Mobility in Databases and Distributed Systems*, IEEE Computer Society, (pp. 961–965).

Hwang, J., Xing, Y., Cetintemel, U., & Zdonik, S. (2007). A cooperative, self-configuring high-availability solution for stream processing. In *Proceedings of the International Conference on Data Engineering*, IEEE Computer Society.

Ilarri, S., Mena, E., & Illarramendi, A. (2008). Location-dependent queries in mobile contexts: Distributed processing using mobile agents. *IEEE Transactions on Mobile Computing*, *5*(8), 1029–1043. doi:10.1109/TMC.2006.118

Imielinski, T., & Nath, B. (1993). Data management for mobile computing. *SIGMOD Record*, *22*(1), 34–39. doi:10.1145/156883.156888

Imielinski, T., & Nath, B. (2002). Wireless graffiti: Data, data everywhere. In *Proceedings of the ACM International Conference on Very Large Databases*, (pp. 9-19).

Kabra, N., & DeWitt, D. (1998). Efficient mid-query re-optimization of sub-optimal query execution plans. In *Proceedings of the ACM SIGMOD International Conference on Management of Data.*

Karimi, H. A., & Liu, X. (2003). A predictive location model for location-based services. In *Proceedings of the 11th ACM International Symposium on Advances in Geographic Information Systems*, (pp. 126–133).

Karnstedt, M., Sattler, K., Hauswirth, M., & Schmidt, R. (2006). Similarity queries on structured data in structured overlays. In *Proceedings of the 2nd International Workshop on Networking Meets Databases*, IEEE Computer Society.

Kriegel, H.-P., Kunath, P., & Renz, M. (2007). Probabilistic nearest-neighbour query on uncertain objects. In *Proceedings of the 12th International Conference on Database Systems for Advanced Applications*, Springer Verlag, (pp. 337–348).

Kuntschke, R., Stegmaier, B., Kemper, A., & Reiser, A. (2005). StreamGlobe: Processing and sharing data streams in Grid-based P2P infrastructures. In *Proceedings of the International ACM Conference on Very Large Databases.*

Labbe, C., Roncancio, C., & Villamil, M. P. (2004). PinS: Peer-to-Peer interrogation and indexing system. In *Proceedings of the International Database Engineering and Application Symposium.*

Lazaridis, I., Porkaew, K., & Mehrotra, S. (2002). Dynamic queries over mobile objects. In *Proceedings of the International Conference in Extending Database Technology.*

Lee, D. L. (2007). On searching continuous k nearest neighbours in wireless data broadcast systems. *IEEE Transactions on Mobile Computing, 6*(7), 748–761. doi:10.1109/TMC.2007.1004

Li, F., Cheng, D., Hadjieleftheriou, M., Kollios, G., & Teng, S.-H. (2005). On trip planning queries in spatial databases. In *Proceedings of the 9th International Symposium on Advances in Spatial and Temporal Databases*, Springer Verlag, (pp. 273–290).

Liu, L., Pu, C., & Tang, W. (1999). Continuous queries for Internet scale event-driven information delivery. *IEEE Transactions on Knowledge and Data Engineering, 11*(4).

Luo, Y., Wolfson, O., & Xu, B. (2008). Mobile local search via p2p databases. In *Proceedings of 2nd IEEE International Interdisciplinary Conference on Portable Information Devices*, (pp. 1-6).

Markopoulos, A., Pissaris, P., Kyriazakos, S., & Sykas, E. (2004). Efficient location-based hard handoff algorithms for cellular systems. In *Proceedings of the 3rd International IFIP-TC6 Networking Conference,* Springer Verlag, (pp. 476–489).

Marsit, N., Hameurlain, A., Mammeri, Z., & Morvan, F. (2005). Query processing in mobile environments: A survey and open problems. In *Proceedings of the 1st International Conf. on Distributed Frameworks for Multimedia Applications*, IEEE Computer Society, (pp. 150–157).

Mokbel, M. F., & Aref, W. G. (2008). SOLE: Scalable on-line execution of continuous queries on spatio-temporal data streams. *The VLDB Journal, 17*, 971–995. doi:10.1007/s00778-007-0046-1

Mokbel, M. F., Xiong, X., & Aref, W. G. (2004). SINA: Scalable incremental processing of continuous queries in spatio-temporal databases. In *Proceedings of the ACM SIGMOD International Conference on Management of Data*, (pp. 623-634).

Mokhtar, H. M. O., & Su, J. (2005). A query language for moving object trajectories. In *Proceedings of the 17th International Conference on Scientific and Statistical Database Management*, (pp. 173–184).

Moreira, J., Ribeiro, C., & Abdessalem, T. (2000). Query operations for moving objects database systems. In *Proceedings of the 8th ACM International Symposium on Advances in Geographic Information Systems*, (pp. 108–114).

Mouratidis, K., & Papadias, D. (2007). Continuous nearest neighbour queries over sliding windows. *IEEE Transactions on Knowledge and Data Engineering, 19*(6), 789–803. doi:10.1109/TKDE.2007.190617

Nascimento, M. A., Silva, J. R. O., & Theodoridis, Y. (1999). Evaluation of access structures for discretely moving points. In *Proceedings of the 1st International Workshop on Spatio-Temporal Database Management*, Springer Verlag, (pp. 171–188).

Paolucci, M., Kawamura, T., Payne, T. R., & Sycara, K. (2002). Semantic matching of Web services capabilities. In *Proceedings of First International Semantic Web Conference.*

Papadias, D., & Sellis, T. (1997). Spatial relations, minimum bounding rectangles, and spatial data structures. *International Journal of Geographical Information Science, 11*(2). doi:10.1080/136588197242428

Papadias, D., Zhang, J., Mamoulis, N., & Tao, Y. (2003). Query processing in spatial network databases. In *Proceedings of the ACPM International Conference on Very Large Databases.*

Papadimos, V., Maier, D., & Tufte, K. (2003). Distributed query processing and catalogs for Peer-to-Peer systems. In *Proceedings of the Conference on Innovative Data Systems Research.*

Pereira, J., Fabret, F., Jacobsen, H. A., Llirbat, F., & Shasha, D. (2001). Webfilter: A high-throughput XML-based publish and subscribe system. In *Proceedings of the International ACM Conference on Very Large Data Bases.*

Pfoser, D., & Jensen, C. S. (1999). Capturing the uncertainty of moving-object representations. In *Proceedings of the 6th International Symposium on Advances in Spatial Databases*, Springer Verlag, (pp. 111–132).

Pitoura, E., & Bhargava, B. (1999). Data consistency in intermittently connected distributed systems. *IEEE Transactions on Knowledge and Data Engineering, 11*(6), 896–915. doi:10.1109/69.824602

Pitoura, E., & Samaras, G. (1998). *Data management for mobile computing.* Boston, MA: Kluwer.

Prabhakar, S., Xia, Y., Kalashnikov, D. V., Aref, W. G., & Hambrusch, S. E. (2002). Query indexing and velocity constrained indexing: Scalable techniques for continuous queries on moving objects. *IEEE Transactions on Computers, 51*(10), 1124–1140. doi:10.1109/TC.2002.1039840

Raman, V., & Hellerstein, J. M. (2002). Partial results for online query processing. In *Proceedings of ACM SIGMOD International Conference on Management of Data.*

Saltenis, S., Jensen, C. S., Leutenegger, S. T., & Lopez, M. A. (2000). Indexing the positions of continuously moving objects. In *Proceedings of the ACM SIGMOD International Conference on Management of Data*, (pp. 331–342).

Selinger, P. G., Astrahan, M. M., Chamberlin, D. D., Lorie, R. A., & Price, T. G. (1979). Access path selection in a relational database management system. In *Proceedings of the ACM SIGMOD International Conference on Management of Data.*

Seshan, S. (1995). *Low-latency handoff for cellular data networks.* Ph.D. thesis, University of California at Berkeley.

Seydim, A. Y., Dunham, M. H., & Kumar, V. (2001). Location dependent query processing. In *Proceedings of the 2nd ACM International Workshop on Data Engineering for Wireless and Mobile Access*, (pp. 47–53).

Sistla, A. P., Wolfson, O., Chamberlain, S., & Dao, S. (1997). Modelling and querying moving objects. In *Proceedings of the 13th International Conference on Data Engineering*, IEEE Computer Society, (pp. 422–432).

Song, Z., & Roussopoulos, N. (2001). K-nearest neighbor search for moving query point. In *Proceedings of the International Symposium on Advances in Spatial and Temporal Databases,* Springer Verlag.

Su, J., Xu, H., & Ibarra, O. H. (2001). Moving objects: Logical relationships and queries. In *Proceedings of the International Symposium on Advances in Spatial and Temporal Databases,* Springer Verlag, (pp. 3–19).

Sun, J., Tao, Y., Papadias, D., & Kollios, G. (2006). Spatio-temporal join selectivity. *ACM Transactions on Information Systems, 31*(8), 793–813.

Tao, Y., & Papadias, D. (2005). Historical spatio-temporal aggregation. *ACM Transactions on Information Systems, 23*(1), 61–102. doi:10.1145/1055709.1055713

Tao, Y., Xiao, X., & Cheng, R. (2007). Range search on multidimensional uncertain data. *ACM Transactions on Database Systems, 32*(3), 15. doi:10.1145/1272743.1272745

Theodoridis, Y. (2003). Ten benchmark database queries for location-based services. *The Computer Journal, 46*(6), 713–725. doi:10.1093/comjnl/46.6.713

Thilliez, M., & Delot, T. (2004). Evaluating location dependent queries using ISLANDS. In *Advanced Distributed Systems* (pp. 125–136). Springer Verlag. doi:10.1007/978-3-540-25958-9_12

Trajcevski, G., Scheuermann, P., Ghica, O., Hinze, A., & Voisard, A. (2006). Evolving triggers for dynamic environments. In *Proceedings of the 10th International Conference on Extending Database Technology*, Springer Verlag, (pp. 1039–1048).

Trajcevski, G., Wolfson, O., Hinrichs, K., & Chamberlain, S. (2004). Managing uncertainty in moving objects databases. *ACM Transactions on Database Systems*, *29*(3), 463–507. doi:10.1145/1016028.1016030

Tzouramanis, T., Vassilakopoulos, M., & Manolopoulos, Y. (1999). Overlapping linear quadtrees and spatio-temporal query processing. In *Proceedings of the 3rd East-European Conference on Advanced Databases and Information Systems.*

Urhan, T., & Franklin, M. J. (2000). Xjoin: A reactively-scheduled pipelined join operator. *A Quarterly Bulletin of the Computer Society of the IEEE Technical Committee on Data Engineering*, *23*(2).

Vazirgiannis, M., & Wolfson, O. (2001). A spatiotemporal model and language for moving objects on road networks. In *Proceedings of the 7th International Symposium on Advances in Spatial and Temporal Databases*, Springer Verlag, (pp. 20–35).

Wiederhold, G. (1992). Mediator in the architecture of future Information Systems. *The IEEE Computer Magazine, 25*(3).

Wolfson, O., Chamberlain, S., Kapalkis, K., & Yesha, Y. (2001). Modelling moving objects for location based services. In *Proceedings of the NSF Workshop Infrastructure for Mobile and Wireless Systems*, Springer Verlag, (pp. 46–58).

Wolfson, O., & Mena, E. (2004). Applications of moving objects databases. In *Spatial databases: Technologies, techniques and trends* (pp. 186–203). Hershey, PA: IDEA Group Publishing.

Wolfson, O., Sistla, A. P., Chamberlain, S., & Yesha, Y. (1999). Updating and querying databases that track mobile units. *Distributed and Parallel Databases*, *7*(3), 257–287. doi:10.1023/A:1008782710752

Wu, W., Yang, F., Chan, C. Y., & Tan, K.-L. (2008). Continuous reverse k-nearest-neighbour monitoring. In *Proceedings of the 9th International Conf. on Mobile Data Management*, IEEE Computer Society, (pp. 132–139).

Xiong, X., Elmongui, H. G., Chai, X., & Aref, W. G. (2004). PLACE: A distributed spatio-temporal data stream management system for moving objects. In *Proceedings of the International Conference on Very Large Databases.*

Xu, B., Ouksel, A. M., & Wolfson, O. (2004). Opportunistic resource exchange in inter-vehicle ad-hoc networks. In *Proceedings of the 5th International Conference on Mobile Data Management.*

Xu, B., Vafaee, F., & Wolfson, O. (2009). In-network query processing in mobile P2P databases. In *Proceedings of the 17th ACM SIGSPATIAL International Conference on Advances in Geographic Information Systems*, (pp. 207-216).

Xu, B., & Wolfson, O. (2003). Time-series prediction with applications to traffic and moving objects databases. In *Proceedings of the 3rd ACM International Workshop on Data Engineering for Wireless and Mobile Access*, (pp. 56–60).

Xu, Z., & Jacobsen, A. (2007). Adaptive location constraint processing. In *Proceedings of the ACM SIGMOD International Conference on Management of Data*, (pp. 581–592).

Yao, Y., & Gehrke, J. (2003). Query processing in sensor networks. In *Proceedings of the First Biennial Conference on Innovative Data Systems Research.*

Yavas, G., Katsaros, D., Ulusoy, O., & Manolopoulos, Y. (2005). A data mining approach for location prediction in mobile environments. *Data & Knowledge Engineering*, *54*(2), 121–146. doi:10.1016/j.datak.2004.09.004

Yu, B., & Kim, S. H. (2006). Interpolating and using most likely trajectories in moving objects databases. In *Proceedings of the 17th International Conference on Database and Expert Systems Applications*, Springer Verlag, (pp. 718–727).

Zhang, J., Zhu, M., Papadias, D., Tao, Y., & Lee, D. L. (2003). Location-based spatial queries. In *Proceedings of the ACM SIGMOD International Conference on Management of Data.*

Zheng, B., & Lee, D. L. (2001). Semantic caching in location-dependent query processing. In *Proceedings of the International Symposium on Spatial and Temporal Databases.*

Zhu, X., Xu, B., & Wolfson, O. (2008). Spatial queries in disconnected mobile networks. In *Proceedings of the ACM International Conference on Geographic Information Systems*.

ADDITIONAL READING

Bobineau, C., Bouganim, L., Pucheral, P., & Valduriez, P. (2000). PicoDBMS: Scaling Down Database Techniques for the Smartcard. *Proceedings of the International Conference On Very Large Databases (VLDB)*, Best Paper Award.

Chaari, T., Ejigu, D., Laforest, F., & Scuturici, V.-M. (2006). Modelling and Using Context in Adapting Applications to Pervasive Environments. *In Proceedings of the IEEE International Conference of Pervasive Services.*

Chaari, T., Ejigu, D., Laforest, F., & Scuturici, V.-M. (2007). *A Comprehensive Approach to Model and Use Context for Adapting Applications in Pervasive Environments. International Journal of Systems and software* (*Vol. 3*). Elsevier.

Chaari, T., Laforest, F., & Celentano, A. (2008). Adaptation in Context-Aware Pervasive Information Systems: The SECAS Project. *International Journal on Pervasive Computing and Communications.*

Collet, C., & the Mediagrid Project members (2004). Towards a mediation system framework for transparent access to largely distributed sources. *In Proceedings of the International Conference on Semantics of a Networked world (semantics for Grid databases),* LNCS, Springer Verlag.

Dejene, E., Scuturici, V., & Brunie, L. (2008). Hybrid Approach to Collaborative Context-Aware Service Platform for Pervasive Computing. [JCP]. *Journal of Computers*, *3*(1), 40–50.

Düntgen, C., Behr, T., & Güting, R. H. (2009). BerlinMOD: a benchmark for moving object databases. *The VLDB Journal*, *18*, 1335–1368. doi:10.1007/s00778-009-0142-5

Grine, H., Delot, T., & Lecomte, S. (2005). Adaptive Query Processing in Mobile Environment. *In Proceedings of the 3rd International Workshop on Middleware for Pervasive and Ad-hoc Computing.*

Gripay, Y., Laforest, F., & Petit, J.-M. (2010). A Simple (yet Powerful) Algebra for Pervasive Environments, *In Proceedings of the 13th International Conference on Extending Database Technology EDBT 2010*, pp. 1-12.

Scholl, M., Thilliez, M., & Voisard, A. (2005). Location-based Mobile Querying in Peer-to-Peer Networks. *In Proceedings of the OTM 2005 Workshop on Context-Aware Mobile Systems*, Springer Verlag.

Thilliez, M., & Delot, T. (2004). A Localization Service for Mobile Users in Peer-To-Peer Environments, *In Mobile and Ubiquitous Information Access. Springer-Verlag, LNCS, 2954*, 271–282.

Thilliez, M., & Delot, T. (2004). Evaluating Location Dependent Queries Using ISLANDS. *In Advanced Distributed Systems: Third International School and Symposium, (ISSADS)*, Springer-Verlag.

Thilliez, M., Delot, T., & Lecomte, S. (2005). An Original Positioning Solution to Evaluate Location-Dependent Queries in Wireless Environments. *Journal of Digital Information Management, 3*(2).

Tuyet-Trinh, V., & Collet, C. (2004). Adaptable Query Evaluation using QBF. *In Proceedings of the of International Database Engineering & Applications Symposium* (IDEAS).

Vargas-Solar, G. (2005). Global, pervasive and ubiquitous information societies: engineering challenges and social impact, *In Proceedings of the 1st Workshop on Philosophical Foundations of Information Systems Engineering (PHISE'05)*, In conjunction with CAISE.

KEY TERMS AND DEFINITIONS

Snapshot Query: is executed once on one or several data producers. It can be a spatio-temporal query or a location-aware query.

Spatio-temporal Query: involves location constraints. (e.g., *give me the name and geographic position of gas stations located along the highway A48*).

Location-aware Query: answer depends on the location of the data producer (e.g., *give me the name and geographic position of the police patrols in my neighborhood*).

Recurrent Query: is executed repeatedly at specific points or intervals of time, as long as a condition is verified, or when an event is notified. It can be a location-dependant query, a stream query or a continuous query.

Location-dependant Query: answer depends on the location of the data consumer. (e.g., *which are the nearest gas stations with respect to my current location?*).

Stream Query: is evaluated on data stream (e.g., *which are the traffic conditions of the highway A48?*).

Continuous Query: has to be re-evaluated continuously until an event is produced. (e.g., *as long as I am driving in highway A48 inform me about the position of the police patrols 100 km around my current position*)

ENDNOTES

1 Partially supported by the OPTIMACS project, which is financed by the French National Association of Research (ANR).

2 The following partners of the OPTIMACS contributed to this chapter. In alphabetical order: C. Bobineau, Grenoble INP, LIG, France; V. Cuevas-Vicenttin, Grenoble INP, LIG, France, N. Cenerario, U. Valenciennes, LAMIH, France; M. Desertot, U. Valenciennes, LAMIH, France, Y. Gipray, INSA, LIRIS, France; F. Laforest, INSA, LIRIS, France, S. Lecomte, U. Valenciennes, LAMIH, France, M. Scuturici INSA, LIRIS, France.

3 Some authors like (Ilarri et al., 2008) define this query as a type of location dependent or location based query (Huang and Jensen 2004). They agree that the different types imply different evaluations strategies. Since our classification focuses on these strategies we separate them in different groups.

4 For this type of query our classification does not consider that the consumer is mobile, in such a case the query becomes continuous

and it is classified accordingly (see the Section describing recurrent queries).

5 Recurrent means something that is performed several times.

6 (Bidoit-Tollu, N. and Objois, M. 2008) proposes a comparison of stream query languages making the distinction between those that use windows for querying streams and those that not. The comparison is done using formal tools and shows the equivalence of both language families.

7 Recall that the equi-join corresponds to a θ join where the operator is the equality.

8 This query type is addressed in the Section describing snapshot queries because it is classified as a snapshot query.

Chapter 2
Context-Aware Smartphone Services

Igor Bisio
University of Genoa, Italy

Fabio Lavagetto
University of Genoa, Italy

Mario Marchese
University of Genoa, Italy

ABSTRACT

Combining the functions of mobile phones and PDAs, smartphones can be considered versatile devices and offer a wide range of possible uses. The technological evolution of smartphones, combined with their increasing diffusion, gives mobile network providers the opportunity to come up with more advanced and innovative services. Among these are the context-aware ones, highly customizable services tailored to the user's preferences and needs and relying on the real-time knowledge of the smartphone's surroundings, without requiring complex configuration on the user's part. Examples of context-aware services are profile changes as a result of context changes, proximity-based advertising or media content tagging, etc.

The contribution of this chapter is to propose a survey of several methods to extract context information, by employing a smartphone, based on Digital Signal Processing and Pattern Recognition approaches, aimed at answering to the following questions about the user's surroundings: what, who, where, when, why and how. It represents a fundamental part of the overall process needed to provide a complete context-aware service.

INTRODUCTION

Context-aware smartphone applications should answer the following questions about the device's surroundings (Dey, 2000): What, Who, Where, When, Why and How. As a consequence, in order to provide context-aware services, a description of the smartphone's environment must be obtained by acquiring and combining context data from different sources, both external (e.g., cell IDs, GPS

DOI: 10.4018/978-1-60960-611-4.ch002

coordinates, nearby Wi-Fi and Bluetooth devices) and internal (e.g., idle/active status, battery power, accelerometer measurements).

Several applications explicitly developed for smartphones will be surveyed in this chapter. In more detail, an overview of the context sources and sensors available to smartphones and the possible information they can provide is proposed in Section "Smartphones: an Overview".

The general logical model of a context-aware service composed of *i)* Context Data Acquisition, *ii)* Context Analysis and *iii)* Service Integration is introduced in Section "Context-Aware Services". A set of possible context-aware services such as Audio Environment Recognition, Speaker Count, Indoor and Outdoor Positioning, User Activity Recognition is listed in the following Sections. Further details concerning the aforementioned Context Analysis phase for specific context-aware services, which have been designed and implemented for smartphone terminals, are introduced as well.

In the specific case of this chapter, all context-aware services are based on sophisticated Digital Signal Processing approaches that have been specially designed and implemented for smartphones. The presented methods have been designed based on the principles set out by the corresponding related literature in the field, while additionally all the described solutions concern specific proposals and implementations performed by the authors.

Specifically, Audio Signal Processing-based services are introduced in Section "Audio Signal Processing based Context-Aware Services". In more detail, Environment Recognition (Perttunen, 2009) and Speaker Count (Iyer, 2006) services are described. Concerning Environment Recognition, both the architecture and the signal processing approach designed and implemented to identify the audio surrounding of the terminal (by distinguishing among street, overcrowded rooms, quiet environment, etc.) will be presented. Speaker Count services will be introduced as well. In detail, determining the number of speakers participating in a conversation is an important area of research as it has applications in telephone monitoring systems, meeting transcriptions etc. In this case the service is based on the audio signal recorded by the smartphone device. The speech processing methodologies and the algorithms employed to perform the Speaker Count process will also be introduced.

An overview of services based on the processing of signals received by smartphones' network interfaces such as GPS receiver, Wi-Fi, Bluetooth, etc. is proposed in Section "Network Interface Signal Processing based Context-Aware Services: Positioning". In particular, Indoor Positioning methods (Wang et al., 2003) have been taken into account. In this case the information required to carry out the positioning process is obtained from multiple sources such as the Wi-Fi interface (in the case of Indoor Positioning) and the GPS receiver (in the case of Outdoor Positioning). In particular, the methods suitable for smartphone implementation will be illustrated with particular emphasis on the Indoor Positioning approaches that have been implemented and tested directly on smartphones.

Finally, possible User Activity Recognition services (Ryder, 2009) that can be provided, starting from raw data acquired directly from the measurements carried out by the smartphone's accelerometer, are introduced in Section "Accelerometer Signal Processing based Context-Aware Services". In this case, additional technical details on the methods for the classification of activities such as walking, running, etc. will be described.

In all Sections where specific context-aware services will be introduced, the design and the implementation aspects of each service will also be detailed, based on the practical expertise, the employed test-beds and the results obtained during specific experimental campaigns that we have conducted. The chapter moreover will focus on the computational load and the energy consumption that is required to provide specific context-aware services in order to take into account the limited computational capacity and energy autonomy of smartphone platforms.

CONTEXT-AWARE SERVICES FOR SMARTPHONES

Smartphones: An Overview

For the next years, several market experts predict a significant growth in the market for converged mobile devices that simultaneously provide voice phone function, multimedia access, PDA capabilities and game applications. These devices will allow expanding the current market by adding new types of consumers. In fact, they will employ these devices for activities very different with respect to classical mobile phone calls usage.

This new trend will drive both Original Equipment Manufacturers (OEMs) and Carriers to meet this growth by providing smart devices and new services for the new class of users. In more detail, in 2003 it was estimated that converged mobile devices, also termed smartphones, made up three percent of worldwide mobile phone sales volume. Nowadays, the smartphone market is continuing to expand at triple digit year-over-year growth rates, due to the evolution of voice-centric converged mobile devices, mobile phones with application processors and advanced operating systems supporting a new range of data functions, including application download and execution.

In practice, smartphones will play a crucial role to support the users' activities both from the professional and private viewpoint. Context-aware services, object of this work, are a significant example of new features available to users. For this reason, before the survey of possible context-aware services for smartphones, a brief introduction concerning the smartphone platform in terms of hardware and software architecture is provided starting from (Freescale Semiconductor Inc., 2008), as well as a survey of the available smartphone Operating Systems.

Smartphone Architecture

From the hardware viewpoint, the first generation of analog cell phones was composed of devices consisted of a discrete single Complex Instruction Set Computing (CISC)-based microcontroller (MCU) core. Its task concerned the control of several analog circuits. The migration from analog to digital technology created the necessity of a Digital Signal Processor (DSP) core.

In fact, more advanced architectures included both cores, thus creating a dual-core system consisting of an MCU and a DSP, which were integrated in a single Application Specific Integrated Circuit (ASIC). Actually, the aforementioned dual-core architectures did not support the feature requirements of converged devices because they were designed only to support communications tasks. As a result, today's smartphone architecture requires additional processing resources. Currently, a discrete application processor is included in the architecture together with the discrete dual-core cellular baseband integrated circuit. Each processor requires its own memory system including RAM and ROM, which complete the computation architecture of a smartphone. Together with the above described architecture, recent mobile devices include wireless networking interfaces, such as Wi-Fi and Bluetooth technology. Each added communication interface, in several cases also very useful to provide context-aware services, requires additional modules for each function, including radio transceivers, digital basebands, RAM and ROM components within the module. In practice, modern smartphones mount a minimum of three, or as many as six, processors, each with its own dedicated memory system, peripherals, clock generator, reset circuit, interrupt controller, debug support and inter-processor communications software. Obviously, the overall architecture requires a power supply system.

A logical scheme of the described smartphone architecture is reported in Figure 1.

Concerning the software, the Cellular Baseband block shown in Figure 1, typically divides its tasks in the same way. In particular, the DSP performs signaling tasks and serves as a slave processor to the MCU, which runs the upper layer (L2/L3) functions of the communication protocol stack. On one hand, the Layer 1 signal processing tasks, handled by the DSP, include equalization, demodulation, channel coding/decoding, voice codec, echo and noise cancellation. On the other hand, the MCU manages the radio hardware and moreover implements the upper layer functions of the network protocol stack, such as subscriber identity, user interface, battery management and the nonvolatile memory for storage for the phone book. The Application Processor block, equipped with an MCU, manages the user interface and all the applications running on a smartphone.

In this Hardware/Software architecture, it is worth noticing that the communication protocol tasks and multimedia workloads may lead to performance conflicts, since they share the smartphone resource. This problem, only mentioned here as it is out of the scope of the chapter, requires a sophisticated internetworking approach and, in particular, advanced inter-processor communications aimed at increasing processing availability and at reducing overheads and power consumption, which result in reduced battery life and usage time for the end user.

A possible low-cost solution to such a problem may be to merge the Application Processor and the Cellular Baseband blocks into a single ASIC consisting of two or three cores. This approach eliminates the performance conflict between the communication protocol and multimedia tasks, although the complexity of the inter-processor communication is not reduced significantly.

Operating Systems Survey

Nowadays, the software functions previously described are obtained by using dedicated Operating Systems (OSs) designed and implemented for smartphone platforms. For the sake of completeness, a list of the currently available OSs is reported below. There are many operating systems designed for smartphones, the main ones being Symbian, Palm OS, Windows Mobile (Microsoft), Android, iPhone OS (Apple) and Blackberry OS (RIM).

Figure 1. Logical scheme of the modern smartphones' hardware architecture

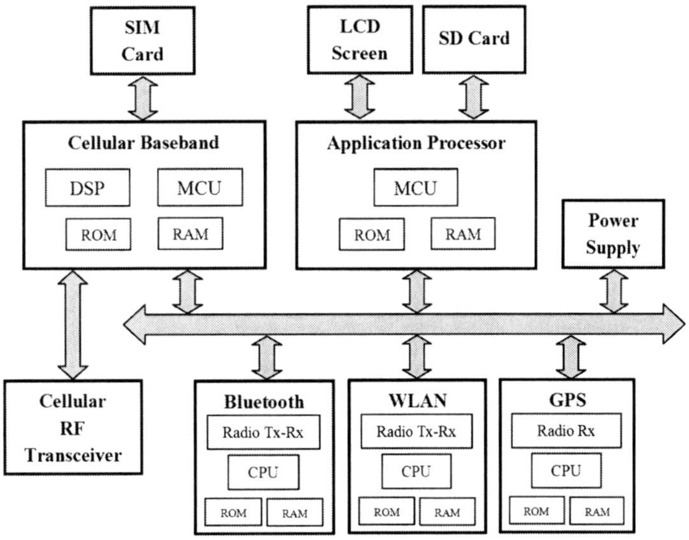

The most common one is Symbian, but its popularity is declining due to the recent diffusion of other OSs such as Android, iPhone and Blackberry. In fact, in recent years iPhone and BlackBerry phones have had a remarkable success, while the popularity of Android (the open source OS developed by Google) is constantly on the rise, after a very successful 2009. In more detail, *Symbian OS* is an open operating system adopted as standard by major global firms producing mobile devices (cell phones, smartphones, PDAs) and is designed to support the specific requirements of data transport generation mobile devices (2G, 2.5G and 3G). In 2005 the first version of the 9.x series (version 9.1) was released and, in particular, in 2006 version 9.3 included multimedia processing features, which are of great interest to the current applications of the smartphone platforms. *Palm OS* was developed in 1996 and released by the American Palm OS PalmSource Inc., later acquired by Japan's Access Systems which immediately reformulated the project with the aim to embrace the power and versatility of the Linux operating system. Despite having been announced for 2007, the new Palm OS at the moment is not yet available. *Windows Mobile* is the Microsoft operating system, including a suite of basic applications, dedicated to mobile devices. In this particular case, the user interface of the OS is very similar to the latest versions of the operating system for desktop and notebook PCs. In 2007 Google planned to develop a smartphone to compete directly with the Apple iPhone. Actually, in the early 2008 Google's management claimed not to be interested in the implementation of hardware, but in the development of software. In fact, Google launched a new OS called *Android*, an open source software platform for mobile devices, based on the Linux operating system. As detailed in the following Section, Android together with Symbian have been employed in our experiments to implement the described context-aware services. *iPhone OS* is the operating system developed by Apple for iPhone, iPod and iPod Touch and it is, in practice, a reduced version of Mac OS X. *BlackBerry OS* is the operating system developed by Research In Motion (RIM) and it is specifically designed for its own devices (BlackBerry).

Context-Aware Services

In this Section, a brief overview of the concept of context-aware services is provided. The overall framework presented here is based on the work reported in (Marengo et al, 2007) and in references therein.

In more detail, the real-time knowledge of a user's context is able to offer a wide range of highly personalized services. It makes services really customized because they are based on the environments, the behavior and other context factors that users themselves are experiencing when the services are provided. In practice, all the information a user may receive, for example by using a smartphone, which is also the source of context data in the case of this chapter, is based on position and geographic area in which users are, on the activities that are taking place and on the users' preferences. In practice, Context-Aware services provide useful information to users starting from the answers to the questions about the device's surroundings: What, Who, Where, When, Why and How.

The contribution of this chapter is to propose a survey of several methods to extract context information, by employing a smartphone, based on Digital Signal Processing and Pattern Recognition approaches, aimed at answering to the aforementioned questions. It represents a fundamental part of the overall process needed to provide a complete context-aware service as briefly detailed in the following.

From a more technical perspective, a system that realizes a complete context-aware service can be divided into three, successive and complementary, logic phases (or stages) listed below taking smartphone terminals as reference: *i)* Context Data Acquisition; *ii)* Context Analysis; *iii)* Service Integration. A scheme of the overall process to provide such service in reported in Figure 2, which is a slightly revised version of the scheme proposed in (Marengo, 2007).

Stage 1: Context Data Acquisition

During this stage, context information is captured and aggregated starting from signals generated by various information sources available (typically sensors or network interfaces).

These sources can provide information concerning the employed network accesses (e.g., using the GSM network rather than UMTS or the Wi-Fi interface), concerning the terminal (e.g., battery level, idle terminal) or information obtained by signals acquired by sensors on the device (e.g., microphone, accelerometer).

At this stage, considering the very limited resources available in a smartphone, in particular from the computational and energetic viewpoint, it is important to realize Context data acquisition approaches able to collect data quickly and to integrate heterogeneous information sources.

Stage 2: Context Analysis

It is the stage where information previously acquired provided by smartphones' sources is processed. This level is very important because it is responsible for the process that starts from "raw" data and ends with the decision of the context in which the device is. In particular, the main functions of this level are the identification of the context of a user and the generation of complete context information, starting from lower level information, i.e. raw data, which is directly captured by the smartphone's sensors.

In this case signal processing and pattern recognition methods play a crucial role. In fact, at this stage smartphones must process the data supplied from the lower level of context and apply the algorithms needed to extract information from such data and provide higher level information.

Stage 3: Service Integration

This is the final stage where the context-aware information is exploited to provide the output of the overall context-aware service. In practice, in this phase, the services are provided to the users. For example, an e-health context-aware service may concern the tele-monitoring of long-suffering users through a smartphone terminal: signals (lower level information) from the microphone, from the accelerometer and from the GPS receiver are captured (Stage *i*); information (higher layer information) about the environment, the movement and the position of the long-suffering users is provided (Stage *ii*); possible feedbacks to the

Figure 2. Stages of a context-aware service realized with smartphones adapted from (Marengo, 2007)

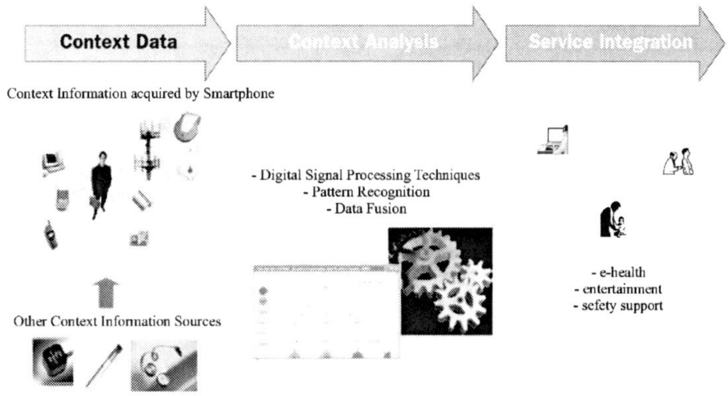

long-suffering users and/or to the medical/emergency personnel of a clinic are provided directly in their own smartphones (Stage *iii*).

AUDIO SIGNAL PROCESSING BASED CONTEXT-AWARE SERVICES

In the next few years, mobile network providers and users will have the new opportunity to come up with more advanced and innovative context-aware services based on the real-time knowledge of the user's surroundings. In fact, context data may also be acquired from the smartphone's audio environment. In general, the classification of an audio environment, the correspondence between two or more audio contexts or the number and the gender of active speakers near the smartphone, together with other possible context features, can be useful information employed to obtain helpful contents and services directly by the mobile users' devices.

Environment Recognition

In this sub-section the implementation and the related performance analysis of an Audio Fingerprinting platform is described. The Audio Fingerprint is a synthesis of the audio signals' characteristics extracted from their power density functions in the frequency domain. The platform and its capabilities are suited to be a part of a context-aware application in which acoustic environments correspondence and/or classification is needed.

In more detail, starting from the state of the art concerning Digital Signal Processing (DSP) and Acoustic Environment Classification (AEC), we implemented a system able to analyze the correspondence among audio signals. The proposed platform, and in particular the software procedure implemented in it, produced encouraging experimental results, in terms of correct correspondence among audio environments, and the computations needed to provide audio signal correspondence, introduced below, are performed in a reasonable amount of time.

The implemented platform is a hardware/software system able to evaluate the correspondence between two or more audio signals. It is composed of N terminals, called Clients, directly connected to a centralized Server. In the proposed implementation, shown in Figure 3, $N = 2$ terminals have been used. In general, the network employed to connect the platform elements may be a Local Area Network (LAN) or other possible network typologies (e.g., Wireless Local Area Network (WLAN) as in the case of our work) may be employed without loss of functionality. All network nodes are synchronized by using the well-known Network Time Protocol (NTP) and a specific reference timing server. Synchronization is a necessary requirement. It allows performing a reliable evaluation of the audio signals correspondence. In fact, when two equal audio signals

Figure 3. Audio fingerprinting platform architecture

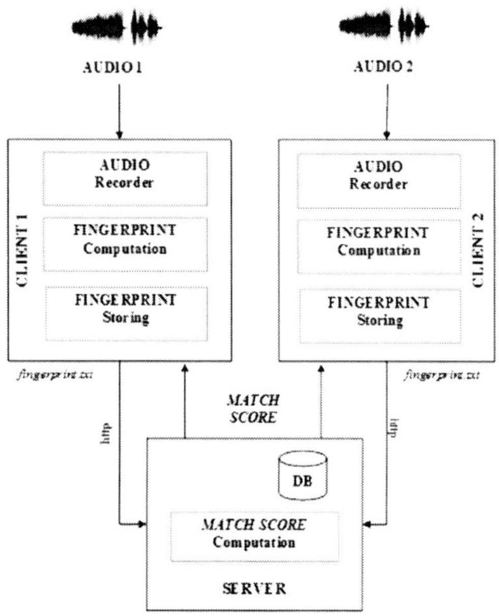

are unsynchronized the system might not detect their correspondence.

In more detail, the aim of the Clients is to record audio signals from the environments where they are placed, to extract the audio fingerprints, as described below, and write it in a textual file. The Clients subsequently send the file containing the fingerprints to the Server by employing the Hyper Text Transfer Protocol (HTTP). The Server node receives the fingerprints transmitted through the network and evaluates their possible correspondence as detailed in the following. To allow the fingerprint transmissions via HTTP, an Apache server has been installed on each node of the network.

The proposed architecture is suited to be used to fulfill two typical context-awareness actions: the environment classification and the environment correspondence. The former application is aimed at recognizing an environment starting from one ore more fingerprints of the recorded audio and comparing them with previously loaded fingerprints, representative of a given environment, stored in a specific Data Base (DB) in the Server node of the platform. The latter action is aimed at establishing if two or more audio fingerprints coincide.

The implemented platform, described in this sub-section, has been configured to fulfill the second action (the audio fingerprints correspondence) and in the specific case of the platform implemented by our research group, the Clients are smartphones. The considered environments, in the case of this implemented architecture, are five: quiet environment (silence); an environment where there is only one speaker; an environment where there is music; noisy environment; a noisy environment where there are also several speakers.

In the architecture shown in Figure 3, the Client part is composed of three fundamental components whose functions are:

- Audio Recording;
- Fingerprint Computation;
- Fingerprint Storing.

Furthermore, the Server component plays a crucial role. It is a typical web server where dynamic PHP pages have been implemented to exchange fingerprints among different client devices and to compute the correspondence between fingerprints. In more detail, the Server has two specific aims:

- Fingerprint Storage (in this case the stored fingerprints have been received from different Clients);
- Fingerprint Correspondence Analysis (it compares different fingerprints and establishes if they are equal as detailed in the following).

In practice, the fingerprints computed by the Clients are sent to the Server, which saves them in its local database (DB) and, finally, a specific function implemented in the Server computes the correspondence between a given fingerprint of the database (or, alternatively, the last received one) and the stored ones. It allows finding the possible correspondence among audio fingerprints.

The employed procedures for the computation of audio fingerprints and of correspondence among fingerprints are described in the following.

Audio Fingerprint Computation

The considered audio fingerprint is a matrix of values representative of the energy of the recorded audio signal computed by considering specific portions of the entire frequency bandwidth of the signal. The method applied in this paper is based on the techniques reported in (Lee, 2006). It represents a revised *Philips Robust Hash* (PRH) approach (Doets, 2006), which has been chosen in this implementation because it is suited to be applied to smartphone platforms due to its limited computational load. The basic idea is to exploit the human hearing system, which can be modeled (Peng, 2001) as a battery of 25 sub-bands contained in the frequency interval between 0 and 20 KHz. In more technical detail, the recorded audio signal is divided into 37 ms frames and *Hann* windowing is applied to each frame. Consecutive frames are overlapped by 31/32 in order to capture local spectral characteristics. This approach follows exactly the proposal reported in (Lee, 2006; Haitsma, 2006) where, through experimental campaigns, the frame length and the overlapping fraction have been found.

The energy of each of the above-mentioned 25 sub-bandwidths is computed for each frame in the frequency domain, by employing its Fourier Transform. The energy of a sub-bands is subtracted to the value of the previous one. The obtained results are stored in a vector of 24 components. This procedure is iterated for each frame and the final result is a matrix with 24 rows (the size of each single energy vector) and a number of columns equal to the number of frames. The final computation needed to extract the audio fingerprint requires the comparison, among columns, of the previously described matrix. In practice, for each row, each element is substituted by 1 or 0, respectively, based on whether it is greater or lesser than the following element.

Correspondence Computation

Concerning the evaluation of the correspondence among extracted fingerprints, in more detail, the considered and implemented procedure is based on the method proposed in (Lee, 2006). In practice, as reported in Figure 4, the method computes a *Match Score*, which is the measure of the correspondence between two audio fingerprints.

The computation is based on the fingerprints of short duration audio fragments. As a consequence, the employed method is implicitly granted a low computational complexity. The previously-defined fingerprint comparison is performed in the frequency domain and not in the time domain. In more technical terms, the Match Score is the maximum value of the two-dimensional cross-correlation between the fingerprint matrixes of the audio fragments. It ranges between 0, which is the value of the Match Score in case of different fingerprints, and 1, which is the value of the *Match Score* in case of comparison among two identical audio fingerprints. To reduce the number of operations needed to compute the two-dimensional cross-correlation, such procedure is carried out by computing the Discrete Fourier Transform (DFT) of the two fingerprint matrixes and by calculating their product, as schematically depicted in Figure 4. This approach has the obvious advantage of significantly reducing the number of operations required to obtain exactly the same results as in the time domain.

Figure 4. Correspondence computation functional block

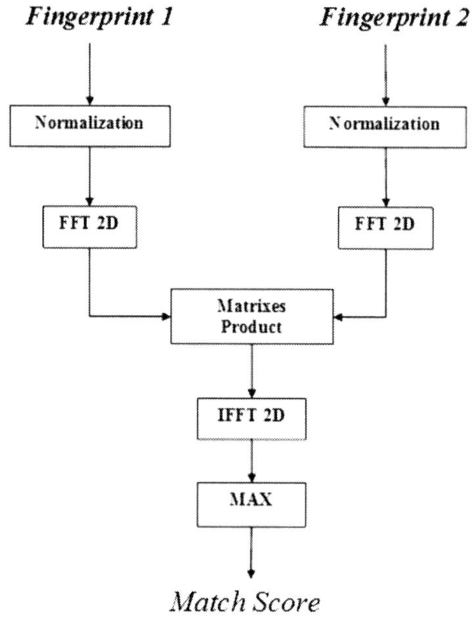

Speaker Count and Gender Recognition

Speaker count is applicable to numerous speech processing problems (e.g., co-channel interference reduction, speaker identification, speech recognition) but it does not yield a simple solution. Several speaker count algorithms have been proposed, both for closed- and open-set applications. Closed-set implies the classification of data belonging to speakers whose identity is known, while in the open-set scenario there is no available *a priori* knowledge on the speakers.

Audio-based gender recognition also has many possible applications (e.g., for selecting gender-dependent models to aid automatic speech recognition and in content-based multimedia indexing systems) and numerous methods have been designed involving a wide variety of context features.

Although for both problems many methods have produced promising results, available algorithms are not specifically designed for mobile device implementation and thus their computational requirements do not take into account smartphone processing power and context-aware application time requirements.

In this Section, on the basis of our previous practical experience, a speaker count method based on pitch estimation and Gaussian Mixture Model (GMM) classification, proposed in (Bisio, 2010) is described. It has been designed to recognize single-speaker (1S) samples from two-speaker (2S) samples and to operate in an open-set scenario. The proposed method produced encouraging experimental results and sample recognition is obtained in a reasonable amount of time. In addition, a method for single-speaker gender recognition was designed as well, and it has led to satisfying results. In this case, the employed OS is Symbian.

Many of the existing speaker count methods are based on the computation of feature vectors derived from the time- and/or frequency- domain of audio signals and subsequent labeling using generic classifiers. While performance varies based on the considered application scenario, the best results exceed 70% classification accuracy.

Audio-based gender recognition is also commonly carried out through generic classifiers, with pitch being the most frequently used feature, although many different spectral features have also been employed. Classification accuracies are better than 90% for most methods.

However, available algorithms are not designed specifically for mobile device implementation and do not take into account smartphone processing power and time requirements of context-aware applications.

Speaker Count and Gender Recognition Approach

As previously mentioned, to give a practical idea of the possibilities offered by smartphone platforms, the implemented method proposed by the authors in (Bisio, 2010) has been taken as reference in the following. As briefly described below, the basic concept of the employed method (Pitch estimation) can be employed for both Speaker Count and Gender Recognition approaches as listed below.

- ***Pitch Estimation***. For voiced speech, pitch can be defined as the rate of vibration of the vocal folds (Cheveignè, 2002), so it can be considered a reasonably distinctive feature of an individual. The basic idea of the proposed speaker count method is that if audio sample pitch estimates have similar values, the sample is 1S. If different pitch values are detected the sample is 2S. In (Bisio, 2010) a pitch estimation method based on the signal's autocorrelation was used because of its good applicability to speech and ease of implementation. Since pitch is linked to the speech signal's periodicity, the autocorrelation of a speech sample will present its highest values at very short delays and at delays corresponding to multiples of pitch periods. To estimate the pitch of an audio frame, the frame's autocorrelation is first computed in the delay interval corresponding to the human voice pitch range (50-500 Hz). The peak of this portion of autocorrelation is then detected and the pitch is estimated as the reciprocal of the delay corresponding to the autocorrelation peak.

- ***Speaker Count***. An audio sample is divided into abutted frames and pitch estimates are computed for each frame. A given number of consecutive frames is grouped together in blocks, in order to allow the computation of a pitch Probability Distribution Function (PDF) for each block. Adjacent blocks are overlapped by a certain number of frames. The values adopted in this paper are summarized in Table 1. A block's PDF is computed by estimating the pitch and computing the power spectrum (via Fourier Transform) for each of the block's frames. For every estimate the value of the PDF bin, which represents a small frequency interval, containing that pitch is increased with the frame's power, obtained from the computed power spectrum, at the frequency corresponding to the pitch estimate.

Compared to computing PDFs by simply executing a "histogram count" (which increases by 1 the value of a PDF bin for every pitch estimate falling into such bin), this mechanism allows distinguishing higher-power pitch estimates with respect to lower-power ones. It leads to more distinct PDFs and, as a consequence, more accurate features.

In order to recognize individual blocks, a feature vector representing the dispersion of its pitch estimate PDF, composed of its maximum and standard deviation, is extracted and used by a GMM classifier to classify the block as either 1S or 2S. Once all individual blocks have been recognized, the audio sample is finally classified through a "majority vote" decision.

- ***Gender Recognition***. In addition to the speaker count algorithm, a method for single-speaker gender recognition was designed as well. It was observed that satisfying results could be obtained by using a single-feature threshold classifier, without resorting to GMMs. In this case, the chosen feature is the mean of the blocks' "histogram count" PDF. In fact, pitch values for male speakers are on average lower compared to female speakers, since pitch can be defined as the vibration rate of the vocal folds during speech and male vocal folds are greater in length and thickness compared to female ones. Individual blocks are classified as "Male" (M) or "Female" (F) by comparing their PDF mean with a fixed threshold computed based on a training set. "Histogram count" PDFs are employed because it was observed that the derived feature was sufficiently accurate. The weighted PDFs, which require the Fourier Transform of individual frames, are not used to significantly reduce the time required by the smartphone application to classify unknown samples.

Experiments and Results

In order to train the GMM and threshold classifiers an audio sample database has been employed. It was acquired using a smartphone, thus allowing the development of the proposed methods based on data consistent with the normal execution of the smartphone applications. The considered situations were 1 male speaker (1M), 1 female speaker (1F), 2 male speakers (2M), 2 female speakers (2F) and 1 male and 1 female speaker (2MF).

Table 1. Experimental setup

Sampling Frequency	22KHz
Frame Duration	2048 samples
Frames per Block	20
Block Overlap	10 frames
PDF bin Width	10 Hz

All audio samples refer to different speakers in order to evaluate classifier performance using data deriving from speakers that did not influence classifier training (open-set scenario). A total of 50 recordings was acquired, 10 for each situation. Half of the recordings was used for training, the other half for testing. The parameters used during experiments have been set to the values shown in Table 1.

Concerning Speaker Count results, different feature vectors were evaluated and comparison of test set classification accuracies was used to select the most discriminating one. A 3-dimensional feature vector performed better than some 2-dimensional ones, but adding a fourth feature does not improve classification accuracy, since it is rather correlated with the others. The feature vector ultimately used for GMM classification, as previously mentioned, comprises the maximum and standard deviation of block PDFs, and it leads to 60% test sample accuracy.

An additional set of experiments ignoring the situations that most of all led to classification errors, i.e. 2M and 2F, was carried out. In fact, these two situations can be misclassified as 1M and 1F, respectively, since same-gender speakers could have pitch estimates close enough in value to lead to 2S PDFs similar to 1S PDFs of the same gender. Therefore a new GMM classifier was designed, in order to distinguish not two classes (1S and 2S) but three classes: 1M, 1F and 2MF. Again, different feature vectors were evaluated, and for each one classification errors involved exclusively class 2MF, i.e. test sample blocks belonging to classes 1M and 1F were never mistaken one for another. The chosen feature vector consists of the mean and maximum of block PDFs, and it leads to 67% test sample accuracy. In order to compare this result with the first set of experiments, classes 1M and 1F can be considered as class 1S and class 2MF as class 2S, producing a 70% test sample accuracy.

Concerning Gender Recognition results, in order to identify the gender of single speakers the threshold on the mean of the "histogram count" pitch PDF was set to the value that led to the best training sample block classification results. The designed classifier leads to 90% test sample accuracy. While both classes are well-recognized, the totality of female samples was correctly classified.

NETWORK INTERFACE SIGNAL PROCESSING BASED CONTEXT-AWARE SERVICES: POSITIONING

Navigation and positioning systems have become extremely popular in recent years. In particular, thanks to an increasingly widespread dissemination and decrease in costs, devices such as GPS receivers are much more efficient for what concerns positioning systems. Obviously, positioning information represents very useful context information which can be exploited in several applications.

The positioning problem may be divided into two families: outdoor and indoor positioning. Several algorithms are available in the literature together with several approaches based on the use of different hardware platforms such as RF (Radio Frequency) technology, ultrasound-, infrared-, vision-based systems and magnetic fields. The RF signal-based technologies can be split into WLAN (2.4 GHz and 5 GHz bands), Bluetooth (2.4 GHz band), Ultrawideband and RFID (Gu, 2009; Moutz, 2009). Concerning the Outdoor positioning, GPS is the most popular and widely used three-dimensional positioning technology in the world. However, in many everyday environments such as indoors or in urban areas, GPS signals are not available for positioning (due to the very weak signals). Even with high sensitivity GPS receivers, positioning for urban and indoor environments cannot be guaranteed in all situations, and accuracies typically range between tens and hundreds of meters. As claimed in (Barnes, 2003), other emerging technologies obtain positions from systems that are not designed for positioning, such as mobile phones or television.

As a result, the accuracy, reliability and simplicity of the position solution is typically very poor in comparison to GPS with a clear view of the sky.

Despite this viewpoint, due to the widespread employment of smartphones, it is interesting to develop possible algorithms suited to be used with those platforms. In particular, based on our previous practical experience, we present in the following the Indoor positioning approaches, based on the Fingerprinting criteria and actually implemented on smartphones, which are introduced to give readers a tangible idea of the possible context-aware applications that such platforms may support.

Indoor Positioning

In more detail, with the increasing spread of mobile devices such as Personal Digital Assistants (PDA), laptops and smartphones, along with a great expansion of Wireless Local Area Networks (WLAN), there is a strong interest in implementing a positioning system which uses similar devices. In addition to this, with a great diffusion of the wireless communications network infrastructure and an increasing interest in location-aware services, there is a need for an accurate indoor positioning technique based on WLAN networks.

Obviously, WLAN is not designed and deployed for the purpose of positioning. However, measurements of the Signal Strength (SS) transmitted by either Access Point (AP) or station could be used to calculate the location of any Mobile User (MU). Many SS-based techniques have been proposed for position estimation in environments in which WLAN is deployed. In the following, the most common approaches in the literature have been described. There are essentially two main categories of techniques which can implement wireless positioning. The first is called trilateration, while the second fingerprinting.

Trilateration

It employs a mathematical model to "convert" the SS received by the terminal in a measure of the distance between the terminal itself and the corresponding AP. Obviously this distance does not provide any information about the direction in which the device is located. For this reason, it is assumed that the terminal is situated upon a circle centered in the considered AP, with a radius equal to the determined distance.

It is worth noticing that the SS is very sensitive to small changes in the position and orientation of the antenna of the terminal, thus making it particularly difficult to determine an analytical relationship linking SS to distance. In particular, the trilateration approach consists of two steps:

- converting SS to AP-MU distance (*Off-Line*);
- computing the location using the relationship between SS and distance (*On-Line*);

In the first step, a signal propagation model is employed to convert SS to AP-MU distance. This is the key of the trilateration approach and must be as accurate as possible. In the second step, least squares or other methods (such as the geometric method) can be used to compute the location. A positioning process ma start from the classical formulation of the propagation loss for radio communications L_F

$$L_F = 10\log(\frac{P_R}{P_T}) = 10\log G_T + 10\log G_R - 20\log f - 20\log d + K$$

where $K = 20\log\left(3\cdot 10^8/4\pi\right) = 147.56$, G_T and G_R are the transmitter and the receiver antennas' gain, respectively. P_R and P_T are the receive power and the transmitted power. f and d are the frequency and the distance, respectively. In an ideal situation (i.e. G_T and G_R equal to 1), it is possible to define the basic transmission loss (L_B) as:

$$L_B = -32.44 - 20\log f_{MHz} - 20\log d_{km}$$

where d_{km} represents distance (in *Km*) and f_{MHz} represents frequency (in *MHz*). All the equations above are referred to a free space situation, without any kind of obstacles. Thus they do not take into account all the impairments of a real environment, such as reflections, refractions and multipath fading.

In order to solve this problem and determine the mathematical relation, without considering physical properties, an empirical model based on regression was assumed. The key idea is to collect several measurements of SS at the same point, at increasing distance from the AP considered. After the acquisition phase, all measures taken at the same point are averaged with the aim to obtain a more stable reference value of SS. The obtained set of {SS-distance} pairs is then interpolated by a polynomial technique, for example by the least-squares method, producing an expression of the distance as a function of the SS. In more detail, empirical studies have proved that a cubic regressive equation results adequate to obtain a model representative of a trade-off between accuracy and computational load.

If this process is repeated for each AP used in the algorithm and the number of APs of the WLAN is at least three, this method allows estimating the distances between the device (the smartphone in the case of this chapter) and all the APs. The positioning process is then concluded by computing the intersection of three circles with radiuses equal to the estimated distances.

Fingerprinting

A positioning system which uses the fingerprinting approach is again composed by two phases: training (*Off-Line*) and positioning (*On-Line*). In the framework of the research activity conducted by the authors, this approach has been preferred for smartphone implementation because of its limited computational complexity. In more detail, the aim of the training phase is to build a database of fingerprints, whose meaning is clarified in the following, which is used to determine the location of the device. To generate the database, it is necessary to carefully define the reference points (RPs), i.e. the points where the fingerprints will be taken, and the concept of fingerprint itself. The RPs must be chosen in the most uniform way possible, in order to cover the entire area of interest as homogeneously as possible.

The acquisitions are made by placing the device in each RP and measuring the SS of all the APs. From all acquisitions, a distinguishing and robust feature called fingerprint is determined for each AP, taking the average value of the measured SS. This feature is then stored in the database. This process is repeated for all RPs.

During the positioning phase (*On-Line*) the device measures the SS of all the APs, i.e. it determines the fingerprint corresponding to its current position. This imprint is then compared with the fingerprints stored in the database by using an appropriate algorithm for comparison, described in the following. Obviously, the final result of this operation is the estimated position of the device. Figure 5, adapted from (Binghao, 2006), schematically summarizes the two phases of the briefly described process.

In the framework of the described fingerprinting approach there are many algorithms to determine the position of the device. The simplest of all is the so-called Nearest Neighbor (NN). This method determines the "distance" between the measured fingerprint $[s_1, s_2 \ldots s_n]$ and those which are in the database $[S_1, S_2 \ldots S_n]$. The "distance" between these two vectors is determined by the general formula below:

Figure 5. Two phases of the fingerprinting approach: (a) training phase and (b) positioning phase adapted from (Binghao, 2006)

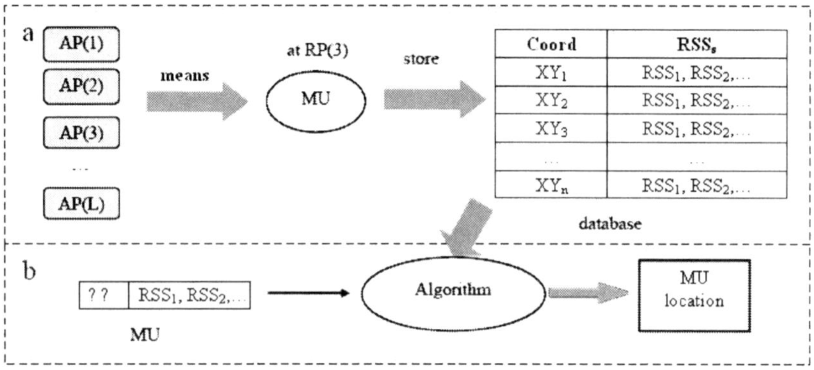

$$L_q = \left(\sum_{i=1}^{n} \left| s_i - S_i \right|^q \right)^{\frac{1}{q}}$$

In particular, the Manhattan and Euclidean distance are obtained with $q = 1$ and $q = 2$, respectively. Experimental tests have shown that the Manhattan distance provides better performance in terms of precision. The NN method defines the Nearest Neighbor to be the RP with the minimum distance, in terms of the equation given above, from the fingerprint acquired by the device. That point is the position produced by the simple NN approach.

Another method for determining the position is to employ the K-Nearest Neighbors (KNN, with $K \geq 2$) that uses the K RPs with the minimum distance from the measured *fingerprint*, and estimates the position of the device by averaging the coordinates of the K points found.

A variant of the this method is the Weighted K-Nearest Neighbors (WKNN), in which the estimated position is obtained by making a weighted average. One of the possible strategies to determine the weights (w_i) could be using the inverse value of the distance, as shown in the equation below:

$$w_i = \frac{1}{L_q}$$

A Probabilistic Approach for the Fingerprinting Method

While the previously described deterministic method achieves reasonable localization accuracy, it discards much of the information present in the training data. Each *fingerprint* summarizes the data as the average signal strength to visible access points, based on a sequence of signal strength values recorded at that location. However, signal strength at a position can be characterized by more parameters than just the average. This led researchers to consider a Bayesian approach to WLAN localization. This had been employed with some success in the field of robot localization (Ladd, 2002). For localization, the Bayes rule can be written as

$$p(l_t / o_t) = p(o_t / l_t)\, p(l_t)\, N$$

where l_t is a position at time t, o_t is an observation at t (the instantaneous signal strength values), and N is a normalizing factor that ensures that all probabilities sum to 1.

In other words, the probability of being at location l_t given observation o_t is equal to the probability of observing o_t at location l_t, and being at location l_t in the first place. During localization, this conditional probability of being at location l_t is calculated for all *fingerprints*. The most likely position is then the localizer's output. To calculate this, it is necessary to calculate the two probabilities on the right hand side of the equation above. The quantity $p(o_t/l_t)$ is known, in Bayesian terms, as the likelihood function. This can be calculated using the signal strength map. For each *fingerprint*, the frequency of each signal strength value is used to generate a probability distribution as the likelihood function. The raw distribution can be used, but as it is typically noisy and incomplete, the data is usually summarized as either a histogram, with an empirically determined optimal number of bins, or as a discrete Gaussian distribution parameterized using mean and standard deviation.

Other representations are also possible; the Bayesian approach allows using any algorithm capable of generating a probability distribution across all positions.

In its simplest version, the Bayesian localizer calculates the prior probability $p(l_t)$ as the uniform distribution over all possible positions. This means that, before each positioning attempt, the target is equally likely to be at any of the position in the *fingerprint* map. In order to achieve higher accuracy, it is possible to compute such probability using the knowledge given by historical information such as user habits, collision detection, and anything else that affects the prior probability that can be modeled probabilistically. For example, Markov Localization (Simmons, 1995) suggests using the transitional probability between positions. This probability is described as

$$p(l_t) = \sum_{l_{t-1}} p(l_t / l_{t-1}) p(l_{t-1})$$

In other words, $p(l_t)$ is the sum of the transitional probability from all positions at $t-1$ to l_t at the current time t, multiplied by the probability of being at those locations at $t-1$. The probability $p(l_{t-1})$ is known from previous positioning attempts.

Test-Bed Description and Preliminary Results

From a practical point of view, certain fingerprinting algorithms have been implemented on a smartphone platform and preliminary results are reported in the following. In more detail, to test the algorithm implementation an *ad hoc* test-bed was set up in the Digital Signal Processing Laboratory at the University of Genoa where the authors are developing their research activity. The room is approximately 8 *m* ×8 *m* in size. In the performed tests five APs have been installed, four of them in the corners of the room and one in the center. All the APs' antennas are omni-directional.

In general, the position of the APs in the room plays a crucial role because it is linked to the accuracy and precision of the system. In particular, (Wang, 2003) shows very clearly that the more APs are installed the better the performance is.

To evaluate the validity of the implemented algorithms, several tests were carried out. In particular, 30 measurements were taken in different parts of the test-bed. For each of these measurements the position was determined using the deterministic fingerprinting algorithm. In particular, all the algorithms previously described (NN, KNN, WKNN) have been compared. The database employed for all the experiments contains 121 RPs, separated 0.6 *m* one from another. The histogram below reports the obtained results.

Figure 6 shows that the simplest and quickest algorithm (i.e. NN) does not provide good results. All other algorithms have a mean error around 1.2 *m*. For this particular set of measures, 6WNN has the best performance in terms of the lowest positioning error (i.e. the distance, expressed in *m*, between the real position and the estimated

Figure 6. Mean and variance of the error for all the algorithms utilized in the fingerprinting positioning system. These results are obtained with a database of 121 RPs and 5 APs

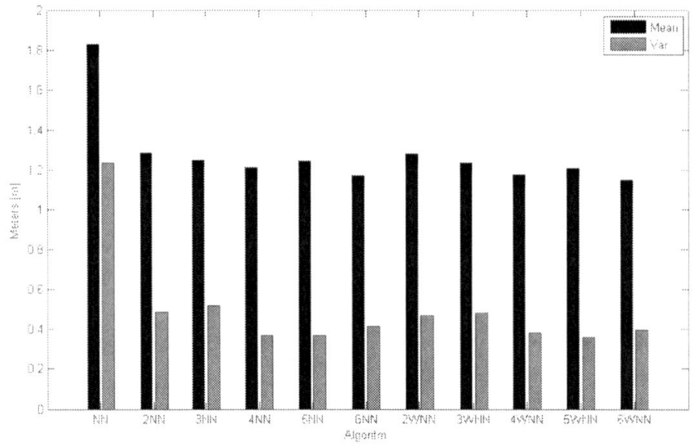

one) and a very low variance. Empirical experiments presented in (Binghao, 2006) prove that the probabilistic approach provides slightly better performance. It indicates that probabilistic methods are relatively robust with respect to naturally occurring fluctuations.

Brief Overview of Other Approaches

For the sake of completeness other common approaches are synthetically described below, as reviewed in (Bose, 2007):

- ***Angle of Arrival*** (AOA) refers to the method by which the position of a mobile device is determined by the direction of the incoming signals from other transmitters whose locations are known. Triangulation techniques are used to compute the location of the mobile device. However, a special antenna array is required to measure the angle.
- ***Time of Arrival*** (TOA) method measures the round-trip time (RTT) of a signal. Half of the RTT corresponds to the distance of the mobile device from the stationary device. Once the distances from a mobile device to three stationary devices are estimated, the position of the mobile device with respect to the stationary devices can easily be determined using trilateration. TOA requires very accurate and tightly synchronized clocks since a 1.0 μs error corresponds to a 300 m error in the distance estimation. Thus, inaccuracies in measuring time differences should not exceed tens of nanoseconds since the error is propagated to the distance estimation.
- ***Time Difference of Arrival*** (TDOA) method is similar to Time of Arrival using the time difference of arrival times. However, the synchronization requirement is eliminated but nonetheless high accuracy is still an important factor. As in the previous method, inaccuracies in measuring time differences should not exceed tens of nanoseconds.

ACCELEROMETER SIGNAL PROCESSING BASED CONTEXT-AWARE SERVICES

The physical activity which the user is currently engaged in can be useful context information, e.g. it may be employed to support remote healthcare monitoring (Leijdekkers, 2007), to update the user's social network status (Miluzzo, 2008) or even to reproduce inferred real-world activities in virtual settings (Musolesi, 2008).

In the following, a smartphone algorithm for user activity recognition is described. It is based on the sensing, processing and classification of data provided by the smartphone-embedded accelerometer and is designed to recognize four different classes of physical activities. It is worth noticing that the described approach has been practically implemented and tested by our research group. It represents a *proof of concept* and as such it can be considered as a useful reference for readers' comprehension.

User Activity Recognition

Four different user activities have been considered. Unless specified differently, the phone is thought to be in the user's front or rear pants pocket (as suggested in (Bao, 2004)) and training data was acquired accordingly. Furthermore, the acquisition of training data was performed keeping the smartphone in four different positions, based on whether the display was facing towards the user or away from him and whether the smartphone itself was pointing up or down. The evaluated classes are:

- ***Sitting***: the user is sitting down. Training data was acquired only with the smartphone in the front pocket, under the assumption that it's unlikely users will keep the smartphone in a back pocket while sitting.
- ***Standing***: the user is standing up, without walking. Satisfactory distinction from *Sitting* is possible due to the fact that people tend to move a little while standing.
- ***Walking***: the user is walking. Training data for this class was acquired in real-life scenarios, e.g. on streets, in shops, etc.
- ***Running***: the user is running. As for *Walking*, training data for this class was acquired in common every-day scenarios.

Sensed Data

The smartphone employed during the work is an HTC Dream, which comes with an integrated accelerometer manufactured by Asahi Kasei Corporation. It's a triaxial, piezoresistive accelerometer which returns the acceleration values on the three axes in m/s^2.

The proposed algorithm periodically collects raw data from the smartphone accelerometer and organizes it into frames. A feature vector is computed for every frame and is used by a decision tree classifier to classify the frame as one of the classes previously listed. Groups of consecutive frames are organized in windows, with consecutive windows overlapped by a certain amount of frames. Every completed window is assigned to one of the four considered classes, based on one of several possible decision policies. Such windowed decision is considered as the current user activity. Therefore, several parameters are involved in the data acquisition. First of all, a frame's duration must be set: shorter frames mean quicker feature computation, but the minimum length required to properly recognize the target activities must be considered as well. The frame acquisition rate must also be determined, i.e. how often must the accelerometer be polled. Higher frame rates imply shorter pauses between frames and a more precise knowledge of the context, but also more intensive computation. On the other hand, lower frame rates provide a less precise knowledge of the context, but also imply a lighter computational load, which is an important requirement for smartphone terminals.

The window size affects the windowed decision which determines the current state associated with the user. Small windows ensure a quicker reaction to actual changes in context, but are more vulnerable to occasionally misclassified frames.

On the other hand, large windows react more slowly to context changes but provide better protection against misclassified frames. The window overlap (number of frames shared by consecutive windows) must also be set. Employing heavily-overlapped windows provides a better knowledge of the context but may also imply consecutive windows bearing redundant information, while using slightly-overlapped windows could lead to signal sections representing meaningful data falling across consecutive windows.

Feature Computation and Frame Classification

In order to determine the best possible classifier, numerous features were evaluated and compared, among which were the mean, zero crossing rate, energy, standard deviation, cross-correlation, sum of absolute values, sum of variances and number of peaks of the data obtained from the accelerometer. The feature vector ultimately chosen is made of nine features, i.e. the mean, standard deviation and number of peaks of the accelerometer measurements along the three axes of the accelerometer.

Once a feature vector has been computed for a given frame, it is used by a classifier in order to associate the frame to one of the classes listed before. As in earlier work (Bao, 2004; Musolesi, 2008; Tapia, 2007; Ryder, 2009), the employed classifier is a decision tree. Using the Weka workbench (a tool dedicated to Machine Learning procedure), several decision trees were designed and compared based on their recognition accuracy. A decision tree was trained for every combination of two and three of the users employed in the dataset creation (see the brief performance evaluation reported below). In order to evaluate the classifiers' performance, a separate test set (made of the dataset portion not used for training) was used for each combination.

Classification Scoring and Windowed Decision

Every completed window is assigned to one of the four considered classes, based on one of several possible decision policies. The simplest of such policies is a majority-rule decision: the window is associated to the class with the most frames in the window. While it is clearly simple to implement and computationally inexpensive, the majority-rule windowed decision treats all frames within a window in the same way, without considering when the frames occurred or the single frame classifications' reliability.

Therefore, other windowed decision policies were evaluated. It must be noted that such policies are completely independent from the decision tree used to classify individual frames.

A first alternative to the majority-rule decision is the time-weighted decision. In a nutshell, it implies giving different weights to a window's frames based solely on their position in the window and assigning a window to the class with the highest total weight. This way a frame will have a greater weight the closer it is to the end of the window, under the assumption that more recent classifications should be more useful to determine the current user activity.

In order to determine what weight to give to frames, a weighting function $f(t)$ was designed according to the following criteria:

- $f(0) = 1$, where $t = 0$ represents the time at which the most recent frame occurred;
- $f(t) \geq 0$ for all $t \geq 0$;
- $f(t)$ must be non-increasing for all $t \geq 0$.

If T_f is the instant associated with a frame and T_{dec} is the instant at which the windowed decision is made, then the frame will be assigned a weight equal to $f(T_{dec} - T_f)$.

Two different weighting functions were compared, i.e. a Gaussian function and a negative

Exponential function. For each function type five different functions were compared by choosing a reference instant T_{ref} and forcing $f(T_{ref}) = p$, where p is one of five linearly-spaced values between 0 and 1.

A second kind of windowed decision policy requires assigning to each frame a score representing how reliable its classification is. As in the case of the time-weighted decision, a window is associated to the class with the highest total weight. Unlike other classifier models, the standard form of decision tree classifiers does not provide ranking or classification probability information. In the literature there are numerous approaches to extend the decision tree framework to provide ranking information (Ling, 2003; Alvarez, 2007). In our work the method proposed in (Toth, 2008) has been implemented.

Such scoring method takes advantage of the fact that each leaf of a decision tree represents a region in the feature space defined by a set of inequalities determined by the path from the tree root to the leaf. The basic idea is that the closer a frame's feature vector is to the decision boundary, the more unreliable the frame's classification will be, under the hypothesis that the majority of badly classified samples lie near the decision boundary.

This scoring method requires the computation of a feature vector's Mahalanobis distance from the decision boundary and an estimate of the correct classification probability. The Mahalanobis distance is used instead of the Euclidean one because it takes into account the correlation among features and is scale invariant. This ensures that if different features have different distributions, the same Mahalanobis distance along the direction corresponding to a feature with greater deviation will carry less weight than along the direction corresponding to a feature with lesser deviation.

The distance of a feature vector from the decision boundary is given by the shortest distance to the leaves with class label different from the label associated to the feature vector. The distance between a feature vector and a leaf is obtained by solving a constrained quadratic program.

Using separate training data for each leaf, an estimate of the correct classification probability conditional to the distance from the decision boundary is produced. Such estimate is computed by using the leaf's probability of correctly and incorrectly classifying training set samples (obtained in terms of relative frequency) and probability density of the distance from the decision boundary conditional to correct and false classification.

The classification score is finally given by the lower bound of the 95% confidence interval for the estimate of the correct classification probability conditional to the distance from the decision boundary.

The confidence interval lower bound is used instead of the correct classification probability conditional to the distance from the decision boundary estimate because the latter may remain close to 1 even for large distances. However, a large distance may not imply a reliable classification but be caused by an unknown sample located in a region of the feature space insufficiently represented in the training set. On the contrary, past a certain distance (which varies with every leaf), the confidence interval lower bound decreases rapidly.

Another windowed decision policy is given by combining the temporal weights and the classification scores into a single, joint time-and-score weight. Fusion is obtained simply by multiplying the corresponding time weight and classification score, since both are between 0 and 1.

By considering the described methods as single approaches and by mixing them it is possible to obtain six approaches. In particular, Majority decision (M), Exponential time weighting (T_e), Gaussian time weighting (T_g), classification score weighting (S), joint classification score / exponential time weighting (S+T_e), joint classification score / Gaussian time weighting (S+T_g). The performance comparison among them is briefly described below. It is worth noticing that what has been described previously is object of ongoing research by the Authors of this chapter and further details about such solutions will be provided in the future.

Brief Performance Evaluation

The dataset employed in the experiments was acquired by 4 volunteers. Each volunteer acquired approximately 1 hour of data for each of the classes listed above, producing a total of almost 17 hours of data. The employed OS was Android. For every combination of two and three users, the dataset was then divided into a training set for classifier training and a distinct test set for performance evaluation purposes. In evaluating the performance of the proposed method, one must distinguish single-frame classification accuracy from windowed-decision accuracy: the former depends solely on the decision tree classifier, while the latter depends on what decision policy was used.

Of all the evaluated classifiers, the one with the best single-frame accuracy produced a 98% correct test set classification average. In more detail, the class with the best recognition accuracy is *Sitting* (over 99% of test set frames correctly recognized), while *Running* is the activity with the lowest test set accuracy (95.2%), with most of the incorrectly classified frames (approximately 4.6% of the total) being misclassified as *Walking*. Such results are extremely satisfactory: in particular, the implemented classifier led to an improvement of the activity recognition accuracy of more than 20% compared to (Miluzzo 2008) which considers the same classes and also uses decision tree classification, although the employed dataset is somewhat smaller.

As for the windowed decision, an additional *ad hoc* sequence, not included in the dataset used for classifier training and testing, was employed to determine the best values for the frame acquisition rate, window size, window overlap and scale parameter for the time-weighting functions briefly described above. Such sequence is made of just over an hour of data, referring to all four considered user activities executed in random order. Windowed decision was applied to the *ad hoc* sequence using 411 different parameter configurations and all six above-mentioned decision policies for each parameter combination. The results can be summed up in Figure 7. Using only the time-based frame classification weighting does not seem to improve performance compared to the majority decision, while employing classification score weighting, by itself or combined with time weighting, led to significant improvements in windowed decision accuracy. Overall, the best parameter configuration led to an 85.2% windowed decision accuracy: it was obtained using 16-second pauses between consecutive frames, 8-frame windows, single-frame window overlap and joint classification score / Gaussian time weighting

CONCLUSION

The proposed chapter is based on the authors' previous research experience and ongoing work and it is aimed at giving an idea of possible context-aware Services for smartphones considering and describing algorithms and methodologies practi-

Figure 7. Percentage of total number of evaluated parameter configurations in which each windowed decision policy gave the best correct windowed decision percentage

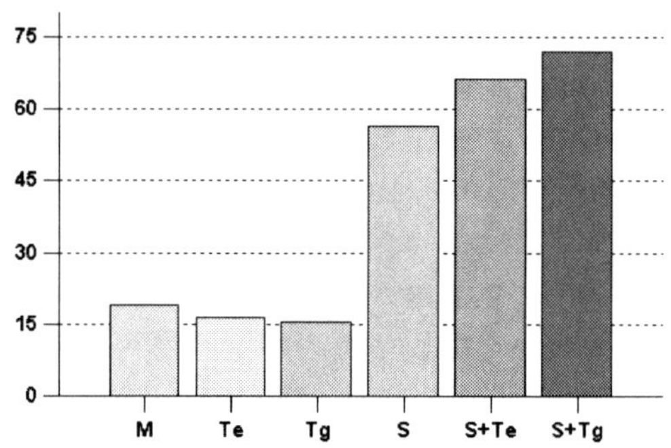

cally designed and implemented for such devices. In more detail, such methods have been exploited to implement particular Context-Aware services aimed at recognizing the audio environment, the number and the gender of speakers, the position of a device and the user physical activity by using a smartphone. The practical implementation of these services, capable of extracting useful context information, is the main technical objective of this work.

Starting from the open issues considered in this chapter and from the literature in the field, it is clear that context awareness needs to be enhanced with new efficient algorithms and needs to be developed in small, portable and diffused devices. Smartphones have the mentioned characteristics and, as a consequence, they may represent the target technology for future Context-Aware services. In this context, the lesson learned by the authors is that an important effort in terms of advanced signal processing procedure that exploit the smartphone feature, sensors and computational capacity need to be done and what has been presented in this chapter represents the first step in that direction.

The development of efficient signal processing procedure over smartphone opens the doors to future application of smartphone-based context-aware services in several fields. Two important sectors may be the safety and the remote assistance. In the first case, information about the audio environment, the position and the movement that the personnel dedicated to the surveillance of a sensitive area, acquired by using their smartphones, may represent a useful input for advanced surveillance systems. In the second case, remote monitoring of patients or elders that need to be monitored can be realized as well. Position, outdoor or indoor (within their domestic ambient), and movements constitute useful input for physicians to monitor the lifestyle of patients or to individuate possible emergency cases.

The evolution of the signal procession procedures for smartphones and the application of them to realize context-aware service for safety and health-care platforms constitute the future direction for the research in the presented field.

ACKNOWLEDGMENT

The authors wish to deeply thank Dr. Alessio Agneessens and Dr. Andrea Sciarrone for their precious support in the implementation and testing phase of this research work and for their important suggestions.

REFERENCES

Alvarez, I., Bernard, S., & Deffuant, G. (2007). Keep the decision tree and estimate the class probabilities using its decision boundary. *Proceedings of the International Joint Conference on Artificial Intelligence*, (pp. 654-660).

Bao, L., & Intille, S. S. (2004). *Activity recognition from user-annotated acceleration data.* In 2nd International Conference, PERVASIVE '04.

Barnes, J., Rizos, C., Wang, J., Small, D., Voigt, G., & Gambale, N. (2003). High precision indoor and outdoor positioning using LocataNet. *Journal of Global Positioning Systems*, *2*(2), 73–82. doi:10.5081/jgps.2.2.73

Binghao, L., James, C. S. R., & Dempster, A. G. (2006). Indoor positioning techniques based on wireless LAN. In *Proceedings of Auswireless Conference 2006.*

Bisio, I., Agneessens, A., Lavagetto, F., & Marchese, M. (2010). Design and implementation of smartphone applications for speaker count and gender recognition. In Giusto, D., Iera, A., Morabito, G., & Atzori, L. (Eds.), *The Internet of things*. New York, NY: Springer Science.

Bose, A., & Foh, C. H. (2007). A practical path loss model for indoor Wi-Fi positioning enhancement. In *Proc. International Conference on Information, Communications & Signal Processing (ICICS)*.

de Cheveignè, A., & Kawahar, H. (2002). A fundamental frequency estimator for speech and music. *The Journal of the Acoustical Society of America, 111*(4). doi:10.1121/1.1458024

Dey, A. K., & Abowd, G. D. (2000). Towards a better understanding of context and context awareness. In *The What, Who, Where, When, Why and How of Context-Awareness Workshop at the Conference on Human Factors in Computing Systems (CHI)*.

Doets, P. J. O., Gisbert, M., & Lagendijk, R. L. (2006). On the comparison of audio fingerprints for extracting quality parameters of compressed audio. *Security, steganography, and watermarking of multimedia contents VII, Proceedings of the SPIE*.

Freescale Semiconductor, Inc. (2008). *Mobile extreme convergence: A streamlined architecture to deliver mass-market converged mobile devices*. White Paper of Freescale Semiconductor, Rev. 5.

Gu, Y., Lo, A., & Niemegeers, I. (2009). A survey of indoor positioning systems for wireless personal networks. *IEEE Communications Surveys & Tutorials, 11*(1).

Haitsma, J., & Kalker, T. (2002). A highly robust audio fingerprinting system. In *Proceedings of the International Symposium on Music Information Retrieval, Paris, France*.

Iyer, A. N., Ofoegbu, U. O., Yantorno, R. E., & Smolenski, B. Y. (2006). Generic modeling applied to speaker count. In *Proceedings IEEE, International Symposium On Intelligent Signal Processing and Communication Systems, ISPACS'06*.

Ladd, A. M., Bekris, K. E., Rudys, A., Marceau, G., Kavraki, L. E., & Dan, S. (2002). *Robotics-based location sensing using wireless ethernet*. Eighth ACM Int. Conf. on Mobile Computing & Networking (MOBICOM) (pp. 227-238).

Lee, Y., Mosley, A., Wang, P. T., & Broadway, J. (2006). *Audio fingerprinting from ELEC 301 projects*. Retrieved from http://cnx.org/content/m14231

Leijdekkers, P., Gay, V., & Lawrence, E. (2007). *Smart homecare system for health tele-monitoring*. In ICDS '07, First International Conference on the Digital Society.

Ling, C. X., & Yan, R. J. (2003). Decision tree with better ranking. In *Proceedings of the International Conference on Machine Learning (ICML2003)*.

Marengo, M., Salis, N., & Valla, M. (2007). Context awareness: Servizi mobili su misura. *Telecom Italia S.p.A. Technical Newsletter, 16*(1).

Mautz, R. (2009). Overview of current indoor positioning systems. *Geodesy and Cartography, 35*(1), 18–22. doi:10.3846/1392-1541.2009.35.18-22

Miluzzo, E., Lane, N., Fodor, K., Peterson, R., Lu, H., Musolesi, M., et al. Campbell, A. T. (2008). Sensing meets mobile social networks: The design, implementation and evaluation of the CenceMe application. In *Proceedings of the 6th ACM Conference on Embedded Network Sensor Systems* (pp. 337–350).

Musolesi, M., Miluzzo, E., Lane, N. D., Eisenman, S. B., Choudhury, T., & Campbell, A. T. (2008). The second life of a sensor - integrating real-world experience in virtual worlds using mobile phones. In *Proceedings of HotEmNets '08, Charlottesville*.

Peng, W., Ser, W., & Zhang, M. (2001). *Bark scale equalizer design using wrapped filter*. Singapore: Center for Signal Processing Nanyang Technological University.

Perttunen, M., Van Kleek, M., Lassila, O., & Riekki, J. (2009). *An implementation of auditory context recognition for mobile devices*. In Tenth International Conference on Mobile Data Management: Systems, Services and Middleware.

Ryder, J., Longstaff, B., Reddy, S., & Estrin, D. (2009). *Ambulation: A tool for monitoring mobility patterns over time using mobile phones*. Technical Report UC Los Angeles: Center for Embedded Network Sensing.

Simmons, R., & Koenig, S. (1995). *Probabilistic robot navigation in partially observable environments*. In The International Joint Conference on Artificial Intelligence (IJCAI'95) (pp. 1080-1087).

Tapia, E. M., Intille, S. S., Haskell, W., Larson, K., Wright, J., King, A., & Friedman, R. (2007). Real-time recognition of physical activities and their intensities using wireless accelerometers and a heart rate monitor. In *Proceedings of International Symposium on Wearable Computers, IEEE Press* (pp. 37-40).

Toth, N., & Pataki, B. (2008). Classification confidence weighted majority voting using decision tree classifiers. *International Journal of Intelligent Computing and Cybernetics*, *1*(2), 169–192. doi:10.1108/17563780810874708

Wang, Y., Jia, X., & Lee, H. K. (2003). An indoor wireless positioning system based on wireless local area network infrastructure. In *Proceedings 6th International Symposium on Satellite Navigation Technology*.

KEY TERMS AND DEFINITIONS

Smartphones: mobile phone with a significant computational capacity: several available sensors and limited energy.

Context-Aware Services: services provided to users obtained by considering the environment in which the users are and by considering the actions that users are doing.

Digital Signal Processing: theory and methodology to process numerical signals.

Pattern Recognition: theory and methodology to recognize a pattern.

Audio Environment Recognition: methodologies obtained from both signal processing and pattern recognition approaches aimed at individuating the environment based on the audio captured by a microphone (such as the smartphones' microphone).

Speaker Count and Gender Recognition: methodologies obtained from both signal processing and pattern recognition approaches aimed at individuating the number of speakers and the related genders based on the audio captured by a microphone (such as the smartphones' microphone).

Indoor Positioning: methodologies obtained from both signal processing and pattern recognition approaches aimed at individuating the position of users in a given environment (outdoor or indoor) based on radio signals captured by radio interfaces available on a given device (such as the smartphones' Bluetooth and WiFi interfaces).

Activity Recognition: methodologies obtained from both signal processing and pattern recognition approaches aimed at individuating the number type of movement that users are doing based on the accelerometer signals generated by an (such as the smartphones' accelerometer).

Section 2
Frameworks and Applications

Pervasive computing environments have attracted significant research interest and have found increased applicability in commercial settings, attributed to the fact that they provide seamless, customized, and unobtrusive services over heterogeneous infrastructures and devices. Successful deployment of the pervasive computing paradigm is mainly based on the exploitation of the multitude of participating devices and associated data and their integrated presentation to the users in a usable and useful manner. The focal underlying principle of pervasive computing is user-centric provisioning of services and applications that are adaptive to user preferences and monitored conditions, namely the related context information, in order to consistently offer value-added and high-level services.

Chapter 3
Building and Deploying Self-Adaptable Home Applications

Jianqi Yu
Grenoble University, France

Pierre Bourret
Grenoble University, France

Philippe Lalanda
Grenoble University, France

Johann Bourcier
Grenoble University, France

ABSTRACT

This chapter introduces the design of a framework to simplify the development of smart home applications featuring self-adaptable capabilities. Building such applications is a difficult task, as it deals with two main concerns a) application design and development for the business logic part, and b) application evolution management at runtime for open environments. In this chapter, the authors propose a holistic approach for building self-adaptive residential applications. They thus propose an architecture-centric model for defining home application architecture, while capturing its variability. This architecture is then sent to a runtime interpreter which dynamically builds and autonomously manages the application to maintain it within the functional bounds defined by its architecture. The whole process is supported by tools to create the architecture model and its corresponding runtime application. This approach has been validated by the implementation of several smart home applications, which have been tested on a highly evolving environment.

INTRODUCTION

Pervasive computing emphasizes the use of small, intelligent and communicating daily life objects to interact with our surrounding computing infrastructure (Weiser, 1991). This new interactive computing paradigm tends to change user experience, especially since new electronic devices progressively blend into our common living environment. This is particularly true in

DOI: 10.4018/978-1-60960-611-4.ch003

our homes where new appliances such as digital photo frames aim to be as much decorative as they are powerful. Electronic devices become less and less perceivable by human beings. To fulfill the vision of a pervasive world, electronic devices must have the ability to communicate and integrate advanced computing features.

Research efforts have, for now, mainly focused on building hardware compatible with the vision of a pervasive world. Consequently, plenty of devices enabling part of this vision are already commercialized, whereas very few interesting applications take advantage of this new computing infrastructure.

Indeed, the complexity of building software exploiting this type of hardware infrastructure is often underestimated. Usual software engineering technologies and tools are not suitable, because several software engineering challenges remain to be solved. Specifically, the high degree of dynamism, distribution, heterogeneity and autonomy of electronic devices raises major concerns when building such applications. The very unpredictable nature of the execution environment brings issues relative to the production of applications capable of handling this uncertainty. The problem tackled in this chapter is the complexity of building smart home applications and particularly applications featuring self-management properties to meet the environment evolution requirements.

In our previous work (Escoffier, 2008), we devised a runtime infrastructure to support smart home applications. This architecture argues for the use of home gateways hosting residential applications following the service-oriented computing (SOC) paradigm (Papazoglou, 2003). The SOC paradigm is based on three major actors: service providers, service consumers and one or more service trader. A service consumer connects to a service provider by asking the trader for a suitable provider. In this work, we consider an approach called Dynamic Service-Oriented Computing, which refers to a subpart of this programming paradigm capable of handling the dynamic appearance and disappearance of service providers available to the consumer, as presented in (Escoffier, 2007). Due to several inherent characteristics, such as technology neutrality, loose coupling, location transparency and dynamics, it is commonly accepted that SOC provides a suitable paradigm to build pervasive applications (Escoffier, 2008).

Nonetheless, while this smart home platform supported the execution of residential applications, it lacked the basic functionalities for designing self-adaptive applications. We therefore propose a model capturing the architectural boundaries of a service-based application. This architecture model is interpreted at a runtime platform to create a running application, which is able to autonomously adapt to contextual changes.

This work follows a particular trend in the autonomic computing domain where the architecture of an application is used as a management policy or strategy (Garlan, 2004; Sicard, 2008) to autonomously adapt the application at runtime. However, current approaches fall short in their ability to handle the application variability. They often propose low level abstraction models to perform application design. On the contrary, the emerging approaches of dynamic software product lines (DSPL) are seeking to use the domain-specific business notion for self-adaptive application design. As a result, the abstraction level of application conception is increased (Hallsteinsen, 2008). At the same time, the adaptive reactions of an application at runtime have no longer aimed at a general or technical purpose, while adapting to changes in accordance with a business-specific goal. In addition, the approaches of dynamic software product lines are supposed to foresee the variations for designed applications as much as possible so as to cope with the adaptation concern. However, very few runtime platforms of DSPL can really support dynamic application execution and evolution.

Our proposition is thus to overcome these limitations by reconciling the dynamic software product line approach and autonomic computing in the context of producing service-based smart home applications. The main contributions of this work are:

- An architecture model dedicated to service-based application with variability composed of:
  1. Service specifications
  2. Links between service specifications
  3. Variation points governing the relation between links
- An open-source tool to facilitate application design
- A runtime infrastructure capable of:
  1. Creating the running application from the application architecture model
  2. Autonomously adapting the running application to maintain conformity between the running application and its architecture model

The rest of this chapter is organized as follows. First, a background section presents H-Omega, an existing smart home platform on which we validate our approach, and motivating examples. This is followed by a section on related work on approaches for self-adaptive applications, autonomic computing and dynamic software product lines. We then present our proposition as a three-phase approach. This proposed approach is architecture-centric and developed by using Model Driven Architecture (MDA) technologies. It is composed of two architecture modeling tools (at the domain and application level) and a runtime infrastructure. However, the main goal of this chapter is focused on presenting the runtime infrastructure. Therefore, we briefly present the relative notions of modeling application architecture, while introducing the runtime infrastructure in details. This is then followed by the presentation of the implementation and validation of our approach. This chapter is concluded by pointing out the lessons learned from this work and giving directions for future works.

BACKGROUND

H-Omega

The work presented in this chapter is based on our previous proposition for a home application server named H-Omega (Escoffier, 2008). This application server constitutes the runtime infrastructure for smart home applications.

Figure 1 shows the internal design of the H-Omega residential server. This computing infrastructure is based on the service-oriented computing paradigm, and therefore, home applications are built using the iPOJO (Escoffier, 2007)

Figure 1. Architecture of the H-Omega gateway

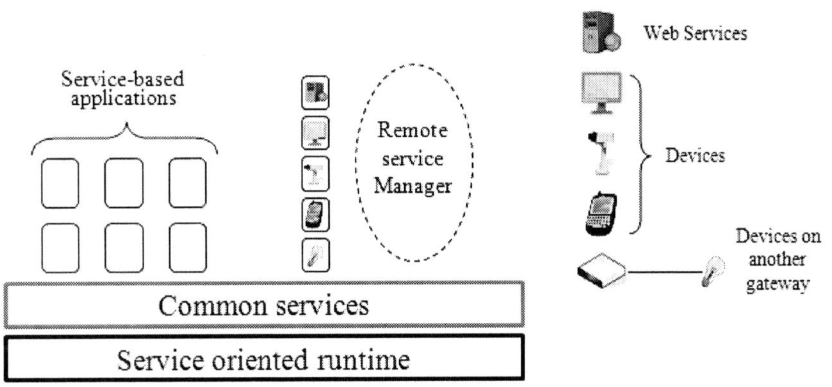

service oriented component model. The services available on the home network are reified as services in the framework by an entity called the remote service manager. These particular services follow the availability of the remote services and take in charge the remote communication. The lifecycle of these proxy services is managed by the remote service manager. More specifically, services offered by UPnP (UPnP Forum, 2008), DPWS (Zeeb, 2007), X10 (Charles, 2005), Bluetooth devices or Web Services (Booth, 2006) are automatically handled by the remote service manager. Application developers can then rely on these services to build their own application without taking care of all the tricky problems of device distribution, heterogeneity and dynamism.

The H-Omega server also provides common services in order to further simplify the development of residential applications. These common services are common, shared functionalities across applications. These provided facilities currently include event communication, scheduling of repetitive tasks, persistence of data and remote administration facilities.

The H-Omega server constitutes an open infrastructure in which service providers can freely deploy and withdraw applications taking advantage of the available devices in the home environment. These applications are remotely managed by the service provider.

Motivating Examples

Our work in this chapter is focused on the development of smart home applications. A set of domestic applications has been implemented based on H-Omega and they provide diverse functionalities, such as offering comfort for daily life, ensuring home security, assisting handicapped or remotely supervising patients at home, or smartly controlling the energy consumption. In this chapter, we present an application the goal of which is to remind people their medical appointments. This appointment reminder makes extensive use of a scheduler service offered by the runtime platform H-Omega. The appointment reminder uses either a speaker or a digital screen with a call bell for showing the appointment details to end-user. Indeed, the two means of communication for showing the appointment information to end-user are alternative. Additionally, some supplementary information, such as, weather forecast, current traffic information or public transport proposition, may be provided to the user, typically by utilizing some Web Services. Normally, this kind of information is not necessary for this type of application, but it is very useful and practical for the end-user in order for her to plan her appointment effectively. In addition, this information may be continuously complemented depending on the available services on the network.

RELATED WORK

Approaches for Self-Adaptive Applications

Self-adaptability will be a basic ability for the future pervasive applications, which normally execute in a highly dynamic environment. Evolution in such dynamic environments may be caused by several different factors, such as environmental conditions, user requirements, technology evolution and market opportunities, as well as resources' availabilities. Due to several inherent dynamic characteristics of the SOC paradigm, service-based applications can be a suitable solution for realizing dynamic and self-adaptive systems.

Actually, self-adaptive applications will have to execute in a constantly evolving environment, while continuously adapting themselves in an automatic manner to react to those changes. In addition, the reconfiguration of the application's behavior or its business logic structure during its execution has to be performed in order to achieve the following dynamic goals (Nitto, 2008), 1) overcoming the mismatches between aggregated services, 2) repairing faults, or 3) reconfiguring the applications in order to better meet their requirements.

Recently, model-driven architecture approaches (Nierstrasz, 2009) have been widely used to facilitate the development of self-adaptive applications. Specifically, application models are used to guide dynamic reconfigurations of an application with respect to its structure or behavior. Andersson et al provided a classification of modeling dimensions for self-adaptive systems (Andersson, 2009). The objective of each modeling dimension is to deal with a particular aspect concerning self-adaptation at runtime. Precisely, this classification has divided the modeling dimensions into four aspects, such as goals, changes, mechanisms and effects. The two former dimensions are considered as factors causing the dynamic changes of the environment. In this respect, the latter dimensions are considered as approaches enabling an application to react correctly with these changes. Moreover, Cheng et al have performed a thorough review of the state-of-the-art to illustrate a synthetic view of existing approaches in software engineering literature regarding self-adaptive systems. They have identified critical challenges and essential views of self-adaptation in (Cheng, 2009), in terms of: modeling dimensions, requirements, engineering and assurances.

While over the past decade we have witnessed significant progress in the manner in which self-adaptive systems are designed, constructed, and deployed, there is still a lack of consensus among researchers and practitioners on some of the fundamental underlying concepts (Cheng, 2009). In particular, these concepts concern mechanisms for reacting to dynamic environmental changes, which are just emerging. Recently, the field of autonomic computing has gained a lot of research attention since due to its several inherent characteristics, such as self-healing, self-protection, self-configuration and self-optimization, it offers a set of mechanisms for dealing with some of the challenges that have been identified for self-adaptive applications.

Autonomic Computing

The autonomic computing term refers to the autonomic nervous system that governs the operation of our body without any conscious recognition or effort on our part (Kephart, 2003). For example, our nervous system regulates our blood pressure, our heartbeat rate and our balance, without involving the conscious part of our brain. An autonomic computing system must therefore respectively allow the user to concentrate on his interests and manage all vital tasks of the lowest level. An autonomic system essentially allows the user to focus on what he wants and not on how to achieve it (Horn, 2001).

One particular trend of autonomic computing consists in providing an architectural model for designing applications, and using this architecture as a reference to create and maintain these applications at runtime. This allows users to concentrate on designing their applications, i.e. building the architectural model, rather than focusing on how to manage these applications. This particular trend is illustrated by two main projects, i.e. Jade (Sicard, 2008) and Rainbow (Garlan, 2004).

Jade is a project developed by the University of Grenoble providing a framework for simplifying the development of autonomic applications. This platform uses an architecture-based approach for the autonomic management of applications. One of the main objectives is to enable autonomic management of legacy applications by encapsulating existing software into components, which comply with a unified administration interface. This project uses a platform based on components called Fractal (Bruneton, 2006). The main benefit of using Fractal's component model is the support of a hierarchic Architecture Description Language (ADL). A particularity of this system is the ability to automatically maintain a knowledge base of the current architecture of the managed system. Thus, autonomic managers benefit from this knowledge and provide self-repair, self-optimization and self-configuration features. The architectural description used by Jade as a basis of the whole autonomic behavior is a fixed ADL formatted representation involving binding and components. The abstraction level of this model is thus relatively low, and the possibility to express variability within applications' architecture is not provided.

Rainbow (Garlan, 2004) is a project developed at Carnegie Mellon University providing self-adapting capabilities to complex systems using an architecture-based approach. This system provides a reusable architecture for the management of adaptation strategies. Rainbow is independent of the execution platform and only relies on a Runtime Manager conforming to a common interface for dynamic reconfiguration of a system. Rainbow developers base the whole reasoning on a model of the current architecture which is kept up-to-date by a set of probes. Rainbow also offers a component that defines an interface for accessing and modifying the application architecture. Thus, Rainbow users have the possibility to build their own autonomic managers based on this architecture. The architecture model used by Rainbow is generic and provides an abstraction from the real architectural style used by the application. Despite this abstraction, this architecture limits the expression of acceptable variability within an application. Indeed, the provided architectural style augments the classical architecture description languages with the concept of operators specifying authorized evolutions of the basic architecture. Nonetheless these evolutions do not really specify the application variability and remain expressed in terms of concrete components and bindings between these components.

The architectural model provided by both approaches limits the flexibility of produced applications, by limiting the variability expression and providing a low abstraction level. These two approaches are thus unsuitable for the production of smart home applications, as the latter require a higher level of flexibility in their architectural description.

Traditional Software Product Lines

Software product lines (SPLs) engineering (Clements, 2001) aims at developing families of similar software systems, instead of integrated software systems satisfying different user requirements. This development paradigm emphasizes reuse of common software assets in a specific domain in order to achieve common development goals, such as shorter time-to market, low costs, and higher quality. The SPLs paradigm has identified two development processes: domain engineering and application engineering. Domain engineering aims to explore commonalities among products in a specific domain, while managing variability among mass-products in a systematic way. These software artifacts, which may be either abstract or concrete, are considered as core assets for re-use, such as reference architectures, production plans and implemented components. Application engineering aims to produce specific products satisfying particular needs by reusing the core assets. A fundamental principle of SPLs is variability management, which allows delaying design decisions concerning variation points as late as possible for building the individual products. A key notion of variability management is binding time, namely when design decisions should be taken for binding variants to the points. Variability management mechanisms are always seeking to bind variation points as late as possible to enable the final product to be quite flexible. However, traditional SPLs approaches typically force the binding time before runtime execution of an application.

Dynamic Software Product Lines

Modern computing and network-based environments are demanding for a higher degree of adaptability for their software systems. For example, applications in the smart home domain are becoming increasingly complex with emerging smart sensors, devices and very large sets of diverse end-user requirements. In addition, various dynamic and uncontrolled evolutions in open environments (involving user needs and available resources) contribute to the complexity of development. Finally, the development of user interface coping with the evolution of software and hardware availability adds to the complexity of development.

The emerging Dynamic Software Product Lines (DSPLs) approach based on SPLs is seeking to produce software capable of adapting to fluctuations in user needs and evolving resource constraints (Hallsteinsen, 2006). The main purpose is to take design decisions regarding variation parts of a specific product or application at runtime, while reconfiguring it for adapting to context change impacting its execution. The key difference compared to traditional SPLs is actually the binding time of variation points. DSPLs aims at binding variation points at runtime, initially when software is launched to adapt to the current environment, but also during the execution to adapt to changes in the environment (Hallsteinsen, 2006). In addition, DSPLs approaches are focused on a single adaptive product instead of considering variability among a set of family products.

As a result, the DSPLs approaches deal with more problems than statically configuring individual products, such as (Lee, 2006):

- Monitoring the current situation (i.e. the operational context) of a product,
- Validating a reconfiguration request considering impacts of changes and available resources,
- Determining strategies to handle currently active services during configuration,
- Performing dynamic configuration while maintaining system integrity.

Various approaches have been proposed in the DSPLs engineering domain for developing adaptive software products. The common point of these approaches is to use variability management technologies for dynamically adapting a specific product to context changes at runtime.

In particular, two proposed approaches have attracted our attention. First, feature modeling (Lee, 2006) has been used to represent common and variable features in the form of a feature graph. This graph aims at showing an overview of relationship among features. The unbound variation features in such graph are used to present configurable parts for dynamic product-specific configuration. The dynamic configuration involves dynamic addition, deletion, or modification of individual product features. Tools supporting such approaches are for now limited to prototypes.

Since the initial purpose of feature-oriented modeling is to specify the requirements of software systems, the feature graph with variability has to foresee all reusable features and their relationships. The main challenges are thus to deal with the evolution of dynamically adaptive systems, such as a newly available feature, unanticipated events causing context change, etc.

On the other hand, several propositions of variability modeling (Hallsteinsen, 2006) can be considered as architecture-centric approaches. These approaches build application architectures consisting of the two following parts:

- Common part: the basis of the application providing main functionalities.
- Variable part: the optional or alternative elements for constructing the application.

In fact, the variable parts are integrated within the common architecture. Such parts may remind to be bound until runtime, while considering services' availability on the runtime platform. Hence, such architecture provides a high-level abstraction for dynamically configuring individual products and adapting to context changes. This architecture corresponds to an extension of individual product architectures in traditional SPLs approaches. These architecture-centric approaches provide a flexible and adaptable structural specification for service-based applications at a high-level of abstraction within a domain-specific boundary.

Technical Challenges for Service-Based Application Development

Service-based applications are normally characterized by their dynamicity, heterogeneity and flexibility. The main challenges for developing this kind of applications are the following:

- **Dynamism management.** The dynamism is an important characteristic of service-based applications. A service can dynamically appear or disappear on the network without any notice beforehand. The integration of multiple technologies in a dynamic environment brings extra work, since it has to verify the availability of heterogeneous services on the network. This is not a simple task. The dynamism can be categorized into two aspects. The first aspect concerns runtime context evolutions, such as services' availability. The second aspect concerns user requirements which can be dynamically adjusted by users.
- **Heterogeneity management.** Service-based applications generally run in distributed and heterogeneous environments. In order to build an application, we seek to use all services satisfying the compositional constraints, regardless of distance or implementation technology. The distribution factor is always a challenging problem when managing communications. Heterogeneity causes the concern of mastering different SOC implementation technologies, which are often quite specific for service discovery and invocation.
- **Service-based application correctness management**. It is very difficult to ensure and verify that the configuration of a service-based application is always conforming to the application architecture with variability definition, while correctly adapting to context changes. Most current approaches are focused on verifying syntactic correctness of service-based applications. The semantic correctness or planned variations in service-based applications are not discussed here, but the interested reader is referred to (Olumofin, 2007) for an in-depth analysis. Moreover, the verifica-

Figure 2. Application for reminding medical appointments

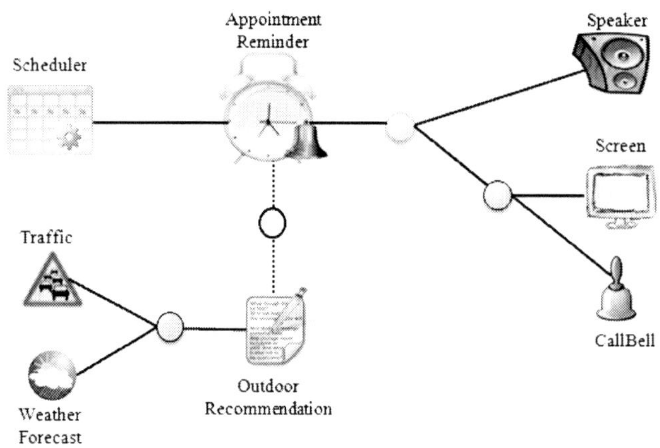

tion of correctness becomes extremely intractable while integrating heterogeneous technologies.

A THREE-PHASE APPROACH FOR SERVICE-BASED APPLICATION DEVELOPMENT

Our work is dedicated to reconciling the two reuse approaches – SOC and SPLs – by proposing a three-phase approach for service-based application development. The three phases are:

1. **Defining a specific domain of service-based applications**. The goal of this first phase is to define a reference architecture and a set of reusable services, as a set of abstract and reusable core assets in the context of the SPLs paradigm, in the specific domain. Services may be implemented in accordance with different technologies and may bring about several versions depending on the runtime platform or the provided functionality. These services allow abstracting a precise implementation as a formalized specification, which is independent of any technology or communication mechanism. A product line architecture (called *reference architecture*) can be seen as a blueprint to guide the assembly of services at an abstract level while guaranteeing its correctness. The reference architecture consists of service specifications, service assembly rules and variability in various forms, for service-based application building. The domain-specific reference architecture aims at providing a common architectural structure, which can describe the main business logic of the targeted domain, for all service-based applications in the targeted domain. The first development phase is similar to the domain engineering phase of the SPLs paradigm but using notions based on the SOC paradigm.
2. **Defining the application architecture.** The objective of this second phase is to define an application architecture to answer a particular need. This architecture, according to the reference architecture is composed of service specifications or implementations. This means that some services are clearly identified by a specific technology version, while others remain abstract specifications independent of any implementation. The definition of variations in the application architecture may be similar to the reference architecture. The application architecture plays the role of explicitly planning and defining architectural variations. These variations enable executing an application derived from its architecture to adapt to expected changes or different customer needs. This phase can be compared to the application engineering phase of the SPLs paradigm. It is completed with the deployment of application architecture on a service-oriented runtime platform.
3. **Executing the application**. The goal of this phase is to execute the application in accordance with its architecture. Design decisions have to be taken at all variation points in the application architecture. In particular, service instances are selected or created during runtime. The application architecture is used to guide the assembly of service-based application. Therefore, all configurations of the executing application must conform to its application architecture. In this chapter, the targeted platform of service-based applications is implemented on top of OSGi/iPOJO, which is extended with facilities for discovering and reifying heterogeneous services (UPnP and WS). iPOJO is used as the pivot technology for our targeted platform. In others words, the integration of heterogeneous services technologies is carried out by our runtime platform.

Our proposed three-phase approach is summarized by the schema illustrated in Figure 3.

This three-phase approach is supported by facilities to make it practically applicable. Particularly, we have developed three tools dedicated to perform each of the phases mentioned above. The first tool allows defining reusable core assets in the form of services and the reference architecture toward a specific domain. The second tool allows defining the application architecture by refining the reference architecture. This tool is automatically derived from abstract artifacts built during the first phase. More precisely, from the definition of domain-specific abstract artifacts, the second development tool is generated automatically by means of a model transformation. Finally, the third tool takes the form of the runtime infrastructure on top of our targeted runtime platform. This tool can handle services arrival and departure on the runtime platform, while taking into account various technologies (in our case, iPOJO, UPnP, and WS). At the end, it should be able to select appropriate services in accordance with the application architecture and build connections between services, which could be heterogeneous or not.

Designing Smart Home Applications

As we presented above, the application architecture design is a challenging task for architects or technicians. We propose an architecture model integrating variability management. A service is considered as the fundamental element to build such architecture. However, the service may be presented in three different forms, namely service specification, service implementation and service instance. Figure 4 illustrates their relationship.

Service specification aims at describing the provided and required functions of services and a set of featuring properties. This specification is independent of any given implementation technology, such as UPnP, DPWS or Web Services. It retains the major features of the service orientation

Figure 3. Proposed three-phase approach

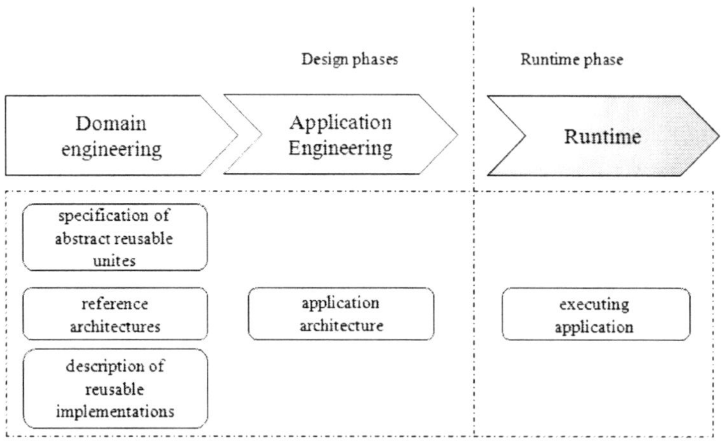

Figure 4. Service specification, implementation and instance

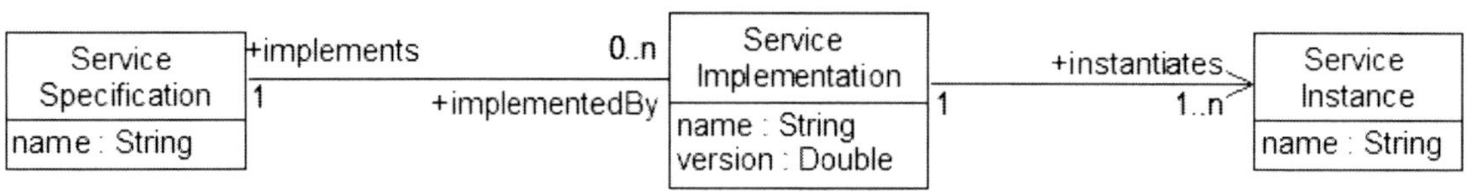

and ignores low-level technological aspects. In our model, an abstract service is defined in the following terms:

- Functional interfaces specify the functionalities provided by services. An interface can define a set of operations.
- Properties, identified by their names and types, can be divided into three categories:
    1. Service properties define static service attributes that cannot be modified when specifying an abstract service composition (e.g. message format property – text or multimedia).
    2. Configurable properties represent dynamic attributes used to configure abstract services during the customized service composition process (e.g. destination of messages sent).
    3. Quality properties define static or dynamic attributes regarding non-functional aspects of service instances, such as security or logging properties.

Service implementation aims at describing an implementation of a service specification in a given service technology. A service implementation can be realized using any service technology such as iPOJO, OSGi, Web Services, UPnP or DPWS. However, in our approach, all service implementations different from iPOJO are realized by means of proxies invoking operations provided by the real service implementation. Thus, developers manage only one implementation model. Several service implementations can be made available for a single service specification. A clear separation has to be maintained between service specification and their implementations, which can subsequently change over time.

Service instance corresponds to a particular configuration of a service implementation. The factory of a service implementation is used to instantiate service instances.

A service specification may have different service implementations. These implementations may differ in their non-functional properties, their version, implemented technologies, etc. Service implementation also enables the creation of multiple instances that can be characterized by different initial configurations.

The architecture plays a leading role for resolving the adaptability of service-based applications. It has to represent architectural characteristics which are essential for all application configurations at runtime. At the same time, it must have adequate flexibility in order to plan variation parts for expected changes of context, thus enabling dynamic adaptation at runtime. Therefore, integration of variability management within an architecture is an effective way, which allows predicting and planning variations during the design phase for domain-specific application development. In this respect, the proposed architecture model can guide architects in defining service bindings and their properties, for building customized applications in the second phase. It can also assist developers in making good design decisions for application creation. For instance, it can prevent the conflict definition about dependencies between services in an application architecture. Finally, it enables to delay design decisions by retaining unbound variation points in the application architecture.

The architecture model (illustrated in Figure 5) is composed of the service specification, the connectors (called ServiceBinding) between services, as well as the variation points. It is expressed exclusively in terms of service-oriented concepts. A Service Binding is identified by a name and a set of properties. Bidirectional properties define data transfer direction. Min(Max)Cardinality properties are used to specify the interval of the number of instances to be bound on a service binding. The dynamic property expresses a design decision that is delayed until runtime. The dynamic property assigned a value of true indicates that one of the two services bound via the Service Binding may bind dynamically one or several instances of the other service at runtime.

We integrate the variability management within the architecture by using variation points defined in traditional SPLs approaches. A variation point identifies part of the architecture where architectural decisions are left open. For instance, a variation point can express the fact that a ServiceA may be connected to two services among ServiceB, ServiceC, and ServiceD, which are variants attached to this variation point. A choice will have to be made at runtime. According to our meta-model, a binding can be mandatory (and), alternative (xor), multiple (or) or optional. The mandatory, alternative, multiple bindings are specified as properties of a variation point, while the optional binding as a property specified through the cardinality (0..n). We defined two types of variation points:

- **PrimitiveVariationPoint** is used to define possible variations from one or several other service bindings between a service specification and its related dependencies. These dependencies are considered as choices associated with this variation point.
- **AdvancedVariationPoint** is used to define possible variations among either one or several variation points, or from one or more service bindings and one or several variation points. It means that this type of variation point describes variations not only on service bindings but also on variation points defined in both types. This leads to a structure of dependency between variation points and service bindings.

Binding a variation point with a selected variant at a moment may impose certain dependencies and constraints on other variation points and variants, e.g. a sequence of variation points with semantic dependencies. For example, a variant selection at one variation point may depend on the result of another design decision at another variation point. In some cases, binding one variant at a variation point may require or exclude a specific variant selection at the same or another variation point. Such dependency is described via the two

Figure 5. The meta-model of the architecture-integrated variability management mechanism

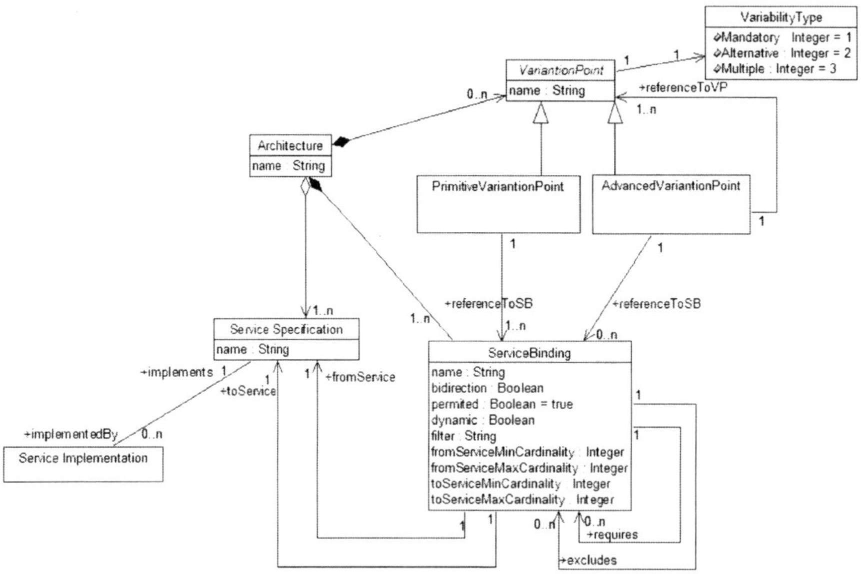

references *requires* and *excludes* surrounding **Service Binding**.

The architecture's flexibility is provided not only by topologic variation points defined above, but also by the notions of service specifications. Each mechanism actually provides different types of variability. We detail the following different types of variability within the architecture, besides the topologic variation points:

- **Service specification** brings about choices among service implementations during the second phase of our proposed approach or at runtime. This may lead to different behaviors, which are adapted to the actual context (in terms of expressed user needs and environment state), while following the expected functionalities;
- **Service implementation** brings about choices among service instances at runtime, based on the properties configured in advance. This allows to adapt dynamically to the current context in terms of service availability;
- **Cardinality definition in service binding** allows introducing explicitly the constraint in terms of the number of service instances, which can be connected dynamically at runtime.

Runtime Infrastructure

The runtime phase aims at automatically creating and managing a service-based application from the model of its architecture. A service-based application consists of appropriate service instances available on the network, and service connections. A concrete architecture consists of service instances corresponding to service specifications, which are used by the application architecture defined during application engineering.

Our runtime infrastructure consists of an interpretation engine and a repository of heterogeneous services including a runtime model, which presents the platform state at runtime. Figure 6 illustrates an overview of this runtime infrastructure.

The repository of heterogeneous services is in charge of monitoring available services on the network, while inspecting the state of runtime platform. All relevant information is stored in the runtime model.

The interpretation engine is a key element allowing the creation and management of executing applications. The interpretation engine receives

Figure 6. Overview of the runtime infrastructure

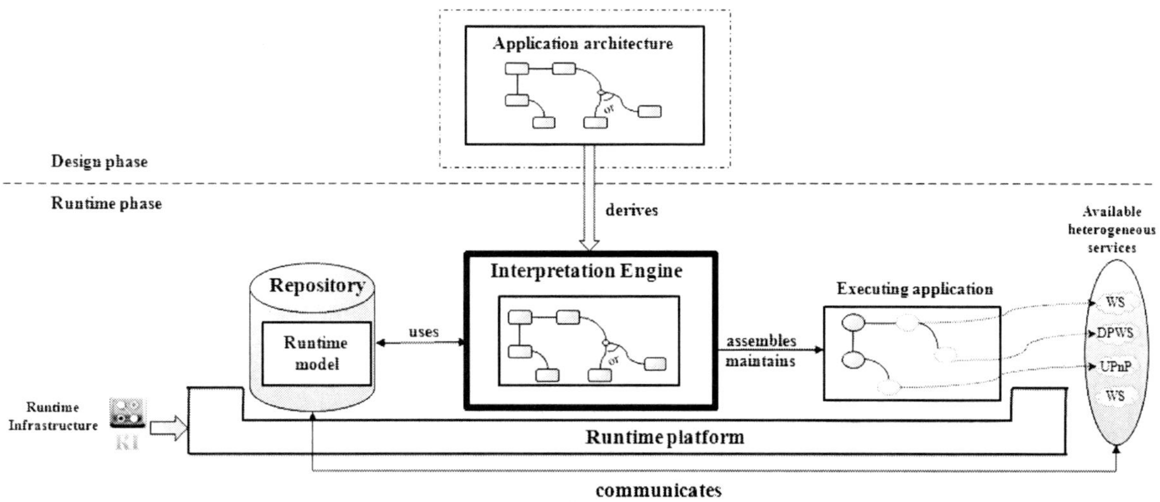

the application architecture, and uses the repository of heterogeneous services with the execution model. This interpretation engine automatically manages the executing application according to the following policies: maximize the overall availability of the application and economize resources of the runtime platform. It selects, creates and assembles service instances according to the application architecture received, while conforming to this policy.

Functionalities of Runtime Infrastructure

In order to fulfill its role, the runtime infrastructure has to be able to:

1. discover services on the network and manage the heterogeneity among services, for instance, the interaction between a Web Service and a service provided by a UPnP device;
2. monitor the current state of the target runtime platform involving the state of executing applications and available services on the network;
3. eliminate all of the variations in the application architecture so as to produce the concrete application architecture at runtime. For instance, the runtime infrastructure can make design decisions at topological variation points in the application architecture. It can also determine which service implementation should be used corresponding to a particular service specification within the application logic architecture. These variation points have to be bound in accordance with the previously defined policies for runtime platform management.
4. build executing applications by dynamically assembling selected service instances in accordance with their specifications within the application architecture;
5. manage the evolution of application performance, while taking into account the impacts of changes caused by the availability of services or resources. This phase is realized by respecting the application architecture and policy management, which can guarantee and verify the correctness of executing an application in accordance with its architecture, as defined in the design phase.

Repository of Heterogeneous Services

The objective of the repository of heterogeneous services is to deal with the dynamism and the heterogeneity of service-oriented architectures. This repository is implemented as a mediator allowing communication among heterogeneous services and services on the runtime platform. In fact, it takes charge of the first two functionalities presented in the previous section.

In our case, the targeted runtime platform is implemented by using the iPOJO platform on top of an OSGi middleware. As a result, all service implementations are developed in accordance with the key technology iPOJO or realized as a proxy to enable access to the external technology. Therefore, the integration of heterogeneous technologies such as UPnP, Web Services and DPWS is realized through the use of proxies.

The repository of heterogeneous services provides several functionalities:

- Discovering available iPOJO services on the runtime platform
- Importing dynamic heterogeneous services (implemented in accordance with another technology). Firstly, the repository has to discover heterogeneous services and then it has to import or automatically generate the specific proxy.
- Storing service implementation deployed on the runtime platform, including iPOJO services implementations and heterogeneous service proxies, into the runtime model. These service implementations are used to create service instances at runtime following the application architecture.

- Storing all service instances connected to the network in the runtime model
- Updating the runtime model and notifying the interpretation engine about changes in the availability of service instances.

Runtime Model

The runtime model within the repository of heterogeneous services is used to store the state of runtime platform. It provides the required information for the interpretation engine. It is composed of the three following parts:

- the list of available service instances on the network
- the list of deployed service implementations on the target runtime platform
- the list of historical architectural configurations of executing applications

The list of available service instances aims at keeping track of service instances on the platform. These service instances are considered as basic elements to build the application at runtime.

The list of deployed service implementations aims at storing service implementations running on the platform. A service implementation may be considered as a factory, which is used by the interpretation engine in order to create its service instances when needed.

The list of historical states of executing applications is designed to store all states of executing applications since their creation. This kind of information is used during the selection of available service instances for building and managing an application in accordance with its previous state. At any time, the state of an executing application can be represented by an architectural snapshot of this application, which must conform to its application architecture. The different snapshots are taken when an event causes modification on the configuration of the running application. When such an event occurs, the new configuration is stored together with the event causing the change and the time that this happened. This information assists the interpretation engine in selecting high quality service during the creation or configuration of the executing application.

Integration of Multiple Service-Oriented Architecture Technologies

As we have previously introduced two different types of service implementations, we have developed a mechanism for integrating multiple technologies based on the "proxy" (Gamma, 18) design pattern. The process for integrating various heterogeneous technologies is slightly different, but the methodology is overall similar. We illustrate the global architecture for the mechanism of multiple technologies integration in Figure 7.

The repository of heterogeneous services uses a technical mediation layer to make the heterogeneity transparent and to reduce the complexity of service selection. In the following sections of this chapter, an external service corresponds to a heterogeneous service or a service provided by a device in a different technology than the one used by our runtime infrastructure.

This technical mediation layer allows firstly discovering, and then notifying on the availability of external services in a dynamic way. It also allows transforming the description of operations of external services (usually in the form of XML files) into Java interfaces. The result of this operation depends strongly on the considered technology and the technical mediation layer responsible for automatic translation. Moreover, the technical mediation layer is extensible in order to provide the necessary flexibility for future integration of other technologies.

In order to enable iPOJO services to collaborate with external services, the repository of heterogeneous services utilizes the technical mediation layer to achieve the following six activities:

Figure 7. The architecture for integrating various service technologies

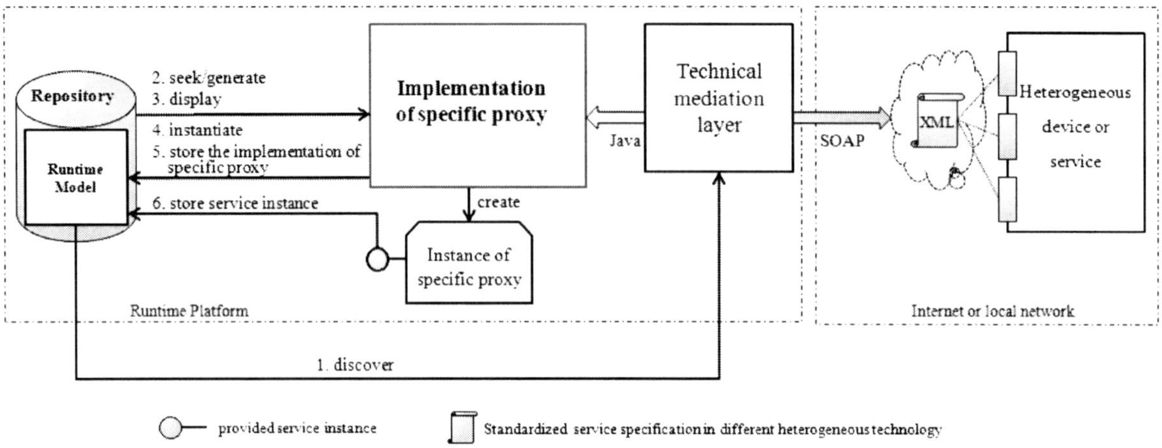

1. discover the availability of external services and notify on the state of these executing services on the network;
2. seek/generate a suitable proxy for invoking the discovered external service. The specific proxies may be previously implemented to invoke operations of external services, according to specific needs. Those specific proxy implementations must be stored in a database (which can be dedicated to a particular technology) local or remote. In the case where no corresponding proxy is available, a specific proxy can be generated automatically from the specification of the external service. For instance, the specification in WSDL for Web Services, is recognized by the technical mediation layer during the service discovery and may generate a specific proxy toward this specification;
3. display the location of the suitable proxy service corresponding to an external service discovered on the targeted runtime platform;
4. instantiate the specific proxy implementation to create an instance of the proxy configured to cooperate with the corresponding external service;
5. store the implementation of a specific service proxy in the runtime model;
6. store service instances of specific proxies within the runtime model.

Interpretation Engine

The interpretation engine plays a key role within the runtime infrastructure. Its objectives are firstly to create an executing application depending on its application architecture, while also considering the current state of the targeted runtime platform by using the repository of heterogeneous services. On the other hand, it must dynamically manage the evolution of the executing application, in accordance with the dynamic context and its application architecture. Both tasks are based on the definition of variations within the application architecture to delay design decisions until runtime.

As soon as all design decisions are taken by the interpretation engine, the corresponded executing application will be built by assembling a set of selected service instances. This selection of appropriated service instances follows a selection strategy. The availability of services used by the executing application is susceptible to change over time. (Similarly, the availability of resources can also change over time.) In order to deal with these dynamic changes, the interpretation engine must take design decisions on variation locations

Figure 8. The application architecture for reminding an appointment with a specialist or a doctor

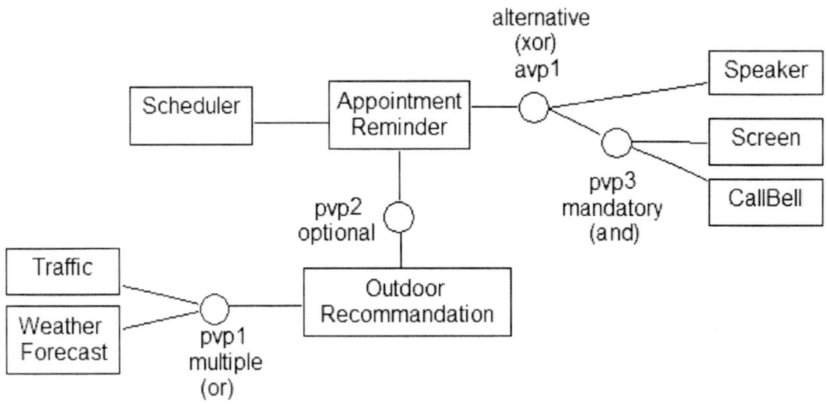

within the application architecture by constantly reapplying the service selection strategy.

The selection strategy of services complies with the following principles:

- maximizing the availability of services composing the executing application,
- economizing resources on the runtime platform.

In fact, the interpretation engine selects the appropriate services among all available service instances on the network or services implementations to create service instances.

To illustrate the concrete activities of the developed interpretation engine, we use the example application that was earlier detailed (see Figure 2) concerning the reminding of medical appointments. Figure 8 shows the architecture of this application.

Creation of Executing Application

The interpretation engine creates the executing application according to the application architecture, while taking into account the state of the targeted runtime platform. In particular, the interpretation engine carries out the selection strategy of services based on the application architecture. The selection of appropriate service instances uses the runtime model. It also generates "glue code" when needed to configure specific service instances. For example, the interpretation engine may generate the code for logging some operations of a particular service instance. Finally, the interpretation engine assembles selected service instances to build the application.

We specify the service selection strategy considering the various type of variability within the application architecture:

- Variations caused by a service implementation. These variations correspond to different configurations for the instantiation of the same implementation. Therefore, when multiple instances of the same service implementation exist, the interpretation engine must make a selection. The implemented strategy for this selection takes into account some characteristics of these instances, such as stability (disconnection rate), reliability (failure rate), frequency and usability of a service instance (users' feedback). In particular, the strategy carried out by the interpretation engine aims at promoting the choice of local iPOJO services compared with other heterogeneous services to increase the reliability of the resulting application at runtime.

- Variations caused by a service specification. These variations correspond to different service implementations for the development of the same service specification. These implementations differ in implemented versions, concrete service technology implemented, non-functional properties and communication mode. The selection strategy favours the selection of service implementations that already have available instances, as well as the implementations corresponding to the latest versions. This strategy is implemented as follows:
    1. Firstly, we observe the available service implementations on the runtime platform as stored in the runtime model.
    2. Secondly, the interpretation engine selects the service implementation with the most appropriate version, which can be compatible with all its dependencies in the application architecture. If several service implementations satisfy the criteria associated with those dependences, the interpretation engine favours the selection of service implementation with the latest version.
    3. Thirdly, if the selected service implementation does not have any available instance on the runtime platform, the interpretation engine should perform the instantiation of this implementation. When the selected service implementation has already available service instances, the interpretation engine can carry out the selection strategy presented above.
    4. Finally, when no service implementation is consistent with the criteria mentioned above, the interpretation engine fails and sends a warning message to the technician who is in charge of installing the application architecture.
- Variations caused by topological variation point defined in the application architecture. This type of variability is represented by the following two concepts of the meta-model of our architecture: *PrimitiveVariationPoint* and *AdvancedVariationPoint*. Both concepts define variations among service specification connections or/and variation points. The interpretation engine must choose the best candidates associated with each variation point among service specifications, according to the variability logic defined as *mandatory, alternative, multiple and optional*. The selection strategy favors the selection of service specifications already having one or more available service implementations. This strategy is implemented as follows:
    1. Firstly, we inspect service implementations corresponding to those abstract specifications of service, which are related to the description of variation points due to the execution model;
    2. Then, the interpretation engine implements the strategy defined in the paragraph above to select service instances so as to select service instances corresponding to selected service implementations. Here, we clarify the two cases below:
- When no service implementation implements the service specifications, the interpretation engine fails, and sends a warning message to developer or technician, who is in charge of installing the application architecture.
- When the strategy cannot differentiate among available service instances according to criteria defined previously, the interpretation engine makes an arbitrary choice.

In our example, at the variation point "avp1" in the presented application architecture with the defined logic "alternative", the service instances, such as "Screen", "CallBell" and "Speaker", are simultaneously available on the network. In this case, the interpretation engine may choose the service instance of "Speaker" at variation point "avp1". It can also choose the service instances "Screen" and "CallBell" at the same time, in order to provide the same functionality. The interpretation engine will do this choice in an arbitrary way. Indeed, the expression of selection criteria can be complex and is beyond the scope of our proposal.

Management of Executing Application Evolution During Runtime

The management of application evolution aims at enabling the application to run continuously, while taking into account the impacts of changes caused by the availability of services and resources. Hence, the interpretation engine has to maintain service-based applications to adapt to those anticipated changes in the dynamic environment.

As mentioned previously, several events may influence service availability, such as intermittent service connectivity, failure of service connection and new installation of services. It should be noted that resources might be considered as services in this section. These changes on the runtime platform are monitored and stored by the repository of heterogeneous services using the runtime model. In addition, the repository of heterogeneous services takes charge of notifying the interpretation engine. The interpretation engine deals with two types of events:

- **The disappearance of a service instance** involved in the running application, e.g. the "WeatherForecast" service provided by BBC disconnected from the Internet. The interpretation engine is essential to find another available service instance, for instance, a "WeatherForecast" service available from CNN can be bounded by reapplying the service selection strategy studied in the previous section. This newly available service instance "WeatherForecast" should be able to supply the full functionality provided by the disappeared service instance. Subsequently, the interpretation engine carries out the mechanism for managing the lifecycle of service instances to enable all dependencies of this added service instance, while disabling dependencies pointing at the disappeared service instance.
- **The appearance of a service instance** answering to a part of application functionality at runtime; for example, a service instance that was disconnected reappears on the network. The interpretation engine may adapt the executing application in order to improve the quality of this application. In our example, the service "OutdoorRecommendation" is an optional service for the purpose of reminding appointments with specialists or doctors. Initially, this service is available to provide an extra service on top of the reminder of appointments with specialists or doctors. It can provide additional information, such as the weather and the current state of traffic, so as to best plan the visit to the doctor. From these different kinds of information, this application may give some useful information to travel, such as how to choose the faster route and means of transport, take the umbrella, etc. When the service is disconnected from the network, it means that the "OutdoorRecommendation" functionality is no longer available on the network. As a result, the application shows to the user only the destination address and the scheduled time for his medical appointment. Once the service "OutdoorRecommendation" reconnects to the network, the interpretation engine

can interpret the evolution of the executing application in order to rejoin this service, "OutdoorRecommendation". This evolution for the executing application is performed by taking the previous configuration from the historical statements of this application within the runtime model on the runtime infrastructure. In this case, the interpretation engine can skip the step of service selection to directly cope with the evolution of the service-based application by retrieving a previous architecture configured for the executing application. This evolution allows the executing application to adapt to changes by coming back to a previous state recorded in the history of the service-based application.

EVALUATION

To evaluate our approach, we developed a prototype of the reminding medical appointments application, using the proposed architecture model to define the architecture shown in Figure 8. The main purposes of this evaluation are to demonstrate that the implemented runtime infrastructure is working correctly, while the execution of this prototype does not introduce additional impacts on the performance of service-based application execution.

We describe a scenario in this section to illustrate how the runtime infrastructure configures this application according to its architecture for dynamic adaptation. These dynamic configurations are caused by successive events of context changes. In the scenario, we discuss two types of events causing the change about service availability, namely "appear" and "disappear". In additions, the performance of the runtime infrastructure is illustrated via a curve of CPU consumption of the framework as a whole in Figure 9. We tested this prototype and the application scenario described hereafter on a laptop computer with a 1.73GHz CPU, 1.5Gb of RAM and a wired access to the Internet. Figure 9 shows the variations of the runtime infrastructure's CPU consumption during the progress of the scenario. Its x-axis and y-axis respectively represent the execution time (in minutes and seconds) and the relative CPU consumption (%).The instants of the application architecture bootstrap and of the other cases of the scenario are pointed out by numbered arrows on the x-axis. The circled numbers on the curve represent the reactions of the CPU consumption

Figure 9. CPU consumption of runtime infrastructure execution

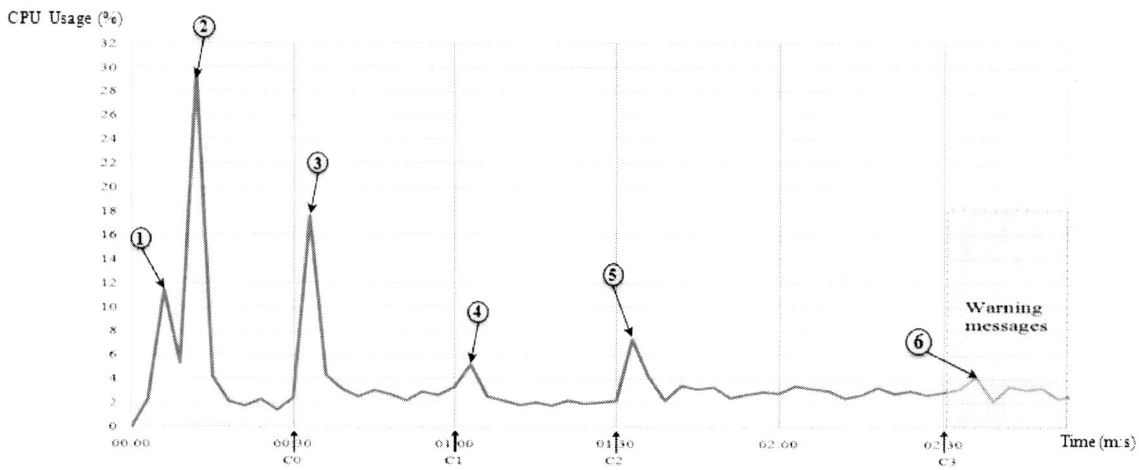

to the context switch, according to the scenario. The remaining parts of the curve represent the CPU consumption of the stabilized framework and application (running before the sixth peak, stopped after).

Let us assume that for the purposes of evaluation the following services are available on the runtime platform when the architecture is deployed:

- Service implementations: "AppointmentReminder", "OutdoorRecommendation";
- Service instances: "Scheduler", "Speaker", "CallBell";
- Unavailable services for the defined architecture: "Traffic", "Weatherforecast", "Screen".

The first point represents the consumption peak caused by the bootstrap of the runtime infrastructure execution. The second point represents the peak caused by the preparation of the scenario initial state.

Dynamic Creation of the Service-Based Application Underlying the Architecture

The architecture of the aforementioned application has been deployed on our runtime infrastructure. First, the interpretation engine takes this architecture and looks for available services in the runtime model, while matching service specifications in the architecture. Secondly, the interpreter uses the "AppointmentReminder" implementation to create a service instance. Finally, it assembles service instances: "Scheduler", created "AppointmentReminder" and "Speaker" for building the runtime application. Although "OutdoorRecommendation" implementation and "CallBell" instances are available and partially fit the architecture specification, they are not used in the initial configuration.

The interpretation engine has not instantiated the "OutdoorRecommendation" implementation since it is an optional element in the architecture. Besides, no service of its dependencies concerning practical information about weather or traffic is available at that time. The interpretation engine has not used the "CallBell" instance, as its utilization required an available "Screen" service.

The CPU consumption for loading application model and creating application has been pointed out by the third peak consumption in the curve of Figure 9.

Dynamic Management Evolution of the Service-Based Application Subject to Variability within the Architecture

- **Case 1:** The "Speaker" service instance disappears and the "Screen" service provided by a UPnP device appears on the network.

Because of the "Speaker" disconnection, the application can no longer use this service for reminding appointments and showing information to end-users. On the other hand, the UPnP digital screen is dynamically detected by the repository of heterogeneous services. This repository firstly searches and selects a corresponding proxy for this device in the remote services' UPnP repository. Then it deploys the selected proxy and stores this proxy service implementation into the runtime model. Finally, it notifies the interpretation engine. As "Screen" is required for "CallBell" to enable communication with end-user, the interpretation engine integrates both service instances into the "old" configuration of the application architecture.

The fourth peak in Figure 9 shows the reaction in CPU consumption during this case (C1). We consider that the CPU overload caused by these changes is low.

- **Case 2:** "WeatherForecast" or/and "Traffic" services appear on the network as Web Services.

Due to the "WeatherForecast" connection, the appointment reminder application can provide the complementary information. First, the repository of heterogeneous services detects it and automatically generates and instantiate an iPOJO proxy to communicate with this Web Service. The runtime model stores the generated proxy, while the interpretation engine is notified of the appearance of a newly available service. At the same time, the interpretation engine uses the "OutdoorRecommendation" service implementation, which is available in the runtime model, in order to create an instance. Finally, the interpretation engine reconfigures the application to integrate the new instances. In the same way, once "Traffic" is connected to the network, the runtime infrastructure generates the corresponding proxy and instantiates it. Indeed, the two services "Traffic" and "WeatherForecast" can be bound together as the defined variation point "pvp1" follows the "multiple (or)" variability type. The service "OutdoorRecommendation" can now provide complete information to end-user.

In Figure 9, the fifth peak is caused by this case (C2) in the curve. The re-computation of the "pvp1" and "pvp2" variation points states implies that the CPU consumption is a bit higher than the one measured during C1, but we can still consider the overload as moderated.

- **Case 3:** "Screen" UPnP device disappears.

The variation point "avp1", following "alternative (xor)" variability logic, defines that the "AppointmentReminder" service requires either the "Speaker" or "Screen" and "CallBell" services. Therefore, the application must be stopped as no acceptable configuration is currently possible. In this case, the runtime infrastructure sends a warning message to highlight this abnormal application situation.

The sixth peak in Figure 9 is caused by this case (C3). The resulting CPU overload can be considered as almost insignificant.

We have also estimated the performance of this prototype in terms of average adaption time for reconfiguring the application in response to context changes, by running 50 times this scenario. We have observed that this reaction time is significantly moderated. As a result, the runtime infrastructure execution does not imply any noticeable overhead at runtime.

CONCLUSION

The approach presented in this chapter capitalized on the advantages of SOC, SPLs and autonomic computing. In this context, the proposition makes use of SPLs to integrate variability into a SOC architecture.

In particular, we believe that our approach provides the following benefits:

- **It simplifies service-based application development**. The implementation of service-based applications is much more accessible for developers, but not for experts in the aspect of heterogeneous technology. The runtime infrastructure takes charge of services' selection in accordance with criteria dedicated by developers and is responsible of generating, customizing or managing code and invocating the appropriate services. This would support developers to focus on business logic of service-based applications' development without any detail about the communication between different heterogeneous services.
- **It takes full advantage of the dynamism inherent in SOC**. Services having to be related to the application are selected automatically at the latest moment. They can

also be modified automatically so as to consider the expected changes at runtime (new environment, new user needs). This dynamic adaptation is driven by the architecture model.

- **The proposed model controlled the evolution of the application**. The provided architecture integrating the variability model enables our runtime infrastructure to safely manage the various evolutions happening at runtime.

This work is opening perspective for future works. We are particularly interested in studying other policies to manage the running applications. Perspectives on finer policy management that can be tailored by the application architecture such as the choice of the best service provider when facing alternatives are attracting our attention. Providing this kind of mechanisms will enable the creation of safer SOC infrastructures, while keeping the adaptability property of such infrastructures.

REFERENCES

Andersson, J., Lemos, R., Malek, S., & Weyns, D. (2009). Modeling dimensions of self-adaptive software systems. In Cheng, B. H. C., de Lemos, R., Giese, H., Inverardi, P., & Magee, J. (Eds.), *Software engineering for self-adaptive systems* (pp. 27–47). New York, NY & Berlin/Heidelberg, Germany: Springer. doi:10.1007/978-3-642-02161-9_2

Booth, D., Haas, H., McCabe, F., Newcomer, E., Champion, M., Ferris, C., & Orchard, D. (2004). Web services srchitecture. *World Wide Web Consortium (W3C) organization standardization.* Retrieved February 11, 2004, from http://www.w3.org/TR/ws-arch/

Bruneton, E., Coupaye, T., Leclercq, M., Quéma, V., & Stefani, J. B. (2006). The FRACTAL component model and its support in Java: Experiences with auto-adaptive and reconfigurable systems. *Software, Practice & Experience, 1*(36), 1257–1284. doi:10.1002/spe.767

Charles, P., Donawa, C., Ebcioglu, K., Grothoff, C., Kielstra, A., & von Praun, C. ... Sarkar, V. (2005). X10: An object-oriented approach to non-uniform clustered. In *Proceedings of the 20th Annual ACM SIGPLAN Conference on Object-Oriented Programming, Systems, Languages, and Applications (OOPSLA'05)* (pp. 519-538). San Diego, CA: Association for Computing Machinery.

Cheng, B. H. C., Lemos, R., Giese, H., Inverardi, P., & Magee, J. (2009). Software engineering for self-adaptive systems: A research roadmap. In Cheng, B. H. C., de Lemos, R., Giese, H., Inverardi, P., & Magee, J. (Eds.), *Software engineering for self-adaptive systems* (pp. 48–70). New York, NY & Berlin/Heidelberg, Germany: Springer. doi:10.1007/978-3-642-02161-9_1

Clements, P., & Northrop, L. (2001). *Software product lines: Practices and patterns*. Boston, MA: Addison-Wesley Professional.

Escoffier, C., Bourcier, J., Lalanda, P., & Yu, J. Q. (2008). Towards a home application server. In *Proceedings the IEEE International Consumer Communications and Networking Conference* (pp. 321-325). Las Vegas, NV: IEEE Computer Society.

Escoffier, C., Hall, R. S., & Lalanda, P. (2007). iPOJO: An extensible service-oriented component framework. In *Proceedings of SCC'07: Proceedings of the IEEE International Conference on Services Computing, Application and Industry Track* (pp. 474-481). Salt Lake City, UT: IEEE Computer Society.

Gamma, E., Hem, R., Jahnson, R., & Vissides, J. (1994). *Design patterns: Elements of reusable object-oriented software*. Boston, MA: Addison-Wesley Professional.

Garlan, D., Cheng, S. W., Huang, A. C., Schmerl, B., & Steenkiste, P. (2004). Rainbow: Architecture-based self-adaptation with reusable infrastructure. *IEEE Computer*, *10*(37), 46–54.

Hallsteinsen, S., Hinchey, M., Park, S., & Schmid, K. (2008). Dynamic software product lines. *IEEE Computer*, *4*(41), 93–95.

Hallsteinsen, S., Stav, E., Solberg, A., & Floch, J. (2006). Using product line techniques to build adaptive systems. In *Proceedings of the 10th International Software Product Line Conference (SPLC'06)* (pp. 141-150) Baltimore, MD: IEEE Computer Society.

Horn, P. (2001). *Autonomic computing: IBM's perspective on the state of Information Technology.* Paper presented at AGENDA, Scottsdale, AZ. Retrieved from http://www.research.ibm.com/autonomic/

Kephart, J., & Chess, D. (2003). The vision of autonomic computing. *IEEE Computer*, *1*(36), 41–50.

Lee, J., & Kang, K. C. (2006). A feature-oriented approach to developing dynamically reconfigurable products in product line engineering. In *Proceedings of the 10th International Software Product Line Conference (SPLC'06)* (pp. 131-140). Baltimore, MD: IEEE Computer Society.

Nierstrasz, O., Denker, M., & Renggli, L. (2009). Model-centric, context-aware software adaptation. In Cheng, B. H. C., de Lemos, R., Giese, H., Inverardi, P., & Magee, J. (Eds.), *Software engineering for self-adaptive systems* (pp. 128–145). New York, NY & Berlin/Heidelberg, Germany: Springer. doi:10.1007/978-3-642-02161-9_7

Nitto, E. D., Ghezzi, C., Metzger, A., Papazoglou, M., & Pohl, K. (2008). A journey to highly dynamic, self-adaptive service-based applications. *Automated Software Engineering*, *3*(15), 313–341. doi:10.1007/s10515-008-0032-x

Olumofin, F. G. (2007). *A holistic method for assessing software product line architectures*. Saarbrücken, Germany: VDM Verlag.

Papazoglou, M. (2003). Service-oriented computing: Concept, characteristics and directions. In *Proceedings of the 4th International Conference on Web Information Systems Engineering (WISE'03)* (pp. 3-12). Roma, Italy: IEEE Computer Society.

Sicard, S., Boyer, F., & Palma, N. D. (2008). Using component for architecture-based management. In *Proceedings of International Conference on Software Engineering (ICSE'08)*, Leipzig, Germany: ACM-Association for Computing Machinery.

UPnP Plug and Play Forum. (2008). *UPnP device architecture,* version 1.1. Device Architecture Documents. Retrieved October 15, 2008, from http://upnp.org/specs/arch/UPnP-arch-DeviceArchitecture-v1.1.pdf

Weiser, M. (1991). The computer for the 21st century. *ACM SIGMOBILE Mobile Computing and Communications Review*, *3*(3), 3–11. doi:10.1145/329124.329126

Zeeb, E., Bobek, A., Bonn, H., & Golatowski, F. (2007). Lessons learned from implementing the devices profile for Web services. In *Proceedings of Inaugural IEEE-IES Digital EcoSystems and Technologies Conference (IEEE-DEST'07)* (pp. 229-232). Cairns, Australia: IEEE Computer Society.

KEY TERMS AND DEFINITIONS

Service-Oriented Computing: Service-Oriented Computing (SOC) is the computing paradigm that utilizes services as fundamental elements for developing applications/solutions.

Autonomic Computing: Autonomic Computing is a concept that brings together many fields of computing with the purpose of creating computing systems that self-manage, such as, self-configuration, self-optimization, self-healing and self-protection.

Software Product Line: A software product line (SPL) is a set of software-intensive systems that share a common, managed set of features satisfying the specific needs of a particular market segment or mission and that are developed from a common set of core assets in a prescribed way.

Dynamic Software Product Lines: Dynamic Software Product Lines (DSPLs) is an emerged approach based on SPLs that aims at seeking to produce software capable of adapting to fluctuations in user needs and evolving resource constraints.

Reference Architecture: A Reference Architecture is a description of the structural properties for building a group of related systems (i.e., product line), typically the components and their interrelationships. The inherent guidelines about the use of components must capture the means for handling required variability among the systems.

Chapter 4
CADEAU: Supporting Autonomic and User-Controlled Application Composition in Ubiquitous Environments

Oleg Davidyuk
INRIA Paris-Rocquencourt, France & University of Oulu, Finland

Iván Sánchez Milara
University of Oulu, Finland

Jukka Riekki
University of Oulu, Finland

ABSTRACT

Networked devices, such as consumer electronics, digital media appliances, and mobile devices are rapidly filling everyday environments and changing them into ubiquitous spaces. Composing an application from resources and services available in these environments is a complex task which requires solving a number of equally important engineering challenges as well as issues related to user behavior and acceptance.

In this chapter, the authors introduce CADEAU, a prototype that addresses these challenges through a unique combination of autonomic mechanisms for application composition and methods for user interaction. These methods differ from each other in the degree to which the user is involved in the control of the prototype. They are offered so that users can choose the appropriate method according to their needs, the application and other context information. These methods use the mobile device as an interaction tool that connects users and resources in the ubiquitous space. The authors present the architecture, the interaction design, and the implementation of CADEAU and give the results of a user study that involved 30 participants from various backgrounds. This study explores the balance between user control and system autonomy depending on different contexts, the user's needs, and expertise. In particular, the study analyses the circumstances under which users prefer to rely on certain interaction methods for application composition. It is argued that this study is a key step towards better user acceptance of future systems for the composition of ubiquitous applications.

DOI: 10.4018/978-1-60960-611-4.ch004

INTRODUCTION

Our everyday living, working and leisure environments are rapidly becoming ubiquitous due to the wide availability of affordable networking equipment, advances in consumer electronics, digital media appliances and mobile devices. This, combined with the increasing importance of web technologies for communication (e.g., Web Services, Cloud Computing and Social Networking) is resulting in the emergence of innovative ubiquitous applications. These applications usually involve multiple resources and Web Services at the same time. Examples of such resources are mobile devices, displays, portable players and augmented everyday objects. Web Services utilize these resources and provide the interfaces through which users can interact and control the ubiquitous environment. Ubiquitous applications differ from traditional applications that are static and bound to resources as specified at design time. Ubiquitous applications, on the other hand, are composed (or realized) from the available resources and Web Services at run-time according to user needs and other context information.

Depending on the degree of autonomy, application composition can be autonomic or user-controlled. A system supporting autonomic composition fully controls all processes (including the application's behavior) and does not assume any user involvement. In contrast, user-controlled composition systems involve users in control. These systems can be further classified as manual composition systems (users themselves control everything) and semi-autonomic composition systems (both users and the system collaborate to control the composition through, e.g., a visual interface). For instance, a semi-autonomic system can rely on a mixed initiative interface which guides users through a sequence of steps that result in a composed application.

In general, systems for autonomic application composition aim to ensure better usability by keeping user distraction during the composition to minimum (although user attention may be distracted while (s)he is using the composed application). These systems focus on abstracting user activities from their system-level realization and allow users to concentrate on what they need, rather than on how these activities have to be realized by the system (Sousa et al., 2006, 2008b; Masuoka et al., 2003). User activities are users' everyday tasks that can be abstractly described in terms of 1) the situation (context) in which the tasks take place, 2) the system functionalities required to accomplish the activities, and 3) user preferences relating to QoS, privacy and other requirements. In order to support the user in these activities, the automatic system captures the user's goals and needs by means of user context recognition facilities (Ranganathan & Campbell, 2004) or through dedicated user interfaces (Davidyuk et al., 2008a; Sousa et al., 2006; Kalasapur et al., 2007). Some systems allow users to express their intent vaguely, for example in their natural language as suggested by Lindenberg et al. (2006). Then, the system reactively or even pro-actively searches for possible ways to compose the required application using the appropriate resources.

In spite of the advantages in autonomic application composition, users might feel out of control, especially when the system does not behave as anticipated or when the resulting application does not match the users' original goal. Moreover, as pointed out by Hardian et al. (2006) and confirmed through user experience tests by Vastenburg et al. (2007), involving users in application control is essential to ensure that users accept autonomous prototypes, especially those intended for home or office automation domains. In addition, our earlier studies on user control for application composition (Davidyuk et al., 2008a) reveal that users still need to be provided with control interfaces even if the system is autonomic and users do not intend to control the composition of each application.

In this chapter, we present CADEAU, a prototype that supports the composition of applications from ubiquitous resources and Web Services. This prototype uses the user's mobile device as the interaction tool that can control the application composition as well as the application itself. This prototype is a complete solution that supports both automatic and the user-controlled composition. CADEAU provides three interaction methods, namely the autonomic, the manual and the semi-autonomic method, which differ from each other in how much the user is involved in the control of the application composition. These methods are offered in order to let the users to choose the most suitable means of interaction according to their needs. As the main contribution of the chapter we present the implementation of the prototype, the example application and the results of a user study. This user study involved 30 participants and aimed to explore the balance between user control and system autonomy in application composition in different contexts, depending on users' needs and experience with technologies. In particular, the study addresses the question of the autonomy domain of the system, i.e. the issues that users allow the system to take decisions on. This study also analyzed the circumstances under which the users prefer to rely on certain interaction methods for application composition. We are not aware of any other user evaluation study of a fully implemented system for application composition.

The chapter begins by reviewing the related work on application composition in ubiquitous environments. Then, we introduce the application scenario and overview the conceptual architecture of both the CADEAU prototype and the example application. Then, we present the interaction methods and the user interfaces of the application. The main contributions of the chapter, which are the implementation of the prototype and the user evaluation study, are then described. Finally, we discuss the main findings of the chapter and outline future work.

STATE OF THE ART

Various solutions that tackle ubiquitous application composition have been proposed. These solutions focus on service provisioning issues (Chantzara et al., 2006; Takemoto et al., 2004), context-aware adaptation (Preuveneers & Berbers, 2005; Rouvoy et al., 2009; Bottaro et al., 2007), service validation and trust (Bertolino et al., 2009; Buford et al., 2006), optimization of service communication paths (Kalasapur et al., 2007), automatic generation of application code (Nakazawa et al., 2004), distributed user interface deployment (Rigole et al., 2005, 2007) and design styles for developing adaptive ubiquitous applications through composition (Sousa et al., 2008a; Paluska et al., 2008). In contrast, the work described in this chapter focuses primarily on providing user control in application composition. Hence, we classify related work in these categories according to the extent of user control: autonomic, semi-autonomic and manual application composition.

Autonomic Composition

Systems in this category usually aim to minimize user distraction while (s)he is composing an application. These systems assume that users do not wish to be involved in the control, and thus all processes are carried out autonomously. Most research on autonomic composition deals with activity-oriented computing (Masuoka et al., 2003; Sousa et al., 2006, 2008b; Ben Mokhtar et al., 2007; Messer et al., 2006; Davidyuk et al., 2008b). These systems take a user-centric view and rely on various mechanisms to capture users' needs and intentions that are automatically translated into abstract user activity descriptions. These descriptions can be provided to the system implicitly through user context recognition facilities (Ranganathan & Campbell, 2004), explicitly through dedicated user interfaces (Sousa et al., 2006; Messer et al., 2006; Davidyuk et al., 2008a) or they can be supplied by application developers at design time (Beauche & Poizat, 2008; Ben Mokhtar et al., 2007). After the system receives an activity description, it carries out the activity by composing an application that semantically matches the original description according to some specified criteria and a matching (or planning) algorithm. Issues related to semantic matching for application composition have been studied, e.g., by Ben Mokhtar et al. (2007) and by Preuveneers & Berbers (2005). Planning algorithms for application composition have been proposed among others by Beauche & Poizat (2008), Ranganathan & Campbell (2004), Rouvoy et al. (2009) and Sousa et al. (2006). The prototype presented in this chapter also builds on the activity-oriented infrastructure and uses a planning algorithm (Davidyuk et al., 2008b) to realize autonomic application composition.

Semi-Autonomic Composition

In general, these solutions assume that the applications are composed as the result of collaboration between users and the system. Semi-autonomic composition may vary from computer-aided instruction to intelligent assistance that involves two-way dialogue with the system (also known as mixed initiative interface). For example, DiamondHelp (Rich et al., 2006) uses a mixed initiative control interface based on the scrolling speech bubble metaphor (i.e. resembles an online chat) which leads the user through a set of steps in order to control or manipulate appliances at home. Another approach that provides a set of interactive tools for composing applications has been developed by Kalofonos & Wisner (2007). Their first tool allows users to see the devices available in the home network and compose applications by simply connecting these devices in this interface. Then, another tool interactively assigns events and actions to all devices chosen by the users and guides them through the process of specifying the application's behavior, after which the application can be started. The semi-autonomic composition used in CADEAU resembles an interface for computer-aided instruction, i.e. users control the composition process by choosing from the options that are dynamically produced by the system.

Manual Composition

These approaches allow the users themselves to decide how applications are composed. In this case, the role of the system is to provide some means of user interaction (e.g. a graphical user interface) through which users can specify the structure and the functionality of their applications. Solutions that focus on application composition for home networks have been suggested by Bottaro et al. (2007), Chin et al. (2006), Gross & Marquardt (2007), Mavrommati & Darzentas (2007), Newman & Ackerman (2008), Newman et al. (2008) and Rantapuska & Lahteenmaki (2008). Manual application composition in the museum domain has been suggested in Ghiani et al. (2009). Somewhat related is the solution proposed by Kawsar et al. (2008). Although their work focuses mainly on the end-user deployment of ubiquitous devices in home environments, they also tackle some application composition issues. In particular, their system allows users to install various devices (i.e. by physically plugging and wiring them) and then to develop simple applications by manipulating smart cards associated with the installed devices. Another approach, presented by Sánchez et al. (2009), uses an RFID-based physical interface that allows users to choose visual resources (that have to be used with an application) by simply touching RFID tags attached to resources.

Applications for delivering multimedia content in ubiquitous spaces based on RFID technology have been proposed, for instance, in the prototypes of Broll et al. (2008) and Sintoris et al. (2007). These solutions, however, focus on the interaction of users with RFID tags and do not support application composition.

Several researchers have studied the issue of balancing user control and autonomy of the system. For example, Vastenburg et al. (2007) conducted a user study in order to analyze user willingness to delegate control to a proactive home atmosphere control system. They developed a user interface which provided three modes of interactivity: manual, semi-automatic and automatic. However, the automatic behavior of their system was "wizard-of-oz", in that it was remotely activated by a human observer during the experiment. Another attempt to address the issue of balancing user control and autonomy solution has been made by Hardian et al. (2008). Their solution focuses on context-aware adaptive applications and attempts to increase user acceptance by explicitly exposing the system's logic and context information used in the application adaptations.

CADEAU differs from the related work presented above, because our prototype supports autonomic, semi-autonomic and manual composition at the same time. Moreover, we are not aware of any other user evaluation experiment of a fully implemented composition system that has studied the balance between user control and system autonomy.

OVERVIEW OF CADEAU

Applications in CADEAU are composed of ubiquitous resources and Web Services. CADEAU supports the resources that provide multimedia, computational or other capabilities. These resources are used and controlled by Web Services. The applications in CADEAU can be composed automatically or manually depending on the extent to which users wish to be involved in control. In the first case the applications are composed according to abstract descriptions provided by the application developers. These descriptions define what ubiquitous resources are needed and what particular characteristics (or capabilities) these resources must have in order to compose these applications. Applications are realized automatically during the composition process, whose primary goal is to produce application configurations, i.e. the mappings of application descriptions to concrete resources. Once an application configuration has been produced, CADEAU reserves the resources and Web Services for the user and executes the application.

Depending on the amount of resources available in the environment together with their characteristics and capabilities, the same application description may correspond to multiple application configurations. Assuming that the resource characteristics vary, some of the application configurations will be more attractive to users than others. For example, if the user needs to watch a high-quality video file, (s)he will prefer the application configuration option which utilizes an external display with higher resolution and faster network connection. In order to address this issue, CADEAU uses the optimization criteria that allow 1) to compare application configurations and 2) to encode the user's preferences regarding various resource characteristics.

User-controlled composition in CADEAU is based on semi-autonomic and manual interaction techniques. The semi-autonomic method also relies on the automatic composition process, but provides a user interface for selecting alternative application configurations produced by CADEAU. Users can browse these configurations, compare them and choose the one that suits them best. The manual method allows users to fully control the application composition through a physical user interface. This interface consists of a NFC-enabled (NFC Forum, 2010a) mobile device and RFID tags which are attached to ubiquitous resources in the environment. A user composes an application by simply touching corresponding tags with his or her mobile device. This action triggers CADEAU to reserve these resources for this user and to start the application.

The general overview of the CADEAU prototype is shown in Figure 1. The main components are the CADEAU server, mobile clients, ubiquitous resources and Web Services. The CADEAU server is built upon the REACHeS system (Riekki et al., 2010) and provides the communication facilities for other components, performs the composition of applications and allocation of resources. In particular, the CADEAU server includes the Composition Engine that is responsible for finding the application configurations matching the user's needs and the situation in the environment. The role of Web Services is to enable the control and interaction with ubiquitous resources. They also implement application logic and provide access to data used in the applications. The mobile clients are used as interaction devices that connect users, resources and the server. The mobile clients are also a part of the CADEAU user interface which consists of (i) the user interface on the mobile devices and external displays and (ii) the physical interface through which the users interact with the ubiquitous environment. While the first play the primary role in CADEAU, the physical interface provides the input for user interaction. In other words, the physical interface in CADEAU bridges the real and digital worlds, so that the user is able to interact with augmented objects and access appropriate ubiquitous resources. The physical interface of CADEAU is made up of RFID tags and mobile devices with integrated RFID readers.

In order to explain the features and illustrate CADEAU, we present an application scenario that we implemented with the prototype and used for the user evaluation study (Davidyuk et al., 2010b). It should be noted, however, that CADEAU supports various kinds of Web Services and resources and the application scenario presented below is only one example.

John is reading a newspaper in a cafeteria. This newspaper has some hidden multimedia content (audio narration, video and images) that can be accessed by touching the newspaper with a mobile phone (see Figure 2). John touches the newspaper titles and, shortly after, CADEAU prompts John to browse the hidden content on a nearby wall display. John browses the list of articles which are linked with multimedia files. He selects the most interesting files by pressing buttons on the mobile phone's keypad. When files are chosen, CADEAU stores files' links in John's mobile phone. Later that day, John decides to watch the videos and listen to the audio narration in a conference room at work. John decides to use a semi-autonomic method to choose appropriate resources. CADEAU proposes several combinations of a display, an audio system and Web servers that host the multimedia files. John chooses the combination named "nearest resources" and starts the application that plays the multimedia files using these resources. John

Figure 1. CADEAU architecture

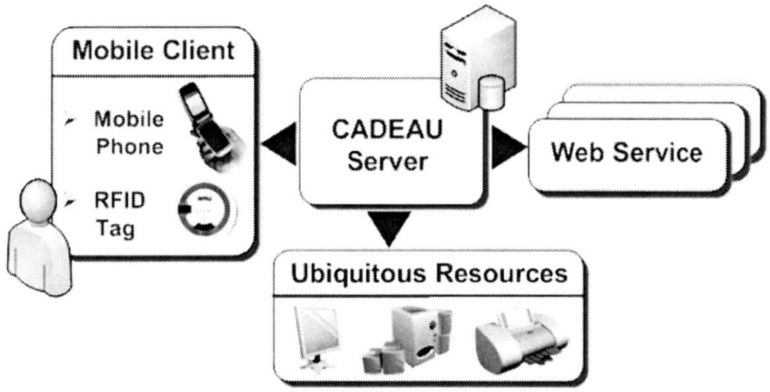

can control the playback (stop, pause, next/previous) by pressing the phone's buttons.

The multimedia information that John accessed in the CADEAU application is organized as shown in Figure 3. All content is categorized by subjects that are mapped to RFID tags in the newspaper. Each subject is related to a cluster of articles which are represented with short textual descriptions that resemble an RSS feed. Users acquire a subject by touching the appropriate tag. Then users browse related articles on an external display. Textual descriptions act as links to the multimedia files (audio, video and image slideshows) that are related to the articles. Thus, if a particular article is chosen while browsing some topic, the user's mobile device acquires links to all multimedia files associated with this article. Among these, the audio narration provides the most important information, while videos and images are supplementary material whose role is to enrich and augment the user experience with the application. The advantage of the audio narration feature stems from the fact that it provides information which is normally printed in the newspaper. Each audio narration consists of two parts, a short version and a long version. The short version narrates the overview of the article, while the long one is a thorough description that goes into greater detail. By default, CADEAU assumes that users listen

Figure 2. The prototype of a smart newspaper with embedded tags (a) and a user interacting with the smart newspaper (b)

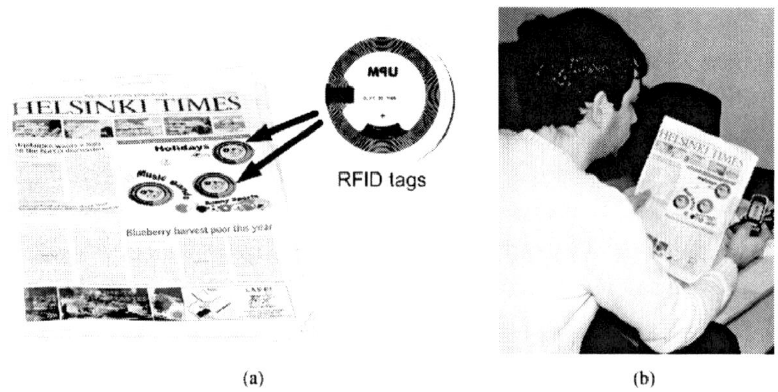

Figure 3. Conceptual structure of the multimedia content in the example application

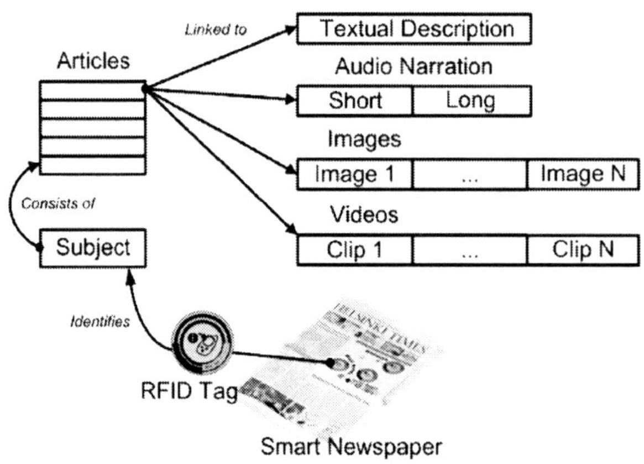

only to the short version of audio. However, if interested, users can request the long version. As video and image files do not have the same importance as audio narration, the playback of audio narrations is controlled separately from the playback of the other types of files.

CADEAU INTERACTION DESIGN

In this section we present the interaction methods supported by CADEAU and explain them using the application presented in the previous scenario as an example. The example application can be functionally divided into collecting and delivering phases, as shown in Figure 4. The goal of the first phase is to allow users to choose multimedia content from the "smart newspaper", while the second phase focuses on delivering this content using multiple ubiquitous resources.

During the collecting phase, users interact with the tags embedded in the newspaper by touching them with their mobile devices. Each of these tags is augmented with a graphical icon and a textual description, as shown in Figure 2a. The action of touching prompts the user to browse the chosen subject on a public wall display (located nearby) using his or her mobile device as a remote display controller. The user interfaces of the wall display and the mobile device are shown in Figures 5a and 5b.

The user interface of the wall display comprises a list of articles that are associated with the subjects chosen by the user (see Figure 3). Users can choose multiple articles. When the user selects an article of interest, the application acquires the article's reference number and adds it to the user's playlist which is stored in the memory of the mobile device. The *collecting* phase ends when the user closes the application.

The second phase of the application scenario, the *delivering* phase, involves using an application in a large ubiquitous environment with multiple resources. In order to help users to choose the right combination of resources, the CADEAU offers three alternative interaction methods, namely, manual, semi-autonomic and automatic. These methods are shown in Figure 6 where they are arranged according to the levels of user involvement and system autonomy that the methods provide. The users can always switch from one interaction method to another as required by the situation in the ubiquitous environment, the application being composed or the user's personal needs. Once the application has been composed by means of any of these methods, it can be used with the chosen

Figure 4. The interaction workflow of the example application

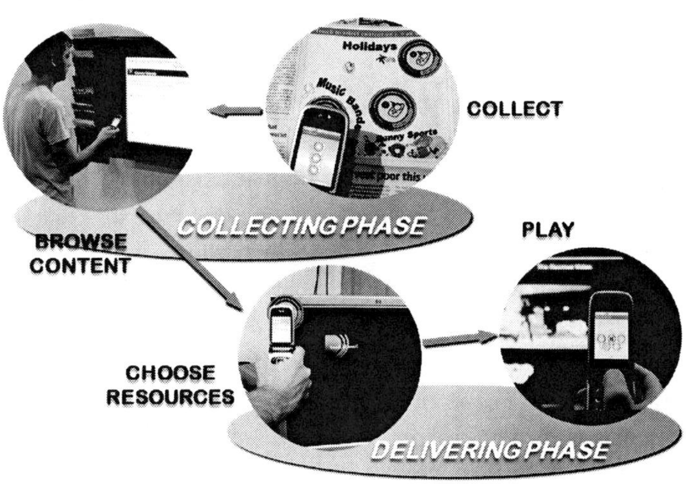

Figure 5. The user interface for browsing on the external display (a) and the remote controller user interface (b)

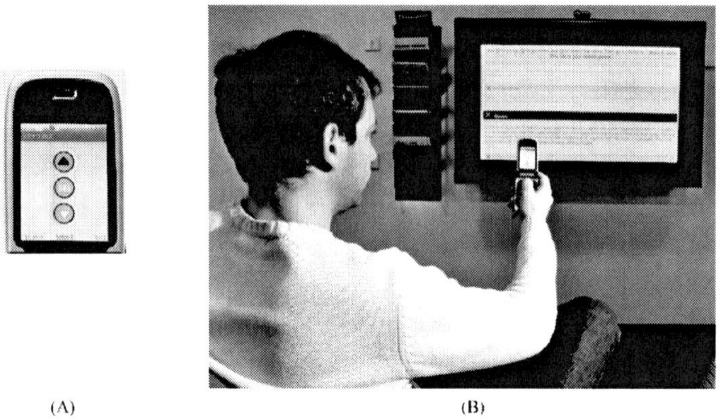

Figure 6. CADEAU interaction methods

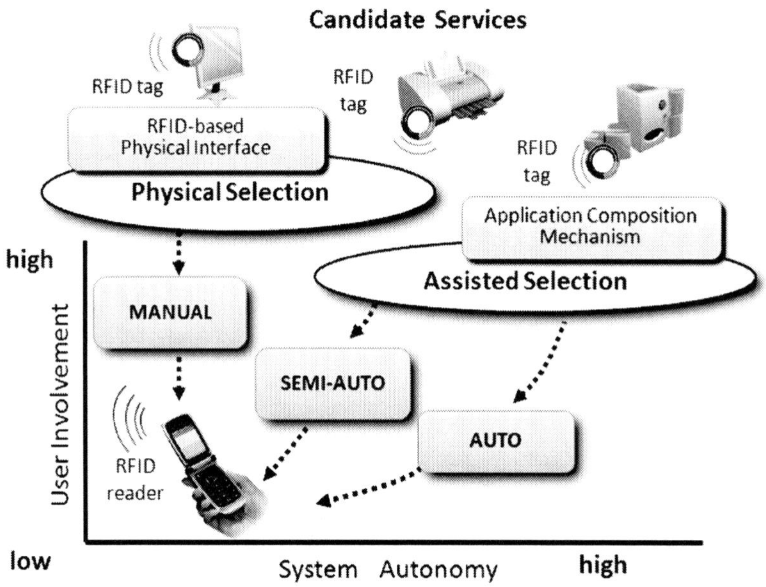

resources. Next, we present the motivation and explain these interaction methods in detail.

The manual method is an interaction technique which addresses the need of the users to fully control the composition of the CADEAU application (see Figure 7). The manual method relies on the physical interface to allow the users themselves to choose the resource instances. Figure 7a demonstrates a user choosing a display resource by touching the attached RFID tag with a mobile device. Whenever a resource tag is touched, it uniquely identifies the resource instance associated with that tag. The CADEAU application requires multiple resource instances to be chosen, hence the interface on the mobile device suggests to the user what other resources are needed in order to compose the whole application.

The user interface on the mobile device plays an essential role in the manual method. It provides feedback to the user's actions (i.e. it visualizes

Figure 7. The user interface for the manual method: user interacting with a display service (a), the mobile phone user interface (b) (shows that two services are selected) and the control panel for the remote services (c)

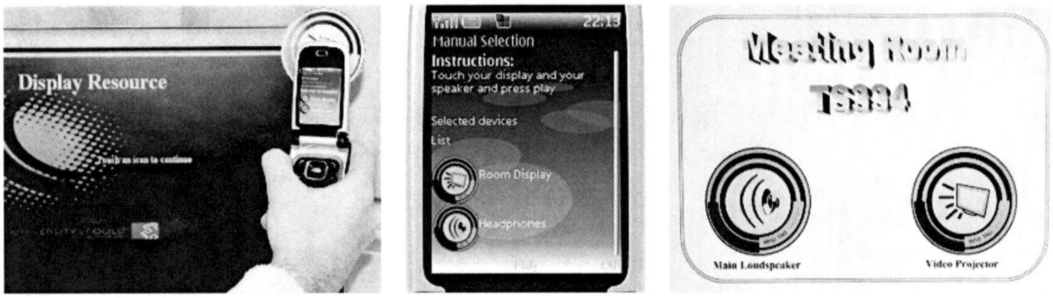

(A) (B) (C)

the information the user collects by touching tags) and also suggests to the user what other resources (or services) (s)he needs to choose before the application can be started. Figure 7b presents the user interface on the mobile device after the user has chosen two resource instances (a display and a speaker resource). The CADEAU application starts as soon as the user chooses the last necessary service instance.

The resource instances that cannot be equipped with tags are represented in the ubiquitous space with remote control panels. Such resources are typically non-visual services that are either abstract (i.e. exist only in a digital world) or are located in places that are hard to reach (e.g., on the ceiling). Figure 7c shows an example of such a control panel for a video projector resource that is mounted on the ceiling of the ubiquitous space.

The semi-autonomic method allows the application composition to be controlled by the Composition Engine as well as by the user. The key role in this interaction method is played by the list of application configurations that appears on the mobile device when a user touches the start tag (see Figure 8a) in the ubiquitous space. Each entry in this list is comprised of a set of service instances required by the application. This list is dynamically produced and organized by the system according to the user defined criteria. Thus, the list always starts with the most attractive application configuration for the user. Figure 8b shows the user interface of the list with three alternative application configurations. In this case, each application configuration is a combination of two resource instances represented by small circular icons. These icons visualize the type of the resource instance (i.e. a display or a speaker) while supplementary textual descriptions (e.g. "closest headset") indicate the instances from the ubiquitous space that are engaged in this particular application configuration.

Often the users are unfamiliar with the ubiquitous space and hence may experience difficulties when associating particular resource instances to their textual descriptions. In addition, the users may need to preview a certain application configuration before starting it. In these cases, users can optionally browse the list of application configurations and identify the resource instances using the keypad of their mobile devices. This action commands the resources in the ubiquitous space to respond to the user: the services providing display capabilities respond by showing a "splash screen" (see Figure 9) while the audio services play a welcoming audio tone. However, users can omit this step and proceed directly to starting the preferable application

Figure 8. Starting the CADEAU application using the automatic method (a), the UI of the semi-autonomic method (b), and the UI of the remote control (c)

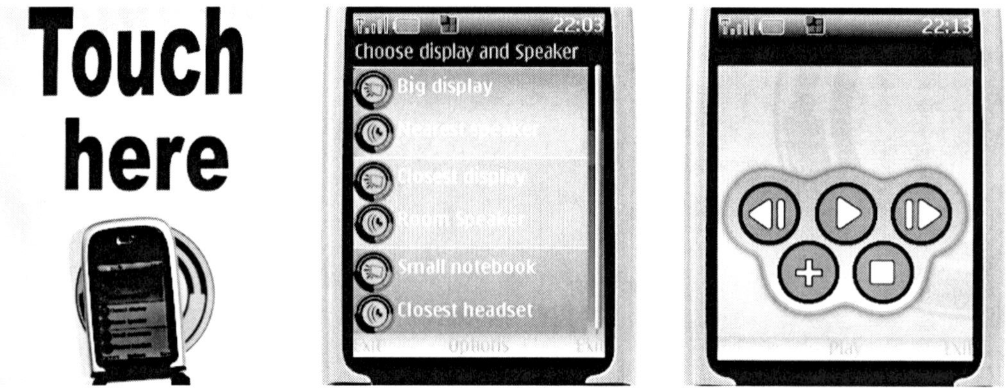

(A) (B) (C)

configuration by highlighting it and pressing the phone's middle button, as shown in Figure 8b.

Sometimes, none of the application configurations offered by the Composition Engine may suit the user, and, in this case, (s)he can switch to the manual method which provides a greater degree of user control.

The automatic method is an interaction technique which is based on the so-called-principle of least effort (Zipf, 1949) and aims to start the application while keeping user distraction to minimum. This method assumes that the user does not want to control the application composition and (s)he prefers to delegate the task of choosing an application configuration to the system. The user starts the application by touching the start tag in the ubiquitous space (see Figure 8a) after which the system responds by automatically choosing and starting an application configuration.

Figure 9. Semi-autonomic method helps users to identify resources in the ubiquitous space

When an application configuration is started by means of one of the methods mentioned above, the application changes the user interface of the mobile device into a remote control, as presented in Figure 8c. Simultaneously, the wall display shows the user interface of the playlist composed by the user during the collecting phase. From this point, the user can control the application by giving commands from his or her mobile device. For example, the user can start, stop and pause playing the items from the playlist, as well as jump to the next or the previous item. The user can also mute, increase and decrease the volume of the speakers. During the playback, the user can optionally listen to the long versions of audio files by pressing the "more" button from his or her mobile device. This command loads the file of longer duration to the playlist. The CADEAU application can be stopped at any time by closing the application from the user interface. This action stops the CADEAU application, erases the playlist and releases the resource instances for the next user.

IMPLEMENTATION

The implementation of the CADEAU prototype is built upon the REACHeS platform (Riekki et al., 2010) and reuses its communication and the Web Service remote control functionalities. CADEAU extends the basic composition mechanism used in REACHeS with the Composition Engine and, in addition, provides interaction methods for controlling the composition process. Figure 10 shows the architecture of the prototype which consists of the mobile clients, the CADEAU server, ubiquitous resources and the Web Services.

CADEAU Architecture

The client-side functionality is implemented using J2ME-MIDlets running on Nokia 6131 NFC mobile devices. The prototype supports Nokia 6131 and 6212 mobile devices which are, to date, the only market available mobile phones equipped with NFC readers. The MIDlets imple-

Figure 10. The architecture of the CADEAU prototype

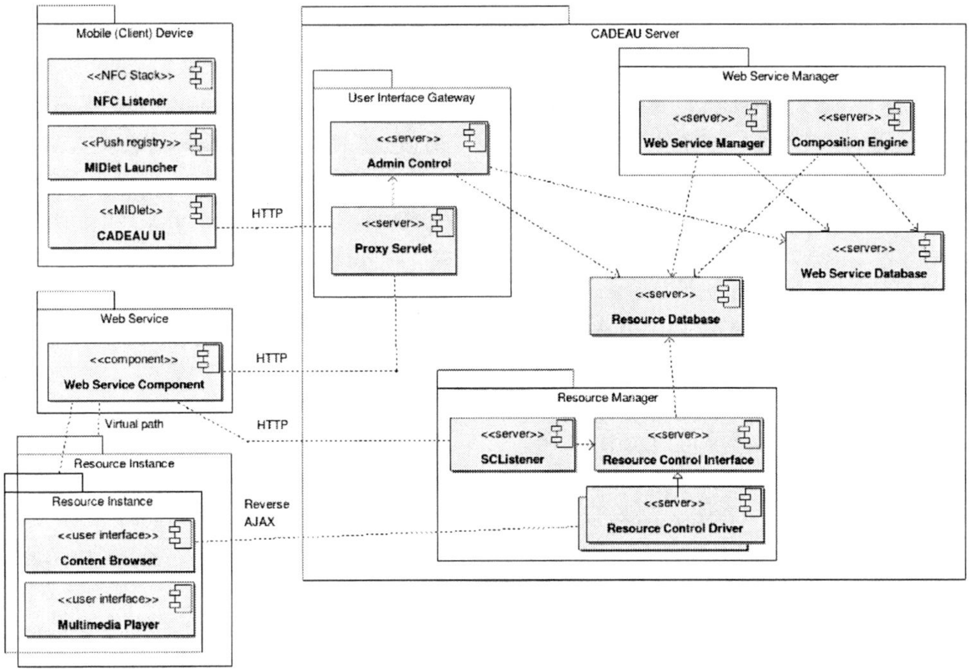

ment the user interface on the mobile device and also implement the interaction with RFID tags. The latter is realized by two components, the NFC Listener and the MIDlet Launcher (part of the mobile device's OS). The NFC Listener is responsible for detecting RFID tags while the MIDlet Launcher maintains the registry of RFID tags and the MIDlets associated with these tags. The NFC Listener component is built using the Java Contactless Communication API JSR-257. When the NFC Listener detects that a tag has been touched, it either (i) triggers the MIDlet Launcher to start the User Interface (UI) MIDlet or (ii) dispatches the information read from the tag directly to the UI MIDlet, if the MIDlet is already started.

The physical interaction is realized using ISO/IEC 14443 RFID tags (Mifire 1k type) that are attached to physical objects (i.e. ubiquitous resources). These RFID tags store data which is used for two purposes: (i) to describe an application that has to be invoked and provide the parameters that are needed for its invocation, and (ii) to specify the parameters that are needed to control the execution of an application (e.g., the events generated by the CADEAU user interface). Data is stored inside memories of tags as NDEF messages (NFC Forum, 2010b) that may consist of multiple NDEF records. Each record contains NDEF flags and a variable payload. In CADEAU, a payload is an ASCII string which encodes a pair of a parameter name and the corresponding parameter value. In particular, these parameters are used in the communication protocol described in the next section. NDEF messages can be read from the memories of tags using an NFC enabled mobile device.

CADEAU Server. As shown in Figure 10, the CADEAU server comprises three subsystems, the User Interface Gateway (UIG), the Web Service Manager (WSM) and the Resource Manager (RM). In addition, the server-side includes the databases that store the information related to the Resource Instances and the Web Services. The server-side functionality is implemented using Java Servlet API 2.2. running on Apache Tomcat 6, although the Composition Engine (part of the Web Service Manager subsystem) is implemented in C++ to achieve better performance.

The goal of the UIG is to provide the communication between the user interface on mobile devices and the other subsystems. The UIG consists of the Proxy Servlet and the Admin Control components. The Proxy Servlet processes the messages sent by the UI MIDlet or a resource instance and dispatches them to the appropriate components in the system. Certain messages are dispatched to the Admin Control component, whose role is to keep the information in the Resource and the Web Service databases up-to-date. The first database stores the information about the available Resource Instances and those which are allocated for each Web Service. The second database contains the information that associates the Web Service instances with the sessions opened by different CADEAU MIDlets. It should be noted that one application may use multiple MIDlets.

The Resource Manager subsystem connects the ubiquitous resources to the server and consists of two components, the Resource Control Driver and the SCListener. The former realizes the Resource Control Interface and implements the resource-specific control and communication protocol. Each ubiquitous resource is assigned with its own Resource Control Driver instance, one part of which is executed within the CADEAU server while the other part of the driver is executed within the Resource Instance.

Specifically, the Resource Control Driver implements a Reverse Ajax protocol based on HTTP Streaming (AJAX public repository, 2010) for Display and Speaker resources. The SCListener is responsible for dispatching commands (i.e. asynchronous messages) from Web Service Components to the appropriate Resource Control Drivers.

A Resource Instance (RI) is a standalone PC embedded into the ubiquitous space whose functionality is used by Web Services. Certain RIs in the prototype (e.g. ones that offer multimedia facilities) are provided with user interfaces that are realized using web browsers and JavaScript. Because the CADEAU prototype does not require deploying any additional software onto the RI's PC, any PC equipped with an Internet connection and a web browser can be turned into a new CADEAU Resource Instance by opening the browser and typing in the HTTP registration request. This triggers the RI's web browser to load the necessary scripts that belong to the Resource Control Driver. After that, the RI can be communicated with and controlled through the Web Service interface.

CADEAU application. The example application that we presented in the overview is implemented as a set of MIDlets on the mobile device, the Content Browser, the Media Web Services, and MIDlets to assist the composition phase. The Content Browser Web Service enables users to browse dynamically generated HTML pages on a remote Display RI. The first phase of the application (i.e. collecting phase) starts when the user chooses a topic by touching an RFID tag in the newspaper. This action initializes the Content Browser and also loads the UI MIDlet so that the user can control the Content Browser from his or her mobile device. Upon receiving a command from the user (i.e. from the UI MIDlet), the Content Browser generates an HTML page and sends it to the dedicated Display RI which loads the page into the web browser (i.e. displays the page to the user). The user navigates on this HTML page and checks and unchecks articles by sending commands from the mobile device. These commands are forwarded to the Content Browser which either generates a new HTML page or commands the RI to update the page that is currently being displayed. User selections are stored in an XML file which is used as a playlist during the second phase of the application (i.e. the delivering phase). The second phase of the application involves the playback of the multimedia content chosen by the user. The multimedia files are stored on multiple Media Web Services which provide access to the files on request. The playback is realized by the Display and Speaker RIs that implement the open source JWMediaPlayer and the JWImageRotator Flash players (LongTail Video, 2010). These RIs support rendering of multimedia files in various formats, support streaming over the network and accept dynamic playlists.

Although the example application presented utilizes only the multimedia facilities, the CADEAU prototype supports other types of ubiquitous resources whose functionality can be accessed using a Web Service.

The CADEAU Communication Protocol

The components of the CADEAU server, the Web Services and the RIs communicate with each other using the HTTP protocol. The messages, sent between the Web Services and the UI MIDlet, are encapsulated into the HTTP GET requests, while the messages, sent between the Web Services and the RIs, are transmitted using the POST requests. The HTTP requests include several parameters in the GET URL, while the POST requests include a message with several commands in the POST body. Each message can accommodate multiple parameters. These parameters are either mandatory or optional (e.g. service-specific) parameters. Example parameters for GET requests are listed in Table 1. The mandatory parameters always specify the recipient of the message (i.e. the target Web Service or the subsystem) and the event to be sent. The events are the administrative commands or the service-specific actions that are used to change the state of the RIs (e.g. to update the UI of the resource).

The administration commands are always dispatched to the Admin Control Component that processes and performs the requested commands (e.g. adds a new RI description to the Resource database). Unlike the administration commands, the service-specific and error messages are dis-

Table 1: The parameters used in the communication between the MIDlets, the UIG and the Web Services

Parameter	Mandatory	Example Value	Description
Service	Yes	MultimediaPlayer	Id of the target Web Service
Event	Yes	Play	Describes the event to be sent to the Web Service
ResourceId	No	000000001	List of RIs to be allocated to a Web Service
IsAsync	No	True	Has to be set to "true", if the event does not require setting up a session
Playlist	No	playlist.xml	The URL of the playlist to be shown at a Display RI

patched directly to the target Web Services and then routed to the RIs through dedicated Resource Control Drivers.

Figure 11 illustrates how the CADEAU subsystems communicate during the browsing phase of the application scenario. As can be seen, the phase starts when the user touches an RFID tag in the newspaper and then presses a button on his or her mobile device to scroll down the displayed HTML page.

The Application Composition Process

The CADEAU prototype supports the user-controlled composition (based on the manual and the semi-autonomic methods) as well as the automatic composition. The composition process of the latter is presented in Figure 12. In this case, the key role is played by the Composition Engine which produces the application configuration according to the predefined optimization criteria. This Composition Engine is based on the application

Figure 11. Communication between the subsystems of the CADEAU prototype

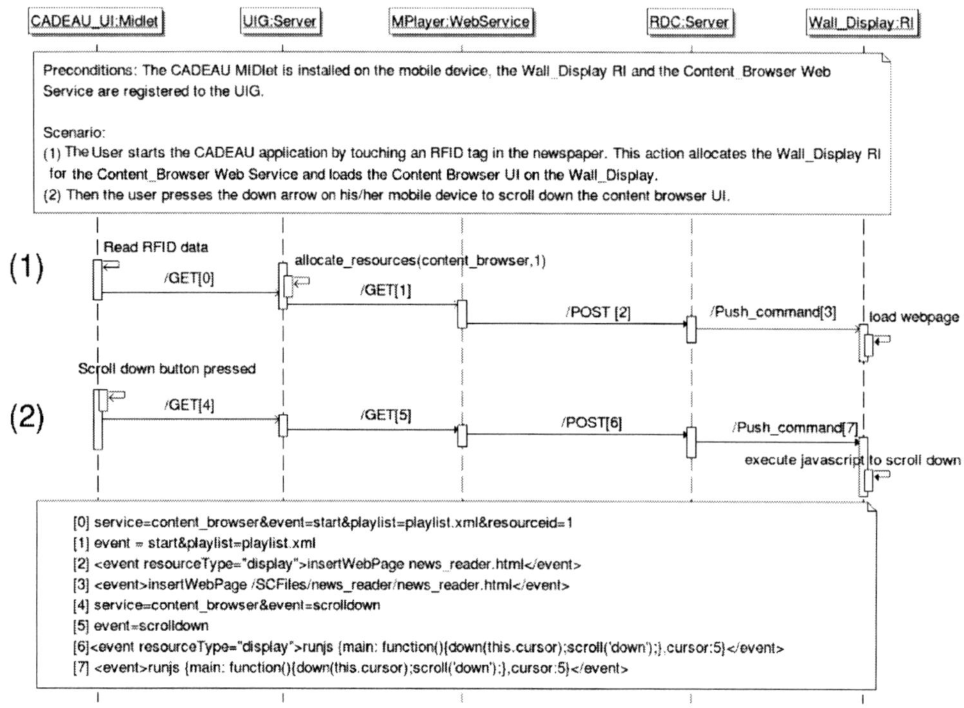

allocation algorithm that we reported earlier in (Davidyuk et al., 2008b). This Composition Engine is implemented as a C++ library that takes two XML files as input, (i) the list of available RIs and (ii) the application model. The first one is created by extracting from the resource database the descriptions of the RIs that are physically located in the same ubiquitous space as the user. This file is dynamically created at the beginning of the composition process. The second file, the application model, is a static XML file which is provided by the application developers. It encodes the structure of the CADEAU application, i.e., it specifies what types of RIs are needed and how they have to be connected. In addition, the application model describes the properties of RIs (e.g., the minimum bandwidth, screen resolution and such) that are required by the application. Example applications and platform model files are presented in Figures 13a and 13b, respectively.

If the semi-autonomic method is used, the Composition Engine produces three alternative application configurations of the same application (see Figure 14). These configurations are displayed on the mobile device for the user, who can browse these configurations and choose the most suitable one. Then, this configuration is sent to the UIG which commands the WSM to reserve the RIs listed in the configuration and, after that, invokes the CADEAU application. If the automatic method is used, the Composition Engine produces only one application configuration which is sent directly to the UIG, as shown in Figure 12.

The composition process of the manual interaction method differs from the other two methods, as it does not use the Composition Engine. Instead, the RIs are chosen and provided to the system when the user touches RFID tags with his or her mobile device. This action commands the UI MIDlet to send the Id numbers of the chosen RIs to the UIG. Then, the UIG requests the WSM to allocate the chosen RIs and, after that, invokes the CADEAU application (see Figure 15).

USER STUDY AND EVALUATION

We followed a design process that involved multiple iterations, including the development of the initial prototype followed by a preliminary usabil-

Figure 12. The composition process of the automatic method

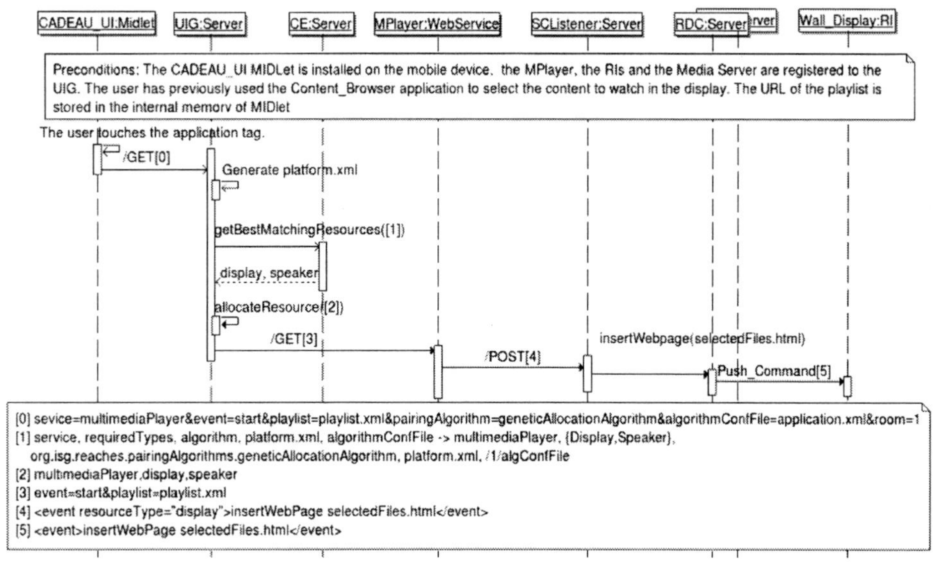

Figure 13. Listing of the application model (a) and the platform model (b) files used in the prototype

```xml
<?xml version="1.0" encoding="UTF-8"?>
<data>
   <Displays>
      <Display id="1">
         <resourceQ>30</resourceQ>
         <bandwidth>20</bandwidth>
         <isDisplay>true</isDisplay>
         <isSpeaker>false</isSpeaker>
         <quality>0</quality>
         <cpu>0</cpu>
      </Display>
   </Displays>
   <Speakers>
      <speaker id="2">
         <resourceQ>30</resourceQ>
         <bandwidth>20</bandwidth>
         <isDisplay>false</isDisplay>
         <isSpeaker>true</isSpeaker>
         <quality>0</quality>
         <cpu>0</cpu>
      </speaker>
   </Speakers>
   <Servers>
      <server id="3">
         <resourceQ>0</resourceQ>
         <bandwidth>20</bandwidth>
         <isDisplay>false</isDisplay>
         <isSpeaker>false</isSpeaker>
         <quality>10</quality>
         <cpu>20</cpu>
      </server>
   </Servers>
</data>
```

(A)

```xml
<?xml version="1.0" encoding="UTF-8" standalone="yes"?>
<data>
<Displays>
      <Display id="259">
            <resourceQ>30.0</resourceQ>
            <bandwidth>30.0</bandwidth>
            <isDisplay>true</isDisplay>
            <isSpeaker>false</isSpeaker>
            <quality>0.0</quality>
            <cpu>0.0</cpu>
      </Display>
                  ...
</Displays>
<Speakers>
      <speaker id="514">
            <resourceQ>50.0</resourceQ>
            <bandwidth>50.0</bandwidth>
            <isDisplay>false</isDisplay>
            <isSpeaker>true</isSpeaker>
            <quality>0.0</quality>
            <cpu>0.0</cpu>
      </speaker>
                  ...
</Speakers>
<Servers>
      <server file="http://www.ee.oulu.fi/
                 ~jiduran/video1.flv" id="100">
            <resourceQ>0.0</resourceQ>
            <bandwidth>30.0</bandwidth>
            <isDisplay>false</isDisplay>
            <isSpeaker>false</isSpeaker>
            <quality>40.0</quality>
            <cpu>20.0</cpu>
      </server>
                  ...
</Servers>
</data>
```

(B)

Figure 14. The composition process of the semi-autonomic interaction method

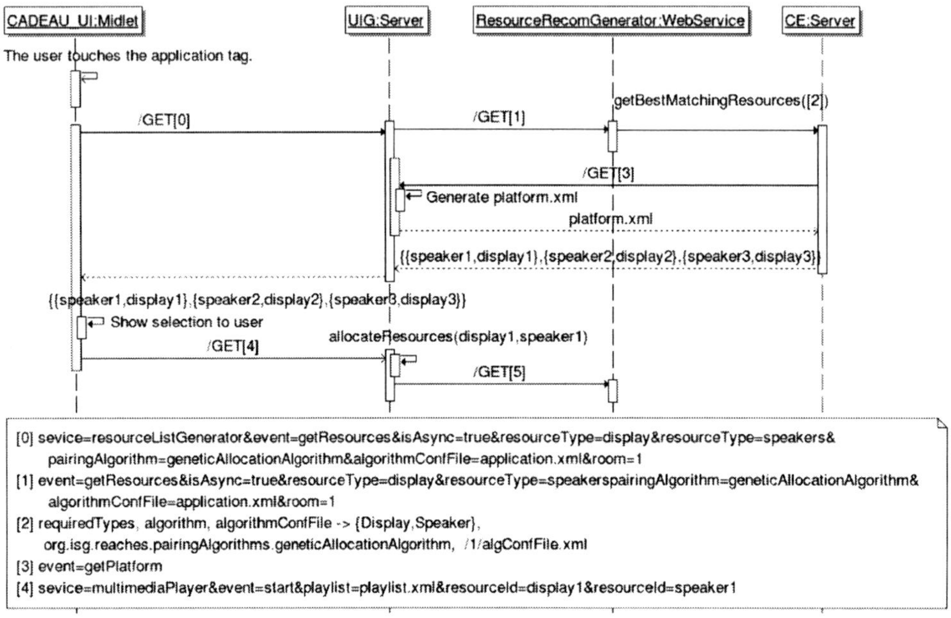

Figure 15. The composition process of the manual interaction method

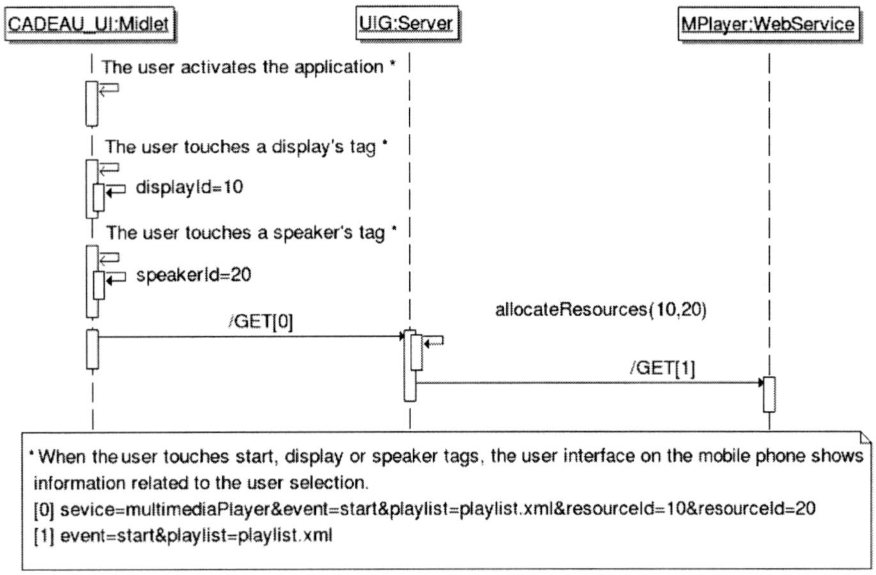

ity study with some experts in IT. Lack of space does not allow us to report the process in detail, nor the intermediate results. However, the resulting CADEAU prototype and the application are described in the sections "CADEAU Interaction Design" and "Implementation", correspondingly. Therefore, in this chapter we describe only the setup, the procedure and our findings from the final user study; this study was conducted with the fully implemented CADEAU prototype.

The primary goal of this user study was to make an assessment of the trade-off between user control and autonomy of the system for application composition, dictated by the user's needs, situation and expertise. This was carried out by comparing the interaction methods and analyzing the factors (e.g. the amount of feedback) contributing to the user's comfort and feeling of control in different contexts. We concentrated our efforts on identifying the issues that were difficult for users to comprehend. The last goal was to gain insights for future research by understanding user experiences, especially the breakdowns perceived by users when they were carrying out tasks in CADEAU.

Methodology

Thirty participants from the local community of the City of Oulu (Finland) took part in the study. These participants were recruited according to their background and previous experience with technologies, and were assigned to one of three focus groups that each consisted of 10 individuals.

The first group, group A, consisted of IT professionals and students studying towards a degree in computer science or engineering. This group represented experts who deal with mobile technologies on a daily basis as well as having some previous experience with ubiquitous applications. These users were chosen in order to give an expert opinion and provide feedback from a technical point of view. The second group, group B, consisted of less computer-savvy individuals who represented average technology users. As they reported later in the survey, 50% of them never or very rarely use mobile phones beyond calling or texting. The participants in the last group (group C) were carefully screened to ensure that their computer skills and experience were minimal and none of them had any technical background.

This group represented a variety of professions, including economists, biology students, a manager, a planning secretary and a linguist. These individuals were chosen to represent conservative users who are less likely to try new technologies and applications. The distribution of gender and age across the participants of these three groups is shown in Table 2. All the users were trying the CADEAU prototype for the first time and two persons had watched the video of the application scenario.

The study was carried out at the Computer Science and Engineering Laboratory at the University of Oulu. Two adjacent meeting rooms were converted into ubiquitous spaces prior to the experiment. Each of these spaces was fitted with 6-8 multimedia devices of different kinds. The experiment began in the nearby lobby, so that the users could see the spaces only during their testing session.

Each participant came to our laboratory individually for a session that took approximately an hour. At the beginning the users were given a short introduction in which the functionality of the system was demonstrated using the newspaper and one display located in the lobby. The users, who were unfamiliar with RFID technology, were given additional explanations and time to practice reading RFID tags using the mobile device. Then, each user was asked to perform first the collecting task and then the delivering task from the CADEAU example application (see the section "Overview of CADEAU" for details). All participants had to perform each task twice, using different interaction methods in the two ubiquitous spaces. That is, each participant used one of the following combinations: manual and autonomic, manual and semi-autonomic or automatic and semi-autonomic. The experiment was organized in such a way that each of the three methods was used an equal number of times in each focus group.

The participants were encouraged to ask questions, give comments, point out difficult issues and think out loud during the experiment. Since most of the users had had little or no experience with similar systems in the past, all the users were explicitly told that they could not break the system or do anything wrong. After the tasks were completed, the users were asked to fill in an anonymous questionnaire and then discuss their experience with the observers. We used the questionnaire to compare the interaction methods while the interview focused on collecting feedback on the concept and the system in general.

Results

Although we did not set a strict time limit for completing the assignments and asked the users to finish when they felt they understood how the application and the system work, the users belonging to group A completed the tasks in a significantly shorter time than users from the other two groups (B and C). This is because, in most cases, the experts omitted the preamble and thus could proceed directly to the experiment with the CADEAU application.

User willingness to delegate control. In this section we present an analysis of user preferences

Table 2. Demography of the user study

Group	Gender		Age		
	M	F	≤25 y.o.	26-30 y.o.	30+
(A) IT experts	70%	30%	30%	40%	30%
(B) Average users	70%	30%		80%	20%
(C) Non-tech. users		100%	60%	30%	10%

towards certain interaction methods in different contexts. This analysis is based on the anonymous questionnaires and the user feedback collected during interviews.

1. **Manual method.** User opinions regarding the manual method were similar across all the focus groups. Users preferred to rely on the manual method when they had already thought about some specific application configuration and hence wanted the system to realize this exact configuration. As an example, one participant described a situation where he was giving a talk and needed a configuration with two display resources cloning each other. This example also points to another important factor - the reliability of the interaction method. Our users felt that the manual method provides the most control. This was best expressed by a non-technical user "I really feel that I control it [*the resource*] when I touch it". Another factor affecting the choice of the manual method was familiarity with the ubiquitous space. The manual method was certainly preferred when users were familiar with the environment and knew the location of each resource. Almost all the users mentioned their homes and work places as such environments. As for the public environments, the users chose to rely on the manual method when they wanted privacy (e.g. when browsing a family photo album in a cafeteria) or when they wished to avoid embarrassing situations involving other individuals. This last finding is in line with the results of the experiments reported by Vastenburg et al. (2007). They concluded that users in general prefer to rely on the manual selection if they are involved in a social activity. As ubiquitous applications can be composed of non-visual resources as well (i.e. content providers, servers, so called "hot spots" and many others), participants were asked whether they prefer to manually choose these resources as well. Surprisingly, users from all three groups answered that they trust the system to choose these resources automatically, and find a configuration that leads to the best overall application quality.
2. **Semi-autonomic method.** Users liked this method as they could control everything on the mobile device without needing to walk anywhere. This feature was also found useful when users wanted to "hide" their intentions (i.e. while preparing to use a resource) in certain cases. As we were told by a non-technical user (she was assigned to compare this and the manual method), she would always prefer the semi-autonomic method as she felt uncomfortable when touching resources in front of bystanders. We hope such attitudes will change when the RFID technology becomes a part of our daily lives. Some of the expert users found this method useful, too. However, they stated that they wanted to know the selection criteria before they could fully trust the method. The fact that the criteria was hardwired in the application seemed to be the major shortcoming of the method. Besides, as an expert user later admitted, he would trust the method more if he were able to use it for longer periods of time. Thus, a better approach would be to run the experiment over the course of several days and compare the initial user evaluation scores with the scores obtained at the end of the experiment. In particular, Vastenburg et al. (2007) observed in their experiment that user confidence and ease of use increase over time. Several users (groups A and B) admitted that the semi-autonomic method is preferable in situations where one is in a hurry. They pointed out that the UI of the method displays the configurations on the mobile phone, so users can quickly take a look before starting the configuration if they are hesitating about the choice proposed by the system. One user suggested that this

method could save his last choice (i.e. the application configuration used in some similar context) and suggest this configuration among the other options. We believe this feature will increase the usefulness of the method in future.

3. **Automatic method.** Although the expert users were cautious about using this method on a daily basis, they found it useful in several situations. For example, someone is entering a ubiquitous space with an open application on his or her device and (s)he is hesitating (or confused) to choose a configuration on his or her own. In that case the system could automatically choose an application configuration after a short delay. However, the majority of the expert users admitted during the interview, that they need to feel that the method is reliable in order to rely on it. According to these users, reliability means for them that the outcome of the method is predictable. As one expert commented, "I need to know what happens next and if this system is still surprising me, this surprise has to be a positive one". The users from group B suggested a public space with many possible combinations of resources as another example situation where this method could be used. But, like in the case with the semi-autonomic method, they requested to know the decision (i.e. the choice) of the system and what information was used by the system to take it, in order for this choice to be corrected if necessary. This confirms theoretical findings reported by Hardian et al. (2008), where the authors suggested exposing the context information and logic to users in order to ensure that the actions (e.g. adaptation to context) taken on behalf of the users were both intelligent and accountable. The non- technical users were more enthusiastic towards the automatic method than their expert colleagues. Some non-technical users suggested that this method could be used in most situations. As one of them commented, "it is just nice when things are done automatically". Although she added that she prefers other methods if she needs to hide her application or its content. The autonomic method was also appreciated for its speed and easiness. These factors were dominant for non-technical users in cases where a person is in a hurry.

Subjective comparison. These results were collected using questionnaires where users had to answer questions like "how easy was the method to use" (1="very difficult", 5="very easy") or "did it require apparent effort in order to understand the method" (1="I did not understand it immediately and it took me a long before I understood it", 5="I understood it immediately and did not have to ask any questions"). The results of the comparison between the three methods are shown in Figure 16.

1. **Easiness.** As can be seen from the graphs, the expert users (group A) graded the automatic method as the easiest to use (4.8 pts), while the manual and the semi-autonomic methods scored the second (4.4 pts) and the third (4 pts) place, respectfully. The non-technical (group C) users gave the automatic method the highest grade (4.6 pts) while the manual method was given the lowest (3.7 pts). The group B users gave approximately the same scores to all three methods. Although the scores received from the experts and the average user groups were somewhat expected, the non-technical users surprisingly gave the lowest grade to the manual method. A possible explanation could be that none of them had any previous experience with RFID technology, thus the users did not feel comfortable using it.
2. **Intuitiveness.** The answers given by the expert and average users followed each other hand in hand, although the average users gave lower overall grades: they chose the

Figure 16. Comparing the manual (left), the semi-autonomic (middle) and the automatic (right) methods across three focus groups (A=experts, B=average users, C=non-technical users)

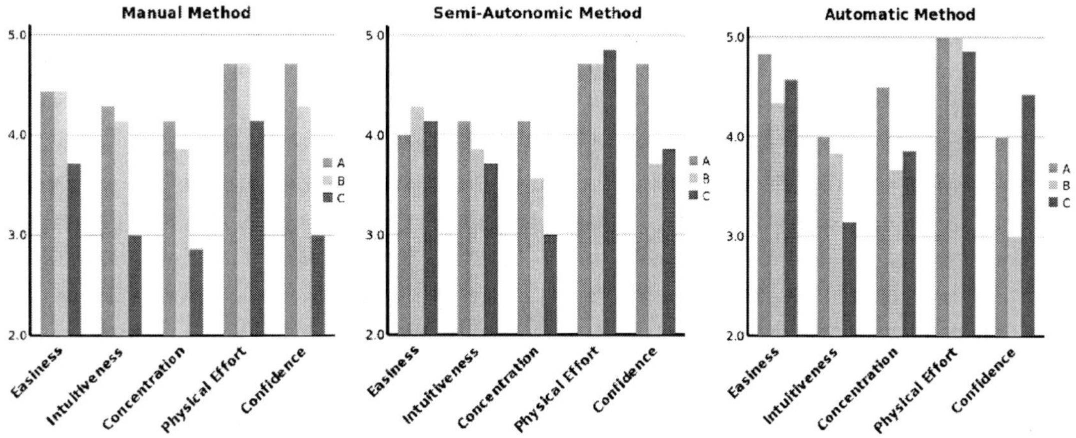

manual method as the most intuitive (4.1 pts) and they gave the lowest grade (3.8 pts) to the automatic method. As one user from this group (B) commented, the automatic method was not very intuitive because its choice criteria was not clear at all. We believe this is caused by the fact that the users did not have access to the optimization criteria on the UI. The non-technical users named the manual method as the least intuitive (3 pts). As in the case with the "easy to use" characteristic, we believe this to be due to a lack of experience and, hence, difficulties with understanding the RFID technology. One user from group C could not complete the assignment using the manual method, but had to interrupt the experiment and ask the observers for explicit instructions on what she has to do.

As was later revealed, she always preferred to use some "default configuration" when she was working on her computer, thus she was confused when she herself had to make a choice in the first place.

3. **Concentration.** The expert users found that the manual and the semi-autonomic methods are equally demanding (4.1 pts) and require higher concentration efforts than the automatic method (4.5 pts). The results of the average user group showed a similar tendency, although these users gave lower grades to all three methods. The answers given by the non-technical users were in line with the results of the other groups.
4. **Physical effort.** We expected our users to choose the manual method as the most demanding and the automatic one as the least demanding in terms of physical effort. Although we guessed right in the case of the non-technical group, the other two groups (A and B) gave equal scores to both the manual and the semi-autonomic methods. As we observed during the experiment, these two groups behaved actively and were walking around to identify resources also when using the semi-autonomic method. On the other hand, the group C users preferred to stay on the spot and were focusing on the mobile phone's UI during the experiment. We believe that this observation is also linked

to the confidence factor, which we discuss next.

5. **Confidence.** We expected the expert users to demonstrate a higher level of confidence with the automatic method because they deal with similar technologies on a daily basis. The non-technical users were supposed to show greater confidence when using the manual method, because we believed that the outcome of this method was easier for them to predict. Finally, we expected the average users to show results similar to the expert users. The results showed quite the opposite picture. The non-technical users expressed the highest level of confidence when using the automatic method (4.4. pts) and gave lower scores to the mixed initiative (3.9 pts) and the manual (3 pts) methods. The expert users were equally confident with both the manual and the semi-autonomic methods (4.7 pts) and gave lower scores to the automatic method (4 pts). The opinion of the average user group was in line with the experts. Surprising was the fact that although the non-technical group found the automatic method mediocre in terms of intuitiveness (3.1 pts) they nevertheless demonstrated the highest confidence (4.4. pts) with this method. This means that the non-technical users were overconfident when using the automatic method. The experts and the average users demonstrated interesting opinions as well. They were in favor of the manual and the semi-autonomic methods. The explanation of this phenomenon is that these two user groups have, in, general, lower trust in the autonomy of systems. This hypothesis was also confirmed during the exit interviews.

Design of RFID icons and physical browsing. The user evaluation of the prototype helped us to pinpoint two important usability related issues. The first is the graphical design of the icons that appear on the front side of RFID tags and the second issue is so called physical browsing.

Icon design is an essential issue that influences the intuitiveness and ease of use of RFID-based interfaces (Sánchez et al., 2009). The role of icon design is to communicate the meaning of tags to users in a precise and non-ambiguous manner. In other words, it allows users to correctly recognize and interpret the action that is triggered when a certain tag is touched. Therefore, we included the evaluation of the icon design as a part of this user study. We were particularly interested in evaluating the icon design of the start tag (see Figure 8a) which users had to touch on entering the ubiquitous space. The designer of the tag aimed to communicate to the users that they need to touch this tag in order to deliver the information that they have in their mobile devices. Hence, our participants were asked in the questionnaire to describe the action that, according to their option, is best associated with this tag. Similarly, users had to describe three other designs. The icon used was correctly described by 70% of the expert users, 40% of the average users, and 80% of the non-technical users. We found this result satisfactory for this prototype, although the icon design could be refined in the next design iteration.

Another issue that we studied was physical browsing, which is the mechanism that helps users to identify Resource Instances in the ubiquitous spaces. This is especially challenging when users need to preview an application configuration (offered by the system) on their mobile device while they are not familiar with the ubiquitous space. Such a mechanism should allow users to associate each application configuration with corresponding resource instances in the environment. The CADEAU prototype implements this mechanism as part of the semi-autonomic method and allows users to preview (or validate) chosen application configurations by clicking the middle button on the mobile phone. This commands the display RIs to show "splash screen" and the audio RIs to play an audio tone. We asked our users to suggest alternative mechanisms to identify resources in ubiquitous spaces. Among the most interesting suggestions were the map-like user interface with a compass, concise textual descriptions on the mobile phone (including, e.g. color and size of the resources), a radar-like user interface and an LED-based panel where all resources are marked. In spite of these suggestions, users generally liked the current validation mechanism implemented in CADEAU.

DISCUSSION AND FUTURE WORK

Although ubiquitous technology aims to be autonomous and invisible, there is still a need for user control and intervention. This is best explained by one participant during the exit interview: "if it [*the application*] does not read my mind, how does it know what I want?". Based on the results of this study developers of ubiquitous technology could take into account the preferences of users who have varying degrees of expertise. For example, the expert users need to understand the details of application operation and therefore they require most of the adaptation and configuration processes to be explicit. The average computer users have similar requirements to the experts and they also expressed less trust in the autonomy of the system. For example, they need to be able to override the system's choices and adjust the selection criteria. However, these users may in certain situations rely on autonomy of the system. Users with little or no experience in technologies seem to be overconfident when using the system and thus prefer to rely on default or autonomic options. These users, however, still need to be able to control the application or the system, if necessary.

Among the other factors that influence willingness to delegate control to the prototype were named privacy, familiarity with the environment, the presence of other persons, time pressure and predictability of the outcome of the system's choices. These factors were almost equally important across the three user groups involved in the experiment. For example, users explicitly prefer to rely on the manual method when they wish to hide the multimedia content from other persons. Depending on how familiar users were with the environment, they tended to rely on the manual method if they were very familiar (e.g. at home, or in the office) and chose the automatic or the semi-autonomic methods in the environments less familiar to them. In the presence of other persons, users in general tried to avoid choices that might lead to unpleasant and embarrassing situations. For example, many users liked the semi-autonomic method as they could hide their intentions when preparing to use certain resources with the application. However, user preferences in this case depended on how confident the user was with the prototype. For example, the expert and average users named the manual method as the most preferable to use when other persons are present. On the other hand, the non-technical users were happy to rely on the semi-autonomic method in this situation. Generally, the expert and the average users tended to use the semi-autonomic and the automatic methods if they were able to predict the behavior of the prototype. Otherwise their preferred method was the manual one. Although the non-technical users admitted that the automatic and the semi-autonomic methods were lacking in intuitiveness, they did not impose high requirements on the predictability of the prototype, as the other user groups did.

Another important finding was the fact that the average users expressed opinions similar to those given by the expert group. The average users however, gave lower overall scores in the long run than those given by the expert users. Thus, as a conclusion, we find it acceptable to rely on the expert opinions when evaluating features related to manual or semi-manual system configuration. On the other hand, we find it unacceptable to rely only on expert or even average users when assessing the automatic (or nearly autonomic) features of a system.

Limitations. One of the limitations of our methodology was the fact that we carried out the experiment in the lab. Although CADEAU is meant to be used in various environments including home, office and public spaces, the lab truly represented only the office space. The findings that were related to other environments and were collected during the interviews were based entirely on the personal experiences and the user's subjective understanding of how CADEAU could be used. A better approach could be to perform field studies. However, such an experiment will require significantly greater time and effort. Another limitation was due to the fact that our users were not given a possibility to try the prototype over several days. Although sufficient for our needs, the approach used in the experiment does not study general trends in time. For example, Vastenburg et al. (2007) demonstrate in their experiments that such factors as user confidence and ease of use have a tendency to increase over time. That suggests that the scores obtained in our study could be in fact higher.

Future work. Several promising directions of future research are identified in this study. One of them is the development of control methods that can be adapted to users with various levels of experience in technologies. That is, rather than having a set of "fixed" control methods that are offered to all users equally, we are interested in developing and evaluating the methods that can be tailored to user expertise and willingness to delegate the control to the system. For example, users themselves could specify the tasks they want to delegate to the system and the tasks they prefer to control manually.

Another issue for future research involves developing a new control method that unites the advantages of the manual and the automatic methods. This new method, the semi-manual method, does not require users to choose all the resources manually. It could work as follows: a user could select some resource instances (s) he wished to use with the application. Then, the missing resources would be assigned and the rest of the configuration would be realized automatically. The major advantage of this new method is that the user could choose the most important resources manually while leaving less important decisions to be made by the system automatically.

An interesting research direction is the end user composition of applications. This subject studies tools, methods and technologies that allow end-users to develop composite applications in a do-it-yourself fashion. The initial steps towards this research are reported in (Davidyuk et al., 2010a).

ACKNOWLEDGMENT

CADEAU is the result of a collaborative effort that has been built thanks to the contribution of many people who supported the authors during the development of the prototype and the writing of this chapter. We wish to thank all those who helped us to successfully complete this project, and in particular:

- *Marta Cortés* and *Jon Imanol Duran* for taking part in the development of CADEAU;
- *Hanna-Kaisa Aikio* and *Hillevi Iso-Heiniemi* for making the audio narration;
- *Jukka Kontinen, Hannu Rautio* and *Marika Leskelä* for their kind support in organizing the user evaluation experiment;
- *Simo Hosio, Tharanga Wijethilake* and *Susanna Pirttikangas* for testing the alpha version of CADEAU and for being patient when the prototype did not work;
- All participants in the user evaluation experiment who kindly agreed to take part in lengthy interviews;
- *Valérie Issarny* and *Nikolaos Georgantas* from the ARLES team (INRIA Paris-Rocquencourt) for their valuable comments regarding the experimental results;

- *Richard James* (from INRIA Paris-Rocquencourt) and *Minna Katila* for English language advice.

This work has been funded by Academy of Finland (as the Pervasive Service Computing project), and by GETA (Finnish Graduate School in Electronics, Telecommunications and Automation).

REFERENCES

AJAX public repository. (2010). *HTTP streaming protocol.* Retrieved June, 8, 2010, from http://ajaxpatterns.org/HTTP_Streaming

Beauche, S., & Poizat, P. (2008). Automated service composition with adaptive planning. In *Proceedings of the 6th International Conference on Service-Oriented Computing (ICSOC'08)*, (LNCS 5364), (pp. 530–537). Springer.

Ben Mokhtar, S., Georgantas, N., & Issarny, V. (2007). COCOA: Conversation-based service composition in pervasive computing environments with QoS support. *Journal of Systems and Software, 80*(12), 1941–1955. doi:10.1016/j.jss.2007.03.002

Bertolino, A., Angelis, G., Frantzen, L., & Polini, A. (2009). The PLASTIC framework and tools for testing service-oriented applications. In *Proceedings of the International Summer School on Software Engineering (ISSSE 2006-2008)*, (LNCS 5413), (pp. 106–139). Springer.

Bottaro, A., Gerodolle, A., & Lalanda, P. (2007). Pervasive service composition in the home network. In *Proceedings of the 21st International Conference on Advanced Information Networking and Applications (AINA'07)*, (pp. 596–603).

Broll, G., Haarlander, M., Paolucci, M., Wagner, M., Rukzio, E., & Schmidt, A. (2008). Collect&Drop: A technique for multi-tag interaction with real world objects and information book series. In *Proceedings of the European Conference on Ambient Intelligence (AmI'08)*, (LNCS 5355), (pp. 175–191). Springer.

Buford, J., Kumar, R., & Perkins, G. (2006). Composition trust bindings in pervasive computing service composition. In *Proceedings of the 4th Annual IEEE International Conference on Pervasive Computing and Communications Workshops (PERCOMW '06)*, (pp. 261–266). Washington, DC: IEEE Computer Society.

Chantzara, M., Anagnostou, M., & Sykas, E. (2006). Designing a quality-aware discovery mechanism for acquiring context information. In *Proceedings of the 20th International Conference on Advanced Information Networking and Applications (AINA'06)*, (pp. 211–216). Washington, DC: IEEE Computer Society.

Chin, J., Callaghan, V., & Clarke, G. (2006). An end-user tool for customising personal spaces in ubiquitous computing environments. In *Proceedings of the 3rd International Conference on Ubiquitous Intelligence and Computing, (UIC'06)*, (pp. 1080–1089).

Davidyuk, O., Georgantas, N., Issarny, V., & Riekki, J. (2010). MEDUSA: A middleware for end-user composition of ubiquitous applications. In Mastrogiovanni, F., & Chong, N.-Y. (Eds.), *Handbook of research on ambient intelligence and smart environments: Trends and perspectives*. Hershey, PA: IGI Global.

Davidyuk, O., Sánchez, I., Duran, J. I., & Riekki, J. (2008a). Autonomic composition of ubiquitous multimedia applications in reaches. In *Proceedings of the 7th International ACM Conference on Mobile and Ubiquitous Multimedia (MUM'08)*, (pp. 105–108). ACM.

Davidyuk, O., Sánchez, I., Duran, J. I., & Riekki, J. (2010). *CADEAU application scenario*. Retrieved June 8, 2010, from http://www.youtube.com/watch?v=sRjCisrdr18

Davidyuk, O., Selek, I., Duran, J. I., & Riekki, J. (2008b). Algorithms for composing pervasive applications. *International Journal of Software Engineering and Its Applications*, *2*(2), 71–94.

Forum, N. F. C. (2010a). *Near Field Communication (NFC) standard for short-range wireless communication technology*. Retrieved June 8, 2010, from http://www.nfc-forum.org

Forum, N. F. C. (2010b). *NFC data exchange format*. Retrieved June 8, 2010, from http://www.nfc-forum.org/specs/

Ghiani, G., Paternò, F., & Spano, L. D. (2009). Cicero Designer: An environment for end-user development of multi-device museum guides. In *Proceedings of the 2nd Int. Symposium on End-User Development (IS-EUD'09)*, (pp. 265–274).

Gross, T., & Marquardt, N. (2007). CollaborationBus: An editor for the easy configuration of ubiquitous computing environments. In *Proceedings of the Euromicro Conference on Parallel, Distributed, and Network-Based Processing*, (pp. 307–314). IEEE Computer Society.

Hardian, B., Indulska, J., & Henricksen, K. (2006). Balancing autonomy and user control in context-aware systems - a survey. In *Proceedings of the 3rd Workshop on Context Modeling and Reasoning (part of the 4th IEEE International Conference on Pervasive Computing and Communication)*. IEEE Computer Society.

Hardian, B., Indulska, J., & Henricksen, K. (2008). Exposing contextual information for balancing software autonomy and user control in context-aware systems. In *Proceedings of the Workshop on Context-Aware Pervasive Communities: Infrastructures, Services and Applications (CAPS'08)*, (pp. 253–260).

Kalasapur, S., Kumar, M., & Shirazi, B. (2007). Dynamic service composition in pervasive computing. *IEEE Transactions on Parallel and Distributed Systems*, *18*(7), 907–918. doi:10.1109/TPDS.2007.1039

Kalofonos, D., & Wisner, P. (2007). A framework for end-user programming of smart homes using mobile devices. In *Proceedings of the 4th IEEE Consumer Communications and Networking Conference (CCNC'07)*, (pp. 716–721). IEEE Computer Society.

Kawsar, F., Nakajima, T., & Fujinami, K. (2008). Deploy spontaneously: Supporting end-users in building and enhancing a smart home. In *Proceedings of the 10th International Conference on Ubiquitous Computing (UbiComp'08)*, (pp. 282–291). New York, NY: ACM.

Lindenberg, J., Pasman, W., Kranenborg, K., Stegeman, J., & Neerincx, M. A. (2006). Improving service matching and selection in ubiquitous computing environments: A user study. *Personal and Ubiquitous Computing*, *11*(1), 59–68. doi:10.1007/s00779-006-0066-7

LongTail Video. (2010). *JW Flash video player for FLV*. Retrieved June, 8, 2010, from http://www.longtailvideo.com/players/jw-player-5-for-flash

Masuoka, R., Parsia, B., & Labrou, Y. (2003). Task computing - the Semantic Web meets pervasive computing. In *Proceedings of the 2nd International Semantic Web Conference (ISWC'03)*, (LNCS 2870), (pp. 866–880). Springer.

Mavrommati, I., & Darzentas, J. (2007). End user tools for ambient intelligence environments: An overview. In *Human-Computer Interaction, Part II (HCII 2007)*, (LNCS 4551), (pp. 864–872). Springer.

Messer, A., Kunjithapatham, A., Sheshagiri, M., Song, H., Kumar, P., Nguyen, P., & Yi, K. H. (2006). InterPlay: A middleware for seamless device integration and task orchestration in a networked home. In *Proceedings of the 4th Annual IEEE Conference on Pervasive Computing and Communications*, (pp. 296–307). IEEE Computer Society.

Nakazawa, J., Yura, J., & Tokuda, H. (2004). Galaxy: A service shaping approach for addressing the hidden service problem. In *Proceedings of the 2nd IEEE Workshop on Software Technologies for Future Embedded and Ubiquitous Systems*, (pp. 35–39).

Newman, M., & Ackerman, M. (2008). Pervasive help @ home: Connecting people who connect devices. In *Proceedings of the International Workshop on Pervasive Computing at Home (PC@Home)*, (pp. 28–36).

Newman, M., Elliott, A., & Smith, T. (2008). Providing an integrated user experience of networked media, devices, and services through end-user composition. In *Proceedings of the 6th International Conference on Pervasive Computing (Pervasive '08)*, (pp. 213–227).

Paluska, J. M., Pham, H., Saif, U., Chau, G., Terman, C., & Ward, S. (2008). Structured decomposition of adaptive applications. In *Proceedings of the 6th Annual IEEE International Conference on Pervasive Computing and Communications (PerCom '08)*, (pp. 1–10). IEEE Computer Society.

Preuveneers, D., & Berbers, Y. (2005). Automated context-driven composition of pervasive services to alleviate non-functional concerns. *International Journal of Computing and Information Sciences*, *3*(2), 19–28.

Ranganathan, A., & Campbell, R. H. (2004). Autonomic pervasive computing based on planning. In *Proceedings of the International Conference on Autonomic Computing*, (pp. 80–87). Los Alamitos, CA: IEEE Computer Society.

Rantapuska, O., & Lahteenmaki, M. (2008). Task-based user experience for home networks and smart spaces. In *Proceedings of the International Workshop on Pervasive Mobile Interaction Devices*, (pp. 188–191).

Rich, C., Sidner, C., Lesh, N., Garland, A., Booth, S., & Chimani, M. (2006). DiamondHelp: A new interaction design for networked home appliances. *Personal and Ubiquitous Computing*, *10*(2-3), 187–190. doi:10.1007/s00779-005-0020-0

Riekki, J., Sánchez, I., & Pyykkonen, M. (2010). Remote control for pervasive services. *International Journal of Autonomous and Adaptive Communications Systems*, *3*(1), 39–58. doi:10.1504/IJAACS.2010.030311

Rigole, P., Clerckx, T., Berbers, Y., & Coninx, K. (2007). Task-driven automated component deployment for ambient intelligence environments. *Pervasive and Mobile Computing*, *3*(3), 276–299. doi:10.1016/j.pmcj.2007.01.001

Rigole, P., Vandervelpen, C., Luyten, K., Berbers, Y., Vandewoude, Y., & Coninx, K. (2005). A component-based infrastructure for pervasive user interaction. In *Proceedings of Software Techniques for Embedded and Pervasive Systems* (pp. 1–16). Springer.

Rouvoy, R., Barone, P., Ding, Y., Eliassen, F., Hallsteinsen, S. O., Lorenzo, J., et al. Scholz, U. (2009). MUSIC: Middleware support for self-adaptation in ubiquitous and service-oriented environments. In *Software Engineering for Self-Adaptive Systems*, (pp. 164–182).

Sánchez, I., Riekki, J., & Pyykkonen, M. (2009). Touch&Compose: Physical user interface for application composition in smart environments. In *Proceedings of the International Workshop on Near Field Communication*, (pp. 61–66). IEEE Computer Society.

Sintoris, C., Raptis, D., Stoica, A., & Avouris, N. (2007). Delivering multimedia content in enabled cultural spaces. In *Proceedings of the 3rd international Conference on Mobile Multimedia Communications (MobiMedia'07)*, (pp. 1–6). Brussels, Belgium: ICST.

Sousa, J. P., Poladian, V., Garlan, D., Schmerl, B., & Shaw, M. (2006). Task-based adaptation for ubiquitous computing. *IEEE Transactions on Systems, Man and Cybernetics. Part C, Applications and Reviews*, *36*, 328–340. doi:10.1109/TSMCC.2006.871588

Sousa, J. P., Schmerl, B., Poladian, V., & Brodsky, A. (2008a). uDesign: End-user design applied to monitoring and control applications for smart spaces. In *Proceedings of the Working IEEE/IFIP Conference on Software Architecture*, (pp. 71–80). IEEE Computer Society.

Sousa, J. P., Schmerl, B., Steenkiste, P., & Garlan, D. (2008b). Activity-oriented computing, chap. XI. In *Advances in Ubiquitous Computing: Future Paradigms and Directions.* (pp. 280–315). Hershey, PA: IGI Publishing.

Takemoto, M., Oh-ishi, T., Iwata, T., Yamato, Y., Tanaka, Y., & Shinno, K. … Shimamoto, N. (2004). A service-composition and service-emergence framework for ubiquitous-computing environments. In *Proceedings of the 2004 Workshop on Applications and the Internet, part of SAINT'04*, (pp. 313–318).

Vastenburg, M., Keyson, D., & de Ridder, H. (2007). Measuring user experiences of prototypical autonomous products in a simulated home environment. [HCI]. *Human-Computer Interaction*, *2*, 998–1007.

Zipf, G. K. (1949). *Human behavior and the principle of least effort.* Cambridge, MA: Addison-Wesley Press.

KEY TERMS AND DEFINITIONS

Service-oriented Computing: is a paradigm that promotes building applications by assembling together independent networking services.

Activity-oriented Computing: promotes the idea of supporting everyday user activities through composing and deploying appropriate services and resources.

Interaction Design: is a discipline that studies the relationship between humans and interactive products (i.e. devices) they use.

Physical user Interface Design: is a discipline that studies user interfaces in which users interact with the digital would using real (i.e. physical) objects.

Ubiquitous Environments: refers to computer environments that are populated with tiny networking devices which support people in carrying out their everyday tasks using non-intrusive intelligent technology.

Chapter 5
Pervasive and Interactive Use of Multimedia Contents via Multi-Technology Location-Aware Wireless Architectures[1]

Pasquale Pace
University of Calabria, Italy

Gianluca Aloi
University of Calabria, Italy

ABSTRACT

Nowadays, due to the increasing demands of the fast-growing Consumer Electronics (CEs) market, more powerful mobile consumer devices are being introduced continuously; thanks to this evolution of CEs technologies, many sophisticated pervasive applications start to be developed and applied to context and location aware scenarios. This chapter explores applications and a real world case-study of pervasive computing by means of a flexible communication architecture well suited for the interactive enjoyment of historical and artistic contents and built on top of a wireless network infrastructure. The designed system and the implemented low cost testbed integrate different communication technologies such as Wi-Fi, Bluetooth, and GPS with the aim of offering, in a transparent and reliable way, a mixed set of different multimedia and Augmented Reality (AR) contents to mobile users equipped with handheld devices. This communication architecture represents a first solid step to provide network support to pervasive context-aware applications pushing the ubiquitous computing paradigm into reality.

INTRODUCTION

In the last few years we witnessed a great advance in mobile devices processing power, miniaturization and extended battery life, making the goal of ubiquitous computing every day more realistic, also thanks to novel networked consumer electronics (NCE) platforms that are capable of supporting different applications such as video streaming, file

DOI: 10.4018/978-1-60960-611-4.ch005

transfer and content delivery. In modern society, computers are ubiquitous and assist in increasing human efficiency and saving time; in particular, two main aspects of the same coin have contributed to the development and implementation of the ubiquitous computing paradigm pushing it into reality: the advancements in technologies and the increased popularity of context-aware applications. The first aspect, consisting in the rapid development of computer technology, has yielded the shrinking of computer size and increasing of processing power; such progress is well realized by wearable computers (Kim, 2003; Starner, 2002); the second one has made context-aware computing more attractive for many groups, research centers and industries (Han et al., 2008; Schilit et al., 2002). In context-aware computing, applications may timely change or adapt their functions, information and user interface depending on the context and client requirements (Kanter, 2002; Rehman et al., 2007).

Taking the vision of ubiquitous computing to another level, we see the development of context-aware ubiquitous systems which take into account a great amount of information before interacting with the environment, and dynamically cater to user needs based on the situation at hand; furthermore, these systems are interconnected by novel mobile wireless and sensing technologies (Machado et al., 2007; Roussos et al., 2005) setting up a new kind of intelligent environment where context-aware applications can search and use services in a transparent and automatic way. Nowadays, many possible wireless networking technologies are available such as wireless local area networks (WLANs) based on the well known IEEE 802.11a/b/g standards or personal area networks (PANs) supporting Bluetooth communication (McDermott-Wells, 2005).

Since context-aware applications necessarily require some kind of mobile wireless communication technology, the transparent integration of different communication standards and equipments has a growing interest in the scientific community; in other words, the current state of mobile communication and consumer electronics can be characterized by the convergence of devices and by the growing need for connecting these devices.

Starting from this existing scenario, the chapter first describes a set of useful localization techniques and services for pervasive computing; then it proposes a real word case-study networking architecture suitable to provide AR and multimedia historical and artistic contents to the visitors of museums or archeological sites equipped with CEs handheld devices. This location-based contents delivery system has been called GITA (Pace et al., 2009) that in Italian language means "*trip*" with the aim of pointing out the main goal and purpose of the designed application.

The architecture uses a two-level (*hard* and *soft*) localization strategy to localize the visitors and to provide them information about what they are viewing, at their level of knowledge, and in their natural language. The soft localization, mainly based on Wi-Fi/GPS and Bluetooth technologies, allows knowing a coarse user's location in order to select and deliver a set of multimedia contents of potential interest, while a more accurate (hard) localization, based on the use of fiducial markers, is used only to support the provision of AR contents. The system also gives the possibility to the users to have a graphical user interface adapted to their CEs devices (e.g. cellular phones, Smartphones, PDAs, UMPC) and to receive useful AR contents.

In particular, the proposed GITA system differs from the works described in the "*State of the art and related works on Location Based Systems and Services*" section because it is able to locate users in both indoor and outdoor environments using and combining, at the same time, different technologies (i.e. Wi-Fi, Bluetooth, GPS and Visual Based) in a flexible and transparent way; moreover the proposed system presents the following improvements:

- it is accurate enough to track movements and to determine the position of a person within the network coverage area offering several precision levels;
- it is inconspicuous for the users and thus it does not force them to carry any additional hardware;
- it is able to track several persons per room with justifiable computational power;
- it is easy to install and unobtrusive (with respect to the environment);
- it is built with inexpensive standard components;
- it is adaptable to the different capabilities of commercial consumer devices.

The chapter is organized as follows: we first present an overview of localization techniques and services that will be supported by the GITA system also giving few hints of recently developed architectures and applications by various researchers; after that, we explain the system operation and the software modules implemented in our case study with the aim of making the communication, within the system, easy, reliable and transparent to the users; finally we show the performance of the implemented testbed with the aim of verifying the effectiveness of the overall architecture. Future extensions, possible research directions and general conclusions are given in the last section of the chapter.

OVERVIEW OF LOCALIZATION TECHNIQUES AND LOCATION BASED SERVICES

Pervasive computing is a rapidly developing area of Information and Communications Technology (ICT) and it refers to the increasing integration of ICT into people's lives and environments, made possible by the growing availability of intelligent devices with inbuilt communications facilities. Pervasive computing has many potential applications, such as health and home care, environmental monitoring, intelligent transport systems, entertainment and many other areas. One of the most challenging problems faced by pervasive computing researchers is how to support services and applications that need to be enjoyed by users having different devices and harmonized with the context and the environment of the users. Seamless communications among intelligent devices could transform ordinary spaces into intelligent environments. A smart environment is different from an ordinary space because it has to perform system perception, cognition, analysis, reasoning, and predict users' status and surroundings. Context awareness is the most fundamental form of such capabilities, since the system should be aware of any information it can use to characterize situations in order to adapt its responses to user's activities.

In such perspective Location Based Services (LBS) and localization techniques play a crucial role in order to effectively support mobile users and context aware applications. In recent years, LBS have generated a lot of interest mostly due to the growing competition between different telecommunication technologies (Bellavista et al., 2008). A successful LBS technology must meet the position accuracy requirements determined by the particular service, at the lowest possible cost and with minimal impact on the network and the equipment.

According to this vision, the current section summarizes the strength of the three localization techniques (i.e. GPS, Wi-Fi, Visual) that have been integrated into the proposed communication system. We remark that the localization procedure represents one of the main features of the GITA system because only by knowing the position of mobile handheld devices it is reasonable to offer a compact set of interesting multimedia contents according to the environment visited by the user.

GPS Localization

GPS (Global Position System) is used in surveying and positioning (tracking and navigating vehicles) for many years (Kaplan, 1996; El-Rabbany, 2006). The basic principle is to measure the distance from the user's receiver to at least 3 satellites (triangulation/trilateration), whose position in orbit is known. An observer on Earth can uniquely locate his position by determining the distance between himself and three satellites whose orbital positions are already known. Distance information is based on the travel time of a satellite signal, obtained by measuring the time difference of arrival, at the GPS receiver, of special ranging codes. Errors in receiver or satellite clocks are present in the distance estimation, which, for this reason is referred to as pseudo-range estimation. Observation geometry affects the quality of the resulting three-dimensional position. Satellites that appear close to one another in the sky provide correlated (redundant) range information: this effect is known as geometric dilution of precision (GDOP). If observations are extended to four (or more) satellites, by receiver design, these geometric effects can be minimized by choosing satellites which maximize the volume of a tetrahedron defined by the points of intersection on a unit sphere (centered on the user) of vectors between the satellite and the ground receiver. This allows for a 2D- and 3D-positioning worldwide, independent of weather conditions and time.

A mobile user with a GPS receiver is provided with accurate latitude, longitude, time and bearing 24 hours a day, worldwide. From a user's point of view, GPS is a passive system making use of the infrastructure that was set up by the US military (NAVSTAR-GPS) or Russian military (GLONASS). In the future, the European system GALILEO (Quinlan, 2005; Peng, 2008) will enrich the existing GPS technologies with improved robustness and better positioning accuracy due to additional active satellites.

There are two primary GPS positioning modes: absolute and relative positioning, and there are several different strategies for GPS data collection and processing, relevant to both positioning modes. For absolute positioning, a single receiver may observe pseudo-distances to multiple satellites to determine the user's location. Of major interest are differential GPS techniques (DGPS) which refer to a relative positioning technology. DGPS employs at least two receivers, one defined as the reference (or base) receiver, whose coordinates must be known, and the other defined as the user's receiver, whose coordinates can be determined relative to the reference receiver by differencing the simultaneous measurements to the same satellites observed by the reference and the user receiver. Using pseudo-distances it is possible to achieve an accuracy of 1-5m for absolute positioning, whereas a relative positioning with pseudo-distances can achieve accuracies of circa 50cm. With carrier phase measurements, accuracies in both static and mobile mode within the range of some millimeters are achievable (Grejner-Brzezinska, 2004).

Although GPS techniques for localization of fixed and mobile users are quite accurate, they can be applied only in outdoor environments because users need to have the satellites in line of sight. Since GPS does not work inside buildings, alternative indoor tracking systems have been proposed; for example in (Graumann et al., 2003) the authors aim at designing a universal location framework by using GPS in an outdoor environment and Wi-Fi positioning for an indoor environment.

Cellular Networks Localization

Mobile communication systems such as GSM (Global Standard for Mobile Communications) or UMTS (Universal Mobile Telecommunication System) are based on a set of cellular networks. Cellular localization (Song, 1994; Varshavsky et al., 2006) takes advantage of the mobile cellular infrastructure present in most urban environments to estimate the position of an object.

Although only one base station is used by the generic mobile phone for communication, usually several base stations can listen to and communicate with a mobile phone at any time. This fact allows a number of localization techniques to be used to estimate the position of the mobile phone. A well known technique called Received Signal Strength Indicator (RSSI) uses the strength of the received signals to derive the distance to the base stations. It is also possible to estimate a distance based on the time it takes for a signal to leave the sender and arrive at the base station (*Time of Arrival – ToA*) or the difference between the times it takes for a single signal to arrive at multiple base stations (*Time Difference of Arrival – TDoA*). Once we have the distances from the mobile phone to at least three base stations, it is possible to compute the position of the mobile phone using such techniques as "*trilateration*" and "*multilateration*" (Boukerche et al., 2007). Although the time of arrival and the signal strength can be directly converted to range measurements, we have to keep in mind, that the radio channel is a broadcast medium subject to interference, multipath and fading causing significant errors, while also making the cellular localization less precise than GPS; for these reasons, the accuracy depends on a number of factors such as the current urban environment, the number of base stations detecting the signal, the positioning algorithm used, etc. In most cases, the average localization error will be between 90m and 250m (Chen et al., 2006), which is not accurate enough for applications well suited for relatively small areas such as office buildings, archeological parks or museums.

Wi-Fi Localization

The widespread adoption of the 802.11 family of standards for wireless LAN as a common network infrastructure enables Wi-Fi-based localization with few additional hardware costs and has thus inspired extensive research on indoor localization in the last few years (Liu et al., 2007; Roxin et al., 2007). Since Wi-Fi-based location systems can be either deterministic or probabilistic in matching RSSI (Received Signal Strength Indication) from mobile devices to a radio map, location fingerprinting has been used for such approaches where information in a database of prior measurements of the received signal strength at different locations is matched with the values measured by a mobile station.

The most common method to establish a position is to determine the distance by either measuring the signal propagation delay or by measuring the signal strength. Due to the structure of modern buildings and the reduced abilities of commercial WLAN network cards and common access points, both of the values cannot be used in practice. Instead an inferring approach has been developed and is commercially available as the EKAHAU positioning engine (www.ekahau.com). The basic idea (Roos et al, 2002) is to utilize a general propagation model and to parameterize this model through a number of test measurements. The mathematical calculation of such a model would be too complex to present here. In short, the mobile client measures the signal strengths of all surrounding access points and delivers these data to the positioning engine which in turn calculates the position by solving a maximum likelihood problem. The system is not affected by the fact that several access points transmit at the same frequency because it uses the integrated signals.

The best Wi-Fi localization systems claim 90% accuracy with an error of less than 1~2 meters (Chan et al., 2006). Some of these systems achieve better accuracy by combining different localization methods. That is, a hybrid system can benefit under situations where one method works poorly while another still works well. For example in (Gwon et al., 2004) the authors proposed algorithms combining Wi-Fi and Bluetooth sensors as information sources and selectively weighting them such that error contribution from each sensor can be minimized to improve the positioning accuracy. Microsoft Research proposed an RF-based indoor location tracking system by processing signal strength information at multiple base stations (Bahl & Padmanabhan, 2000). In addition, a more synthetic description of indoor positioning systems previously developed can be found in (Kim & Jun, 2008), although Wi-Fi localization techniques can be used also in outdoor environments subject to an accurate WLAN deployment.

Visual-Based Localization

A great deal of research has been done on visual-based localization systems and two prominent types have emerged. One analyzes an environment's scenery, matching the result with captured images and the other uses "*Fiducial Markers*" placed in the environment (Fiala, 2005; Fiala 2010). Fiducial markers are useful in many situations where object recognition or pose determination is needed with a high reliability, where natural features are not present in sufficient quantity and uniqueness, and where it is not inconvenient to affix markers. Example applications include indoor augmented reality, hand-held objects for user pose input, message tags to trigger a behavior, or generic pose determination in industrial settings.

A fiducial marker system consists of some unique patterns along with the algorithms necessary to locate their projection in camera images. The patterns should be distinct enough so as not to be confused with the environment. Ideally the system should have a library of many unique markers that can be distinguished one from another. The image processing algorithms should be robust enough to find the markers in situations of uncontrolled lighting, image noise and blurring, unknown scale, and partial occlusion. Preferably, the markers should be passive (not requiring electrical power) planar patterns for convenient printing and mounting, and should be detectable with a minimum of required image pixels to maximize the range of usage.

In (Behringer, et al., 2002) the authors matched images with models of the surroundings, while an efficient solution to real-time camera tracking of scenes that contain planar structures has been proposed in (Simon & Berger, 2002).

Although some of these solutions were designed for outdoor augmented reality, they are also adaptable for indoor localization. The advantage of these systems is that they do not need any beacons that might not fit inside a room. On the other hand, a limitation of these systems is that if the environment changes, the system loses its point of reference, and the tracking will fail. For this reason, other researchers have experimented with fiducial markers, which can also provide positional data. Some systems use markers that are based on ARToolkit (Kato & Billinghurst, 1999); these markers have a square frame, and by taking advantage of two opposing edges of the frame, a camera's position can be calculated. Many researchers have developed localization systems using ARToolkit markers (Thomas et al., 2000; Kalkusch et al., 2002; Baratoff et al., 2002; Zhang et al., 2002). In particular (Kim & Jun, 2008) proposes a vision-based location positioning system using augmented reality techniques for indoor navigation.

The GITA system proposed in this chapter, automatically recognizes a location from image sequences taken from indoor environments, and it realizes augmented reality by seamlessly overlaying the user's view with location information. Fiducial markers will be also used in the GITA system, as show in in a forthcoming section, in order to obtain a fine localization mechanism that will enable the provision of augmented reality contents.

State of the Art on Location Based Systems and Services

Location Based Systems for both indoor and outdoor localization using wireless technologies were studied extensively and described to a great extent in the related literature over the last decade; several projects based on WLAN localization have been proposed but many of the WLAN management and monitoring systems are not widely available today and they simply approximate the location of the client with the location of the AP that the client is associated with.

A famous indoor localization project, RADAR (Castro & Muntz, 2000), developed by Microsoft, uses pattern matching of received signal strength at a client from landmarks, such as APs, to locate a Wi-Fi client. It adopted the k-nearest neighbor (KNN) algorithm and inferred the user's location by computing the Euclidean distance between the user and the sampled points. Ekahau (www.ekahau.com) improves the location algorithm adopted by RADAR using probabilistic evaluation parameters other than distance. In the offline phase it stores the probability of the signal strength sampling signal every ten seconds in four directions. In the online phase, it computes the probability of acquired samples to infer user location.

LANDMARC (Jin et al., 2006) is another indoor localization system based on radio frequency identification (RFID) technology. This method utilizes active RFID tags for indoor location sensing employing the idea of having extra fixed location reference tags to improve the overall accuracy of locating objects and to minimize the presence of fixed RFID readers spread in the environment. Accuracy of this approach is highly dependent on the density of the deployed reference tags and readers, nevertheless, it is not possible to spread a great number of active tags and readers within a museum or a historical place because they need a capillary power supply distribution; moreover, this solution is not comfortable for the users because they need to be equipped with an additional device able to communicate with the RFID tags. An evolution of the LANDMARC architecture is proposed in (Siadat & Selamat, 2008) using passive RFID tags which are planted in various areas within the targeted environment and are read by an RFID reader attached to a mobile device for the purpose of service discovery. One of the advantages of this approach is that the passive RFID tag does not consume power. In fact, there is no need for an extra power supply because passive RFID tags have zero power consumption and the RFID reader is attached to a mobile device that is already powered.

In addition, there are also positioning systems based on the *Widespread Bluetooth technology* that estimate the distance between the sensor nodes based on signal strength measurements; a first recent example of these systems (Subramanian et al., 2007) consists of a scalable indoor location service based on a cost-effective solution. Another case study is given by (Rashid et al., 2008); in this work the authors present a system that can be used with any current mobile phone to provide location based information/advertisements to any mobile phone, equipped with Bluetooth technology, without any necessity of installing client side software. Even though these solutions are simple to be implemented, they cannot be used in outdoor environments such as archaeological parks because of the limited coverage range. Furthermore, the accuracy of all of these systems based on RF signals for localization is more or less diminished because of multipath propagation. To overcome this problem Fontana et al. proposed to use ultra wideband (UWB) signals for the propagation time measurements (Fontana et al., 2003). Due to the shortness of the measurement pulses, the directly received signal can be distinguished more easily from reflected signals. However, due to the high signal propagation speed and the required high sampling frequencies, costly hardware is truly necessary, thus making the whole system architecture very expensive and less attractive for customers.

Location Based Systems are used to provide location based services consisting in *"...services that take into account the geographic location of a user"* (Junglas & Spitzmüller, 2005) or in *"... business and customer services that give users a set of services starting from the geographic location of the client"* (Adusei et al., 2004). Starting from these specific definitions, a detailed classification of Location Based services has been proposed by the research community; in particular, (Junglas & Spitzmüller, 2005) and (Barkhuus & Dey, 2003) distinguished two classes that are generally named *position-aware* and *location-tracking services*.

These two kinds of services can be identified and distinguished basically by the role of the requester and the recipient of the requested information. In *position- aware* services, information is received by the user who is at the same time the requester; therefore, the requesters may provide their actual location information in order to receive location dependent information. One example for this kind of service is the calculation of the shortest route to some point of interest. In contrast to that, *location-tracking services* receive requests from and provide location information to external third-party applications which act on behalf of the users. In this case, the requester and the receiver are not necessarily the same. Another distinction is that position-aware applications respond to each single service request whereas location-tracking applications' processes are activated once to collect and process location information of several users.

Another possible way of classification is to distinguish whether a location-based service is *reactive* or *proactive* (Küpper et al., 2006). Whereas reactive location-based services only deliver location information upon the users' request, proactive services operate on sessions and react to predefined events. According to (Bellavista et al., 2008), reactive and proactive services are closely related to position-aware and location-tracking applications. Whereas reactive location-based services rely on users' interaction, proactive applications can operate more autonomously. Once they are started they detect and react to location changes, by triggering certain actions and changing states. The possible interaction patterns are various and are usually based on proximity detection of users or other target objects. The decisive distinction between reactive and proactive services is that reactive services provide to users only a synchronous communication pattern, whereas proactive services allow users to communicate asynchronously. One popular example represents the widespread use of car navigation systems that process the cars' actual position information that is received from a satellite. The location information is processed directly on the navigation device and for example instantly displayed on a map on the screen. The basic functionality of car navigation systems, that is the internal processing of received GPS position information demonstrates a typical example of position-aware services.

Finally, the actual number of users being part of an active session allows to distinguish between *single* and *multi-target location-based services*. It is clear that location-based services that are capable of tracking multiple users or objects at once may also be included to the single-target location-based services. A distinction that makes probably more sense is given by (Bellavista et al., 2008). Simple scenarios may for example have only one implemented functionality such as displaying the actual location of the user being tracked on a map. On the other hand, the focus of multi-target applications is rather on interrelating positions of several users that are tracked in one or possibly several sessions.

According to presented classifications of location based services, the proposed GITA system can be considered as a Multi-Target, Reactive, Position-Aware architecture whose potential will be investigated in the next section.

SYSTEM ARCHITECTURE

The overall architecture of the GITA system is based on the cooperation of an edge wireless network and a core wireless/wired network as shown in Figure 1. The edge side is based on Wi-Fi, GPS and Bluetooth technologies, while the core network supports the integration of the previous technologies within a fixed Ethernet local area network and a wireless IEEE 802.11a/b/g WLAN. The proposed architecture can provide both connectivity and localization services, the former are used to support the delivery of multimedia contents toward user's terminals, while the latter are needed to localize the area of interest close to each user.

The localization infrastructure uses a two levels (*hard* and *soft*) localization strategy to localize the visitors and to provide them information about what they are viewing, at their level of knowledge, and in their natural language. The *soft* localization strategy, preparatory to the *hard* one, is mainly based on Wi-Fi/GPS and Bluetooth technologies, it allows knowing a coarse user's location in order to select and deliver a set of multimedia contents of potential interest taken from a Geo-Referenced Data Base. The *hard* localization is visual based and makes use of fiducial markers to support the provision of AR contents. When a generic user decides to enjoy Augmented Reality applications, the *hard*-Visual-Based Localization strategy can compute the position of the user in respect to the observed object making the client application ready to execute the correct local rendering process. In this way, the previously downloaded AR content can be superposed to the real scene.

The communication protocol between the different devices belonging to the GITA system represents the main issue of the proposed network architecture.

Figure 1. Overall GITA system architecture

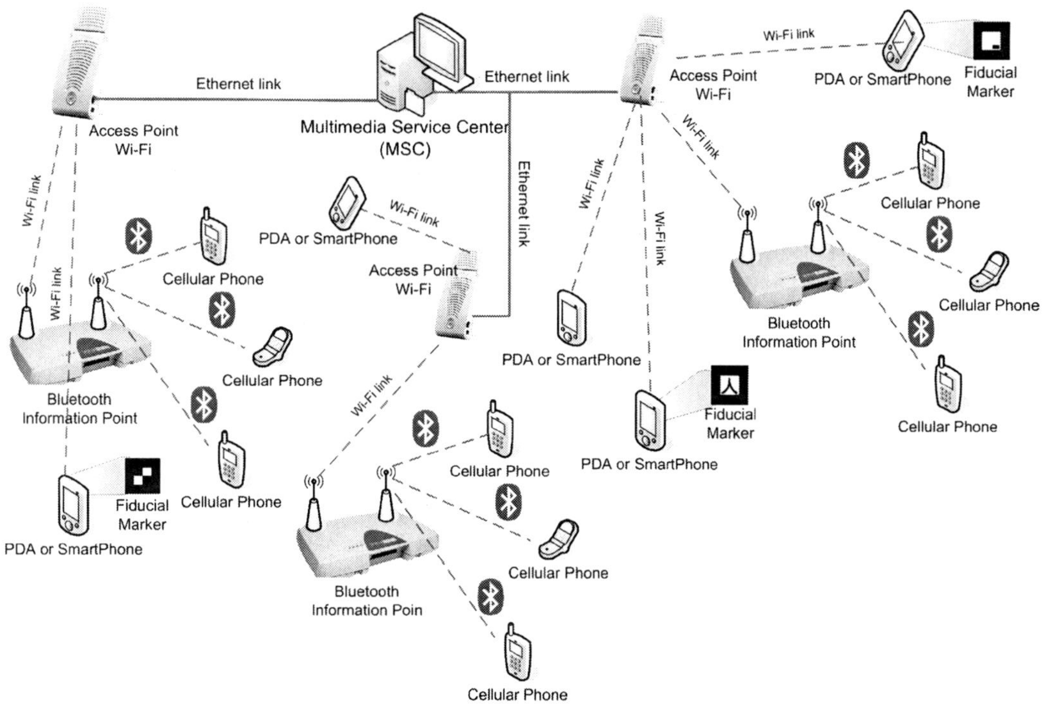

The key entities within the GITA system are the Handheld Devices (HDs), the Bluetooth Information Points (BIPs) and the Multimedia Service Center (MSC). These devices are based on different communication standards and technologies but they need to communicate to each other in order to offer a flexible and reliable communication architecture to the customers; furthermore they consist of different subsystems that will be detailed in the following sections.

Handheld Devices

Handheld devices can be enhanced portable CEs such as PDAs, SmartPhones or low cost cellular phones. Enhanced devices are usually equipped with both Wi-Fi and Bluetooth interfaces (PDA, SmartPhone) thus they can download multimedia contents stored on the MSC using the wireless network. Thanks to the Wi-Fi interface, these devices can be localized through the localization software installed on the MSC and therefore they just receive the multimedia contents concerning the artworks close to their area. Basic cellular phones are generally equipped only with a Bluetooth interface and can be considered as very simple handheld devices. They can receive small amounts of data from the BIPs and, in this last simple scenario, the execution of the localization procedure is unnecessary because the BIPs are fixed and only cellular phones within the BIP coverage area can receive multimedia contents. BIPs are installed during the network deployment phase and the coverage area can be set with an appropriate power tuning.

Bluetooth Information Points (BIPs)

BIPs are particular access points equipped with both Wi-Fi and the Bluetooth wireless interfaces. These devices can offer connectivity to the handheld devices through the Bluetooth interface within a small coverage area (up to 10m) and mobile clients can download multimedia contents, stored on the MSC, through the multi-hop WLAN infrastructure. The generic BIP is able to push multimedia contents directly to enabled devices (Mobile Phone, Smartphone…) using Bluetooth (McDermott-Wells, 2005) standard profiles such as *Generic Object Exchange Profile* (GOEP) and *Object Push Profile* (OPP). BIPs are the only way to communicate with low cost cellular phones.

Multimedia Service Center (MSC)

The Multimedia Service Center is the control center of the GITA system. It hosts multimedia contents within a Geo-Referenced Data Base and delivers Location Based Services (LBS) to handheld devices within a museum or historical area. The MSC also hosts the server side of software modules for localization purposes; it provides accurate real-time localization and tracking of handheld devices collecting Wi-Fi and GPS information coming from mobile clients. When a mobile client is in proximity of an interesting area, the MSC, being aware of its position, notifies it of the availability of a set of multimedia contents. Since multimedia content delivery is performed on demand, the generic user, upon examination of the content list, can decide to download, or not, one or more of the suggested contents.

Software Modules within System Architecture

In order to provide reliable and flexible communication and localization services between the different devices, specific software modules have been designed to be installed on both client and server side.

According to the proposed architecture, the client side represents the mobile handheld device whilst the server side represents the MSC.

The modules have been programmed using *Visual Studio.NET* as an integrated development programming environment that supports multi-platform applications; thus, it is possible to develop

Figure 2. Software modules within GITA architecture

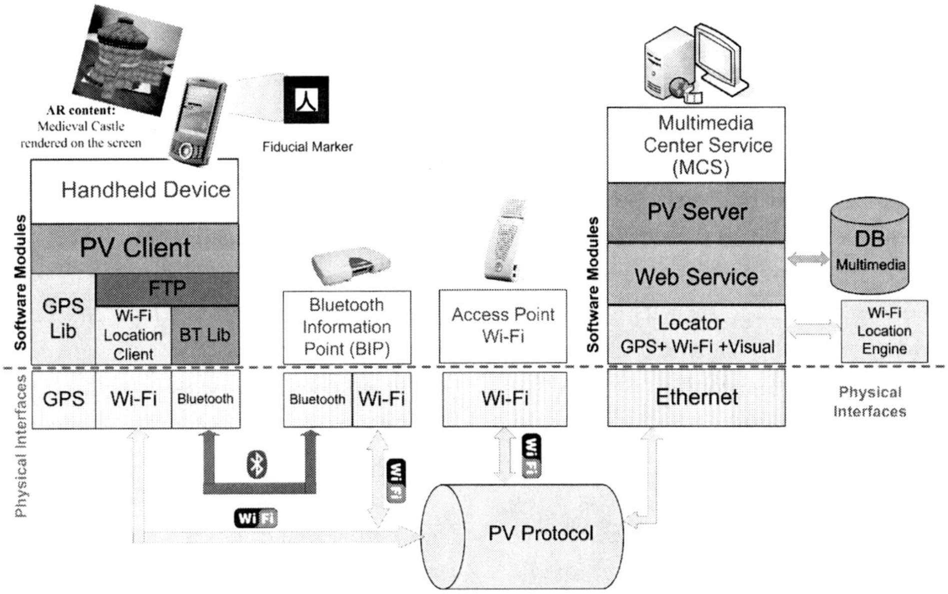

programs for servers, workstations, Pocket PCs, Smartphones and as Web Services. Figure 2 shows the software modules and the communication interfaces designed for GITA.

In the following subsections we explain the main features of each module and the operation of the personal viewer communication protocol (PVP) that has been designed for our system.

1. Personal Viewer Protocol (PVP)

The PVP allows the communication between the service center and the mobile handheld devices using a socket architecture. It has been developed as software libraries that need to be installed on both client and server side in order to link up the exchanged communication data format. Once the connection has been established using the socket paradigm (*ip address* and *destination port*), data are encapsulated in an XML (*eXtensible Markup Language*) string to be send over the communication channel. The overhead introduced by this solution is very small because each XML string is composed only by the following four fields:

- User ID (1 byte)
- Operation code (1 byte)
- User Position (2*8 bytes)
- DATA (variable length)

Concerning the user's position, we need a structure to store the 2 fields (latitude, longitude) provided by standard GPS devices. These fields can be used also for Wi-Fi localization, but in that case latitude and longitude values will be translated into X and Y coordinates on a map representing the network's coverage area.

We would like to remark that we chose XML because it is a generic language that can be used to describe any kind of content in a structured way, separated from its presentation to a specific device (Hunter et al., 2007); in this way, the proposed structure can be easily extended or modified according to the system needs.

2. Software Modules within the Client Side

The *Wi-Fi Location Client* is a software library designed to send the signal power values of the mobile handheld device to the MSC. These data will be used by the locator module within the MSC to localize the mobile user.

GPS Lib is a software library for sending the GPS position to the MSC; this library can be used only if the client is equipped with a GPS antenna. The GPS co-ordinates will be used by the localization software implemented on the server in order to discover the exact position of a generic user within the network coverage area. This position will be used for executing an efficient query on the multimedia database in order to retrieve a list of downloadable multimedia contents close to the generic user.

FTP is a software library used to offer a file transfer service to the mobile user; once the user has received the list of downloadable multimedia contents, he can simply download the desired content by selecting it on the touch screen.

BT Lib module implements both GOEP and OPP standard Bluetooth profiles to exchange binary objects with target devices. Both profiles are based on the OBEX (*OBject Exchange*) protocol that was originally developed for Infrared Data Association (IrDA) and lately adopted by the Bluetooth standard. OBEX is transport neutral, as with the hypertext transfer protocol (HTTP), which means that it can work over almost any other transport layer protocol; furthermore, OBEX is a structured protocol which provides the functionality to separate data and data attributes (Bakker et al., 2002; Huang et al., 2007).

3. Software Modules within the Service Center Side

Locator GPS+Wi-Fi+Visual is an application designed for the server architecture. This module mainly allows to localize the client according to the signal power level values received from the handheld device through the PV protocol, but also using other localization means. According to the received data, the handheld device can be localized through the Wi-Fi network (indoor or outdoor localization), the GPS signal (outdoor localization) or the fiducial markers (visual-based localization) This application is strictly linked to the Wi-Fi Location Engine module in which are implemented the algorithms for the Wi-Fi localization.

The *Wi-Fi Location Engine* is a software module for real-time localization (RTLS). It is based on RSSI (Received Signal Strength Information) with fingerprinting method which enables us to locate the mobile terminal; this software communicates with all the Wi-Fi-based (802.11 a/b/g) access points in the network area to locate an object.

In order to use the *Wi-Fi Location Engine* module, we must first define a new positioning model by inserting the floor plan of our chosen environment. Then we define paths and trails for our model. These paths are the routine paths within which we may wish to track specified objects. Subsequently, we must calibrate our model, executing a training phase, by walking around the area along those paths that we have defined for collecting data by measuring the received power from different accessible access points. Every few meters we can gather information by reading the received power from access points. In this way, we can build our database of observed signal strength as we walk through all the routine paths in the network area and collect data. The more data we collect, the more accurate our location estimation can be. After collecting the data, we can locate the desired target which can be either a laptop or a PDA.

The *Web Service* is a software module that provides the needed interface for querying the multimedia database through a dedicated Web Service. Using this Web Service architecture the system is more flexible because the multimedia database can be stored on a different computers or in a remote repository as well. We used WSDL (*Web Services Description Language*) for implementing the web service description in a general and abstract manner.

TESTBED AND RESULTS

In this section we show the deployment of the proposed communication architecture, we illustrate the devices chosen for the testbed and we verify the effectiveness of the system in terms of localization accuracy and network reliability.

The testbed evaluation presented in this chapter has been conducted in the indoor environment even if the GITA system can be used, as already explained, in both outdoor and indoor environments. The motivation behind this choice is mostly due to the lack of the specific authorization for installing the overall network communication system in a big outdoor area, such as an archaeological or a natural park. In order to overcome this limitation, at present, we are setting up an outdoor testbed in our university campus even though we would like to remark that the indoor localization issues are more severe than the outdoor ones, in which the GPS techniques have proven to guarantee a satisfactory accuracy level. In particular, we experienced big difficulties in the training phase of the Location Engine Module for outdoor environments where many propagation effects can disturb the channel making it very unstable and changeable. In indoor environments, the localization technique using Wi-Fi technology greatly benefits from multipath effects, whilst in outdoor these effects are very small and the localization accuracy is hence highly reduced. Thus in outdoor settings, GPS technology is more stable and it overcomes the Wi-Fi one in supporting a more useful localization.

We deployed the network architecture illustrated in Figure 1 using the hardware listed in Figure 3.

We installed the Wi-Fi and Bluetooth access points in two different environments:

- a floor of our building according to the position illustrated in Figure 4a in which the overall area covered by the Wi-Fi network is about 190 square meters.
- the archaeological museum of *"Capo Colonna"* placed in Crotone (Italy) and composed by 3 big rooms of about 750 square meters each as shown in Figure 4b.

Wi-Fi access points were initiated to work on different channels using the configuration which gives us the least interference between channels. Two of them were working on channel eleven, the next two were working on channel six and the last was working on channel one. The access points with the same working channel were placed as far as possible from each other.

After that, we installed the software modules described in the previous section on the handheld devices and on the MSC; then we executed the survey phase for training the localization software.

We stored different multimedia contents on the MSC; each content is associated with a pair of coordinate values (X,Y) according to its position on the map. Every room in our testbed contains different multimedia contents; thus, the generic users can receive a list of multimedia contents close to their own position in the visited room.

Localization Accuracy

We verified the reliability of the whole system architecture evaluating the accuracy of the localization process. We have chosen four and five points for the office and the museum environments respectively, as shown in Figure 4a and 4b, to carry out the position measurements in order to evaluate the position error with respect to the power link strength.

The horizontal and vertical position errors were measured and combined together in order to evaluate the overall error. We named as the origin the upper left corner of the map, so if the estimated location is to the right of the actual location the error would be considered as a positive value and if it was to the left of actual points, error was considered as a negative value. The same procedure has been applied for Y-direction,

Figure 3. Devices used for network deployment

5 Wi-Fi Access Point Alcatel OmniAccess AP60/61 Standard wireless: 802.11a\b\g	
3 Smartphone HTC P3300 equipped with Wi-Fi, GPS and Bluetooth interfaces	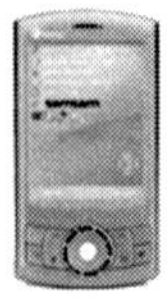
1 Samsung Q1 Ultra Mobile PC (UMPC) equipped with Wi-Fi and Bluetooth 2.0 interfaces	
3 Access Point Bluetooth Blue Giga Wrap access server equipped with Wi-Fi and Bluetooth 2.0 interfaces	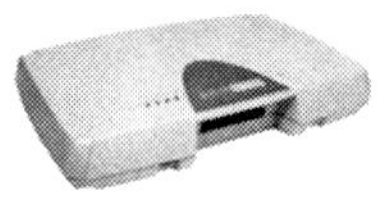

where positive error meant that the estimated point is higher up in the map comparing to the actual location and negative if the estimated location is lower. We executed 50 measurements for each point in order to average the effect of the wireless link fluctuations. The position error of each sample has been computed as the difference between the real value and the value provided by the localization software; we evaluated the position error on both X and Y map directions individually, and then we evaluated the modulus of the distance error defined as:

$$E_{X,Y} = \sqrt{X_{err}^2 + Y_{err}^2}$$

Finally we computed mean and variance of the 50 measurements carried out for each location point and we plotted the cumulative distribution function (CDF) of the position error. Figure 5 shows the obtained results for point A of the office environment; the dashed line represents the theoretical trend of the CDF whilst the solid line has been obtained plotting the measured values of all samples.

In particular, it is possible to observe that an error position probability of 2.5m is very low (less than 10%) whilst the probability to have a position error of 1.5m is very high (about 50%). Figure 6 shows the relation between the position error and the quality of the wireless link; as a natural result, the error position is drastically reduced if the link quality is elevated. We obtained quite similar results for the testing points of the two different environments; these measurements are summarized in Figure 7 and validate the good operation

Figure 4. Wi-Fi and Bluetooth Access Points within the testbed area: a) Office – b) Museum

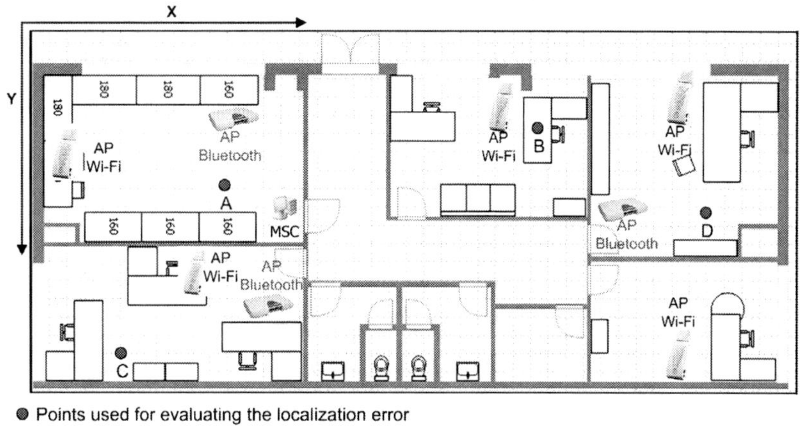

(a)

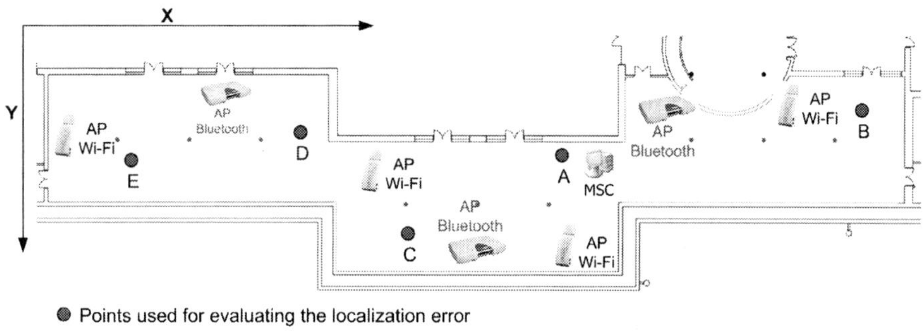

(b)

of the localization software. According to these results, each mobile user with a handheld device can be localized inside the testbed area with an accuracy of about 2,5m (worst case); this precision level is enough to localize users inside each room offering them a list of downloadable multimedia contents inherent to artworks enclosed in the room and next to the users.

We would like to remark that, even if the localization accuracy provided by the GITA system is quite close to the one supported by other wireless systems (Chen et al., 2006), our objective is not focused on the accuracy improvement but in the designing of a localization platform where location services are always available. Our architecture supports and integrates different localization techniques (i.e. Wi-Fi, GPS, Bluetooth, Visual Based through Fiducial markers) offering different degrees of precision according to the context and the environment in which users are operating. Thanks to this technology integration, a generic user is free to move in any environment

Figure 5. CDF Error Module – Point A – Office environment

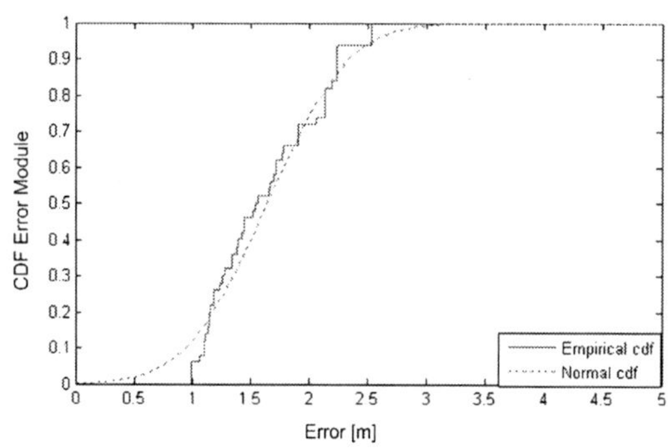

Figure 6. Mean error value according to the quality over wireless link – Point A – Office environment

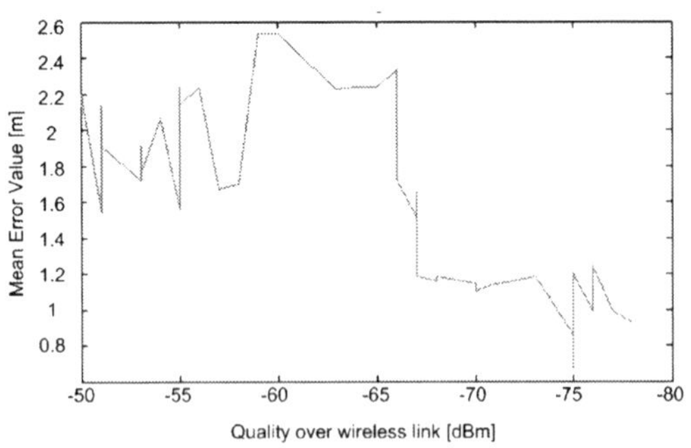

being always localized and able to enjoy multimedia and/or AR contents in a transparent way. For example: i) GPS technology is available only outdoor and only for terminals equipped with a specific antenna, ii) Wi-Fi localization needs enabled terminals and could be utilized in both indoor and outdoor environments even if it performs better in indoor ones, iii) low cost cellular phones cannot be localized neither with GPS nor with Wi-Fi; hence, we counter this inconvenience by integrating the Bluetooth technology using BIPs. In addition, our system is able to support AR applications on enhanced devices (PDA, SmartPhone) equipped with on board camera. The representation of AR objects needs fine localization accuracy in order to compute the exact position of the observer in respect to the observed object. We obtained this desired precision using a visual localization solution based on fiducial markers, as explained in the next section.

Visual-Based Localization and Augmented Reality

In the GITA architecture we also used fiducial markers associated to an artwork in order to provide hard users localization and augmented reality contents delivery. In particular, we programmed an ARToolkit based application that can be installed on enhanced handheld devices equipped with a camera and Windows Mobile operating system. Once the mobile device has been soft localized, it receives a set of downloadable multimedia contents also including compressed data that will be used by the client for rendering the scene. When the camera captures the fiducial marker, the visual based localization system computes the position of the user in respect to the observed object and the client software executes a local rendering process adding the AR content previously downloaded to the real scene.

We improved the ARToolkit system by adding the possibility to reuse the finite number of fiducial markers that are associated to a specific position using a Geo-Referenced Data Base; in this way, AR contents are related to both fiducial marker and the client position.

Figure 8 shows an example of the software operation. Different augmented reality contents such as the Greek column, the Tank and the Castle can be associated to different fiducial markers placed in particular locations within the specific environments.

Figure 7. Position errors

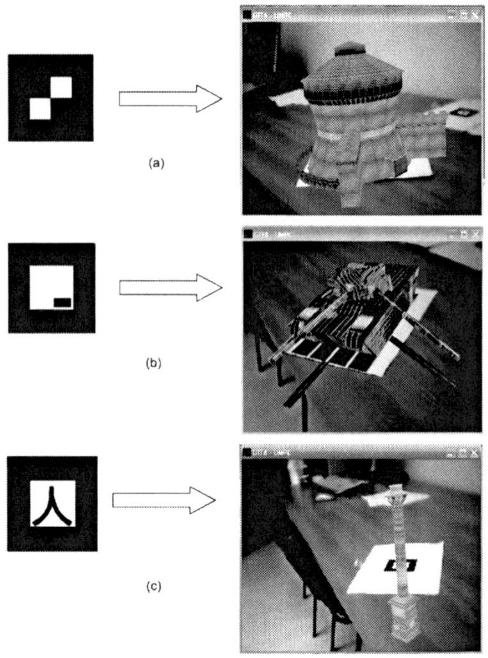

Figure 8. Augmented reality content: Fiducial Marker (left side) - a) Castle - b) Tank – c) Greek column

Position	X Precision	Y Precision	X Mean Error (m)	Y Mean Error (m)	Mean Module Error (m)
Office Environment					
A	99,17%	72,0%	0,68	2,08	2,19
B	93,6%	97,6%	0,47	0,35	0,59
C	84,3%	79,3%	1,05	1,20	1,59
D	85,8%	74,4%	1,25	2,21	2.54
Museum Environment					
A	86,5%	78,9%	1,15	1,71	2,06
B	84,9%	75,2%	1,31	1,98	2.37
C	94,8%	97,5%	0,67	0,45	0,81
D	82,5%	78,4%	1,27	1,63	2,07
E	89,17%	71.2%	0,38	2,48	2,51

C. GITA Application Details

In this section we show a few screenshots of the software application (client side and server side) designed for the GITA system and used for implementing the contents download procedure.

Figure 9 (left side) illustrates the software application running on the mobile handheld device. It is possible to note how the application supports several features; each client has a *personal ID* number and a socket connection needs to be established providing the correct IP address and logical port of the listening server. At the same time the client, in order to download multimedia contents can be logged on a FTP server by entering personal account details (user-password). All these information can be provided to the customers during the registration phase when they buy the ticket for the museum or for the archaeological park. In outdoor environments the client can also use the GPS localization checking the "*Only GPS*" check box. The software application used for the testbed can also provide other useful information, such as general GPS information and Wi-Fi position coordinates using the tab at the bottom of the screen. The right-hand side of Figure 9 shows the list of downloadable multimedia contents close to the generic mobile user; this list is periodically updated according to the current user position. Figure 10 shows the main interface of the software module running on the MSC. This module uses both Wi-Fi and GPS information received by the mobile devices in order to localize users and provide a list of multimedia contents that are associated with locations close to them. Furthermore, it is possible to set the maximum number of mobile devices to be connected to the network and the refresh position period in order to make the system more reactive to fast direction variations of the mobile clients.

In conclusion, Figure 11 summarizes information about each handheld device within the GITA system. The list of active devices is periodically updated and it is always possible to know users positions using any available GPS or Wi-Fi technology. Each device in the list has been tagged with a different color in order to be identifiable on the map in a fast and easy way.

Figure 9. Software application designed for the handheld device

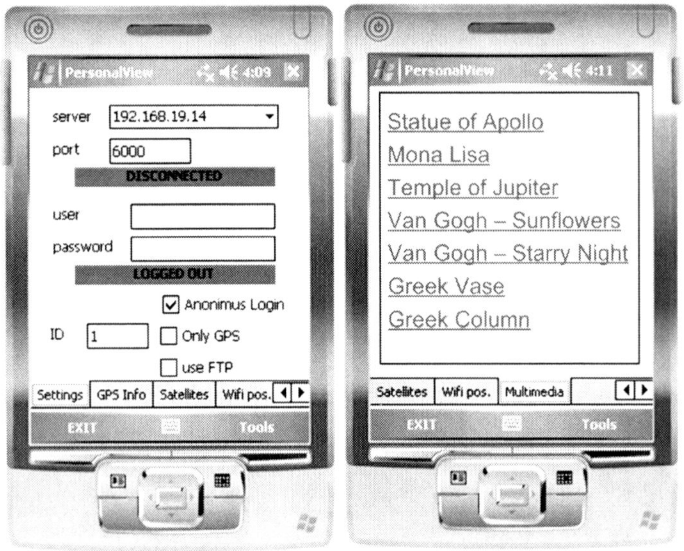

Figure 10. Software application running on multimedia service center

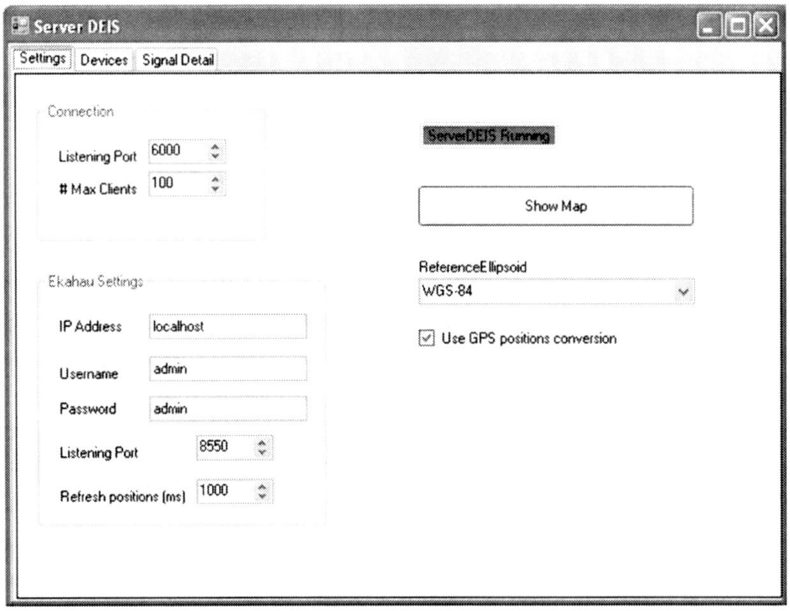

We would like to remark that the screenshot shown in this example has no information about GPS position because the test has been conducted in indoor environment. The Wi-Fi position of each client obtained through the Wi-Fi location engine is expressed by a pixel unit in respect to the map.

Figure 11. Handheld devices connected to the system

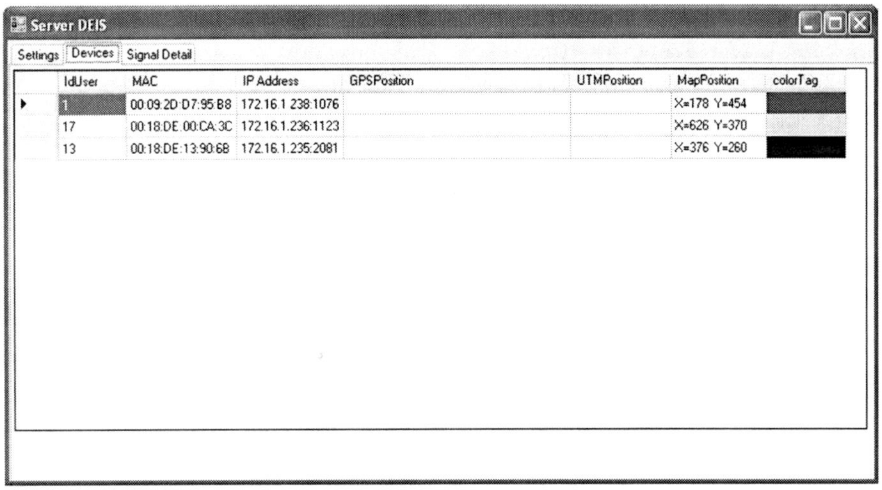

CONCLUSION AND FUTURE RESEARCH DIRECTIONS

In this chapter we presented the GITA system, an integrated communication architecture able to localize mobile users equipped with consumer electronics handheld devices within a well known area offering them multimedia or augmented reality contents. The GITA system combines different wireless technologies such as Wi-Fi, Bluetooth and GPS in a transparent way, thus, it can be easily adopted in museums or archaeological parks. At present time, we are planning to validate the overall architecture using an outdoor testbed in which the integration between Wi-Fi and GPS localization could improve the system's performance and the localization accuracy.

In the future, it is also expected that there will be hybrid networks for communication where there will be seamless roaming between cellular networks (GSM, UMTS) and WLANs depending on availability, cost-service requirements, and so on. Thus, it may be expected that there will be hybrid positioning technologies, too. A major issue for the future will be to cross the borders between the different existing technologies. Therefore a network infrastructure needs to be developed allowing to combine signals from different sensors and to compute best feasible positions taking all available sensors at that time and place into consideration. Adjustment theory and Kalman filtering (Yan et al., 2009) might be the appropriate mathematical framework for such hybrid position computations.

REFERENCES

Adusei, K., Kaymakya, I. K., & Erbas, F. (2004). *Location-based services: Advances and challenges*. IEEE Canadian Conference on Electrical and Computer Engineering- CCECE (pp. 1-7).

Bahl, P., & Padmanabhan, V. N. (2000). *RADAR: An in-building RF-based user location and tracking system* (pp. 775–784). IEEE INFOCOM.

Bakker, D., Gilster, D., & Gilster, R. (2002). *Bluetooth end to end*. New York, NY: John Wiley & Sons.

Baratoff, G., Neubeck, A., & Regenbrecht, H. (2002). *Interactive multi-marker calibration for augmented reality applications*. International Symposium on Mixed and Augmented Reality – ISMAR (pp.107-116).

Barkhuus, L., & Dey, A. K. (2003). Location-based services for mobile telephony: A study of users' privacy concerns. *Proceedings of the International Conference on Human-Computer Interaction - INTERACT- IFIP.* (pp. 1-5). ACM Press.

Behringer, R., Park, J., & Sundareswaran, V. (2002). *Model-based visual tracking for outdoor augmented reality applications*. International Symposium on Mixed and Augmented Reality - ISMAR (pp.277-278).

Bellavista, P., Kupper, A., & Helal, S. (2008). Location-based services: Back to the future. *IEEE Pervasive Computing / IEEE Computer Society [and] IEEE Communications Society*, *7*(2), 85–89. doi:10.1109/MPRV.2008.34

Boukerche, A., Oliveira, H. A., Nakamura, E. F., & Loureiro, A. A. (2007). Localization systems for wireless sensor networks. *IEEE Wireless Communications – Special Issue on Wireless Sensor Networks, 14*(6), 6–12.

Castro, P., & Muntz, R. (2000). Managing context for smart spaces. *IEEE Personal Communications*, *7*(5), 44–46. doi:10.1109/98.878537

Chan, L., Chiang, J., Chen, Y., Ke, C., Hsu, J., & Chu, H. (2006). *Collaborative localization enhancing WiFi-based position estimation with neighborhood links in clusters*. International Conference Pervasive Computing - (Pervasive 06), (pp. 50–66).

Chen, M., Haehnel, D., Hightower, J., Sohn, T., LaMarca, A., & Smith, I. … Potter, F. (2006). Practical metropolitan-scale positioning for gsm phones. *Proceedings of 8th Ubicomp*, (pp.225–242).

EKAHAU. (2010). *EKAHAU positioning engine 2.0*. Retrieved July 10, 2010 from http://www.ekahau.com/

El-Rabbany, A. (Ed.). (2006). *Introduction to GPS: The Global Positioning System* (2nd ed.). Artech House, Inc.

Fiala, M. (2005). *ARTag, a fiducial marker system using digital techniques.* IEEE Conference on Computer Vision and Pattern Recognition - CVPR (pp.590-596).

Fiala, M. (2010). Designing highly reliable fiducial markers. *IEEE Transactions on Pattern Analysis and Machine Intelligence*, *32*(7), 1317–1324. doi:10.1109/TPAMI.2009.146

Fontana, R. J., Richley, E., & Barney, J. (2003). *Commercialization of an ultra wideband precision asset location system*. IEEE Conference on Ultra Wideband Systems and Technologies, (pp.369–373).

Graumann, D., Hightower, J., Lara, W., & Borriello, G. (2003). *Real-world implementation of the location stack: The universal location framework.* IEEE Workshop on Mobile Computing Systems & Applications - WMCSA (pp.122-129)

Grejner-Brzezinska, D. (2004). Positioning and tracking approaches and technologies. In Karimi, H. A., & Hammad, A. (Eds.), *Telegeoinformatics: Location-based computing and services* (pp. 69–110). CRC Press.

Gwon, Y., Jain, R., & Kawahara, T. (2004). *Robust indoor location estimation of stationary and mobile users* (pp. 1032–1043). IEEE INFOCOM.

Han, L., Ma, J., & Yu, K. (2008). *Research on context-aware mobile computing*. International Conference on Advanced Information Networking and Applications - AINAW (pp. 24-30).

Huang, A. S., & Rudolph, L. (2007). *Bluetooth essentials for programmers*. Cambridge, UK: Cambridge University Press. doi:10.1017/CBO9780511546976

Hunter, D., Cagle, K., & Dix, C. (2007). *Beginning XML*. Wrox Press Inc.

Jin, G. Y., Lu, X. Y., & Park, M. S. (2006). *An indoor localization mechanism using active RFID tag*. IEEE International Conference on Sensor Networks, Ubiquitous, and Trustworthy Computing (pp.40-43).

Junglas, I. A., & Spitzmüller, C. (2005). *A research model for studying privacy concerns pertaining to location-based services*. Hawaii International Conference on System Sciences - HICSS (pp. 180-190).

Kalkusch, M., Lidy, T., Knapp, M., Reitmayr, G., Kaufmann, H., & Schmalstieg, D. (2002). *Structured visual markers for indoor pathfinding*. International Workshop on Augmented Reality Toolkit (pp.1-8).

Kanter, T. G. (2002). HotTown, enabling context-aware and extensible mobile interactive spaces. *IEEE Wireless Communications*, *9*(5), 18–27. doi:10.1109/MWC.2002.1043850

Kaplan, E. D. (Ed.). (1996). *Understanding GPS principles and applications*. Artech House, Inc.

Kato, H., & Billinghurst, M. (1999). *Marker tracking and HMD calibration for a video-based augmented reality conferencing system*. ACM International Workshop on Augmented Reality - IWAR (pp.85-94).

Kim, J., & Jun, H. (2008). Vision-based location positioning using augmented reality for indoor navigation. *IEEE Transactions on Consumer Electronics*, *54*(3), 954–962. doi:10.1109/TCE.2008.4637573

Kim, J. B. (2003). A personal identity annotation overlay system using a wearable computer for augmented reality. *IEEE Transactions on Consumer Electronics*, *49*(4), 1457–1467. doi:10.1109/TCE.2003.1261254

Küpper, A., Treu, G., & Linnhoff-Popien, C. (2006). Trax: A device-centric middleware framework for location-based services. *IEEE Communications Magazine*, *44*(9), 114–120. doi:10.1109/MCOM.2006.1705987

Liu, H., Darabi, H., Banerjee, P., & Liu, J. (2007). Survey of wireless indoor positioning techniques and systems. *IEEE Transactions on Systems, Man and Cybernetics. Part C, Applications and Reviews*, *37*(6), 1067–1080. doi:10.1109/TSMCC.2007.905750

Machado, C., & Mendes, J. A. (2007). *Sensors, actuators and communicators when building a ubiquitous computing system*. IEEE International Symposium on Industrial Electronics - ISIE (pp.1530-1535).

McDermott-Wells, P. (2005). What is Bluetooth? *IEEE Potentials*, *23*(5), 33–35. doi:10.1109/MP.2005.1368913

Pace, P., Aloi, G., & Palmacci, A. (2009). A multi-technology location-aware wireless system for interactive fruition of multimedia contents. *IEEE Transactions on Consumer Electronics*, *55*(2), 342–350. doi:10.1109/TCE.2009.5174391

Peng, J. (2008). *A survey of location based service for Galileo system*. International Symposium on Computer Science and Computational Technology – ISCSCT (pp. 737-741).

Quinlan, M. (2005). *Galileo - a European global satellite navigation system* (pp. 1–16). IEE Seminar on New Developments and Opportunities in Global Navigation Satellite Systems.

Rashid, O., Coulton, P., & Edwards, R. (2008). Providing location based information/advertising for existing mobile phone users. *Journal of Personal and Ubiquitous Computing*, *12*(1), 3–10. doi:10.1007/s00779-006-0121-4

Rehman, K., Stajano, F., & Coulouris, G. (2007). An architecture for interactive context-aware applications. *IEEE Pervasive Computing / IEEE Computer Society [and] IEEE Communications Society*, *6*(1), 73–80. doi:10.1109/MPRV.2007.5

Roos, T., Myllymaki, P., Tirri, H., Misikangas, P., & Sievanen, J. (2002). A probabilistic approach to WLAN user location estimation. *International Journal of Wireless Information Networks*, *9*(3), 155–164. doi:10.1023/A:1016003126882

Roussos, G., Marsh, A. J., & Maglavera, S. (2005). Enabling pervasive computing with smart phones. *IEEE Pervasive Computing / IEEE Computer Society [and] IEEE Communications Society*, *4*(2), 20–27. doi:10.1109/MPRV.2005.30

Roxin, A., Gaber, J., Wack, M., & Nait-Sidi-Moh, A. (2007). *Survey of wireless geolocation techniques* (pp. 1–9). IEEE Globecom Workshops.

Schilit, B. N., Hilbert, D. M., & Trevor, J. (2002). Context-aware communication. *IEEE Wireless Communications*, *9*(5), 46–54. doi:10.1109/MWC.2002.1043853

Siadat, S. H., & Selamat, A. (2008). *Location-based system for mobile devices using RFID*. Asia International Conference on Modeling & Simulation – AMS (pp. 291-296).

Simon, G., & Berger, M. O. (2002). Pose estimation for planar structures. *IEEE CG & A*, *22*(6), 46–53.

Song, H. L. (1994). Automatic vehicle location in cellular communications systems. *IEEE Transactions on Vehicular Technology*, *43*(4), 902–908. doi:10.1109/25.330153

Starner, T. E. (2002). Wearable computers: No longer science fiction. *IEEE Pervasive Computing / IEEE Computer Society [and] IEEE Communications Society*, *1*(1), 86–88. doi:10.1109/MPRV.2002.993148

Subramanian, S. P., Sommer, J., Schmitt, S., & Rosenstiel, W. (2007). *SBIL: Scalable indoor localization and navigation service*. International Conference on Wireless Communication and Sensor Networks - WCSN (pp. 27-30).

Thomas, B., Close, B., Donoghue, J., Squires, J., Bondi, P. D., Morris, M., & Piekarski, P. (2000). *ARQuake: An outdoor/indoor augmented reality first person application*. International Symposium on Wearable Computers - ISWC (pp.139-146).

Varshavsky, A., Chen, M. Y., De Lara, E., Froehlich, J., Haehnel, D., & Hightower, J. … Smith, I. (2006). *Are GSM phones the solution for localization?* IEEE Workshop on Mobile Computing Systems and Applications - WMCSA (pp.20-28).

Yan, J., Guorong, L., Shenghua, L., & Lian, Z. (2009). *A review on localization and mapping algorithm based on extended Kalman filtering* (pp. 435–440). International Forum on Information Technology and Applications – IFITA.

Zhang, X., Fronz, S., & Navab, N. (2002). *Visual marker detection and decoding in AR systems: A comparative study.* International Symposium on Mixed and Augmented Reality –ISMAR (pp.97–106).

KEY TERMS AND DEFINITIONS

Ubiquitous Computing (UC): it is a post-desktop model of human-computer interaction in which information processing has been thoroughly integrated into everyday objects and activities.

Mobile Positioning (MP): it is a technology used by telecommunication companies to approximate the location of a mobile terminal, and thereby also its user.

Location Based Service (LBS): It is an information and entertainment service, accessible with mobile devices through the mobile network and utilizing the ability to make use of the geographical position of the mobile device.

Augmented Reality (AR): it is a term for a live direct or indirect view of a physical real-world environment whose elements are merged with (or augmented by) virtual computer-generated imagery creating a mixed reality.

Multimedia Contents Delivery (MCD): it is the delivery of media "contents" such as audio or video or computer software and games over a delivery medium such as broadcasting or the Internet.

Context-Aware Computing (CAC): it refers to a general class of mobile systems that can sense their physical environment, i.e., their context of use, and adapt their behavior accordingly.

Service-Oriented Architecture (SOA): it is a flexible set of design principles used during the phases of systems development and integration.

Fiducial Marker (FM): it is an object used in the field of view of an imaging system which appears in the image produced. In applications of augmented reality or virtual reality, fiducial markers are often manually applied to objects in a scene so that the objects can be recognized in images of the scene.

ENDNOTES

[1] This work was supported by the Italian University and Research Ministry – (MIUR) under Grant DM 593-DD-3334/Ric-30/12/2005.

Chapter 6
Model and Ontology-Based Development of Smart Space Applications

Marko Palviainen
VTT Technical Research Centre of Finland, Finland

Artem Katasonov
VTT Technical Research Centre of Finland, Finland

ABSTRACT

The semantic data models and ontologies have shown themselves as very useful technologies for the environments where heterogeneous devices need to share information, to utilize services of each other, and to participate as components in different applications. The work in this chapter extends this approach so that the software development process for such environments is also ontology-driven. The objective is i) to support the incremental development, ii) to partially automate the development in order to make it easier and faster, and iii) to raise the level of abstraction of the application development high enough so that even people without a software engineering background would be able to develop simple applications. This chapter describes an incremental development process for the smart space application development. For this process, a supporting tool called Smart Modeler is introduced, which provides i) a visual modeling environment for smart space applications and ii) a framework and core interfaces for extensions supporting both the model and the ontology-driven development. These extensions are capable of creating model elements from ontology-based information, discovering and reusing both the software components and the partial models through a repository mechanism supported by semantic metadata, and generating executable program code from the models.

INTRODUCTION

The work reported in this chapter is performed in the framework of the SOFIA project (Liuha et al., 2009) which contributes to the development of devices and applications capable of interacting across vendor and industry domain boundaries. Consider, for example, a car environment. Typi-

DOI: 10.4018/978-1-60960-611-4.ch006

cally, a board computer and possibly an entertainment system exist in a modern car. In addition, one or more smart-phones can be brought in by the driver and the passengers. The listed devices will possess some pieces of information about the physical world, for example, location and speed of the car, the current activities and context of the passengers, and so on. Unfortunately, although many applications on the intersection of these datasets are imaginable, information sharing between applications running on different kinds of computing devices is not easy at present. For example, it would be useful to have a simple application that automatically mutes the sound system of the car when one of the smart-phones inside the car is receiving a call. However, it is a very difficult task to compose this kind of applications at present. There is a need both for the methods that provide an easy access to the information and services available in physical environments and for the development methods that facilitate the composition of applications that are based on information and services available in various kinds of physical environments.

The ubiquitous computing paradigm aims at providing information and services that are accessible anywhere, at any time and via any device (Weiser, 1991). The SOFIA project contributes to this idea and develops a solution to overcome the barriers of heterogeneity and lack of interoperability and to enable devices to share information, to utilize services of each other, and to participate as components in different kinds of smart space applications. Additionally, the solution is targeted for distributed applications that consist both of the local components and of the components residing in the network. The idea behind the GLObal Smart Space (GLOSS) is to provide support for interaction amongst people, artifacts and places while taking account of both context and movement on a global scale (Dearle et al., 2003). Furthermore, in the Web of Things vision, the physical world becomes integrated with computer networks so that the embedded computers or visual markers on everyday objects allow things and information about them to be accessible in the digital world (Guinard & Trifa, 2009). The SOFIA project pursues the target of making information in the physical world universally available to various smart services and applications, regardless of their location, which aligns well with the GLOSS and with the Web of Things vision, too. As concrete results, the aim of the SOFIA project is to develop both the InterOperability Platform (IOP) and the supporting Application Development Kit (ADK) toolset for the IOP in order to facilitate the smart space application development. This chapter relates to the latter effort.

The IOP is based on an architecture (depicted in Figure 1) consisting of three layers (Lappeteläinen et al., 2008). Firstly, the devices connected through networks and gateways form the *Device World* that is the lowest layer in the architecture. Secondly, the middle layer, the *Service World*, consists of applications, services, and other software-based entities. Thirdly, an information-level world, the *Smart World*, is the highest layer in the architecture. In the IOP, it is assumed that most of the interaction between devices is based on information sharing rather than on service invocations. The following lists the most important elements of the IOP:

- **Semantic Information Broker (SIB):** is an information-level entity for information storing, sharing and governing. The architecture used in the IOP follows the *blackboard* architecture in order to provide a cross-domain search extent for applications of a smart environment. It is assumed that a SIB exists in any smart environment (e.g. in a car). Physically, the SIB may be located either in the physical environment in question or anywhere in the network. In addition, the information in a SIB can be made accessible to applications and components on the network. The IOP relies on the advantages of the semantic data model, i.e. Resource Description Framework

Figure 1. The layers of the IOP architecture

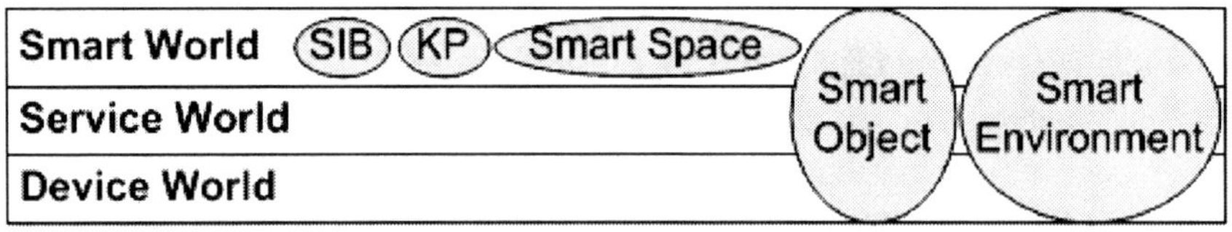

Figure 2. The ADK will produce glue code that both links together existing information-level and service-level entities and defines the business logic for the smart space application

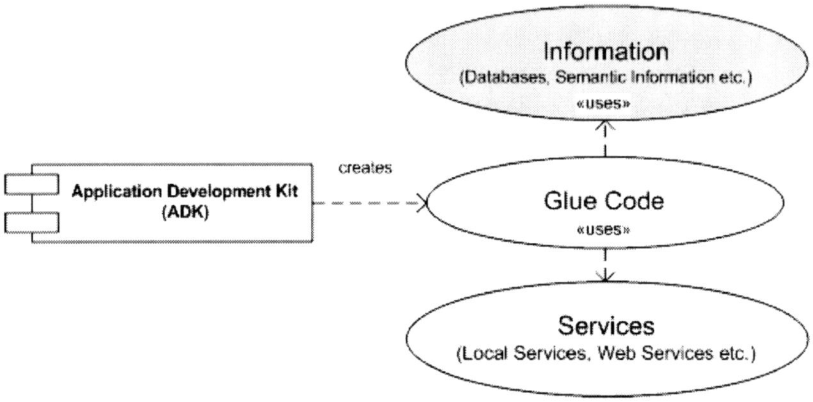

(RDF) (W3C, 2004b), and the ontological approach to knowledge engineering. This means that a SIB is basically a lightweight RDF database that supports a defined interaction protocol that includes add, remove, query and subscribe functions.

- **Knowledge Processor (KP):** is an information-level entity that produces and/or consumes information in a SIB and thus forms the information-level behavior of smart space applications.
- **Smart environment:** an entity of the physical world that is dynamically scalable and extensible to meet new use cases by applying a shared and evolving understanding of information.
- **Smart space:** A SIB creates a named search extent of information, which is called *smart space*. As opposed to the notion of a smart environment which is a physical space made smart through the IOP, the notion of a smart space is only logical: smart spaces can overlap or be co-located.
- **Smart object**: A device capable of interacting with a smart environment. A smart object contains at least one entity of the Smart World: a KP or/and a SIB. In addition, it may provide a number of *services* both to the users and the other devices (these services conceptually belong to the Service World).

The objective of the ADK is to integrate cross-domain tools to support the incremental development of smart space applications for the IOP. In a smart space application, there is a need for ontologies and for some *glue code* that both links together existing information-level and service-level entities and also defines the business logic of a smart space application (depicted in Figure 2). This means that (at least) three kinds of stakeholders participate in the development of the smart space applications:

1. **Ontology developers:** they develop ontologies for smart space applications. However, the issues related to the ontology development (see e.g. Noy & McGuinness, 2001) are not in the scope of this chapter and, thus methods and tools related to the ontology development are not discussed in more detail in this chapter.
2. **Professional developers and programmers:** they develop the glue code, as well as new components if not yet available, for smart space applications. The professional developers and programmers have a lot of knowledge of the software engineering issues. However, these developers may not have previous and extensive knowledge of the domain for which they are developing smart space applications.
3. **End-users and domain-experts:** they have a lot of knowledge regarding the target application domain and its requirements. Unfortunately, the end-users and domain-experts do not often have much experience related to software engineering. Methods and tools are needed to hide complexities of the software development from the end-users and domain-experts and thus to enable them to participate in the glue code development.

The goal of the ADK is to provide support for different kinds of stakeholders participating in the development of the smart space applications. We believe that the development of the glue code can be significantly facilitated through tool support. The clear separation between the information level and the service level in the IOP, and a higher position of the former, means that the ontologies used at the information-level for the run-time operation of a smart space application have an obvious value also for the development phase of the smart space applications. Therefore, the ADK follows the *Ontology Driven Software Engineering (ODSE)* approach (Ruiz & Hilera, 2006) and utilizes ontologies for the software architecture development, for the system specification, and for the discovery of appropriate software components. In addition, an important benefit of the ontology-driven approach in ADK is that it enables people without an extensive software engineering background (e.g. end-users or domain-experts) to effectively participate in the development or modification of applications for a smart space.

This chapter describes an ODSE approach that supports the incremental development of smart space applications and the *Smart Modeler* that is a part of the ADK toolset. The Smart Modeler raises the level of abstraction of the smart space application development by enabling the developers to graphically create a model of a smart space application and then automatically generate executable program code for the created model. Various ontology-driven extensions to the Smart Modeler enable further automation of the process. For example, such extensions can generate model elements based on domain ontologies, import sub-models from repositories for re-use, and do ontology-driven discovery for software components that are appropriate to be integrated into the smart space application.

This chapter is organized as follows. Firstly, an overview of ontology driven software engineering is discussed. Then, an approach towards incremental development process is described for the aforementioned smart space applications. Subsequently, the Smart Modeler tool and a sensor application example are presented in following sections. Finally, the conclusions are drawn and future research directions are presented in the last Section of this chapter.

ONTOLOGY-DRIVEN SOFTWARE ENGINEERING

The Ontology Driven Software Engineering (ODSE) paradigm promotes the utilization of the great potential of ontologies for improving both the processes and the artifacts of the software engineering process (Ruiz & Hilera, 2006). For example, the Object Management Group (OMG) has developed the Ontology Development Metamodel (ODM) (OMG, 2009b) intended to bring together software engineering languages and methodologies such as the Unified Modeling Language (UML) (OMG, 2009) with Semantic Web technologies such as RDF (W3C, 2004b) and Web Ontology Language (OWL) (W3C, 2004). In addition, a working group of the World Wide Web Consortium (W3C) has published a note (W3C, 2006) to outline the benefits of applying knowledge representation languages, such as RDF and OWL, in systems and software engineering practices.

The *ODSE* can be considered as an extension to the *Model-Driven Engineering (MDE)* approach (Schmidt, 2006; Singh & Sood, 2009). The goal of the MDE approach is to increase the level of abstraction to cope with complexity. In addition, the MDE insulates business applications from technology evolution through increased platform independence, portability and cross-platform interoperability, encouraging the developers to focus their efforts on domain specificity (W3C, 2006).

In the MDE process, the models are used for both the design and the maintenance purposes and as a basis for generating executable artifacts for downstream usage. The following steps are typically included in a MDE process (e.g. Singh & Sood, 2009):

1. **Creation of a Computation-Independent Model (CIM):** that is a perception of the real world that models the target software system at the highest level of abstraction. For example, this step can produce UML sequence diagrams for the use cases of the target software system.
2. **Creation of a Platform-Independent Model (PIM):** It is based on the CIM. The PIM can contain a UML's class diagram, state-transition diagrams, and so on. However, it is important to note that the PIM does not contain information specific to a particular platform or a technology that is used to realize it.
3. **Creation of a Platform-Specific Model (PSM):** The PIM combined with a *Platform Profile* is transformed into the PSM that is refined to provide more information on the target operating system, programming language, and so on.
4. **Generation of a program code:** This step will generate the executable program code from the PSM.

Unfortunately, the first two steps of the MDE process, creation of the CIM and PIM, are fully manual and the connection between them is rather loose. The ODSE tries to solve this problem by including the use of ontologies in the MDE process. The most common ontology use in the ODSE is to utilize a domain ontology in the place of the CIM and use it for generating some parts of the PIM (Soylu & de Causmaecker, 2009), resulting in some level of automation. In particular, many approaches such as (Vanden Bossche et al., 2007) focus on transforming the domain ontology directly into the hierarchy of the classes of a software application. The ontology is also used for automated consistency checking of the PIM or PSM (W3C, 2006).

The target of our work is to support much wider utilization of ontologies. Based on the review of ontology classifications given in (Ruiz & Hilera, 2006) and putting it in the context of the ODSE, we consider that four groups of ontologies exist:

1. **Ontologies of software:** define concepts for the software world itself, e.g. "component", "method", etc.
2. **Domain ontologies:** define concepts of the application domain, e.g. "user", "car", etc.
3. **Task ontologies:** define the computation-independent problem-solving tasks related to the domain, e.g. "adjust", "sell", etc.

4. **Behavior ontologies:** define some more abstract concepts for describing the behavior of software, e.g. "resource", "produces", "precondition", etc.

Although the domain ontologies are the most common ontologies, the importance of defining task ontologies is also argued in (de Oliveira et al., 2006). For example, task ontologies can support creation of the PSMs. A generic task defined in a task ontology is firstly imported into the CIM and then linked to some domain ontology concepts as task parameters, e.g. creating "adjust car speed" specific task. Finally, by matching the task description with the annotations of software components (for the target platform) residing in a repository, a proper component implementation for the given task can be found and included into the PSM. Such component annotations, like a method parameters description (i.e. *software metadata*) have to refer to concepts of software ontology, task ontology, domain ontology, and also behavior ontology. By the term "behavior ontologies" we refer here to ontologies that introduce a set, normally very limited, of concepts to be used when describing the logic of software behavior and/or interaction between software and its environment.

It is important to note that the semantic annotations of software components can be used, and are used, outside the ODSE. For example, the process of mashing-up of composite applications presented in (Ngu et al., 2010) uses the semantic annotations of software components. The overall ODSE process used in our work is depicted in Figure 3. The following lists the four important benefits of ontologies stemming from such a process:

- **Communication:** Shared ontology can act as a "boundary object", i.e. something that is understood by people coming from different social worlds.
- **Specification:** Ontology is utilized in the place of a CIM in the MDE process to facilitate the requirements specification and design specification of the system.
- **Search:** Appropriate software components are discovered based on semantic descriptions of them.

Figure 3. The Ontology Driven Software Engineering (ODSE) process

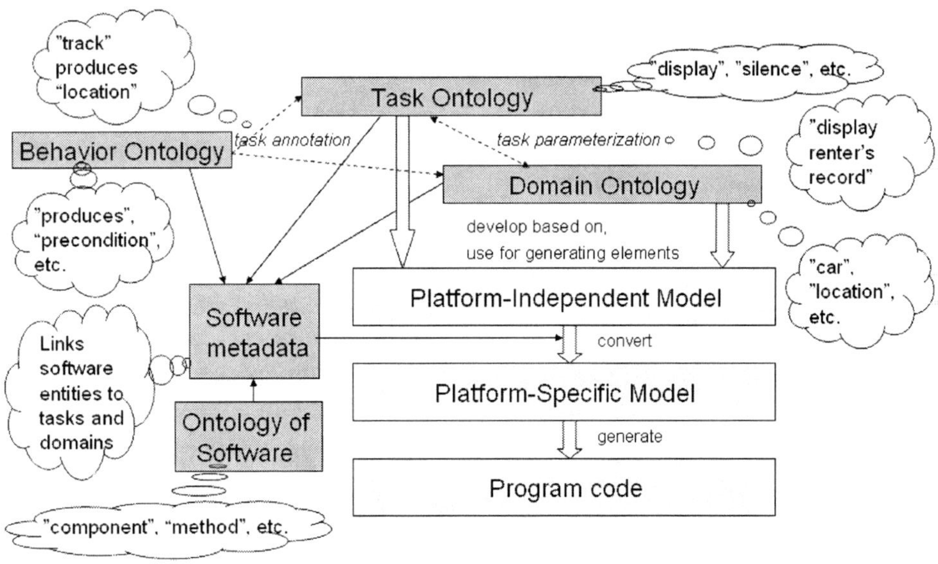

- **Verification:** Ontology is used as a basis for verification (e.g. consistency checking) of the requirements or/and design of the system.

As said before, the level of automation and domain orientation brought by the use of ontologies also enables people without an extensive software engineering background to more effectively participate in either the development or the modification of smart space applications.

THE INCREMENTAL DEVELOPMENT OF SMART SPACE APPLICATIONS

A smart environment is a very dynamic execution environment – information, services, and smart objects existing in the smart environment may change during run-time. This must be taken into consideration while a development process is selected for the smart space application development. For example, in the waterfall model, customers must commit to a set of requirements before design begins and the designer must commit to particular design strategies before implementation (Sommerville, 2000). In this sense, the incremental development process (Mills, 1980) is better for smart space applications because it gives the customers and developers some opportunities to delay decisions on their detailed requirements until they have had some experience with the system.

As described before, both the MDE and the ODSE approaches are capable of increasing the level of abstraction of the application development. There are (at least) two ways to model a smart space application:

1. **Top-down modeling of a smart space application:** this produces a scenario model to outline the components (i.e. KPs and SIBs) and the behavior of the smart space application. In practice, the scenario is an interaction sequence that specifies messages that are passed between different kinds of KPs and SIBs in a specific use case(s) of the smart space application. On the downside, it is difficult to take the dynamic nature of a smart space application in consideration in a scenario model that is typically based on the assumption that certain KPs and SIBs exist and interact in the smart space. One possibility to avoid this problem is to provide separate use case descriptions for each possible KP/SIB configuration in the scenario model. Unfortunately, it requires a lot of effort to create the use case descriptions for a big number of KP/SIB configurations.
2. **Bottom-up modeling of a smart space application:** this does not try to model the overall behavior of a smart space application but focuses on a single smart object at a time and models how its KPs interact with the SIBs. The benefit of this approach is the fact that it does not make any assumptions related to other smart objects in the smart space but it only specifies how the KPs of a single smart object publish and consume information of the smart space. The drawback of this approach is the fact that it does not specify the interaction between different smart objects. In other words, it does not provide a representation for the overall behavior of the smart space application.

As a summary, we think that both the top-down and the bottom-up modeling techniques are needed in the development of the smart space applications. The top-down modeling supports team work; it outlines the overall behavior of the smart space application and thus facilitates communication between different stakeholders. The bottom-up modeling produces a more concrete description of the behavior of a single smart object and its KPs and thus facilitates the implementation of the parts of the smart space application.

A suitable development process that supports both the top-down and the bottom-up modeling and the incremental development of smart space applications was not available for our purposes. Thus we decided to use the incremental development process (Mills, 1980) as a starting point and to adapt it for the smart space applications by using the following principles as a base:

- **Smart objects as increments:** The smart space application is based on the smart objects and on the software that is installed in the smart objects. The software development is performed for a single smart object at a time. Therefore, each smart object represents a development increment for the application that brings new KPs and/or SIBs into it. In addition, it is assumed that ready-made smart objects (i.e. increments) may exist to be used in the smart space application.
- **Support for dynamic increments:** The smart space is a very dynamic environment. New smart objects may either emerge to or leave from the smart space. This means that the increments of the smart space application change dynamically. Thus the process is designed to support development of smart space applications that are based on *dynamic increments*. Two kinds of dynamic increments exist (Figure 5): i) the *mandatory increments* are increments that are always needed in the smart space application and ii) the *optional increment sets* are collections of increments that add optional features to the smart space application. An example of a mandatory increment is a smart object containing the business logic of the smart space application. The optional increments are smart objects such as displays and audio devices that enhance the usability of the smart space application.
- **Ontology Driven Software Engineering:** The process is based on the ODSE approach (described in previous Section) that facilitates implementation of software for smart objects that will provide increments for smart space applications.

This all produced an incremental development process (depicted in Figure 4) that supports both the top-down modeling and the bottom-up modeling of smart space applications.

The steps of the process presented in Figure 4 are described briefly in the following list:

1. **Define outline requirements:** The aim of this step is to collect requirements and to do top-down modeling for the smart space application. Practically this means that Computation-Independent Models (CIMs) such as UML sequence diagrams are specified for the use cases of the smart space application. The sequence diagrams will outline both the overall information-level behavior and the KPs and SIBs of the smart space application. The goal of the specified sequence diagrams is to facilitate communication between different stakeholders that participate in the smart space application development.
2. **Assign requirements to the increments:** The purpose of this step is to define the increments of the smart space application. Firstly, both the name and the KPs/SIBs that belong to the increment are specified for each increment. Secondly, the increments are classified into the mandatory and the optional (less important) increments.
3. **Design an architecture for the smart space application:** The goal of this step is to produce a Platform-Independent Model (PIM) that specifies an architecture for the smart space application. The architecture will specify the mandatory increments and the optional increment sets for the application. As much as possible interaction between KPs is assumed to happen through a SIB. However, services may be needed in a smart space application, too. For example, the KPs

Figure 4. The incremental development of smart space applications

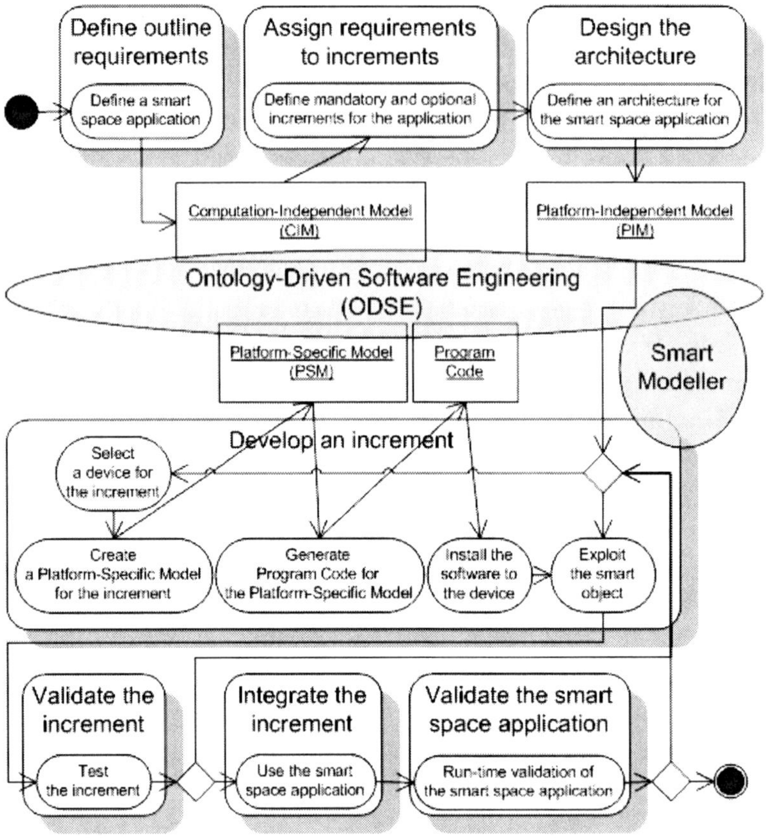

may publish and consume services through service registries. Therefore, the services (e.g. see Figure 5) that the KPs will publish and consume in the smart space application are presented in the architecture model, too.

4. **Develop an increment:** The development of increments starts from the most important (mandatory) increments and continues to the increments that provide optional features for the smart space application. If a ready-made increment exists, it is exploited in the smart space application. Otherwise a device that is suitable (e.g. a device that has enough memory and processing power) for the system increment is first selected, then a Platform-Specific Model is created for the increment, subsequently a program code is generated for the PSM, and finally the created software is installed to the selected device. This procedure will produce an increment that is later exploited in the smart space application.
5. **Validate the increment:** The increment is tested before being used in the smart space application. This testing means a run-time testing assuring that the software that is installed to the smart object will behave as assumed. The process continues to step 6 if all the mandatory increments exist. Otherwise, the process returns to step 4.
6. **Integrate the increment:** The smart object is used together with the other mandatory and optional smart objects in the target smart space.
7. **Validate the smart space application:** This step evaluates the overall behavior of the

Figure 5. An example of the architecture of a smart space application that contains both the mandatory and the optional increments

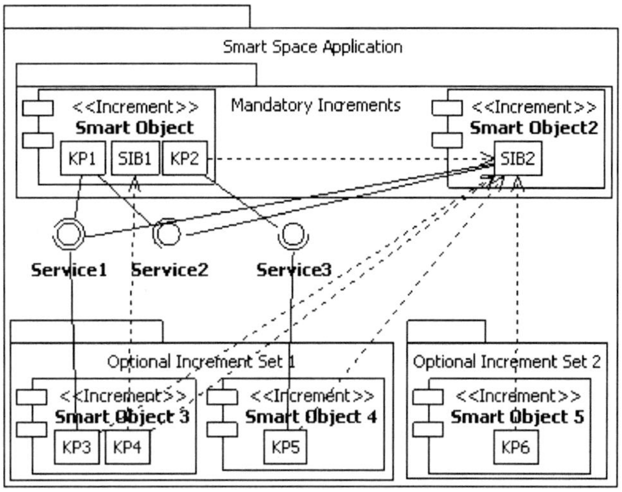

smart space application while the different smart objects participate in the execution of the application. The development process will continue until all the specified increments for the smart space application have been developed.

SMART MODELER

A suitable tool that supports both the Ontology Driven Software Engineering and incremental development of smart space applications was not available for our purposes. Thus we decided to develop the *Smart Modeler* that is a part of the ontology-driven ADK developed in the SOFIA project. The initial aim of the Smart Modeler is to facilitate implementation of software for smart objects. The Smart Modeler provides both the visual composition approach for smart space applications and the support for the ODSE and for the incremental development of smart space applications (see Figure 4). In addition, the Smart Modeler facilitates reuse of software components and partial models in the smart space application development. The reuse of software components and models is supported by *repositories*, which are RDF data storages themselves.

Design Principles

The end-users and domain-experts have a lot of knowledge of the target application domain and its requirements. Thus it would be very beneficial if the end-users and domain-experts could participate in the development of the smart space applications. The main goal of the Smart Modeler is to provide an integrated development environment for smart space applications, to support Ontology Driven Software Engineering, and to raise the level of abstraction of the smart space application development so that also the end-users and domain-experts could develop smart space applications. In order to achieve this, the Smart Modeler is designed to support:

1. **Graphical modeling of smart objects:** The Smart Modeler enables the developer to graphically compose a smart space application of basic building blocks and then to

automatically generate executable program code for it. In the IOP architecture, KPs form information-level behavior for smart space applications. Modeling of this behavior is the principal goal of the Smart Modeler.

2. **Reuse of models and software components:** The process supports the incremental development of smart space applications. Both model-level and component-level reuse is supported by repositories. The end-user can export models/components from the smart object model to the repositories and later import models/components from the repositories to the new smart object models. The models are stored as RDF graphs to the repositories.
3. **Hierarchical models:** A smart object model can contain a lot of elements. It is possible to compose element composites of parts of smart object models. An element composite is presented as a single element and thus it hides the complexity of the parts of a smart object model. In addition, if needed, the element composite can be later reviewed and its elements can be edited for the smart space application in question.
4. **Tool-level extensibility:** The software has to consist of a common framework and a set of extensions, so that new extensions can be easily introduced when needed. Various extensions to the Smart Modeler enable further automation of the process, contributing to the ease and speed of the development.
5. **On-the-fly development:** It should be possible to utilize the entities of the smart space such as semantic information brokers and different kinds of service registries in the application development. New extensions can be introduced to support utilization of SIBs and service registries available in the physical space in which the developer is located in.
6. **Openness and all-in-one package approach:** The software is to be based on open-source components and will be published as open-source.
7. **Interoperability with other tools:** To support interoperability, standard-based solutions are preferred. For example, the Smart Modeler is capable of importing/exporting smart object models as RDF graphs. Thus tools that are able to read the RDF format are capable of utilizing the information that is provided in the smart object models.

Architecture

Figure 6 depicts the overall architecture of the Smart Modeler that is designed for the above discussed requirements. The architecture consists of three main parts:

1. **Smart Modeler:** contains three core components that are marked with a gray color in Figure 6. The core components are: i) a framework, ii) a smart object model, and iii) a visual editor that provides basic editing facilities for smart object models.
2. **Extensions:** containing extension modules that provide new functionalities to be used in the visual editor of the Smart Modeler. An *extension* can be, for example, a tool/wizard that speeds up and automates the model

Figure 6. The architecture of the smart modeler

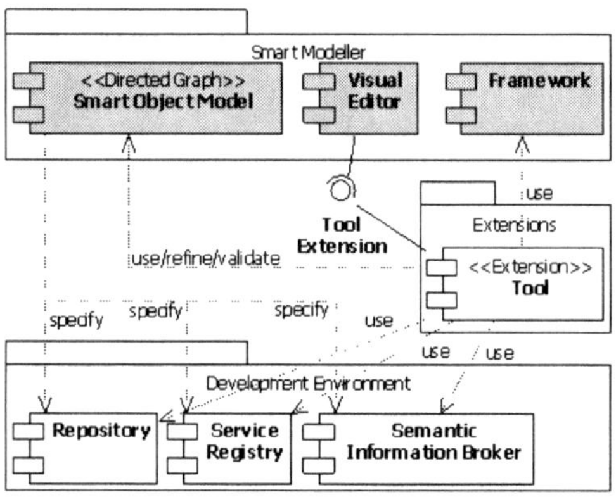

and ontology-driven development of smart space applications. The Smart Modeler's framework provides a directed graph representation for smart object models and an extension point and core interfaces for tool extensions. The goal of the directed graph representation is to provide easy access to the information provided in smart object models and thus to facilitate implementation of new *extension* modules.

3. **Development Environment:** The Smart Modeler and tool extensions are executed in a development environment that contains (possibly not all of them): i) repositories, ii) semantic information brokers, and iii) service registries. The goal of the repositories is to support reuse of software components and models in smart space applications. More precisely, the repositories can contain existing software components and models to be reused in new smart space applications. The SIBs and service registries provide access to the information and services existing in the physical space where the developer is currently located in. The usage of repositories, SIBs, and service registries is based on the tool extensions in the Smart Modeler. For example, a tool extension can enable the end-user to search out ready-made elements for smart objects from the repositories and to reuse these parts in new smart object models. Furthermore, a tool extension can provide access to the local service registries and SIBs and facilitate the developer to create a smart space application for the physical space where the developer is currently located in. The elements of the smart object model (described in the next Section) specify the repositories, SIBs, and service registries to be used in the development of smart space applications. This means that the smart object model does not just specify the elements of the smart space application; the smart object model can also configure the tool environment.

Later, Figure 8 will depict how the implementation of the Smart Modeler is deployed in an actual environment.

A Meta-Model for Smart Objects

Similarly to an RDF graph, a smart object model created with the Smart Modeler is also a directed graph. The Smart Modeler is based on the meta-model for smart objects (depicted in Figure 7) that specifies the basic building blocks for the visual composition of IOP-based smart space applications. The meta-model consists of two kinds of entities: *elements* and *connectors* (marked with a grey color in Figure 7). All kinds of elements have a *name* attribute, and for many of them it is the only attribute defined – because the main part of information in the model is contained in the connectors between elements. However, additional attributes are defined for some elements.

The meta-model of the Smart Modeler consists of three kinds of elements: there are elements related to the IOP architecture (Smart Object, SIB, KP, Service, and Ontology), elements belonging to an ontology of software (Action, Parameter, Variable, and Condition), and elements facilitating the development of software (Repository, Composite, and Composite Port). The following lists the elements that are related to the IOP:

1. **Smart Object:** a device capable of interacting with a smart environment and participating in a smart space application. It may contain Knowledge Processors and SIBs and offer services for other smart objects. It has no additional attributes.
2. **Semantic Information Broker:** an entity capable of storing, sharing and governing the information as RDF triples. Additional attributes are *IP*, *port*, and *smart space name*.

Figure 7. A meta-model for smart objects

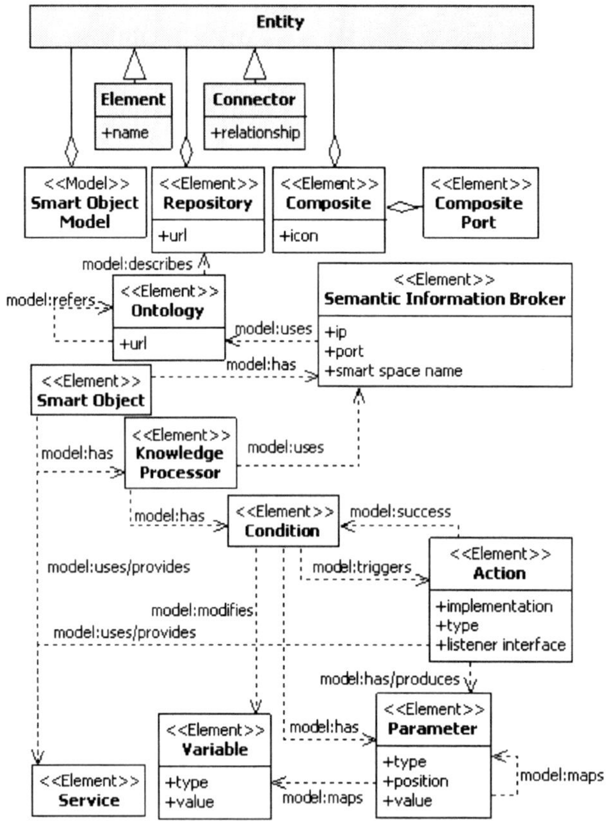

3. **Knowledge Processor:** entity producing and/or consuming information in a SIB. It has no additional attributes.
4. **Ontology:** a local or online document consisting of RDF Schema (RDF-S) and possibly of Web Ontology Language (OWL) definitions. *url* is the only additional attribute.
5. **Service:** a service or a service registry that is available for a smart object or its parts. The provider and consumer of a service can be located in different smart objects, different KPs of one smart object, or even parts of one KP. The service is only a logical entity because an Action providing the Service and another Action consuming the Service must always exist. It has no additional attributes.

The next elements of the meta-model are related to the ontology of software:

6. **Action:** either a specific action (e.g. a Java method) or a generic action (a task) that a KP performs. For a specific action, additional attributes are *implementation* (e.g. System.out.println), *type* (currently, there are the following types defined: method, constructor, expression, and inline) and optionally *listener interface* (e.g. an IAlarmListener interface).
7. **Condition:** In terms of states-events-transitions, a Condition corresponds to a transition. Therefore, roughly speaking, Condition elements are used to specify what

Figure 8. The deployment of the smart modeler

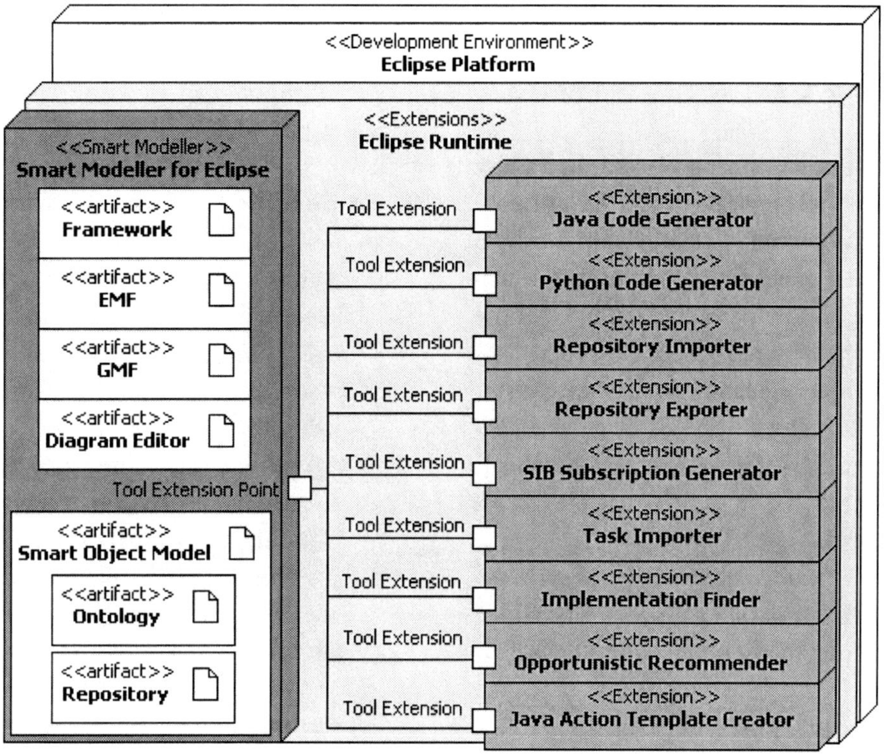

Actions are to be executed upon occurrence of certain events. A connector with an Action as the source and a Condition as the target corresponds to an event. The additional attributes are *logical expression*, and *filter expression* that can be used to define the precise condition under which the transition occurs.

8. **Parameter:** Either an input or output parameter of an Action or otherwise a constituent of a Condition. Additional attributes are *type*, *position* (to define the order in a method signature), *value* (if a constant).
9. **Variable:** A persistent data storage element of a KP. Additional attributes are *type* and *value* (an initial value).

Finally, the aim of the following elements of the meta-model is to facilitate the development of smart space applications:

10. **Repository:** an RDF storage that contains pre-configured model elements (following this meta-model) and their groups that can be re-used in modeling. There are extensions for both importing and exporting elements from/to a Repository. *url* is the only additional attribute.
11. **Composite:** a sub-model consisting of other elements and connectors between them. The objective of a composite is to increase usability of diagram editing and to enable modeling at even higher levels of abstraction. Composite can be expanded to show its contents or alternatively collapsed and

presented as just an icon. *icon* is the only additional attribute.

12. **Composite Port:** an input or output port of a Composite representing an element inside a composite. It has no additional attributes.

The purpose of a Connector is to define a link between two model elements. It has one attribute *relationship*. The value of relationship attribute affects the visual appearance of a connector in a diagram. In the following we list the most of the meaningful links between model elements.

A **Smart Object** element can be connected to:

- **A KP or a SIB (*model:has* relationship):** specifying a KP or a SIB that the Smart Object hosts.
- **A Service (*model:uses* or *model:provides* relationship):** defining a service provided or consumed by the smart object.

A **Knowledge Processor** element can be connected to:

- **A SIB (*model:uses* relationship):** indicating that the KP consumes/produces information from/to the SIB.
- **A condition (*model:has* relationship):** specifying a start-up Condition for the KP. The Code Generators use it as a starting point in the creation of program code for the behavior of KP.

An Action element can be connected to:

- **An input parameter (*model:has* relationship):** specifying an input parameter for the Action.
- **An output parameter (*model:produces* relationship):** specifying an output parameter for the Action.
- **A condition (*model:success* relationship):** indicating the Condition that becomes true as result of the Action execution Instead of *model:success,* there can also be a name of the method in the listener interface that the Action uses for posting events.
- **A service (*model:uses* or *model:provides* relationship):** defining a service utilized or provided by the action.

A Condition element can be connected to:

- **A parameter (*model:has* relationship):** specifying a constituent of a Condition, i.e. some data item generated by a *model:produces* relationship of an Action led to this Condition.
- **An action (*model:triggers* relationship):** specifying an Action triggered when the Condition becomes true.
- **A variable (*model:modifies* relationship):** specifying a Variable where the value of a parameter is to be stored.

A Parameter element that specifies an output parameter/return value of an Action can be connected to:

- **An input parameter of another Action (*model:maps* relationship):** defining the mapping or wiring between the output parameter/return value of the Action and the input parameter of another Action.
- **A variable (*model:maps* relationship):** defining the mapping or wiring between the parameter and the variable.

An Ontology element can be connected to:

- **Another ontology element (*model:refers* relationship):** denoting that the Ontology refers to concepts from a more general, upper-level ontology.
- **A repository (*model:describes* relationship):** specifies that this Ontology element is a Task ontology and that the specific im-

plementations for some of its tasks can be searched for in the Repository.

A Semantic Information Broker element can be connected to an Ontology element (*model:uses* relationship) – indicating the ontology, on which the data in the SIB is based. The forthcoming subsection will describe how an extension of the Smart Modeler uses this link for the automated generation of SIB subscriptions.

A Composite Port can be connected to any element inside the same Composite – defining that the Composite Port acts as the representative of the element. Any link drawn to/from the port is the same as a link drawn to/from the element itself.

The Implementation and Extensions of the Smart Modeler

We chose to implement the Smart Modeler in Java on top of the Eclipse Integrated Development Environment (http://www.eclipse.org/) that is an open, extensible, and well-standardized environment for different kinds of software development tools (Figure 8). The Eclipse platform provides an extensible framework upon which software tools can be built (Rubel, 2006). In addition, the Eclipse-based implementation enables interoperability with many other available tools as well as ready-made extensibility framework thanks to the Eclipse's component-based architecture. The Smart Modeler is based on the Eclipse Graphical Modeling Framework (GMF) (Eclipse Foundation, 2010) that provides a generative component and run-time infrastructure for developing graphical editors. GMF, in turn, is based on both the Eclipse Modeling Framework (EMF) and the Graphical Editing Framework (GEF). First, the meta-model of the Smart Modeler was implemented by using EMF Ecore. Secondly, a set of additional GMF-specific specifications was added, including the palette of creation tools, the labels that are used in the diagram, and so on. Thirdly, the GMF framework was used to generate the readily working code for the diagram editor.

The Eclipse component-based architecture makes it easy to extend the generated diagram code with a set of *extension points*, through which *plug-ins* can be connected. The *tool extension point* was inserted to enable the interface towards custom plug-ins capable of programmatically modifying the diagram or utilizing the information encoded in it for some purpose. All the Smart Modeler extensions were then implemented and connected by using this extension point. In addition, it is important to note that new extensions can always be added later, also by 3rd parties. The following kinds of extensions are currently provided for the Smart Modeler and for the smart space application development:

1. **Java Code Generator:** extension is capable of generating a Java implementation for a modeled KP. A new Java project with a name corresponding to the KP's name in the model is first created for the KP. The extension will then copy the implementations of actions and any additional non-Java resources (such as images, RDF documents) other than the diagram files found in the modeling project into the generated project. Finally, the required libraries are copied or linked to the project.
2. **Python Code Generator:** the same as the Java Code Generator, only outputs Python code. We are considering implementing code generators for other programming languages as well, including C++ and ANSI C for embedded devices and JavaScript for the KPs providing Web interfaces.
3. **Repository Importer:** extension is applicable to a Repository element only. When executed, the extension first shows a dialog listing all the graphs (collections, elements and connectors) defined in the repository and, then, inserts the selected graph into the model.

4. **Repository Exporter:** extension is applicable to any model element, or to a collection of elements including connectors. When executed, the extension shows a dialog listing all the repositories of the model, then creates a single graph of the selected elements and connectors, and finally exports the created graph into the selected Repository.
5. **SIB Subscription generator:** extension is applicable to an Ontology element only. When invoked, the extension first shows a dialog window for selecting a type of subscription to be generated. Alternatives are currently: i) any new triple, ii) new instance of a class, iii) changed value of a property. If either ii) or iii) are selected, the extension shows another dialog, where it lists all the corresponding classes and properties that are defined in the ontology. Finally, the extension adds to the model a Composite containing all the needed elements for managing a SIB subscription and a minimum set of CompositePorts: for starting a subscription, for receiving notifications, and for the received data values.
6. **Task Importer:** extension is applicable to an Ontology element only. The extension shows a dialog window listing all the generic tasks defined in the task ontology. After, a user selects one, an Action element is added to the model with the task URI in the Implementation attribute.
7. **Implementation Finder:** extension is applicable to an Action element (to a generic task) only. When executed, the extension lists all implementations (graphs) matching the given generic task in a dialog window, and after one is selected, adds it to the model. This extension searches through all the Ontology-Repository connected pairs in the model.
8. **Opportunistic Recommender:** extension is applicable to an Ontology element only. When executed, this plug-in performs the following process:
   - Checks whether any of the tasks defined in the Task Ontology has a *produces* annotation (class of the entity produced).
   - If so, checks whether a realization of this task is a part of the current model.
   - If so, checks whether there is any other task in the Task Ontology that has a *requires* annotation with the same entity class.
   - If so, checks whether any of the Repositories connected to the Task Ontology contains an implementation for this task.
   - If so, it proposes to the user to include the implementation into the model (a dialog window listing all the possible implementations for the task is displayed for the user's benefit).
   - If the user agrees, it inserts the elements related to the selected implementation of the task into the model (allowing the user to specify the location on the diagram where to place the elements) and automatically connects (control flow and parameters mappings) the inserted elements.
9. **Java Action Template Creator:** extension is applicable to an Action element only. The extension generates a template for an action implementation, if a non-existing implementation is defined for an Action element in the model. The generated method interface of the action will contain the input or/and output Parameters (including a return value) that are linked to the Action in the model. The extension splits the implementation attribute into package name, class name, and method name and, then, generates the method, the Java source code file for the class that will contain the needed method, and finally the required package folders.

More details about our *software metadata framework*, which is the enabler for the Opportunistic Recommender and Implementation Finder extensions, can be found in (Katasonov, 2010).

EXAMPLE: THE COMPOSITION OF A SIMPLE SENSOR APPLICATION

The application domain of the example application consists of sensors providing measurements (e.g. temperature) and of actuators, through which some parameters of the environment can be controlled (e.g. lighting). Actuators have status, e.g. "on" and "off", and this status is reflected using the *gc:hasStatus* property in the SIB of the environment. The simple sensor application is designed to perform the following tasks: i) there is a KP that subscribes to the SIB for data matching the pattern given, and ii) when the SIB will deliver an update, a dialog will pop up showing the text "Actuator's status changed: ex:ActuatorA on".

Figure 9 depicts a simple example model for the sensor application that is displayed in the visual editor of the Smart Modeler. Firstly, the model defines a repository element and ontology elements for "GC Repository", and "Tasks Ontology". Secondly, the model specifies a reactive "GCMonitor" KP using both the "GC" SIB and its associated "GC ontology". Thirdly, the composite "Changed <hasStatus>" element contains an action that has subscription to the SIB with the pattern *?resource gc:hasStatus ?value*. The action will produce an update delivered by the SIB as an output to the "Ev:Added" port of the composite. Fourthly, the "Ev:Added" port is connected to a "Show in Dialog" action that is triggered to open a dialog window to display an update delivered by the SIB.

Without going much into the details, the following steps are included in the modeling process:

1. Inserting a Repository element to an empty diagram, and setting its *Url* attribute.
2. Executing the *Repository Importer* extension to import the same Repository but extended with an associated Task Ontology.
3. Invoking the *Repository Importer* extension to import the SIB with the Domain Ontology.
4. Insertion of a KP and Condition elements to the model. Connecting the KP to the SIB and Condition elements. The relationships are set automatically to the connectors.
5. Invoking the *SIB Subscription Generator* extension, selecting "Changed value of a Property" and then selecting *gc:hasStatus* property. The Composite will be added. Connecting its "Action" port to the Condition.
6. Invoking the *Task Generator* extension to import *task:InformUser* task.
7. Executing the *Implementation Finder* extension and selecting from the presented list "*Show in Dialog*" action – other options can for example include the standard function of printing out to the output stream. This will add the Action and its Parameters to the model.
8. Setting constant value for the Parameter *s1* and then connecting *s2* and *s3* to the data ports of the subscription Composite. Connecting the event port of the Composite to the Action itself. The model is ready to be used after this step.
9. Invoking *Java Code Generator* plug-in to generate Java code for the modeled KP. This will create a new Java project for the KP, copy the implementations of actions and any additional non-Java resources (such as images, RDF documents) other than the diagram files found in the modeling project into the generated project and finally copy or link the required libraries to the project.
10. The project is ready to be deployed and executed in a real smart environment.

Figure 9. A model for a simple sensor application

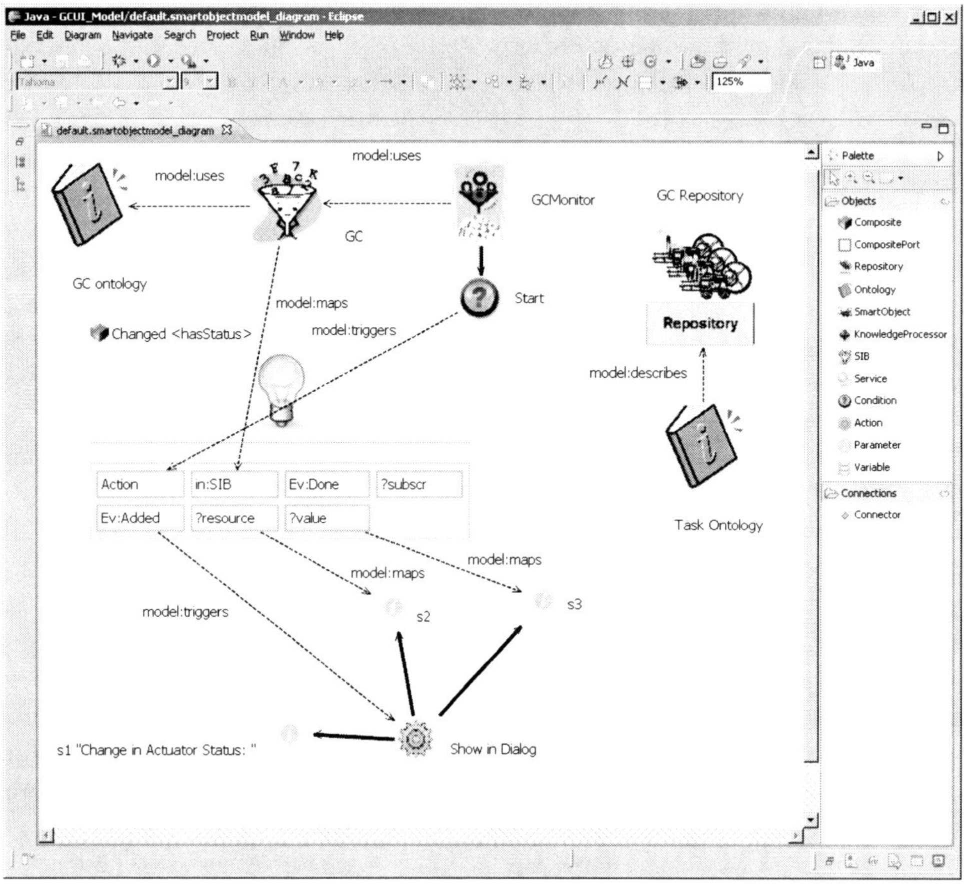

CONCLUSION AND FUTURE RESEARCH DIRECTIONS

This chapter described an ontology-driven approach supporting the incremental development of software applications for smart environments. In comparison to the traditional way of software development, the presented approach partially automates the development processes, facilitates reuse of components through metadata-based discovery, and raises the level of abstraction of the smart space application development. The goal of this all is to make the development easier and faster and to enable also the non-programmers to develop smart space applications. As the sensor application example in the previous Section showed, as long as existing software components are sufficient, the development may not involve any coding. In addition, the software composition is made much faster through ontology/metadata support. We think that such an example process (i.e. the numbered list that described a composition process for the sensor application) could already be performed by a person without software engineering background. Furthermore, we believe that the "wizard" mechanism can make this process even easier to use. Identifying the processes that can be reasonably automated through wizards and realizing such wizards is one direction for the future work.

We think that it is important to provide tools that cover all the phases of the smart space application development. In this chapter, we described the Smart Modeler tool that currently supports bottom-up modeling of smart space applications and facilitates the implementation of software for smart objects. The top-down modeling produces models (i.e. sequence diagrams) for the overall behavior of the smart space applications. There is a need for extensions that would facilitate the automatic utilization of these models in the Smart Modeler. Furthermore, there is also a need for tools supporting the dynamic testing of both the smart objects and the applications that are based on multiple smart objects. For example, there is a need for extensions that could insert test bed / test case generation features to the Smart Modeler.

An interesting approach to programming is used in Scratch (Resnick et al., 2009): the program entities are like Lego bricks; they have different shapes and can be attached to each other only if it would make a syntactic sense. Although this approach is not applicable directly to the Smart Modeler tasks, studying into how to make the development process similarly intuitive and inherently less error-prone is another important direction for the future work. In (Resnick et al., 2009), significant stress is also placed on the notion of *tinkerablility*, i.e. ability to connect fast some elements together and to immediately see what will happen. Introducing such tinkerability to the Smart Modeler would involve creating some kind of a simulation framework to enable developers to see how the modeled smart space applications would function when deployed. The development of such a simulation framework is one more possible direction for the future work.

The ontologies and metadata of components are the main inputs to our development process and these can be published in some way in a smart environment. An interesting and promising scenario would form then a case in which a person entering the environment composes an application matching his needs *on-the-fly*. An important direction for the future research is to provide tool-support for such a scenario in SOFIA. Also, our goal is to develop further the *opportunistic* way for a software composition, a very simple case of which is implemented in Opportunistic Recommender extension (see also Katasonov, 2010). Both the *opportunistic* way of utilizing the metadata of components and the task ontologies are included in our future research topics that we study in our endeavor into the *ontology-driven composition of software*, which is our main longer-term research direction, even beyond the SOFIA project.

ACKNOWLEDGMENT

This work described in this chapter is performed in the SOFIA project which is a part of EU's ARTEMIS JU. The SOFIA project is coordinated by Nokia and the partners include Philips, NXP, Fiat, Elsag Datamat, Indra, Eurotech, as well as a number of research institutions from Finland, Netherlands, Italy, Spain, and Switzerland.

REFERENCES

W3C. (2000). Extensible Markup Language (XML) 1.0 (2nd ed.). In T. Bray, J. Paoli, C. M. Sperberg-McQueen, & E. Maler (Eds.), *W3C recommendation*. Retrieved July 4, 2010, from http://www.w3.org/TR/REC-xml

W3C. (2004). OWL Web ontology language overview. In D. L. McGuinness, & F. Van Harmelen (Eds.), *W3C recommendation*. Retrieved July 4, 2010, from http://www.w3.org/TR/owl-features/

W3C. (2004b). Resource Description Framework (RDF): Concepts and abstract syntax. In G. Klyne, & J. J. Carroll (Eds.), *W3C recommendation*. Retrieved July 4, 2010, from http://www.w3.org/TR/rdf-concepts/

W3C. (2004c). RDF Vocabulary Description Language 1.0: RDF schema. In D. Brickley, & R. V. Guha (Eds.), *W3C recommendation*. Retrieved July 4, 2010, from http://www.w3.org/TR/rdf-schema/

W3C. (2006). *Ontology driven architectures and potential uses of the Semantic Web in systems and software engineering.* Retrieved July 4, 2010, from http://www.w3.org/2001/sw/BestPractices/SE/ODA/

de Oliveira, K. M., Villela, K., Rocha, A. R., & Travassos, G. H. (2006). Use of ontologies in software development environments. In Calero, C., Ruiz, F., & Piattini, M. (Eds.), *Ontologies for software engineering and software technology* (pp. 276–309). Springer-Verlag. doi:10.1007/3-540-34518-3_10

Dearle, A., Kirby, G., Morrison, R., McCarthy, A., Mullen, K., & Yang, Y. … Wilson, A. (2003). *Architectural support for global smart spaces.* (LNCS 2574). (pp. 153-164). Springer-Verlag.

Eclipse Foundation. (2010). *Graphical modeling framework.* Retrieved July 4, 2010, from http://www.eclipse.org/modeling/gmf/

Guinard, D., & Trifa, V. (2009). *Towards the Web of things: Web mashups for embedded devices.* Paper presented at Workshop on Mashups, Enterprise Mashups and Lightweight Composition on the Web (MEM 2009), Madrid, Spain.

Katasonov, A. (2010). Enabling non-programmers to develop smart environment applications. In *Proceedings IEEE Symposium on Computers and Communications (ISCC'10)* (pp. 1055-1060). IEEE.

Lappeteläinen, A., Tuupola, J. M., Palin, A., & Eriksson, T. (2008). *Networked systems, services and information.* Paper presented at the 1st International Network on Terminal Architecture Conference (NoTA2008), Helsinki, Finland.

Liuha, P., Lappeteläinen, A., & Soininen, J.-P. (2009). Smart objects for intelligent applications – first results made open. *ARTEMIS Magazine, 5*, 27–29.

Mills, H. D. (1980). The management of software engineering, part I: Principles of software engineering. *IBM Systems Journal, 19*, 414–420. doi:10.1147/sj.194.0414

Ngu, A. H. H., Carlson, M. P., Sheng, Q. Z., & Paik, H.-Y. (2010). Semantic-based mashup of composite applications. *IEEE Transactions on Services Computing, 3*(1), 2–15. doi:10.1109/TSC.2010.8

Noy, N. F., & McGuinness, D. L. (2001). *Ontology development 101: A guide to creating your first ontology.* (Stanford Knowledge Systems Laboratory Technical Report KSL-01-05 and Stanford Medical Informatics Technical Report SMI-2001-0880). Stanford, CA: Stanford University.

OMG. (2009). *Unified Modeling Language* (UML), version 2.2, Retrieved July 4, 2010, from http://www.omg.org/cgi-bin/doc?formal/09-02-02.pdf

OMG. (2009b). *Ontology Definition Metamodel*, version 1.0, Retrieved July 4, 2010, from http://www.omg.org/spec/ODM/1.0/

Resnick, M., Maloney, J., Monroy-Hernandez, A., Rusk, N., Eastmond, E., & Brennan, K. (2009). Scratch: Programming for all. *Communications of the ACM, 52*(11), 60–67. doi:10.1145/1592761.1592779

Rubel, D. (2006). The heart of Eclipse. *ACM Queue; Tomorrow's Computing Today, 4*(6), 36–44. doi:10.1145/1165754.1165767

Ruiz, F., & Hilera, J. R. (2006). Using ontologies in software engineering and technology. In Calero, C., Ruiz, F., & Piattini, M. (Eds.), *Ontologies for software engineering and software technology* (pp. 49–102). Springer-Verlag. doi:10.1007/3-540-34518-3_2

Schmidt, D. C. (2006). Model-driven engineering. *IEEE Computer, 39*(2), 25–31.

Singh, Y., & Sood, M. (2009). Model driven architecture: A perspective. In *Proceedings IEEE International Advance Computing Conference* (pp. 1644–1652). IEEE.

Sommerville, I. (2000). *Software engineering* (6th ed.). Harlow, UK: Addison-Wesley.

Soylu, A., & de Causmaecker, P. (2009). Merging model driven and ontology driven system development approaches: Pervasive computing perspective. In *Proceedings 24th International Symposium on Computer and Information Sciences* (pp. 730–735). IEEE.

Vanden Bossche, M., Ross, P., MacLarty, I., Van Nuffelen, B., & Pelov, N. (2007). Ontology driven software engineering for real life applications. In *Proceedings 3rd International Workshop on Semantic Web Enabled Software Engineering (SWESE 2007)*. Springer-Verlag.

Weiser, M. (1991). The computer for the 21st century. *Scientific American*, (September): 94–104. doi:10.1038/scientificamerican0991-94

KEY TERMS AND DEFINITIONS

eXtensible Markup Language (XML): The XML is a textual data format that describes a class of data objects called XML documents and partially describes the behavior of computer programs which process them (W3C, 2000). The XML 1.0 Specification (W3C, 2000) specifies both the structure of the XML and the set of rules for encoding documents in a machine-readable form. The XML is widely used for the representation of arbitrary data structures. For example, the RDF data models are represented as XML documents.

Knowledge Processor (KP): An information-level entity that produces and/or consumes information in a SIB and thus forms the information-level behavior of smart space applications.

Ontology: A representation of terms and their interrelationships (W3C, 2004b).

Resource Description Framework (RDF): The RDF is a framework for representing information in the Web (W3C, 2004b). The RDF provides both the data model for objects (i.e. *resources*) and relations between them and the simple semantics for this data model. The data model can be represented in an XML syntax.

RDF Schema (RDF-S): The RDF-S is a vocabulary description language that provides mechanisms for describing groups of related resources and the relationships between these resources (W3C, 2004c). These resources are used to determine characteristics of other resources, such as the domains and ranges of the properties. The RDF-S is a semantic extension of the RDF and the RDF Schema vocabulary descriptions are written in the RDF.

Semantic Information Broker (SIB): An information-level entity for storing, sharing and governing the semantic information. It is assumed that a SIB exists in any smart environment. Physically, the SIB may be located either in the physical environment in question or anywhere in the network. Furthermore, the access to the SIB is not restricted to the devices located in the physical environment. In addition, the information in a SIB can be made accessible to applications and components on the network.

Smart environment: An entity of the physical world that is dynamically scalable and extensible to meet new use cases by applying a shared and evolving understanding of information.

Smart object: A device capable of interacting with a smart environment. A smart object contains at least one entity of the Smart World: a KP or/and SIB. In addition, it may provide a number of *services* both to the users and the other devices.

Smart space: A SIB creates a named search extent of information, which is called as *smart space*. As opposed to the notion of a smart environment which is a physical space made smart through the IOP, the notion of a smart space is only logical: smart spaces can overlap or be co-located.

Unified Modeling Language (UML): The UML is a widely accepted and easily extensible modeling language that supports modeling of business processes, data structures, and the structure, behavior, and architecture of applications (OMG, 2009).

Web Ontology Language (OWL): An ontology language that can be used to explicitly represent the meaning of terms in vocabularies and the relationships between those terms (W3C, 2004). The OWL facilitates greater machine interpretability of Web content than that supported by XML, RDF, and RDF Schema (RDF-S) by providing additional vocabulary along with a formal semantics (W3C, 2004). In addition, the OWL provides three increasingly-expressive sublanguages: the OWL Lite, OWL DL, and OWL Full.

Section 3
Pervasive Communications

Pervasive environments built on principles of ubiquitous communications will soon, therefore, form the basis of next generation networks. Due to the increasing availability of wireless technologies and the demand for mobility, pervasive networks that will be increasingly built on top of heterogeneous devices and networking standards will progressively face the need to mitigate the drawbacks that accordingly arise regarding scalability, volatility, and topology instability. Novel trends in pervasive communications research address such concerns include autonomic network management, re-configurable radio and networks, cognitive networks, use of utility-based functions, and policies to manage networks autonomously and in a flexible and context-driven manner, to mention a few.

Chapter 7
Self-Addressing for Autonomous Networking Systems

Ricardo de O. Schmidt
Federal University of Pernambuco, Brazil

Reinaldo Gomes
Federal University of Pernambuco, Brazil

Djamel Sadok
Federal University of Pernambuco, Brazil

Judith Kelner
Federal University of Pernambuco, Brazil

Martin Johnsson
Ericsson Research Labs, Sweden

ABSTRACT

Autoconfiguration is an important functionality pursued by research in the contexts of dynamic ad hoc and next generation of networks. Autoconfiguration solutions span across all architectural layers and range from network configuration to applications, and also implement cross-layer concepts. In networking, the addressing system plays a fundamental role as long as hosts must be uniquely identified. A proper identification is the base for other network operations, such as routing and security issues. Due to its importance, addressing is a challenging problem in dynamic and heterogeneous networks, where it becomes more complex and critical. This chapter presents a review and considerations for addressing autoconfiguration, focusing on the addressing procedure. Several self-addressing solutions for autonomous networks are surveyed, covering a wide range of possible methodologies. These solutions are also categorized according to the methodology they implement, their statefulness, and the way they deal with addresses duplication and/or conflicts. Special considerations regarding conformity to IPv6 are also presented.

DOI: 10.4018/978-1-60960-611-4.ch007

INTRODUCTION

The idea of autonomous computer systems relies heavily on the concept of autoconfiguration in computer networks. The automation in the process of communication establishment is one of the most important topics for the Next Generation of Networks (NGN). Autoconfiguration mechanisms for dynamic networks may vary from self-addressing procedures to network layer routing self-stabilization, like those proposed in Forde, Doyle & O'Mahony (2005). The addressing system may be seen as one of the main challenges in this process. Automatic distribution and management of addresses is critical to an autonomous communication system, since addressing is one of the fundamental keys to ensure the correct networking operation. In addition, this challenge increases when considering mobile nodes, intermittent connections and policy-based networks.

In future, considering the Ubiquitous Computing concepts, nodes will be able to connect and disconnect from a network, independently of its technologies or network's topology, and without any manual intervention, e.g. from a network administrator or final user. By using a robust mechanism for automatic bootstrapping a node will be able to configure itself, through possibly contacting another existing node and getting connected to an existing network, or creating a new network. In all suggested autoconfiguration approaches, addressing is seen as an important first milestone.

Several parameters must be considered in the context of a successful address configuration strategy. Applicability scenarios may vary from military operations, purely composed by ad-hoc networks, to complex ubiquitous commercial solutions (e.g., telecommunication industry), where many distinct networks can cooperate, interconnecting users and providing them with the required services at any time and irrespective of their location. Further definitions on scenarios of similar future networking are given in the websites of the projects 4WARD (4WARD, 2010), Ambient Networks (Ambient Networks, 2010), *Autonomic Network Architecture* (ANA, 2010), *Designing Advanced network Interfaces for the Delivery and Administration of Location independent, Optimized personal Services* (DAIDALOS, 2010) and *European Network of Excellence for the Management of Internet Technologies and Complex Services* (EMANICS, 2010).

This chapter is organized as follows. A short background of autoconfiguration is presented in the next section. Then, the parameters and considerations regarding the implementation of autoconfiguration solutions are described, and also the proposed taxonomy for classification of self-addressing approaches is presented. Next, the performance metrics to be considered when designing a self-addressing solution for a specific networking scenario, and/or evaluating a self-addressing approach, are described. Several solutions of self-addressing are surveyed, covering a wide range of methodologies already proposed as solution for this problem. In addition, special emphasis is given to both proposals that modify the current Internet protocol stack and to special considerations for IPv6. Finally, future research directions are drawn, based on the current research projects on self-addressing and autoconfiguration, and final considerations are presented concerning the problem statement and the already proposed solutions for self-addressing.

Background

Network technologies have been converging to attend the requirements of Pervasive and Ubiquitous Computing. These concepts bring new challenges to existing networking architectures such as the need for the management of a very dynamic and heterogeneous network. Due to its complex nature, such management is a cumbersome task for system administrators. Auto-managed technologies are a welcome new capability that creates a degree of ambient intelligence, where a network and its elements are mostly able to configure themselves.

Applicability of Autoconfiguration

According to Williams (2002), examples of dynamic network applicability scenarios, where autoconfiguration issues are desirable, include: home networks, ad hoc networks at conferences and meetings, emergency relief networks, VANETs – Vehicular Ad hoc Networks (networks composed by automobiles, airplanes, trains, etc), and many others. These scenarios may vary from a simple two-node data configuration exchanging through a wireless LAN connection, to thousands of heterogeneous ones involving different network topologies, communicating through different technologies, and accessing a vast number of services.

As defined by the project Ambient Networks (2010), the scenarios for a future generation of networking involve many complex characteristics, such as:

- Different radio technologies;
- Autoconfiguration of dynamic network composition, ensuring connectivity, resource management, security, manageability, conflict resolution, and content handling;
- Emergency networks set up to deal with spontaneous operations and needed to coordinate information exchange in real-time critical missions, such as fire rescue team work, police public security actions, military operations, etc. These networks are seen as *zero-conf networks* that should be able to setup and work with: minimum human intervention, almost no prior setup, and little or no infrastructure support;
- Dynamic agreements providing access to any network including support for an end-to-end QoS concept;
- Advanced multi-domain mobility management of users and user groups, over a multitude of heterogeneous wireless access networks, including personal area and vehicular networks;
- Self-management not only for network nodes, but also for newly composed/created networks.

Due to their complex peculiarities, the scenarios for a future generation of computer networks demand "auto", also known as "self", technologies for configuration and management of the communication structure. However, new solutions should be designed by taking into account some important parameters. These parameters should guide the proposals for standardization and ensure correctly and efficiently dealing with autoconfiguration problems. They are also relevant for defining guidelines regarding security issues. The next sections present the requirements definition and security-related considerations for dynamic networks autoconfiguration.

Self-Addressing and Autoconfiguration

Self-addressing concepts have a very close relationship with autoconfiguration ones. The main reason for this is because the former is part of the set of technologies that may form a complete autoconfiguration solution for networking systems. According to some points presented above, and also discussions that follow in next sections of this chapter, self-addressing can be considered as a fundamental part of autoconfiguration, given its prime responsibilities in networking systems when providing hosts with valid identification information and enabling communication among them.

An autonomous networking system may be composed by several technologies operating at different layers, like intelligent signaling and routing protocols, self-addressing protocols, self-healing procedures, self-management operations, etc. This chapter focuses on self-addressing protocols and how they can contribute to the support of autoconfiguration in autonomous networks. However, due to their close relation, it is impossible to discuss self-addressing concepts and techniques without approaching autoconfiguration concepts and, therefore, in the following several times self-addressing schemes are reported as part of more general autoconfiguration frameworks and/or architectures.

DESIGN ISSUES AND CLASSIFICATION

Design Issues

Existing mechanisms, like DHCP (*Dynamic Host Configuration Protocol*) (Droms, 1997) and (Droms, 2003), SLAAC (*Stateless Address Autoconfiguration*) (Thomson, Narten & Jinmei, 2007), NDP (*Neighbor Discovery Protocol*) (Narten, Nordmark, Simpson & Soliman, 2007) and DHCP-PD – (*DHCP – Prefix Delegation*) (Troan & Droms, 2003), provide only partial solutions with regard to the goals above mentioned. This means that, for example, they are unable to deliver when dealing with specific dynamic, multi-hop and distributed nature of ad hoc networks. Thus, additional work is still needed to fully contemplate such goals.

Despite the fact that it is an ongoing work, the IETF (*Internet Engineering Task Force*) working group AUTOCONF (2010) has already established a number of goals that should be seen to any autoconfiguration mechanism. According to Baccelli (2008), among these, there is the configuration of unique addresses for nodes and, when working with IPv6, the allocation of disjoint prefixes to different nodes. Furthermore, Baccelli (2008) and Williams (2002) also consider that autoconfiguration solutions should additionally:

- Configure a node's IP interface(s) with valid and unique IP addresses within a network;
- Configure disjoint prefixes for routers within the same network;
- Be independent from the routing protocol in use, i.e. the mechanism should not require a routing protocol to work properly and should not depend on routing functionality. However, Baccelli (2008) states that the solution may leverage the presence of routing protocols for optimization purposes;
- Provide support mechanisms and/or functionality to prevent and deal with addresses conflict, which can be originated for instance from networks merging together, local pre-configuration or node misconfiguration;
- Consider the particular characteristics of dynamic and heterogeneous networks such as their multi-hop nature, the potential asymmetry of links, and the variety of devices;
- Generate low overhead of control messages;
- Achieve their goal(s) with low delay or convergence time;
- Provide backward compatibility with other standards defined by the IETF;
- Not require changes on existing protocols on network interfaces and/or routers;
- Work in independent dynamic networks as well as in those connected to one or more external networks;
- Consider merging and disconnection of networks;
- Consider security issues;
- Be designed in a modular way, where each module should address a specific subset of the requirements or scenarios.

Security Considerations

With regard to autoconfiguration mechanisms, an important security issue to be considered is that of maintaining the confidentiality and the integrity of some data being exchanged between end-points in the network, e.g. servers and clients. This task is equivalent to that of ensuring end-to-end security in other types of networks. Therefore, according to Baccelli (2008), existing security enabled techniques are applicable.

Overall, current protocols for dynamic networks assume that all nodes are well-behaving and welcome. Consequently, the network may fail when allowing malicious nodes to get connected to it. Baccelli (2008) states that specific malicious behavior includes:

- Jamming, resulting in DoS (Denial of Service) attacks, whereby malicious nodes inject high levels of traffic in the network, increasing the average autoconfiguration convergence time;
- Incorrect traffic relaying, e.g. man-in-the-middle attacks, by which the attacker can:
    - Intercept IP configuration messages and cause operation failure;
    - Generate altered control messages likely to damage the addressing integrity;
    - Fake a router node participating in addressing tasks, also violating addressing integrity;
    - Generate incorrect traffic (e.g. server, router or address spoofing), that can also lead to impersonation, whereby a non-legitimate node can spoof an IP address;
    - Perform replay attacks by maliciously retransmitting or delaying legitimate data transmissions.

As the use of cryptographic solutions for secure autoconfiguration requires the presence of a higher entity in the network, this is not applicable in most cases where dynamic networks are used. Such dynamic network scenarios either lack any higher authority in the network or, may not trust it a priori. Despite this, dynamic networks remain the best choice regardless of affecting convergence time.

According to Baccelli (2008), another important issue concerning dynamic networks is the nodes behavior. The so called "selfish node", i.e. a node that preserves its own resources while consuming resources from other nodes by accessing and using their services (Kargl, Klenk, Schlott & Weber, 2004), can cause non-cooperation among the network nodes during the addressing procedures, hence affecting such mechanisms. Therefore, any secure solution for autoconfiguration mechanisms should consider the particularities of: (a) network nodes behavior; (b) other existing protocols operating in the network; (c) nodes limited resources; and (d) dynamic network deployment scenarios.

Classification of Addressing Approaches

Concerning the problem of addressing in dynamic networks, many solutions have already been put forward. According to already existent informal classifications, these can be roughly divided into three main categories: *stateless*, *stateful* and *hybrid* approaches. It is important to note that the term "state" in addressing context is related to the status of a specific address. This status may assume two values: free or allocated. Therefore, being aware of addresses state within a network prevents new nodes from being configured with conflicting information (i.e., duplicated addresses).

Stateless approaches, also known as conflict-detection approaches, allow a node to generate its own address. According to Thomson, Narten & Jinmei (2007), the stateless approach is implemented when a site is not concerned with the addresses other nodes are using, since they are unique and routable. To ensure this, the addresses could be generated by combining local information and information provided by available routers in the network (e.g., the network prefix). The information provided by routers is usually gathered from periodic routing advertisement messages. Using the local and gathered information, the node then creates a unique identification to its interface(s). If no routers are available within a given network, the node may only create a link-local address. Despite the fact that the usage of link-local addresses in self-addressing is one of the most questionable implementations within the IETF working group AUTOCONF, they are sufficient for enabling communication among the nodes attached to the same link.

A simpler alternative for stateless addressing approaches is random address selection. Some mechanisms do not implement a deterministic formula for generating an address. Instead, they define/calculate a range from where a node picks up one. Consequently, some duplicate address detection procedure is also needed. For example, such range may be determined by the IPv4 link-local prefix as defined by IANA (*Internet Assigned Numbers Authority*): 169.254/16 (IANA, 2010; IANA, 2002; and Cheshire, Aboba & Guttman, 2005).

The main drawback of stateless approaches is that they require a mechanism for duplicate address detection (DAD). Even the solutions that adopt some mathematical calculus for address generation, such as by combining information or by estimating the network size, at some moment will need to perform DAD to guarantee address uniqueness. Some stateless solutions are composed only by a DAD procedure and, therefore, are known as pure DAD approaches (e.g., Strong DAD, which is presented next).

Depending on the underlying algorithm used for generating random numbers, many stateless approaches based on random address selection from a given range may not perform as intended. This is due to limitations inherent to the random function used. According to Moler (2004), Random Number Generators, like those in the MATLAB and Statistics Toolbox software, are algorithms for generating pseudo-random numbers with a given distribution.

Some solutions implement pseudo-random functions that combine data, from different sources, attempting to generate a quasi-unique value. A good pseudo-random number generation algorithm must be chosen so that different nodes do not generate the same sequence of numbers and ultimately, the same addresses, which would create a loop of subsequent conflicts. Moreover, algorithms for pseudo-random number generation should not use the real-time clock or any other information which is (or may be) identical in two or more nodes within the network, as stated in Cheshire, Aboba & Guttman (2005). It means that for a set of nodes, which were powered at the same time, the algorithm may generate the same sequence of numbers, resulting in a never-ending series of conflicts when probing their self-generated addresses.

Approaches which follow the stateful paradigm consider the existence of at least one entity responsible for addressing in the network. Such solutions may also often implement schemes where the network nodes are allowed to actively take part in address assignment procedures. The main advantage of a stateful approach over a stateless one is that the former does not require DAD mechanisms. Therefore, stateful mechanisms can also be categorized as conflict-free solutions.

Some solutions build a local allocation table to store information about the state of addresses. Usually such table is updated passively, i.e. with information extracted from routing packets and/or packets from the addressing mechanism itself. Others divide a starting pool of addresses among the nodes in the network. These in turn may differ in that some of them implement a technique where the pool of addresses is divided among all nodes in the network, whereas others assume that just part of the nodes will take part in the addressing tasks.

Stateful approaches have some known weaknesses. When sharing the role of addressing among all nodes, some level of synchronization may be required. If each node keeps an address allocation table, the information held by them must be shared with other nodes within the network. In this way, all nodes will have coherent updated addressing information knowing at any time the addresses in use and those available for possible future assignments.

Efficiency with regard to address conflict resolution comes at the price of having an exhaustive control by the addressing mechanism over its resources. When dividing a pool of addresses among network nodes, these must remain in touch in order to determine, for example, whether the network is still having available addresses for allocation, to execute the recovery of unused resources and, probably, to create information backups avoiding single points of failure.

Control overhead may differ drastically among the stateful approaches. Depending on the considered scenario, one may however be willing to pay the price due to advantages such as address conflict-free guarantee, and possibly having a wider area of applicability. Considering scenarios of the Next Generation of Networks, stateful approaches seem to fit better in the core of complex networking scenarios, due to strong requirements on addressing integrity, while stateless mechanisms fit better in more isolated networks, connected or not to the core networks. As example, one can consider the existence of a networking scenario with a cellular network and a mobile data network coexisting and being managed by a single structure. Addressing must be provided in both networks, independently of the topology or devices technologies and, in this particular situation, the cooperation between two addressing strategies would be the best solution: a stateful protocol for the more stable cellular infrastructure and a stateless protocol for the more dynamic data network.

Hybrid addressing approaches combine stateless and stateful techniques into a single solution. Usually, these solutions implement node's locally allocation table and one or more DAD procedures. Their objective is to be as efficient as possible while ensuring a 100% conflict-free addressing within the network. However, by implementing a combination of stateless and stateful methodologies the overhead generated by a hybrid solution can be considerably high.

Figure 1 presents a proposed taxonomy for addressing solutions. At the top level, the approaches are divided into one of the three main classes: (a) stateless ones, where nodes are not aware of the addresses state within their network; (b) stateful ones, which implement some kind of control over the addressing space/resources enabling all nodes, or only part of them, to be aware of the addresses state; or (c) hybrid, which implement a combination of stateless and stateful techniques.

The stateless approaches can in turn be divided in two different categories: random selection and mathematical effort. The former implements a simple random address selection from a predefined range and then performs DAD. Otherwise, mathematical solutions attempt to calculate an address that has a high probability of being unique within the network, sometimes making use of

Figure 1. Simple taxonomy for self-addressing mechanisms

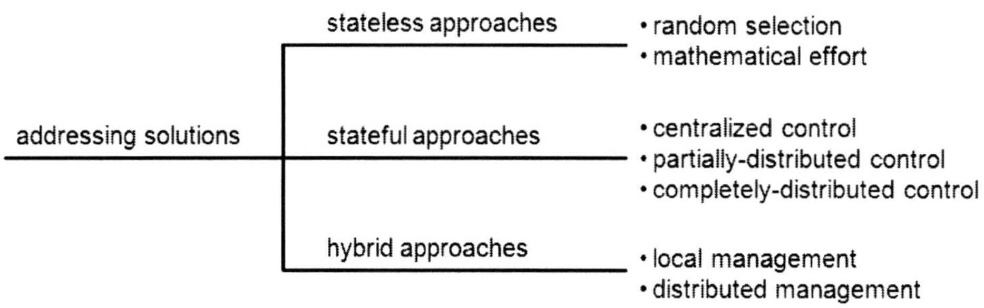

predefined information. However, even with an effort to select an exclusive address, those solutions eventually need to perform DAD.

Stateful approaches can be divided in three different categories: centralized, partially-distributed and completely-distributed approaches. In centralized approaches the state of addressing resources are kept within only one responsible entity, as is the case with the basic DHCP for example. Differently, partially-distributed solutions divide the addressing tasks among part of the nodes within a network, while completely-distributed approaches share the addressing issues within all network nodes.

Hybrid solutions can also be divided into two different categories: locally or distributed allocation management. In locally managed solutions every node in the network implements an allocation table. In distributed solutions the allocation table can be kept by one or more authority within the network. All hybrid solutions implement preventive and/or passive duplicate address detection.

Several self-addressing solutions are presented next exemplifying approaches for each of the categories. In addition to the solutions next presented in this chapter, one can find other references to addressing protocols and schemes for autonomous networks in the documents periodically published within the IETF working group Autoconfiguration (AUTOCONF, 2010).

Performance Metrics

When designing an addressing protocol for dynamic networks, basic considerations for autoconfiguration, as above mentioned, must be respected. According to the solution's applicability, one performance metric can be seen as more important than others in order to achieve its goals. Three basic quantitative metrics for judging the merit of addressing solutions are proposed. Such metrics can promote meaningful comparisons and assessments of each approach. In this section, we do not consider security related metrics. The retained metrics are formally defined as follows:

- *Address uniqueness:* represents to what extent a solution dedicates its efforts to avoid address duplication;
- *Configuration latency:* measures the necessary time for a new node to get configured with a valid and unique address within a network when the address is self-generated or provided by an addressing authority;
- *Control overhead:* this metric quantifies the message overhead that is necessary to promote a more reliable addressing integrity. Stateless solutions usually require less control messages to be exchanged among the network nodes than stateful ones which, for example, may need to synchronize allocation tables. However, the inverse may also be true depending, for example, on the DAD procedure implemented by the stateless approach. It may be the case that a solution implements not only the addressing basic tasks, but also the mechanisms to be triggered when facing critical situations like network partitioning and merging. Such mechanisms increase the control overhead.

The optimization of all metrics is very hard to achieve. In designing an addressing solution, one must have clear goals. In the following we discuss how one metric can be optimized even if sometimes at the expense of another one.

Address Uniqueness vs. Configuration Latency

Regarding stateless approaches, the configuration latency performance metric is related to the time a node takes for calculating its own address, plus the time for testing the calculated address within the other nodes in the network. For mechanisms implementing DAD procedures, a good address uniqueness degree has the cost of higher configuration latency. This is because it may be necessary to execute proactive DAD more than once to ensure a higher level of conflict-free reliability. Proactive DAD means the execution of conflict detection procedures on behalf of a selected or generated address before configuring the node with such address, while reactive or passive DAD are executed after the node's interface configuration.

Stateless mechanisms that implement mathematical efforts in order to ensure address uniqueness or to postpone the execution of DAD procedures, may guarantee uniqueness at the cost of low configuration delays. However, depending on the applicability scenario, for example considering very densely populated networks, reactive DAD procedures may degrade the network's performance by injecting addressing control traffic.

On the other hand, in stateful approaches, i.e. the ones that implement distributed addressing servers, the availability of such servers determines the configuration latency. As the addressing integrity is a servers' responsibility, the bigger the number of servers deployed in the network, the lower is the time for getting configured with a valid address. However, this time also depends on the solution adopted for deploying the servers at strategic locations within the network.

Address Uniqueness vs. Control Overhead

Sometimes it would be preferable to exercise a lower control overhead. However, for both stateless and stateful approaches, a lower overhead means a lower control over the addressing scheme. It certainly results in problems with address uniqueness. For example, to decrease the overhead in stateless mechanisms one may opt for implementing weaker DAD procedures, which in turn may result in failures when proving address exclusivity.

Under stateful approaches, for example, a reduced overhead may imply limiting the communication among the addressing authorities, compromising the addressing integrity. For ensuring a higher reliability of addressing uniqueness, stateless approaches must implement strong mathematical approaches or exhaustive DAD procedures, while stateful ones should guarantee the communication among the entities which are responsible for storing addressing information.

Configuration Latency vs. Control Overhead

Understandably most stateful approaches are likely to generate more control overhead than stateless ones. On the other hand, configuration may be faster with the former. Proactive DAD solutions usually implement flooding through broadcast messages in order to validate a tentative address. This procedure is typically performed more than once to ensure better uniqueness reliability. In addition, stateless approaches by mathematical effort also need to perform proactive or reactive DAD to guarantee certain dependability. As more DAD procedures are required, more control overhead is generated and, consequently, the configuration latency becomes higher either in terms of waiting time in proactive DAD or of data transmission delay in reactive DAD.

Stateful solutions, i.e. the ones that implement distributed servers, need to synchronize the addressing information to ensure network integrity. Depending on the optimization of servers' distribution, a starting node can easily and quickly be configured with a valid and unique address. However, this advantage may impose a higher control overhead.

Self-Addressing Solutions

In this section, we present the related work on self-addressing. Several approaches are surveyed and classified according to the above presented taxonomy. The selected solutions, which are thoroughly described, are believed to fully represent their respective classes, covering different methodologies and techniques for performing autonomous addressing.

Stateless Approaches

As above explained stateless approaches are those that does not keep track of the addressing resources of a network. Nodes are provided with a mechanism for generation and attribution of their own addresses. In the following different methodologies of stateless addressing solutions are presented.

Strong DAD

The Strong DAD (Perkins, Malinen, Wakikawa, Belding-Royer & Sun, 2001) is the simplest mechanism for duplicate address detection. According to the classification presented in Figure 1, this protocol fits in the stateless approaches with random selection of addresses and posterior execution of a duplicate detection procedure. A first node running Strong DAD randomly picks two addresses: a temporary address and a tentative one (i.e., the one to be claimed). The tentative address is selected from the range FIRST_PERM_ADDR – 65534, from 169.254/16 (IPv4 only). The temporary address is selected from the range 0 – LAST_TMP_ADDR (IPv4 only), and will be the source address of the node while performing the uniqueness check.

Address checking consists of two messages: Address Request (AREQ), from the starting node, and Address Reply (AREP), from a configured node. After selecting the addresses, the starting node sends an AREQ to the tentative address. It waits for an AREP during a pre-defined period of time. If no AREP is returned, the starting node retries the AREQ, with the same tentative address, up to a pre-defined time. If, after all retries, no AREP is received, this node assumes that the tentative address is not in use, i.e. it is unique within the network. Then, it configures its interface with the address and assumes to be connected.

When a configured node receives an AREQ message, it first checks its cache to see whether it has already received an AREQ from this source with this tentative address. If an entry is found, the node just discards the packet. Otherwise, the node enters the values of these fields into a temporary buffer. Considering that the node's neighbors will also rebroadcast the same packet, the node will realize it has already received the AREQ and then will not reprocess the packet.

Next, the configured node enters in its routing table a new route, with the packet's source as destination. The packet's last hop, i.e. the node from which the configured node received the AREQ, is set as the route's next hop. This way, a reverse route for the AREQ, with a pre-defined lifetime, is created as the packet is retransmitted through the network. This reverse route is used when a unicast AREP message is sent to the starting node.

Then, the configured node checks if its own IP address matches the tentative address on the AREQ message. If not, the node rebroadcasts the packet to its neighbors. On the other hand, if the node has the same IP address than the one claimed in the received AREQ, the configured node must reply to the packet. To do so, it sends a unicast AREP message to the AREQ's source node. The reverse route created by the AREQ is now used to route the AREP packet to the starting node.

When receiving an AREP in response to its AREQ, the initiating node randomly picks up another address, from the range FIRST_PERM_ADDR – 65534, and sends another request claiming the new selected tentative address. Then, the algorithm is repeated until the starting node either gets configured with a valid and unique address or reaches the maximum permitted number of retries. More information about the Strong DAD mechanism, packet formats and particularities for IPv4 and IPv6, can be found in (Perkins, Malinen, Wakikawa, Belding-Royer & Sun, 2001).

Weak DAD

Since Strong DAD is not applicable in unbounded delays networks, due to it timeout-based DAD, Weak DAD (Vaidya, 2002) was proposed as an alternative addressing mechanism to the former. Weak DAD can be used independently or in combination with other schemes, like the one proposed in Jeong, Park, Jeong & Kim (2006), which specifies a procedure for enabling mobile nodes to configure their interfaces with IPv4 or IPv6 and handle address duplications with Weak DAD procedures. The categorization of Weak DAD in one of the subcategories presented in Figure 1 for stateless approaches depends directly on the combined mechanism for address selection/generation. The main characteristic of Weak DAD, as a stateless approach, is that it relaxes the requirements for detecting duplicate addresses. That is, it does not require the detection of all conflicts in the network. Weak DAD imposes that a packet sent to a specific destination must be routed to this destination and not to a node X, different from the packet's destination, even if the destination and the node X have the same address.

As an example of how the Weak DAD operates, let us consider two distinct networks X and Y. A packet sent from the node A to node D in the network X, travels via nodes B and C. Let us also consider that in the network Y another node, named K has selected the same IP address as node D in the network X. If the networks X and Y merge with each other in the near future, forming the network Z, the nodes D and K will have the same IP address, resulting in an address conflict in the network Z. Therefore, the previous route from node A to node D may be injured, since the intermediate nodes may forward the packet to node K instead. This means, that while before the merging the packets were routed from node A to node D, now they may be routed from node A to node K. Weak DAD suggests that duplicate addresses can be tolerated within a network as long as packets still reach their intended final destination correctly.

To do so, Weak DAD requires some changes in the routing protocol that will operate in the network. It can be considered as a disadvantage of this solution since it depends on other technologies operating on the network. Nevertheless, its scheme, as presented in Vaidya (2002), considers the following design goals:

- Address size cannot be made arbitrary large. Therefore, for instance, MAC address cannot be embedded in the IP address;
- IP header format should not be modified. For instance, we do not want to add new options to the IP header;
- Content of routing-related control packets (such as link-state updates, route requests, or route replies) may be modified to include information pertinent to DAD;
- No assumptions should be made about protocol layers above the network layer.

The Weak DAD approach assumes that each node in the network is pre-assigned with a unique key. The MAC address can be used as the node's key. Although these addresses may sometimes be duplicated on multiple devices, as discussed in Nesargi & Prakash (2002), MAC addresses remain among the best choices when it comes to unique identifiers for nodes' interfaces. Alternatively, the nodes can use another identifier or procedure to generate a key, since this key has a small probability of being duplicated or generated more than once.

Given the unique key, and considering IPv6, a unique IP address can be created simple by embedding this key in the IP address. However, when considering IPv4, the number of bits of the IP address is smaller, and embedding the key may not be possible. The latter case is presented in Vaidya (2002). Therefore, the Weak DAD uses the key for the purpose of detecting duplicate IP addresses within the network, without actually embedding this key in the IP address.

Weak DAD was designed to work with link-state routing protocols. Basically, the routing protocol maintains a routing table at each node with an entry for each known node in the network. In each entry, the table contains the destination node and the next hop addresses. Using the link-state information from the routing packets, the nodes update their routing tables and determine the network topology, which is helpful for choosing the shortest path (i.e. lowest cost) route to the destination.

Instead of having a routing table containing only the IP address of the destination node and its respective next hop, the node will contain a routing table with the IP address and the key of the destination node and the IP address of its respective next hop. As well as with the routing table, the link-state packet must also be modified to carry the information of the IP address and key of both destination node and next hop.

With this modification, Weak DAD attempts to ensure that a packet, considering the example above presented, that is sent from node A to node D, through nodes B and C, will never reach the wrong destination K due to the existent address conflict. Instead, node A and the intermediate nodes in the route path to node D, will forward the packet following the nodes' key. In addition, the address conflict can be detected by the node A, for instance, when this node receives the link-state packets with routes to nodes D and K, and then a resolution protocol may be triggered to deal with such address conflict.

In Vaidya (2002), the author also presents the solution for the conflict detection and resolution as well as its possible solution. Moreover, it also defines a hybrid DAD scheme, i.e. how the Weak DAD is combined with another timeout-based mechanism, and describes the case of performing Weak DAD with the Dynamic Source Routing (DSR) protocol.

Passive DAD

The Passive DAD, or PDAD (Weniger, 2003), is part of a more complete solution called PACMAN, presented below as a hybrid addressing solution. PDAD is another mechanism that requires support of routing protocols. Although it is a disadvantage, this solution does not require modification to the routing protocol. In particular, PDAD takes advantage of routing protocol control messages. It allows a node to analyze incoming routing protocol packets to derive hints about address conflicts. To do so, PDAD implements a set of algorithms that are triggered depending on the routing protocol the network is running. PDAD can operate with link-state or reactive routing protocols, but different algorithms need to be implemented for each type of protocol. The classification of PDAD, according to Figure 1, is directly connected to the PACMAN solution due to its conjunction operation. Given that the generation of address in PACMAN is done by using a probabilistic algorithm, PDAD can be considered as a stateless approach using mathematical efforts. More information on PACMAN is given in the hybrid solutions section.

According to Weniger (2003), PDAD algorithms are applied to routing packets with the objective of exploring events that either:

- Never occur in case of unique address, but always in case of a duplicate address. In this case, the conflict is certain if the event occurs at least once;
- Rarely occur in case of a unique address, but often in case of a duplicate address. In this case, there is a probability of the conflict existence. Then, a long-term monitoring (e.g., to detect if the event occurs again) may be necessary.

According to Weniger (2005), PDAD algorithms derive information about a sender's routing protocol state at the time the packet was sent from incoming routing protocol packets. This state can be compared with the state of the receiver or with the state of another node, which can be obtained from previously received packets from this address. This way, the node stores information about the last routing packet received, from a specific address, in a routing packet information table.

In addition, the author considers a model of a classic link-state routing protocol, where the protocol periodically issues link-state packets. Each packet contains the originator's address, a sequence number, and a set of link-states consisting of the addresses of all neighbors. These packets are flooded in the network and forwarded on the application layer. Considering on-demand routing protocols, due to their passive nature, PDAD can only detect address conflict among nodes which participate in routing activities, i.e. in route discovery and maintenance procedures.

Examples of algorithms implemented with the PDAD solution, as presented in Weniger (2005), are:

- PDAD-SN (*Sequence Number*): this algorithm exploits the sequence numbers (SN) in the routing protocol packets. Each node in the network uses a SN incremented by itself only once within a predetermined interval. In Weniger (2005) a better explanation of how PDAD estimates this interval for incrementing the SN can be found. A node may detect the possibility of an address conflict when receiving a packet from the address *X* with a lower sequence number than the last packet received by the same address. This means that since each packet is forwarded once and never reaches the same node twice, then both packets with the same address *X* were generated by different nodes in the network. This algorithm can be used with link-state and reactive routing protocols;
- PDAD-SND (*Sequence Number Difference*): this algorithm also exploits the SN in the routing packets and can also be used with link-state and reactive routing protocols. Differently from the PDAD-SN, this algorithm identifies possible conflicts when the SNs have a considerable difference in their increment. PDAD considers that there is a possible address conflict when the difference between two SNs, from the same origin, is higher than the possible increment within the time defined by $t1 - t2 + td$, where $t1$ and $t2$ being the points in time when, respectively, packets 1 and 2 were received, and td the estimated time between each SN increment;
- PDAD-SNE (*Sequence Number Equal*): this algorithm detects the existence of a possible address conflict in the network when an intermediate node receives a routing protocol packet from two different nodes with the same originator's address and sequence number. However, the link-state information will differ from each other, indicating that actually the packets are not from the same source. This algorithm can be used with link-state and reactive routing protocols;
- PDAD-NH (*Neighbor History*): it is a specific algorithm for link-state routing protocols and it exploits bidirectional link-states. It considers the node's neighbors to detect possible address conflicts and requires that nodes store information about their recent neighbors in a table. For instance, if a node receives a link-state packet with its own address in the link-state information, the packet originator's address must have been a node's neighbor at least during the last period of a predetermined interval. If the node identifies that the originator's address has not been its neighbor, it assumes that its own address is duplicated in the network. Other algorithms exploring the link-state information and the node's neighborhood are explained in Weniger (2005);

- PDAD-SA (*Source Address*): this algorithm can be used by link-state and reactive routing protocols and it utilizes the packet's IP header. Considering a protocol that forwards application layer packets, the IP source address is always the address of the last hop. Therefore, an address conflict can be detected if a node receives a routing packet with the IP source address equal to its own address;
- PDAD-RNS (*RREQ-Never-Sent*): it is a specific algorithm for reactive routing protocols and it detects a possible address conflict in the network when a Route Request message (RREQ) is received by a receiver's originator address, but the latter has never sent a RREQ to this destination. Therefore, another node with the same address must have sent the RREQ message;
- PDAD-RwR (*RREP-without-RREQ*): this algorithm can be used with reactive routing protocols only and it detects a possible conflict when a node receives a Route Reply message (RREP), but this node has never sent a RREQ message to the specific destination;
- PDAD-2RoR (*2RREPs-on-RREQ*): this algorithm is also specific to reactive routing protocols and uses the duplicate message cache information. It assumes that a RREQ's destination only replies once. Therefore, if the RREQ originator receives more than one RREP from the same destination, it concludes that an address conflict was detected within the network.

The work in Weniger (2005) offers details of PDAD algorithms application in the following routing protocols, and their respective evaluation: Fisheye State Routing (FSR), Optimized Link-State Routing (OLSR), and Ad hoc On-demand Distance Vector (AODV).

AIPAC

AIPAC stands for Automatic IP Address Configuration (Fazio, Villari & Puliafito, 2006). The objective of this stateless protocol is to perform addressing and manage possible conflicts occurrences, while operating with a reduced number of control packets. It also provides a mechanism for handling networks merging and partitioning. Its authors divided address autoconfiguration in four parts: (1) initial configuration of nodes; (2) networks merging management; (3) networks partitioning management; and (4) gradual networks merging management.

Differently to Strong DAD, initial address configuration on AIPAC does not rely on temporary addresses, but it defines a relation between two nodes: the initiator (an already configured node in the network), and the requester (the new node). The requester relies on the initiator for obtaining a unique address within the network. When a node is started it selects a Host Identifier (HID) and broadcasts messages requesting to join a network. If no reply is obtained, this node assumes to be the very first one in the network, and then selects its own IP address and a Network ID (NetID). When receiving a response from an already configured node to its requests, the new node waits for this initiator in order to negotiate on its behalf within the network a valid and unique address. AIPAC establishes that the IP addresses must be chosen from the range of $n=2^{32}$ possible values. AIPAC defines that an address for a new node must be selected randomly from a range of allowed addresses, based on Strong DAD (Perkins, Malinen, Wakikawa, Belding-Royer & Sun, 2001). According to Figure 1, this characteristic classifies AIPAC as a stateless approach of random selection of addresses.

To check the availability of a selected address, the initiator broadcasts a message with the chosen address. The nodes that receive this message check whether the requested IP address matches any of their own addresses. If not, they rebroadcast the same message. Otherwise, the node that identified a conflict address for the generated address sends a message back to the initiator. Upon receiving this information, the initiator restarts the same process by selecting a new address from the same range. However, if no reply message is received, the initiator assumes the address to be available for assigning to the requester. Finally, it sends the selected address to the requester that configures its interface with it.

To manage networks merging and partitioning, AIPAC uses the concept of Network ID (NetID), similar to the one defined in Nesargi & Prakash (2002). Different networks that come in contact can be detected through their different NetIDs, which are carried by their nodes. AIPAC limits itself to the detection of a presence of more than a dynamic network and falls short of taking any actual actions for dealing with possible addresses conflicts immediately. Instead, as a reactive protocol, it waits until the nodes need to transmit data packets. It makes AIPAC suitable for scenarios with networks that use reactive routing protocols. AIPAC passively uses the routing protocol route discovery packets to detect address duplication.

AIPAC requires modification of the routing protocol packets by adding the node's NetID into the route reply packets. If a node receives several route replies with different NetIDs, it concludes that the destination address is duplicated. Then the source node triggers a procedure notifying the nodes that have conflicting addresses enforcing them to proceed in reconfiguration or negotiation for solving such problem. This mechanism for conflict detection and correction is not applicable for scenarios of networks partitioning and re-merging.

Attempting to deal with re-merging problems, AIPAC implements a procedure where nodes store information about their neighborhood. This information is gathered from bidirectional neighbor packet exchange. If a node has not received replies from one of its neighbors during a predetermined period of time and, consequently, the neighbor has also not received the node's periodic messages, the nodes assume that there is a possibility of network partitioning. Therefore, the neighbor with the highest IP address triggers a procedure for route discovery towards that neighbor. If no route is found the node concludes that network partitioning has occurred, selects a new NetID, and distributes this new configuration to the nodes within its network. Doing so, it avoids the problem of re-merging two networks with the same NetID. However, a node departure may be misinterpreted as a network partitioning and the procedure for reconfiguring the network may be unnecessarily executed increasing the addressing control costs, i.e. traffic and delay.

Moreover, AIPAC assumes that, after two or more networks merge into one, it is more convenient and desirable that the new network has a single NetID. The reason for this is the fact that the more fragmented a system is the higher is the probability that duplicate addresses may occur. The AIPAC gradual merging mechanism allows a heterogeneous system to become more uniform by decreasing the number of different networks. If there is the tendency of real merging between two networks, the system focuses on the NetID of the network with a higher number of nodes or a higher density of nodes. More information about the AIPAC protocol can be found in Fazio, Villari & Puliafito (2004) and Fazio, Villari & Puliafito (2006).

Stateful Approaches

Stateful approaches are those that maintain any type of register of addresses in use within the network. The nodes are able to check the address availability with local or distributed addressing authorities. In the following different stateful solutions are detailed.

Prophet Allocation

Prophet Allocation (Zhou, Ni & Mutka, 2003) is a proposed scheme that addresses allocation in large scale MANETs. According to its authors, Prophet is a low complexity, latency and overhead mechanism, and is capable of dealing with the problem of network partition and merging. This solution was named Prophet Allocation because the very first node of the network is assumed to know in advance which addresses are going to be allocated. According to Figure 1, the basis of the algorithm is stateful with completely-distributed addressing control, where a sequence consisting of numbers is obtained in a range R through a function f(n). The initial state of f(n) is called a seed, where each seed leads to a different sequence with the state of f(n) updated at the same time. The function *f(n)* is given by

$$f(n) = (a \cdot s \cdot 11) \bmod 7$$

where a and s are the node address and the node state respectively.

In Prophet Allocation every node is identified by a tuple [address, state of f(n)]. To better understand the operation of Prophet Allocation, let us consider an example where the very first node A, at the initial time t1, uses the value 3 as both its IP address and seed, i.e. A[3,3]. When a node B joins the network, node A obtains the value 1 for B through f(n). Then, at t2, A changes its state of f(n) to 1, i.e. A[3,1], and assigns 1 to B. At time t3, nodes C and D join the network through, respectively, nodes A and B. Using f(n), node C is assigned the value 5 from A, and node D gets configured by B with value 4. Both nodes A and B change their state of f(n), respectively, to the values 5 and 4, i.e. A[3,5] and B[1,4].

Considering that the addressing space for the example presented above is [1,6], i.e. from 1 to 6, the next round of allocation, said time t4, will result in a conflict. According to the authors, address claiming is not necessary with Prophet. Conflicts will indeed occur, but the minimal interval between two occurrences of the same number is extremely long. Another point the authors assume is that, when a new node is assigned an "old" address, the previous node that was using this address has likely already left the network. Nevertheless, the authors consider as an alternative to avoid address conflicts the execution of a DAD procedure when identifying the possibility of conflicts occurrence.

Prophet Allocation is said to easily handle situations of networks partitioning and re-merging. Considering a scenario with network B, which used to be part of the network A, a merging process to network A would not be a problem. As the sequences of each network are different, the new addresses, allocated during the time the networks were separated, remain different among the partitions. Therefore, no address conflict will occur if the networks merge again. As well as in AIPAC, to handle merging between two or more distinct networks, Prophet Allocation implements the idea of Network ID (in this case refereed as NID). The NID is known to the network during the address allocation process, and the merging can be detected by analyzing modified routing protocol packets.

In Zhou, Ni & Mutka (2003), more detailed information about Prophet Allocation is presented. The design of the function f(n) is detailed, as well as a finite state machine that is used to explain the states of a node through the mechanism functionalities is described. In addition, performance comparisons between Prophet Allocation and other addressing mechanisms and simulation results are also presented.

SooA

SooA stands for *Self-organization of Addresses*, and it is introduced in Schmidt, Gomes, Sadok, Kelner & Johnsson (2009). According to the classification presented in Figure 1, it is a stateful protocol, with partially-distributed addressing control, that implements allocation and management of addressing resources. SooA was designed to be a more comprehensive solution for self-addressing. Its functionalities are quite similar to those found in DHCP and its extensions. However, according to the authors, SooA implements procedures and relations between network nodes which allow the protocol to operate in a wide variety of scenarios, mainly those described as NGN scenarios (e.g., complex network composed by different topologies and technologies).

One of the main advantages of SooA is that it is an independent solution. This means that the protocol does not rely in any other technology in the network, such as routing protocols. Consequently, SooA does not require modification to other existing protocols and/or applications. This characteristic makes SooA more suitable for scenarios of autonomous networks, where technologies can be negotiated between nodes and applied to the network without requiring reconfiguration (e.g., routing protocol negotiation).

SooA is a stateful and partially distributed solution, where one or more nodes are responsible for executing addressing operations in the network. These nodes are called *addressing servers* (or just *server*). Each addressing server is provided with a pool of valid and unique addresses. The addressing server uses the resources from this pool to allocate configuration information to new nodes. A new node is configured in the network after contacting an addressing server and being provided with a valid and unique address. Upon receiving a valid and unique address from the server and configuring its interface with such information, the new node becomes a client for that addressing server. A client's interface can be attached to only one addressing server, i.e. the one that provided it with the addressing information. It is important to state that a new node can reach a server directly (i.e. one hop communication) or indirectly (i.e. two or more hops communication). In the second situation, the protocol implements a mechanism similar to the one found in *DHCP Relay* where it allows clients (i.e. already configured nodes) to perform intermediate negotiations between their own addressing server and a new node.

A second situation in SooA's allocation procedure is that an active addressing server may decide for the creation of a new addressing server in the network instead of accepting a new client connection. According to the authors, this decision can be driven by different situations, depending on the implementation and applicability scenario. One possible reason is that the addressing server has a maximum addressing workload that it can assume, e.g. a maximum number of active client connections. Another reason could be the cost of the connection of the new node, e.g. the distance of the new node from the server in number of hops. Upon receiving a request for configuration from a new node, and identifying that it is reaching its maximum allowed workload, the server sends to the new node the configuration information that is necessary to become a new addressing server in the network, i.e. a pool of not allocated and unique addresses, which is a portion of the existing server's pool. This way, the protocol implements a distribution on the addressing responsibility through the network nodes, and also creates a father-child relation between these servers that are used to maintain the addressing integrity.

The basic allocation functionality of SooA is supplemented by the allocation management procedure. It is executed for both allocations between servers and clients and allocations between father servers and child servers. This procedure is composed basically by a periodical exchange of messages between the entities in the addressing structure, which allows the protocol to manage nodes departures and/or failures and, consequently, the resources retrieval ensuring more integrity on addressing.

As the protocol operates with servers as responsible for addressing issues, it has the problem of single points of failure, i.e. in situations of servers' failure the addressing in the network can be compromised. Attempting to solve such problems, the authors proposed a functional module for replicating the addressing information in the network. To do so, each server must select two of its clients to become its backups. A first level backup must directly contact the server periodically to receive updates of addressing procedures done, and then also forward the information received to a second level backup. The existence of the second level backup is due to information redundancy. Upon identifying a critical situation of server failure, the backup node assumes the server's position (the first level backup has the priority), and becomes the new server replacing the failed one, ensuring addressing integrity, and eliminating the need for nodes reconfiguration.

Currently, SooA is an ongoing project. Therefore, there are several modules under development and implementation, which will improve the basic protocol functionality with characteristics of scalability, integrity, self-healing, and even ensuring a certain level of security in addressing, making the protocol a more robust solution. More information about the protocol can be found in Schmidt, Gomes, Sadok, Kelner & Johnsson (2009).

IPAS

The work presented in Manousakis, Baras, McAuley & Morera (2005) proposes a framework for autoconfiguration of host, router and server information. It includes the automatic generation and maintenance of a hierarchy, under the same architectural, algorithmic and protocol framework. This framework is composed of two parts: (a) the decision making part, which is responsible for obtaining network and hierarchy configuration, according to the network performance objectives; and (b) the communication part, that is responsible for distributing the configuration decisions and collecting the required information used by the decision making part. Concerning configuration of interfaces, and according to Figure 1, IPAS can be classified as a stateful approach with centralized control.

The communication part of the framework consists of the Dynamic Configuration Distribution Protocol (DCDP), Dynamic and Rapid Configuration Protocol (DRCP), and Yelp Announcement Protocol (YAP). These modules are part of the IPAS (IP Autoconfiguration Suite) that is responsible for the network configuration. The modules DRCP and DCDP constitute the core of the autoconfiguration suite.

The autoconfiguration suite functionality can be seen as a feedback loop. It interacts with the ACA (Adaptive Configuration Agent) distributing new configuration, from the Configuration Information Database, through the DCDP. In every node, the DRCP configures the interface within a specified subnet. When configured, the interface reports its configuration information, through YAP, to the Configuration Information Server. Finally, the server stores this configuration information in the Configuration Information Database, which will be accessed by the ACA to start the cycle again.

According to the authors, the DCDP is robust, scalable, has low-overhead, and is lightweight (minimal state) protocol. It was designed to distribute configuration information on address-pools and other IP configuration information such as DNS Server's IP address, security keys, or routing protocol. To be deployed in scenarios such as military battlefields, DCDP is able to operate without central coordination or periodic messages. It also does not depend on routing protocols for distributing its messages.

The DCDP relies on the DRCP to configure the node's interface(s) with a valid address. The DRCP is responsible for detecting the need for reconfiguration due, for example, to node mobility or conflicting information. The authors also state that DRCP allows for: (a) efficient use of scarce wireless bandwidth; (b) dynamic addition or deletion of address pools for supporting server fail over; (c) message exchange without broadcast; and (d) clients to be routers. In each sub-network there is at least one DRCP server, and the other nodes are set to be DRCP clients.

As far as node configuration is concerned, a node starts operating the DRCP protocol and takes the role of a DRCP client. Its first task is to discover a server in the network. To do so, the client waits for an advertisement message, and if it is not received within a predetermined interval, the client broadcasts a message attempting to discover a configured server. Again, if the client has not received such a message within a predetermined period of time, it goes to the pre-configuration state and, upon realizing it fills the requirements for becoming a server, it changes its status to assume the server position. A node is able to become a server if it, for example, carries a pool of valid addresses or receives such configuration information from an external interface. Otherwise, if this client does not fill the requirements to assume a server position, it returns to the initial state and continues its search for a server by broadcasting messages.

In a second case, upon receiving an advertisement message from a valid server, the client goes to a binding state, where it sends a unicast message to the server and waits for its reply. If the client receives a reply from the server, the client immediately configures its interface with the configuration information sent by the server within the reply message. After assuming the configuration, the client must periodically renew its lease with the server through a request-reply message exchange. If, for some reason, the renewal fails, the client starts another configuration procedure.

In addition to the allocation operations, a server executes preemptive DAD to all the addresses of its pool, i.e. for both attributed and available addresses. According to the authors, this DAD procedure contributes to the recovery of unused addresses. However, such procedure may result in an increasing traffic overload and latency for nodes configuration.

In order for the DRCP configuration process to work properly, predefined configuration information must be provided. Using the DCDP this predefined information is disseminated through the network. For instance, the communication between DCDP and DRCP is used when a server needs a pool of addresses. In this situation, a request is done from the DRCP to the DCDP. The latter executes the necessary procedures to get a new pool and then returns such information to the DRCP. To do so, the DCDP allows the communication between other nodes in the network and also the communication between the node and the network manager.

The IP Autoconfiguration Suite is a much bigger project than the basic description above presented. This framework has other important components which are fundamental to its functionality. The brief description presented here introduced how IPAS handles the initial configuration of nodes, which involves addressing configuration. More information about this framework and related work can be found in McAuley, Das, Madhani, Baba & Shobatake (2001), Kant, McAuley, Morera, Sethi & Steiner (2003), Morera, McAuley & Wong (2003), Manousakis (2005) and Manousakis, Baras, McAuley & Morera (2005).

Hybrid Approaches

Hybrid approaches are those that implement a combination of stateless and stateful techniques. Usually, these solutions are composed of three steps: (a) self-generation of address; (b) proactive DAD; and (c) registration of the generated and attributed address. In the following some key hybrid solutions are detailed covering different methodologies.

HCQA

The HCQA (*Hybrid Centralized Query-based Autoconfiguration*), proposed in Sun & Belding-Royer (2003), is considered to be the first hybrid approach for addressing autoconfiguration. According to the solutions classification presented in Figure 1, this approach is considered as a hybrid approach with distributed address management, because it uses the Strong DAD protocol and a single and centralized allocation table to improve address consistency. Consequently, it is classified as a hybrid approach with central management of addresses. As part of the Strong DAD operation, at the initialization phase a node chooses a temporary address and a tentative one from distinct ranges. This first step succeeds when the tentative address is proved to be within the network and it is found not to be in use yet.

In a second step, the node must register this successfully tested address within an Address Authority (AA) in the network. To do so, the node waits for an advertisement from the AA. Upon receiving the advertisement, the node sends a registration request to the AA and waits for its confirmation. The node may use the address only after receiving this confirmation. Upon concluding the registration, the node initiates a timer for repeating this process periodically.

The network's AA is the first node which obtains a unique IP address, and it also selects a unique key to identify the network, e.g. its own MAC address. This network identifier is broadcasted periodically by the AA. If a node does not receive AA's broadcast for a predetermined period of time, it assumes that there is a network partitioning and becomes the new AA by generating a new network identifier. Upon receiving a new network identifier, a node must register itself within the new AA without changing its own address. However, the unnoticed departure of the AA node from the network, for example due to connection failure, may generate problems when other nodes assume the AA position. Similarly to other solutions presented in the previous, HCQA identifies networks merging by detecting the presence of two or more different network identifiers. Only the AA nodes are involved in the process of address conflict detection by exchanging their respective allocation tables.

The first node that registers its address with an AA is automatically selected to be the AA's backup. This is done to ensure a higher level of addressing integrity. Every time a new node registers its IP address, the AA reports an update with this new information to its backup.

In a research report about addressing mechanisms, Bachar (2005) states that HCQA extends the stateless approach Strong DAD, guaranteeing address conflict detection and proposing an effective solution for dealing with network partitioning and merging. However, the implemented conflict detection mechanism by exchanging AA information, may generate high control traffic in the network. In addition, the dependability on a single central entity for addressing creates a scenario with a single point of failure and, consequently, it becomes a solution that is not fault-tolerant enough considering scenarios with high dynamicity.

MANETconf

MANETconf (Nesargi & Prakash, 2002) is a distributed dynamic host configuration protocol designed to configure nodes in a MANET. This mechanism establishes that all nodes in the network must accept the proposed address for a new node as long as such address is not in conflict with another address in use within the network. This means that a starting node will be configured with a proposed address that has been checked with the network. In order to ensure a more effective address testing, MANETconf determines that all nodes in the network must store information regarding the state of addresses in use within the network which, according to Figure 1, categorizes this protocol as a hybrid solution with local management of addresses. It includes the set of all allocated IP addresses in the network and the set of all pending IP addresses (i.e. addresses that are in the process of being allocated to other nodes). The procedures for randomly selecting an address and testing such address with the other nodes characterize stateless functionalities, and the local tables for storing information about IP addresses define the stateful characteristics of the protocol. Therefore, by mixing these, MANETconf is considered to be a hybrid solution.

In MANETconf the network is started when the very first node executes the neighbor search procedure and obtains no responses from configured nodes. Consequently, this node configures itself with a randomly selected IP address. Upon receiving a reply from a configured neighbor, the new node selects the neighbor as its initiator, and sends a unicast request message to this initiator. Then, the initiator selects an address that is neither in the allocated address set nor in the pending address set, and adds this address to its own table of pending allocation addresses. The initiator initiates the procedure for claiming the address with the other network nodes by broadcasting a request message to its neighbors. Upon receiving this message, a configured neighbor checks if the claimed address matches with the information in its allocated and pending tables. If so, this node sends a negative reply to the initiator. Otherwise, the receiver adds the information in its table of pending addresses as a tuple [initiator, address] and replies to the initiator with an affirmative message.

The initiator node assumes that the testing procedure was successfully concluded upon receiving only positive answers from other nodes. Then, the initiator assigns the successfully tested address to the requester node, inserts this address in the table of allocated addresses, and informs others about the assignment made so that they can update the information on their own tables. Otherwise, if the initiator receives at least one negative reply to its request, it restarts the process by selecting and testing a new address.

As an address recovery procedure, when a node is able to inform about its departure from the network, it floods the network with a message allowing the others to erase its allocation information. Upon receiving such message, a node simply removes the leaving node's address from the table of allocated addresses, freeing this address for future assignments.

Situations of concurrent addresses assignments are solved considering the initiators' IP address. The initiator configured with the lower IP address has higher priority in the allocation process. Upon receiving an initiator request for an already requested address, an intermediate node checks the initiators' IP addresses. If the concurrent request message comes from a lower priority initiator, the node sends a negative reply to this initiator. Otherwise, if the intermediate node receives the concurrent request from the higher priority initiator, both initiators will be replied positively. However, according to the authors, among multiple conflicting initiations, only the highest priority initiators will receive all affirmative responses, while all other initiators will receive at least one negative reply, enforcing them to restart the testing procedure.

In addition, MANETconf defines a procedure to handle situations where initiator and requester lose the communication between each other during the addressing process due to, for example, nodes mobility. Upon noticing that it has lost the communication with its initiator, the requester node selects an adjacent configured node as its new initiator, and informs this node about its former initiator. The new initiator sends a message to the former one to inform it regarding the migration of the requester node. When the former initiator finishes the process of address testing in behalf of the requester, it sends the configuration information to the new initiator. The new initiator forwards the information to the requester so that this one configures its interface accordingly.

In summary, the previous discussion illustrates the basic functionality of MANETconf. The work in Nesargi & Prakash (2002) presents strategies for improving the protocol in order to make it more robust against situations like initiator node crashing, abrupt node departure, message loss and networks merging and partitioning. Moreover, some security-related considerations are also presented.

PACMAN

PACMAN stands for Passive Autoconfiguration for Mobile Ad Hoc Networks and was proposed in Weniger (2005). It is defined as an approach for the efficient distributed address autoconfiguration in MANETs, and according to the classification of Figure 1, it is a hybrid solution with local management of addresses. It uses cross-layer information from ongoing routing protocol traffic, without requiring modifications to the routing protocol, and utilizes elements of both stateless and stateful paradigms of addressing approaches, consequently, constituting a hybrid solution.

PACMAN has a modular architecture. The *address assignment* component is responsible for the self-generation of addresses, by selecting them through a probabilistic algorithm, and the local allocation table maintenance. The so called *routing protocol packet parser* has the objective of extracting information from incoming routing packets. This information is sent to the *PACMAN manager*, which is an entity responsible for delegating the information to the respective components.

The module of *Passive Duplicate Address Detection (PDAD)*, above presented, is responsible for address conflict detection. The advantage of PDAD is that such mechanism does not generate control messages to search for addresses conflicts. Instead, address monitoring is done by analyzing incoming routing protocol packets. Upon detecting an address conflict, PACMAN triggers the *conflict resolution* component, which is responsible for notifying the conflicting node. The *address change management* component can inform communication partners about the address change in the network and, consequently, it may prevent transport layer connections failure.

PACMAN address self-generation is done through a probabilistic algorithm. Using the information of a predefined conflict probability, an estimation of the number of nodes and an allocation table, the algorithm calculates a virtual addressing space. It randomly selects an address from this virtual space and, using the information on its local allocation table, it ensures the address has not already been assigned to other node. If no local conflict is detected, the selected address is immediately assigned by the node. As long as each node is responsible for assigning an address to itself, not depending on a global state, PACMAN defines that each node is free to choose its virtual address space size.

According to the authors, the probability of address conflicts is almost null and, if it happens it is resolved by the PDAD component in a timely manner. To evaluate the probability of address conflict, the value of this probability is calculated. At this time, an analogy with the well-known birthday paradox (Sayrafiezadeh, 1994) can be made. The equation for calculating the conflict probability, defined in Weniger (2005), considers the number of nodes and the size of the addressing space. The authors also state that, regarding the desired conflict probability as a predefined quality-of-service parameter, and given that the number of nodes within the network is known, the optimal virtual address space size can be calculated by each node through the defined equation.

Furthermore, PACMAN reduces even more the conflict probability when considering the concept of allocation table, maintained with cross-layer information from the routing protocol. However, assuming a scenario with a reactive routing protocol, the allocation table may not be up to date with information from the recently connected nodes. In such scenario, the previously mentioned equation is not able to express the correct conflict probability anymore and, consequently, a second equation for estimating the conflict probability is defined in Weniger (2005). This equation considers the two abovementioned parameters, i.e. addressing space size and number of nodes, plus the number of hidden allocated addresses. This third parameter can be estimated from the allocation table where, if the number of hidden allocation addresses is equal to the number of nodes, then the allocation table is empty, and when the number of hidden allocated addresses is zero, it means that all the allocated addresses are known and the conflict probability is zero.

Considering that the maximum number of uniquely identified nodes, within a predetermined network, strongly depends on the size of the available addressing space, PACMAN also proposes a component for IP address encoding. This component has the goal of encoding addresses on ongoing routing packets in order to decrease the routing control overhead. The encoded addresses are used below the network layer, and decoded back to the original IP address to the higher layers. This also allows compatibility with the IP addressing architecture. In Weniger (2005) more information regarding the complete PACMAN solution can be found, as well as details on the proposed address encoding component, and the integration with PDAD.

New-Layer Approaches

Some of the proposed addressing mechanisms assume more radical approaches by implementing completely new paradigms. New-layer solutions, like the popular *Host Identity Protocol*, are those that propose changes in the current Internet protocol stack. Most of these are focused on IPv6 addressing. However, the implementation of such mechanisms is not simple since changing the current protocol stack would demand a lot of effort and consequently changes in current communication technologies. In the following, one of the most known solutions that implement a new-layer solution is detailed.

HIP

This solution introduces a new namespace called *Host Identity* (HI) and a new protocol layer, the *Host Identity Protocol* (HIP), located between the internetworking and transport layers to allow end system transparent mobility. According to its developers, the Internet currently has two namespaces: *Internet Protocol* (IP) and *Domain Name Server* (DNS). Despite the fact that these namespaces are active in the Internet and are part of its growth, these technologies have some weaknesses and semantic overloading, namely functionality extensions that have been greatly complicated by these namespaces. The HI fills an important gap between IP and DNS.

In Moskowitz & Nikander (2006), the motivation for the creation of a new namespace is provided. In this respect, currently the Internet is built from computing platforms (end-points), packet transport (internetworking) and services (applications). Moskowitz & Nikander (2006) argue that a new namespace for computing platforms should be used in end-to-end operations, across many internetworking layers and independently of their evolution. This should support rapid re-addressing, re-homing, or re-numbering, and being based on public key cryptography, the namespace could also provide authentication services and anonymity. In addition, according to Moskowitz & Nikander (2006), the proposed namespace for computing systems should have the following characteristics:

- It should be applied between the application and the packet transport structures;
- It should fully decouple the internetworking layer from the higher ones by replacing the IP addresses occurrences within applications;
- The names should be defined with a length enabling its insertion into the datagram headers of existing protocols;
- It should be computationally affordable (e.g. packet size issue);
- The collision of names, similar to the problem of address conflicts, should be avoided as much as possible;
- The names should have a localized abstraction which could be used in existing protocols;
- The local creation of names should be possible;
- It should provide authentication services;

- The names should be long-lived, as well as replaceable at any time.

In HIP, IP addresses still work as locators, but the HIs assume the position of end-point identifiers. HIs are slightly different from interface names because they can be simultaneously accessed through different interfaces. A HI is the public key of an asymmetric key pair and it should support the RSA/SHA-1 public key algorithm (Eastlake, 2001) and the DSA algorithm (Eastlake, 1999).

Another element proposed within HIP is the *Host Identity Tag* (HIT). The latter is the hashed encoding of the HI, 128 bits long, and is used in protocols to represent the HI. The HIT has three basic properties: (a) the same length of an IPv6 address, which enables the use in address-sized fields of current APIs and protocols; (b) self-certifying features, i.e. it is hard to find a HI that matches a specific HIT; and (c) the probability of collision between two or more hosts is very low.

According to the authors, the HIP payload header could be carried in every IP datagram. However, as HIP headers are relatively large (40 bytes), it should be compressed in order to limit these to be present only in control packets used to establish or change the HIP association state. A HIP association, used to establish the state between the *Initiator* and *Responder* entities, is a four-packet handshake named *Base Exchange*. The last three packets of this exchange constitute an authenticated Diffie-Hellman (Diffie & Hellman, 1976) key exchange for session key generation. During this key exchange, a shared key is generated and further used to draw the HIP association keys.

HIP is a much wider solution than the brief description presented above. Particularly, HIP has many extensions and considerations for security-related issues, which constitute it as being a very interesting approach. More information about this proposal, and other important mechanisms attached to it, can be found in the references Aura, Nagarajan & Gurtov (2003), Moskowitz & Nikander (2006), and Moskowitz, Nikander, Jokela & Henderson (2008).

Special Considerations for IPv6

IPv6 (Deering & Hinden, 1998; and Hinden & Haberman, 2005) is the addressing structure planned for next IP based networks. For some solutions presented here, like Strong DAD, it is not complex to implement the support for IPv6 given that it would only be necessary to change the size of the protocol messages, due to the different address size from IPv4. It is important to consider IPv6 when designing a new solution. However, since the Internet still operates mainly over IPv4, such mechanism must also handle with this addressing structure. More complete solutions operate using both addressing structures IPv4 and IPv6. As the addressing space of IPv6 is bigger than that of IPv4, theoretically it is easier to assign unique IPv6 addresses to hosts within a local network. A possibility for allocating locally unique addresses with IPv6 is using the structure presented in (Hinden & Haberman, 2005), which is composed of the following elements. The Prefix is used to identify the Local IPv6 unicast addresses, and it is set to FC00::/7. The L value is set to 1 to indicate that the prefix is locally assigned. The 40-bit Global ID is used to create a globally unique prefix. The 16-bit field Subnet ID is the identifier of the subnet within the site. And the 64-bit Interface ID is the unique identifier of the host interface, as defined in (Hinden & Deering, 2006).

The DHCP for IPv6 (Droms, Bound, Volz, Lemon, Perkins & Carney, 2003) is an example of solution specifically designed to handle IPv6 addressing structure. This protocol enables DHCP servers to give IPv6 configuration parameters to the network nodes. It is sufficiently different from DHCPv4 in that the integration between the two services is not defined. According to the authors, DHCPv6 is a stateful counterpart to IPv6

Stateless Address Autoconfiguration, proposed in (Thomson, Narten & Jinmei, 2007).

The *IPv6 Stateless Address Autoconfiguration* (SLAAC) and DHCPv6 can be used simultaneously. SLAAC defines the procedure a host must take to autoconfigure its interface with IPv6. The entire solution is composed of three sub-modules: (a) the auto-generation of a link-local address; (b) the auto-generation of a global address through stateless autoconfiguration procedure; and (c) the execution of Duplicate Address Detection procedure to assure the IP addresses uniqueness.

According to Thomson, Narten & Jinmei (2007), the solution's advantages are that it does not require any manual configuration of hosts, minimal configuration of routers, and no additional servers. The stateless mechanism in SLAAC allows the node to auto-generate its own addresses through the combination of local information and information from routers (e.g. subnet prefixes periodically advertised by routes). More information about this approach can be found in Thomson, Narten & Jinmei (2007) and related documents of Narten, Nordmark, Simpson & Soliman (2007) and Narten, Draves & Krishnan (2007).

Another interesting approach is the *Optimistic Duplicate Address Detection* for IPv6, proposed in Moore (2006). This solution is an adaptation of the solutions in Narten, Nordmark, Simpson & Soliman (2007) and Thomson, Narten & Jinmei (2007). It mainly tries to minimize the latency of successful autoconfiguration and to reduce the network disruption in failure situations. Other mechanisms for self-addressing and autoconfiguration with IPv6 can be found in Draves (2003) and Bernardos, Calderon & Moustafa (2008). Also, it is important to consider the definitions by IANA (2010) regarding IPv6 addressing architecture.

FUTURE RESEARCH DIRECTIONS

Self-addressing is still a hot topic of research in computer networks, and it is even catalyzed by numerous projects in the context of NGN. An autoconfiguration solution, considering the majority of applicability scenarios defined in the documentations of such projects, is not complete without a mechanism that allows devices to configure themselves with a tentative valid and unique address within a determined network. The research lines in this area are dictated by the several projects (research consortiums) which plan to develop technologies and architectures for the NGN. In addition, the IETF working group Autoconfiguration (AUTOCONF, 2010) also indicates important topics that must be considered to research in self-addressing.

The projects Ambient Networks, 4WARD, ANA, DAIDALOS and EMANICS, just to name a few, are good examples of leading research consortiums which have their focus, or at least part of it, on autoconfiguration technologies to support autonomous networks in complex NGN scenarios.

The documents within the IETF group AUTOCONF, even though mainly focused on MANETs application scenarios, can be used as guidelines for the definition and development of self-addressing technologies. The main goal of this group is the description of an addressing model considering network's features and other applications which may be operating in this network. The group has worked to define the first documents of this addressing model, and other documents have already been published as *internet-drafts* defining other points and opening new research lines.

Therefore, analyzing the current work towards autoconfiguration, it is possible to identify new research lines in self-addressing and also the revision of already proposed methodologies. The NGN will also bring new situations and networking scenarios which will challenge researchers to always come up with fresh ideas to solve problems in the context of self-addressing and autoconfiguration.

FINAL CONSIDERATIONS

With the work done in this survey, we can conclude that current operating protocols for nodes configuration, like DHCP, have limited applicability when considering the characteristics of the scenarios for the future generation of computer networks. Attempting to fill this gap, some protocols and mechanisms for self-addressing in dynamic networks have already been proposed. Working groups connected to the IETF have defined guidelines and requirements that must be followed and attended when designing auto-configuration and self-addressing approaches.

Proposed solutions for auto-configuration, focusing in self-addressing, partially attend the requirements of scenarios with dynamic and heterogeneous networks. There are solutions that appeal for structures supported by stable mechanisms, which we did not consider in this survey due to its semi-autonomous nature.

Some approaches for self-addressing are only locally applicable and do not consider complex situations as networks merging and partitioning. Those solutions that implement a stateless paradigm can be a good choice for ad-hoc networks. However, such solutions will always need to be supported by Duplicate Address Detection mechanisms. There are also addressing solutions that depend on a specific technology in the network, e.g. the routing protocol as stated in Mase & Adjih (2006), imposing limits on the mechanism applicability, i.e. only to scenarios with the required specifications. In addition, other solutions implement mathematical approaches ensuring that the interval between two occurrences of the same IP address is too long to be considered a real problem. However, in scenarios for the future generation of computer networks the network may range from two nodes to thousands of them. Therefore, the duplicate address problem must be in depth considered.

It was observed that most of the existing solutions for auto-configuration and self-addressing did not consider the peculiarities of complex scenarios, involving many heterogeneous nodes, often spread over a large geographical area, and divided in many sub-networks topologies. Another weakness in most of the existing approaches is that they do not consider scenarios where IPv4 and IPv6 already coexist. On the other hand, a complete solution like HIP may be too complex to be implemented and included within the current Internet structure and technologies. It will take a considerable period of time and efforts to perform the changes required by the HIP proposed architecture.

Other solutions for self-addressing, not described here, can be found within the documents of the IETF working group AUTOCONF (2010), ZEROCONF (2010), and MANET (2010), and also in the survey done in Weniger & Zitterbart (2004) and Bernardos, Calderon & Moustafa (2008).

REFERENCES

Ambient Networks. (2010). *The Ambient Networks Project, EU framework programme 6 integrated project (FP6)*. Retrieved June 1, 2010, from http://www.ambient-networks.org/

ANA. (2010) *Autonomic Network Architecture, EU framework programme 6 integrated project (FP6)*. Retrieved June 1, 2010, from http://www.ana-project.org/

Aura, T., Nagarajan, A., & Gurtov, A. (2005). *Analysis of the HIP Base Exchange protocol*. Paper presented at 10th Australian Conference on Information Security and Privacy (ACISP 2005). Brisbane, Australia.

AUTOCONF. (2010) *IETF WG MANET Autoconfiguration*. Retrieved June 1, 2010, from http://tools.ietf.org/wg/autoconf/

Baccelli, E. (2008). *Address autoconfiguration for MANET: Terminology and problem statement. Internet-draft*. IETF WG AUTOCONF.

Bachar, W. (2005). *Address autoconfiguration in ad hoc networks. Internal Report, Departement Logiciels Reseaux, Institut National des Telecommunications*. Paris, France: INT.

Bernardos, C., Calderon, M., & Moustafa, H. (2008). *Ad-hoc IP autoconfiguration solution space analysis. Internet-draft*. IETF WG AUTOCONF.

Cheshire, S., Aboba, B., & Guttman, E. (2005). *Dynamic configuration of IPv4 link-local addresses*. (IETF RFC 3927).

DAIDALOS. (2010). *Designing advanced network interfaces for the delivery and administration of location independent, optimized personal services, EU framework programme 6 integrated project (FP6)*. Retrieved June 1, 2010, from http://www.ist-daidalos.org/

Deering, S., & Hinden, R. (1998). *Internet protocol, version 6 (IPv6) specification*. (IETF RFC 2460).

Diffie, W., & Hellman, M. (1976). New directions in cryptography. *IEEE Transactions on Information Theory*, *22*(6), 644–654. doi:10.1109/TIT.1976.1055638

Draves, R. (2003). *Default address selection for Internet protocol version 6 (IPv6)*. (IETF RFC 3484).

Droms, R. (1997). *Dynamic host configuration protocol*. (IETF RFC 2131).

Droms, R., Bound J., Volz, B., Lemon, T., Perkins, C., & Carney, M. (2003). *Dynamic host configuration protocol for IPv6 (DHCPv6)*. (IETF RFC 3315).

Eastlake, D. (1999). *RSA keys and SIGs in the Domain Name System (DNS)*. (IETF RFC 2536).

Eastlake, D. (2001). *RSA/SHA-1 SIGs and RSA KEYs in the Domain Name System (DNS)*. (IETF RFC 3110).

EMANICS. (2010) *European network of excellence for the management of Internet technologies and complex services, EU framework programme 6 integrated project (FP6)*. Retrieved June 1, 2010, from http://www.emanics.org/

Fazio, M., Villari, M., & Puliafito, A. (2004). Merging and partitioning in ad hoc networks. In *Proceedings of the 9th International Symposium on Computers and Communications (ISCC 2004)*, (pp. 164-169).

Fazio, M., Villari, M., & Puliafito, A. (2006). AIPAC: Automatic IP address configuration in mobile ad hoc networks. *Computer Communications*, *29*(8), 1189–1200. doi:10.1016/j.comcom.2005.07.006

Forde, T. K., Doyle, L. E., & O'Mahony, D. (2005). Self-stabilizing network-layer auto-configuration for mobile ad hoc network nodes. In *Proceedings of the IEEE International Conference on Wireless and Mobile Computing, Networking and Communications, 3*, (pp. 178-185).

Hinden, R., & Deering, S. (2006). *IP version 6 addressing architecture*. (IETF RFC 4291).

Hinden, R., & Haberman, B. (2005). *Unique local IPv6 Unicast addresses*. (IETF RFC 4193).

IANA. (2002). *Special-use IPv4 addresses*. (IETF RFC 3330).

IANA. (2010). *Internet assigned number authority*. Retrieved June 1, 2010, from http://www.iana.org/

Jeong, J., Park, J., Jeong, H., & Kim, D. (2006). *Ad hoc IP address autoconfiguration. Internet-draft*. IETF WG AUTOCONF.

Kant, L., McAuley, A., & Morera, R. Sethi, A. S., & Steiner, M. (2003). Fault localization and self-healing with dynamic domain configuration. In *Proceedings of the IEEE Military Communications Conference (MILCOM 2003), 2*, (pp. 977-981).

Kargl, F., Klenk, A., Schlott, S., & Weber, M. (2004). Advanced detection of selfish or malicious nodes in ad hoc networks. In *Proceedings of the 1st European Workshop on Security in Ad-hoc and Sensor Networks (ESAS)*, (pp. 152-165).

MANET. (2010). *IETF WG mobile ad-hoc network*. Retrieved June 1, 2010, from http://tools.ietf.org/wg/manet/

Manousakis, K. (2005). *Network and domain autoconfiguration: A unified framework for large mobile ad hoc networks*. Doctoral Dissertation, University of Maryland, 2005. Retrieved from http://hdl.handle.net/1903/3103

Manousakis, K., Baras, J. S., McAuley, A., & Morera, R. (2005). Network and domain autoconfiguration: A unified approach for large dynamic networks. *IEEE Communications Magazine, 43*(8), 78–85. doi:10.1109/MCOM.2005.1497557

Mase, K., & Adjih, C. (2006). *No overhead autoconfiguration OLSR. Internet-draft*. IETF WG MANET.

McAuley, A., Das, S., Madhani, S., Baba, S., & Shobatake, Y. (2001). *Dynamic registration and configuration protocol (DRCP). Internet-draft*. IETF WG Network.

Moler, C. B. (2004). *Numerical computing with MATLAB*. Retrieved from http://www.mathworks.com/moler/chapters.html

Moore, N. (2006). *Optimistic Duplicate Address Detection (DAD) for IPv6*. (IETF RFC 4429).

Morera, R., McAuley, A., & Wong, L. (2003). Robust router reconfiguration in large dynamic networks. In *Proceedings of the IEEE Military Communications Conference (MILCOM 2003), 2*, (pp. 1343-1347).

Moskowitz, R., & Nikander, P. (2006). *Host Identity Protocol (HIP) architecture*. (IETF RFC 4423).

Moskowitz, R., Nikander, P., Jokela, P., & Henderson, T. (2008). *Host identity protocol*. (IETF RFC 5201).

Narten, T., Draves, R., & Krishnan, S. (2007). *Privacy extensions for stateless addresses autoconfiguration in IPv6*. (IETF RFC 4941).

Narten, T., Nordmark, E., Simpson, W., & Soliman, H. (2007). *Neighbor discovery for IPv6*. (IETF RFC 4861).

Nesargi, S., & Prakash, R. (2002). MANETconf: Configuration of hosts in a mobile ad hoc network. In *Proceedings of the 21st Annual Joint Conference of the IEEE Computer and Communications Societies, 2*, (pp. 1059-1068).

Perkins, C. E., Malinen, J. T., Wakikawa, R., Belding-Royer, E. M., & Sun, Y. (2001). *IP address autoconfiguration for ad hoc networks. Internet-draft*. IETF WG MANET.

Sayrafiezadeh, M. (1994). The birthday problem revisited. *Mathematics Magazine, 67*, 220–223. doi:10.2307/2690615

Schmidt, R. de O., Gomes, R., Sadok, D., Kelner, J., & Johnsson, M. (2009). An autonomous addressing mechanism as support for auto-configuration in dynamic networks. In *Proceedings of the Latin American Network Operations and Management Symposium (LANOMS 2009)*, (pp. 1-12).

Sun, Y., & Belding-Royer, M. E. (2003). *Dynamic address configuration in mobile ad hoc networks*. Technical Report, University of California at Santa Barbara. Rep. 2003-11.

Thomson, S., Narten, T., & Jinmei, T. (2007). *IPv6 stateless address autoconfiguration*. (IETF RFC 4862).

Troan, O., & Droms, R. (2003). *IPv6 prefix options for dynamic host configuration protocol (DHCP) version 6*. (IETF RFC 3633).

Vaidya, N. (2002). Weak duplicate address detection in mobile ad hoc networks. In *Proceedings of the 3rd ACM International Symposium on Mobile Ad Hoc Networking & Computing*, (pp. 206-216).

4WARD. (2010). *The 4WARD Project, EU framework programme 7 integrated project (FP7)*. Retrieved June 1, 2010, from http://www.4ward-project.eu/

Weniger, K. (2003). Passive duplicate address detection in mobile ad hoc networks. In *Proceedings of the IEEE Wireless Communications and Networking (WCNC 2003), 3*, (pp. 1504-1509).

Weniger, K. (2005). PACMAN: Passive autoconfiguration for mobile ad hoc networks. *IEEE Journal on Selected Areas in Communications, 23*(3), 507–519. doi:10.1109/JSAC.2004.842539

Weniger, K., & Zitterbart, M. (2004). Address autoconfiguration in mobile ad hoc networks: Current approaches and future directions. *IEEE Network, 18*(4), 6–11. doi:10.1109/MNET.2004.1316754

Williams, A. (2002). *Requirements for automatic configuration of IP hosts. Internet-draft*. IETF WG Zeroconf.

ZEROCONF. (2010) *IETF WG zero configuration*. Retrieved June 1, 2010, from http://tools.ietf.org/wg/zeroconf/

Zhou, H., Ni, L., & Mutka, M. W. (2003). Prophet address allocation for large scale MANETs. In *Proceedings of the 22nd Annual Joint Conference of the IEEE Computer and Communications Societies, 2*, (pp. 1304-1311).

KEY TERMS AND DEFINITIONS

Network Address: a 32-bit or 64-bit identification used to uniquely identify a node's interface within a network.

Autonomous Network: a networking system which is capable of configuring, organizing and managing itself without or with very little intervention of a network administrator or manager.

Autoconfiguration: the ability a system or an entity has of starting and configuring its parameters by itself.

Self-addressing Protocol: a protocol, usually designed for ad hoc networks, which is responsible for providing nodes in a network with valid and unique layer 3 addresses (i.e., IP addresses), without relying in a stable or fixed structure, allowing these nodes to configure their own interface(s).

Chapter 8
A Platform for Pervasive Building Monitoring Services Using Wireless Sensor Networks

Abolghasem (Hamid) Asgari
Thales Research & Technology (UK) Limited, UK

ABSTRACT

At the core of pervasive computing model, small, low cost, robust, distributed, and networked processing devices are placed, which are thoroughly integrated into everyday objects and activities. Wireless Sensor Networks (WSNs) have emerged as pervasive computing technology enablers in several field, including environmental monitoring and control. Using this technology as a pervasive computing approach, researchers have been trying to persuade people to be more aware of their environment and energy usage in the course of their every day life. WSNs have brought significant benefits as far as monitoring is concerned, since they are more efficient and flexible compared to wired sensor solutions. In this chapter, the authors propose a Service Oriented Architecture for developing an enterprise networking environment used for integrating enterprise level applications and building management systems with other operational enterprise services and functions for the information sharing and monitoring, controlling, and managing the enterprise environment. The WSN is viewed as an information service provider not only to building management systems but also to wider applications in the enterprise infrastructure. The authors also provide specification, implementation, and deployments of the proposed architecture and discuss the related tests, experimentations, and evaluations of the architecture.

INTRODUCTION

Accurate monitoring of the buildings, systems and their surroundings has normally been performed by sensors dispersed throughout the buildings. Existing building systems are tightly coupled with the sensors they utilize, restricting extensibility of their overall operation. The emergence of Wireless Sensor Networks (WSNs) has brought significant

DOI: 10.4018/978-1-60960-611-4.ch008

benefits as far as environmental monitoring is concerned, since they are more efficient due to the lack of wired installations compared to their wired counterparts, while additionally they allow for flexible positioning of the sensor devices. Pervasive computing environments such as intelligent buildings require a mechanism to easily integrate, manage and use heterogeneous building services and systems including sensors and actuators. Any WSN system, viewed as a system offering a building service, should be designed in such a manner, so as to allow its straightforward integration to the general networking infrastructure where any other applications can utilize the data gathered by the WSN.

Achieving this integration necessitates an overall building services framework architecture that will be open and extensible, allowing for dynamic integration of updated or advanced building services addressing the diversity of the offered building services and the scalability issues related to any specific building applications.

The most prominent approach towards realizing the above goal is that of Service Oriented Architectures (SOAs) open framework (Erl, 2005). In the case of SOAs all architectural elements are decoupled and considered as service providers and consumers. Service discovery and access to the services is performed in a dynamic manner, ensuring a generic and extensible design. Web Services (Stal, 2002) constitute the most significant technological enabler of SOAs due to the interoperability that they offer and the fact that they can easily support the integration of existing systems.

SOAs are essentially a means of developing distributed systems, where the participating components of those systems are exposed as services. A service can be defined (Sommerville, 2007, p. 747) as "a loosely coupled, reusable software component that encapsulates discrete functionality, which may be distributed and programmatically accessed." The motivation for constructing a SOA is to enable new, existing, and legacy pieces of software functionality to be put together in an ad-hoc manner to rapidly orchestrate new applications in previously unpredicted ways to solve new problems. This can result in highly adaptive enterprise applications (Malatras, 2008a).

The usage of SOA is as follows. The service provider registers the offered services to a service registry, which is accessed by a service consumer that wishes to interact with a service that satisfies certain requirements. The service registry informs the service consumer on how to access a service that satisfies its selection criteria, by returning the location of an appropriate service provider. The service provider and consumer from that point onwards exchange messages in order to agree upon the semantics and the service description that they are going to be using. The service provisioning subsequently takes place, with the consumer possibly expecting some response from the provider at the completion of the process.

The SOA architecture is broken down into a set of enterprise middleware services, a set of application services and a service bus. These are described in details in (Malatras et al., 2008a). This architecture is generic enough allowing for different types of applications to be integrated, provided they are capable of exposing appropriate services on the service bus. Characteristic examples of applications include security systems, business and operational functions, ambient user interfaces to display building related information, Wireless Sensor Networks (WSNs) to monitor and collect building-related information, and services offered by building management systems and building assessment tools, etc.

The remaining of this chapter is structured as follows. Next section briefly reviews the related works in the area of service-oriented frameworks as well as wireless sensor networks. Then, a discussion of the proposed WSN architecture in the overall SOA framework for building services integration is given. Specification of the proposed architecture is also briefly described. Two developed services, i.e., operational health monitoring and security of WSN are then explained. The system level deployments are provided. Following this, further elaborations are presented on the functionality tests, experimentations, system-level evaluations and obtained results from environmental monitoring. Finally, the chapter is concluded and future directions are given.

RELATED WORK

An aspect that has been neglected in most middleware-based solutions is the importance of incorporating BMSs and automation systems in the overall enterprise-networking environment. In recent years, there has been a wider shift towards the adoption of enterprise-wide architectures, driven by the SOA paradigm, in the building management realm (Craton, Robin, 2002), (Ehrlich, 2003). Under this prism, IT and building management convergence is logically promoted, while allowing for open, flexible and scalable enterprise-wide architectures to be built. Furthermore, following this stream will enable the much desirable accessibility of overall facilities management over the Internet. Such a research direction has also been implied by recent work in (Wang et al., 2007).

Recent surveys of wireless sensor networks can be found in (Garcia et al., 2007), (Yick, 2008). Research work in the area of WSNs has moved from the traditional view of sensor networks as static resources, from which data can be obtained, to the more innovative view of systems engineering in general, where everything is considered in a service-oriented perspective (Botts et al., 2008), (King et al., 2006), (Kushwaha et al., 2007), (Chu et al., 2006), (Ta et al., 2006), (Moodley, Simonis, 2006). This allows WSNs to be regarded as service providers, i.e. information services, and consequently more advanced, dynamic, reusable and extensible applications and operations to be provided to the service consumers. Enterprise application integration is therefore additionally facilitated, particularly with BMSs for control and management.

The benefits of exposing sensor nodes and sensor networks as service providers in a generalized SOA motivated the emergence of the Sensor Web Enablement (SWE) activity by the Open Geospatial Consortium (OGC, 2010). This is essentially a set of standards that allow for exposing sensor networks as Web Services making them accessible via the Web. While SWE work is a valuable starting point, it is too generic to be directly applicable, and requires tailoring to be adapted to the building and facilities management domains despite its benefits. Our work takes advantage of certain principles set out by SWE, such as abstraction, separation of operations in reusable objects and applies them to the building services management realm, also taking into account the particular domain's inherent characteristics, e.g. space categorization and coexistence with existing BMSs and building services.

In (Chu et al., 2006) a set of web services is introduced for collecting and managing sensor data for environmental and spatial monitoring. This work has a confined scope regarding the use of sensors, while it sidesteps integration issues with enterprise-wide applications, which is the most important benefit of the SOA paradigm. Service oriented architectures at a different level, concerning the core WSN activities such as sensing, processing, etc., is studied at (Kushwaha et al., 2007). While this work is useful, our efforts focus on exposing the WSN as a service to the overall enterprise building and facilities management system. On the contrary, the Atlas platform (King et al., 2006) relates more closely to the approach we plan to undertake regarding the overall framework for the web enablement of WSNs. We distinguish ourselves from this work however, since our architecture is not confined with specific hardware platforms as Atlas does and hence allow for different and diverse sensor platforms to be used.

SOA-BASED WSN ARCHITECTURE FOR ENVIRONMENTAL MONITORING IN BUILDINGS

In this section, we propose an architectural framework for WSN and its integration with other applications over an SOA infrastructure. Wireless sensor networks (Akyildiz et al., 2002), (Chong, Kumar, 2003), (Garcia et al., 2007), (Yick et al., 2008) are a major disruptive technology not only in the sensor technology arena, but also in the way sensors can rapidly be deployed and used. The unit costs are still high. The size and energy consumption are the foremost constraints that WSN platforms have to reconcile, and it this set of constraints that is driving their advancement in design and operation. A sensor node or mote is made up of five main component types, namely the processor, the sensors, the communication radio, the power and peripherals. A WSN is made up of two types of devices: wireless sensor nodes as core of the sensor network and gateways. A gateway device connects the wireless sensor network to wider networks and is used to support the scalability of management operations, as well as the overall WSN reliability and survivability.

The functionality of the WSN in relation to SOA architecture can be decomposed in two complementing aspects, namely:

- WSN services exposed to the applications (service consumers) by means of the enterprise middleware.
- WSN tasking to enable configuring sensor nodes for data collection by means of the tasking middleware (Malatras et al., 2008b).

The WSN architecture assumes the role of service provider as far as data collection and information management is concerned. This justifies the need for a WSN service interface to be defined and exposed to the SOA infrastructure, in order to hide the complexity and heterogeneity of the underlying WSNs. The architecture that we propose for this purpose has to additionally cater for the monitoring and data management aspects. These functional requirements are addressed by a tasking middleware that is responsible for handling the translation of requests for information as received from applications/clients and translating them into WSN-specific data queries. The clients need not to be aware of the WSN internal operations, hence the importance of the tasking middleware.

A typical use case scenario of the proposed WSN architecture involves the following. When an application/service wishes to obtain specific WSN monitored information, it accesses the respective WSN service interface requesting so. The WSN service is discovered by accessing the Service Registry, which provides details on available service interfaces that satisfy certain selection criteria. Upon receiving a client request, the WSN service assigns this request to the tasking middleware that directly operates on top of the sensor nodes and performs the actual data collection and possibly processing. The outcome of this operation, i.e. the corresponding sensed data, is then forwarded to the WSN service that is stored in the data-base and then the processed information is posted back to the original requester.

As stated, the WSN architecture is implemented over the both sensor platforms, i.e. the sensor node and the gateway, while at a higher layer of abstraction the Server entity (also called Virtual Gateway) is responsible for managing the WSN nodes. The high level layered architecture of the WSN infrastructure is shown in Figure 1. The functionality for both the sensor nodes and the gateways is almost identical apart from the fact that the gateway has an additional feature, i.e. gateway coordination and the sensor nodes have the tasking middleware employed.

The overall WSN is divided into WSN zones where each zone covers a specific area/space. A gateway essentially is a network-bridging device, which connects a WSN zone to the Intranet/enterprise network. In that sense, it does not par-

Figure 1. Functional layered architecture for WSN

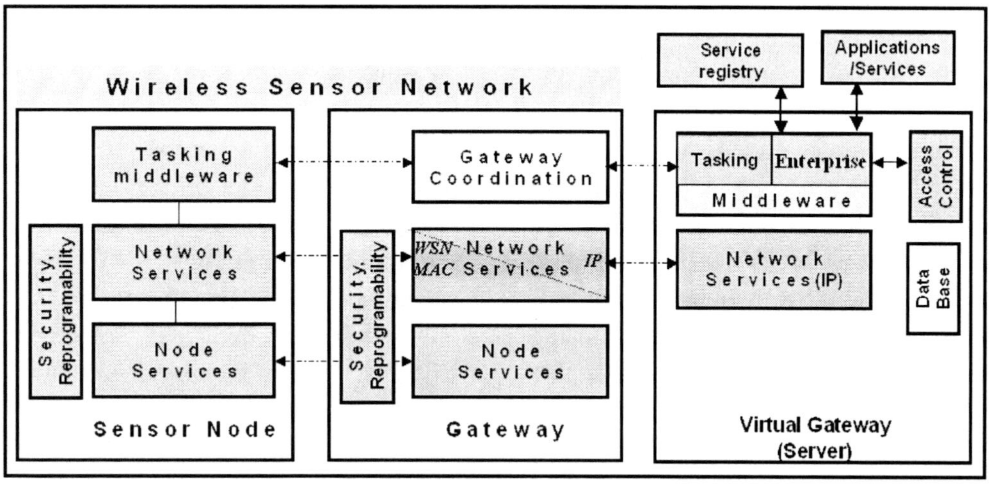

ticipate in the tasking of sensors; it rather relays data from the WSN to the enterprise network and vice versa. To ensure scalability and reliability of a WSN zone we consider that there might be the need to have more than one gateway for a single WSN zone, since for example the number of nodes could rise significantly or the main gateway could potentially fail. Another reason is to allow for survivability of the WSN i.e., having diverse routes where not all nodes should use the same path to route their data towards the gateway, which would drain the resources of particular nodes rapidly and hence lead to node failures.

Nevertheless, conceptually the WSN should be viewed from external entities as having a single point of access to ensure consistency and have manageable administration. For every WSN zone therefore one of the gateways assumes the role of the Master Gateway (MGW) and the remaining gateways, if any, are deemed as Secondary Gateways (SGW). Both the MGW and SGWs manage their respective assigned sensor nodes, but the MGW is moreover responsible for coordinating all gateway activities within a zone through an appropriately defined gateway coordination protocol and serving as the single point of access to the WSN for communication with external entities. The gateway coordination protocol is responsible for informing the Server of any changes in the WSN, e.g. MGW and SGW status.

As shown in Figure 1, the network service layer deals with the communication aspect of the sensor network such as addressing, routing and data transport. It also relies mainly on the radio/enterprise network interface components for communication at wireless MAC or IP levels.

The node services are the functions, which are local to the devices. Both sensor node and gateway contain the same basic computing functions, namely processing, storage and a radio function. The gateway additionally has an external network interface, to connect to the wider network (e.g., Intranet), so that the corresponding WSN can be accessed remotely and also to allow for the inter-gateway communication (MGW to SGWs). Sensor nodes contain a number of additional node services, not present in the gateway, such as a sensing, a power management and a positioning function.

The Server is made aware of various WSNs available in the enterprise building and their respective MGWs and SGWs by accessing a topology map. When applications/services require interaction with the WSN system as a whole, this occurs through the relevant WSN service interface that interacts with the Server. The Server is equipped with an enterprise middleware layer, which is responsible for communicating with the WSN service interface of the SOA. It has to be clarified that the Server itself is not part of the WSN, but is used to access and interact with the WSN. The Server resides outside the WSN and communicates with the MGWs, in order to expose data gathered by the WSN to high-level applications. The Server has nevertheless the functionality for the tasking middleware, in order to be able to instruct the sensor nodes (that also have this functionality) on data collection and reporting as per the client requests. A back-up Server has also been considered for stability and reliability reasons (so as for the Server not to constitute a single point of failure).

The tasking middleware is the architectural entity that implements the functionality exposed by the WSN service interface. It is actually client-server architecture with the client side residing on sensor nodes and the server side existing on the Server. The tasking middleware receives as input high-level service requests (known as WSN queries) from enterprise entities via the enterprise middleware, i.e. WSN WS interface, determines at the Server what data and processing are required to provide the service, tasks the relevant sensor nodes to perform sensing and processing (known as sensor tasks), collects the resulting data at the sensor node, sends the data back to the Server where it might be contextually processed and stored in a database for keeping records and finally responds to the original service request.

Specification of the Architecture

The WSN service interface is exposed in an overall SOA. We used a web services service model due to its wide-acceptance and the fact that they enable easy and straightforward deployment of applications over enterprise networks and the Internet in general, as required by the proposed architecture and are supported by well-established standards. Web services constitute a means for various software platforms to interoperate, without any prerequisite regarding platforms and frameworks homogeneity being necessary.

A WSN environment is essentially a collection of resources (i.e. sensors) that continuously monitor their environment (i.e. get measurements). We have therefore defined a REST-based (REpresentational State Transfer) style SOA to enable integration of the WSN with enterprise services. REST-based WS (Fielding, 2000) lack the complexity of SOAP-based WS (SOAP, 2008) and form an open and flexible framework, allowing scalable and dynamic resource monitoring (Landre, Wesenberg, 2007), (Pautasso, 2008).

The WSN Web Services are rooted at the following base URI: http://{hostname}/REST/{version}/. The {hostname} parameter must be replaced with the name of the server hosting the WS, and the {version} parameter must be replaced with the version number of the service. When a client wishes to interact with the WSN architecture over the SOA, the client issues the appropriate HTTP method, namely GET (to query an existing resource), POST (to create a new resource), DELETE (to remove an existing resource), and PUT (to update an existing resource). When a client wishes to retrieve the results from a particular DomainTask resource, then the client issues an HTTP GET request to the URI http://{hostname}/REST/{version}/DomaintaskResult/id where id is the unique identifier of that result and the corresponding data is returned using an XML representation.

The actual functionality behind the WS interface is implemented by the Server entity, which was discussed previously. It is at the Server where the required processing takes place, prior to the tasking of the WSN to collect data. The gateway entities serve as network bridging devices between the WSN and the Server.

Clients have access only to the DomainTask resource exposed through the WSN WS interface and the other resources are used internally by the WSN architecture, namely the Server. The DomainTask represents a high level tasking of the WSN that is described in terms that are more familiar to the building management domain than the WSN domain. It is the job of the Server of the WSN architecture to take a DomainTask as input and translate this into one or more SensorTasks that can deliver the data required to fulfill a DomainTask. The SensorTask resource is a lower level tasking of the WSN that is specified in terms that are familiar to this domain. SensorTasks can cause one or more Sensors to be configured to deliver data. The SensorTask may perform processing and aggregation of data received from Sensors before data delivery. The base SensorTask type is abstract, with specializations existing to describe periodic data collection tasks and conditional, or alarm based, data collection tasks. Each SensorTask is assigned to a sensor node of the WSN architecture. The sensor nodes report data back to the Server via their respective gateway.

The Sensor resource represents a sensing component of the WSN. It provides a mechanism for getting information about the capabilities of the sensors that comprise the WSN, including sensor type, position, and power status. The Space resource represents a textual description of a space, i.e. a zone, of the building environment, e.g. a room, a block, etc.

The format of the resource representations used by the WSN architecture has been formally described in (Asgari, 2008). Resource representations are used both by clients when sending a request to a Server, and by the Server when returning a response to a client. The data model is formally specified using an appropriate XML Schema Definition; further details can be found in (Asgari, 2008). By implementing the specified architecture, sensor information is made available to BMSs and other information consumers via the enterprise-based networking infrastructure.

WSN OPERATIONAL HEALTH AND SECURITY SERVICES

Health Monitoring Application

Operational health monitoring of WSN is becoming an essential part of these networks. A WSN health monitoring application is distinct from the sensor data visualization as each is aimed at different audiences i.e., the WSN health monitor is intended to aid those who set-up and maintain the network, while the sensor data visualization is aimed at building/facilities managers for building monitoring or the building occupants for comfort monitoring and awareness. Health monitoring should provide an indication of sensor node failures, resource exhaustion, poor connectivity, and other abnormalities. There are several problems that may result in the WSN gateway not receiving sensor data, for example, low battery voltage or poor connectivity to the gateway. It is very time consuming to resolve such problems if there is no means of monitoring the operation of the WSN. This necessitates the development of an easy to understand, visual method of monitoring the health of the WSN in real-time.

A number of works has already been reported in the literature. MOTE-VIEW is a client-tier application developed by Crossbow designed to perform as a sensor network monitoring and management tool (Turon, 2005). NanoMon is software developed for WSN monitoring which is also capable of visualizing the history of received sensed data as well as network topology (Yu et al., 2007). In (Ahamed et al., 2004) a middleware service is proposed for monitoring of sensor networks by using sensor agent nodes equipped with error/failure information forwarding capability. An execution and monitoring framework for sensor network services and applications, called ISEE is also proposed in (Ivester, Lim, 2006). One of the ISEE modules provides a consistent graphical representation of any sensor network. A work on using heterogeneous collaborative groupware to monitor WSNs is presented in (Cheng et al., 2004). We have also developed an application that is capable of monitoring the operational health of a deployed WSN and displaying the results through a browser-based user interface. This work focuses on providing a network health monitoring service that complies and utilizes the REST-based web services SOA style. The sensor nodes collect environmental data and periodically send the updates, which are stored by the Server in a database.

The health monitoring application uses data that is stored in the database and provided by the Server to identify several types of possible operational problems in the WSN, as listed below:

- The battery level of a mote is below a configurable threshold.
- The time-stamp of the most recent measurement from a sensor is older than a configurable number of milliseconds.
- No measurements have been received from a sensor.

The health monitoring application is implemented, as an enterprise Java web application that exposes a REST interface through which the Server can provide required sensor information. It runs inside a standard servlet container, e.g. Apache Tomcat (Apache, 2008). The application can be configured to automatically analyze the health of the WSN at regular intervals, and it is also possible to manually initiate a check of the WSN through the user interface. The application is configured via a properties file (i.e., located at i3con-manager/WEB-INF/application.properties). The configurable properties are shown below:

- bimResource – the location of the XML resource that describes the topology and structure of the deployed WSN, e.g. file:i3con_margaritas_deployment_01.xml. This file is the same format as used by the Server. The structure of a deployed WSN is shown in Figure 2.
- moteLowBatteryWarningLevel – the battery level in volts below which a mote battery is considered too low.
- sensorMeasurementTooOldWarningInterval – the age in milliseconds above which the most recent measurement from a sensor is considered too old.
- autoRefresh – true if the Health Monitoring application should automatically check the health of the WSN at regular intervals, otherwise false.
- autoRefreshInterval – if autoRefresh is true this is the period in milliseconds at which the health of the WSN will be checked.

This health monitoring application has been deployed and is in use in a WSN testbed and in a real building, which will be described in the next section.

Security Service

In this section, we briefly discuss the WSN security as an important and related aspect to the health of WSN. Recent surveys of security in WSN are given in (Wang et al., 2006a), (Zhou et al., 2008). Given the vulnerabilities of WSNs, security is a highly desirable and essentially a necessary function, depending on the context and the physical environment in which a sensor network might operate (Perrig, 2004).

Since WSNs use wireless communications, they are vulnerable to attacks, which are rather simpler to launch when compared to the wired environment (Perrig et al., 2001). Many wired networks benefit from their inherent physical security properties. However, wireless communications are difficult to protect; they are by nature a broadcast medium, in which adversaries can easily eavesdrop on, intercept, inject, and alter transmitted data. In addition, adversaries are not restricted to using sensor network hardware. They can interact with the network from a distance by using radio transceivers and powerful workstations. Sensor networks are vulnerable to resource consumption attacks. Adversaries can repeatedly send packets to waste the network bandwidth and drain the nodes' batteries. Since sensor networks are often physically deployed in less secure environments, an adversary can steal nodes, recover their cryptographic material, and possibly pose as one or more authorized nodes of the network.

Approaches to security should satisfy a number of basic security properties, i.e. availability, data access control, integrity, message confidentiality and control the access to task the sensor and retrieve the data in the presence of adversaries (Luk et al., 2007). Service and network availability is of great concern because energy is a limited resource in sensor nodes that is consumed for processing and communications. Equipped with richer resources, the adversaries can launch serious attacks such as resource consumption attacks and node compromise attacks. Link layer access control implies that the link layer protocol should prevent unauthorized parties from joining and participating in the network. Legitimate nodes should be able to detect messages from unauthorized nodes and reject them. Closely related to message authenticity is message integrity. Data integrity guarantees that data should arrive unaltered to their destination. If an adversary modifies a message from an authorized sender while the message is in transit, the receiver should be able to detect this tampering. Confidentiality means keeping information secret from unauthorized parties. It is typically achieved with encryption preventing the recovery of whole/partial message by adversaries. Data encryption guarantees that sensitive data are not revealed to third parties, intruders, etc. Data is encrypted for coping with attacks that target sensitive information relayed and processed by the WSN. Access control service is to provide a secure access to WSN infrastructure for sensor tasking and data retrieval.

As far as implementation of the proposed architecture is concerned, data encryption, data integrity and access control have been selected as the most prominent security functions to be considered. The first two can be provided as middleware services, i.e., they do not affect existing interfaces and are transparent to the communication between sensor nodes. Both of these security functions have also been designed and implemented in a testbed environment and reported in (Asgari, 2008).

WSN Access Control Service

The requirement is set to create a general access control mechanism that provides secure access to data. As previously described, the proposed solution defines a REST web services API to provide clients with a mechanism to task (i.e. configure) and query the WSN. Sensor tasking and querying are distinct operations that clients must only be allowed to perform if they have been granted the necessary rights to do so. This requires the REST web service to enforce a level of access control that can authenticate clients and ensure that they have authority to make a particular request. A WSN access control mechanism has been implemented that provides authentication of REST clients and restricts access to specific resources based on a combination of URL patterns and roles assigned to the client. The implementation is based on the Spring Framework's security project (Spring, 2009), which provides comprehensive application-layer security services to Java based applications.

Spring Security provides support for authentication (i.e. the process of establishing that a client is who they say they are), and for authorization (i.e. the process of establishing that a client is allowed to perform an operation). A wide range of authentication mechanisms is supported, including HTTP BASIC authentication (Franks et al., 1999), OpenID (OpenID, 2010) and HTTP X.509 (Pkix, 2009). We used HTTP Digest authentication (Franks et al., 1999), which ensures that client passwords are not sent in clear text. It should be noted that Spring Security does not provide transport-layer security, however it can be used in conjunction with an appropriate transport layer security mechanism (e.g. HTTPS) to provide a secure data channel in addition to authentication and authorization. The Spring Security authorization mechanism can be used to control access to class methods, object instances, and HTTP resources (identified via a URL pattern).

Two client roles have been defined for the REST API. Clients who are granted the role ROLE_WSN_QUERY are permitted to query WSN data. Clients who are granted the role ROLE_WSN_TASK are allowed to perform tasking operations on the WSN network. Clients who are granted both roles are allowed to perform WSN query and tasking operations. Spring Security can be configured to obtain client details from a variety of sources, for example an in-memory map, or a relational database. The access control mechanism required for the system prototype is expected to support a limited number of clients. For this reason the client details (i.e. username, password, and assigned roles) are stored in an in-memory map that is configured during application start-up from an XML configuration file. This provides the flexibility necessary to configure and change users after the system has been deployed.

WSN SYSTEM LEVEL DEPLOYMENTS

The WSN system was initially deployed as a testbed in our premises at one of its building blocks. The selected monitoring environment was made up of an open plan area and office spaces equipped with Crossbow sensor nodes (Crossbow, 2009) each with a number of embedded sensing units. The testbed was used for testing hardware platforms of gateway and sensor nodes, debugging software codes, setting up the Server, verification and integration tests, and performing initial proof-of-concepts. The deployed testbed has constantly been in use and consistently updated with software packages as they are upgraded with bug fixes and new developed features. The deployed WSN system in the testbed has been made operational and has been collecting environmental data since March 2008.

Subsequently, a real deployment has been carried out in a state of art building (called Margaritas) in Madrid. Figure 2 shows the deployed system in this building. The aim for this deployment was to exploit the integrated enterprise building systems architecture using a number of applications/services including Wireless Sensor Networks, an Information Display Panel PC, and a Mobile Browser. The WSN system provides information for building occupants/manager through the Panel PC and mobile browser. Displayed information includes measurements obtained from WSN including temperature, humidity, light intensity, presence, and CO2 level, electricity, cold and hot water consumptions.

Figure 3 shows the layout for the location of sensors in a two-bedroom apartment and Figure 4 shows the actual positions of devices in a one-bed room apartment. Figure 5 shows the exterior view of Margaritas building. Each apartment is equipped with two types of sensor platforms; one platform with Temperature-Humidity-Light (THL) sensing units and one with Carbon Dioxide-Presence (CO2PIR) sensing units. The THL sensor unit is made up of a single board MTS400 sensor platform from Crossbow (Crossbow, 2009), which integrates directly with their wireless radio and MPR2400 processing platform. The CO2PIR sensor platform consists of external CO2 and PIR sensors, connected to Crossbow's MDA300 prototyping board, which integrates directly with the MPR2400. In Figure 3, the shaded area in front of the CO2PIR sensor unit indicates the estimated coverage area of the presence sensor. The locations of the CO2PIR sensor platform and the gateway unit are confined to the proximity and availability of mains power (due to their relatively high power consumption).

Figure 2. The deployment architecture in Margaritas building

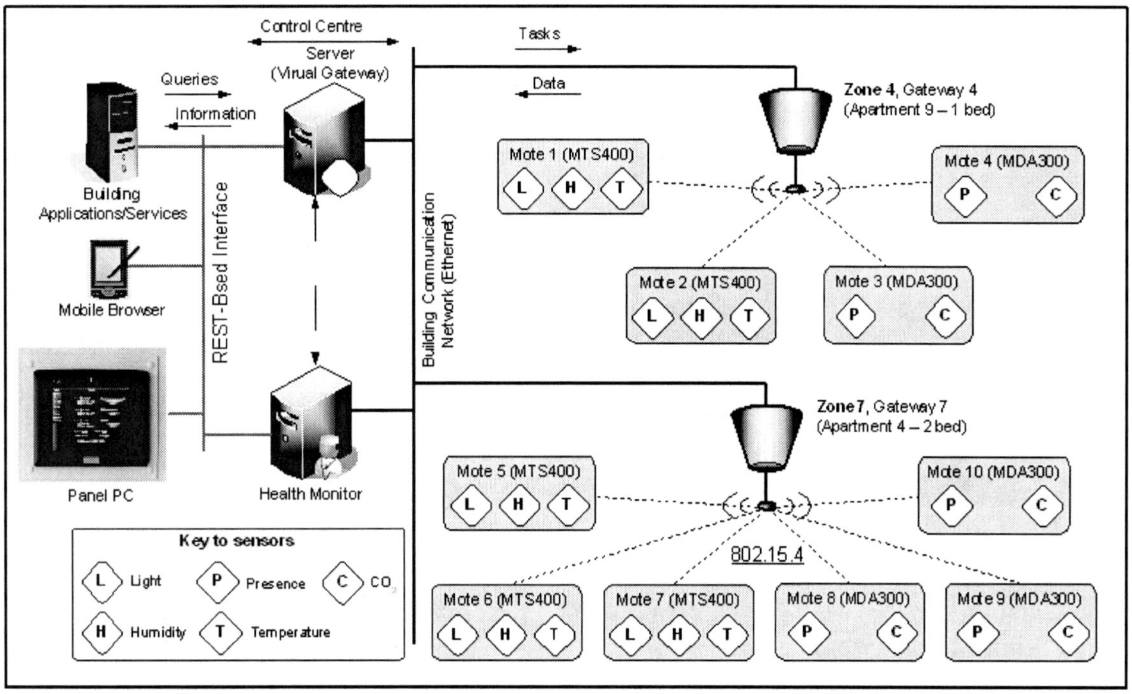

Figure 3. Location of sensors and gateway in the 2-bedroom apartment

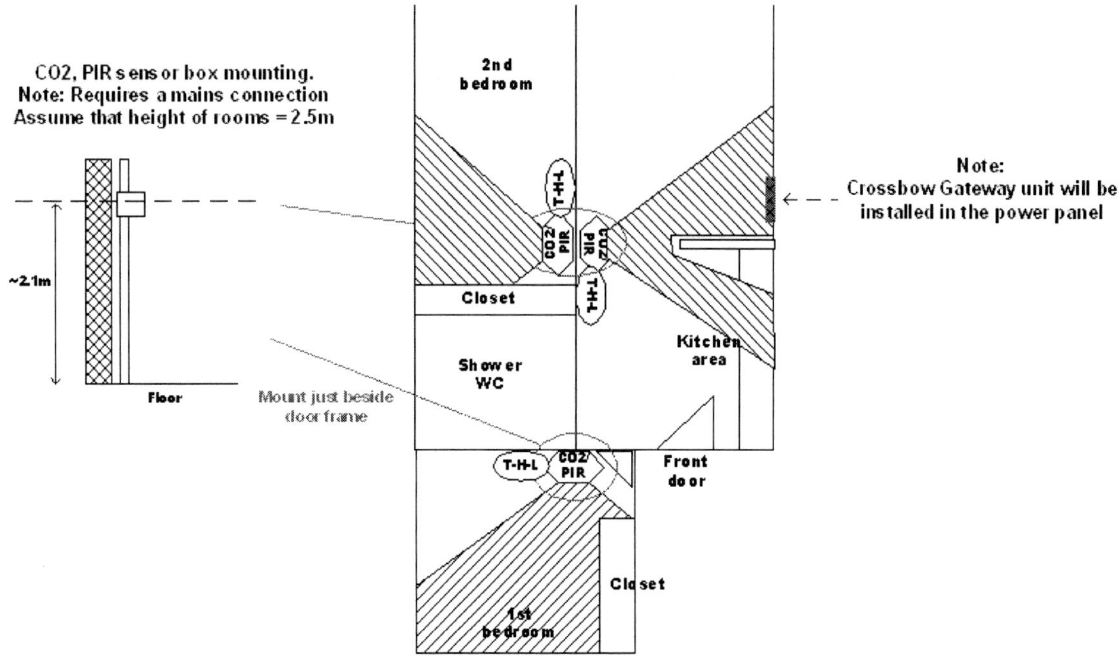

T-H-L: Temperature, Humidity, Light Sensor

Figure 4. WSN deployment in a one-bedroom apartment

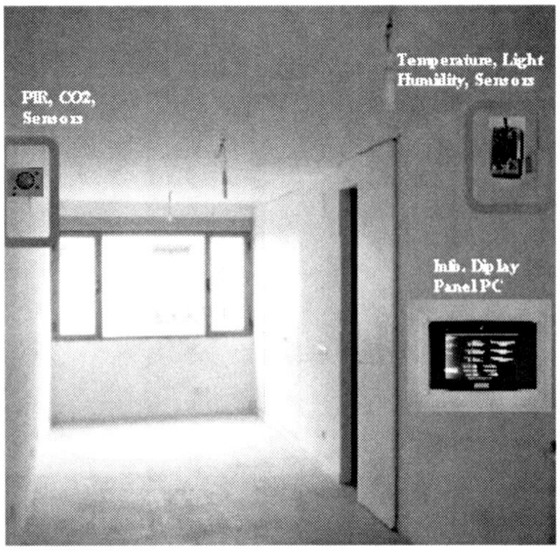

The deployed system has been expected to assist in deducing some measures in term of the improvement to the consumption of energy and building maintenance by making use of data collected by wireless sensors dispersed in the building. Building performance indicators have been used as these have been defined in appropriate standards (e.g. setting temperature between 20 and 25 °C, depending on the season). An overall energy assessment of the apartment is deduced based on the environmental conditions setting, measured data by the appropriate sensors, and the measured consumed energy. The raw data and processed information are displayed on the PC panel and the mobile browser interface for the attention of the occupant and building manager so as to promote energy conservation.

EXPERIMENTATION FOCUS, TESTS, EVALUATIONS, AND ENVIRONMENTAL MONITORING

A number of experimentations and tests have been performed that are divided into the following categories:

Figure 5. Margaritas building in Madrid

- Component level verification tests (hardware and software components)
- Integration tests (both at system and application levels)
- System level verification tests (the whole SOA-based WSN infrastructure)
- System level performance evaluations (the whole WSN infrastructure)
- Building monitoring tests and results

The component and system level verification, validation, and functionality tests as well as testing the related applications were carried out in the testbed described in the following sections.

COMPONENT LEVEL VERIFICATION TESTS

The emphasis of these tests was set to prove the functionality and validating the correct behavior of the components by passing on the known input to each component and verifying the resultant output against the expected output.

Testing the enterprise middleware involved the following steps:

- Verifying the correct interpretation and processing of a new sensor query issued by a client application; two independent clients were used; a developed I3CON WSN Portal, and an HTTP tool named cURL (cURL, 2010). In the event when the enterprise middleware correctly processes a sensor query, a sensor task will be created and transferred to the tasking middleware. This was verified by checking the debug statements in the programming code for the tasking middleware.

- Verifying the correct interpretation of sensor responses; tasking middleware periodically sends sensor data messages to the enterprise middleware. The enterprise middleware will persist the data once it receives it, completes any required post-processing of the raw data, and stores it in a data-base. The verification that the sensor responses have been processed correctly was viewed by querying the database.
- Verifying the retrieval of existing sensor data; the testing process of the retrieval of sensor data involved the use of WSN Portal and the cURL tool.

The tasking middleware is responsible for receiving sensor task(s) from the enterprise middleware, formatting it appropriately for the sensor network communications protocol, and delivering it to the correct sensor. The sensor node then sends the sensor data response through the tasking middleware, so that it can be forwarded to the enterprise middleware. The testing process involved creating dummy sensor tasks that were sent by the enterprise middleware to the tasking middleware, and then waiting for the responses. The expected (asynchronous) 'response' from the tasking middleware was the presentation of sensor responses, in the appropriate format, and at the appropriate periodicity, as determined by the sensor task parameters. The resulting responses, in the form of formatted messages, were printed out and verified manually that the responses are correct.

The testing of the tasking middleware also involves testing the wireless sensor networking protocol. The networking protocol is provided by the use of Crossbow's XMesh networking software library, which plugs directly into the tasking middleware. The tasking middleware is responsible for determining, from the parameters in the sensor task received from the enterprise middleware, the appropriate WSN gateway to send a sensor message to. The WSN is divided into a number of zones in order to achieve scalability. XMesh accepts a correctly formatted message that includes the destination address of the message, and its payload, in order to forward it to the appropriate sensor node. It assumes that the message has been delivered to the correct WSN gateway (the root node of a zone), in order to route the message. The verification process was performed by physically connecting a Crossbow debugging platform (MIB510) onto a sensor node. This allowed one to view debug messages output from the sensor node, as it processes any messages. The content of the message can be printed out to ensure the message has been received by the correct node and decoded correctly.

The sensor hardware verification process also involves the use of the MIB510 platform and by connecting it to the sensor platform (MPR2400) in order to print debugging statements. The objective of the debugging statements was to show that the environmental sensors, e.g. temperature, react to changing environmental conditions. All the sensors' data can be converted on the sensor platform to display in SI derived units, instead of just raw ADC values. Each of the sensors was set to sample periodically, and converted data displayed through the debugging interface. Sensors were calibrated and the converted sensor data was checked to be in the appropriate range.

- THL sensors: The correct functioning of ambient temperature and humidity was tested through simple breathing onto the sensors. Ambient light was tested by cov-

ering the sensor with an opaque paper, to simulate light and dark. Additionally, the light sensor is checked against a calibrated light meter.
- CO2PIR sensors: The correct functioning of the CO2 sensor is exercised through breathing lightly onto the sensor receptor. The presence sensor is exercised using an opaque paper to simulate movement.

Integration Tests

System level integration tests include enterprise middleware, tasking middleware, WSN, user interface, health monitoring application, etc. The integration activities have also been carried out for making use of WSN infrastructure by a set of external applications. These tests verified that these applications and WSN infrastructure inter-work and function collectively. The integration efforts performed are as follows:

- A developed Panel PC display has been integrated with our WSN infrastructure at Margaritas building. The PC Panel is placed in each apartment and is able to display indoor and outdoor conditions.
- In both the testbed and Margaritas building deployments, the REST-Based interface of WSN infrastructure has been successfully used by a Mobile Browser application that displays sensor information.

System Level Verification Tests

The emphasis of these tests is proving the functionality and validating the correct behavior of the entire WSN system infrastructure. There have been the following observations when the entire system was put in place for operation:

- The sensors has been tasked with reporting period of 15 minutes intervals, therefore it's trivial to verify whether data has been reported consistently. It has been observed that data has sporadically been missing from the data-base meaning that the WSN gateways has not been received the data.
- Sensors' batteries have been draining at inconsistent rates and with no WSN health monitoring system initially in place, sensor nodes were shutting down without being noticed.
- Mains power outages can occur sporadically, which renders the system non-operational.

The above issues do not, however, discredit the functionality of the system. For the first point above, it is believed that the layout of our office space, the materials used in its construction, the constant movement of employees, wireless signals issued from other sources that affected the reliability in receiving some of the messages. The continuing operation of the network after the missing messages demonstrates that the system has been robust. For the second and third points, however, with the use of health monitoring application it has been quite practical to pin point the sensors' and system's operational failures.

System Level Performance Evaluations

The purpose of the system level performance evaluations is to determine whether the overall objectives of the proposed system have been realized. The overall aim for the SOA-based architectural framework has been to create an appropriate building services environment that can capitalize from a number of principles. These are to maximize benefits, reduce the costs, be reliable and provide continuous availability, be scalable, stable and usable. Some of the above principles must also be considered for the WSN networking environment. These principles are further explained below in both SOA-based framework for building services and WSN networking.

It may not be possible to thoroughly and conclusively evaluate the stated system-level performance principles and attributes as our proof-of concept testbed as well as deployed system in the real enterprise building have had limited size and scope. But where it has been possible, some assessments have been carried out using the both environments to prove the functionality and concepts.

SOA-Based Approach Principles

Benefits/Costs

The Benefits/Costs analysis assesses what improvements to the building and its operation are attributable to the new proposed SOA approach, along with a measure of the cost that is incurred in providing the benefit. We envisaged and shown that the proposed SOA-based system facilitates the use of advanced applications in a transparent manner. In addition, the benefits of utilizing this framework are considered as cost reductions in integrating applications, ease of maintenance, provision of superior flexibility and improvement of agility to respond to dynamic conditions are among the most prominent advantages that can be observed. That is, new applications can use the plug in and play environment exploiting the SOA-enabled system as long as they adhere to the defined interfaces. Applications are loosely coupled and operate independently in a flexible manner. However, there are costs associated with it, such as the cost and overhead associated with establishing the SOA-based system and developing applications and software in particular.

In general, the total cost of constructing intelligent buildings and providing advanced building services, as reported in (Wong et al., 2005), is higher than that for conventional buildings. This is simply because the intelligent building utilizes more applications of advanced technological materials and smart components in building services systems compared to traditional buildings.

In (Wong et al., 2005) various methods and techniques for the evaluation of investments in intelligent buildings are examined, such as net present value method, lifecycle costing analysis and cost benefit analysis. The authors of (Wong et al., 2005) argue for the adoption of an assessment methodology that adopts both qualitative and quantitative viewpoints throughout the building's lifespan.

Reliability

In a SOA-based building services environment, reliability includes two aspects: availability and accessibility of services. Availability is the aspect of whether a service is present or ready for immediate use. This can be represented by a probability value. Accessibility is the aspect that represents the capability of serving a request, which may be expressed as a probability measure to indicate the success rate. Accessibility can be measured according to the degree of meeting the user demands.

It should be noted that there is possible situations where a service is available but not accessible. The reliability assessments should therefore be conducted to show how these aspects are realized (Liu et al., 2007). We tried to specify and design the entire system by taking into account both aspects and having redundant and back-up components.

Scalability

Scalability is a generic word that defines the ability of a system, a technique, etc. to be deployed and consistently used at large-scale, whatever the criteria that define the scale.

In the context of SOA-based building services environment, the scalability of a system is the ability of effectively deploying the system at the scale of a large enterprise offering a number of services to a large number of applications and population size where the system consistently serves the service requests in spite of possible variations in the volume of requests. Exploiting SOA creates a building services environment that potentially allows adding in large-scale new services and applications incrementally. As the size of enterprise network increases, the response time should still remain reasonable. The response time includes the time taken by the service consumers to get their requested service that is provided in normal conditions or when a change has occurred (failure, addition of a new application/interface, retrieval of an interface, etc.). In case of our deployed system, the scalability should be evaluated against the following:

- Response time of the Server to handle service requests for retrieving data from the database and passing it to clients
- Response time of the Server for recording sensor data in the database.

It has not been possible to perform relevant scalability tests in our deployments due to their size limitations. But with high-spec servers, we believe the Server can reasonably cope with large deployment environments with respect to response times.

Stability

Stability evaluation verifies that a system, given its specified dynamics/responsiveness, is operating in a way that keeps/drives the system to a stable state of operation, in a representative set of conditions. That is the expected behavior is indeed realized without oscillations. It may not be possible to prove stability by tests, but it should be possible to identify any severe instability. Stability is a primary concern during the system operation. This is to avoid oscillations between actions of different entities that may incur or between states the system can or cannot provide the targeted performance. For example, a service provider (WSN) can be potential source of instability where a service consumer (BMS) reacts to network stimuli, e.g., sensor measured data or continuous alarm notifications, which could result in unstable operation. The main aspects that the stability assessments should address are the following:

Speed of reaction, otherwise the reaction may be too late to be effective.

- Stable state must be re-established.
- Other parts of the system must not become unstable as a consequence of any other component instability/failure.

We will perform stability checks when we integrate a BMS to the WSN infrastructure in a planned deployment in the second half of 2010.

Usability

Usability evaluation demonstrates that a system can operate as expected (according to its functional objectives) in terms of policy-based and/or tuning parameters upon which it may depend. Here, usability should be addressed in terms of having a policy framework that gives a building manager some control over the configuration and tuning of building services. According to the policy-based framework, this control should be taken with a level of precaution that the building manager considers acceptable to take, in order not to cause, as a result, dissatisfaction of users and any contract violation as well as to avoid overwhelming the system. It is to provide a degree of satisfaction (being analogous to the comfort level) to the user population. A number of other usability criteria are also identified and are taken into account such as ease of use, ease of configuration, quality of documentation, etc. The deployed system in Margaritas building is currently being assessed by occupants and building manager on its usability.

Wireless Sensor Networking Aspects

Benefits/Costs

The benefits associated with intelligent buildings exploiting advanced technological facilities (e.g., WSNs) should include the ease of integration, ease and reduction of maintenance costs, flexibility, reducing energy consumption for minimizing the on-going expenses, and creating a better environment for improving productivity.

In order to reduce the integration and maintenance cost, wireless sensors have been installed during the fit-outs without putting any burden during the construction and the need for wiring. Only, WSN gateways needed to be connected to the building communication network.

There are several problems that may result in the WSN gateway not receiving sensor data, for example, low battery voltage or poor connectivity to the gateway. It is very time consuming to resolve such problems if there is no means of monitoring the operation of the WSN. This necessitated the development of an easy to understand, visual method of monitoring the health of the WSN in real-time. We have developed an application that is capable of monitoring the operational health of a deployed WSN and displaying the results through a browser-based user interface as was explained in Chapter 5. This health monitoring application is regarded an essential part of WSN. It is intended to aid those who set-up and maintain the network and provides an indication of sensor node failures in reporting, resource exhaustion battery level), poor connectivity, and other abnormalities. Any sensor/gateway failures can be easily recognized and replaced or their battery can be changed.

Flexibility and agility are considered for the WSN where the sensor platforms can be added/removed at any time, or re-tasked depending on the needs, etc. The node addition/removal should not disrupt the network operation. These have been considered in our deployed WSN system as the network self-organizes itself as explained in the next section.

The environmental data visualization user interface is aimed at building/facilities managers or the building occupants for comfort monitoring and awareness. This has been helping the occupant to be more vigilant and the manager to study the energy consumption and make a comparison with where the application is not used. The user interface is currently in use in Margaritas building in Madrid and the impact of awareness for energy consumption is under study there.

Currently, the cost of WSN deployment (hardware and associated software) is still very high. This can be due to the fragmented and research focused deployments and the high development cost for WSN applications (Merrill, 2010). When assessing and evaluating one should not neglect the fact that any financial analysis should consider the entire building lifecycle, not only the initial construction costs. Furthermore, certain aspects of such an analysis are intangible, e.g. the well being of the occupants and the productivity level of the workers in an office environment, both of which should be enhanced through the deployment of WSNs in intelligent buildings. While the latter aspects cannot be directly reported in the financial analysis of a building, they should not be disregarded since they are key factors to satisfying a viable occupancy level for the building.

Reliability and Robustness

A reliable data delivery assures the data has reached its intended destination. Reliability should be considered at different levels as below:

Routing and Networking: In our WSN environment, we used the XMesh routing protocol (XMesh, 2008); a multi-hop, ad-hoc, mesh networking protocol developed by Crossbow for wireless sensor networks. Surveys of other routing protocols for WSNs are reported in (Akkaya, Younis, 2005), (Garcia et al., 2009). XMesh is a self-forming and self-healing network routing protocol and provides improved reliability by the use of multi-hoping. This means that sensor nodes can leave or join the network at any time without adversely affecting the operation of the network provided the network is dense enough to have alternative routes allowing the protocol to recover. The network also recovers form node failures due to faults/poor connectivity/low battery. XMesh provides the ability to transmit and receive data between the base station, also known as the WSN gateway, and any nodes in its network, i.e., an any-to-base and base-to-any network communications.

In the deployed networks, an independent instance of XMesh is run in each of WSN zones confining the routing changes and overheads to each zone and making the entire network scalable. Therefore, the gateway provides a bridge between the enterprise IP network and the 2.4GHz wireless sensor network. Each WSN gateway is only able to communicate with sensor nodes that 'reside' in its network group/zone. In this configuration, each WSN gateway communicates only with sensor nodes programmed to communicate in a specific 2.4GHz wireless channel. Frequency channel separation is a means for providing additional reliability, as it will reduce interference between sensor nodes from different WSN network groups. Additionally, this will help in the scalability of the network, if a large network is deployed.

Transport: Two schemes are used for transport layer reliability i.e., hop-by-hop and end-to-end. For hop-by-hop reliability, nodes infer loss through a gap in the sequence numbers of sent packets. Hop-by-hop reliability scheme cannot recover losses when topology changes or when the intermediate nodes cashes overflow. End-to-end reliability is defined as reliable upstream or downstream data transfer between a sensor node and its gateway. For end-to-end reliability, the destination node initiates an end-to-end recovery requesting for missing packets. A survey of transport protocols for WSNs is given in (Wang et al., 2006b). End-to-end reliability uses more link bandwidth usage then the hop-by-hop scheme. Providing end-to-end reliability comes at a cost of packet retransmissions and the use of scarce wireless bandwidth that might not be necessary for non-mission critical data. In our deployed WSN topology whereby sensor nodes are positioned closed to their gateways and frequency channel separation are meant to support packet transport, improve reliability and robustness without the additional cost.

By the way, Crossbow's XMesh protocol stack provides, as an optional service, end-to-end reliability. In the event that a data packet is sent as reliable and arrives at its destination, the XMesh stack will automatically send an ACK (acknowledgment). Conversely, if the sender of a data packet does not receive an ACK within a pre-defined period, it will attempt to re-send the data packet. This occurs for a pre-defined number of attempts before the sender gives up, and flags it up to the sending application. In addition, XMesh by default is reliable hop-by-hop at the link layer communications. Every data transmission between neighbors is acknowledged by the upstream receiver to the sender hop node. Otherwise, the sender hop node will retry re-transmission for up to 7 times, then giving up. A complete failed transmission will only be reported to the application layer, at the originating node – forwarding nodes will drop the message quietly.

WSN Network System: This is to find out about network behavior organizing itself and in delivery of packets in terms of time and quality. The deployed WSN system has been augmented with a recovery system, where all sensors in the WSN are re-tasked to re-start sensor sampling, when the enterprise middleware is started from fresh. The WSN system re-organizes itself after a mains power failure, which affects the WSN gateways because of a built-in capability of XMesh. It is possible to measure lost packets from the database entries where we expect a sample every e.g., 15 minutes. XMesh claims that it synchronizes the entire network with the gateway, but only in an epoch basis – the time when WSN's gateway is powered up is zero. Therefore, some measures of packet latency can be obtained.

Scalability

An important issue in designing the WSN architecture is that of scalability and robustness, because of existence of potentially large number of sensors in a building and their limited radio transmission ranges. It is typically necessary to expand the network, add sensors, and potentially manage a large number of gateways. In addition, large-scale multi-hop wireless networks can be overwhelmed by relay traffic in which the increased relaying of the traffic can exceed the capacity. Network coding, per-hop data aggregation and in-network processing, adaptive sampling, and network partitioning can limit the traffic. To avoid excess of traffic in the wireless medium, as explained below we used network partitioning where we can limit the number of sensor nodes in each zone.

We assumed that the building consists of multiple logical zones/spaces each one having a WSN dedicated for its monitoring needs. A zone gateway is used to connect one of these WSNs to the enterprise network. Each zone gateway manages the sensor nodes that are under its zone of responsibility. Each sensor node has a unique identifier making it easier to identify and manage them as they are placed in an ad-hoc manner. Zone gateways are connected to the Server via enterprise network. The Server is responsible for managing and controlling the array of zone gateways. High-level applications are made aware of the zones that are specified descriptively (e.g. Apartment-9) and not of WSN gateways. The enterprise applications that access the WSN service need a certain degree of abstraction from the underlying complexity and the specifics of the zone/space assignments, and use a single point of contact (the Server) to WSN-related activity in the building as a whole.

The size of each of the WSN zones is hard limited by the size of the address space available for addressing individual sensor nodes, currently limited to 16 bits. Therefore, it allows theoretically up to 216 unique sensor devices to connect to one gateway and potentially large number of gateways that permits large number of sensor devices, in the whole network in total. Practically, there are limits to the size of the network zone, in the form of limited wireless bandwidth that impacts the number of message transmissions in the network for any period of time. Another limitation is the ability of each hop node to cache messages whilst in the process of forwarding them, essential in a carrier sensing multiple access wireless networks. In reality, the largest Crossbow XMesh network (zone) that has been deployed so far is reported to be in the order of 100-plus sensor nodes. It should be noted that the number of WSN gateways in the whole network depends on the IP networking domain used at the enterprise networking part and its limitations and expansion aspects. Anyway, it is not likely for the high –spec Server to suffer from processing high number of sensor data packets relayed from large number of gateways.

Usability

For practical use and real deployments, sensor networks must consist of off-the-shelf components (in our case Crossbow devices used) that are relatively easy to understand, configure, deploy, and maintain. This has been the case for our deployments. The network should allow its continuous use without intervention. Thus, it should also be possible (as in our case) to restart the network in case of any system failure or error where the network can self-configure itself.

Power Management in Sensors

Long-term operation of sensors and sensor networks require careful power management. Power management is an essential function within the WSN nodes as the power source (typically, two AA batteries in our case) for sensor devices are very limited. Given the deployment and power consumption constraints, all sensor devices may not be mains powered. For example, some of the sensors, e.g. CO2 sensors, require main power due to their power consumption. This does not negatively impact but the usefulness of wireless communications. Additionally, given size constraints, the batteries cannot be large, and to keep operational expenditure costs down, battery replacement must be infrequent. This creates one of the main challenges of the WSN field, which is the scarcity of energy and should be considered when developing any solution targeted for WSNs.

In order to achieve a meaningful life expectancy for deployment of sensor nodes, energy can be conserved by enforcing strategies to selectively deactivate (put to sleep) some unused parts of the device when such actions will lead to energy savings (the energy costs of powering down and powering up must be offset, etc.). Many functions/services on the platforms are candidates for duty cycling, but the benefits and impact on the node's overall performance will be different for each one (Malatras et al., 2008b). In particular, the duty cycling of the radio has a significant power benefit, as many radio designs require comparable power draws whether the device is transmitting, receiving data, or just listening to the channel. However, duty cycling the radio also has a crucial impact on the fabric of the network, as neighboring devices can only communicate if their radios are on at the same time. Solutions to this prominent issue can be divided into two classes: either transmitting preambles before any data message that are longer than the maximum time a node can be asleep (Polastre et al., 2004). This ensures that a neighbor node will always hear some part of the preamble and can remain awake to hear the subsequent message; or employing some synchronization strategy to ensure neighboring nodes are awake at the same time (Ye et al., 2004). A combined approach is often applied (Dam, Langendoen, 2003), whereby a level of synchronization allows the use of a shorter preamble. The length of the required preamble is therefore inversely related to the synchronization precision.

Building management application requirements must be considered in order to set the tradeoffs between power saving and node availability. For periodic reporting services, the WSN can be permanently asleep between reports (apart from occasional network and node management activities) and therefore run very efficiently. The implication of adopting this trade-off is however that re-tasking the network will be a slow process, as control messages can only be disseminated during the awake periods. If rapid re-tasking is required (for example the ability to deliver high granularity information in time and space when an incident occurs, within seconds of the request being issued), then the network duty cycles must be short enough to propagate the task throughout the networks within the time constraints. The power requirement of operating with this trade-off is much higher, as the devices must be awake more frequently to listen for transmission. The standard approach is to determine the optimal trade-off for the particular application requirements and to deploy the WSN operating service accordingly. A much more flexible alternative can be envisaged, whereby the trade-off is set dynamically in a context aware fashion, as described in (Murray, 2008). By implementing basic context processing and decision making into the WSN nodes, the duty cycling regime can be changed proactively, in all or part of the network, if an incident is detected. This advanced level of power management allows significant power savings while supporting rapid re-tasking.

XMesh has a built-in low-power mode that can be switched on upon programming the sensor nodes, which significantly extends the life of a typical sensor node. The strategies employed include putting the processor to sleep when there's no task for processing (which happens by default anyway) and duty-cycling the radio. The default setting allows a data transmission every 3 minutes and radio listening rate of 8 times per second.

When there's no transmission, the radio goes into a 'sleep' mode. When this mode is switched on in our deployments, it is found that XMesh performs relatively robustly at these settings with no specific issues detected.

Remote Management

Remote management is necessary to re-task nodes, reprogram the nodes, update any operating software, find/fix bugs, etc. A review of reprogramming approaches is given in (Wang et al., 2006c). Power control is also necessary to power up the WSN infrastructure in case of power cuts and failures. Since nodes are uniquely identified, network operational health monitoring application allows monitoring the network and locating problems and finding any node failures. At the WSN sensor node level, it is possible to remotely re-program nodes by using an optional module in XMesh. However, in practice, this is rarely, used in a static deployment environment. In order to reduce the impact on the limited storage and memory on the sensor nodes, this feature is not enabled in our deployments.

In terms of managing the enterprise Server and the software packages deployed on it, remote management is achieved through a combination of Microsoft Windows' Remote Desktop tool, FTP client/server, and web tools. The Remote Desktop tool allows emulating remotely the local desktop interactivity. FTP clients are used to transfer files between the remote machine and a local machine. Web tools, such as a web browser, allow a local user to interact with the deployed Web Services – for instance, to create new task or cancel current tasks. In the event of a mains power cut, it is envisioned that a machine on the deployed network automatically powers itself up upon the restoration of power.

Environmental Monitoring in a Real Building

The environmental monitoring is designed for a number of uses; occupant/building manager awareness, human comfort and energy efficiency. The sensor data has been collected and is made accessible through a number of means as below.

Non-graphical interfaces: These interfaces are designed as machine-to-machine interfaces, therefore, are more suitable for use programmatically.

- MySQL database (MySQL, 2009) interface; this interface is only accessible directly on the machine that hosts the MySQL database where the sensor data is stored, or from another computer on the same LAN but not remotely from the Internet.
- REST-based Web Services interface; this interface is accessible from both the LAN and the Internet.

Graphical interfaces: The interfaces below are designed for human interaction.

- A developed WSN Portal user interface for users with access to a Flash-compatible web browser, where raw current and historical data can be viewed in graphical plots.
- A user interface designed for handheld devices, where raw current and historical data can be viewed in tabular form.

The panel PC installed in individual apartments of the Margaritas building designed for viewing by the apartment's occupant, where raw current and historical data can be viewed, and some analysis can be invoked. Figures 6 to 11 show the range and types of sensor data that can be viewed using the WSN Portal.

Figure 6. Temperature and humidity in kitchen of Apartment 9 (26/11 to 30/11/2009)

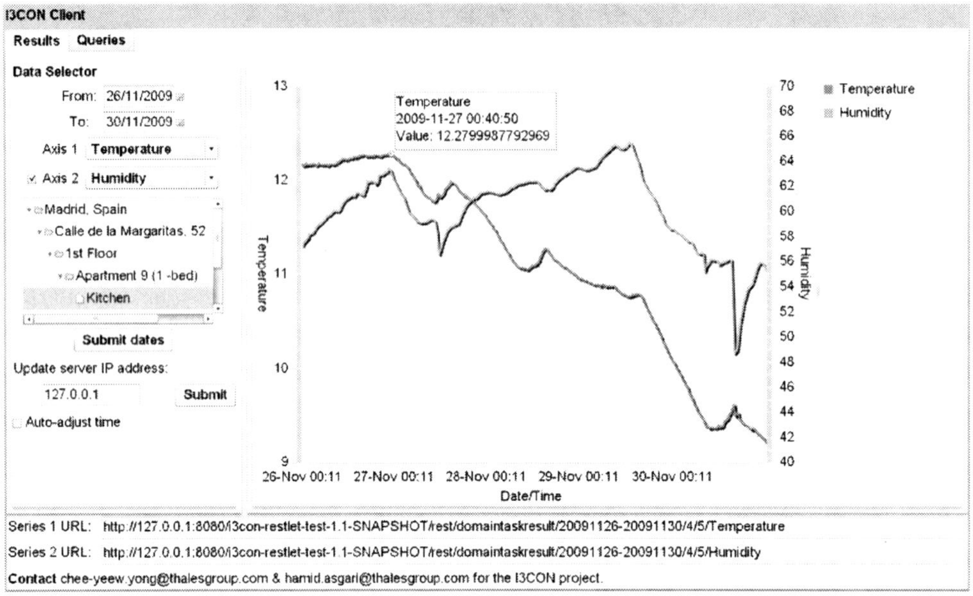

Figure 7. Presence detected in kitchen of Apartment 9 (01/10 to 01/12/2009)

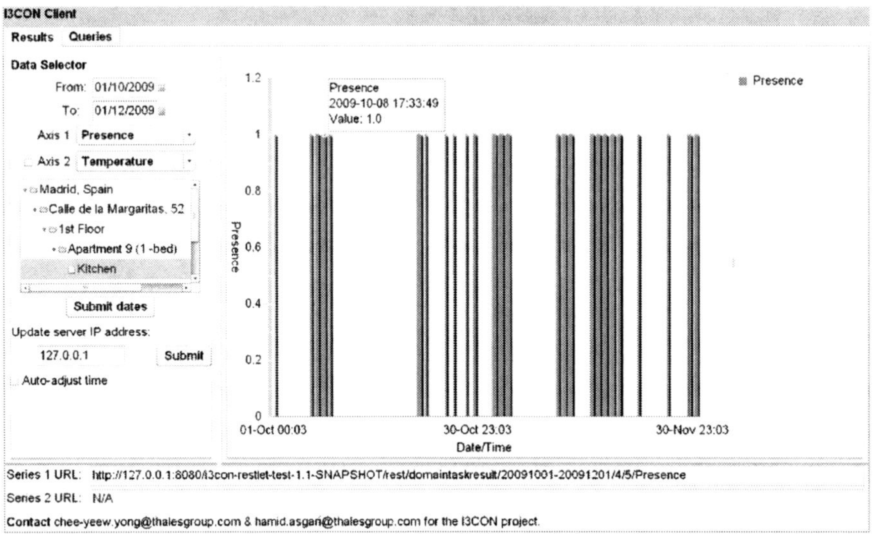

CONCLUSION

We have discussed in this chapter an architectural framework that enables the integration of wireless sensor networks in an overall enterprise building architecture. The benefits that can be reached by utilizing service-oriented enterprise architectures are numerous, hence the need to move towards such approaches. Reductions in cost, flexibility and agility to respond to dynamic conditions are among the most prominent advantages that can be observed.

Figure 8. CO^2 levels measured in all 3 deployed areas in Apartment 4, (11/11 to 26/11/2009).

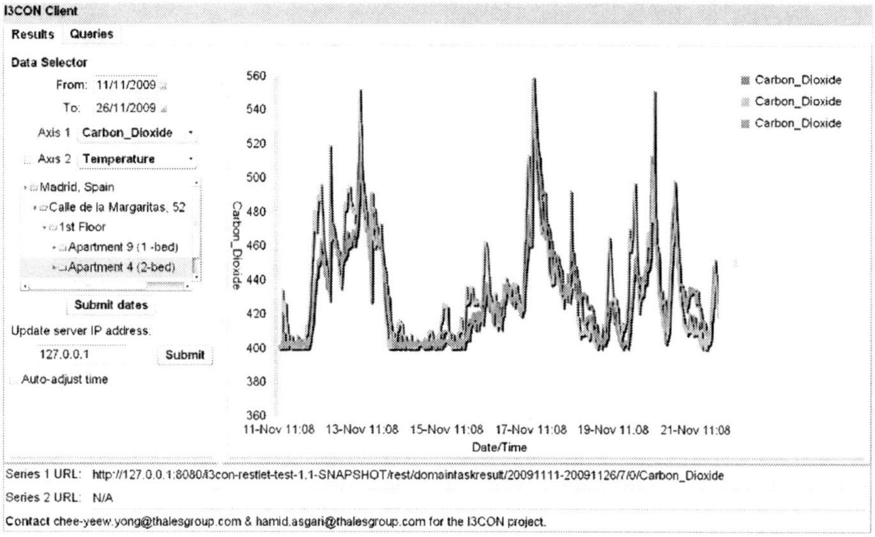

Figure 9. Outdoor temperature as logged in Plaza Castilla, (the nearest weather station to Margaritas building), Madrid (01/11 to 01/12/2009)

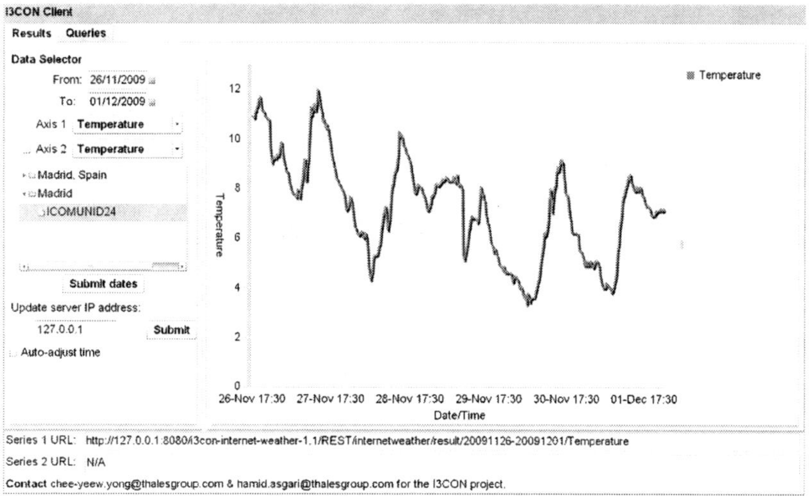

We have discussed related issues and based on the requirements we have provided a functional architecture and a corresponding specification for the proposed WSN architecture. Scalability, extensibility and reliability that are extremely important in the wireless domain have been taken into account, while in parallel security should also be supported. We elaborated on developed a service-oriented architecture to expose WSN-related information to the overall enterprise architecture utilizing a tasking middleware that are actually responsible for data collection and processing.

We have implemented and deployed the entire system in a real building and currently assess-

Figure 10. Outdoor temperature and precipitation (rain) as logged in Plaza Castilla, Madrid (26/11 to 30/11/2009)

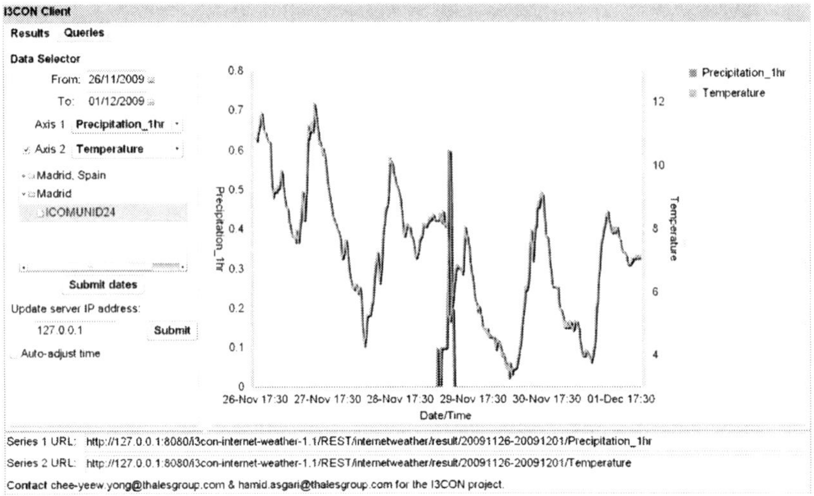

Figure 11. Various environmental sensed data displayed on the panel PC

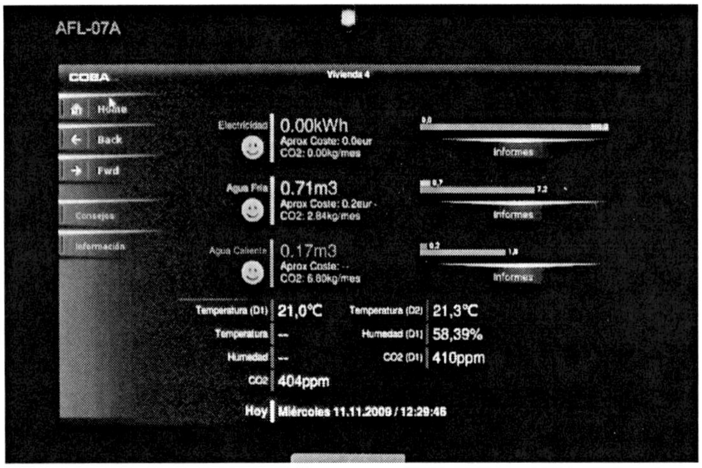

ing its overall impact and performance to the building users. We have thoroughly discussed on the functionality tests, experimentations, and system-level evaluations and provided some environmental monitoring results. The purpose of the system level evaluations was to determine whether the overall objectives of the proposed architecture have been realized. The overall aim for the SOA-based architecture has been to create an appropriate building services environment that can maximize benefits, reduce the costs, be reliable and provide continuous availability, be scalable, stable and usable. Finally a further deployment is planned in the second half of 2010 with the aim of integrating a BMS into our SOA platform where the BMS can utilize the wireless sensor data. Some further tests including stability checks will be performed when we integrate the BMS to the WSN infrastructure.

ACKNOWLEDGMENT

The work described in this chapter has been carried out in the NMP I3CON FP6 (NMP 026771-2) project, which is partially funded by the Commission of the European Union. The author would like to acknowledge the contributions of his colleagues especially Chee Yong, Mark Irons, and Apostolos Malatras (former colleague) in Thales Research & Technology (UK) Ltd. and others project colleagues especially from EMVS – "Empresa Municipal De La Vivienda Y Suelo De Madrid" (Madrid municipal city council), Intracom Ltd. in Greece, and Lonix Ltd. in Finland.

REFERENCES

Ahamed, S. I., Vyas, A., & Zulkernine, M. (2004). Towards developing sensor networks monitoring as a middleware service. In *Proceedings of the 2004 International Conference on Parallel Processing Workshops - ICPPW'04* (pp. 465–471).

Akkaya, K., & Younis, M. (2005). A survey on routing protocols for wireless sensor networks. *Ad Hoc Networks*, *3*(3), 325–349. doi:10.1016/j.adhoc.2003.09.010

Akyildiz, I. F., Weilian, S., Sankarasubramaniam, Y., & Cayirci, E. (2002). A survey on sensor networks. *IEEE Communications Magazine*, *40*(8), 102–114. doi:10.1109/MCOM.2002.1024422

Apache. (2008). *Apache Tomcat software*. Retrieved June 2008 from http://tomcat.apache.org/

Asgari, H. (Ed.). (2008). *I3CON project deliverable D3.42-1, sensor network and middleware implementation and proof of concept*. Retrieved July 20, 2010 from http://ww.i3con.org/

Botts, M., Percivall, G., Reed, C., & Davidsson, J. (2008). *OpenGIS ® sensor Web enablement: Overview and high level architecture. LNCS GeoSensor Networks book* (pp. 175–190). Berlin/Heidelberg, Germany: Springer.

Cheng, L., Lin, T., Zhang, Y., & Ye, Q. (2004). Monitoring wireless sensor networks by heterogeneous collaborative groupware. In *Proceedings of the ISA/IEEE Sensors for Industry Conference* (pp.130 – 134).

Chong, C.-Y., & Kumar, S. P. (2003). Sensor networks: Evolution, opportunities and challenges. *Proceedings of the IEEE*, *91*(8), 1247–1256. doi:10.1109/JPROC.2003.814918

Chu, X., Kobialka, T., Durnota, B., & Buyya, R. (2006). Open sensor Web architecture: Core services. In *Proceedings of 4th International Conference on Intelligent Sensing and Information Processing - ICISIP* (pp. 98-103), IEEE Press.

Craton, E., & Robin, D. (2002). *Information model: The key to integration*. Retrieved July 20, 2010 from http://www.automatedbuildings.com/

Crossbow. (2009). *Crossbow technology company: Product related information*. Retrieved July 20, 2010 from http://www.xbow.com/Products/wproductsoverview.aspx

CURL. (2010). *cURL and libcurl, tool to transfer data using URL syntax*. Retrieved July 20, 2010 from http://curl.haxx.se/

Ehrlich, P. (2003). Guideline for XML/Web services for building control. In *Proceedings of BuilConn 2003*. Retrieved July 20, 2010 from http://www.builconn.com/

Erl, T. (2005). *Service-oriented architecture: Concepts, technology and design*. New York, NY: Prentice Hall PTR.

Fielding, R. T. (2000). *Representational State Transfer (REST)*. Unpublished PhD thesis. Retrieved July 20, 2010 from http://www.ics.uci.edu/~fielding/pubs/dissertation/rest_arch_style.htm

Franks, J., Hallam-Baker, P., Hostetler, J., Lawrence, S., Leach, P., Luotonene, A., & Stewart, L. (1999). *RFC 2617 - HTTP authentication: Basic and digest access authentication*. IETF Standards Track.

Garcia-Hernandez, C. F., Ibarguengoytia-Gonzales, P. H., Garcia-Hernandez, J., & Perez-Diaz, J. A. (2007). Wireless sensor networks and applications: A survey. *International Journal of Computer Science and Network Security*, *7*(3), 264–273.

García Villalba, L. J., Sandoval, O,. Ana, L., Triviño Cabrera, A., & Barenco Abbas, C. J. (2009). Routing protocols in wireless sensor networks. *MDPI - Open Access Publishing Sensors, 9*(11), 8399-8421.

Ivester, M., & Lim, A. (2006). Interactive and extensible framework for execution and monitoring of wireless sensor networks. In *Proceedings of 1st International Conference on Communication System Software and Middleware - Comsware 2006* (pp.1-10).

King, J., Bose, R., Yang, H., Pickles, S., & Helal, A. (2006). Atlas: A service-oriented sensor platform, hardware and middleware to enable programmable pervasive services. In *Proceedings 2006 of 31st IEEE Conference on Local Computer Networks-LCN* (pp. 630-638). IEEE Press.

Kushwaha, M., Amundson, I., Koutsoukos, X., Neema, S., & Sztipanovits, J. (2007). OASiS: A programming framework for service-oriented sensor networks. In *Proceedings of 2nd IEEE International Conference on Communication Systems Software and Middleware – COMSWARE* (pp. 7-12). IEEE Press.

Landre, W., & Wesenberg, H. (2007). *REST versus SOAP as architectural style for Web services.* Paper presented at the 5th International Workshop on SOA & Web Services, OOPSLA, Montreal, Canada.

Liu, Z., Gu, N., & Yang, G. (2007). A reliability evaluation framework on service oriented architecture. In *Proceedings of 2nd International Conference on Pervasive Computing and Applications - ICPCA 2007* (pp. 466-471).

Luk, M., Mezzour, G., Perring, A., & Gligor, V. (2007). MiniSec: A secure sensor network communication architecture. In *Proceedings of 6th International Conference on Information Processing in Sensor Networks - IPSN 2007* (pp. 1-10).

Malatras, A., Asgari, A. H., & Baugé, T. (2008b). Web enabled wireless sensor networks for facilities management. *IEEE Systems Journal*, *2*(4), 500–512. doi:10.1109/JSYST.2008.2007815

Malatras, A., Asgari, A. H., Bauge, T., & Irons, M. (2008a). A service-oriented architecture for building services integration. *Emerald Journal of Facilities Management*, *6*(2), 132–151. doi:10.1108/14725960810872659

Merrill, W. (2010). Where is the return on investment in wireless sensor networks? *IEEE Wireless Communications*, *17*(1), 4–6. doi:10.1109/MWC.2010.5416341

Moodley, D., & Simonis, I. (2006). *A new architecture for the sensor Web: The SWAP framework.* Paper presented at the 5th International Semantic Web Conference (ISWC'06), Athens, GA, USA.

Murray, B., Baugé, T., Egan, R., Tan, C., & Yong, C. (2008). *Dynamic duty cycle control with path and zone management in wireless sensor networks.* Paper presented at the IEEE International Wireless Communications and Mobile Computing Conference, Crete, Greece.

MySQL. (2009). *MySQL DB official homepage*. Retrieved July 20, 2010 from http://www.mysql.com/?bydis_dis_index=1

OGC. (2010). *Open Geospatial Consortium Inc., official homepage*. Retrieved July 20, 2010 from http://www.opengeospatial.org/

Open, I. D. (2010). *OpenID standard*. Retrieved July 20, 2010 from http://en.wikipedia.org/wiki/OpenID

Pautasso, C., Zimmermann, O., & Leymann, F. (2008). RESTful Web services vs. big Web services: Making the right architectural decision. In *Proceedings of the ACM 17th International Conference on World Wide Web - WWW 2008*, Beijing, China.

Perrig, A., Szewczyk, R., Wen, V., Culler, D., & Tygar, J. D. (2001). Spins: Security protocols for sensor networks. *Wireless Networks*, *8*(5), 521–534. doi:10.1023/A:1016598314198

Perrig, J., Stankovic, A., & Wagner, D. (2004). Security in wireless sensor networks. *Communications of the ACM*, *47*(6), 53–57. doi:10.1145/990680.990707

Pkix. (2009). *IETF public-key infrastructure* (X.509) (pkix) *Working Group*. Retrieved July 20, 2010 from http://www.ietf.org/dyn/wg/charter/pkix-charter.html

Polastre, J., Hill, J., & Culler, D. (2004). Versatile low power media access for wireless sensor networks. In *Proceedings of the 2nd ACM SenSys Conference* (pp. 95–107), Baltimore, USA.

SOAP. (2008). *W3C SOAP 1.2 specification*. Retrieved July 20, 2010 from http://www.w3.org/TR/soap12-part1/

Sommerville, I. (2007). *Software engineering* (8th ed.). New York, NY: Addison- Wesley Pubs.

Spring. (2009). *Spring framework's security project*. Retrieved July 20, 2010 from http://static.springframework.org/spring-security/

Stal, M. (2002). Web services: Beyond component-based computing. *Communications of the ACM*, *45*(10), 71–76. doi:10.1145/570907.570934

Ta, T., Othman, N. Y., Glitho, R. H., & Khendek, F. (2006). Using Web services for bridging end-user applications and wireless sensor networks. In *Proceedings of 11th IEEE Symposium on Computers and Communications - ISCC'06* (pp. 347-352), Sardina, Italy: IEEE Press.

Turon, M. (2005). MOTE-VIEW: A sensor network monitoring and management tool. In *Proceedings of the 2nd IEEE Workshop on Embedded Network Sensors - EmNets'05* (pp. 11-18). IEEE press.

van Dam, T., & Langendoen, K. (2003). An adaptive energy-efficient MAC protocol for wireless sensor networks. In *Proceedings of the 1st ACM SenSys Conference* (171–180), Los Angeles, CA: ACM Press.

Wang, C., Sohraby, K., Li, B., Daneshmand, M., & Hu, Y. (2006b). A survey of transport protocols for wireless sensor networks. *IEEE Network Magazine*, *20*(3), 34–40. doi:10.1109/MNET.2006.1637930

Wang, O., Zhu, Y., & Cheng, L. (2006c). Reprogramming wireless sensor networks: Challenges and approaches. *IEEE Network*, *20*(3), 48–55. doi:10.1109/MNET.2006.1637932

Wang, S., Xu, Z., Cao, J., & Zhang, J. (2007). A middleware for Web service-enabled integration and interoperation of intelligent building systems. *Automation in Construction*, *16*(1), 112–121. doi:10.1016/j.autcon.2006.03.004

Wang, Y., Attebury, G., & Ramamurthy, B. (2006a). A survey of security issues in wireless sensor networks. *IEEE Communications Surveys & Tutorials*, *8*(2), 2–23. doi:10.1109/COMST.2006.315852

Wong, J. K. W., Li, H., & Wang, S. W. (2005). Intelligent building research: A review. *Automation in Construction*, *14*(1), 143–159. doi:10.1016/j.autcon.2004.06.001

XMesh. (2008). *XMesh routing protocol for wireless sensor networks*. Crossbow Company. Retrieved July 20, 2010 from http://www.xbow.com/Technology/MeshNetworking.aspx

Ye, W., Heidemann, J., & Estrin, D. (2004). Medium access control with coordinated, adaptive sleeping for wireless sensor networks. *IEEE/ACM Transactions on Networking*, *12*(3), 493–506. doi:10.1109/TNET.2004.828953

Yick, J., Mukherjee, B., & Ghosal, D. (2008). Wireless sensor networks survey. *Computer Networks*, *52*(12), 2292–2330. doi:10.1016/j.comnet.2008.04.002

Yu, M., Kim, H., & Mah, P. (2007). NanoMon: An adaptable sensor network monitoring software. In *Proceedings of IEEE International Symposium on Consumer Electronics - ISCE 2007* (pp. 1 – 6).

Zhou, Y., Fang, Y., & Zhang, Y. (2008). Securing wireless sensor networks: A survey. *IEEE Communications Surveys & Tutorials*, *10*(3), 6–28. doi:10.1109/COMST.2008.4625802

KEY TERMS AND DEFINITIONS

Wireless Sensor Network (WSN): A WSN consists of spatially distributed autonomous sensors to cooperatively monitor physical or environmental conditions.

Service oriented Architecture (SoA): SoA is a means of deploying distributed systems, where the participating components of those systems are exposed as services.

Building Management System (BMS): A BMS is a computer-based system installed in buildings that controls and monitors the building's mechanical and electrical equipment such as ventilation, lighting, power systems, fire systems, and security systems.

WSN Health Monitor: An application intended to provide an indication of sensor node failures, resource exhaustion, poor connectivity, and other abnormalities.

System Level Evaluations: The purpose of the system level evaluations is to verify, validate, assess and prove the functionality of the complete devised system in order to determine whether the overall objectives of the system have been realized.

Chapter 9
Level Crossing Sampling for Energy Conservation in Wireless Sensor Networks:
A Design Framework

Hadi Alasti
University of North Carolina at Charlotte, USA

ABSTRACT

In pervasive computing environments, shared devices are used to perform computing tasks for specific missions. Wireless sensors are energy-limited devices with tiny storage and small computation power that may use these shared devices in pervasive computing environments to perform parts of their computing tasks. Accordingly, wireless sensors need to transmit their observations (samples) to these devices, directly or by multi-hopping through other wireless sensors. While moving the computation tasks over to the shared pervasive computing devices helps conserve the in-network energy, repeated communications to convey the samples to the pervasive computing devices depletes the sensors' battery, quickly.

In periodic sampling of the bandlimited signals, many of the consecutive samples are very similar and sometimes the signal remains unchanged over periods of time. These samples can be interpreted as redundant. For this, transmission of all of the periodic samples from all of the sensors in wireless sensor networks is wasteful. The problem becomes more challenging in large scale wireless sensor networks. Level crossing sampling in time is proposed for energy conservation in real-life application of wireless sensor networks to increase the network lifetime by avoiding the transmission of redundant samples. In this chapter, a design framework is discussed for application of level crossing sampling in wireless sensor networks. The performance of level crossing sampling for various level definition schemes are evaluated using computer simulations and experiments with real-life wireless sensors.

DOI: 10.4018/978-1-60960-611-4.ch009

INTRODUCTION

A Wireless Sensor Network (WSN) is an emerging category of wireless networks that consists of spatially distributed wireless devices equipped with sensors to monitor physical or environmental conditions, such as temperature, sound, vibration, pressure, pollutants, etc. in various locations (Akyildiz et al, 2001). Energy conservation is one of the most challenging problems for major categories of WSN. Pervasive sensor networks have been proposed for different applications such as healthcare (Jea et al, 2007; Lin et al, 2007) and equipment health monitoring (Nasipuri et al, 2008; Alasti, 2009), when wireless sensors are cooperating with the other available computing devices in a pervasive computing task to find an appropriate solution. In applications in which the sensors should sense the signals and work as the part of pervasive computing system, energy conversation becomes more complicated.

To conserve energy, various schemes such as adaptive medium access control (MAC) (Ye & Estrin, 2004), efficient routing protocols (Trakadas et al, 2004), cross layering designs (Sichitiu, 2004), and distributed signal processing (Alasti, 2009) have been discussed. As discussed in various related work, the energy consuming operations in WSN are usually categorized in three major groups: communication, computation, and sensing. A comparative study shows that for a generation of Berkeley sensor nodes, the ratio of the required energy for single bit communication over the required energy for processing of a bit ranges from 1000 to 10000 (Zhao & Guibas, 2004). This huge ratio clearly shows that to have a WSN with longer life-time, the successful protocols, signal processing algorithms and network planning schemes should shift the network's operating mode from communication-dominant to computation-dominant mode. For instance, a considerable part of the network's energy is wasted on inefficient multi-hopping and packet collisions in the network. This energy loss may be reduced by signal processing schemes like localized in-network information compression (Zhao& Guibas, 2004), and collaborative signal processing (Alasti, 2009; Zhao& Guibas, 2004).

Another major challenge that is critical for designing protocols and algorithms for WSNs is scalability. Network scalability is the adaptability of the network's protocols and algorithms to the variation of the node density for maintaining a defined network's quality. As also defined in (Swami et al, 2007), a network is scalable if the quality of service available to each node does not depend on the network size. As the network size increases, the higher traffic load of the network exhausts the in-network energy faster, a situation that affects the quality of service.

This chapter is focused on the application of level crossing sampling (*LCS*) for energy conservation to increase the life-time of the WSN. Transmission of the periodic samples of all of the sensors in the network with multi-hopping exhausts the in-network energy, shortly. At times, when the signal does not change significantly, sampling and transmission through the network, extravagantly wastes the in-network energy. A scheme is proposed to enable smart selection of the sampling instance, based on the instantaneous bandwidth of the signal, which effectively reduces the number of transmissions and relaying. This scheme shifts the operating mode of the network from communication dominant toward computation dominant and is energy friendly, but nonetheless needs complex algorithms and processing. *LCS* has recently received attention for energy saving in specific applications such as mobile devices (Qaisar et al, 2009). In this chapter we present the design and implementation of *LCS* based sampling in a real-life wireless sensor network. Various design issues of *LCS* are presented such as considerations for determining the number of levels, level-selection, and appropriate sampling periods that are needed for achieving higher energy efficiency without loss of useful information at wireless sensors.

The organization of the chapter is as follows: The motivation section justifies the use of *LCS* for wireless sensor networks in pervasive environments. In the background section, a reported energy consumption regime of real-life WSN with periodic sampling is firstly reviewed. Then, the advantages and the difficulties of using *LCS* based sampling instead of periodic sampling that have been discussed in the related academic literature are reviewed.

After that the *LCS* problem statement is given and the optimal sampling levels for minimization of the reconstruction error when the probability density function (*pdf*) of the signal is known is discussed. Practically, having the *pdf* of the signal is a non-realistic assumption in WSN. Accordingly, a tractable, heuristic approach based on having a few of the statistical moments of the signal is discussed.

The minimum sampling rate for acceptable recovery of the signal with *LCS* condition is discussed in a subsequent section. Technically, wireless sensors are digital microcomputers that record and process the sensor readings at discrete times. Implementation of *LCS* for proper reconstruction of the sensor observations needs to be aware of the characteristics of the signal. The *LCS* sampling problem is discussed and a couple of examples are given for introducing the design framework.

After that the performance of *LCS* based sampling is presented based on the numerical and experimental results. To evaluate the performance and the cost of *LCS*, the reconstruction error and the average sampling rate are obtained using computer simulations. The performance and cost of *LCS* with optimally spaced levels, heuristic *LCS* scheme and uniformly spaced levels are compared. Additionally, experimental results of comparing the performance and cost of *LCS* with an application case study of periodic temperature sensing with the *MICAz* wireless sensors from *Crossbow Technology Inc.* is presented as supportive results, prior to concluding the chapter.

Motivation

Wireless sensors are inexpensive, low power devices with limited storage, bandwidth and computational capabilities. In applications of wireless sensor networks, such as health monitoring, sometimes the signals of multiple sensors from different locations should be monitored and analyzed over time. Announcing an upcoming urgent condition requires the simultaneous analysis of multiple signals of different sensors, which is hardly possible to do in power-limited wireless sensors networks.

In pervasive computing environments, various devices embedded in the surroundings are public and shared among multiple users. These devices can be used to perform the required computation, analysis and the planning of related tasks. In a pervasive environment, wireless sensors send their observations directly or with multi hopping to the closest sink that can be one of these public and shared devices.

Despite that taking over the computation tasks to the pervasive environment increases the sensor network lifetime, repeated and unnecessary transmissions respectively act in a diminishing way. Transmission of periodic sensor observations when the signals vary slowly or remain unchanged does not convey new information, although it consumes the in-network energy of wireless sensors. Irregular sampling is a possible solution to this problem.

Appropriately selecting the instantaneous sampling rate needs storage and computational capability, two features that the wireless sensors are normally short of. Using pervasive computing solutions to find the appropriate instantaneous sampling rate at each of the sensors is not feasible as it needs instantaneous knowledge of the sensor observations.

Level crossing sampling is a subset of irregular sampling based on sampling at the crossing instance of a set of pre-defined levels. As the sampling levels are known beforehand, no computation is required. A few subsets of sampling levels are stored in the wireless sensor platform and according to the accuracy and granularity requirements set by the pervasive environment, the wireless sensors switch between the existing subsets for higher or lower accuracy.

Using level crossing sampling provides higher energy efficiency and less risk of contention due to the reduction of a set of unnecessary transmissions. It is also expected that using level crossing sampling provides a slightly more secure network by reducing the risk of tampering.

Background

The conventional approach of periodic sampling of analog signals is usually motivated by the need for perfect reconstruction of the signal from its samples, i.e. by sampling the signal at the *Nyquist* rate or higher. However, periodic sampling may not be appropriate for many applications of WSNs, where reduction of communication cost is a critical requirement. In such applications, non-uniform sampling provides an excellent solution to conserve communication costs by sacrificing some accuracy of signal reconstruction. The basic idea is to suppress or slow down transmissions when the samples do not carry much information, e.g. signal has not changed much. This is particularly important for temporally sparsed (bursty) and variable bandwidth signals. For such cases, periodic sampling usually results in redundant samples that should be eliminated before transmission or storage to maintain efficiency. Non-uniform sampling with sampling intervals that vary according to the short-term bandwidth of the signal is an effective solution for achieving efficiency in such applications. One of the main challenges in non-uniform sampling is the choice of sampling instants that should be defined based on the short-term characteristics of the random signal. *LCS* has been proposed to resolve this issue by sampling the signal when the signal crosses a set of predefined levels (Qaisar et al, 2009; Sayiner et al, 1996; Marvasti, 2001).

LCS is a subclass of non-uniform sampling based on sampling at the crossing points of a set of levels. Figures 1a and 1b visually compare the periodic sampling and *LCS*. In these figures the dark crossbars show the sampling instance of the signal in time. Unlike periodic sampling, in *LCS* the new sample is taken when the amplitude value of the signal crosses either the higher or the lower amplitude level of the most recently crossed amplitude level. Accordingly, when the signal's amplitude does not change or varies slightly about the most recent crossed amplitude level, no sample is taken. Figure 1b shows *LCSH* (LCS and Hold) which is equivalent to the pulse amplitude modulation (*PAM*). In this chapter, *LCSH* is defined for the comparative study of the reconstruction error for various types of sampling levels, such as uniformly or non-uniformly spaced levels.

LCS has been studied under several different names including event-based sampling, magnitude driven sampling, deadbands, and send-on-delta (Miskovicz, 2006). Although the subject has been investigated for many years, its potential received renewed attention in recent years due to applications where signals with variable characteristics are present, such as in voice-over IP (*VOIP*) and sensor systems.

An experimental study of low power wireless mesh sensor networks with the *MICAz* wireless platforms proved that as the network size increases, regardless of the battery type the network's lifetime sharply decreases due to the higher number of route update requests and transmission of redundant data (Nasipuri et al, 2008). Using *LCS* is an approach to stop a number of transmissions.

The performance of *LCS* based *A/D* converter is highly affected by reference level placement. Guan et al (Guan et al, 2008) showed that it is possible to sequentially and adaptively implement these levels. Based on this idea, they proposed an adaptive *LCS A/D* converter which sequentially updates the reference sampling levels to properly

Figure 1. Comparative illustration of (a) periodic sampling and (b) level crossing sampling (LCS) with zero-order spline reconstruction, i.e. level crossing sampling and hold (LCSH)

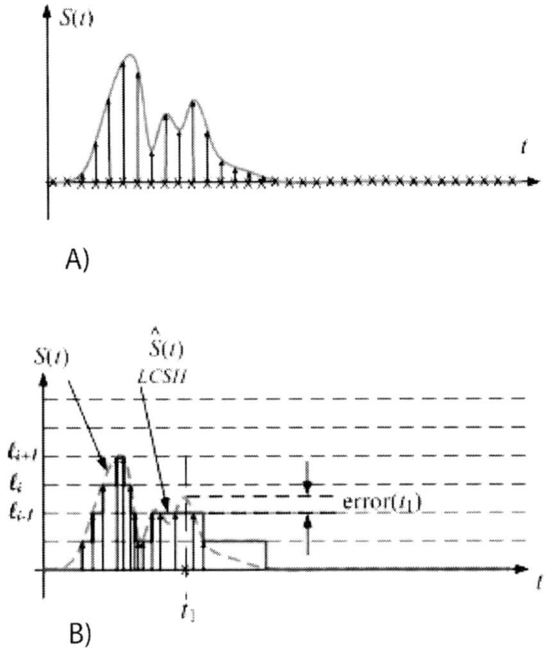

decide where and when to sample. They analytically proved that as the length of the signal's sequence increases, their adaptive algorithm's performance approaches its best possibility.

The speed of sampling of the signal for proper *LCS* depends on the bandwidth of the signal. When the signal's bandwidth changes with time are unknown, the sampling speed should be adaptively found. Using short-time Fourier transform (STFT) with constant time-frequency resolution is very common in analysis of the time-varying signals. Qaisar et al proposed a computationally reduced adapted STFT algorithm for level-crossing sampling (Qaisar et al, 2009). In their algorithm the sampling frequency resolution and the window of STFT is adapted based on the characteristics of the signal. As the sampling rate is adapted, the processing power of the *LCS* based *A/D* converter has been significantly reduced. In another related work of these authors, to filter the non-uniformly spaced samples of the *LCS* output, an adaptive rate finite impulse response (*FIR*) filter was proposed and its computational complexity was reduced (Qaisar et al, 2007). The proposed adaptive algorithm was proposed for power limited mobile systems for applications where the signal's amplitude remains constant for a long period of time.

Guan & Singer (2006) studied the use of oversampled *A/D* converter along with low resolution quantization for reconstruction of a specific class of non-bandlimited signals. They showed that the studied sampling scheme outperforms the periodic sampling. They also studied the sampling of finite rate innovation signals using *LCS* and proposed an algorithm for perfect reconstruction of this category of signals after *LCS* (Guan & Singer, 2007).

The processing of non-stationary signals after *LCS* was studied by Greitans (Greitans, 2006). The difficulty of signal reconstruction due to non-uniformly spaced samples and the time-varying statistical properties of the signal were reviewed. The shortcomings of STFT, such as the appearance of spurious components and the drawbacks of wavelet transform which include low spectral resolution at high frequencies and low temporal resolution at low frequencies, were also reviewed. Clock-less signal dependent transforms were proposed to improve the reconstruction performance. It was concluded that because the spectral characteristics of the non-stationary signals vary with time, the signal dependent transform should be adapted locally.

Greitans & Shavelis also discussed the signal reconstruction after *LCS* using cardinal spline for *LCS* samples of speech signal (Greitans & Shavelis, 2007). It was shown that in many of the cases the applied reconstruction approach works properly, but not always. Using the non-uniformly spaced reference levels was mentioned as a tentative solution to this problem.

Sayiner et al introduced a *LCS* based *A/D* converter, where issues like speed, resolution and hardware complexity were investigated (Sayiner et al, 1996). For evaluation of the quality of the sampling, the reconstruction root mean square of the error was calculated after zero and first order polynomial interpolation of the non-uniformly spaced samples and then uniform sampling. In addition to polynomial interpolation, decimation was used for increasing the overall resolution of the converter. They suggested a modest decimation factor.

Application of *LCS* for efficiently sampling the bursty signals was studied in an information theoretical framework by Singer and Guan (Singer & Guan, 2007). They showed that while *LCS* has less total sampling rate, it can convey the same amount of information as periodic sampling. The idea was proposed for data communication and compression. They proposed to use the probability density function of the signal in designing the *LCS A/D* conversion reference levels for optimal *LCS*.

Mark and Todd proposed and discussed a systematic framework for reference level sampling of the random signals at quantized time (Mark & Todd, 1982). The main concentration of the work was on data compression. They proposed a structure for the non-uniform predictive encoder and decoder and applied their proposed algorithm in an image compression example.

A quick look into the reviewed related work shows that these researches were focused on two areas: firstly how *LCS* reduces the unnecessary samples to have a good enough signal reconstruction; and secondly how to reconstruct the original signal from the *LCS* based samples.

LCS Problem Statement

LCS is a sampling method based on sampling the signal at a fixed set of amplitudes values in time, as shown in Figure 1b. *LCS* involves challenging design issues such as selection of the number of levels and their corresponding values. These factors are critical for determining the accuracy of reconstructing the signals from its samples as well as estimating the average communication cost. In addition, a key constraint is the maximum number of levels that is physically possible to use in the hardware-constrained low-cost wireless sensors. Hence, we focus on the analysis of *LCS* with arbitrary level spacing in order to meet the requirements of signal reconstruction error, average sampling rate, and maximum number of levels. We first obtain the optimum set of levels that minimize the mean square error (*MSE*) between the reconstructed signal and the original signal, which are obtained from knowledge of the probability density function (*pdf*) of the bandlimited stationary signal. We show that, for a specified number of levels, the *pdf*–aware *LCS* with optimum levels results in less reconstruction *MSE* than that with uniform *LCS*. We then propose a μ-law based non-uniform *LCS* that is similar in concept to the μ-law based level selection scheme (Sayood, 2000). The proposed μ-law based *LCS* can be designed under some basic assumptions on the characteristics of the signal.

The concept of *LCS* in comparison to periodic sampling is illustrated in Figure 1b. In *LCS*, the signal is sampled at the points at which the signal crosses *M* predefined levels $\left\{\ell_i\right\}_{i=1}^{M}$. Consequently, sampling instances in *LCS* are no longer uniform, but are determined by the characteristics of the signal itself. Also, unlike periodic sampling there is no concrete mechanism for perfect reconstruction of the original signal for *LCS* using non-iterative methods. In this chapter, we assume a piece-wise constant or the zero-order-spline reconstruction of the signal. This is equivalent to a level-crossing sample and hold (*LCSH*) operation from the level crossing samples of the signal (see Figure 1b). *LCSH* is the flat-top reconstruction of the signal from its *LCS* based samples. This simple method, although not as fine as reconstruction methods that use higher order splines, allows us to get a good enough solution for the *MSE*.

The reconstruction error signal between the *LCSH* and original signals is defined by:

$$\varepsilon_S(t) = S(t) - \hat{S}(t) \tag{1}$$

where $S(t)$ is the original signal and $\hat{S}(t)$ is *LCSH* with level-crossing set $\{\ell_i\}_{i=1}^{M}$ at time instance *t*. Because of the stochastic behavior of the signal and its samples, the error power changes randomly with time. The *MSE* is then given by:

$$E[\varepsilon_S^2(t)] = \int_{-\infty}^{\infty} \varepsilon_S^2(t) f_\varepsilon(\varepsilon; t) d\varepsilon \tag{2}$$

where $f_\varepsilon(\varepsilon; t)$ is the *pdf* of the error signal at time instance *t*. Our objective is to minimize the *MSE* by better tracking of the dynamics of the signal, which can be obtained by appropriate selection of the levels. Note that the average number of samples obtained from *LCS* also depends on the chosen sampling levels, which we address later.

Error Analysis

The reconstruction *MSE* in (2) can be rewritten as:where $E[\varepsilon_{S,i}^2(t)]$ is the *MSE* between level ℓ_i and ℓ_{i-1}, and p_i is the probability that the signal resides inside level-interval ℓ_i and ℓ_{i-1}, $i = 1, 2, \ldots, M$.

The marginal *pdf* of the signal between each two neighboring levels is:

Note that at upward crossing of the signal at level ℓ_i (see Figure 2), *LCSH* takes value ℓ_i until the signal crosses ℓ_{i+1} and the error will be $\varepsilon_{S,i}(t) = S(t) - \ell_i$. When the signal crosses downwards at the level ℓ_{i+1} and resides between levels ℓ_i and ℓ_{i+1}, the error will be $\varepsilon_{S,i}(t) = S(t) - \ell_{i+1}$. Based on this observation we write:

$$f_{\varepsilon,i}(\varepsilon) = f_{\varepsilon,i}(\varepsilon \mid \text{up-crossing}).\ \Pr(\text{up-crossing}) + f_{\varepsilon,i}(\varepsilon \mid \text{down-crossing})\ .\ \Pr(\text{down-crossing}) \tag{6}$$

Hence (3) can be written as:

(7)

Simplifying (7) leads to (8):

$$E[\varepsilon_S^2(t)] = \int_{\ell_0}^{\ell_1} (\ell_1 - s)^2 f_S(s)\ ds + \int_{\ell_M}^{\ell_{M+1}} (\ell_M - s)^2 f_S(s)\ ds + \sum_{i=2}^{M} \frac{1}{2} \left\{ \int_{\ell_{i-1}}^{\ell_i} (\ell_{i-1} - s)^2 f_S(s) + (\ell_i - s)^2 f_S(s)\ ds \right\} \tag{8}$$

which gives the *MSE* for an arbitrary set of levels.

Optimizing Levels for Minimizing MSE

We now obtain the solution to the optimum set of levels which leads to the minimal *MSE* by setting the partial derivatives of *MSE* for all ℓ_i to zero, according to equation (9). It should be noted that *MSE* is a continuous function in the valid domain of the levels $\{\ell_i\}_{i=1}^{M}$ and the

Figure 2. Illustration of error between signal and LCSH

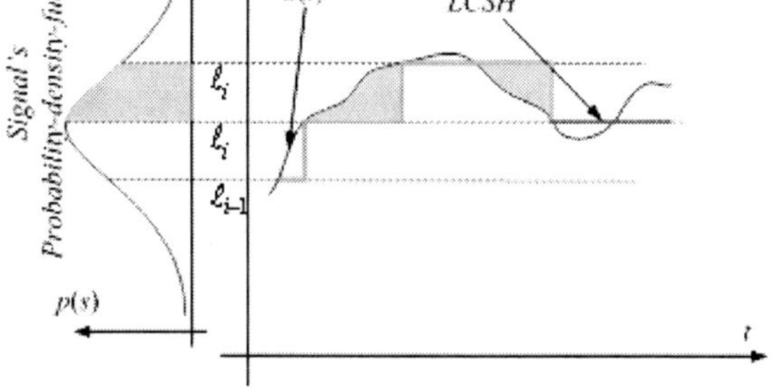

global minima of *MSE* is one of the solutions of equation (9).

$$\frac{\partial E[\varepsilon_S^2(t)]}{\partial \ell_i} = 0, \quad 1 \le i \le M \tag{9}$$

This results in M simultaneous non-linear integral equations, as follows:

$$\ell_1 = \frac{\int_{\ell_0}^{\ell_1} x\, f_S(x)\, dx + \int_{\ell_0}^{\ell_2} x\, f_S(x)\, dx + \frac{1}{2} f_S(\ell_1)(\ell_2 - \ell_1)^2}{\int_{\ell_0}^{\ell_1} f_S(x)\, dx + \int_{\ell_0}^{\ell_2} f_S(x)\, dx} \tag{10}$$

$$\ell_i = \frac{\int_{\ell_{i-1}}^{\ell_{i+1}} x\, f_S(x)\, dx}{\int_{\ell_{i-1}}^{\ell_{i+1}} f_S(x)\, dx}, \quad 1 < i < M$$

$$\ell_M = \frac{\int_{\ell_M}^{\ell_{M+1}} x\, f_S(x)\, dx + \int_{\ell_{M-1}}^{\ell_{M+1}} x\, f_S(x)\, dx - \frac{1}{2} f_S(\ell_M)(\ell_M - \ell_{M-1})^2}{\int_{\ell_M}^{\ell_{M+1}} f_S(x)\, dx + \int_{\ell_{M-1}}^{\ell_{M+1}} f_S(x)\, dx}$$

Note that (10) indicates that the optimal set of levels is such that each level is located at the ensemble mean value of the signal between its two immediate neighboring levels. These equations can be solved numerically, for instance by using an iterative approach. For the details concerning the derivation of (10) see appendix A.

Proposed μ-law Based Approach

It is obvious that derivation of the optimum levels as described above requires knowledge of the *pdf* of the signal. In the absence of such information, we propose a sub-optimal *LCS* scheme where the non-uniform sampling levels are chosen under the assumption that the signal *pdf* is unimodal and symmetric, with the peak of the *pdf* lying at the mean value of the signal distribution. This is a valid assumption for most realistic signals, and allows us to define non-uniform sampling levels that are more concentrated near the mean of the signal distribution, and hence, expected to capture the dynamics of the signal more effectively than uniform *LCS*. We propose to use a μ-law based levels $\{\mu_i\}_{i=1}^{M}$ as defined below, which are based on standard μ-law expansion formula used for non-uniform quantization in pulse code modulation (*PCM*) (Sayood, 2000).

$$U_i = \frac{2\left(\frac{\ell_{M+1} - \ell_0}{M} i + \ell_0 - \frac{\ell_{M+1} + \ell_0}{2}\right)}{\ell_{M+1} - \ell_0}$$

$$\mu_i = \left[\frac{\operatorname{sgn}(U_i)}{\mu}\left[(1+U_i)^{\mu} - 1\right]\right] \frac{\ell_{M+1} - \ell_0}{2} + \frac{\ell_{M+1} + \ell_0}{2}, \quad i = 1,2,\ldots,M \tag{11}$$

In this equation U_i is the *i*th uniform level and ℓ_0 and ℓ_{M+1} are the expected lower and upper bounds within the range of the signal.

Level-Crossing Sampling Design Problem

According to the general non-uniform sampling theorem, the required sample volume for unique representation of a bandlimited signal should not be less than the *Nyquist* rate (Marvasti, 2001). Then assuming M sampling levels, the average *LCS* rate R_{LCS} should be more than twice of the bandwidth (*BW*) of the signal. Rice extensively studied the behavior of filtered Gaussian noise and formulated a set of important parameters (Rice, 1945). Level crossing rate as the rate at which the signal meets a specific amplitude level is one of these parameters. According to Rice's results and the general non-uniform sampling theorem, the mean level crossing sampling rate of the signal *x* at the sampling levels $\{\ell_i\}_{i=1}^{M}$ should satisfy equation (12).

$$R_{LCS} = \sum_{i=1}^{M} \int_{-\infty}^{\infty} |x'| \, f(x' \mid x = \ell_i) \, d\,|x'| \quad > \quad 2\,BW \tag{12}$$

Specifically for Gaussian signal, equation (12) is simplified to equation (13).

$$R_{LCS} = \sum_{i=1}^{M} \frac{1}{\pi} \sqrt{\frac{-R''(0)}{R(0)}} \quad \exp(-\frac{\ell_i^2}{2R^2(0)}) \quad > \quad 2\,BW \tag{13}$$

Equation (13) is in term of the autocorrelation function of the signal and the second order derivative of this function. It can be simplified by using the definition of the *rms* bandwidth of the signal. By using the definition of *rms* bandwidth (BW_{rms}) according to (14) (Gardner, 1990), and then using the definition of the autocorrelation function of the signal $R_X(t)$ according to equation (15), equation (14) will change to (16) that clearly shows the term of BW_{rms} in equation (13).

$$BW_{rms} = \sqrt{\frac{\int_{-\infty}^{\infty} f^2 S_X(f) df}{\int_{-\infty}^{\infty} S_X(f) df}} \tag{14}$$

$$R_X(t) = \int_{-\infty}^{\infty} S_X(f) \ \exp(j2\pi f t) \ df \tag{15}$$

$$BW_{rms} = \sqrt{\frac{\frac{-1}{4\pi^2} R''(0)}{R(0)}} = \frac{1}{2\pi} \sqrt{\frac{-R''(0)}{R(0)}} \tag{16}$$

Accordingly, the average level crossing rate is connected to the BW_{rms} as follows:

$$R_{LCS} = 2BW_{rms} \sum_{i=1}^{M} \ \exp(-\frac{\ell_i^2}{2\sigma^2}) \tag{17}$$

In equation (17), σ is the standard deviation of the Gaussian signal. According to the general non-uniform sampling theorem, R_{LCS} should be greater than the average *Nyquist* sampling rate,

$$BW_{rms} \sum_{i=1}^{M} \ \exp(-\frac{\ell_i^2}{2\sigma^2}) \ > BW \tag{18}$$

Then, normalized average level-crossing rate should satisfy equation (19).

$$\overline{R}_{LCS} = \sum_{i=1}^{M} \ \exp(-\frac{\ell_i^2}{2\sigma^2}) \ > \frac{BW}{BW_{rms}} \tag{19}$$

For simplicity, by approximating the power spectral density of the signal with flat-top spectra according to (20), the relationship between BW_{rms} and the signal's bandwidth is simplified to $BW_{rms} = \frac{1}{\sqrt{3}} BW$.

$$S(f) = \begin{cases} L & |f| \le BW \\ 0 & \text{otherwise} \end{cases} \tag{20}$$

Accordingly, the average *LCS* rate in terms of the signal's bandwidth and the selected set of levels is calculated according to (21).

$$R_{LCS} = \frac{2}{\sqrt{3}} BW \sum_{i=1}^{M} \ \exp(-\frac{\ell_i^2}{2\sigma^2}) \tag{21}$$

Then the levels $\{\ell_i\}_{i=1}^{M}$ should be chosen so that normalized level crossing sampling rate as defined in (22), becomes larger than the specified limit in (22).

$$\bar{R}_{LCS} = \frac{R_{LCS}}{BW} = \sum_{i=1}^{M} \exp(-\frac{\ell_i^2}{2\sigma^2}) > \sqrt{3} \quad (22)$$

LCS Design Examples

The problem is finding a set of sampling levels $\{\ell_i\}_{i=1}^{M}$ which satisfy equation (22). For this the following statements are assumed:

- The signal is bandlimited, stationary Gaussian $N(0,1)$
- The dynamic range of the signal is assumed to be known
- The power spectral density function of the signal is assumed to be flat-top

Case 1: *LCS* Using Uniformly Spaced Levels

In the signal dynamic range interval $(\frac{-\Delta}{2}, \frac{\Delta}{2})$, the M uniformly spaced level

$$U_i \ , \ U_i = -\frac{\Delta}{2} + (i-1)\frac{\Delta}{M-1} \quad , \quad i = 1,2,\ldots,M$$

should be chosen so that it satisfies equation (22).

For this, M should be found so that:

$$\bar{R}_{LCS} = \sum_{i=1}^{M} \exp(-\frac{(-\frac{\Delta}{2} + (i-1)\frac{\Delta}{M-1})^2}{2}) > \sqrt{3} \quad (23)$$

Case 2: *LCS* Using μ-Law Based Levels

For μ-law based *LCS*, the levels are defined according to (11) and for that, the minimum number of acceptable sampling levels *M*, which satisfies the proper sampling criteria should be chosen so that:

$$\bar{R}_{LCS} = \sum_{i=1}^{M} \exp(-\frac{\left\{\left[\frac{\mathrm{sgn}(U_i)}{\mu}\left[(1+U_i)^{\mu} - 1\right]\right]\frac{\Delta}{2}\right\}^2}{2}) > \sqrt{3} \quad (24)$$

As a result, we conclude that the number of sampling levels for proper *LCS* sampling using uniform and μ-law based *LCS* should be at least 8 and 5, respectively. This result is illustrated in Figure 3.

Minimum Sampling Period for Proper *LCS* Using Periodic Sampler

For applications where sensors have already been designed for periodic sampling, adjusting sampling period for *LCS* and discarding the irrelevant samples so that the sampler in consecutive sampling instances does not miss any sampling levels is important. In the rest of this section, periodic sampling rate issue for implementation of *LCS* is discussed. Selection of the sampling period is a function of the instantaneous slope of the signal.

As signal changes randomly with time, we need to use the statistical characteristics of the signal. If the minimum spacing between the two neighboring sampling levels is $d_{\min}$ and the sampling period is δ (see Figure 4), the maximum sampling slope should satisfy equation (25).

$$|S_{Max}| < \frac{d_{\min}}{\delta} \quad (25)$$

With Gaussian assumption, the instantaneous slope will be Gaussian too. It is known from basic probability that the zero mean Gaussian random variable x with standard deviation σ_x with probability of 99.95 percent is in the interval $(-4\sigma_x \ , \ 4\sigma_x)$. Similarly, with the same probability the slope of the Gaussian signal is in the in-

Figure 3. Normalized level crossing rate for uniform and μ-law LCS

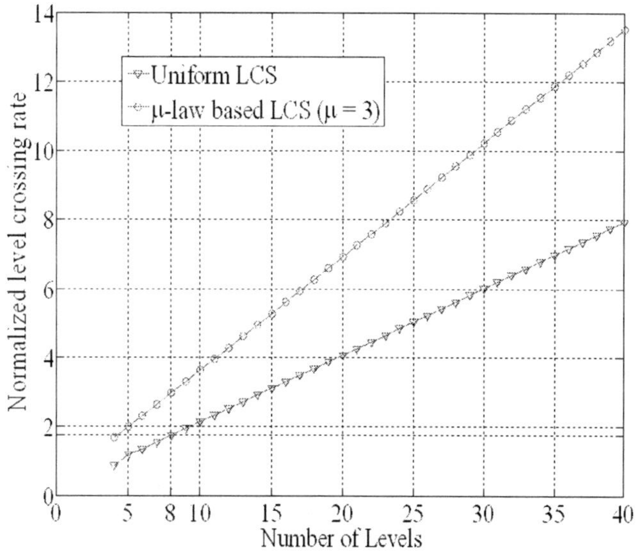

terval $(-4\sigma_{x'}, 4\sigma_{x'})$, where $\sigma_{x'}$ is the standard deviation of the slope of the Gaussian signal x. With this approximation and by using equation (25), δ is bounded as shown in (26).

$$\delta < \frac{d_{min}}{4\sigma_{x'}} \quad (26)$$

For simplification again let us assume that the signal has a bandlimited flat-top power spectral density like $S(f)$ in (20). Then there is the following relationship between the standard deviation of the signal and its slope:

Figure 4. Schematic of the LCS when sampler probes the signal periodically

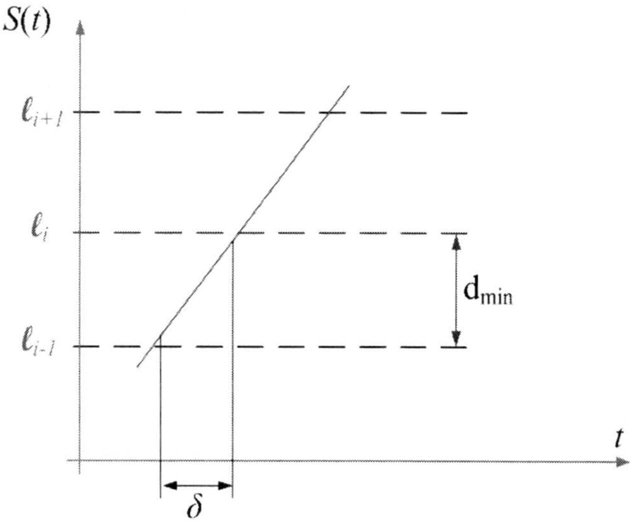

$$\sigma_{x'}^2 = \frac{(2\pi \ BW)^2}{3} \sigma_x^2 \tag{27}$$

By using (26) and (27), the minimum sampling period δ should not be more than the specified limit in equation (28).

$$\delta < \frac{d_{\min}}{4\sigma_{x'}} = \frac{\sqrt{3}\ d_{\min}}{8\pi \ BW} \frac{1}{\sigma_x} \tag{28}$$

NUMERICAL AND EXPERIMENTAL RESULTS

In this section, we first evaluate the performance of the *LCS* based sampling and compare the reconstruction error with *LCSH* and cardinal spline for the three *LCS* schemes using simulations and numerical analysis. The performance evaluation also includes the trade-off issue between the reconstruction performance and the sampling cost of *LCS*. These computer simulations were performed using MATLAB. Later, we present experimental results of implementation of *LCS* based sampling using *MICAz* wireless sensor platforms. Experimental results were first obtained during the turn on and turn off process of the home's AC fan from which we get comparative performance results of different *LCS* schemes in temperature sensing.

Numerical Results

To evaluate the performance of the *LCS* schemes, we use computer simulations to determine their reconstruction *MSE* and average sampling rate obtained for a temporally sparsed (bursty) Gaussian signal, using three level-definition schemes: uniformly spaced levels, the proposed μ-law based levels, and the optimal set of levels as obtained from solving the equations in (10). For these simulations, we use a bursty Gaussian signal that is generated by adding 50 sinusoids with random amplitudes and frequencies in the range of the assumed bandwidth. We use an activity factor of 0.1, which implies that the signal has no variations for 90% of the time. The amplitude of the random signal is normalized, and its average power σ_x^2 is obtained numerically in the simulations.

Optimal μ

We first investigate the effect of μ on the reconstruction *MSE* obtained with the proposed μ-law based *LCS* scheme. First, we investigated the variation of the reconstruction *MSE* (with *LCSH*) using the μ-law based *LCS* versus μ, for different numbers of levels *M* for the synthetic Gaussian signal. It is observed that for correlated Gaussian signal the lowest reconstruction *MSE* is obtained for $\mu = 3.5$ for all *M*. On all subsequent performance evaluations we use this value in μ-law based *LCS*.

Reconstruction Error

Reconstruction error and sampling rate (cost) are two constraints in the *LCS* design problem. Selection of the levels based on (22) implicitly implies that the samples will uniquely represent the signal. However, sampling below the Nyquist rate is also desirable when the cost is a critical constraint of the problem and the reconstruction error will not be high. Study of the reconstruction error in terms of the number of levels for different level definition schemes can be a good approach to study the effect of under and over *Nyquist* sampling on reconstruction error.

In the previous section, after a few theoretical assumptions, the relationship between the minimum sampling rate and the set of levels was inspected.

In this section the effect of three level definition schemes on the reconstruction error of the bandlimited Gaussian signal is inspected. Figure 5, illustrates the reconstruction *MSE* of *LCS* using *LCSH* for these level definition schemes:

uniformly spaced levels, μ-law based levels, and optimal levels based on (9) using numerical analysis and simulations. The reason for using *LCSH* is that firstly, the optimal levels are designed based on minimizing the error when this *LCSH* is used and secondly, it is also good to compare the reconstruction error of the other level definition schemes with the reconstruction error of the optimal scheme. As this figure shows, the reconstruction error of μ-law based *LCS* for any specific number of levels is between optimal and uniform *LCS.*

We next evaluate the reconstruction *MSE*s of the three level selection schemes for the bandlimited Gaussian signal described above. For each scheme, the reconstruction is performed by passing the samples through cardinal spline (Greitans & Shavelis, 2007) with adapted tension. The corresponding *MSE*s obtained for different values of *M* using computer simulations are shown in Figure 5.

The results show that the reconstruction *MSE* obtained using the proposed μ-law based levels is very close to the optimum reconstruction *MSE*, particularly at higher values of *M*. For any desired *MSE*, the μ-law based *LCS* requires much fewer numbers of levels than *LCS* with uniform levels. For instance, to get reconstruction error equal to *MSE*=0.3×10^{-2}, the number of sampling levels required with uniform levels is 34, whereas it can be achieved with only 19 levels and 15 levels using μ-law based and optimum levels, respectively.

The comparison of the required number of levels required with the different level selection schemes for various *MSE* values is depicted on the left side of Figure 6. Note that fewer numbers of levels do not necessarily imply a lower average sampling rate, as depicted by the sampling efficiencies of the three *LCS* schemes for different *MSE* values that are plotted on the right side of Figure 6. In this figure, the sampling efficiency (γ) is $\gamma = \frac{R_{Nyquist}}{R_{LCS}}$ where $R_{Nyquist}$ and R_{LCS} are the *Nyquist* and average *LCS* sampling rate, respectively. In fact, Figure 6 indicates that selection of uniform levels is most efficient in terms of the average sampling rate. However, this is achieved by using a larger number of levels. So, it may be concluded that "when the number of sampling levels can be high enough, uniform *LCS* which

Figure 5. Reconstruction error of LCSH and Cardinal spline with adapted tension for the three schemes: uniform, μ-law based and optimal LCS

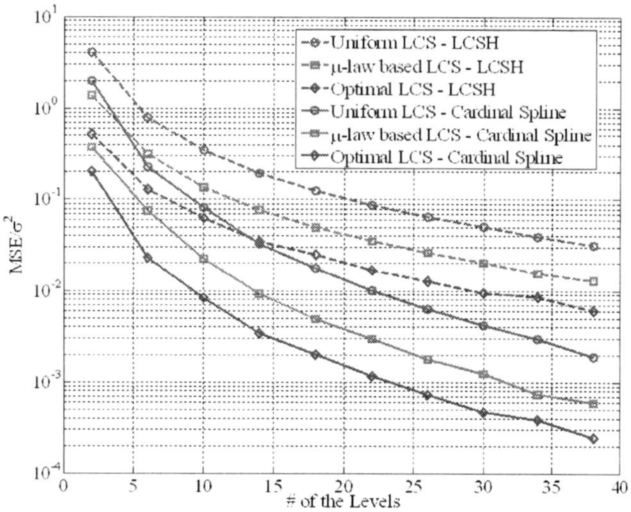

leads to the highest sampling efficiency is the most appropriate level definition scheme".

Experimental Validation and Evaluation of *LCS*

To experimentally investigate the efficiency of *LCS* and compare it with periodic sampling, three *LCS* schemes were implemented with the *MICAz* wireless sensor platform from *Crossbow Technology Inc* (Crossbow, 2010).

Wireless Sensor Platform

The *MICAz* is an Atmel based 8-bit ATMega128L wireless platform that contains a 2.4GHz IEEE 802.15.4 (Gutierrez et al, 2004) compliant RF transceiver and 4KB of RAM. The *MICAz* motes run on TinyOS, which is an open source operating system specifically designed for embedded sensor network devices (Crossbow, 2010). It features various component libraries that include sensor drivers along with network protocols (Levis & Gay, 2009). Since *TinyOS* is open source, it is possible to extend the functionality of the pre-distributed drivers to meet the needs of the developer.

Sensing Board

The *MDA320* data acquisition board (*DAQ*) that is mounted on the *MICAz* along with a simple resistive temperature device (*RTD*) board with 2 *RTD*s was used for temperature sensing. The sensed voltage was launched to one of the A/D inputs of *MDA320 DAQ*. The *MDA320CA* is designed as a general measurement platform for the *MICAz* and *MICA2*. It has eight single ended analog-to-digital input channels, three differential analog channels, eight digital input channels, and one counter channel.

To appropriately sense and sample the temperature, it was oversampled at 1 Min interval sampling periods. Whenever the samples cross any of the levels, the new sample value was sent to the base station, provided the previous crossed level and the recent one are not the same.

Figure 6. The required number of levels and the sampling efficiency for different MSE in performance comparison of different LCS schemes after Cardinal spline filtering

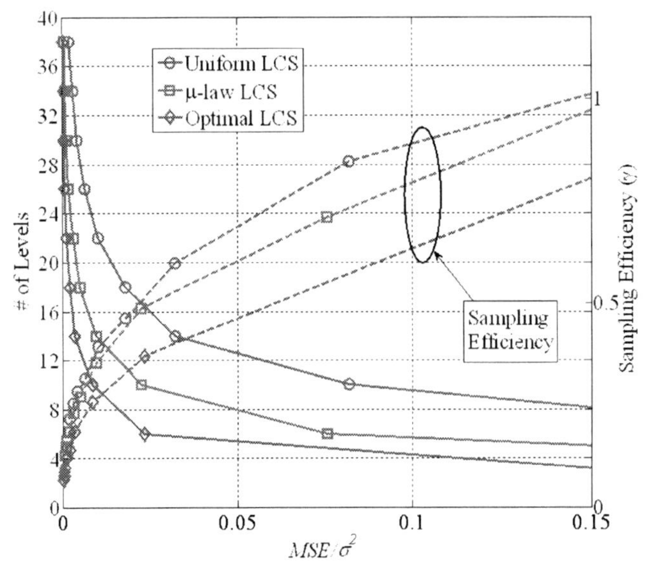

Test Scenario

To experimentally study the effect of different level definition schemes on the sampling efficiency of *LCS*, three types of levels for sensing temperature in the range of 20 to 60 degree Celsius were defined. Three wireless sensor nodes were programmed for sampling based on *LCS* using each of these three types of levels. These three nodes sensed the outside temperature of an AC compressor fan. To compare the performance and the cost of the *LCS* schemes to periodic sampling, a fourth node with the same parts was programmed to sense the temperature periodically with period of 1 minute.

The sampled data was sent to the base-station which had a *MICAz* mote as base-station, a *MIB520* as gateway which was connected to a computer through a USB cable, and, xlisten, the open source data logger, and a computer. The network used XMESH (Powell & Shim, 2009) protocol over IEEE 802.15.4 physical and data link layer protocol. The three sets of levels were defined based on the following three schemes:

A- Uniform LCS: Based on the previous analysis, for sampling a normalized Gaussian temperature, at least 8 uniformly spaced levels are required. This result is valid for a normalized Gaussian temperature, the dynamic range of which is approximately 10. For sampling the temperature with Gaussian statistics in the range of 40 degrees with the same sampling precision, the number of levels should be 4 times more, which means 32 levels.

B- μ-law based LCS: We showed that for uniquely representing the normalized Gaussian signal based on its samples from *LCS*, the number of sampling levels in μ-law scheme should not be less than 5. For sampling in the selected temperature range (20 °C to 60 °C) with the same justification of part A, the number of levels should not be less than 20.

C- Mixed Mode Sensing LCS: In behavioral study and monitoring of a phenomenon, the usual variation range of the quantities is not very interesting and it is normally preferred to focus on the critical ranges. With this assumption, to study the effect of high temperatures with good accuracy, the variation range of temperature was divided into two parts: 20 °C to 40 °C as the normal variation range, and 40 °C to 60 °C as the critical sampling range. The normal variation range was sampled with uniformly spaced *LCS* with coarse levels, and the critical sensing range was sampled with oversampled μ-law based *LCS*. The number of levels in the uniform *LCS* and μ-law based *LCS* were chosen 4 and 12, respectively.

Measurement Results

The plot of the number of the received packets is shown in Figure 7. The figure shows how *LCS* trades off between the performance and cost. The summary of the results from the figure are:

- When the bandwidth of the signal is not known exactly, but the amplitude range is known, *LCS* based sampling help to reduce the sampling cost. This result is very helpful for sampling of roughly known signals using wireless sensor networks.
- The reconstruction performance of *LCS* using μ-law based levels leads to better reconstruction performance in comparison to uniform and the mixed mode *LCS*, provided the number of levels is chosen appropriately, the mean value of the signal is known exactly and proper μ value is selected.

To compare the sampling performance of the introduced schemes, cardinal spline with adapted tension is used. Periodically oversampled signal is used as the reference and the sampling error is

Figure 7. The number of the received packets in different scenarios

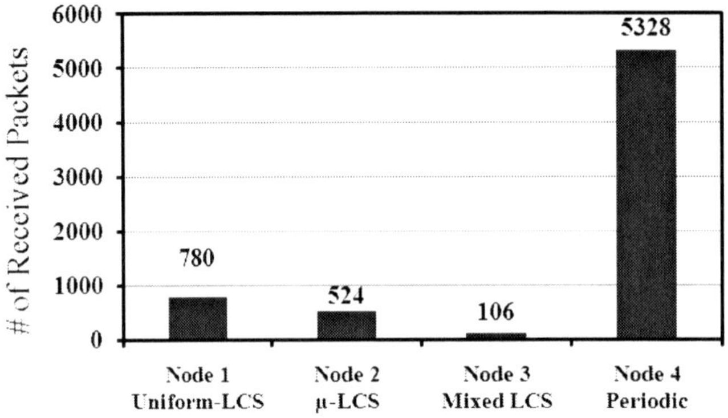

found after that interpolation of the spline curve is fitted. Accordingly, the error at time t_i is calculated based on the equation (29). In (29) ΔT is the period of the periodic samples S_p.

$$e(t_i) = | S_{LCS}(t_i) - S_P(t_n) | \quad , \qquad n = \arg\min | t_i - n\Delta T | \tag{29}$$

To compare the quality of the signal after Cardinal spline reconstruction from the *LCS* based samples of the three introduced schemes, the root mean square of error (*RMSE*) was calculated. From these calculations, the *RMSE* of the μ-law based *LCS* and Mixed mode *LCS* were 1.26 and 3.11 times larger than that of *RMSE* of Uniform *LCS*. Based on these results, μ-law based *LCS* and uniform *LCS* have almost the same performance and the mixed mode sensing has the highest error. For this comparison, the *RMSE* is calculated from (30).

$$RMSE = \sqrt{\frac{1}{t_{end} - t_0} \int_{t_0}^{t_{end}} e^2(t)dt} \tag{30}$$

BATTERY CONSUMPTION AND LIFETIME CALCULATIONS

To study the energy usage of wireless sensor network, a basic approach for performing the analytical calculations of average energy consumption in a wireless sensor node is measurement of its current consumption under various activity periods or events (such as packet transmit, receive, sense, etc.) and then determining the occurrences of each of these events at the node under the assumed network characteristics. These events are packet transmission, packet reception by all *N* related neighbors, route update packet transmission and receptions, and channel sensing process. Practically, in a wireless sensor network with standard XMESH protocol, *N* = 7. The amount of current consumption for these events and their duration are reported in (EPRI, 2008; Alasti, 2009). Table 1 shows the approximate duration of each of these activities from this reference.

Using these data, the current consumption in the *MICAz* mote with mounted *MDA320 DAQ* is estimated from equation (31) where I_x and T_x represent the current drawn and the duration of an event *x*, respectively, as listed in Table 1, and I_{RUI} and T_D represent the route update interval (*RUI*) and data transmit intervals used, respectively (Nasipuri et al, 2010).

$$I = I_{R_t} \frac{T_{R_t}}{T_{RUI}} + I_{D_t} \frac{T_{D_t}}{T_D} + N(I_{R_r} \frac{T_{R_r}}{T_{RUI}} + I_{D_r} \frac{T_{D_r}}{T_D}) + I_S \frac{T_S}{T_{D_t}} + 8I_P T_P \tag{31}$$

Table 1. MICAz mote in the temperature sensing application (EPRI, 2008)

Event	Current (mA)	Duration (ms)
Route update transmit R_t	27	180
Route update receive R_r	20	180
Data transmit D_t	27	185
Data receive D_r	20	185
Sensing S	10	10
Processing P	8	3

With these assumptions the estimated battery life of the working wireless sensors for the three discussed *LCS* based sampling schemes (uniform, μ-law, and mixed modes) are illustrated in Figure 8. In this graph the route-update is 2 hours and the sampling period is 15 Min. In the network, nodes with periodic sampling scheme sample and transmit their observations every 15 minutes and the *LCS* based nodes sample every 15 minutes and transmit if any of the level is crossed within 15 minutes. In this figure, it is assumed that each of the wireless sensors uses a 5000 mAH battery.

Figure 8 shows that the battery life of wireless sensors with uniform and μ-law *LCS* are at least 2.7 times more than the battery life of the nodes with periodic sampling. It also shows that the battery life of the nodes with μ-law *LCS* is more than the ones with uniform *LCS*, which conflicts with the result obtained in the numerical results section. This is due to two reasons: firstly, the statistical distribution of the sampled quantity was not Gaussian and the assumed μ was not proper; secondly, the mean value of the sampled quantity was unknown and was selected approximately.

CONCLUSION

A *LCS* design framework for application in wireless sensor networks in pervasive computing environment is proposed and discussed in this chapter. The optimum set of levels to have the minimum reconstruction error is investigated. μ-law based *LCS* is proposed that unlike optimal *LCS* which needs the *pdf* of the signal, needs only a few of the signal's statistics. The reconstruction error of the *LCS* based samples of correlated normalized Gaussian signals with sample and hold reconstructor is achieved numerically and using computer simulations for optimal, μ-law based, and uniform *LCS*.

The minimum required number of levels for uniquely representing the *LCS* based sampled signal is investigated. It is shown that under certain conditions, the minimum required number of levels is independent from the spectral characteristics of the signal.

The minimum required periodic sampling rate for *LCS* based sampling is obtained on the characteristics of the signal. It is shown that this rate is proportional to the bandwidth, the power of the signal and the minimum spacing between the levels.

The reconstruction error and the cost of *LCS* based sampling with uniform, μ-law based and a mixture of these two schemes is experimentally tested and compared with periodic sampling. It is shown that the performance of μ-law based sampling is poorer than that of uniform *LCS* after cardinal spline, but uniform *LCS* has a slightly higher cost. This result does not match with the numerically achieved result which can be attributed to the difference between the statistics of the signal and the assumptions such as poor estimation of the statistical mode of the signal's distribution. Mixed mode *LCS* is applied by simultaneously using uniform and μ-law based *LCS* on two different ranges. The experimental results showed that the mixed mode *LCS* has much smaller cost in

Figure 8. Estimation of the battery-life for the three LCS based sampling schemes

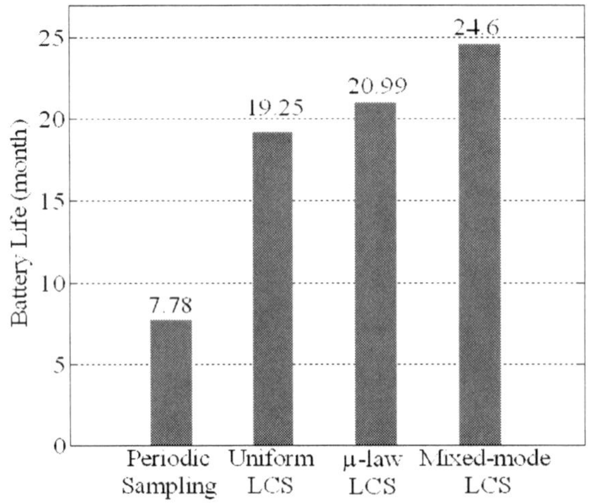

comparison to the uniform and μ-law based *LCS* schemes, but it has higher reconstruction error.

Comparison between the battery-life of the *MICAz* nodes with *LCS* based sampling and periodic sampling in the network shows that *LCS* is able to dramatically increase the network lifetime.

ACKNOWLEDGMENT

The author wants to appreciate Dr. Apostolos Malatras, the Editor of the book and also the unknown reviewers for the valuable correcting comments on this chapter. The author likes to thank Professor Asis Nasipuri for his correcting comments, supports and enlightening discussions.

REFERENCES

Akyildiz, I. F., Su, W., Sankarasubramaniam, Y., & Cayirci, E. (2001). Wireless sensor networks: A survey. *Elsevier Journal of Computer Networks*, *38*(4), 393–422. doi:10.1016/S1389-1286(01)00302-4

Alasti, H. (2009). *Level based sampling techniques for energy conservation in large scale wireless sensor networks*. Unpublished doctoral dissertation, University of North Carolina, Charlotte.

Crossbow. (2010). *Crossbow Technology, Inc. official website*. Retrieved July 5, 2010 from http://www.xbow.com

EPRI report. (2008). *Substation-wide monitoring through applications of networked wireless sensor devices- phase-II: Scalability and sustainability studies*.

Gardner, W. A. (1990). *Introduction to random processes: With applications to signals and systems*. New York, NY: McGraw-Hill.

Greitans, M. (2006). Processing of non-stationary signals using level-crossing sampling. In *Proceedings of International Conference on Signal Processing and Multimedia Applications*, (pp. 170-177).

Greitans, M., & Shavelis, R. (2007). Speech sampling by level-crossing and its reconstruction using spline-based filtering. In *Proceedings of EURASIP Conference on Speech and Image Processing, Multimedia Communications and Services* (pp. 292-295), Maribor, Slovenia.

Guan, K. M., Kozat, S. S., & Singer, A. C. (2008). Adaptive reference levels in a level-crossing analog-to-digital converter. *EURASIP Journal of Advances in Signal Processing*.

Guan, K. M., & Singer, A. C. (2006). A level-crossing sampling scheme for non-bandlimited signals. In *Proceedings of International Conference on Acoustic, Speech and Signal processing*: *Vol. 3*, (pp. 381-83). Toulouse, France.

Guan, K. M., & Singer, A. C. (2007). Opportunistic sampling by level-crossing. In *Proceedings of IEEE international conference on acoustic, speech and signal processing (ICASSP '07)*: Vol 3, (pp. 1513-1516). Honolulu, Hawaii.

Gutierrez, J. A., Callaway, E. H., & Barrett, R. L. (2004). *IEEE 802.15.4 low-rate wireless personal area networks: Enabling wireless sensor networks. Standard Information Network*. IEEE Press.

Jea, D., Yap, I. S., & Srivastava, M. B. (2007). *Context-aware access to public shared devices*. Presented at the First International Workshop on Systems and Networking Support for Health Care and Assisted Living Environments.

Levis, P., & Gay, D. (2009). *TinyOS programming*. Edinburgh, UK: Cambridge University Press. doi:10.1017/CBO9780511626609

Lin, C. K., Jea, D., Dabiri, F., Massey, T., Tan, R., Sarrafzadeh, M., et al. Montemagno, C. (2007). *The development of an in-vivo active pressure monitoring system*. Presented at the 4th International Workshop on Wearable and Implantable Body Sensor Networks.

Mark, J. W., & Todd, T. D. (1982). A nonuniform sampling approach to data compression. *IEEE Transactions on Communications*, *29*, 24–32. doi:10.1109/TCOM.1981.1094872

Marvasti, F. (Ed.). (2001). *Nonuniform sampling: Theory and practice*. New York, NY: Kluwer Academic.

Miskovicz, M. (2006). Efficiency of level-crossing sampling for bandlimited Gaussian random process. In *Proceedings of IEEE International Workshop on Factory Communication Systems*, (pp. 137-142). ANIPLA-Torino.

Nasipuri, A., Alasti, H., Puthran, P. H., Cox, R., Conrad, J. M., Van der Zel, L., et al. Graziano, J. (2010). *Vibration sensing for equipment's health monitoring in power substations using wireless sensor*. Presented at IEEE Southeastcon, Charlotte, NC.

Nasipuri, A., Cox, R., Alasti, H., Van der Zel, L., Rodriguez, B., McKosky, R., & Graziano, J. A. (2008). *Wireless sensor network for substation monitoring: design and deployment*. Demo presented at Sensys, Raleigh, NC.

Powell, S., & Shim, J. P. (2009). *Wireless technology: Applications, management, and security (Lecture Notes in Electrical Engineering)*. Springer.

Qaisar, S. M., Fesquet, L., & Renaudin, M. (2007). Adaptive rate filtering for a signal driven sampling scheme. In *Proceedings of IEEE International Conference on Acoustic, Speech and Signal processing*: *Vol. 3*, (pp. 1465-1468).

Qaisar, S. M., Fesquet, L., & Renaudin, M. (2009). An adaptive resolution computationally efficient short-time Fourier transforms. *EURASIP. Research Letters in Signal Processing*, 12.

Rice, R. O. (1945). Mathematical analysis of random noise. *The Bell System Technical Journal*, *24*, 46–156.

Sayiner, N., Sorensen, H. V., & Viswanathan, T. R. (1996). A level-crossing sampling scheme for A/D conversion. *IEEE Transactions on Circuits and Systems*, *43*, 335–339. doi:10.1109/82.488288

Sayood, K. (2000). *Introduction to data compression*. San Francisco, CA: Morgan Kaufmann.

Sichitiu, M. (2004). *Cross-layer scheduling for power efficiency in wireless sensor networks.* Paper presented at IEEE INFOCOM, Hong Kong.

Singer, A. C., & Guan, K. M. (2007). Opportunistic sampling of bursty signals by level-crossing – an information theoretical approach. In *Proceeding of Conference on Information Science and Systems*, (pp. 701-707). Baltimore, MD.

Swami, Q. Z. A., Hong, Y.-W., & Tong, L. (Eds.). (2007). *Wireless sensor networks: Signal processing and communications. Chichester/West Essex.* UK: John Wiley & Sons.

Trakadas, T. Z. P., Voliotis, S., & Manasis, C. (2004). Efficient routing in pan and sensor networks. *ACM SIGMOBILE Mobile Computing and Communications Review*, *8*(1), 10–17. doi:10.1145/980159.980165

Ye, J. H. W., & Estrin, D. (2004). Medium access control with coordinated adaptive sleeping for wireless sensor networks. *IEEE/ACM Transactions on Networking*, *12*(3), 493–506. doi:10.1109/TNET.2004.828953

Zhao, F., & Guibas, L. (2004). *Wireless sensor networks: An information processing approach.* San Francisco, CA: Morgan Kaufmann.

KEY TERMS AND DEFINITIONS

Wireless Sensor Networks: A number of tiny wireless nodes with small amount of storage and computational capability that have been deployed for specific mission such as monitoring a large area, in a distributed way.

Energy Conservation: Efforts for reducing the amount of energy consumption.

Level Crossing Sampling: A scheme for sampling the signal at specific amplitude values in time. Level crossing sampling is a subset of non-uniform sampling.

Periodic Sampling: Sampling the signal in time periodically that often supports *Nyquist* sampling rate criteria.

Optimization: Choosing the best element(s) or setting(s) for minimization of a cost function or maximization of an assumed profit. Optimization is usually along with trade off between a few other costs.

***MICAz* Wireless Sensor:** A wireless sensing platform from Crossbow Technology Inc. with educational and industrial attributes that works in ISM band.

APPENDIX

Optimal Levels for Level Crossing Sampling

The optimal set of levels is the particular solution of equation (9) that minimizes the equation (8). Equation (8) is repeated here in (A-1). For this, we take the partial derivative of the equation A-1 with respect to each of the levels and then put it equal to zero as is shown in (A-2) to find its optimal roots.

$$E[\varepsilon_S^2(t)] = \int_{\ell_0}^{\ell_1} (\ell_1 - s)^2 f_S(s)\ ds + \int_{\ell_M}^{\ell_{M+1}} (\ell_M - s)^2 f_S(s)\ ds\ + \sum_{i=2}^{M} \frac{1}{2} \left\{ \int_{\ell_{i-1}}^{\ell_i} (\ell_{i-1} - s)^2 f_S(s) + (\ell_i - s)^2 f_S(s)\ ds \right\} \qquad \text{(A-1)}$$

$$\frac{\partial E[\varepsilon_S^2(t)]}{\partial \ell_i} = 0, \quad 1 \le i \le M \qquad \text{(A-2)}$$

Equation (A-1) is re-written as follows:

$$E[\varepsilon_S^2(t)] = \int_{\ell_0}^{\ell_1} (\ell_1^2 + s^2 - 2s\ell_1) f_S(s)\ ds + \int_{\ell_M}^{\ell_{M+1}} (\ell_M^2 + s^2 - 2s\ell_M) f_S(s)\ ds\ + \frac{1}{2} \sum_{i=1}^{M-1} \left[2\int_{\ell_i}^{\ell_{i+1}} s^2 f_S(s)\ ds + (\ell_i^2 + \ell_{i+1}^2) \int_{\ell_i}^{\ell_{i+1}} f_S(s)\ ds - (\ell_i + \ell_{i+1}) \int_{\ell_i}^{\ell_{i+1}} s f_S(s)\ ds \right] \qquad \text{(A-3)}$$

When the level is not the first and the last level, the partial derivative of the (A-1) with respect to the level is as follows:

$$\left.\frac{\partial E[\varepsilon_S^2(t)]}{\partial \ell_i}\right|_{i \ne 1, M} = \ell_i \int_{\ell_{i-1}}^{\ell_{i+1}} f_S(s)\ ds - \int_{\ell_{i-1}}^{\ell_{i+1}} s\ f_S(s)\ ds + \frac{1}{2} \ell_{i-1}^2\ f_S(\ell_i) - \ell_i\ \ell_{i-1}\ f_S(\ell_i) - \frac{1}{2} \ell_{i+1}^2\ f_S(\ell_i) + \ell_{i+1}\ \ell_i\ f_S(\ell_i) \qquad \text{(A-4)}$$

$$\ell_i = \frac{\int_{\ell_{i-1}}^{\ell_{i+1}} s\ f_S(s)\ ds + \frac{1}{2} f_S(\ell_i) \left[(\ell_{i+1} - \ell_{i-1})(\ell_{i+1} + \ell_{i-1} - 2\ell_i) \right]}{\int_{\ell_{i-1}}^{\ell_{i+1}} f_S(s)\ ds}, \quad i = 2, 3, \ \ldots, M \qquad \text{(A-5)}$$

Equation (A-5) shows the level with respect to itself and the other neighboring levels. In this equation then the second term of the numerator becomes too small because of $(\ell_{i+1} + \ell_{i-1} - 2\ell_i)$, then this term is ignored in comparison to $\int_{\ell_{i-1}}^{\ell_{i+1}} s\ f_S(s)\ ds$. Hence, (A-5) is simplified to (A-6), which is the *Lloyd-Max* equation (Sayood, 2000).

$$\ell_i = \frac{\int_{\ell_{i-1}}^{\ell_{i+1}} s\, f_S(s)\, ds}{\int_{\ell_{i-1}}^{\ell_{i+1}} f_S(s)\, ds} \quad , i = 2,3, \ldots, M \tag{A-6}$$

We repeated the same process for the first level as follows:

$$\begin{aligned}\frac{\partial E[\varepsilon_S^2(t)]}{\partial \ell_1} &= \ell_1 \int_{\ell_0}^{\ell_1} f_S(s)\, ds + \frac{1}{2}\ell_1^2\, f_S(\ell_1) - \int_{\ell_0}^{\ell_1} s\, f_S(s)\, ds - \frac{1}{2}\ell_1^2\, f_S(\ell_1) \\ &+ \ell_1 \int_{\ell_0}^{\ell_2} f_S(s)\, ds - \int_{\ell_0}^{\ell_2} s\, f_S(s)\, ds - \frac{1}{2}\ell_2^2\, f_S(\ell_1) + \ell_1 \ell_2\, f_S(\ell_1)\end{aligned} \tag{A-7}$$

$$\frac{\partial E[\varepsilon_S^2(t)]}{\partial \ell_1} = 0 \quad \Rightarrow$$

$$\ell_1 = \frac{\int_{\ell_0}^{\ell_1} s\, f_S(s)\, ds + \int_{\ell_0}^{\ell_2} s\, f_S(s)\, ds + \frac{1}{2}(\ell_1 - \ell_2)^2 f_S(\ell_1)}{\int_{\ell_0}^{\ell_1} f_S(s)\, ds + \int_{\ell_0}^{\ell_2} f_S(s)\, ds} \tag{A-8}$$

And for the last level, we repeat the same process:

$$\begin{aligned}\frac{\partial E[\varepsilon_S^2(t)]}{\partial \ell_M} &= \ell_M \int_{\ell_{M-1}}^{\ell_{M+1}} f_S(s)\, ds + \frac{1}{2}\ell_1^2\, f_S(\ell_1) - \int_{\ell_{M-1}}^{\ell_{M+1}} s\, f_S(s)\, ds + \frac{1}{2}\ell_{M-1}^2\, f_S(\ell_M) \\ &+ \ell_M \int_{\ell_M}^{\ell_{M+1}} f_S(s)\, ds - \frac{1}{2}\ell_M^2\, f_S(\ell_M) - \int_{\ell_M}^{\ell_{M+1}} s\, f_S(s)\, ds + \frac{1}{2}\ell_M^2\, f_S(\ell_M)\end{aligned} \tag{A-9}$$

$$\frac{\partial E[\varepsilon_S^2(t)]}{\partial \ell_M} = 0 \quad \Rightarrow$$

$$\ell_M = \frac{\int_{\ell_M}^{\ell_{M+1}} s\, f_S(s)\, ds + \int_{\ell_{M-1}}^{\ell_{M+1}} s\, f_S(s)\, ds - \frac{1}{2}(\ell_M - \ell_{M-1})^2 f_S(\ell_M)}{\int_{\ell_M}^{\ell_{M+1}} f_S(s)\, ds + \int_{\ell_{M-1}}^{\ell_{M+1}} f_S(s)\, ds} \tag{A-10}$$

The optimal levels are the roots of the M simultaneous integral equations of (A-6), (A-8) and (A-10).

Section 4
Security and Privacy

Pervasive computing incorporates a significant number of security concerns, since amongst all else, it implies the sharing of data and information amongst users of possibly different administrative domains and of no prior awareness of each other. Secure information management becomes, therefore, an absolute necessity in pervasive environments. Another security concern involves the adaptability of pervasive systems and their functionality in terms of dynamic and context-driven re-configuration, since both these aspects can be easily exploited by malicious users to adversely affect the operation of the system. Additionally, for any pervasive application to provide services customized to user needs and preferences, users should share personal information to that application to make it context-aware, thus raising privacy concerns.

Chapter 10
Dependability in Pervasive Computing

Frank Ortmeier
Otto-von-Guericke-Universität Magdeburg, Germany

ABSTRACT

The paradigm of Pervasive Computing is that in a near future many objects of day to day life will be equipped with some kind of computing and communication capability. This will allow for a whole new generation of support, planning, and assistance systems. The great benefit is that they will offer support and guidance in everyday life and/or normal working processes. Although the possibilities seem unlimited, dependability issues most often form rigid limits. Because the systems are so smoothly integrated into normal life, they are expected to be robust against intended manipulations, failure-tolerant, to guarantee functional requirements and/or to be traceable and understandable (for the human user). This set of functional requirements makes Pervasive Computing systems special. There are few to no other domains where an application has to meet so many requirements from so many different facets of dependability at the same time (i.e. security, safety, reliability, functional correctness, and user-trust). In addition, the adaptive nature of many Pervasive Computing systems makes them very difficult to analyze and predict.

This chapter is targeted at developers of Pervasive Computing systems, who have to specify and meet dependability requirements. It gives an overview on different aspects of dependability, important terms and concepts, lists common analysis and design methods for meeting dependability requirements in Pervasive Computing scenarios, and shortly discusses different classes of Pervasive Computing systems and their impact on dependability issues.

DOI: 10.4018/978-1-60960-611-4.ch010

INTRODUCTION

Pervasive Computing can be seen as an enabler technology for many new and exciting applications. Indicative examples of envisaged applications include the following: a smart shopping list, which automatically adds items with low supplies to the list; a digital personal assistant, which provides useful information on the basis of the user's current context and needs (e.g. time schedules); a medical diagnostics system, which supervises vital functions of patients at all times and therefore allows much better diagnostics; a similar system could also be used to monitor heart patients and trigger emergency calls. Even closer in the future are systems, which allow continuous monitoring and tracking of goods. Just think of smart production, logistic or transportation systems. If for example luggage was to be equipped with RFID tags, long and time-consuming check-in procedures could be omitted, lost luggage would be reduced and customs would be simplified.

All these systems offer a lot of new interesting and useful possibilities, but would not be possible without Pervasive Computing technologies. However, as with every new system (generation) the question of dependability arises as soon as the idea of the system has sprung. Dependability can be typically divided into a number of aspects, namely (functional) correctness, safety, security, reliability, availability, transparency and traceability. It is interesting to note, that for most existing systems only a very limited number of aspects of dependability are relevant. For example a train control system must be able to tolerate component failures and fulfill its function at all times. Thus it must be safe, reliable and available. Aspects like security, transparency and traceability play little to no role. On the other hand, e-shopping systems need to be secure, transparent and traceable. Safety and reliability are not of much concern (as these systems have virtually no inherent potential for damage).

This is different for Pervasive Computing systems. Most Pervasive Computing systems come with requirements from all aspects of dependability. The reason for this lies in the nature of Pervasive Computing itself. Typically Pervasive Computing systems are very tightly connected with specific users (let it be directly such as a medical diagnostic system or indirectly such as a smart logistics system, which handles personal luggage at airports). Pervasive Computing systems often gather and store information on behavior, context, habits and plans of their users. This information forms the basis for many of the benefits that the system can offer to the users. For example, a heart attack warning system can only trigger emergency calls, if it knows the person it is monitoring and its position. Check-in procedures can only be circumvented, if pieces of luggage carry information about their owner respectively their target destination. Additionally, Pervasive Computing systems often rely on wireless communication. Considering these issues in parallel automatically raises requirements in terms of security, transparency and traceability. Secondly, Pervasive Computing systems are commonly embedded in the environment not only for gathering information, but also for making decisions or at least for decision support. Regarding safety, any decision can be either harmful or not. As a rule of thumb, the closer the connection to the physical world is, the higher the potential for a safety relevant impact will be. A lost emergency signal from a patient's heart monitoring system might cost her live; wrong loading of transportation containers could make airplanes very instable and cause severe problems during flight. In addition, intended attacks and manipulations of the systems can cause severe consequences (let it be monetary or in the form of injuries or deaths). For example consider the case of smuggling dangerous luggage into airplanes by means of abusing the check-in system. Therefore, in general Pervasive Computing systems also need to be safe, reliable and functionally correct.

Besides the need for meeting requirements from many different aspects of dependability, Pervasive Computing also implies restrictions on methods that can be applied. One reason is that in many application scenarios energy and computation power is a very limited resource. So for example, cryptography is not always feasible. Another reason is that very often such systems rely on some sort of learning mechanism, which allows them to dynamically adapt to new situations and function in changing environments. Although this feature is highly desirable, it brings a lot of restrictions on how the systems can be validated or verified. Unfortunately, there is no generic out-of-the-box solution for guaranteeing dependability for Pervasive Computing available yet. As a matter of fact such a solution does not even exist for traditional IT systems. However, there exist a lot of approaches for different facets of dependability.

This chapter will give an overview on available methods for analyzing dependability and explain their applicability to Pervasive Computing. The Section "Aspects of Dependability" presents a classification of different dependability requirements. Following this classification, important concepts and references to widely applied methods and tools are provided. Afterwards, the following section explains different "Types of Pervasive Computing Systems" and outlines their relationship to dependability requirements and applicable methods before concluding the chapter.

Aspects of Dependability

Although very frequently used, the term "dependability" is a very broad concept, subsuming numerous, sometimes even contrary to each other sub-terms. Some people, institutions and/or organizations call a system dependable if it does not fail for a long time and is constantly and consistently available (for example Chen et al. (2009) call some distributed information systems dependable, if they are mostly available). Others call a system dependable if it does not cause harm even if some of its sub-components are faulty (for example a safety braking mechanism in a modern train). For example, the International Electrotechnical Commission (IEC, 2003) defines dependability as "*the collective term used to describe the availability performance and its influencing factors: reliability performance, maintainability performance and maintenance support performance*". Other standardization committees – such as the International Federation for Information Processing (IFIP, 2010) – define dependability as "*the trustworthiness of a computing system which allows reliance to be justifiably placed on the service it delivers*". Dependability is also often identified with trustworthiness. However, the IT community often sees trustworthiness as a system property, which states that the system may not be manipulated to gain an advantage (for example an electronic payment system). This is clearly a security property and is thus a much too strict definition for the term dependability. Avizienis, et al. (2001, 2004) point out, that both aspects are (equally) important. However, they do not see individual users and their subjective impression on the system as part of dependability. In particular, for Pervasive Computing the user should play a central role in dependability discussions. The reason is that many Pervasive Computing systems transparently assist users and guide their actions. If users distrust the system and ignore its advice, the potential benefit of the whole system and its user adoption are both at stake.

All these definitions are useful from a standardization point of view; from an engineering point of view they are often too vague or leave out important domain-specific facets. A system designer needs specific methods, approaches and tools, which help her achieving dependability goals. She has to break down the term dependability into precise sub-terms from which requirements can be derived. For every sub-term there exist a number of efficient approaches and methods to help system developers. This chapter aims at help-

Figure 1. The five aspects of dependability: Functional correctness, Safety, Reliability, Security and User-Trust

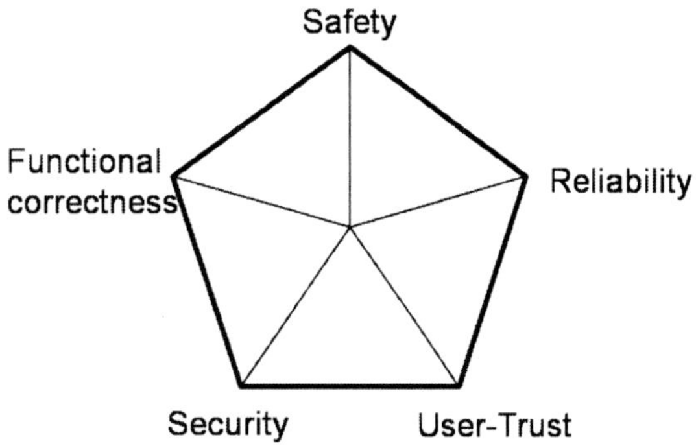

ing designers in this respect by providing them with a structured literature and method overview. In this chapter dependability is divided into five major aspects, where each aspect corresponds to a number of related methods and approaches. Functional correctness means the system adheres to its specification or fulfills the intended functionality. Safety means that the system does not do any harm to humans or the environment. Reliability subsumes all quantitative, safety related aspects. This covers risk associated with the system as well as quantitative approximations of failure rates or availability questions. User-Trust includes all issues, which are related to the question whether an individual user subjectively gauges the system to be dependable. In this context, it also includes aspects such as the traceability and transparency of the system. Figure 1 shows the aforementioned five aspects of dependability.

Multi-dimensional data can very easily be displayed in Kiviat- or star diagrams. The Kiviat-diagram in Figure 1 shows the five aspects of dependability: Safety, Reliability, Security, User-Trust and Functional correctness. Each axis of the diagram represents a corresponding aspect. The relative importance of each aspect is depicted on this axis, where biggest importance is depicted as being closer to the edge and no importance at all is denoted as being the center of the diagram. Such a star diagram may be used in very early design stages.

Each one of these dependability aspects is the domain of a lot of research work being carried out. As a result, for each aspect various methods, tools and approaches have been developed. In the following sub-sections for each aspect a brief definition is given, common terms and methods are sketched (with references for further readings) and a discussion on important specifics of Pervasive Computing (with respect to the aspect of dependability) is presented. This overview provides developers of Pervasive Computing systems with useful suggestions on how dependability issues may be addressed in their specific scenarios with state-of-the-art methods.

Functional Correctness

This is often also expressed as: the system adheres to its specification. A specification in this context is a precise (maybe even formal) description of the intended functionality of the system. For example, the specification of a list sorting algorithm is, that for any result list RL for a each pair (RL^i, RL^{i+1}) in this list $RL^i \leq RL^{i+1}$ holds.

General Terms and Methods

There exist many different notations for system specification. Very common notations include predicate logic or – in particular for object oriented software development – object constraint logic (Object-Management-Group, 2006). These are in particular useful for specifying properties which hold after termination or are by default invariant. Properties, which vary through time (e.g. X=0 until Y=1) can be expressed using temporal logics. Temporal logics can be divided into discrete time and continuous time logics. Another, orthogonal partitioning is that of only universal properties (e.g. in all possible futures) versus universal and existential properties (e.g. there exists at least one possible future). The most common logics are Computational Tree Logic (discrete time; existential and universal), Linear Temporal Logics (discrete time, universal), and Duration Calculus (continuous time, universal). A good overview on these (and other) temporal logics is given in Emerson (1990).

To analyze a given system, the most popular approaches are static analysis (for example Ball et al., (2006) and Vistein et al., (2009)), model checking (for example Clarke et al., (1999) and Merz (2001)) and interactive verification (for example Bäumler et al., (2004)). Static analysis is a very efficient and powerful method. The core idea is to deduce properties merely from the structure of the program (and not using any knowledge about explicit program runs or executions). Its main drawbacks are that only a limited scope of properties can be analyzed and that static analysis always has to deal with false-positives and false-negatives. The former describe situations, where the method unjustly says that the system violates a property, while the latter falsely interpret the system as being consistent with the specification (common tools: Mygcc (Volanschi, 2006), Coverity Prevent (Coverity, 2010) or Microsoft's Static Driver Verifier (Bach et al., 2006)). The idea of model checking is, to analyze all possible runs of the system. Model checking can deal with an infinite number of runs (of possibly infinite length). In many cases model checkers can also provide the designer with witness runs respectively counter examples. A witness is a possible scenario in which a certain situation occurs (for example correct activation and later deactivation of a backup system) and a counter example is a scenario in which a certain property does not hold (for example a possible intrusion scenario, in which an attacker gains control of the system). However, model checking is always very vulnerable to the state explosion problem. Interactive verification tools are – in theory – capable of analyzing systems of any size. The core idea is to analyze a system at a semantic level and make use of abstraction, generalization and induction to formulate requirements as theorems in a formal specification language and to prove these theorems. In practice, these methods (and the according tools) are often very much targeted at one specific domain. Applying them to a new domain often comes with a lot of effort and requires expert knowledge (common tools for interactive verification include: KIV (KIV, 2010), PVS (PVS, 2010), ISABELLE (Isabelle, 2010)).

Functional Correctness and Pervasive Computing

While showing functional correctness is relatively easy for pure algorithmic questions, it typically is much harder for Pervasive Computing systems. One reason is that such systems typically do not terminate but are rather reactive. Another reason is that, very often the specification is intuitively clear but on a closer look only relatively vague and context dependent. One of the most important reasons is that the intended functionality of a Pervasive Computing system very often depends on its current context and user. While some users of a system might call it a design error if they are confronted with some information that the system has gathered, others might call it a design error if they are not given the same information. It is also possible that according to the current situation different specifications might seem to be intuitively correct. For example privacy issues might be violated, if a home sensor networks is about to report a fire. At the same time, they shall not be violated if it is just reporting missed visitors. All the aforementioned problems highlight specification difficulties.

But Pervasive Computing systems are not only harder to specify. They are also much harder to analyze. Model checking often runs into state explosion problems and interactive approaches become very time-consuming and difficult. Static analysis methods are often not expressive enough to answer the interesting questions. A general recommendation for one method or another cannot be given. As a rule of thumb, interactive approaches are preferable if many similar components are involved and model checking is preferable if the number of components is not too large and the components are not identical.

Safety

A more formal definition for the safety is "a property of a system that it does not endanger human life or the environment" (Storey, 1996). From this definition it is clear that software alone is never safety critical. Safety is a system level property and can only be specified and analyzed on system level. A system, which has no capability of doing any harm, is by definition safe.

General Terms and Methods

Safety is often further distinguished into primary safety, functional safety and indirect safety (Storey, 1996). Primary safety means, that the system does not cause harm when it is working as intended. In other words: The system is not malicious by design. Functional safety states, that the system fulfills its intended (safety) function. This is in some sense a specialization of functional correctness, where the intended/wanted property is a safety relevant property. Indirect safety means, the system does not cause any harm even if some components fail or if there are disturbances in the environment. Just think of an airplane, which must not crash, if a single velocity gauge fails. Indirect safety is the main focus of most safety analysis methods. Some important terms in safety analysis are: Accident, incident and hazard. An accident is a situation where harm occurred (person hit by car because of loss of brakes). An incident is a situation where harm could have occurred (but didn't because of some lucky environment conditions; e.g. the person managed to jump aside). A hazard is a situation in which an accident or incident may occur (e.g. the loss of brakes while traveling at medium or high speed). Hazards are the primary focus in safety analysis. Hazards at the system level are equivalent to failures at the component level. In this context, a failure is a situation where a specific component fails to fulfill its intended functionality. For a more detailed overview please consult Storey (1996).

In safety analysis one distinguishes between risk and hazard analysis. Risk analysis tries to measure and estimate what possible harm can be done. The most often used technique is Preliminary Hazard Analysis and particularly its extension to software-hardware systems (Lawrence, 1995). It is done in very early design stages and gives a very rough impression on the hazards that the system might bring. In a second step, the corresponding risk is rated in terms of its potential impact. This is typically done in relatively coarse categories (ranging from "minor" to "catastrophic").

As far as hazard analysis is concerned, there exists a very broad variety of – often domain specific – analysis methods. The shared goal of these methods is to determine causal relationships between component failures and system hazards. This is then used to derive some kind of probability estimation on the likelihood of occurrence of the hazard. The most popular hazard analysis method is failure modes and effects analysis.

Failure Modes and Effects Analysis (FMEA) is a forward, bottom-up method, which starts with component failures as input and tries to predict possible propagation of these failures through the system. There is an abundance of literature on FMEA available. It is recommended to either start directly with a standard for the domain that one is addressing or begin with one of the FMEA introduction books (for example McDermott (1996)). In contrast to this approach, fault tree analysis (FTA) starts with a given hazard and iteratively decomposes it into sub-hazards until the desired granularity has been reached. A good overview on FTA can be found in the) fault tree handbook by Vesley et al. (2002).

Most hazard analysis methods are more or less only methodological guidelines. They purely rely on knowledge and expertise of the engineer. In the last 10 years advances in formal methods also allowed for newer model based analysis methods. The basic idea of these approaches is to deduce cause consequence relationships from an executable, precise model of the system and its environment. Formal fault tree analysis (Schellhorn et al., 2002), deductive cause-consequence analysis (Ortmeier et al., 2006) and failure injection (Bozzano et al., 2003) are three popular techniques of this category. These methods are more costly but also yield much more precise results.

Safety and Pervasive Computing

Safety in Pervasive Computing is both especially important and difficult to guarantee. The difficulty lies in the distributed and dynamic nature of the systems. Behavior in distributed, asynchronous systems is typically relatively hard to predict. For pervasive systems this is even harder, because the systems very often heavily depend on interaction with their environment. Therefore, a precise understanding of environmental relations and effects is required. In particular different time scales and relaxation times make such systems very hard to analyze. For the special case when hazardous situations can be detected locally, it is possible to add (local) supervisors to each component. These observers monitor passively the component and bring it into a failsafe state, whenever it might trigger a hazard. Unfortunately, very often hazards cannot be detected locally. In this case model based analysis methods could help. The latter are capable of detecting flaws and weaknesses in concurrent systems. In practice often complexity and state explosion problems make them difficult in the context of Pervasive Computing. This can be eased by clever abstraction and use of symmetry. Abstraction is a technique, where complex models are substituted by less complex models for analysis purposes. An example is, that instead of using exact 2D/3D coordinates in an automatic luggage handling system abstract, logical positions might used be used for analysis. Exploiting symmetry means, that for example only a limited number of pieces of luggage is used for analysis. It must not be forgotten, that such methods also raise the question of adequacy of the used model. Model based approaches are only correct with respect to the used models. The more abstract the analyzed models are, the higher the chance of a discrepancy between the model and reality.

In general, it can be recommended to use some sort of risk reduction method when using Pervasive Computing for safety critical systems. This can be done by moving from a fully autonomous system to a decision support system, where a human has the ultimate responsibility. Another option is to add diverse, redundant systems for increasing safety.

Reliability

Reliability and safety are closely related to each other. While safety addresses more qualitative aspects (e.g.: What harm can be done? What must happen, such that harm is being done?), reliability addresses quantitative aspects (e.g. How much harm will be done? How probable is the occurrence of harm?). Sometimes reliability is also used in a more general context. In this understanding reliability is very close to the term availability. Reliability then is a measure on how probable it is that the system will fulfill a required functionality when it is requested.

General Terms and Methods

The result of most reliability analyses is a (set of) real value(s). This number is often interpreted as the probability of a system failure. However, probability values are very easily misunderstood. The understanding of reliability as a probability makes sense only if within the system some kind of finite "demands/requests" can be identified, for example the loss of a critical radio messages within a given time interval (if an infinite interval is considered the probability will simply be 1). However, many safety critical systems are reactive. This means that they do not terminate but rather continuously monitor and/or control some safety critical equipment. For such systems failure probabilities do not make sense, because for an infinite time interval this probability will always be 1. There exist two popular solutions to this problem. The first one is to only consider a priori fixed, finite time intervals and calculate the probability of system failure for this interval. The other is to calculate failure rates or stochastic means. Concerning the latter, the most important metrics are mean-time-to-failure (MTTF) and mean-time-between-failures (MTBF). The former describes the (stochastic) mean time until the first system failure should be expected, while the latter describes the average time between two system failures. Both numbers are used frequently in practice, because they can also be used as decision support (for example: planning maintenance intervals). A frequently occurring mistake is to mix probabilities and rates. This is very tempting, because it seems intuitively correct and in many case yields seemingly correct results. Nevertheless, this is only by chance and not mathematically justified. Thus it will often lead to (hidden) misjudgments.

Most methods for measuring reliability rely on – previously completed – qualitative safety analysis (see the previous section on safety and derive stochastic information from the results of this analysis. Widely known methods include quantitative fault tree analysis and event tree analysis (Vesley et al., 2002). Another approach is empirical data. Real field data is only possible if reliability is understood as availability (see above). If the reliability of some safety critical function is to be measured, this is not feasible. Firstly the resulting probabilities are so small, that stochastic significance can only be achieved with exorbitant long testing periods and – secondly – the harmful situation can often not be accepted to happen (just think of an airplane crash). In this situation, simulation-based and model-based approaches can help. For example failure injection in combination with Monte Carlo based simulation or probabilistic model checking (common tools to perform these methods include MRMC (Markov Reward Model Checker, 2010) or Prism (Kwiatkowska, 2002)).

Reliability and Pervasive Computing

Most Pervasive Computing systems are not highly safety critical. As a consequence measuring reliability by field testing seems possible. In practice, this often turns out to be difficult. The problem is that due to the dynamic and adaptive nature of the system a good, representative testing environment can often not be defined. The fact that Pervasive Computing systems are often a combination of many heterogeneous sub-systems also worsens field testing for measuring reliability.

Many Pervasive Computing systems are reactive. Therefore, traditional methods of measuring MTTF and MTBF are only to a limited extend applicable. The reason is that by design many Pervasive Computing systems are able to recover from some (local) disturbances or loss of components automatically. Here, methods from self-healing systems or Organic Computing might be useful. For more information on Organic

Computing see the Organic Computing Initiative's Website (2010).

Security

Security aims at making systems tamper-proof against intended manipulations. People or entities who try to manipulate a system are usually called "attackers". Attackers can either be humans or malicious programs running on any kind of computer. A system is called secure (against a pre-defined attacker) with respect to some requirements, if these requirements hold despite any of the attackers actions.

General Terms and Methods

Security or to be more precise information security comes in many different flavors. Traditionally, it subsumed three aspects: confidentiality, integrity, and availability. With the growing importance of E-Commerce and with it the necessities of means to buy and pay goods online, additional principles have been added: non-deniability, consistency and authenticity. Although they offer slightly different views, it can be discussed whether these principles are really new or only variants of existing ones. Some researchers even claim, that all of them can be reduced to the problem of authenticity. Authenticity here means, that it is possible to decide without doubt for any given data packet who the originator of the data is. A good overview on security may be found in Anderson (2008).

One of the most crucial factors for security is what type of capabilities an attacker has. A very common model for attacker's capabilities is the Dolev-Yao model (1983). The basic idea of this model is, (1) the attacker can read any data being sent between two individuals, (2) the attacker can only read encrypted messages, if she knows the correct key, and (3) the attacker does not forget previous knowledge. In larger scenarios, security requirements are not always total (e.g. privacy does not require, that only sender and receiver may read some data) but are defined on hierarchies and groups. Common – but somewhat old – models are Bell and La Padula (1973) and Biba (1977). Newer models – like non-interference (see for example Roscoe, (1994)) – also take hidden channels into account.

Security analysis can be divided into protocol and program analysis methods. The first one aims at guaranteeing that during interaction between two parties no attacks are possible, while the second one should show that manipulation of a single program is not possible. For the first group formal protocol verification has been shown to be very effective (Grandy et al., 2006). For the second group program verification, static analysis, proof-carrying-code or information-flow-control are popular methods (Livshits (2006), Mantel et al. (2006)). Note that analysis of cryptography itself is mostly a pre-requisite and not focus of these methods.

Security and Pervasive Computing

Pervasive Computing systems are very vulnerable to security issues for a number of reasons. The first (obvious) reason is that they are highly distributed and rely heavily on wireless communication. Another one is that individual components only have very limited memory and computing power, which restricts possible security mechanisms. Furthermore, the whole system often consists of heterogeneous components from numerous suppliers. Therefore, pre-defined cryptographic keys or unique identifiers are often not or only to a limited extend applicable.

But probably the most important reason is that most Pervasive Computing systems require input from various sensors. In reality, it is very often possible (sometimes even very easy) to manipulate these sensors – either directly by compromising their control software or indirectly by putting certain stimuli into the environment, which confuse the sensor. It is very hard to make a system robust against such attacks. One possibility is to try to detect such manipulations automatically. This makes a very precise model of the environment and/or redundant sensors necessary. Both approaches are very hard to realize, because the first option requires very precise models of the environment and of dependencies between environment and sensors; the second option obviously increases costs a lot. Another approach is to integrate the user. This allows for much easier detection of possible misuse, as the user is the one who assumes decisions. But it comes at the price of reducing the pervasive character of the system. If for example integration of new components into a private home network always requires the user to authenticate the new component with a PIN, then the pervasive, support character of the system is weakened. This might be acceptable; if such an authentication is only necessary once, but not if it has to be redone every day or every time the component is powered on/off.

From a technological point of view, a priori analysis seems most suitable for Pervasive Computing. Most online approaches such as proof-carrying-code might not be applicable, because of performance restrictions. In order to secure communication channels with cryptography, specific network protocols have been developed, which allow generating common, group-wide network keys with constant extra effort. This is in particular useful, as it directly addresses the problems of limited computation power and dynamic topology changes (Byun et al., 2006). To compensate for sensor manipulation, mechanisms from the fields of data fusion and data aggregation can potentially help. These will allow the Pervasive Computing system to detect sensor anomalies and react accordingly. Important relevant approaches for this can be found in the field of trust networks (Golbeck et al., 2003). The core idea here is to let the system's sensors to observe each other. By comparing sensor data with each other as well as history data, it is often possible to detect sensor manipulation (or sensor failure). A good overview on security in Pervasive Computing is given in (Clark et al., 2006).

User-Trust

This aspect is often mixed up with the others. For example, if a user is concerned about privacy of her data, then one might assume that this is a security issue. However, in reality the objective security aspects and the subjective user trust are independent (and often not even related). Normally, it is not possible for a user to follow the arguments of a security analysis. She rather has to believe, that the system keeps her data private. The opposite effect is of course also possible: a system might have the user's trust while being unsafe or not secure from an objective point of view.

General Terms and Methods

Already in 1989, Davis proposed a (generic) model for technology acceptance (Davis, 1989), which basically claims that user acceptance is a product of perceived usefulness and perceived ease of use. While this acceptance model is still valid, newer studies claim, that user trust is prerequisite for user acceptance (Schmidt-Belz, 2005). According to this claim, user trust could even be described as one of the most important factors for bringing Pervasive Computing systems to market. Despite early assumptions, that user trust is very much dependent on the type of presentation of information (e.g. text, speech, video personas, etc.), this research showed that it is much more dependent on the quality of the information. It is very difficult to define, what quality of information means in this context. The PIE (Program-Interpretation-Effect) model (Dix et. al, 1985) provides a method for formal specification. This models advocates distinction between real actions of the system and information presented to the user. A system acts traceably/understandably (according to Dix's model) if there exists a prediction function, which allows deriving at any time the system's actions from the displayed information. The good thing about this approach is that it is based on a solid formal foundation.

User-Trust and Pervasive Computing

User-Trust has many facets such as usefulness and correctness, but it also incorporates traceability and credibility. For Pervasive Computing systems usefulness and correctness are often very closely related to the dependability aspect of functional correctness. Pervasive Computing systems are by their nature very often specified with respect to their users needs in specific situations. So, in the context of Pervasive Computing these requirements might already be covered (at least to some extent) by functional correctness. Traceability is a different issue. Traceability implies that the user understands why a specific information or advice is given. Credibility implies that the user has the impression of high quality of the presented information or advice. Wrong advice is always accounted much more than good advice. As a consequence, it is of utmost importance to the Pervasive Computing system to always present correct, good advice. This can be very tricky because what is correct and what is not typically depends very much on the user. A way to ease this problem is to increase traceability whenever the uncertainty about desired actions is increasing. Users tend to accept errors more likely when they can understand (Paymans et al., 2004), why the system misbehaved. Besides empirical studies, developers of Pervasive Computing systems might find the PIE method useful. Although it has been designed for dialog interaction in pure IT-systems, extension and transfer to Pervasive Computing scenarios seems very feasible.

Another very important question in the context of user trust in Pervasive Computing is the question of responsibility in case of system failure. Many Pervasive Computing systems consist of components from various suppliers, which form some network and interact with each other. In such a network, failure of individual components can easily make others fail too. Although this is not directly a technical question, Edwards and Grinter (2001) found out that it is part of the seven most important challenges for paving the way to user acceptance of Pervasive Computing systems. As a matter of fact, Edwards and Grinter (2001) even relate aspects such as reliability more to the subjective perception rather than to objective measurements. Following this argument, the way individual components are built might change in future. For example, self-protection mechanisms could then become an integral part of most components.

TYPES OF PERVASIVE COMPUTING SYSTEMS

In general, Pervasive Computing systems must meet requirements from all aspects of dependability. Deciding on which aspect is of what level of importance can only be performed at a domain- or even application-specific level. Graphically, requirements for a given system can be illustrated as a pentagram within the dependability Kiviat-plot (see Figure 1). Each edge then describes the importance of the dependability aspect. If the edge is very close to this corner, this means that the corresponding aspect is very important. If it is very close to the center it means it is less important.

Building such a diagram for a given system is often neither easy nor not subject to discussion. This section presents generic guidelines, which system developers might find useful.

The following sub-sections present a classification of Pervasive Computing systems by arranging them in four dimensions: user-centric vs. object-centric, decision support vs. autonomy, mobile vs. stationary, and static vs. self-adapting. Experience shows, that there often exists a correlation between these dimensions and priority of dependability aspects. Note that this type of generic recommendation can never replace a thorough requirements analysis. But – as said above – it can help decide in very early design stages, which aspect is most promising to look into first and which one can be postponed a little. This advice is of course not mandatory but should be conceived as a generic design guideline.

User-Centric vs. Object-Centric Systems

User-centric Pervasive Computing systems are most often some kind of assistance system. They range from simple PDA-like calendar and time planning applications, to ubiquitous, integrated – maybe location-based – communication assistants. These systems have in common that most information within these systems is directly related to end users. In contrast, object-centric systems often provide some data for technical applications. Traditional examples include traffic prediction/guidance or automated monitoring of logistic or production processes. Data in these systems is very often focused on unanimated objects.

Relation to dependability: Summarizing safety and functional correctness dominate object-centric systems while security and user trust have highest priority in user-centric systems. This is depicted in Figure 2. The ellipses show locations where the center of gravity of an object-centric respectively a user-centric system lies. User-centric applications often have requirements where the plot's center of gravity is in the lower-left half of the dependability pentagram. Object-centric system's center of gravity is often found in the upper half.

Decision Support Systems vs. Autonomous Systems

Decision support systems typically have no or only very limited control capabilities. They most often gather, aggregate and interpret data for a (human) user. The ultimate decision is then being made by this user/operator. One example is traffic or logistic guidance. The Pervasive Computing system might gather information on traffic or goods flow, aggregate this data, predict potential jams and present the results to a control center. But, the last decision about changing routes is being made by an operator. Autonomous systems may not rely at all on humans to help them decide. An example could be a system, which filters and aggregates messages for its user. For being useful, the system must not always ask its user for advice, but is expected to handle spam or commercial e-mails automatically.

Relation to dependability: Figure 3 shows the Kiviat-plot for decision support and autonomous systems. Decision support systems often tend be more focused on user-trust (i.e. traceability) and reliability (i.e. they should be available when their user needs them). For autonomous systems correctness and safety is often the prime requirement. If the system is able to take actions on its own, it must be assured that it does nothing wrong and – even more important – that it does not cause harm.

Mobile, Ad-Hoc Systems vs. Stationary Systems

When talking about Pervasive Computing, many people automatically think of mobile and in most cases ad-hoc networks. While this is true for many systems, there also exist a broad variety of

Figure 2. User-centric vs. Object-centric systems

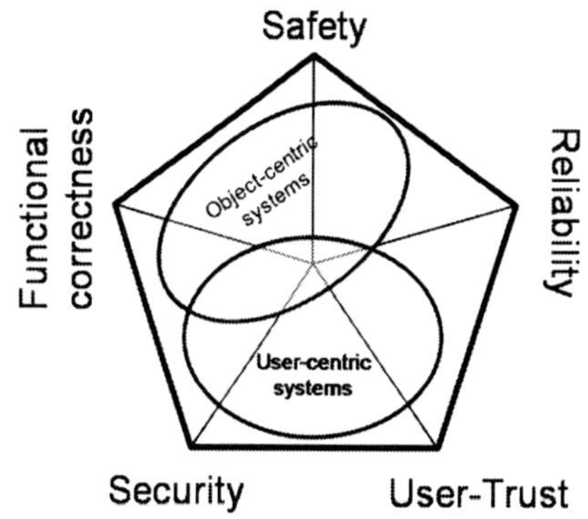

Figure 3. Decision support vs. autonomous systems

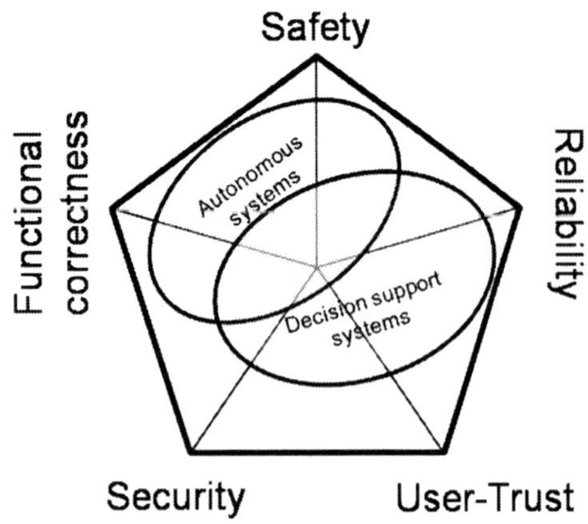

Figure 4. Mobile vs. stationary systems

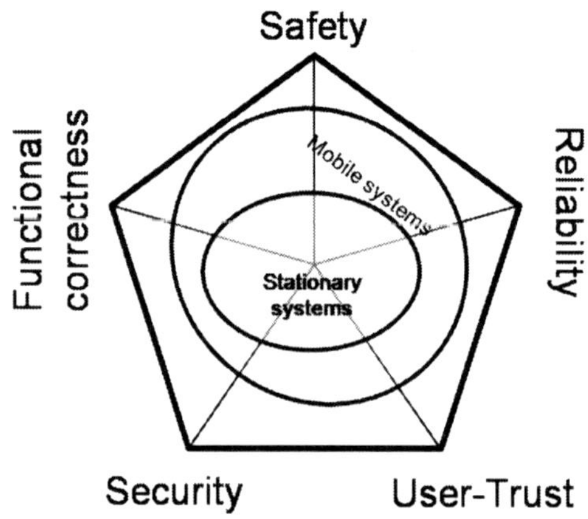

scenarios, where components are stationary. Just think of support systems in production automation, where machinery, personal and task planning scheduling are all interconnected. In this scenario, positions of participating sub-systems rarely or never change.

Relation to dependability: Stationary systems are typically easier to maintain and can thus be repaired more easily. As a consequence reliability is not as important for stationary systems as it is for mobile ones. Security also becomes less important, as possible attacker/intruder scenarios are restricted, because the locations of sub-systems are restricted. Figure 4 depicts this situation graphically.

Static vs. Self-Adapting Systems

A static system is a system, which has been designed for a certain purpose to work in a specified environment. Of course, any system can be designed for a very broad environment to fulfill multiple purposes. The difference to a self-adapting system is, that the designer of a static system must "foresee" all possible environments and purposes. A self-adapting system typically observes its environment and chooses actions accordingly. Very often this is achieved by integration of some kind of learning algorithm. So system behavior is dependent upon its environment and its history. The same system might behave differently in the same situation, only because it has been working in different environments in the past.

Relation to dependability: In theory, self-adapting systems are superior to static systems from a dependability point of view. The reason is that they can react to disturbances, failures and/or attacks. They are also capable of adapting to new environments. In reality, the problem with self-adaptation is that very often unwanted (maybe even dangerous) changes in behavior occur. As a consequence functional correctness and safety are very important for self-adapting systems (see Figure 5). The same holds for user trust (if any users are involved). If users do neither understand why a system acts as it does nor can they predict how it will (re-)act in a given situation, then acceptance for the system will be very low. Therefore self-* systems tend to come with higher requirements in terms of functional correctness and user-trust. On the other hand, not being able to compensate at runtime for faults and disturbances in the environment makes reliability more important for static systems.

Figure 5. Static vs. self-adapting systems

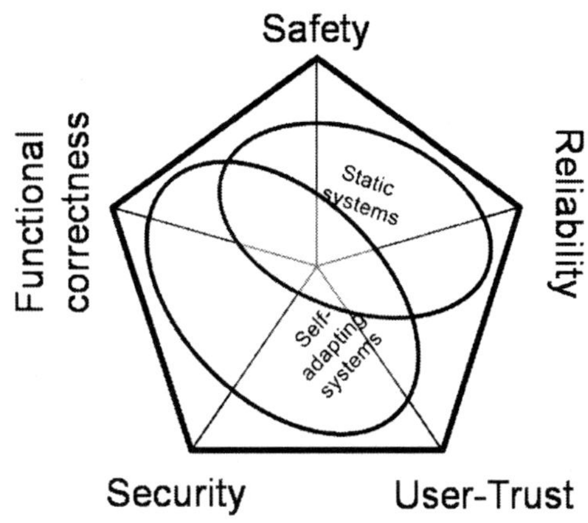

CONCLUSION

Pervasive Computing brings many exciting and promising new possibilities. Dependability is a key prerequisite for any new technical system. However, it is both more important and more difficult to achieve for Pervasive Computing systems. It is more important, because the ubiquitous nature of the system makes them capable of continuously influencing our behavior and our actions. Users will only accept this, if they trust the system. Legal authorities will only allow this, if they are sure that no harm is being done. Companies will only develop and sell such systems, if they have trust in the functional correctness of the system (and that they will not be made liable for any misbehavior).

Dependability is also much more difficult to achieve as many Pervasive Computing systems must fulfill simultaneously requirements from many different aspects of dependability. The abstract concept of dependability subsumes numerous sub-terms. This chapter presented a classification of dependability requirements, which might be in particular useful for Pervasive Computing systems. The classification follows different design and analysis domains. Dependability is here understood as functional correctness, safety, security, reliability and user-trust. Pervasive systems typically share requirements from each of these aspects. This chapter offers developers a brief overview on each aspect of dependability, with links to common tools and possibly interesting further readings.

Definition and ranking of dependability requirements is always a difficult task – even if just one aspect must be considered. This is especially true for Pervasive Computing systems, because of (a) the lack of norms for such systems and (b) their (relatively unique) property that most/all aspects of dependability have to be addressed at the same time. A possible orientation on which aspects are most important can be derived from the type of Pervasive Computing system. To assist developers in this respect, a classification of the Pervasive Computing domain into four dimensions together with their effect on dependability requirements is presented in this chapter. This might serve as a guideline for specification of dependability requirements analysis.

As a summarizing statement, it should be noted that – in addition to any specification problems – dependability of pervasive systems is in particular hard to analyze and guarantee. The nature of Pervasive Computing makes some methods either not applicable or very difficult to adapt. For each aspect of dependability, some methods might be promising, some might be difficult and others might not be applicable at all. In any case, developers will face the situation that they need to meet very high and diverse dependability requirements, while existing techniques are often difficult to apply. But possibly (eventually) research will come up with one (or more) integrated tailor-made approaches for dependability in Pervasive Computing.

REFERENCES

Avizienis, A., Laprie, J.-C., & Randell, B. (2001). *Fundamental concepts of dependability*. Newcastle University Technical Report. Retrieved March 30, 2010, from http://www.cs.ncl.ac.uk/research/trs/papers/739.ps

Avizienis, A., Laprie, J.-C., Randell, B., & Landwehr, C. (2004). Basic concepts and taxonomy of dependable and secure computing. *IEEE Transactions on Dependable and Secure Computing*, *1*(1), 11–33.

Ball, T., Bounimova, E., Cook, B., Levin, V., Lichtenberg, J., & McGarvey, C. … Ustuner, A. (2006). Thorough static analysis of device drivers. In *Proceedings 1st ACM SIGOPS/EuroSys European Conference on Computer Systems* (pp. 73-85), ACM press.

Bäumle, S., Balser, M., Knapp, A., Reif, W., & Thums, A. (2004). Interactive verification of UML state machines. In K.-K. Lau & R. Banach (Eds.), *Formal methods and software engineering* (pp. 434–448). Springer.

Bell, D. E., & Leonard, J. (1973). *Secure computer systems: Mathematical foundations*. MITRE Corporation. Retrieved March 30, 2010, from http://www.albany.edu/acc/courses/ia/classics/belllapadula1.pdf

Schmidt-Belz, B. (2005). User trust in adaptive systems. In *Proceedings of GI-Workshop on Lernen, Wissenstransfer, Adaptivität*. Retrieved March 30, 2010, from http://www.dfki.de/lwa2005/

Biba, K. J. (1977). *Integrity considerations for secure computer systems*. Mitre Corporation Report TR-3153. Bedford Massachusetts.

Bozzano, M., & Villafiorita, A. (2006). The FSAP/NuSMV-SA safety analysis platform. *Springer International Journal on Software Tools for Technology Transfer (STTT), 9*(1), 5-24.

Byun, J. W., Lee, S. M., Lee, D. H., & Hong, D. (2006). Constant-round password-based group key generation for multi-layer ad-hoc networks. In *Proceedings Third International Conference on Security in Pervasive Computing* (pp. 3-17). Springer.

Chen, Y., Romanovsky, A., Gorbenko, A., et al. (2009). Benchmarking dependability of a system biology application. In *Proceedings 14th IEEE International Conference on Engineering of Complex Computer Systems* (pp. 146-153). IEEE Computer Society.

Clarke, E. M., Grumberg, O., & Peled, D. A. (1999). *Model checking*. Cambridge, MA: MIT Press.

Davis, F. D. (1989). Perceived usefulness, perceived ease of use and user acceptance of information technology. *Management Information Systems Quarterly*, *13*(3), 319–339.

Dix, A. J., & Runciman, C. (1985). Abstract models of interactive systems. In *Proceedings HCI '85: People and Computer: Designing the Interface* (pp. 13-22). Cambridge, UK: University Press.

Dolev, D., & Yao, A. (1983). On the security of public key protocols. *IEEE Transactions on Information Theory*, *29*(2), 198–208.

Edwards, W. K., & Grinter, R. E. (2001). *At home with ubiquitous computing: Seven challenges* (pp. 256–272). London, UK: Springer-Verlag. Proceedings of the 3rd International conference on Ubiquitous Computing

Emerson, E. A. (1990). Temporal and modal logic. In J. Leeuwen (Ed.), *Handbook of theoretical computer science (vol. B): Formal models and semantics* (pp. 995-1072). Cambridge, MA: MIT Press.

Golbeck, J., Bijan, P., & Hendler, J. (2003). Trust networks on the Semantic Web. In M. Klusch, et al. (Eds.), *Cooperative information agents VII* (pp. 238–249). Heidelberg/ Berlin, Germany: Springer.

Grandy, H., Haneberg, D., Reif, W., & Stenzel, K. (2006). Developing provably secure m-commerce applications. In G. Muller (Ed.), *Emerging trends in information and communication security (ETRICS)* (pp. 115–129). Heidelberg/ Berlin, Germany: Springer.

Kwiatkowska, M. Z., Norman, G., & Parker, D. (2002). Probabilistic symbolic model checking with PRISM: A hybrid approach. In *Proceedings 8th International Conference on Tools and Algorithms for the Construction and Analysis of Systems*. ACM Press.

Livshits, B. (2006). *Improving software security with precise static and runtime analysis*. Unpublished doctoral dissertation, Stanford University, USA. Retrieved March 30, 2010 from http://research.microsoft.com/en-us/um/people/livshits/papers/pdf/thesis.pdf

Lawrence, J. D. (1995). *Software safety hazard analysis*. Publication of Livermore National Laboratory. Retrieved March 30, 2010 from www.osti.gov/bridge/servlets/purl/201805-VM21Vg/webviewable/

Mantel, H., Sudbrock, H., & Krausser, T. (2006). Combining different proof techniques for verifying information flow security. In *Proceedings 16th International Symposium on Logic Based Program Synthesis and Transformation* (pp. 94-110). Heidelberg/ Berlin, Germany: Springer.

Storey, N. (1996). *Safety critical systems*. Boston, MA: Addison Wesley Longman Publishing.

McDermott, R. E., Mikulak, R. J., & Beauregard, M. R. (1996). *The basics of FMEA*. New York, NY: Taylor & Francis Productivity Press.

Merz, S. (2001). Model checking: A tutorial overview. In F. Cassez, et al. (Eds.), *Modeling and verification of parallel processes* (pp. 3–38). Heidelberg/ Berlin, Germany: Springer.

Van Mulken, S., Andre, E., & Muller, J. (1999). An empirical study on the trustworthiness of life-like interface agents. In *Proceedings of the HCI International '99 (the 8th International Conference on Human-Computer Interaction) on Human-Computer Interaction: Communication, Cooperation, and Application Design*. Volume 2 (pp. 152-156). Hillsdale, NJ: Lawrence Earlbaum Ass.

Object Management Group. (2006). *Object constraint logic 2.0 formal specification*. Retrieved March 30, 2010 from http://www.omg.org/technology/documents/formal/ocl.htm

Ortmeier, F., Reif, W., & Schellhorn, G. (2006). *Deductive cause-consequence analysis*. Paper presented at IFAC World Congress, Istanbul, Turkey.

Paymans, T. F., Lindenberg, J., & Neerincx, M. (2004). Usability trade-offs for adaptive user interfaces: Ease of use and learnability. In *Proceedings of 9th International Conference on Intelligent User Interfaces*. ACM Press.

Roscoe, A. W., Woodcock, J. C. P., & Wulf, L. (1994). Non-interference through determinism. In *Proceedings of the Third European Symposium on Research in Computer Security* (pp. 33-53). London, UK: Springer-Verlag.

Schellhorn, G., Thums, A., & Reif, W. (2002). Formal fault tree semantics. In *Proceedings of 6th World Conference on Integrated Design & Process Technology*. ACM Press.

Vesley, W., Dugan, J., Fragola, J., Minarick, J., & Railsback, J. (2002). *Fault tree handbook with aerospace applications*. NASA Office of Safety and Mission Assurance. Retrieved March 30, 2010 from http://www.hq.nasa.gov/office/codeq/doctree/fthb.pdf

Vistein, M., Ortmeier, F., Reif, W., Huuck, R., & Fehnker, A. (2009). An abstract specification language for static program analysis. In *Proceedings of 4th International Workshop on System Software Verification*. Elsevier.

Volanschi, N. (2006). A portable compiler-integrated approach to permanent checking. In *Proceedings 21st IEEE/ACM International Conference on Automated Software Engineering*. IEEE Press.

ADDITIONAL READING

Anderson, R. J. (2008). *Security Engineering: A Guide to Building Dependable Distributed Systems*. Wiley Publishing.

Clark, J. A., Paige, R. F., Polack, F. A. C., & Brooke, P. J. (Eds.). (2006). *Security in Pervasive Computing*. Heidelberg: Springer Berlin.

Coverity Inc. Website (2010). Retrieved March 30, 2010 from http://www.coverity.com/products/static-analysis.html

German Organic Computing Initiative Website (2010). Retrieved March 30, 2010 from http://www.organic-computing.de/

International Electrotechnical Commission Website [IEC 191-02-03] (2003). Retrieved March 30, 2010 from http://dom2.iec.ch/iev/iev.nsf/display?openform&ievref=191-02-03

International Federation for Information Processing Working group 10.4 - [IFIP 10.4] (2003). Retrieved March 30, 2010 from http://www.dependability.org/wg10.4/

Isabelle Theorem Prover (2010). Retrieved March 30, 2010 from http://www.cl.cam.ac.uk/research/hvg/Isabelle/

Karlsruhe Interactive Verifier (2010). Retrieved March 30, 2010 from http://www.informatik.uni-augsburg.de/lehrstuehle/swt/se/kiv/

Markov Reward Model checker Website (2010). Retrieved March 30, 2010 from http://www.mrmc-tool.org/trac/

Prism Model Checker (2010). Retrieved March 30, 2010 from http://www.prismmodelchecker.org/

PVS Specification and Verification System (2010). Retrieved March 30, 2010 from http://pvs.csl.sri.com/

KEY TERMS AND DEFINITIONS

Functional Correctness: A property of the system, which ensures that the system fulfills its intention correctly. This is often given as a (formal) specification of the intended system behavior.

Safety: A property of a system, which ensures, that no harm to human or environment is done. In contrast to functional correctness even behavior in the presence of component failures is considered.

Reliability: A quantitative measure of a system`s possible safety violation. This is typically given as the probability of the system causing harm.

Security: A property of a system, which ensures that no malicious manipulation of the system is possible. This ranges from protection of data to unauthorized control.

User-Trust: A user (subjective) opinion on dependability aspects. The most important aspects are safety, reliability and security.

Chapter 11
Secure Electronic Healthcare Records Distribution in Wireless Environments Using Low Resource Devices

Petros Belsis
Technological Education Institute Athens, Greece

Christos Skourlas
Technological Education Institute Athens, Greece

Stefanos Gritzalis
University of the Aegean, Greece

ABSTRACT

The continuous growth of wireless technologies introduces a paradigm shift in the way information may be treated. Especially in the medical domain, Information Systems may gain benefits from the utilization of wireless devices which gain continuously in terms of resources. Existing legislation in US and EU countries introduces a lot of new challenges. Above all else, the information exchanged should be encrypted, and verified to reach the intended recipient. The authors of this chapter discuss the challenges hindering the efforts to disseminate in an accurate and secure manner medical information over wireless infrastructures. They present based on the results of two projects partially funded by the EU, an architecture that allows secure dissemination of electronic healthcare records. The chapter presents the architecture based on software agent technologies and enables query and authentication mechanisms in a transparent to the user manner. The chapter also discusses the security oriented choices of the approach and argues based on experimentation that the architecture efficiently supports a sufficient number of users.

DOI: 10.4018/978-1-60960-611-4.ch011

INTRODUCTION

Recent advances in mobile technologies have led to a continuous raise in the degree of integration of mobile devices to many different types of Information Systems. Among else, the medical domain is a field that is of particular interest for the potential benefits that mobile applications can exhibit in this domain. As mobile devices become more powerful, they are integrated as a non high-cost solution in many environments.

The medical domain can benefit a lot by their deployment, since the use of handheld devices may provide doctors and expert medical personnel with accurate information independently of the exact location provided that they are moving within a wireless environment which usually covers the clinic (Belsis et al 2008) in which they belong to.

From this point of view, access to information becomes ubiquitous since there is no need to approach or connect to a fixed point to access the necessary information. In the past this was not so easy to achieve, since it was necessary to access a specific stable point for this purpose; on the other side with today's technologies a lot of the necessary functionalities are provided by mobile devices.

For instance, a doctor may acquire valuable information about a patient's condition while approaching a patient using a mobile device which collects data from a sensor attached to the patient; accordingly, the doctor using the same device may collect more information by querying a database for stored details regarding the health condition of this patient. This treatment model becomes beneficial in case of emergency situations, or alternatively in emergency camps and in any other case characterized by lack of fixed, wired infrastructures.

The benefits related with the deployment of similar infrastructures are manifold; among them we can distinguish: provision of better and faster e-healthcare services, lower costs, easier expansion and scalability of the proposed architectures, to name the most important. However, there are several factors in terms of security that need to be considered, related with the sensitivity of data and imposed by the legislative framework in most of the western countries. These factors have to do with the incorporation of appropriate characteristics in the developed architectures, as well as with the embodying of appropriate security solutions that guarantee the security properties of medical information. Among the main design and implementation challenges we can distinguish (Vassis et al, 2008):

- The capability to provide information to doctors independently of their exact location;
- Achievement of information integration using interoperable standards for medical information storage and exchange;
- The ability to ensure that no sensitive medical information will be disclosed to unauthorized parties.

Mobile environments integrate a variety of heterogeneous applications, and demand flexible management of resources, available to wirelessly interconnected users and devices. Policy based management has supported efficiently the secure management of target resources which often span the borders of an organizational domain. Static oriented security management solutions fail, since there is no central administration available and due to several factors such as the large number of participant users and the mobility of users and devices; hence, there is a necessity for flexible, context related applicability of access control decisions.

The volatility of these environments makes developers forced to deal with contradictory requirements:

- The necessity to provide access from anywhere to anyone authorized to use medical related information,

- Ensuring at the same time non-disclosure of treatment-related information to non-authorized persons.

These restrictions direct our choices towards the creation of an appropriate architecture and towards the selection of appropriate security technologies that comply with the strict privacy and security restrictions related with medical wireless infrastructures.

The structure of the book chapter is as follows: after a brief introduction in this section, the next one presents related work in context and a brief comparison with our approach, while we proceed by discussing the security requirements and describes the security models applied; the policy based model is also described and the role of the different software modules is analyzed. We subsequently present the agent based platform that allows automated, transparent to the user dissemination of medical information; it also describes issues and solutions in respect to the interoperability features. The remaining of the chapter describes a use case scenario and also discusses in brief some parameters measured from experimental evaluation tests, having detailed on particular network management issues. The last section presents a brief discussion and also concludes the paper.

BACKGROUND

There is a lot of ongoing work that focuses on the provision of improved e-health services. A lot of research efforts from both the academia and the industrial sector are focusing towards the provision of high quality services that minimize the needs for binding health professionals to patients, but do not lower on the other side the quality of health related services. Special focus is needed in order to ensure the security properties of medical information processed through the system's modules.

AMON (Anliker et al, 2004) is a project that uses wearable devices to monitor vital patient parameters and transmits them using GSM/UMTS cellular infrastructure. As a target group the project uses patients with chronic cardiac and respiratory illnesses. The Monitor device, which is a basic component of the AMON project, utilizes sensors to gather information and analyses it using an expert system to provide fast treatment in cases of emergency. It focuses on the acquisition of several patient indications which are sent to authorized medical personnel. The main focus of this research project is to perform the necessary research, development and validation for an advanced wearable, personal health system.

The MobiCare project (Chakravorty, 2006) is a system for both in-house and open areas patient monitoring that allows remote monitoring of patients vital parameters using wearable devices and transmits the data using GPRS technology. It enables continuous monitoring for chronically ill patients. It also utilizes a programmable architecture that enables introduction, configuration and customization of diverse medical sensors to a patient sensor network. Client devices can be updated with new medical features, applications and services that are tailored to meet the requirements of patients and the health providers. Its platform allows also easy configuration of services, thus allowing to effectively address the requirements of the patient's medical monitoring needs – the most significant challenge in mobile healthcare.

Wireless mediCenter (Wireless medicenter, 2006) is a system for management of electronic medical records and delivery through secure LANs or high-speed wireless connections. It provides different portals for doctors and patients in order to achieve classification of access permissions. The restriction though to connect through the portal is a serious burden to the user.

The m-Care project (Brazier, 2006) aims at providing secure access through a WAP based architecture. Users and access rights related information is kept in an MS-SQL Server database. In our approach we have enabled a policy based approach which facilitates interoperation with other systems while it also provides a highly distributed nature to our system. PatientService (Choudhri et al, 2003) is a trust-based security architecture that enables medical records management in pervasive environments. In this approach access to medical information is provided to a set of users which hold a PDA that keeps the policy in a smart card. In our approach we issue the request from the PDA while the policy evaluation is not performed by the PDA itself. Moreover, we attempt to evaluate our approach by performing simulation experiments.

Our proposed architecture introduces a hybrid approach that utilizes different wireless interfaces for the transmission of medical data, namely using Wi-Fi and GSM interfaces to send patient data to the hospital. We also introduce robust encryption approaches that as an added benefit also minimize the consumption of resources, which is essential when the network uses portable devices with limited resources. For interoperability issues, we have selected standard, well-defined protocols to codify the medical record's parameters, which is achieved using interoperable protocols and appropriate encoding and encryption standards. Specific attention has been paid to the high security and privacy requirements regarding the transmission of sensitive information, in accordance with the imposed EU legislation.

SYSTEM REQUIREMENTS FOR WIRELESS MEDICAL INFRASTRUCTURES

The development of large scale and high speed Information Systems (IS) as well as the emergence of high performance networked systems did not come without drawbacks. One of the most important challenges is to handle the security challenges and to confront the attacks caused by outside intruders as well as insiders. Managing the resources of a framework in terms of security is a big challenge that requires a lot of effort on both the design as well as the implementation of countermeasures against possible attacks. Security policies are a common approach that is adopted to a high extent towards this direction. A policy can be considered to consist of a set of authoritative statements that determine the set of acceptable options in future selection processes (Kokolakis et al, 2000). Relative to security, a policy can determine the set of acceptable actions, prohibitions and rights that are defined within the borders of an organization. A part of a security policy is determining the access control rights for each individual. Several challenges arise on this field, due to the very large number of subjects (resources) that need to be administered and due to the very large number of users. The Role Based Access Control (RBAC) (Ahn and Sandhu, 2000) (Sandhu et al, 2000) model seems to be dominant and widely accepted in most of the commercial environments and software platforms. The main principle of RBAC is related with the fact that usually users with similar roles need to be accredited for the same actions, and need to have the same access rights. By classifying users to roles and accordingly by relating individuals with a role, the security management is simplified dramatically. For example, each time somebody enters the organization, we simply classify her to one of the predefined roles. Accordingly, when somebody leaves the organization, we do not need to manually withdraw all the access rights for every resource she was assigned to have access rights.

Things can become more complicated in mobile environments since new users enter and leave constantly. In addition, devices are characterized by low computing resources and power. Medical information on the other hand is highly sensitive; thus, we have to design our system so as to demand less processing and network bandwidth resources, without though decreasing our strict privacy requirements. Among the main requirements for our architecture we can distinguish the following:

- **Privacy preservation**. Unauthorized disclosure of medical information may lead to disastrous results. EU and US legislation has been put in force to ensure privacy preservation of medical data. Except from appropriately protecting medical databases, transmission of medical information should also be performed in a reliable and secure manner. We have thus employed efficient encryption techniques based on both symmetric and public key cryptography methods, so as to achieve data protection without demanding excessive processing power. In order to transmit data over wireless channels, we first exchange a shared key using strong encryption based on singing the messages with the private keys of the two parties, and then continue using shared key encryption so as to achieve a lightweight implementation.
- **Network topology instability**: Node mobility and node failure are problems that we have to deal with in the considered scenarios. In order to enable constant connectivity for as long as possible, we have decentralized many of our processing and communication tasks, avoiding thus the existence of single points of failure. Towards this direction we have adopted the DLS (distributed lookup server approach) (Malatras et al, 2005a) (Malatras et al, 2005b) according to which a number of nodes act collectively as a centralized node. When a node is about to stop transmitting, it passes all of its information to its neighbors in order to ensure incessant operation.
- **Interoperability**: In order to enable interoperation of our system with other medical systems and architectures we have adopted the HL7 standard for information encoding and exchange. For secure transmission and in compliance with the guidelines of the HL7 standard that instruct the use of secure protocols, one of the IP Security protocol (IPSec), Secure File Transfer Protocol (SFTP) or Secure Socket Layer Protocol (SSL) can be used for encrypting medical records.
- **Access control management**: In order to apply access control, we have adopted the Role Based Access Control Model (RBAC), due to its simplicity and wide acceptance as a security standard. Access Control is performed in the medical database using a policy based approach (Vassis et al, 2009). A policy approach allows determination of privileges according to business roles; accordingly, these privileges may be encoded in a suitable policy language and each request is directed towards special purpose modules, which reason over a specific request and either authorize or reject the request. Security policies, provide a flexible means to automate the security management procedures as well as to enable the enforcement of access control decisions on distributed systems. Security policies can be codified in several special purpose languages, some of which provide codification in XML format, which makes them preferable, as they provide support for various platforms, and also makes them highly interoperable. The use of policies can simplify the management of distributed systems, which contain a large number of objects which often span across organizational boundaries. A more challenging option arises when it comes to adapting to this framework resources from different domains which cooperate on the grounds of a common basis.

Mobile e-health environments pose a number of significant challenges from a security perspective. In order to retain fundamental security properties such as availability, confidentiality and integrity, several implementation oriented choices were made in our approach:

Table 1. Enabling time – periodicity within pre-specified time intervals

<Rule RuleId=”EveryoneDuringWorkingHours” Effect=”Allow”>
<Condition FunctionId=” Function#time-in-range”> <Apply FunctionId=”function:time-one-and-only”> <EnvironmentAttributeDesignator DataType=http://www.w3.org/2001/XMLSchema#time AttributeId=” environment:current-time”/></Apply>
<AttributeValue DataType=” http://www.w3.org/2001/XMLSchema#time”> 08.00</AttributeValue>
<AttributeValue DataType=” http://www.w3.org/2001/XMLSchema#time”>17:00:00 </AttributeValue>
</Condition></Rule>

- In order to enable a scalable authorization and authentication solution, the RBAC (Sandhu et al, 2000) model was chosen as the most appropriate one. This choice was made for several reasons: a) it is standardized, b) it is supported by most commercial applications, c) it reflects organizational hierarchy and enables easy mapping of privileges to organizational roles and therefore codification of security parameters and classification of roles to security privileges becomes a simpler task.
- Security policies were chosen in order to automate security management of infrastructures. Security policy languages enable determination of access control rules in a suitable format, both machine and human interpretable. Therefore, by configuration of appropriate files, security management becomes an automated process, which eliminates the security administrator burden.
- For confidentiality purposes and non-repudiation, Public Key Infrastructure techniques were deployed. Therefore for our framework, a policy server storing the security credentials and the associated with him/her access rights for each role was set up for each domain.

In our case due to the specific features in respect to mobility the RBAC needs to be extended, by incorporating in the role specification scheme domain specific attributes such as the domain's IP range, or it has to be extended so that time-enabled periodicity can be defined for roles (Table 1).

In our approach we utilize the Extensible Access Control Markup Language (XACML) (XACML, 2007). XACML is a policy language that supports prohibitions, obligations, and resolution of conflicts. Its expressiveness and XML (Extensible Markup Language) codification support allow its integration on a variety of environments, such as web-service based environments, distributed autonomous systems, and with some modifications to be applied also to pervasive environments. Among XACML's strong points, we can highlight the following:

- It is standardized and it is open, allowing extensions that enable interoperation between various platforms
- It is codified in (XML) which tends to dominate as codification standard and is operating system independent.
- It allows extensions as to support the needs for a variety of environments.
- It allows context based authorization, which is a big advantage for the scenarios that we envisage.

A XACML policy management system consists of several modules, with different roles each (Figure 1). In a mobile environment, the basic XACML module would demand adjustment to the topology-specific characteristics, as well as to the limited resource and processing power capability of the participating devices.

Figure 1. The policy based module

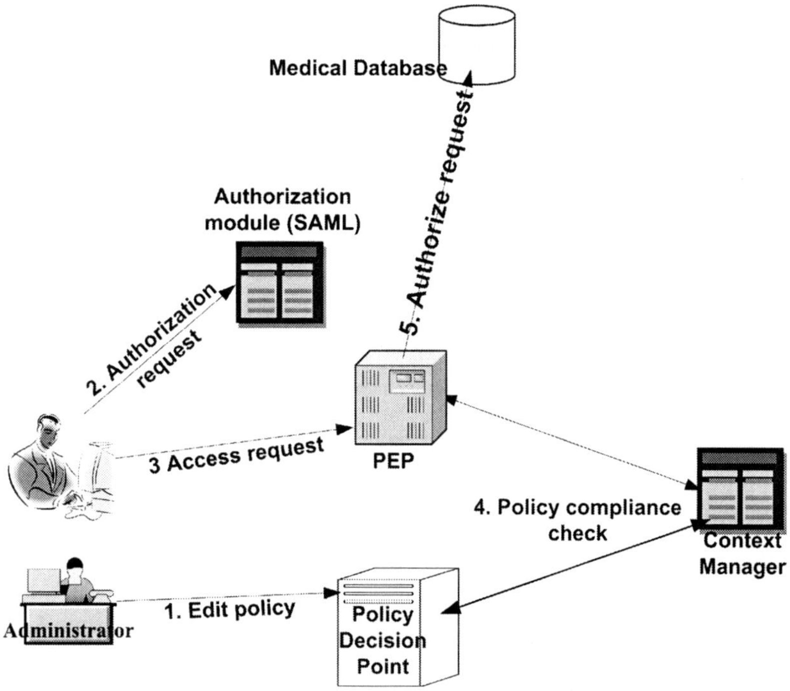

An overview of the XACML operational model is provided in the following. We can distinguish two main modules, namely the Policy Enforcement Point (PEP) and the Policy Decision Point (PDP). These two modules are responsible for reasoning about authorization requests as well as for policy enforcement. In the absence of a centralized authorization infrastructure, the policy based module is responsible for distributed security management. The implemented security module is based on the standardized IETF model. A more detailed description of the functionalities as well as of the tasks performed by each one of the modules is given in the following. More specifically, the different modules are:

- The authorization module, which identifies the user's id using X.509 certificates, and next issues SAML (Hughes et al, 2007) assertions that can be further used to assist the doctor's interaction with the system, providing thus single sign-on functionality to the system.
- The Policy Enforcement Point (PEP), which enforces the decision, after examining the XACML reply messages sent by the PDP.
- The Policy Decision Point (PDP), which loads the policy and reasons over the request, expressed by means of an XACML message sent to the PDP by the PEP.
- The context handler which facilitates policy decisions in respect to specific context related variables, for example the domain name that a user belongs to.

A given use case scenario that is based on the XACML model is the following (Figure 1): First the administrator edits the policy in XML format and makes it available at the PDP. Considering a user who wants to request a resource, the first thing necessary is to obtain an authentication SAML compliant assertion. This is obtained

Table 2. (a) (left) An Excerpt from a XACML request message. The requester's attribute is highlighted, as well as the requested resource. (b) (right) XACML response message

<Request> <Subject> <Attribute > AttributeValue>secretary@aegean.gr </AttributeValue> </Attribute> </Subject><Resource> <Attribute><AttributeValue> file://record/StudentlRecords/PeterKenn </AttributeValue></Attribute> </Resource> <Action><Attribute> <AttributeValue>read</AttributeValue> </Attribute></Action> </Request>	<Response> <Result> <Decision>NotApplicable </Decision> </Result> </Response>

through the authentication module. Then the user's request for a resource is directed from the user's device to the Policy Enforcement Point. The latter issues a related request and directs it to the context handler which constructs an XACML request message, which is further directed to the PDP for evaluation (for example see Table 2 for the structure of the message). The PDP checks the user's permissions and the request and issues a decision. This decision is further directed to the PEP which enforces the decision from the PDP.

Table 2a indicates excerpts from the XACML messages, which describe the requester and object, while Table 2b describes an XACML response. The attributes of the requester are highlighted in Table 2a (left) as well as the resource requested.

AGENT BASED ARCHITECTURE

The security module as described above facilitates security management; still, it is essential for non expert users to be able to interact and retrieve the necessary information in a transparent manner to the user. For this purpose, the use of software agents gives an ideal solution (Zafeiris et al, 2005). Software agents are applications that may act as delegates to the user's actions (FIPA, 2005). For example the authentication and authorization process can be simplified if a software agent retrieves the user's credentials and interacts with the system on the user's behalf. Therefore, in order to facilitate the identification and retrieval of medical information by medical personnel, in a secure manner and with low response times and transparently to the user, we have created an agent based application. Two software agents have been installed on each device; one that is responsible for the identification of the relevant information by querying the medical database and a second that is responsible to perform all the security related operations, or more specifically to handle access control decisions as a delegate of the device owner (the doctor or medical personnel).

When a doctor requests a medical record, the agent handles the query by looking for the requested information in different locations within the distributed environment. For every database there are different agents that are ready to communicate and interoperate with the user's agent. Next, the security agent is invoked which handles the security related tasks between the device and the policy management system which handles the security related tasks. For the software agents development we have used the JADE (Java Agent Development Framework) (Bellifemine et al, 2007) software agent management software and especially the LEAP (Lightweight Extensible Agent Platform) module targeted specific for mobile devices. We will briefly discuss the un-

Figure 2. Overview of the agent based architecture. Interoperation between different distributed locations is performed by means of different agent based applications.

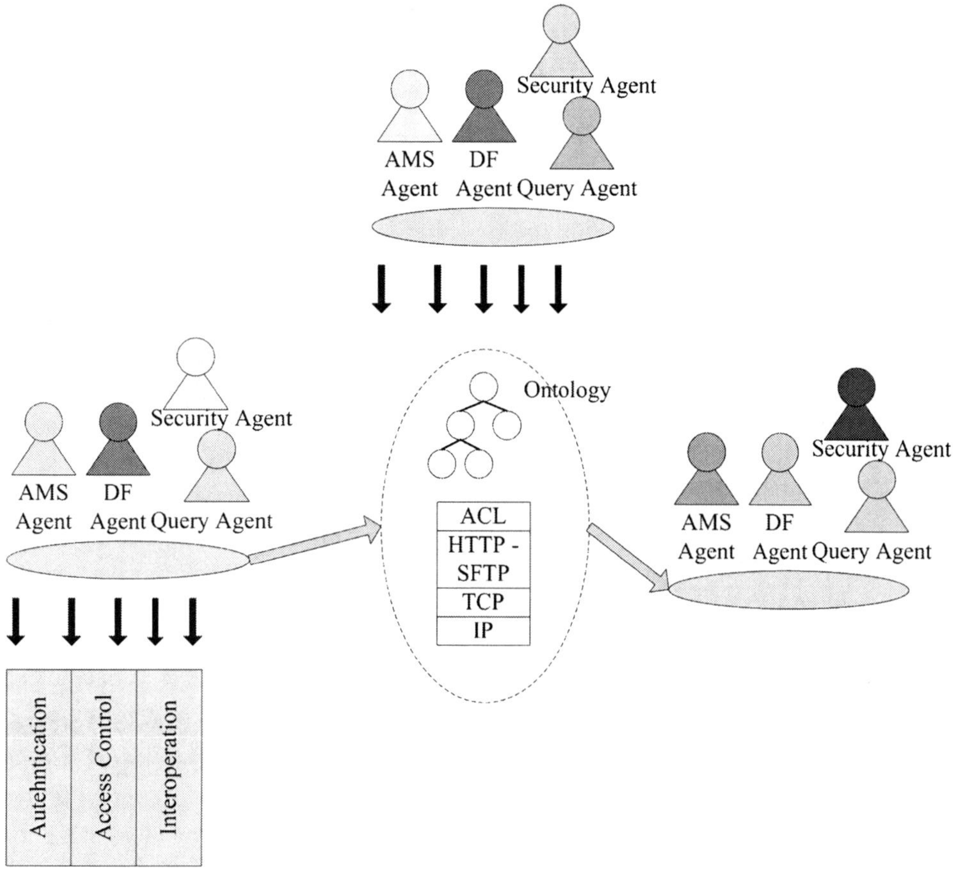

derlying architecture of the JADE platform (Fig. 2): the JADE platform allows the creation of a distributed agent architecture. Therefore, each agent communicates with other agents in this distributed environment and they communicate exchanging messages in the standardized Agent Communication Language (ACL). In order to facilitate the communication, the messages are encoded in an ontology that facilitates the interoperation between them.

The agent platform provides also several additional agents that facilitate interoperation between different agents from different domains: the Agent Management System (AMS) is a software agent that controls the cooperation between agents and the directory facilitator (DF) one that provides directory services to the other agents. In order to lower the resource demands so that our platform operates well in devices with limited resources, we have used the LEAP component of the JADE platform that is suitable for resource constrained devices.

Exploiting Medical Codification Standards for Interoperability

Many efforts during the last years have dealt with the development of medical standards for the codification of medical information; lately, the HL7 has been adopted as a widely accepted standard. In this respect and in order to achieve interoperation of our approach with other standardized systems,

Table 3. An example of an HL7 message

```
MSH|^~\&|Sys|Hosp|HL7Connect|Hosp|2
0050313173613||ADT^A01^ADT_A01|00
00000403|P|2.3.1EVN|A01|20050313173614149|||a017
PID|||8665^^^PH||NGO^ELENA^^^Ms||19750514|F|||42SYG ST
REET^^ATH^VIC^3000PV1||I|2D^13^1^^^^^^Ward 3 Wouth|||
|TESTDR^TEST^PETER^^DR|||ORT||||||||14201|COM|
```

we have selected the HL7 standard to encode and exchange medical information. Table 3 displays an example of a patient admission HL7 message, resulting from a request from a doctor's wireless device (PDA). This message may be easily transformed in XML which facilitates interoperation with most types of applications nowadays. Most of the medical applications nowadays support creation, codification and retrieval of HL7 messages. Thus, except from the security parameters in our research we have attempted to measure the effects of the information overhead caused by a combination of the following factors: i) the use of the HL7 standard to encode the medical information, ii) cryptography to align with the privacy requirements and the use of the agent based applications on the user's device. In the following paragraphs we further analyze the technical details related with the development of our framework and we perform simulations measurements that encounter all the aforementioned parameters to ensure the effective operation of our platform.

SYSTEM USE CASE SCENARIO

Our architecture enables remote monitoring of patients while they are at home, where through a wireless interface and a DSL connection the data can be sent to the hospital or through a GSM device when the patient is outside from his/her home. This enables to continuously monitor the condition of a patient without it being necessary to hospitalize him/her.

Now imagine the following use case scenario: A patient has attached on his/her body a number of sensors that measure several vital parameters. Using a mobile device, these parameters are collected every few minutes. A device attached to the patient's body equipped with several different wireless interfaces is responsible to collect them. For example while the patient is at home, an IEEE 802.11 wireless interface is used to collect all the values. Then the device sends the data to the hospital through a DSL interface. In order to ensure interoperability with other applications at the hospital, the information is encoded in HL7 format. For this purpose we have used the HL-7comm application (Litherland, 2009) which is Java based. In order to ensure the confidentiality of the transmitted information all the information is encrypted using the SSL protocol.

Now imagine that the patient is not within his domestic environment. Similarly to the previous case, the devices collect the vital parameters, but in this case there is neither DSL connectivity nor Wi-Fi coverage. In this case the GSM interface is used and it sends through a GSM provider the messages to the Hospital Gateway. The GSM network supports by default strong encryption methods. In case that the vital parameters of a patient exceed some threshold an alert is produced that notifies the medical personnel to take some kind of action. If the situation demands so, an ambulance is sent at the patient's location to transfer him/her to the hospital. In another case, the hospital personnel may call the patient at home or at his/her mobile to notify on a recommended course of action.

We will now explain the architecture of the system at the hospital's side. The doctors carry each a PDA device that is able to collect messages and inform them about events that require their attention. In order to receive these messages through an automated process that does not require their involvement, this process is performed through the software agents developed for this reason. Therefore when a doctor needs to be informed about a patient's condition, the appropriate agent is retrieving the medical files associated with the specific patient; prior though to bringing the files, the authorization process needs to be completed. For this reason the authorization process is performed in two phases. First, the authentication module, using a challenge response protocol and the doctor's public key, attempts to verify whether the device owner is really a doctor. The security agent at the doctor's device replies after decrypting the challenging message using the doctor's private key which is stored in the device. In order to protect the device from potential theft, we ensure that the doctor's private key is protected using a PIN mechanism. After the doctor has been authenticated, the authentication module issues a SAML assertion that allows the doctor to further interact with the system, achieving thus a single sign on process. Next, the policy management module is invoked, the main responsibility of which is to perform authorization specific processes. All the requests to access a specific file are forwarded to the Policy Decision Point. This checks the request according to the existing policies and in case that the requester should be allowed to view the files, it sends a XACML message to the PEP which allows the request. In order to further ensure that all the messages are exchanged in a secure manner we employ a hybrid encryption approach. First, a shared key is exchanged using asymmetric key encryption. This is done to ensure that the shared key will by no means be intercepted. Then since asymmetric encryption would demand a lot of network and device resources, we use the shared key to handle all communications. Therefore we ensure the robustness of our architecture and we ensure that all communications are safe while we also ensure that the system will respond fast and without excessive consumption of device resources.

NETWORK MANAGEMENT ISSUES

Using a network that builds upon wireless devices demands more advanced ways to handle network management issues than the ones that a fixed network would require. Within the hospital range, we consider different types of wireless nodes that participate in the network. First, we consider the central nodes (CN's) that store the medical data and are responsible for authentication and access control enforcement and two types of mobile nodes with different processing and access control capabilities: the Manager Nodes (MN's) which are assigned with more advanced tasks and Terminal Nodes (TN's) which lack in respect to MN's in resources and are assigned secondary tasks. The CN's are responsible for the operation of the policy management module and are responsible to maintain the medical database; they are characterized by adequate processing as well as network bandwidth capabilities. They have also installed the different policy management modules: the Policy Decision Point (PDP) and the Policy Enforcement Point. Authentication is performed through an LDAP server which evaluates the medical personnel's credentials (encoded as X.509 certificates) and issues a SAML assertion which can be further used for identification in every future transaction with the access control enforcement module, providing thus a Single Sign-On (SSO) mechanism. In respect to mobile nodes, we distinguish two organizational roles which characterize also the operation of each node: a) Manager Nodes (MN) are devices with more processing capabilities and RAM memory and are held by doctors; b) Terminal Nodes (TN) are devices with less processing power capabilities and are supplied with a lightweight implementation that allows simple operations, like informing a medical assistant about a patient's medication and when it should be scheduled.

The software installed on MN's includes a local PDP and PEP module which allow enforcement of local (as recorded in the device) policies, enabling thus access to the device's local repository to other doctors. On the contrary, TN's perform only simple operations, such as informing nursing personnel about an emergency or providing details about a patient's pharmaceutical prescription and

Figure 3. Overall system architecture. The beacon transmits signed messages that are domain specific

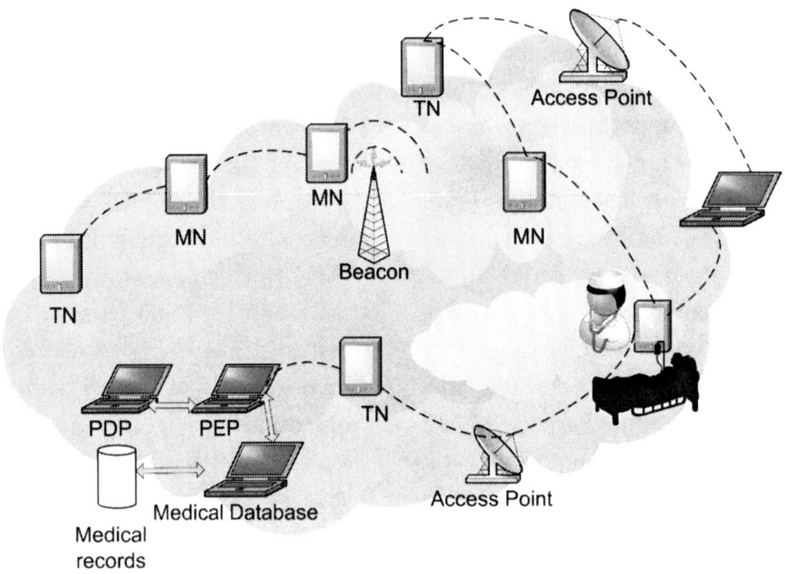

the time that this medication is scheduled; a TN is never allowed to access sensitive medical data.

Both TN and MN nodes are able to identify whether they reside within the clinic or in an unknown environment, with the aid of a beacon (Figure 3) which sends signed messages identifiable by each device when compared to a number of stored signed (within the smart card) messages. Thus, we prevent unauthorized transmission or reception from the device when it resides outside pre-settled space boundaries.

PERFORMANCE EVALUATION

In order to evaluate our architecture we have performed several initial experiments. For an initial test scenario, we concluded to the following results. Initially we measured the time that a monitoring message takes from the moment that it is recorded from the sensor attached to the patient at home until it reaches its final destination at the hospital database. This needs on average 8 seconds from the time of its birth, to the time that is recorded to the database. An alarm generated from the patient's home needs about 2 seconds to be transmitted to the nurse's / doctor's PDA. The delay between the 'birth' of a monitored value above a certain threshold, to the time the alarm message triggered by this value comes to the doctor's PDA is on average 12 seconds. These delays observed in the message transmission, are very small compared to the time needed for the doctor to see the message and proceed to the appropriate action (this can take more than 2-3 minutes, according to the person). These results are satisfactory in order to provide treatment to a number of patients, if we consider that we do not need to hospitalize them if they do not face some immediate danger for their health and still whenever necessary we can be notified and take action in short time intervals.

GENERAL REMARKS AND DISCUSSION

In this chapter we presented a wireless architecture that enables transparent identification and secure dissemination of medical information. Several issues and challenges have been described and diverse solutions have been provided; the most notable of these challenges are:

- Security management, using an automated policy-based framework
- Use of appropriate techniques that ensure confidentiality while they do not consume excessive resources in the network which comprises mobile low resource devices.
- Enabling transparent to the user identification of medical records
- Integration of transparent authorization and authentication processes.

In order to achieve the first task, we implemented a policy based management module which uses the XACML framework to enforce access control decisions within the distributed environment. We have selected a Java based framework to develop software agents that act as delegates of the user to identify the relevant medical information, as well as to enforce the policy decisions. In order to manage the strict security requirements we have implemented a hybrid encryption approach that uses asymmetric encryption to exchange the shared key and then uses this key to encrypt all further communications. Thus, we allow secure information exchange within our framework without excessive consumption of the limited resources from the participating mobile devices.

We distinguish different organizational roles and provide the users with different capabilities; therefore both doctors and supporting personnel may perform the necessary tasks, by providing them also only with the necessary capabilities.

We have presented an architecture that consists of different interoperating modules which could be in general classified in two categories: i) the first consists of the modules that handle patient monitoring tasks using sensors and various wireless interfaces to efficiently transmit messages to the hospital; ii) the second category consists of the modules that handle encoding of messages to the database, and notify the doctor at his/her PDA using a software agent based application and a policy based management approach.

The prototype architecture incorporates different networking technologies such as Bluetooth, Wi-Fi, and 3G. In order to ensure that our platform interoperates with other medical applications we have selected the HL7 standard to encode medical information. We have described our implementation choices and in particular those that handle the advanced security and privacy requirements. The presence of large number of users and mobile devices in the described scenarios has directed our security implementation choices towards a policy based approach resulting in an efficient and in an automated manner flexible management. The presence of agents has further facilitated a transparent interaction between users and the system modules.

We presented an initial evaluation resulting from experimentation that shows that the system response times are acceptable.

FUTURE RESEARCH DIRECTIONS

A lot of ongoing work is devoted to the e-health domain. A lot of international projects are funded towards this direction by the EU (ISHTAR, Trust-Health, MEDSEC, EUROMED-ETS, PRIDEH, RESHEN, and HARP). Among the main challenges we can distinguish the security and interoperability issues as well as network management issues in mobile environments. We are currently experimenting with the different parameters that affect the network performance as well as the effect of the presence of the sensors in the network and overall preciseness and delay due to the presence of heterogeneous devices.

REFERENCES

Ahn, J. G., & Sandhu, R. (2000). Role-based authorization constraints specification. [TISSEC]. *ACM Transactions on Information and System Security*, *3*(4), 207–226. doi:10.1145/382912.382913

Anliker, U., Ward, V., Lukowitcz, P., Tröster, G., Dolveck, F., & Baer, M. (2004). AMON: A wearable multiparameter medical monitoring and alert system. *IEEE Transactions on Information Technology in Biomedicine*, *8*(4), 415–427. doi:10.1109/TITB.2004.837888

Bellifemine, F. L., Caire, G., & Greenwood, D. (2007). JADE software agent development platform. Retrieved June 10, 2010, from http://jade.tilab.com/

Belsis, P., Vassis, D., Skourlas, C., & Pantziou, G. (2008). Secure dissemination of electronic healthcare records in distributed wireless environments. In S. Anderssen, et al. (Eds.), *Proceedings of 21st International Congress of the European Federation for Medical Informatics,* (pp. 661-666), IOS Press.

Brazier, D. (2006). *The m-care project*. Alpha Bravo Charlie Ltd. Retrieved June 10, 2010, from http://www.m-care.co.uk/tech.html

Chakravorty, R. (2006). Mobicare: A programmable service architecture for mobile medical care. In *Proceedings of IEEE PerCom Workshops* (pp. 532-536), IEEE Press.

Choudhri, A., Kagal, A., Joshi, A., Finin, T., & Yesha, Y. (2003). *PatientService: Electronic patient record redaction and delivery in pervasive environments*, Paper presented at the Fifth International Workshop on Enterprise Networking and Computing in Healthcare Industry (Healthcom), Santa Monica.

FIPA. (2005). *Foundation for Intelligent Physical Agents: FIPA specifications*. Retrieved June 10, 2010, from http://www.fipa.org/specifications/index.html

Hughes, J., & Maler, E. (2004). *Technical overview of the OASIS security assertion markup language* (SAML) V2.0. Retrieved June 10, 2010, from http://xml.coverpages.org/SAML-TechOverviewV20-Draft7874.pdf

ISHTAR Consortium (Ed.). (2001). *Implementing secure healthcare telematics applications in Europe – ISHTAR*. Amsterdam, The Netherlands: IOS Press.

Kokolakis, S., & Kiountouzis, E. (2000). Achieving interoperability in a multi-security-policies environment. *Computers & Security*, *19*(3), 267–281. doi:10.1016/S0167-4048(00)88615-0

Litherland, M. (2009). *HL & Comm*. Retrieved June 10, 2010, from http://nule.org/wp/?page_id=63

Malatras, A., Pavlou, G., Belsis, P., Gritzalis, S., Skourlas, C., & Chalaris, I. (2005a). Deploying pervasive secure knowledge management infrastructures. *International Journal of Pervasive Computing and Communications Troubador Publishing*, *1*(4), 265–276. doi:10.1108/17427370580000130

Malatras, A., Pavlou, G., Belsis, P., Gritzalis, S., Skourlas, C., & Chalaris, I. (2005b). Secure and distributed knowledge management in pervasive environments. In *Proceedings of IEEE International Conference on Pervasive Services, Santorini - Greece*, IEEE Press.

Sandhu, R., Ferraiolo, D., & Kuhn, R. (2000). The NIST model for role-based access control: Towards a unified standard. In *Proceedings of the Fifth ACM Workshop on Role-Based Access Control (RBAC '00)* (pp. 47–63). ACM Press.

Vassis, D., Belsis, P., Skourlas, C., & Gritzalis, S. (2009). End to end secure communication in ad-hoc assistive medical environments using secure paths. In G. Pantziou (Ed.), *Proceedings of the PSPAE 2009 1st Workshop on Privacy and Security in Pervasive e-Health and Assistive Environments, in conjunction with PETRA 2009 2nd International Conference on Pervasive Technologies related to Assistive Environments*. ACM Press.

Vassis, D., Belsis, P., Skourlas, C., & Pantziou, G. (2008). A pervasive architectural framework for providing remote medical Treatment. *Proceedings of 1st International Conference on Pervasive Technologies Related to Assistive Environments, ACM International Conference Proceeding Series; Vol. 282, article No. 23,* ACM Press.

Wireless Medicenter. (2006). Retrieved June 10, 2010, from http://www.wirelessmedicenter.com/mc/glance.cfm

XACML. (2007). *XACML extensible access control markup language specification* 2.0. Organization for the Advancement of Structured Information Standards (OASIS). Retrieved June 10, 2010, from http://www.oasis-open.org

Zafeiris, V., Doulkeridis, C., Belsis, P., & Chalaris, I. (2005). *Agent-mediated knowledge management in multiple autonomous domains.* Paper presented at Workshop on Agent Mediated Knowledge Management, Univ. of Utrecht Netherlands.

ADDITIONAL READING

Belsis, P., & Gritzalis, S. (2004, December). *Distributed autonomous Knowledge Acquisition and Dissemination ontology based framework*, Paper presented at Workshop on Enterprise Modeling and Ontology: Ingredients for Interoperability, University of Vienna, Vienna Austria

Belsis, P., Gritzalis, S., & Katsikas, S. (2005). A Scalable Security Architecture enabling Coalition Formation between Autonomous Domains. In *Proceedings of the 5th IEEE International Symposium on Signal Processing and Information Technology (ISSPIT'05), Athens, Greece*. IEEE Computer Society Press.

Belsis, P., Gritzalis, S., Malatras, A., Skourlas, C., & Chalaris, I. (2005). Sec-Shield: Security Preserved Distributed Knowledge Management between Autonomous Domains. In J. Lopez, G. Pernul, (Ed.) *Proceedings of the DEXA'05 TrustBus'05 2nd International Conference on Trust, Privacy, and Security in the Digital Business* (pp. 10-20). Lecture Notes in Computer Science LNCS 3592

Bonatti, P., De Capitani di Vimercati, S., & Samarati, P. (2002). An algebra for composing access control policies. [TISSEC]. *ACM Transactions on Information and System Security*, *5*(1), 1–35. doi:10.1145/504909.504910

Chousiadis, C., Mavridis, I., & Pangalos, G. (2002). An authentication architecture for healthcare information systems. *Health Informatics Journal*, *8*, 199–204. doi:10.1177/146045820200800406

European Parliament and the Council of the EU. (1995). Directive 95/46/EC on the Protection of Individuals with regard to the Processing of Personal Data and on the Free Movement of Such Data, *Official Journal of the European Communities*, L281/38.

Gatzoulis, S., & Iakovidis, I. (2007). Wearable and Portable e-health systems. *IEEE EMB Magazine*, *26*(5), 51–55. doi:10.1109/EMB.2007.901787

Gritzalis, S., Belsis, P., & Katsikas, S. (2007). Interconnecting autonomous medical domains: a security perspective. *IEEE EMB Magazine*, *26*(5), 23–28. doi:10.1109/EMB.2007.901783

Houston, T. (2001). Security issues for implementation of e-medical records. *Communications of the ACM*, *44*(9), 89–95. doi:10.1145/383694.383712

ITU-T Recommendation X.509. (2005). Information Technology - Open systems interconnection The Directory: Public-key and attribute certificate frameworks. Retrieved June 10, 2010 from http://www.itu.int/rec/T-REC-X.509-200508-I/en

Kokolakis, S., Gritzalis, D., & Katsikas, S. (2002). Draft Standard for High Level Security Policies for Healthcare Information Systems. In Allaert, F.-A., Blobel, B., Louwerse, K., & Barber, B. (Eds.), *Security Standards for Healthcare Information Systems* (pp. 37–61). Amsterdam: IOS Press.

SEISMED Consortium (Ed.). (1996). *Data Security for Health Care* (*Vol. I-III*). IOS Press.

Sharmin, M., Ahmed, S., & Khan, A. (2006). Healthcare Aide: Towards a Virtual Assistant for Doctors Using Pervasive Middleware, In *Proceedings of IEEE PerCom Workshops* (pp. 490-495), IEEE Press.

Springer. Blobel, B., & Nordberg, R. "Privilege Management and Access Control in Shared Care IS and EHR", In Proceeding of the MIE 2003.

Zhang, L., Ahn, G.-J., & Chu, B.-T. (2002). A role-based delegation framework for healthcare information systems. In *Proceedings of SACMAT'02*, ACM Press.

KEY TERMS AND DEFINITIONS

Electronic Healthcare Records: digital records of individuals or groups of people containing information related to health issues.

Security: Retaining confidentiality, integrity and availability properties of a piece of information.

Policy Based Management: the process of defining actions executed upon the presence of specific conditions in order to enable automated management of network resources in a network..

Chapter 12
Privacy in Pervasive Systems: Legal Framework and Regulatory Challenges

Antonio Liotta
Technische Universiteit Eindhoven, The Netherlands

Alessandro Liotta
Axiom - London, UK

ABSTRACT

Data protection legislation has developed in a digital communication context that is changing dramatically. Infrastructure-based, networked systems are increasingly interconnecting and interoperating with infrastructure-less or even spontaneous networks, which are important elements of pervasive systems. These are also characterized by an autonomic, self-managed behavior that undermines the role of central management entities such as network and service providers. In this context, meeting the demanding requirements of privacy laws becomes a serious challenge, because once the user's data crosses a managed boundary, it is impossible to clearly determine and transfer responsibilities. This chapter revisits the important elements of privacy regulations with the purpose of highlighting the hurdles posed onto pervasive systems. The analysis in this chapter indentifies imperative research and technological issues.

INTRODUCTION

The treatment of personal information has become a sensitive topic for businesses, governmental authorities and individuals. During the past years, the number of data security breaches occurred has significantly increased, raising great concern in the public opinion. Consumers expect that appropriate technical measures are in place at all times to avoid unauthorized access to their personal data.

The new century is seeing deep technology improvements in the communications arena. This represents, at the same time, a great opportunity for the users, who are now able to benefit from a

DOI: 10.4018/978-1-60960-611-4.ch012

wider variety of services available via different devices, but also a greater threat to their privacy.

Data protection regulations have been in place for several years in almost all countries around the world, but their effectiveness is now being questioned by individuals and businesses in the light of the potential impact that new technologies may have on the individuals' private life.

To this respect, pervasive computing is expected to represent a new challenge for the society (Hansmann, 2003). The intrusiveness of such new communications technology together with the lack of control that (unlike the more traditional networked systems) characterizes its networks, if not addressed adequately, may result in a loss of individuals' trust in pervasive technology. The need to gain customers' confidence and the obligation to comply with all applicable regulations will then impose a great pressure on businesses willing to invest in such technology.

In this chapter, we give an overview of the privacy legislation and its potential impact on the commercial development of pervasive computing, through the analysis of court cases in Europe. We also give a first cut consideration of the potential conflicts between privacy regulations, data retention obligations and copyright infringement protection that may arise in a global environment from the application of pervasive systems, and how these issues are to be seen as topics to put to the attention of businesses, researchers and regulators.

Our review unveils key shortcomings of the current legal framework specifically in relation to pervasive systems. Data protection legislation has developed in a digital communication context that is changing dramatically. Particularly, the role and responsibilities of data controllers, network operators, and service providers are blurred in a pervasive system where networks span across different domains, organizations and countries. Also, several portions of the network tend to be self-managed rather than being under the direct control (and responsibility) of a named entity.

By contrast to a more conventional (non-pervasive) networked system, where it is relatively easier to determine who is responsible for privacy compliance and can transfer those responsibilities among data processors, in pervasive systems this is not always possible. The very idea of pervasiveness is associated with the concepts of "ubiquity", "transparency", "distribution", and "autonomic management". Pervasive networks include not only infrastructure-based technologies (such as WiFi, cellular systems, ADSL), which rely on management entities that can be held responsible for the data flow. Pervasive networks are increasingly made of infrastructure-less (or spontaneous) network elements (such as ad hoc networks, MANETs, or sensor networks) (Sarkar, 2007), in which cases the user's terminal has the potential to transparently store or relay data belonging to other users.

Hence, the very nature of a pervasive system clashes head-on with the very essence of privacy regulatory principles. In order to fully appreciate the controversial legal issues surrounding pervasive systems, this chapter focuses on the current data protection legal framework.

The following section provides the necessary background, introducing key data protection concepts and definitions. We then present the eight fundamental principles underlying the Data Protection Directive. These are further illustrated with the aid of four case studies. Having introduced the relevant legal framework, we finally place it in the context of pervasive systems, which helps understanding the hurdles and risks of pervasive systems (in their current form and their future development), giving an indication of the most crucial technological and research issues.

DATA PROTECTION OVERVIEW

Background

The right to a private domain was first recognized at international level in Article 12 of the Universal Declaration of Human Rights adopted by the General Assembly of the United Nations in 1948[1].

But it is between 1970 and 1980, when computing systems started to spread, bringing with them an increase in the amount of information that could be stored, categorized, classified or transmitted, that a deeper interest in the protection of privacy has arisen (Jay & Hamilton, 2003).

The capacity of new technologies to process data at an unprecedented speed and extent has raised (and continues raising) concerns around the world about potential violations of individuals' privacy.

Almost every country has now adopted measures aimed at protecting personal data from unlawful access. Although each national set of regulations may present different specifications, there are strong commonalities of reasons, approaches and measures among the various legislations, while systems, networks, technologies that generate cross-border data flows potentially need to be compliant in each and every jurisdiction in which they operate.

The European Union (EU) framework is certainly one of the most stringent among the data protection regulation systems applied around the world. For this reason (as well as for practical reasons) we have decided to take it as a comprehensive example to analyze the general legal issues relating to privacy. Taking the EU framework as a model to assess regulatory compliance of pervasive systems may also result advantageous for global businesses that should comply with the highest standards of regulations in order to make sure that the technology used may be adapted to be compliant with regulations worldwide.

Data Protection Concepts

Before starting the analysis of the Data Protection Principles, it is important to understand some key concepts used in the European legislation that relate to privacy, in order to appreciate the scope and application of the legislation.

Personal Data

The EU privacy legislation applies to personal data. Personal data is "any information relating to an identified or identifiable natural person ("data subject"); an identifiable person is one who can be identified, directly or indirectly, in particular by reference to an identification number or to one or more factors specific to his physical, physiological, mental, economic, cultural or social identity"[2]. It is evident how the definition of personal data is very broad. Consequently, the scope of privacy regulations expands depending on the interpretation that authorities may from time to time give to such definition. Regulators have for example considered personal data information regarding bank account details, shopping profiles, fingerprints, which may identify the data subject (Jay & Hamilton, 2003). The Data Protection Directive[3] gives the criteria to apply in order to determine whether the data provided are sufficient to identify a person (and be considered personal data). Recital 26 provides that "to determine whether a person is identifiable, account should be taken of all the means likely reasonably to be used either by the controller or by any other person to identify such person"[4]. For this reason, IP addresses may also be considered personal data depending on the way such data is used, processed or combined with other data. By way of example the UK Information Commissioner's Office (ICO)[5] considered that when information about a web user is built up over a period of time even without the intention to link that information with the name, address or e-mail address of that web user, that information is considered personal data[6].

Processing Personal Data

The definition of the activity of processing personal data is also a broad one. It comprises "any operation or set of operations which is performed upon personal data, whether or not by automatic means, such as collection, recording, organization, storage, adaptation or alteration, retrieval, consultation, use, disclosure by transmission, dissemination or otherwise making available, alignment or combination, blocking, erasure or destructing"[ii]. The list of conducts provided under the Data Protection Directive is not meant to be exhaustive and it intends to capture all types of manipulation of personal data.

Data Controller

Data controller is "the natural or legal person, public authority, agency, or any other body which alone or jointly with others determines the purposes and means of the processing of personal data" [ii]. The definition of data controller is relevant as this is the person that (more than others) has the burden of complying with the data protection obligations. In order to understand when a person performing data processing operations is deemed to be a data controller, the key element to be assessed is the capacity to determine the purposes and means of the processing. Any person who has, at any time, such capacity will be considered a data controller hence responsible for the compliant processing activity (Jay & Hamilton, 2003). Such capacity may be exercised by one person alone or shared with others, in which case all those persons will be considered data controllers under law. For the purposes of telecommunications service providers, it is important to clarify that "where a message containing personal data is transmitted by means of a telecommunications or electronic mail service, if the sole purpose is the transmission of that message, the controller in respect of the personal data contained in the message will normally be the person from whom the message originates rather than the person offering the transmission services"[7].

Data Processor

While data controller is the person who determines the purposes and means of the processing, data processors are those natural or legal persons which process personal data on behalf of the data controller.

Data Protection in Europe

The European Convention for the Protection of Human Rights and Fundamental Freedoms[8] provides that "everyone has the right to respect for his private and family life, his home and his correspondence".

In the early 1970s, each European country started adopting national legislations to regulate the protection of individuals' privacy. Data Protection regulations were adopted in national Constitutions or ordinary legislation.

However, although those national laws had common roots in the international conventions, setting a common and certain regulatory framework on data processing among European countries started to be seen as a fundamental step to achieve a common market where data could flow within the European Community (EC).

Between 1995 and 2006, the EC adopted the following directives on data protection:

- Directive 95/46 of the European Parliament and the Council of 24 October 1995 on the protection of individuals with regard to the processing of personal data and on the free movement of such data (Data Protection Directive);
- Directive 2002/58/EC of the European Parliament and the Council of 12 July 2002 concerning the processing of personal data and the protection of privacy in the elec-

tronic communications sector (e-privacy Directive); and

- Directive 2006/24/EC of the European Parliament and the Council of 15 March 2006 on the retention of data generated or processed in connection with the provision of publicly available electronic communications services or of public communications networks and amending the e-privacy Directive (Data Retention Directive).

The directives provided a common set of general rules and principles applicable in all EU member states. In accordance with the directives, each member state has then adopted national legislations implementing those principles and setting the various national administrative procedures. A complex regulatory system has thus been created constituting a web of national authorities competent on data protection issues, subject to a common European framework.

Despite the efforts made by the European institutions to harmonize the data protection regulations applicable throughout the EU member states, the complexity of the European system and the inconsistency among the policies undertaken by the various national authorities are evident when considering certain legal issues that have already arisen in relation to the development of new technologies (Wright, Liotta & Hodgkinson, 2008). Peer-to-peer (P2P) is an example of an existing fragmentation of approaches taken within the EU (Liotta & Liotta, 2008).

The main European legislation applicable to data protection is the Data Protection Directive, which we will analyze highlighting the principles that may affect the deployment of pervasive systems.

Data Protection across Continents

The Data Protection Directive applies not only to data controllers established in any of the EU member states, but also to a data controller not established in the European Community territory if "for the purposes of processing personal data [the data controller] makes use of equipment, automated or otherwise, situated in the territory of [a] EC member state, unless such equipment is used only for purposes of transit through the territory of the Community"[9].

Transfers of data among member states of the European Economic Area (EEA)[10] are not subject to specific requirements (except for the compliance with any applicable national legislation), while the Data Protection Directive bans data transfers to countries or territories outside the EEA unless the laws and practices of that country or territory ensure an "adequate level of protection"[11] to EU data protection standards.

This provision has raised complex compliance issues to international businesses that intend to put in place global operations involving flows of personal data (Ustaran, 2004). The recitals of the Data Protection Directive give some insight on the reasons behind this provision. While the EC recognizes the fact that cross-border flows of personal data are necessary to the expansion of international trade, it also considers privacy as a fundamental right of the individuals and as such European regulations intend to protect it also when personal data are processed abroad.

The Data Protection Directive allows the European Commission to determine which third countries ensure adequate protection, and the Commission has so far declared that transfers to Switzerland, Canada (to a certain extent), Argentina, Guernsey, Jersey the Isle of Man and the Faroe Islands are compliant with the directive. Transfers to the USA are subject to the US based recipient of the data (the importer) to be registered with the US Department of Commerce and to comply with the so called Safe Harbor Principles[12].

Transfers to countries outside the EEA in respect of which the EC Commission has not declared the adequacy of their legislation to ensure data protection will be subject to the express consent of the data subject or to contractual obligations to be entered into between the EEA based data exporter and the foreign data importer, a process that can require significant resources.

The Eight Data Protection Principles

Any project that involves the use of intrusive technology processing personal information gives rise to privacy concerns.

It is then necessary to assess the technology used and ensure that its design, purpose and operation comply with the principles of data protection. To conduct such evaluation, various data protection authorities have adopted specific guidelines[13], but in order to fully understand the issues involved, we will give an outline of the main data protection principles under the Data Protection Directive.

Legitimate Processing

Data processing has to be legitimate. In particular, personal data may be processed only if: "(1) the data subject has unambiguously given his consent; (2) the processing is necessary for the performance of a contract; (3) the processing is necessary to comply with a legal obligation; (4) the processing is necessary to protect vital interests of the data subject; (5) the processing is necessary to perform tasks carried out in the public interest; or (6) the processing is necessary for legitimate interests pursued by the controller or a third party"[14].

What businesses generally tend to do to comply with this principle, is obtaining the consent of the individual whose data is to be processed. Nonetheless the interpretation of "consent" is very strict and the law requires that it is given unambiguously and freely. In other words, the consent must not be given under pressure and the data subject should be fully aware of the meaning of his consent while giving it. There should also be no consequences or discrimination if the consent is refused as such consequences would be considered as an unjustified hardship.

The other circumstances in which the processing is considered legitimate will depend on the particular contractual or legal situation in which the processing is conducted. If the processing is "necessary" for the controller to perform his obligations under the contract, or under national legislation, then the processing is legitimate. For example a travel agent disclosing the information collected to a hotel or an airline company would be made to perform the agent's obligations with its customer. Disclosing information in compliance with a legal order adopted by local authorities would also be considered legitimate.

Fair and Lawful Processing

The processing must be transparent as to the use that the controller will make of the data. Data subjects must always be aware of such use. This means that collecting personal data of an individual without his prior knowledge (e.g. recording telephone conversations without the speakers' knowledge, save in exceptional cases) is not allowed. The processing must also be compliant with national laws (lawful).

Purpose of the Processing

Personal data must be "collected for specified, explicit and legitimate purposes and not further processed in a way incompatible with those purposes"[15].

The processing must have one or more clear and defined purposes, while a vague and uncertain reason would not be sufficient. The purpose will have to be determined before the data is collected and has to be notified to the competent data protection authority.

If additional uses are made of the personal data which are not compatible with the original purpose(s) declared, the additional uses will be considered new processing that the data controller will have to notify to the authorities and the data subjects. The compatibility test will have to be conducted on a case-by-case basis. For example, using the information collected from bank account holders to market holiday services would not be compatible with the original purpose of the data processing.

Adequacy of the Data

The personal data must be adequate, relevant and not excessive in relation to the purposes for which they are collected and further processed. In other terms there has to be a link between the information collected and the purpose for which it has been collected and processed. Any irrelevant data must then be discarded.

Accuracy of the Data

The personal data collected must be accurate and, where necessary, kept up to date. Every reasonable step must be taken to ensure that data which are inaccurate or incomplete, having regard to the purposes for which they were collected or for which they were further processed, are erased or rectified.

Ability to Identify the Data Subject

"Personal data must be kept in a form which permits identification of data subjects for no longer than is necessary for the purposes for which they are collected and further processed"[16].

Once the purpose for which the data were processed has been achieved, in the event that the data need to be stored for other reasons (commercial or other), it should be made anonymous so that it loses its "personal" characteristic. Special exemption is made for data kept for historical, statistical and scientific purposes.

Confidentiality and Security of Processing

"Any person acting under the authority of the controller or the processor, including the processor himself, who has access to personal data must not process them except on instructions from the controller"[17]. Furthermore, data controllers "must implement appropriate technical and organizational measures to protect personal data against accidental or unlawful destruction or accidental loss, alteration, unauthorized disclosure or access, in particular where the processing involves the transmission of data over a network, and against all other unlawful forms of processing. Having regard to the state of the art and the cost of their implementation, such measures shall ensure a level of security appropriate to the risks represented by the processing and the nature of the data to be protected. The data controller must, where processing is carried out on his behalf, choose a processor providing sufficient guarantees in respect of the technical security measures and organizational measures governing the processing to be carried out, and must ensure compliance with those measures"[18].

The confidentiality and security of the data collected, processed and transmitted is perhaps the issue that more than others causes concerns about new technologies.

The Directive provides for two specific obligations that the controller has to comply with. He must ensure that the members of his staff, third parties working under his authority (e.g. subcontractors) and other data processors follow his instructions in processing the data. The data controller is also responsible for the protection and security of the data processed directly or indirectly (through third parties processors) by him. To this end, the controller must put in place "appropriate technical and organizational measures" to prevent unlawful or unauthorized access or disclosure of the data, with a particular attention to the case of transmission of the data over a network.

As Recital 46 of the Data Protection Directive clarifies, the protection of the rights and freedoms of the data subjects with regard to the processing of personal data requires that appropriate technical and organizational measures be taken, both at the time of design of the processing system and at the time of the processing itself, particularly in order to maintain security and prevent any unauthorized processing.

The measures to be applied will have to take into account the means used to process the data (and the risks involved) as well as the nature of the data processed. Medical data or other sensitive information for example will have to be processed with a higher level of security measures[19]. Data controllers will also have an obligation to apply state of the art techniques to ensure data security, having regard to the cost of implementing such measures.

Applying this rule to a pervasive system characterized by a variety of equipments processing (or potentially processing) personal data, not always under the direct control of the data controller, may represent a strong legal challenge to the deployment of this technology.

Where the data controller makes use of third party processors or does not have a direct control of the equipment used to store and process the data, it will still be responsible for the security of such data. This responsibility may be contractually transferred onto the processors, but the controller's liability would still persist towards the regulators and the data subjects. Furthermore, a flaw in the security systems (at any stage) would inevitably cause reputational damage to the data controller.

The tendency of regulators in Europe and worldwide is for a tight interpretation of the provisions on security measures to be put in place and for a very severe approach to security breaches that occur. The new Telecoms Directive of 25 November 2009 has also introduced an obligation on providers of public communications networks and businesses providing publicly available electronic communications services (e.g. Internet Services Providers (ISPs)) to notify any security breaches to the competent authorities where the breach has had a significant impact on the operation of networks or services[20][21].

Although the European Data Protection Supervisor (EDPS), an independent supervisory body devoted to promoting data protection good practice in the EU institutions, had called for data security breach notification to apply also to semi-public and private networks as well as to all providers of information society services which process sensitive personal data, including on-line banking and insurers, on-line businesses, on-line providers of health care services, etc.[22], the EU Parliament and the Council have decided to limit such obligation only to public electronic communication networks.

The fines imposed by national regulators to public administrations and businesses as a consequence of security breaches have also grown exponentially in the past years following the consumers' perception of the value attributed to their personal information[23].

Information to be Given to the Data Subjects

Data controllers must provide the data subjects with certain information including: a) the identity of the controller; b) the purposes of the processing; c) the categories of data concerned (where the data is not obtained directly from the data subject); d) information regarding the recipients or categories of recipients of the data; and e) any further information necessary to guarantee the fair processing of the data.

The application of this rule is instrumental to the compliance with the "fair processing" principle analyzed above.

Case Studies

The way courts, regulators, national legislators, policy makers, advisory groups and other professionals interpret and implement data protection regulations is certainly important to understand how in practice everyday life is regulated and how new technologies, as well as the behavior of businesses, public authorities and individuals are governed and restricted by law.

Although the potential impact that pervasive systems may have on privacy has yet to be fully explored by case law, the experience that the society has matured in relation to the use of the internet, cookies, search engines, monitoring technology, P2P, and to the intrusive consequences caused by these technologies on the private sphere, can help understanding how the institutions may react to a more thorough expansion of pervasive computing.

While privacy regulations had at first been adopted to restrict the illegal activities of governments and powerful corporations, privacy threats are now experienced in everyday life, as new intrusive technologies may be used to silently monitor everybody's private life for a variety of purposes (Zittrain, 2008).

Cookies, Search Engines and Google Map

The use of the internet and the implementation of certain tools that provide value added services to users, have raised several issues as to their implications on privacy. Three examples that any internet user is familiar with can show how difficult it is to establish the borders of certain technologies in order for them to be privacy compliant.

Cookies are hidden information exchanged between an Internet user and a web server. The information is automatically stored in a file on the user's hard disk when the user connects to a web site. The original purpose of cookies is to facilitate Internet surfing although they can also be used (and are used) to retain information on Internet habits of users for advertising or other purposes. To restrict the potential negative effects on privacy, the e-privacy Directive provides that users should have the opportunity to refuse to have a cookie stored on their equipment and that they must be provided with clear information on the purpose and use of cookies by the relevant website provider[24 25].

Search engines also raised privacy issues, and the Article 29 Working Party (an advisory group to the European Commission) has published an opinion on the applicability of privacy regulations to search engines (Article 29 Working Party 2008).

The Working Party considered that data protection legislation applies to certain activities conducted by search engines, including the collection of IP addresses and search histories and caching of third party web pages. Search engines are also banned from retaining personal data longer than strictly necessary to serve the specified and legitimate purpose for which personal data were collected. Such data retention should not in any case exceed 6 months. More intrusive activities such as behavioral advertising may be conducted only prior user's consent.

Google's new Google Maps service has also raised concerns in some EU countries as to its compliance with privacy[26].

Peer-to-Peer Technology

P2P has been the object of several commercial disputes and court cases, involving the illegal file sharing of audiovisual files, causing significant loss of revenue to the entertainment industry worldwide (Wright, Liotta & Hodgkinson, 2008; Liotta & Liotta, 2008; Dogan, 2005). The media and entertainment industry responded to this threat (among other ways) by developing and adopting technologies that allow copyright owners to monitor Internet use and track relevant illegal activities. These new tools, such as watermarking, filtering and other monitoring software, have been scrutinized by various regulators and courts, some of which have raised doubts as to their compliance with privacy principles.

In the Peppermint case, the Italian Data Protection Authority has stated that the activity of monitoring P2P users for the purposes of prosecuting potential copyright infringements is inconsistent with data protection legislation[27].

In particular, in this case, a German record company (Peppermint Jam Records) had instructed a Swiss company specialized in anti-piracy software solutions (Logistep) to monitor, track and store information in relation to the use of certain P2P networks around Europe (including in Italy).

Having tracked illegal file sharing activity undertaken by certain IP addresses located in Italy, Peppermint requested the court of Rome to order the Italian ISPs providing the relevant internet access services (Telecom Italia and Wind) to disclose the identities of the users corresponding to those IP addresses. The court of first instance ordered the ISPs to undertake such disclosure, while the court of appeal (in line with the Data Protection Authority's opinion) rejected such request on the basis of data protection violations[28 29]. Both Peppermint and Logistep were considered to have been unfairly processing personal data without the data subjects being aware of or having consented to such activity. On the other hand, the ISPs were neither obliged nor entitled to disclose such data to third parties without the data subjects' consent.

Contrary to the Italian Peppermint case, a Belgian court not only considered filtering technology legal, but ordered an ISP to adopt and implement specific filtering technology in order to detect illegal P2P activity and block it[30].

The European Court of Justice (ECJ) has also had the opportunity to clarify the extent to which privacy rights prevent the disclosure of personal data for the purposes of pursuing online infringements. In the Promusicae case, the ECJ stated that data protection directives impose an obligation on ISPs to retain and disclose personal data only for reasons of national security or for the purposes of criminal prosecution, while civil claims would not justify such disclosures unless national legislation provides otherwise[31].

Watermarking

Digital watermarking is "a general-purpose technology with a wide variety of possible applications"[32], generally used to embed information inside a digital media file in order to identify that file (Sohn, 2008).

Whereas general watermarking application does not generally raise privacy issues, the so-called "individualized watermarking" may cause some concerns. Individualized watermarking are those applications in which the data contained in the watermarks is linked to a specific transaction, device or circumstance so that any use of the file will always be referable to an identifiable individual.

In this case, the privacy principles may apply and in particular, the data subject should be made aware of such tool and its purposes should be made clear.

RFID

Radio Frequency Identification (RFID) is a technology that allows automatic identification of objects, animals or persons using radio frequencies (Glover & Bhatt, 2006; Yan, 2008). It is based on the use of micro-chips (tags) that capture information regarding the object, animal or person to be identified, and transmit it via wireless networks to devices that will store and process such information[33].

From a privacy point of view, RFID raises important questions as to the possible consequences of its developments and implementation[34]. If applied to the retail sector by tagging consumer products, consumers' personal data are likely to be processed each time that they acquire a tagged product, as the tagged product itself may be used as an identifier of the consumer. For example a tagged watch would always identify its wearer, continuously capturing information about him. The nature of the product to be tagged will of course determine the sensitivity of the information that can potentially be acquired and retrieved, increasing privacy concerns[35].

Furthermore, RFID systems make it extremely hard to identify the data controllers, as during the lifetime of a tag the controller could change several times depending on any additional services required.

Finally the difficulty in securing the wireless network supporting the RFID data transmission combined with the lack of transparency of the data processing raise serious issues on the compatibility of this technology with privacy regulations[xxxiv].

Privacy and Pervasive Systems

From a pervasive system point of view, the principles, concepts, and requirements of privacy law presented above pose serious challenges. By their very nature, pervasive systems are achieved by interconnecting heterogeneous, networked environments and deploying network-neutral applications. In a pervasive system, the network is unaware of what the application is doing and vice-versa (Loke, 2006). Data across different administrative domains, often transparently to the managers of those domains, and there is considerable use of resource virtualization and sharing. Privacy challenges may be illustrated by means of simple examples i.e., by considering some elementary components of a pervasive system.

Mobile Ad Hoc Networks

Mobile Ad Hoc Networks (MANETs) represent a good example of an autonomic, infrastructure-less network (Lang, 2008), where the role of network administrator is considerably diminished. User terminals interconnect directly and spontaneously and collectively form a network whereby the data path from source to destination is formed by the terminal rather than relying on specialized routing equipment. Under these circumstances, the user's data is relayed by ordinary user terminals which store and forward data on behalf of other users, making it very difficult (if not impossible) to identify the data controller legally responsible for data protection compliance.

It is also not possible to determine the path followed by users' data and ensure its privacy. For instance, if Terminal A sends personal data to Terminal B via Terminals C, D, and E it will not be possible to ensure that C, D or E do not misuse this data. To make things even more difficult, the path from A to B cannot be predetermined since this depends on the particular relative location of the users connected to the network.

In MANETs, nodes usually move and paths are re-computed continuously. Routing algorithms are distributed and autonomic, so there is no way to know whether data is illicitly cached or misused in any other way by an intermediate node.

The question as to whether and how it would be possible to modify the design of a MANET in order to meet the requirements of the privacy law is still open and generates a wealth of technical and research issues.

Wireless Sensor Networks

Just as MANETS, wireless sensor networks form spontaneously and in most cases do not require any central controller or administrator (i.e. they are infrastructure-less networks) (Karl & Willig, 2007). Sensor systems may exchange information among them for the purposes of data fusion, correlation or enhancement. Depending on the type of data, privacy issues may be more or less sensitive. In the most extreme case, IP digital cameras can be considered as forming a sensor system. Imagine the privacy issues arising when camera feeds are transcoded, pre-processed or relayed at intermediate nodes for purposes as varied as face recognition, tailored advertisement or, simply, due to technical constraints (e.g. to reduce the data volume).

To mitigate privacy concerns, there is a strong tendency in research and development to employ sensors that do not capture clear images. Sensing technologies are nevertheless evolving fast and with them, privacy concerns cannot be ignored.

Peer-to-Peer Networks

Peer-to-Peer (P2P) networks address the need to build a network overlay tailored to specific application requirements and regardless of the underlying physical network (topology, technology, and heterogeneity) (Subramanian & Goodman, 2005). As for MANETs, P2P networks are self-managed and use the users' terminals to cache and relay data. Technically, this is achieved at the application layer, rather than at the link and routing layers. However, the privacy issues are analogous since it is very hard to determine data misuse by the users whose terminal acts as a relay.

P2P Content Distribution

P2P networks are the foundation of several low-cost (hence popular) content distribution applications, including P2P file sharing, P2P video-on-demand, and P2P IPTV (Oram, 2001). These applications have a ubiquitous reach, provided that the user has a terminal that is somehow connected to the Internet (even through a MANET).

Similarly to MANETs and P2P networks, P2P content distribution applications make the roles of data controllers and data processors blurred. There is also a question as to whether P2P applications should be allowed to trace or profile the user's behavior for the purpose of overlay management and copyrights protection. Currently, P2P platforms are not able to provide the necessary level of security and privacy protection, owing to their distributed and automated nature.

Resource Virtualization and Sharing

Resource virtualization and sharing platforms, such as grid (Chakrabarti, 2007), represent another vehicle towards pervasiveness. Storage and computational grids virtualize the resources available on individual users' terminals and make those resources available to other users. This virtualization process allows the creation of huge storage and processing capabilities but requires users' data to be temporarily or permanently stored and processed onto alien users' machines.

The arising issues are twofold. First, the data of individual users transit through or remain onto foreign machines and it is, in this way, exposed to privacy breaches. The second problem is that the hosting machine actually acts as storage and/or processor, which makes him responsible for the security of foreign data. What makes things even more sensitive is that, machines connecting to a grid system are not usually located in the same country and are, therefore, subject to different privacy regulations.

CONCLUSION

Our review of the privacy regulations identifies a neat clash with pervasive systems, as exemplified by the case studies described in this chapter. Looking at the wealth of recent court cases, it is clear that there is a definite trend towards a solid interpretation of the current privacy legislation. The recent developments suggest that legal constraints on pervasive systems are not going to diminish, which in turn poses a range of challenges to technologists and researchers.

The main aim of this chapter was to help those involved in designing and investigating future systems familiarize with the requirements imposed by privacy law. The solutions proposed so far do not meet those requirements, challenging the applicability and viability of current pervasive systems, including pervasive networks, services, and applications. Future systems and protocols should better harmonize distribution and resource sharing paradigms with privacy protection mechanisms.

Our analysis shows also another important issue: the dichotomy between privacy and other regulatory requirements. For instance, copyrights protection in a pervasive system (e.g., in the context of a P2P application) is a major technical problem, which conflicts with privacy interests.

The issue of allowing network operators and service providers to meet their regulatory obligations whilst at the same time respecting privacy is another challenge exacerbated by pervasiveness. Within an ordinary network environment, the operator is required to perform legal intercepts and retain a record of connections. How to deploy such functionality in a pervasive system is still an unsolved issue that will require a harmonization between technology, privacy and other regulatory requirements.

REFERENCES

Article 29 Working Party. (2008). *Opinion on data protection issues related to search engines*. Retrieved July 4, 2010, from http://ec.europa.eu/justice_home/fsj/privacy/index_en.htm

Chakrabarti, A. (2007). *Grid computing security*. Springer.

Dogan, S. (2005). Peer-to-peer technology and the copyright crossroads. In Subramanian, R., & Goodman, B. D. (Eds.), *Peer to peer computing: The evolution of a disruptive technology* (pp. 166–194). Hershey, PA: IGI Global.

Glover, B., & Bhatt, H. (2006). *RFID essentials*. O'Reilly.

Jay, R., & Hamilton, A. (2003). *Data protection law and practice*. London, UK: Thomson Sweet & Maxwell.

Karl, H., & Willig, A. (2007). *Protocols and architectures for wireless sensor networks. Wiley. Hansmann, U. (2003). Pervasive computing: The mobile world*. Springer.

Lang, D. (2008). *Routing protocols for mobile ad hoc networks - classification, evaluation and challenges*. VDM Verlag Dr. Mueller E.K.

Liotta, A., & Liotta, A. (2008). P2P systems in a regulated environment: Threats and opportunities for the operator. *BT Technology Journal*, *26*(1), 150–157.

Loke, S. (2006). *Context-aware pervasive systems*. Auerbach Publications. doi:10.1201/9781420013498

Oram, A. (2001). *Peer-to-peer: Harnessing the power of disruptive technologies*. O'Reilly Media.

Sarkar, S. K. (2007). *Ad hoc mobile wireless networks: Principles, protocols and applications*. Auerbach Publications. doi:10.1201/9781420062229

Sohn, D. (2008). *Privacy principles for digital watermarking*. Center for Democracy and Technology. Retrieved July 4, 2010, from http://www.cdt.org/copyright/20080529watermarking.pdf

Subramanian, R., & Goodman, B. D. (Eds.). (2005). *Peer to peer computing: The evolution of a disruptive technology*. Hershey, PA: IGI Global.

Ustaran, E. (2004). *Data exports in data protection handbook*. London, UK: The Law Society.

Wright, T., Liotta, A., & Hodgkinson, D. (2008). *E-privacy and copyright in online content distribution: A European overview*. World Data Protection Report. BNA International.

Yan, L. (2008). *The Internet of things: From RFID to the next-generation pervasive networked systems*. Auerbach Publications.

Zittrain, J. (2008). *The future of the Internet and how to stop it*. London, UK: Penguin.

KEY TERMS AND DEFINITIONS

Privacy: The state of being free from intrusion or disturbance in one's private life or affairs.

Personal Data: Any information relating to an identified or identifiable person.

Processing of Personal Data: Any set of operations performed upon personal data, whether or not by automatic means.

Data Controller: Anybody whom, alone or jointly with others, determines the purposes and means of the processing of personal data.

Data Processor: Anybody who processes personal data on behalf of the data controller.

MANETS: Mobile Ad Hoc Networks, whereby no infrastructure or network administration is necessary.

Peer-to-Peer Networks: applications that realize virtual network mechanisms on top of physical networks and independently from the actual network technology.

Sensor Networks: networks formed of sensors that can communicate directly or indirectly.

ENDNOTES

1 Under Art. 12 of the Declaration "No one shall be subjected to arbitrary interference with his privacy, family, home or correspondence, nor to attacks upon his honor and reputation. Everyone has the right to the protection of the law against such interference or attacks".

2 Directive 95/46 of the European Parliament and the Council of 24 October 1995 on the protection of individuals with regard to the processing of personal data and on the free movement of such data.

3 EC Directive 95/46.

4 The way national legislators have adopted the definition given under the Data Protection Directive and translated it into their own legislations varies. An example, which is demonstrative of the scope of application that national authorities may give to privacy is given by the UK Data Protection Act 1998 under which 'Personal data means data which relate to a living individual who can be identified (a) from those data; or (b) from those data and other information which is in the possession of or is likely to be in the possession of the data controller'.

5 The ICO is the UK Data Protection authority.

6 ICO's Legal Guidance on the UK Data Protection Act 1998. Retrieved 1st March 2010 from www.ico.gov.uk

7 Recital (47) of the Data Protection Directive.

8 The European Convention for the Protection of Human Rights and Fundamental Freedoms was signed in Rome between the 47 countries members of the Council of Europe on 4 November 1950.

9 Article 4 of the Data Protection Directive.

10 The EEA comprises the 27 EU Member States, Iceland, the Principality of Liechtenstein and the Kingdom of Norway.

11 Article 25 of the Data Protection Directive.

12 For a detailed analysis of the requirements to be complied with in order to join the US Safe Harbor regime, see http://www.export.gov/safeharbor/.

13 See for example the Privacy Impact Assessment Handbook adopted by the UK Information Commissioner's Office.

14 Article 7 of the Data Protection Directive.

15 Article 6 of the Data Protection Directive.

16 Article 6(e) of the Data Protection Directive.

17 Article 16 of the Data Protection Directive.

18 Article 17 of the Data Protection Directive.

19 For an example of legislation providing for a detailed distinction of security measures applicable on the basis of the nature of the data to be processed, see the new Spanish Regulations adopted with Royal Decree 1720/2007 of 21 December 2007 implementing the Spanish Organic Law 15/1999 of 13 December 1999 on the Protection of Personal Data.

20 Directive 2009/140/EC of the European Parliament and of the Council of 25 November 2009 amending Directives 2002/21/EC on a common regulatory framework for electronic communications networks and services,

2002/19/EC on access to, and interconnection of, electronic communications networks and associated facilities, and 2002/20/EC on the authorization of electronic communications networks and services. The Directive will have to be adopted by each EU Member State by 25 May 2011.

21 A similar legislation on data breach notification has already been adopted by 40 of the US States. The State of Virginia is reported to be the 40th US State to have enacted legislation imposing security breach notification obligations.

22 Press Release of 14 April 2008 on the EDPS Opinion on e-Privacy Directive review which provides comments on the EC Commission proposal of 13 November 2007 considering further improvements to it. The limited scope of the Directive was also criticized by the Article 29 Working Party (a European advisory group).

23 The UK Parliament should pass new legislation in April 2010 giving the Information Commissioner Office the authority to impose fines of up to £500,000 for the case of breaches of the Data Protection Act.

24 Directive 2002/58/EC of the European Parliament and the Council of 12 July 2002 concerning the processing of personal data and the protection of privacy in the electronic communications sector.

25 ICO's Guidance on the Privacy and Electronic Communications (EC Directive) Regulations 2003. Retrieved 1st March 2010 from www.ico.gov.uk

26 The European Data Protection Supervisor has been reported to declare that 'making pictures in every street is certainly going to create some problems'. It is still to be seen if Google will decide to launch the service in Europe and whether it intends to apply any tools to protect the identity of passers-by (e.g. face-blurring technology). In the USA, the community of North Oaks (Minnesota) has already demanded Google to erase the images of the city.

27 Resolution of the Garante per la Protezione dei Dati Personali in the cases Peppermint v Telecom Italia and Peppermint v Wind, of 28 February 2008.

28 Peppermint v Wind Telecomunicazioni spa, Orders of the court of Rome of 22 September 2006 (1st instance) and 26 October 2007 (appeal).

29 Peppermint v Telecom Italia spa, Orders of the court of Rome of 9 February 2007 (1st instance) and 14 July 2007 (appeal).

30 SCRL Société Belge des Auteurs v Scarlet SA (formerly Tiscali), decision of the court of Brussels of 29 June 2007 (1st instance).

31 Case C-275/06, Productores de Música de España v Telefónica de España SAU, ECJ Decision of 29 January 2008.

32 See the guidelines released by the Center for Democracy & Technology (CDT). The CDT is a non-profit public policy organization dedicated to promoting the democratic potential of today's open, decentralized global Internet.

33 Communication from the Commission to the European Parliament, the Council, the European Economic and Social Committee and the Committee of Regions on 'Radio Frequency Identification (RFID) in Europe: steps towards a policy framework' of 15 March 2007.

34 Opinion of the European Data Protection Supervisor on the Communication from the Commission to the European Parliament, the Council, the European Economic and Social Committee and the Committee of Regions on 'Radio Frequency Identification (RFID) in Europe: steps towards a policy framework' of 15 March 2007, of 23 April 2008.

35 Consider for example a smartcard used for travels that will retain information about holiday habits of the card holder.

Section 5
Evaluation and Social Implications

A key theme of the book is evaluation of pervasive computing systems and the study of factors that enable its adoption and acceptance by users. Despite being of paramount importance for the success of the pervasive computing paradigm, this aspect is by and large neglected in most current research work, and the work presented in this book aims at partially filling this gap and also instigating further research in this direction.

Chapter 13
Factors Influencing Satisfaction with Mobile Portals

Daisy Seng
Monash University, Australia

Carla Wilkin
Monash University, Australia

Ly-Fie Sugianto
Monash University, Australia

ABSTRACT

Smart phones are increasingly used in commercial sectors to facilitate mobile transactions. Herein the advancements of mobile technology and network engineering have been instrumental in the proliferation of pervasive computing using mobile devices. As a result portal technology has emerged to provide users in both Web and mobile contexts with a single point of access and personalization to Information Systems. The shortcomings of existing instruments in capturing the diversity in user opinions about satisfaction with mobile portals mean that the development of a new instrument for measuring user satisfaction in this context is invaluable. This chapter documents the first stage in this journey, namely the content validation process. Drawing upon related theoretical and empirical research, the authors identify an initial pool of factors that affect user satisfaction with mobile portals. Then, using multiple focus groups, the authors refine these factors in preparation for the next stage, which involves development of the items.

INTRODUCTION

The vision of taking computing off the desktop and interlacing it into daily life has become reality. This has been facilitated by the emergence of devices with integrated computing capability and much improved wireless and battery technology. Here, for many people, smart phones have become a significant and integral part of daily life due to their compact size, affordable price, and internet capabilities and functionality like mobile portals. In fact, owing to their affordable price and functionality, mobile phone users outnumber fixed-line telephone users in many countries. According to the International Telecommunication Union the number of worldwide mobile phone subscribers

DOI: 10.4018/978-1-60960-611-4.ch013

increased exponentially from 1.16 billion in 2002 to 3.35 billion in 2007 (ITU, 2007). This figure is expected to hit 5.2 billion by 2011 (Malik, 2008). Given this growth in the utilization of these devices, it is surprising that there is a lack of research that shows how satisfied users are with aspects like mobile portal use.

The concept of satisfaction occupies a central position in business because of its positive impact on market value and accounting returns (Anderson et al., 1994, 2004; Ittner and Larcker, 1996). Here past research indicates that consumer/user satisfaction is a reliable predictor of post-purchase phenomena such as future purchase intention, re-use, brand loyalty and attitude to change. Further, it is a key driver when recommending products and usage to others (Patterson and Spreng, 1997; Wang et al., 2001; Eggert and Ulaga, 2002; Anderson et al., 2004; Howard, 1974; Churchill and Surprenant, 1982). Within the field of marketing consumer satisfaction has long been one of the most widely researched topics. SERVQUAL, an instrument developed in the mid eighties to measure the gap between customer expectations for and perceptions of service quality, is one example of a seminal measure of satisfaction (Parasuraman et al., 1985, 1988). As research into the use of Information Systems (IS) is concerned with, amongst other things, consideration of human behaviors, researchers investigating this discipline often borrow measures and theoretical perspectives from related disciplines like marketing and adapt them to this arena (e.g. DeLone and McLean, 1992; Pitt et al., 1995). For example, researchers have adapted and applied the SERVQUAL instrument to assess user's satisfaction with website service quality, which has resulted in new measures like WEBQUAL (Barnes and Vidgen, 2001).

With respect to user satisfaction with mobile portals, currently there is a dearth of literature that directly examines this. A common proxy measure for user satisfaction is system success (Wang and Liao, 2007). As the success of mobile portals is dependent upon their ability to satisfy user requirements, it is unsurprising to find that smart phone developers and wireless network portal providers are keen to develop mobile portals in ways that increase the experience for users. From a practical standpoint this makes investigation into measuring user satisfaction with mobile portals critically important. From a theoretical standpoint, by exploring the theoretical underpinning of *user satisfaction* and providing a meaning of the construct in the context of mobile portals, we make a contribution here as well.

Although a number of widely accepted and employed scales for measuring user satisfaction in IS research already exist, for example Bailey and Pearson's (1983) measure of computer user satisfaction, Ives et al.'s (1983) refinement of this to measure user information satisfaction and Doll and Torkzadeh's (1988) refinement of Ives et al.'s instrument to measure end-user computer satisfaction, these scales are inappropriate for measuring user satisfaction with mobile portals for the following reasons. Firstly, the former two scales were built to gauge user satisfaction with overall IS in a traditional computing environment where users interact with developers and operational staff; whilst the third scale was developed to measure user satisfaction with specific IT applications in an end-user computing environment where users' interactions are governed through computer interfaces. Secondly, mobile portals are designed specifically for compact devices (like smart phones). Lastly, mobile portals have unique characteristics (such as ubiquity, convenience, localization, personalization, and device optimization) and device limitations (including small screen size and key pads, memory and disk capacity, and limited computational power) that make them different to non-compact devices. In particular, the screen size limitation of these devices greatly affects users' experience, which in turn impacts users' satisfaction (Jones et al., 2002; Findlater and McGrenere, 2008). All in all the experience of using smart phones is fairly unique compared to using other computing devices and applications. Given the shortcomings of existing scales to capture diversity in user opinions regarding their unique experience with mobile portals, coupled with the increasing popularity of smart phones in today's society, more work is required in this area.

Consequently, the ultimate aim of this study is to develop and validate a new instrument for measuring user satisfaction with mobile portals (henceforth referred to as MPUS). The delivery of a simple to administer instrument will allow practitioners to ascertain the success, in terms of user's satisfaction, of their company's current mobile portal and create the opportunity to use these results to identify areas for improvement. Further, researchers can also apply this instrument to different groups of users to compare their levels of satisfaction. This chapter reports on the first stage of this journey in creating the new instrument. Specifically, the objectives of the chapter are threefold:

- To examine the meaning of the terms 'mobile portal' and 'user satisfaction within the context of a mobile portal';
- To identify, from a users' perspective, the factors that influence user satisfaction; and
- To document the content validation process component of our attempt to introduce a new instrument to measure user satisfaction with mobile portals.

In achieving these objectives this chapter is organized as follows. We commence by providing an overview of *mobile portals* and a definition of *user satisfaction*. Next we present a conceptual model that summarizes the existing user satisfaction scales in IS research and provide an initial pool of factors, drawn from the literature, that affect user satisfaction with mobile portals. We then outline the research approach and design before summarizing our findings from the focus groups and providing a comparison of these findings with our initial pool of factors. Finally we offer suggestions for future research before concluding the chapter.

MEANINGS OF THE TERMS MOBILE PORTAL AND USER SATISFACTION

The concepts mobile portal and user satisfaction are difficult to define. Yet given their centrality to research that investigates user's experiences with the performance of a system, what is required is a definition of each. Thus, looking at the term 'mobile portal', the term 'mobile' generally refers to either an electronic device used for mobile telecommunication or the capability of being moved readily from place to place. Whilst there is no unique definition of the term 'portal', in the IS field it generally refers to a gateway, entry point or webpage for accessing content and services on the internet. Smith (2004) argues that the concept of portal should not be limited to the internet, and provides a comprehensive definition of portal as *"an infrastructure providing secure, customizable, personal sable, integrated access to dynamic content from a variety of sources, in a variety of source formats, wherever it is needed"* (p.4). Further, a portal differs from a traditional webpage in that a traditional webpage primarily provides static information while a portal *"provides seamless access to a variety of goods and services via a single interface based on a predefined profile of preferences"* (Lazar, 2000 p.52).

A portal is not the point of destination; rather it is the point of entry in search for information and services. This point is accentuated by the different types of portals and their accompanying definition present in the literature (see Table 1). Two points should be noted from this table: firstly, the existence of different portals for different group of users; and secondly, the recurring reference to the degree of personalized and customized information available on them. Interestingly, the definitions of a mobile portal provided in Table

Table 1. Types and Definitions of Portals in the Literature

Portal Type	Definition	Author(s)
Business Portal	An application which is able to provide business users with one-stop shopping for any information they need inside or outside the enterprise.	Eckerson (1999)
Business to Employee (B2E) Portal	A customized, personalized, ever-changing mix of news, resources, applications and e-commerce options that becomes the desktop destination for everyone in the organization and a primary vehicle by which people do their work.	Ransdell (2000)
Corporate Portal	A website targeted at a specific audience that provides content aggregation and delivery of information that is relevant to the audience, collaboration and community services. Further, it provides application access for the target audience, which is delivered in a highly personalized manner.	Benbya et al. (2004)
Enterprise Portal	A single-point web browser interface used within organizations to promote the gathering, sharing, or dissemination of information throughout the enterprise.	Detlor (2000)
Enterprise Information Portal	An application that enables companies to discharge both internally and externally stored information. Further, it provides users with a single gateway to the personalized information required to make informed business decisions.	Shilakes and Tylman (1998)
Internet Portal	A gateway to the world wide web, which offers an amalgamation of services like search engines, online shopping information, email, news, weather reports, stock quotes, communication forums, maps and travel information.	Vlachogiannis et al. (2007)
Mobile portal	High-level information/service aggregators or intermediaries that play a key role in facilitating mobile internet access for users.	Barnes (2002)
Mobile Portal	A wireless web page that helps portable device users to interact with mobile content and services. It is characterized by a greater degree of personalization and localization.	Clarke and Flaherty (2003)
Web portal	A gateway to the information and services available on the Web. More specifically it provides a gateway to services on both the public Internet and on corporate intranets.	Uden and Salmenjoki (2007)

1 below do not conform to the portal definitions provided by Lazar (2000) and Smith (2004) above.

Portals can also be classified according to category, which helps to clarify the features and characteristics of each. Herein Davydov (2001) identified three major categories of portals: public, corporate and personal portals. Essentially public portals are generally known as Internet portals or web portals. They aim to become the first destination page for users of large screen devices (e.g. computers, wired-laptops and wireless laptops) whenever they want to access information on the Web (Tatnall, 2005). Corporate portals are categorized into Enterprise Information Portals and Role Portals. As with public portals they are designed to be accessed from large screen devices but exclusively by business users. Personal portals are generally customized for personal use and are further divided into pervasive and appliance portals. Mobile portals belong to the pervasive portal category where the portals are embedded in WAP-enabled mobile phones, smart phones, wireless PDAs and personal information devices (Tatnall, 2005). While these devices, due to their physical size, offer users mobility as they are compact enough to be carried everywhere, they suffer from limitations like small screens, complicated text input mechanisms and shorter battery life compared to large screen devices. As a result, mobile portals are characterized by a much greater degree of customization and personalization than both public and corporate portals. This is required in order to tailor access to users' needs and habits so that only the right, concise information is presented at the right time (Muller-Veerse, 2000; Siau et al., 2001; Barnes, 2002).

In the context of this study, 'mobile portal' refers to *the customized, personalized user interface of wireless small screen mobile devices that allow users to seamlessly access mobile content and mobile services*. Small screen mobile devices include WAP-enabled mobile phones, PDAs and smart phones. These devices, due to their physical size, offer users mobility as they are compact enough to be carried almost everywhere and their efficient power supplies mean they can be kept switched on most of the time (Barnett et al., 2000; Takeyasu, 2009).

According to the Global Mobile Suppliers Association (2002), the mobile services provided by mobile portals may be separated into eight main categories: *entertainment* (for instance, games, horoscope, jokes, music and video); *information* (for example, financial and sport news and weather); *lifestyle* (for instance, information on health services, movies, restaurants and nightlife); *messaging* (for example, blogs, mobile e-mail, mobile instant messaging, multimedia messaging and SMS); *mobile commerce* (for instance, auctions, banking, shopping and stock trading); *personal information management* (for example, address books, calendar, contacts and photo albums); *portal characteristics* (for instance, devise optimization, location-based services and personalization); and *travel* (for example, flight listings, hotel listings, traffic updates and travel guides). Mobile portals also allow users to access the mobile internet for web browsing.

Moreover, the mobile portals that are available on these devices can deliver information and services anytime and anywhere, thus providing users with greater value-for-time than users of other web-based portals. As a result, mobile portals differ from web-based portals in five dimensions: ubiquity; convenience; localization; personalization; and device optimization (Tsalgatidou et al., 2000; GMSA, 2002; Clarke and Flaherty, 2003; Serenko and Bontis, 2004; Turel and Serenko, 2007).

Ubiquity is the ability of small screen mobile device users to access information or services and perform transactions from virtually anywhere at any time regardless of location and to be reachable in anyplace at anytime (Muller-Veerse, 2000; Watson et al., 2002; Parsons, 2007). Mobile portals create the ability to leverage ubiquity by providing services to users that are specified during the personalization process like alert notifications regarding schedule changes to airline flights, auction alerts, bidding modifications, email notifications and stock market updates.

Convenience is the dexterity and accessibility provided by mobile portals to their users who are no longer restricted by time or place in obtaining services in contrast to users of other web-based portals who are restricted by locations that provide internet access (Dholakia and Rask, 2002). Similar to the wireless connectivity integrated into small screen mobile devices, data stored in these devices are always available at hand. Mobile portals act as time savers in situations where users are stuck in traffic or queues by allowing them to access services that they would do anyway had they not been 'stuck' in these unforeseen circumstances. This translates into improved quality of life thus leaving more time for work and leisure. Further, by making services more convenient, customers may become more satisfied and loyal (Clarke and Flaherty, 2003; Serenko and Bontis, 2004).

Localization is the ability of small screen mobile devices to identify the geographical location of users and provide them with location-specific information and services that are timely, accurate, and relevant to their needs and requests. In contrast, other web-based portals identify users via their IP address or email address (Dholakia and Rask, 2002). Information and service requirements may include restaurant bookings, hotel reservations, location of the nearest petrol station and movie listings (Tsalgatidou et al., 2000). Mobile portals, therefore, not only serve as a point of consolidation of customer information but also disseminate location-relevant information about local services, businesses and opportunities.

Personalization concerns the presentation of individually tailored information on the mobile portal based upon the user's profile, needs and preferences. This is easy to achieve as the small screen mobile device is carried by a single user. Further, as mobile device usage can be analyzed, personalized service and targeted marketing efforts are possible. Such personalized content is vital because relevant information must always be a single 'click' away. However, because of the resolution available on mobile phones, together with their poor navigability and small screen size, this single click access is not easy to achieve thus restricting the amount of information that can be shown and also their 'surfability' (Barnett et al., 2000; Parsons, 2007).

Device optimization concerns the ability to automatically generate content of a mobile portal based upon device configurations (screen size, memory and CPU), characteristics of the communication channel available (bandwidth) and the languages and protocols that are supported. Given service providers are aware of these details they may optimize the content of their portal(s) to individual users in order to achieve faster transmission speed, simple navigation, intuitive-to-use graphical user interfaces and consistent page layouts (Serenko and Bontis, 2004).

Whilst these unique characteristics can be achieved, users of small screen mobile devices suffer from the following limitations compared to large screen devices: small screens and small key pads; complicated text input mechanisms; shorter battery life; less computational power; limited memory and disk capacity; higher risk of data storage and transaction errors; lower display resolution; graphical limitations; less surfability; and unfriendly user-interfaces (Siau et al., 2001). As a result information displayed on these devices must be highly concise, relevant and accurate. Further, the interesting range of search visualization and manipulation schemes available for large screen devices are not appropriate for small screen mobile devices (Jones et al., 2002) due to the limitations of these devices.

Having defined what a 'mobile portal' is, we now turn our attention to the term 'user satisfaction'. User satisfaction is considered the most critical criterion in evaluating system success or effectiveness (Power and Dickson, 1973; Bailey and Pearson, 1983; Ives et al., 1984; Doll and Torkzadeh, 1988; DeLone and McLean, 1992; Gelderman, 1998; DeLone and McLean, 2003). Herein user satisfaction could be defined as a user's post-usage evaluation of a product or service. Ives et al. (1983 p.785) defined user satisfaction as *"the extent to which users believe that the information system available to them meets their information requirements"*, while Doll and Torkzadeh (1988 p.261) provided a much more limited definition describing it as *"the affective attitude towards a specific computer application by someone who interacts with the application directly"*.

According to Turkyilmaz and Ozkan (2007), more recent studies of satisfaction focus on cumulative satisfaction where it is defined as a *"customer's overall experience to date with [the] product or service provider"* (p.673). This approach to satisfaction is said to provide a more direct and comprehensive measure of a customer's consumption utility and their subsequent behavior and economic performance (Fornell et. al., 1996). Given users of mobile portals interact directly with these portal in ways that are similar to the way in which they interact with a specific computer application, in the context of this study 'user satisfaction with a mobile portal' is defined as *the user's overall affective attitude towards the mobile portal.* Recall from the discussion presented above, as a mobile portal is embedded in the device itself, user satisfaction with a mobile portal includes both evaluation of the hardware and software associated with the device.

Having defined what we mean by user satisfaction with a mobile portal, we now progress towards our aim of providing a measure of this construct. In doing so we argue that user satisfaction with mobile portals can be better understood by identifying factors (or different dimensions) that influence this, which is the focus of our discussion presented below.

Figure 1. Preliminary conceptual model of mobile portal user satisfaction (MPUS)

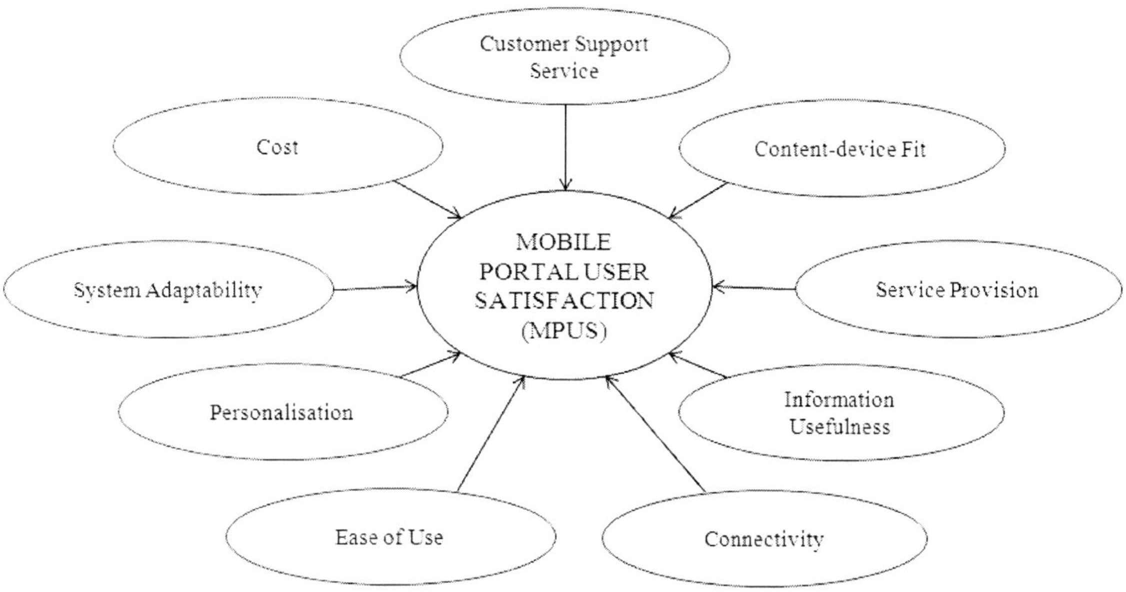

TOWARDS A CONCEPTUAL MODEL OF MOBILE PORTAL USER SATISFACTION

In identifying the list of factors that potentially affect user satisfaction with mobile portals, we reviewed numerous existing user satisfaction instruments reported in the IS literature. This led to the compilation of a list of factors that contribute to user satisfaction with overall IS, web-based IS, IS service quality and web quality. Leveraging off this list we subjectively formulated an initial pool of factors that potentially affect user satisfaction with mobile portals.

Next, we examined these factors against the unique characteristics and device limitations of mobile portals outlined in earlier section. When relevant, factors from the existing literature were adapted, otherwise new factors were defined. Based on this process the following nine factors of MPUS were derived: *Customer Support Service; Content-device Fit; Services Provision; Information Usefulness; Connectivity; Ease of Use; Personalization; System Adaptability;* and *Cost* (see Figure 1). Of the nine factors identified, four of these were added to specifically address mobile portals: *Services Provision; Personalization; System Adaptivity* and *Cost*. A brief description of these nine factors can be found below.

Customer Support Service. The extent to which: (1) the customer support services provided (for example, FAQ services and search facilities) are perceived by users to be adequate; and (2) the customer support service staff are perceived to be assuring, empathetic and responsive to user enquires. In our study the *Customer Support Service* factor encompasses various factors related to service quality identified in past research including: *Assurance* and *Empathy* (Kettinger and Lee, 1994); *Service Quality* (Wang and Liao, 2007); and *Support* (Raymond, 1987).

Content-device Fit. The ability of the mobile portal to present information in a format that is compact, relevant and accurate based on users' specific needs (personalization) and physical location (location-sensitive information). This factor is important for the following reasons. Firstly, the limitation of small screen mobile devices means information presented to users must be both relevant and compact, as opposed to complete (one of the main emphases in "content quality" in the past (Kettinger and Lee, 1994; Wang and Liao, 2007)). Secondly, the availability of location-sensitive information to users is a distinguishing aspect of mobile portals. Hence it is important that this information is accurate.

Service Provision. This factor refers to the type of mobile services available to users. The delivery of mobile services to users relies on private network providers. Such services are usually available in specific regions, and are typically simpler, more personalized, location-specific and time-sensitive (Zhang et al., 2002). Further, for users to be satisfied with mobile portals, there must be a wide range of mobile services available for them to conveniently choose from at anytime from anywhere.

Information Usefulness. The ability of mobile portals to assist users in performing their activities. Tojib and Sugianto (2008) indicated that this factor is a good indicator of user satisfaction. For users to be satisfied with the mobile portal, the information or services made available to them must not only be "rich" but also useful. Despite the vast range of information/services provided, users may be dissatisfied if a particular service they need is unavailable.

Connectivity. The ability of the mobile portal to be connected from anywhere at anytime. This factor is critical to mobile portals because (1) the mobility of mobile devices means that they are physically small enough to be carried at all times, and (2) mobile portals that are connected by wireless networks imply that users are not restricted to locations with internet access. Woo and Fock (1999) referred to this factor as *Transmission Quality and Network Coverage*.

Ease of Use. Given the limitations of small screen mobile devices, this refers to the extent to which the mobile portal is perceived to be user-friendly or easy to navigate. The *Ease of Use* factor has been shown to be a good indicator of user satisfaction by many researchers including Bailey and Pearson (1983); Doll and Torkzadeh (1988); Ho and Wu (1999); Otto et al. (2000); Cho and Park (2001); Muylle et al. (2004); and Wang and Liao (2007).

Personalization. The ability of the mobile portal to allow users to personalize or customize: (1) the layout of the mobile portal; (2) the information received based on the users' specific needs; and (3) the preferred language. Personalization is regarded as a key issue for mobile portal users because of the limitations of the user interfaces available in mobile devices'. Here size and resolution impact the environment in which users conduct communication, information searches and transactions. Thus, for users to be satisfied with mobile portals, personalized content is vital and relevant information and services must always be a single 'click' away (Barnes, 2002; Constantiou et al., 2006).

System Adaptability. This factor refers to the degree to which mobile portal providers adapt the information and the way it is presented through the different device capabilities (for example, varying screen sizes) to users with different network technologies. This factor relates closely to the 'device optimization' characteristic of mobile portals. The ability of mobile portal providers to optimize the content of their mobile portals to individual users ensures faster transmission speed, simpler navigation, intuitive-to-use graphical user interfaces and consistent page layouts, all of which affect user satisfaction (Serenko and Bontis, 2004).

Cost. This factor refers to the cost of accessing information or using services and network connections. Network costs include the cost of data transmission and network services. Further, data transmission cost depends on the size of the transported data packets (Fox, 2000). As a result, users' perception of price or cost will have an impact on their satisfaction with mobile portals.

Next we report on how these factors were validated.

THE USE OF FOCUS GROUPS TO ACHIEVE CONTENT VALIDATION

Given the ultimate aim of this study is to develop a reliable and valid instrument to measure user satisfaction with mobile portals in a rigorous manner, for the instrument to be successful, it must produce consistent and error free results and measure what it is meant to measure. The challenge is that developing a reliable and valid instrument is a complex process (Segars, 1997). Consequently, to assist with this process we use Churchill's methodology (1979), which is a widely used approach for developing multi-item instruments. Our focus in the remainder of this chapter is on reporting results from an early step in this process concerned with content validation in specifying the domain construct. Herein multiple rounds of focus groups were employed to ensure that the right factors that define user satisfaction with mobile portals were identified.

The focus group method involves group discussions that explore specific sets of issues (Barbour and Kitzinger, 1999). It is distinguished from the broader category of group interviews by the explicit use of group interactions to generate data (Stewart et al., 2007). Instead of asking each person a question in turn, in focus groups the moderator encourages participants in the group to interact with one another when discussing a particular topic by asking questions, exchanging anecdotes and commenting on each others' experiences and points of view. Focus groups can be used at virtually any point in a research program (Lewis, 2000). They are particularly useful at early stages of exploratory research when little is known about the phenomenon of interest. In situations like this they can be used to explore the issues and topics people are concerned with in a particular domain (Hansen et al., 1998). This also makes them ideal as a starting point when designing a survey questionnaire. The use of focus groups in this study gave us the benefit of producing key information quickly and more cost-effectively than had individual interviews been used. Information obtained included: consensus about the definition of a mobile portal; from the population of interest, a list of factors that affect user satisfaction with mobile portals; and a refined definition of each factor. Morgan (1997) and Smithson (2000) asserted that focus groups are not simple, nor quick to implement. A considerable amount of time and effort is needed to design and implement focus group research. Key factors that should be taken into account in using focus groups include: group composition, recruitment, group size, total number of focus groups and procedures followed in conducting the sessions. We outline, in Table 2 below, the way in which these factors were operationalised in this study.

SUMMARY OF THE FINDINGS

In all three focus groups, group dynamics were evident in the responses provided to the open-ended questions. In terms of discussion related to the meaning of user satisfaction with mobile portals, the resultant view was consistent with our initial expectations. Satisfaction with mobile portals relates to the overall feeling of satisfaction with using the mobile portal as a whole, which encompasses both the hardware and software aspects of the device.

At the conclusion of the focus groups seventeen factors affecting user satisfaction with mobile portals were identified. Of the seventeen factors, two factors (*Coverage* and *Speed of Response*) were grouped as *Ease of Use* while another two (*Personalization* and *Multi-language Support*) as *Personalization*. The *Service Provision* factor listed earlier was not identified in any of the focus groups. Of the remaining fourteen factors, six factors were new compared to those detailed in earlier section. The new factors included:

Table 2. Operalisation of the Key Factors

Key Factor	Operalisation of it in Our Study
Group composition	Given focus groups are carried out to gain specific types of information, caution is required in recruiting participants to ensure they satisfy the following two criteria: (1) they must be able and willing to provide the desired information; and (2) they must be representative of the population of interest (Hansen et al., 1998). In the focus groups we ran the participants can be categorized as either being: an expert, a researcher in a closely related area, or a mobile phone user. Experts were selected from leaders involved with portal implementations or the telecommunications industry. Researchers included those that had conducted research in the area of user satisfaction, mobile commerce, electronic commerce, portal implementation and/or IS implementation. Mobile phone users included those who used device for more than just making calls and sending SMS.
Recruitment	In this study potential participants were contacted through personal contacts either by telephone or email where the aims and objectives of the research were outlined and a mutually agreeable time arrived at. Reminder emails were also sent out.
Group size and total number of focus groups	The research context determines the correct number of focus groups and the number of participants. Where focus groups are used for exploratory purposes or for generating ideas for a larger study, two to four groups are sufficient (Hedges, 1985; Morgan, 1988). With respect to size, the ideal group size comprises between six and ten participants (Hansen et al., 1998), although when the participants have ample experience to share on a particular topic, four to six participants is preferable (Stewart et al., 2007). In our study we ran three focus groups on the following dates: 22 January 2010; 13 February 2010; and 24 February 2010. The first session comprised of nine participants (two experts, three researchers and four users) while there were seven participants in both the second (three experts, two researchers and two users) and third (two experts, one researcher and four users) sessions. The discussions in all focus groups were highly interactive.
Conducting the focus group	All three focus groups were conducted in a similar way by an independent facilitator who had no involvement in the research. In each session the facilitator followed a guide stipulated by the researchers, with only minor refinements being made to it as the sessions progressed. At the commencement of each session participants were given a pack comprising a plain language statement that outlined the project, a consent form, blank sheets of paper and a pen. The facilitator then began by welcoming the participants. After introductions he briefly described the purpose of the focus group, covered the formalities and thanked them for their participation. Then, following a broad guide he encouraged participants to discuss open-ended questions like what they understood mobile portals to be, their use of and experience with them and what they liked and disliked about them. This resulted in the identification of some factors, which participants were subsequently asked to rank from most important to least important. Each session lasted approximately 2 hours, with a short break in the middle wherein refreshments were provided.

- **Backups:** The ease with which data can be fully backed-up from the mobile portal to secondary storage.
- **Battery Hours:** The length of battery hours in providing power to operate the device.
- **Multi-Tasking:** The ability to switch from one application to another without terminating.
- **Reliability of Device:** The ability and durability of the device to perform its function.
- **Security:** The ability to perform transactions securely from the device.
- **Synchronization:** The ability to synchronies applications in the device, like the calendar, with other (including web-based) applications.

As depicted in Figure 2, the fourteen factors that affect mobile portal user satisfaction include: *Customer Support Service; Content-device Fit; Information Usefulness; Connectivity; Ease of Use; Personalization; System Adaptability; Cost; Backups; Battery Hours; Multi-tasking; Reliability of Device; Security;* and *Synchronization*. The next step for us in our journey is to develop items that are capable of tapping into aspects of user's satisfaction with these factors.

Figure 2. Conceptual model of mobile portal user satisfaction (MPUS)

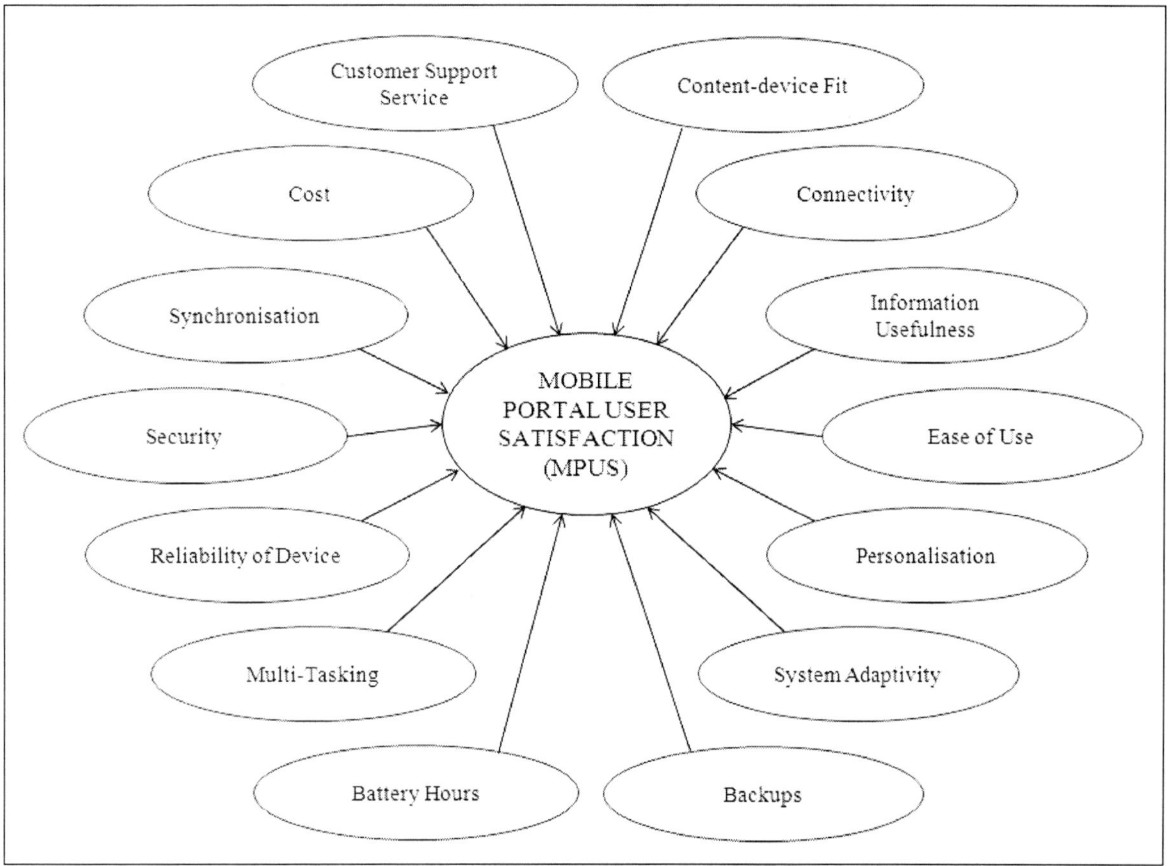

FUTURE RESEARCH

Given that we have identified and validated the factors which affect user satisfaction with a mobile portal, the next logical step, as per Churchill's methodology, is to generate items that measure aspects of these factors. To achieve this, a deductive approach will be employed. The deductive approach requires an understanding of the phenomenon under investigation together with a thorough review of the literature to develop the theoretical construct. This knowledge then guides the composition of items that measure aspects of the factors outlined in Figure 2. Where appropriate, in formulating the items, preference will be given to adapting items from existing IS scales since employing items that have already been empirically tested can enhance reliability and validity of the resultant instrument. Where deficiencies are identified new items will be composed by drawing upon the relevant IS literature. Once the items are developed the Q-methodology will be employed to group related items and see whether the fourteen factors identified above will fall out.

Q-methodology is an approach that provides a foundation for systematically and rigorously studying human subjectivity in a quantitative manner (Stephenson, 1953; McKeown and Thomas, 1988; Brown, 1993). It studies patterns of subjective perspectives across individuals by requiring them to independently rank these items. These individual rankings are then subjected to factor analysis. By correlating people Q factor analysis gives information about similarities and differences in viewpoint on a particular respondent. Based on the outcomes of the Q-methodology the refined items will be formatted into a coherent questionnaire. From this an online survey, which is a medium for survey delivery that has gained popularity over the years, will be used to collect data for both our exploratory and confirmatory studies. The aim of our exploratory study is to identify the underlying factors of the MPUS instrument and to retain the best items, while our confirmatory study will examine the factor structure. Finally, we will employ statistical methods for investigating the reliability and validity of the instrument.

CONCLUSION

This chapter has defined the terms 'mobile portal' and 'user satisfaction with a mobile portal', which provide the context for the study. Mobile portal was defined to mean *the customized, personalized user interface of wireless small screen mobile devices like smart phones that allow users to seamlessly access mobile content and mobile services*. On the other hand, user satisfaction with a mobile portal was defined as *the user's overall affective attitude towards the mobile portal.* Leveraging these and drawing upon related theoretical and empirical research, nine factors that affect user satisfaction with mobile portals were identified. They included: *Customer Support Service; Content-device Fit; Service Provision; Information Usefulness; Connectivity; Ease of Use; Personalization; System Adaptability*; and *Cost*. These factors were subsequently validated using three focus groups, which resulted in the removal of *Service Provision* and the identification of six other factors, namely: *Backups; Battery Hours; Multi-tasking; Reliability of Device; Security;* and *Synchronization.* With these factors in hand we are now able to progress to the next step of Churchill's methodology, which is concerned with generating items to measure aspects of the factors.

REFERENCES

Anderson, E. W., Fornell, C., & Lehmann, D. R. (1994). Customer satisfaction, market share, and profitability. *Journal of Marketing, 58*(3), 53–66. doi:10.2307/1252310

Anderson, E. W., Fornell, C., & Mazvancheryl, S. K. (2004). Customer satisfaction and shareholder value. *Journal of Marketing, 68*(4), 172–185. doi:10.1509/jmkg.68.4.172.42723

Bailey, J. E., & Pearsons, S. W. (1983). Development of a tool for measurement and analyzing computer user satisfaction. *Management Science, 29*(5), 530–545. doi:10.1287/mnsc.29.5.530

Barbour, R. S., & Kitzinger, J. (1999). *Developing focus group research: Politics, theory and practice*. London, UK: Sage Publications.

Barnes, S. J. (2002). The mobile commerce value chain: Analysis and future developments. *International Journal of Information Management, 22*(2), 91–108. doi:10.1016/S0268-4012(01)00047-0

Barnes, S. J., & Vidgen, R. (2001). An evaluation of cyber-bookshops: The WebQual method. *International Journal of Electronic Commerce, 6*(1), 11–20.

Barnett, N., Hodges, S., & Wiltshire, M. J. (2000). M-commerce: An operator's manual. *The McKinsey Quarterly, 3*, 163–173.

Benbya, H., Passiante, G., & Belbaly, N. A. (2004). Corporate portal: A tool for knowledge management synchronization. *International Journal of Information Management, 24*(3), 204–220. doi:10.1016/j.ijinfomgt.2003.12.012

Brown, S. R. (1993). A primer on Q methodology. *Operant Subjectivity, 16*(3/4), 91–138.

Cho, N., & Park, S. (2001). Development of electronic commerce user-consumer satisfaction index (ECUSI) for internet shopping. *Industrial Management & Data Systems, 101*(8), 400–405. doi:10.1108/EUM0000000006170

Churchill, G. A. (1979). A paradigm for developing better measures of marketing constructs. *JMR, Journal of Marketing Research, 19*(4), 491–504. doi:10.2307/3151722

Churchill, G. A., & Surprenant, C. (1982). An investigation into the determinants of customer satisfaction. *JMR, Journal of Marketing Research, 19*(4), 491–504. doi:10.2307/3151722

Clarke, I. III, & Flaherty, T. B. (2003). Mobile portals: The development of m-commerce gateways. In Mennecke, B. E., & Strader, T. J. (Eds.), *Mobile commerce: Technology, theory and applications* (pp. 185–201). Hershey, PA: IRM Press (an imprint of Idea Group Inc.). doi:10.4018/9781591400448.ch010

Constantiou, I. D., Damsgaard, J., & Knutsen, L. (2006). Exploring perceptions and use of mobile services: User differences in an advancing market. *International Journal of Mobile Communications, 4*(3), 231–247.

Davydov, M. M. (2001). *Corporate portals and e-business integration*. New York, NY: McGraw-Hill.

DeLone, W. H., & McLean, E. R. (1992). Information Systems success: The quest for the dependent variable. *Information Systems Research, 3*(1), 60–95. doi:10.1287/isre.3.1.60

DeLone, W. H., & McLean, E. R. (2003). The DeLone and McLean model of information systems success: A ten year update. *Journal of Management Information Systems, 19*(4), 9–30.

Detlor, B. (2000). The corporate portal as information infrastructure: Towards a framework for portal design. *International Journal of Information Management, 20*(2), 91–101. doi:10.1016/S0268-4012(99)00058-4

Dholakia, N., & Rask, M. (2002). *Configuring mobile commerce portals for customer retention*. Retrieved December 17, 2008 from http://ritim.cba.uri.edu/wp2002/pdf_format/M-Commerce-M-Portal-Strategies-Chapter-v04.pdf

Doll, W. J., & Torkzadeh, G. (1988). The measurement of end-user computing satisfaction. *Management Information Systems Quarterly*, (June): 259–274. doi:10.2307/248851

Eckerson, W. W. (1999). *Plumtree blossoms: New version fulfils enterprise portal requirements*. Boston, MA: Patricia Seybold Group.

Eggert, A., & Ulaga, W. (2002). Customer perceived value: Substitute for satisfaction in business markets? *Journal of Business and Industrial Marketing, 17*(2/3), 107–118. doi:10.1108/08858620210419754

Findlater, L., & McGrenere, J. (2008). Impact of screen size on performance, awareness, and user satisfaction with adaptive graphical user interfaces. *Proceeding of the Twenty-Sixth annual SIGCHI Conference on Human factors in computing systems* (pp. 1247-1256), Florence, Italy.

Fornell, C., Johnson, M. D., Anderson, E. W., Cha, J., & Byrant, B. E. (1996). The American customer satisfaction index: Nature, purpose, and findings. *Journal of Marketing, 60*(4), 7–18. doi:10.2307/1251898

Fox, J. (2000). A river of money will flow through the wireless Web in coming years. All the big players want is a piece of the action. *Fortune, 142*(8), 140–146.

Gelderman, M. (1998). The relation between user satisfaction, usage of information systems and performance. *Information & Management, 34*(1), 11–18. doi:10.1016/S0378-7206(98)00044-5

Global Mobile Suppliers Association. (2002). *Survey of mobile portal services* Q4 2002. Retrieved February 13, 2009 from http://www.gsacom.com/downloads/MPSQ4_2002.php4

Hansen, A., Cottle, S., Negrine, R., & Newbold, C. (1998). Media audiences: Focus group interviewing. In Hansen, A., Cottle, S., Negrine, R., & Newbold, C. (Eds.), *Mass communication research methods* (pp. 257–287). Basingstoke, UK: Macmillan Press.

Hedges, A. (1985). Group interviewing. In Walker, R. (Ed.), *Applied qualitative research* (pp. 71–91). Aldershot, UK: Gower.

Ho, C. F., & Wu, W. H. (1999). Antecedents of customer satisfaction on the Internet: An empirical study of online shopping. *Proceedings of the 32nd Hawaii International Conference on Systems Sciences* (HICSS-32), January 5-8, 1999, Maui, Hawaii. IEEE Computer Society, (pp. 1-9).

Howard, J. A. (1974). The structure of buyer behavior. In Farley, J. U., Howard, J. A., & Ring, L. W. (Eds.), *Consumer behavior: Theory and application* (pp. 9–32). Boston, MA: Allyn & Bacon.

International Telecommunication Union. (2007). *Mobile cellular, subscribers per 100 people*. Retrieved January 10, 2009 from http://www.itu.int/ITU-/icteye/Indicators/Indicators.aspx#

Ittner, C. D., & Larcker, D. F. (1996). Measuring the impact of quality initiatives on firm financial performance. In Fedor, D. B., & Ghosh, S. (Eds.), *Advances in the management of organizational quality* (pp. 1–37). London, UK: JAI Press.

Ives, B., Olson, H., & Baroudi, J. J. (1983). The measurement of user information satisfaction. *Communications of the ACM, 26*(10), 785–793. doi:10.1145/358413.358430

Ives, B., Olson, H., & Baroudi, J. J. (1984). User involvement and MIS success: A review of research. *Management Science, 30*(5), 586–603. doi:10.1287/mnsc.30.5.586

Jones, M., Buchanan, G., & Thimbleby, H. (2002). Sorting out searching on small screen devices. In Paterno, F. (Ed.), *Mobile HCI 2002, LNCS 2411* (pp. 81–94). Heidelberg/ Berlin, Germany: Springer-Verlag.

Kettinger, W. J., & Lee, C. C. (1994). Perceived service quality and user satisfaction with information services function. *Decision Sciences, 25*(5), 737–766. doi:10.1111/j.1540-5915.1994.tb01868.x

Lazar, I. (2000). The state of the Internet. *IT Professional, 2*(1), 52. doi:10.1109/6294.819940

Lewis, M. (2000). Focus group interviews in qualitative research: A review of the literature. *Action Research E-Reports, 2*. Retrieved February 24, 2009 from http://www.fhs.usyd.edu.au/arow/arer/002.htm

Malik, O. (2008). *Mobile subscribers forecast to top 5 billion-mark by 2011*. Retrieved January 10, 2009 from http://gigaom.com/2008/08/06/mobile-subscribers-forecast-to-top-5-billion-mark-by-2011/

McKeown, B., & Thomas, D. (1971). *Q methodology*. London, UK: Sage Publications.

Morgan, D. L. (1988). *Focus groups as qualitative research*. Newbury Park, CA: Sage.

Morgan, D. L. (1997). *Focus group as qualitative research* (2nd ed.). Thousand Oaks, CA: Sage Publications.

Muller-Veerse, F. (2000). *Mobile commerce report*. London, UK: Durlacher Research Ltd.

Muylle, S., Moenaert, R., & Despontin, M. (2004). The conceptualization and empirical validation of website user satisfaction. *Information & Management*, *41*, 543–560. doi:10.1016/S0378-7206(03)00089-2

Otto, J. R., Najdawi, M. K., & Caron, K. M. (2000). Web-user satisfaction: An exploratory study (industry trend or event). *Journal of End User Computing*, *12*(4), 3. doi:10.4018/joeuc.2000100101

Parasuraman, A., Zeithaml, V. A., & Berry, L. L. (1985). A conceptual model of service quality and its implications for future research. *Journal of Marketing*, *49*(3), 41–50. doi:10.2307/1251430

Parasuraman, A., Zeithaml, V. A., & Berry, L. L. (1988). SERVQUAL: A multi-item scale for measuring consumer perceptions of service quality. *Journal of Retailing*, *64*(1), 12–40.

Parsons, D. (2007). Mobile portal technologies and business models. In Tatnall, A. (Ed.), *Encyclopedia of portal technologies and applications* (pp. 583–587). Hershey, PA: IGI Global. doi:10.4018/9781591409892.ch098

Patterson, P., & Spreng, R. (1997). Modeling the relationship between perceived value, satisfaction and repurchase intentions in a business-to-business service context: An empirical examination. *International Journal of Service Industry Management*, *8*(5), 414–434. doi:10.1108/09564239710189835

Pitt, L., Watson, R., & Kavan, C. (1995). Service quality: A measure of information systems effectiveness. *Management Information Systems Quarterly*, (June): 173–187. doi:10.2307/249687

Powers, R. F., & Dickson, G. W. (1973). MIS project management: Myths, opinions, and reality. *California Management Review*, *15*(3), 147–156.

Ransdell, E. (2000). *Portals for the people*. Retrieved February 8, 2009 from http://www.fastcompany.com/magazine/34/ideazone.html

Raymond, L. (1987). Validating and applying user satisfaction as a measure of MIS success in small organizations. *Information & Management*, *12*, 173–179. doi:10.1016/0378-7206(87)90040-1

Segars, A. H. (1997). Assessing the unidimensionality of measurement: A paradigm and illustration within the context of information system research. *International Journal of Management Science*, *25*(1), 107–121.

Serenko, A., & Bontis, N. (2004). A model of user adoption of mobile portals. *Quarterly Journal of Electronic Commerce*, *4*(1), 69–98.

Shilakes, C. C., & Tylman, J. (1998). *Enterprise information portals*. New York, NY: Merrill Lynch Inc.

Siau, K., Lim, E. P., & Shen, Z. (2001). Mobile commerce: Promises, challenges, and research agenda. *Journal of Database Management*, *12*(3), 4–13. doi:10.4018/jdm.2001070101

Smith, M. A. (2004). Portals: Toward an application framework for interoperability. *Communications of the ACM*, *47*(10), 93–97. doi:10.1145/1022594.1022600

Smithson, J. (2000). Using and analyzing focus groups: Limitations and possibilities. *International Journal of Social Research Methodology*, *3*(2), 103–119. doi:10.1080/136455700405172

Stephenson, W. (1953). *The study of behavior: q-technique and its methodology*. Chicago, IL: University Chicago Press.

Stewart, D. W., Shamdasani, P. N., & Rook, D. W. (2007). *Focus groups: Theory and practice* (2nd ed.). Thousand Oaks, CA: Sage Publications.

Takeyasu, K. (2009). Mobile marketing. In Cater-Steel, A., & Al-Hakim, L. (Eds.), *Information system research methods, epistemology, and application* (pp. 328–341). Hershey, PA & New York, NY: Information Science Reference.

Tatnall, A. (2005). Portals, portals everywhere. In Tatnall, A. (Ed.), *Web portals: The new gateways to Internet information and services* (pp. 1–14). Hershey, PA: Idea Group Publishing.

Tojib, D. R., & Sugianto, L. F. (2008). User satisfaction with business-to-employee (B2E) portals: Conceptualization and scale development. *European Journal of Information Systems*, *17*(6), 649–667. doi:10.1057/ejis.2008.55

Tsalgatidou, A., Veijalainen, J., & Pitoura, E. (2000). *Challenges in mobile electronic commerce*. Retrieved September 29, 2008, from http://cgi.di.uoa.gr/~afrodite/IeC_Manchester.PDF

Turel, O., & Serenko, A. (2007). Mobile portals. In Tatnall, A. (Ed.), *Encyclopedia of portal technologies and applications* (pp. 587–593). Hershey, PA: IGI Global. doi:10.4018/9781591409892.ch099

Turkyilmaz, A., & Ozkan, C. (2007). Development of a customer satisfaction index model: An application to the Turkish mobile phone sector. *Industrial Management & Data Systems*, *107*(5), 672–687. doi:10.1108/02635570710750426

Uden, L., & Salmenjoki, K. (2007). Evolution of portals. In Tatnall, A. (Ed.), *Encyclopedia of portal technologies and applications* (pp. 391–396). Hershey, PA: IGI Global. doi:10.4018/9781591409892.ch066

Vlachogiannis, E., Velasco, C. A., Gappa, H., Nordbrock, G., & Darzentas, J. S. (2007). Accessibility of Internet portals in ambient intelligent scenarios: Re-thinking their design and implementation. In *Universal access in human-computer interaction. Ambient interaction* (pp. 245–253). Heidelberg/Berlin, Germany: Springer. doi:10.1007/978-3-540-73281-5_26

Wang, Y. S., & Liao, Y. W. (2007). The conceptualization and measurement of m-commerce user satisfaction. *Computers in Human Behavior*, *23*, 381–398. doi:10.1016/j.chb.2004.10.017

Wang, Y. S., Tang, T. I., & Tang, J. T. E. (2001). An instrument for measuring customer satisfaction toward websites that market digital products and services. *Journal of Electronic Commerce Research*, *2*(3), 89–102.

Watson, R. T., Pitt, L. F., Berthon, P. Z., & Inkham, G. M. (2002). U-commerce: Extending the universe of marketing. *Journal of the Academy of Marketing Science*, *30*(4), 329–342. doi:10.1177/009207002236909

Woo, K., & Fock, H. K. Y. (1999). Customer satisfaction in the Hong Kong mobile phone industry. *The Service Industries Journal*, *19*(3), 162–174. doi:10.1080/02642069900000035

Zhang, J. J., Yuan, Y., & Archer, N. (2002). Driving forces for m-commerce success. *Journal of Internet Commerce*, *1*(3), 81–105. doi:10.1300/J179v01n03_08

KEY TERMS AND DEFINITIONS

Content-Device Fit: the ability of the mobile portal to present information in a format that is compact, relevant and accurate based on users' specific needs (personalization) and physical location (location-sensitive information).

Connectivity: refers to the ability of the mobile portal to be connected from anywhere at any time.

Mobile Portal: the customized, personalized user interface of wireless small screen mobile devices that allow users to seamlessly access mobile content and mobile services.

Personalization: refers to the ability of the mobile portal to allow users to personalize or customize: (1) the layout of the mobile portal; (2) the information received based on the users' specific needs; and (3) the preferred language.

System Adaptability: the degree to which mobile portal providers adapt the information and the way it is presented through the different device capabilities (for example, varying screen sizes) to users with different network technologies.

Ubiquity: the ability of small screen mobile device users to access information or services and perform transactions from virtually anywhere at any time regardless of location, and to be reachable in anyplace at anytime.

User Satisfaction with a Mobile Portal: the user's overall affective attitude towards the mobile portal.

Chapter 14
Socio-Technical Factors in the Deployment of Participatory Pervasive Systems in Non-Expert Communities

Andreas Komninos
Glasgow Caledonian University, Scotland

Brian MacDonald
Glasgow Caledonian University, Scotland

Peter Barrie
Glasgow Caledonian University, Scotland

ABSTRACT

This chapter discusses the design and development of an interactive mobile tourist guide system according to the principles of Pervasive Computing laid out by Hansmann (2004) and presents solutions to the technical issues encountered in the development of a multi-tiered system that encompasses a wide ecology of devices. The chapter further presents the non-technical issues encountered during a live trial of the system and uses the experience gathered from this deployment to present evidence that Hansmann's (2004) four principles require the addition of a fifth principle, which is defined and based on hedonic values. In this view, the latter are crucial to the successful adoption of mobile and pervasive systems.

INTRODUCTION

Rural communities face increasing pressure and difficulties that arise from an over-reliance on a declining agricultural sector, ageing populations and poor access to services. Many rural communities are finding that tourism is an increasingly lucrative business and have adapted to provide better accommodation and recreation facilities to attract tourists. Development incentives and funding packages have helped rural communities set up and improve the levels of tourism-related services. However, while Web and Mobile technologies for tourism have become a primary tool for planning and organising tourism in economically developed urban centres, a clear divide between the online

DOI: 10.4018/978-1-60960-611-4.ch014

presence of rural tourism businesses and service provision (information, booking, enquiries) exists.

In developed countries, the presence of IT equipment and Internet connectivity in rural tourism businesses is at high levels. Findings from previous research (Deakins et al., 2004; Pease et al., 2005; Huggins & Izushi, 2002; Buick, 2003; Duffy, 2006) suggest that while rural businesses understand the potential benefits of adopting ICT and innovation in their operations, particularly the "image" benefits that technology innovation offers to potential customers, there appear to be barriers preventing the integration of innovation. Literature identifies the main barriers to ICT used to be the lack of IT training, cost of relevant hardware and software, security concerns, and dependency on external experts. Major barriers highlighted are also the fear of technology itself and the fear of displaying ignorance of IT especially to peers.

With research in the provision of information on mobile devices (Cheverst et al., 2008; Parikh & Lazowska, 2006; Jones et al., 2005; Cheverst et al., 2000; Dearden & Lo, 2005; Dunlop et al., 2004; Kenteris et al., 2009; Vansteerwegen & Van Oudheusden. 2006) feeding increasingly in to mainstream tourism, the barriers of IT training and external expert dependency are increasingly important; at the moment, it is almost impossible for a rural business to integrate and market itself on mobile platforms. In this chapter, we present the design and development of a participatory pervasive computing system based on Bluetooth beacons that transmit up-to-date map-based tourist information to visitors' mobiles. The information is maintained and updated by local businesses through a simple web interface, with each business responsible for their own content. The system is designed to remove the barrier of IT training by making use of existing skills (web browsing) and also to address the problem of reliance on external experts as the system automatically configures and compiles itself.

We name this system with the initials MiniGIST (Miniature Geographic Information System for Tourism) and introduce the system in a Scottish rural community. This chapter explains the multi-tiered architecture of the system that allows the integration of diverse device ecology and affords the participation of non-expert users into the process of ubiquitous creation and acquisition of information. The chapter discusses lessons learnt in the process of designing, developing and evaluating the MiniGIST system and examines these lessons under the principles of Pervasive Computing proposed by Hansmann (2004).

TECHNOLOGY AND MOBILITY IN TOURISM

The introduction of technology, particularly the Internet, into tourism, has had a profound effect in the provision of services in the sector. This transformation has come from the facilitation of communication and exchange of information regarding the services offered by businesses and destinations over the web to prospective tourists. The subject of information systems in tourism has been the epicentre of research by numerous scholars and practitioners, although most research seems to pivot around purely business science or computer science points of view, with few studies examining the impact of information systems in tourism by combining the two perspectives.

In order to gain an understanding of the importance of technology and mobility within tourism both the growing use of mobile devices and information software, and the adoption of ICT by businesses must be examined. Whilst some people are still hesitant to adopt mobile devices it has been found that as the mobile market continues to expand, increasing numbers of users will seek out software within the tourism industry as an additional means of information (Dunlop et al., 2004, p. 60). Similar studies have also shown that there is an increasing adoption of ICT within small rural businesses (Deakins et al., 2004, p. 148), yet research still supports the suggestions that rural companies are still facing issues regarding their adaption to the "information age", and are by and large less innovative and slower to adopt new technologies than their industry equivalents in urban environments (Huggins & Izushi, 2002 p.113). Although it has been proven that both users and developers are equally interested in the creation and use of mobile software it appears unclear as to what stake business individuals have in the area. Research has highlighted that the barriers that businesses face regarding ICT usage, cost of equipment, IT training, the display of fear or ignorance to their peers and the dependency on experts, all contribute to the reluctance of small businesses to embark on the integration of technology in to their company (Duffy 2006, p.182). It has also been suggested that it is simply due to the lack of understanding of the possible benefits available to local companies if they were to exploit such technology, that they may not recognise the value and potential of such systems (Pease et al., 2005, p. 4).

In order for small rural businesses to benefit from technology it must be recognised by local companies that there is a need to utilize technologies to become more responsive to the market and that the sharing of information would maximise the value of information and knowledge. However in relation to tourist destinations, levels of co-operation and incorporation of the required sharing of information has been low (Pease et al., 2005, p.4). Collaboration by the local business community may assist in the overall promotion of the local area and enhance the tourist industry as a whole.

Another vital point of consideration is the issue of the provision of accurate, localised data (Pease et al. 2005 p.3). This has been noted by several researchers who all agree that "the most important elements of successful tourist information systems are the availability of quality data content" and the attainment of dynamic up to date information is something that cannot be obtained by paper guides/leaflets" (Dunlop et al., 2004, p.59). While development studies have provided city visitors with a hand-held context-aware tourist guide, utilising modern technology solutions, they too identified the need for dynamic, up to date, reliable information (e.g. Cheverst et al., 2008; Vansteerwegen & Van Oudheudsen, 2006), as there appears to be a void regarding the creation and control of information (Dearden & Lo, 2004 p.112). To ensure the creation of mobile information will not only assist tourists but also be advantageous to the local businesses involved, local companies must overcome the technology barriers they face and take control of the data presentation which intends to improve the local industry. As noted by such researchers as Huggins & Izushi (2002, p. 121) "the key to the success of any ICT programme is the engagement of local communities in the very early stages so that they facilitate the sense of 'ownership' and the development of a self-managed learning process". The training, content and information management must be controlled by the companies themselves in order to ensure that the companies are not only benefitting substantially in relation to their expended efforts but also to ensure that the tourists are being provided with up to date, reliable information.

The MiniGIST System

Inspired by previous research, but particularly the gap identified from literature in the existence of a system in which the stakeholders (businesses and communities) could be afforded some degree of control of the information presented about them, we designed in 2006 a participatory system called MiniGIST (Miniature Geographic Information System for Tourism). In summary, the MiniGIST system allows the on-site dynamic delivery of map-based tourist information (currently text-based but easily extensible to include multimedia).

The project's primary targets were:

Table 1. Participant ratings

	*	**	***	****	*****	Total score
Accommodation	1	0	5	11	17	145
Food	1	0	10	10	13	136
Local Attraction	3	6	8	6	11	118
Entertainment	1	8	5	7	13	125
Banking	4	7	10	7	6	106
Healthcare	8	6	7	5	8	101
Transport	2	2	8	12	10	128

1. To provide dynamically updated, live tourist information to the modern-age tourist by exploiting the mobile devices they carry with them at a nominal cost to the tourist;
2. To encourage and facilitate the engagement of local communities and local businesses in the tourism industry with modern technologies, such as location based services and mobile advertising;
3. To stimulate tourism business growth and enhance the visitor experience through the provision of mobile and location-based services that increase awareness of the tourism-related businesses and their services.

Preliminary Research

In order to support the design and development of an appropriate architecture and client interfaces, we carried out some initial research in order to determine firstly, the types of updatable content that tourists would be keen on accessing through the system and secondly, the connectivity methods that would be most appropriate to allow tourists access to the desired content. We interviewed 34 people (tourists currently on holiday and people who indicated a general interest towards tourism) and asked several questions relating to their perception of importance of the most prominent categories of tourist information as identified by literature (Accommodation, Food, Local attractions, Entertainment, Banking services, Healthcare facilities, Transport), as well as the types of devices that they carried with them during holidays and their usage of the mobile internet. Our participants were mostly between 18-30 (74%) and residents in the UK (88%). In terms of looking for information, most of our respondents used the Internet as a source of information (76%). A further 44% indicated that they also used guide books and 34% also depended on other sources of information such as recommendations, newspaper articles, friends etc.

We asked our participants to use a "star rating" to indicate the importance of each category of tourist information, with one star being "least important" and five stars being an absolute must-have. The results are summarised in Table 1.

As it can be seen, the most important category (using a simple scoring system of 1 point per star, multiplied by the frequency of responses) is Accommodation, followed by Food, Transport, Entertainment and Local Attractions. Banking and Healthcare proved to be divisive, with the participant body apparently ambivalent regarding their importance.

With regard to local services such as Accommodation and Food, we also asked the participants what kind of information they felt would be of importance. The results highlighted that costs and special offers were very important, along with contact details and directions to venues (Figure 1).

We also asked the participants what type of devices they take with them on holiday, and found

Figure 1. Information on Local Services

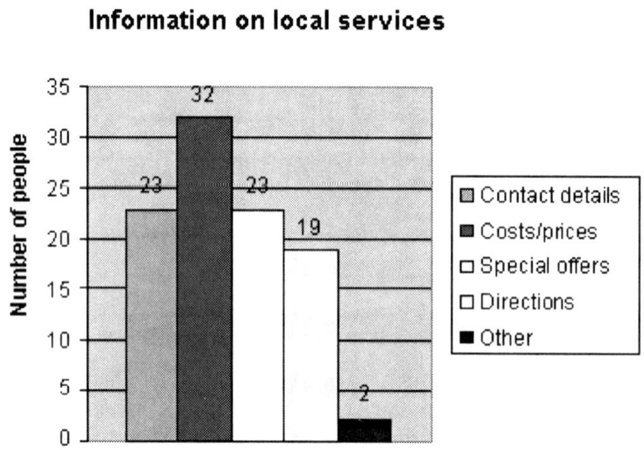

that 50% carried a web enabled mobile or PDA, 17% a laptop, 35% a non-web enabled mobile or PDA, and 12% indicated nothing as a response. With regard to how often they used the internet on their mobile devices, out of the 17 users who responded that they did use it, two indicated that this was done very rarely (once a month or less), seven did so rarely (4-5 times a month), six used it sometimes (2-3) in the week, one person indicated they used it often (every other day) and one more person indicated that they used it every day. We also queried people on whether they thought that the cost of access limited their use of the mobile internet and found that 35% said cost was not a factor, a further 35% indicated that it was a factor both in their country of residence and abroad, 0% indicated that it was a factor only when abroad while a further 30% indicated this question did not apply to them since they did not use the mobile internet (no suitable device). As such, a significant 65% of the respondents indicated that their main barrier to accessing mobile information was either a lack of suitable equipment, or the cost of access.

MiniGIST High-Level Architecture Overview

While our initial thoughts were to create a web-based architecture to allow tourists mobiles to connect over GPRS or 3G networks to access information, it was decided after these findings, to abandon this mode of connectivity for something more ubiquitously available. We adopted the concept of an "access point" – fixed locations within an area of interest – to deliver data to tourists' mobiles. These access points consist of a Bluetooth enabled computing device (this can be anything from a PC, laptop, kiosk or dedicated ruggedized miniature computer). Bluetooth is a short-range radio protocol mostly used for the transfer of small amounts of data across mobile devices (such as photos or songs). Bluetooth is, in a sense, the lowest common denominator for communication in mobile devices, as it is found on almost every model of mobile device produced in the last years and incurs no cost to the user.

To receive the tourist information, tourists connect their mobile phone with the access point wirelessly, via a very simple "pairing" process. Once the phone and access point are connected, the access point automatically sends the data (application and content) to the tourist's phone, at absolutely no cost to the tourist. The access points can alternatively be configured to look for Bluetooth devices in their vicinity and automatically send the data to them ("push" mode), without tourists explicitly instantiating the connection. Examples of Access Points are shown

Figure 2. MiniGIST Deployment Architecture

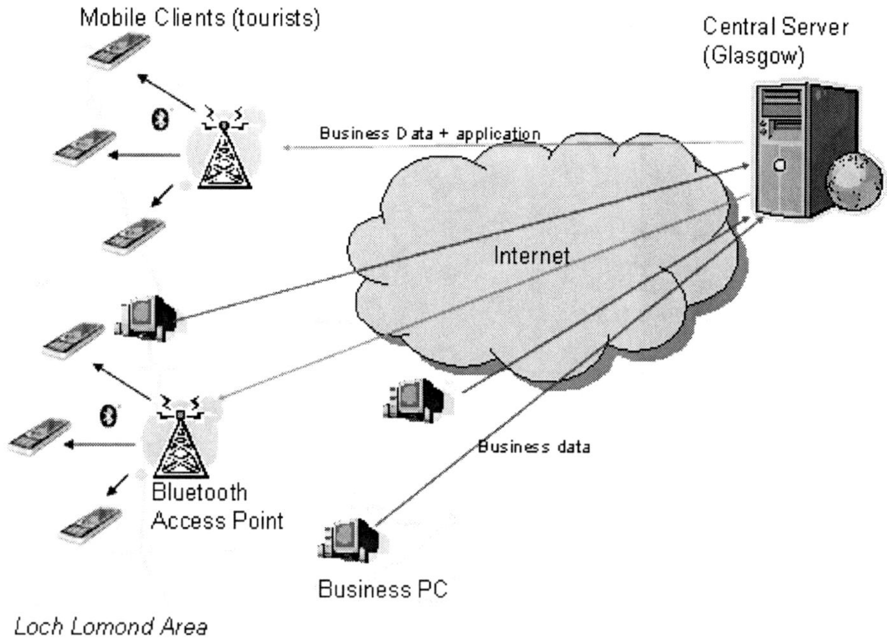

further in this chapter. The system has a range of approximately 8-10 meters.

In this architecture (Figure 2), businesses connect to the MiniGIST central server over their existing internet connections and using a simple website interface, can update their information and details as often as they like. This information is propagated to Access Points at pre-set time intervals through the day (e.g. every hour or twice daily). Access Points are dispersed through a particular geographic location of interest and are connected to our central database server through an internet connection (ADSL, cable, Wi-Fi or 3G/GPRS).

An access point can be a dedicated piece of equipment. However, any business PC can also serve as access point, with the addition of an inexpensive USB Bluetooth device. This way, a business can act as an information generator as well as an information provider. This architecture makes the MiniGIST system extremely low-cost in terms of its maintenance and operation. In a situation where most business PCs also act as access points, there is practically no cost for the system operation as the system utilizes existing Internet connections at business premises. Furthermore, dedicated hardware for the access points can be purchased for as little as £200, making even standalone hardware solutions relatively inexpensive. The system thus provides a high margin for profitability through subscription fees, charges for updates and/or advertisement, depending on the business model agreed upon by its operators.

Development of the Mobile Client User Interface

We chose to build a map-based system to provide the tourist information, as preliminary focus groups indicated that this would be the preferred mode of information delivery, compared to traditional menu-based list interfaces. One finding that became quickly apparent from these initial design consultations was the fact that users were having difficulty with existing Pan-and-Zoom interfaces,

Figure 3. Mobile Client Interface from the Callander Prototype

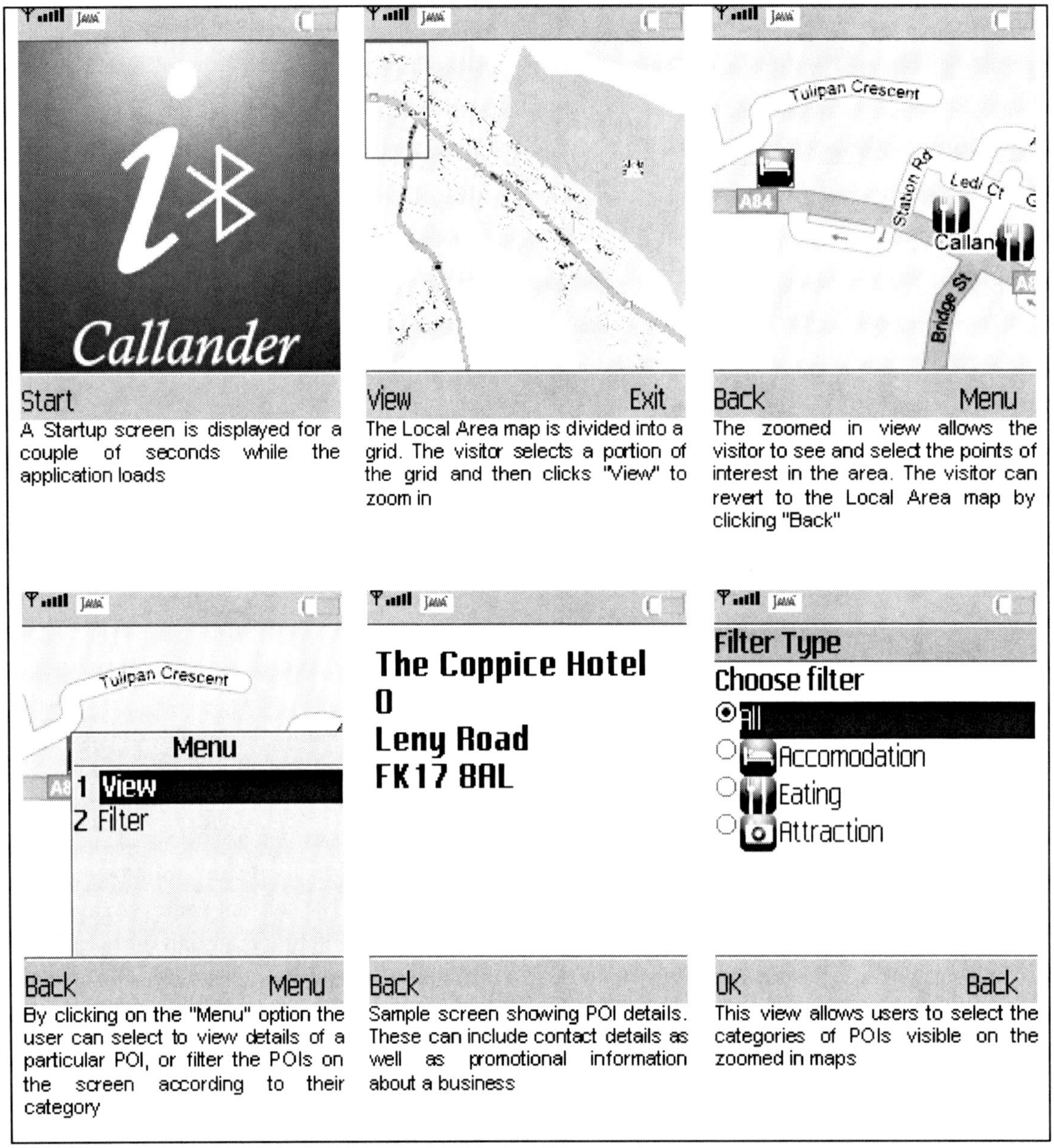

such as these encountered in applications like Nokia Maps. Users were becoming frustrated with the continuous pressing of directional buttons (D-pad) for panning and * or # buttons for zooming. We designed thus a novel zoomable interface, in which the map was split in grid-based segments. A user can select a segment (see Figure 3) with the D-pad on their device or stylus, and then press the central "selection" button of the D-pad or tap the screen to "zoom into" that segment. A user can then zoom out to the previous high-level view and select another segment to zoom into. This concept of "jumping" into and out of the map can be infinitely recursive, so that each view can be split into segments and zoomed into further, although for simplicity, our prototype implemented two "levels of detail", one high level map, plus one level of zoomed in segments. The screenshots in Figure 3 show the mobile client interface from our prototype and illustrate the simplicity and intuitive nature of the application. The application runs on most mobile phone makes and models, including touch-screen based devices (supports stylus tapping).

Evaluation of the Mobile Client User Interface

Since a prototype of our zoomable interface had been built prior to the preliminary research described earlier, we took the opportunity to ask each of the respondents of that survey to undertake a set of three simple information finding tasks using our prototype and asked them for their subjective opinions on the usability of the interface. When questioned if they perceived that the client was quick to learn to use, 32% agreed strongly, 42% agreed, 20% were unsure and 6% disagreed. In questioning their perception of ease of use of the novel zooming system, 35% said they strongly agreed that it was easy, 62% agreed, 3% (one person) was unsure, while nobody disagreed with this statement. The participants were somewhat less sure about the ease of use of the cyclical selection system for the POIs on the map which required them to use the device's Directional Pad in order to highlight one (12% strongly agreed it was easy, 50% agreed, 18% were unsure, and 20% disagreed). In summary, these results gave us confidence that our design directions were appropriate and we continued with implementing the project's back end infrastructure and stakeholder interface for updating and maintaining information.

MiniGIST Server Implementation

The MiniGIST Server consists of a MySQL database which is responsible for storing and maintaining business data. Data from the database is distributed to the Access Points in XML format, upon request from the access points. The Server Website is implemented in HTML and PHP5. Data that appears on the website and data elements, such as login usernames and passwords, are obtained directly from the database through appropriate PHP5 code embedded in the web documents.

When a business wishes to register for the MiniGIST system for the first time, they fill in basic contact details on the MiniGIST website (business name, desired password, a contact name and contact details) (Figure 4). Upon registration of these basic details, an email to the MiniGIST system administrators is automatically generated. Once the administrators are satisfied that the request is genuine and that it originates from an authorised representative of the business, the request is approved through the website (administrators can login and manage requests on a special section of the site visible only to them). Upon approval, the business can then log on to the website and change its basic details or its business details (e.g. address, special offers, prices etc.). Subsequently, any data entered by the businesses is exported to the Access Points in XML format. The access points are responsible for packaging this XML and the mobile application code packages and prepare the final application to be pushed towards the mobile devices. This process of "pulling" the XML data from the server and preparing the mobile application for distribution can be scheduled to take place at regular intervals, as deemed appropriate by the deployment scenario. Finally, in order to facilitate updates to the mobile application code, the Server holds a copy of the latest mobile client and AP application code, which the access points pull (if an updated version exists on the server) along with the XML data. Updates overwrite the application code stored locally in each access point.

MiniGIST Server Website

Using a simple login system on our secure server website, businesses can change their information as often as required to provide the latest infor-

Figure 4. New Business Registration Process (above) and MiniGIST Server Data Flows (below)

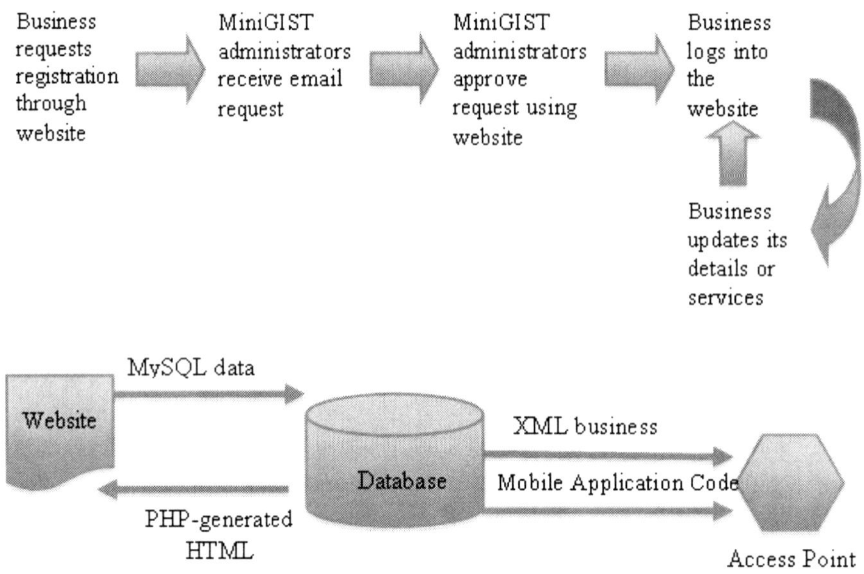

mation to tourists. Updating the information on the web server is also extremely simple, using a web form. The server brings up the information as previously stored and businesses only need to change the parts that need to be updated and then save the update (Figure 5).

MiniGIST Sample Access Points and Mobile Clients

Any PC running Windows XP, with the.NET and Java2SE runtime environment installed, with integrated or external USB Bluetooth hardware can serve as an access point. Figure 6 shows a self-contained, dedicated access point hardware device that runs our access point software under Windows CE, although this device was not used during the Callander pilot project). Our access point software starts automatically when the PC boots and runs in the system tray (Figure 7). The access point software has no user interface apart from a right-click pop up menu that allows a user to enter "admin" mode or exit the program. Admin mode is password protected and is not meant for use by access point operators (businesses). This mode allows a technical person to configure an access point by selecting how ofter it is to receive updates from the central server, and troubleshoot it, by providing manual options for downloading the database info, building the mobile client and sending it to a selected mobile device. Additionally, the pop-up menu allows businesses to explicitly send the mobile app to a device, in the case that the device is not being automatically detected by the access point software (manual mode).

The access points can be configured to distribute data in two modes, Push or Pull. In either mode, a connection to the user's device is established, the mobile client is sent across and then the AP immediately terminates the connection (to prevent misuse of the connection for malicious purposes). The users are prompted that the access point wants to send some data to their device and are given an option to accept or discard the transmitted package. The precise wording of the message depends on the device as each manufacturer implements their own generic message for all incoming Bluetooth transmissions. The mes-

Figure 5. Screenshots highlighting the simplicity of the MiniGIST server business site. Login (left) and MiniGIST server business details input and update screen (right)

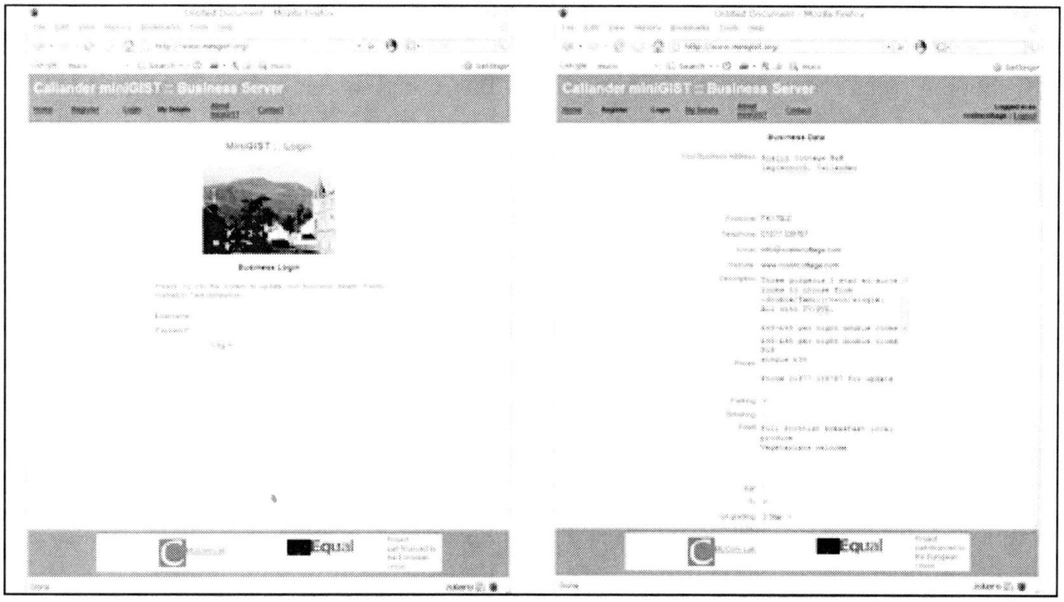

Figure 6. A miniaturized, screen-less standalone unit that can act as a MiniGIST access point. The unit is ideal for installation at indoor locations and can be secured on walls or fitted inside protective covers

sages are typically of the format *"<DeviceName> wants to send some information to your device. Accept?"*. By giving a suitable *DeviceName* to the Access Point (e.g. "Tourism Information Point") the message can inspire confidence to users that this is a genuine request, increasing the likelihood of its acceptance. The mobile application is then typically stored as a message on the user's inbox (depending on the manufacturer of the device). Users of some devices are immediately prompted if they want to install the application (e.g. Sony Ericsson devices) but for other devices, they are required to navigate to their message Inbox and manually install the application (e.g. Nokia). Finally it should be mentioned here that the APs log the outcome of the connection and transmission process with the MiniGIST server by first logging the name and MAC address of the Bluetooth device that has attempted a connection with the APs and then whether transmission was successfully completed or not, following each connection. Provision is also made, if required, to log the name of the AP to which a connection is attempted. This allows the close monitoring of a deployment area to potentially scan for problems in transmission and analyse usage statistics such as number of downloads, number of unique devices connected to the system, repeat downloads, frequently discovered APs etc. The distribution modes of the access points in more detail work as follows:

Push Mode: In this configuration, the access point scans continuously for Bluetooth enabled devices in its vicinity. Once a device is discovered, the access point immediately sends the mobile client application across to that device. In order to prevent constant transmission to a device that has already accepted or declined a communication (e.g. in the case that a user remains in the vicinity of the AP for some time), the access point can log recent connection attempts to devices and not make any further attempts to connect for a configurable period of time (e.g. 2 hours). While this function can help reduce the likelihood of "spamming" devices, it has one drawback in the sense that if a connection is inadvertently refused or terminated, the user will not be able to re-establish it until the pre-configured period of time has elapsed. The main advantage of Push Mode is that it keeps interaction with the system to a minimum in the sense that users only have to enable the Bluetooth function of their device and locate themselves in the vicinity of an access point. Additionally, this is a self-advertising mode that means that serendipitous discovery of the service is much more likely than Pull mode, described below, reducing the reliance on clear labelling of the AP's presence and promotional material (leaflets etc).

Pull Mode: In this configuration, the access point remains passive and waits for users to discover and connect to it. Upon attempting to connect, users are required to input a 4-digit passcode (set to 0000 for all access points). Once a connection has been established, the access point immediately sends the mobile client across and terminates the connection once the data has been transmitted. This method requires more input from users and also that they are familiar with the process of discovering and pairing with other Bluetooth

Figure 7. The MiniGIST server, running on a standard PC acting as an access point. The server runs discreetly in the background, with only one icon (circled) in the system tray denoting that it is active. The MiniGIST access point icon provides some control options when right-clicked

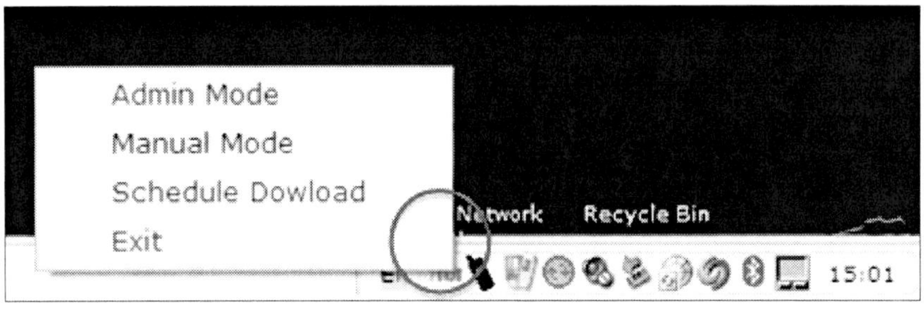

devices. Additionally, it requires users to have knowledge of the 4-digit passcode, although this is set to 0000 which is a universal standard for pairing to Bluetooth accessories such as headsets, speakers, keyboards etc. This constraint can also be mitigated through the use of clear labelling on the access point and inclusion of the passcode in marketing and promotional material. The main advantage of this mode is that "spamming" is completely avoided and that users remain in complete control of the frequency and timing of connections, which has the added benefit of allowing for easy repetition of the process in the case an error occurs during transmission. However, this method of distribution is much more reliant on clear labelling, information and promotion of the system, as serendipitous discovery of the AP services is much less likely that Push Mode.

DEPLOYMENT AND EVALUATION OF MINIGIST

To test the developed system in a field trial, a suitable location had to be found. In May 2008, we launched the MiniGIST system in the town of Callander in Stirlingshire, Scotland, for a pilot demonstration. The roll-out was conducted in collaboration with Callander Enterprise, a local business association representing a significant proportion of businesses located in Callander. Additionally the roll-out was supported by Stirling Council. The system was rolled out for a period of six months.

Securing Participation

In preparation for the roll-out, it was important to try to form a critical mass of businesses that would be part of the initial data set. If too few businesses participated in the scheme, tourists would be unlikely to find the system of any use, thus would be unlikely to download or make much use of it. Additionally, it was important to find local "champions" for the system, businesses who would be willing to take the first step forward in trialling the system out and hopefully convincing other businesses to join at a later stage.

A presentation of the system during one of the regular Callander Enterprise meetings was carried out to inform local businesses of the system's functionality and its advantages, where initial interest in the system was judged to be encouraging and the project was given the green light for a roll-out. To facilitate the participation of businesses in the scheme and in order to achieve the required critical mass, we funded the purchase of USB Bluetooth dongles to the first 10 participating businesses. Additionally, we offered to install the Bluetooth dongles and access point software on the computers of those businesses who would be part of the initial scheme.

Even though 10 USB dongles were donated, we found that some businesses had computers that were actually already Bluetooth-enabled. As such, we were successful in recruiting a total number of 16 businesses as a starting point (Table 2 and Figure 8). Two local champions for the system were additionally identified, one of which was the Chairman of Callander Enterprise. To support the launch of the system, Stirling Council provided £1000 towards the design and print costs of promotional material for the launch. The launch material consisted of posters promoting awareness of the system and its existence, leaflets containing more information about the system and instructions for tourists on how to connect to the access points and how to download and use the mobile client and window stickers denoting businesses participating in the pilot project.

Technical and Promotional Preparation

One of the key decisions that had to be taken during the deployment of the system was whether to use the "Push" or "Pull" mode for the access points. Upon consultation with local businesses and given

Table 2. Type and Number of businesses participating in Callander Launch Scheme

Business Type	Number of Businesses
Accommodation	3
Eating & Drinking	7
Shop	5
Attraction	1

Stirling Council's support for the production of promotional material, it was deemed best to use the "Pull" mode for access points and strong emphasis to be placed on the advertisement of the service. Another issue that was discussed during consultations was the inclusion of information for planned events in Callander. The MiniGIST client supports a time-context aware mechanism that allows the display of events that are happening within a pre-determined timeframe from the time of use, while still allowing users to search for events further in the future or in the past. Events were mostly of three types, some that were organised by local businesses themselves (e.g. live bands), some that were organised by the local authorities (e.g. Jazz festival) and some that were organised by the local Callander Enterprise group. During consultation, it became quickly apparent that entering events and maintaining information about them would be difficult as uncertainty arose on whether events should all be managed centrally by Callander Enterprise or individually by local businesses. While it was decided initially that the former method would be most desirable, the fact that no representative of Callander Enterprise felt they could manage this task individually, coupled with strong opposition from some local businesses led to the decision of excluding this type of information from the pilot phase and that we would continue with the remaining information types identified by the preliminary study.

Given the decision to adopt Pull mode for the access points, a professional designer was hired to design promotional and informational material to help promote awareness of the system. The material consisted of an A3-size poster

Figure 8. Map of Callander showing the geographic distribution of the participating pilot scheme businesses marked with colour-coded stars

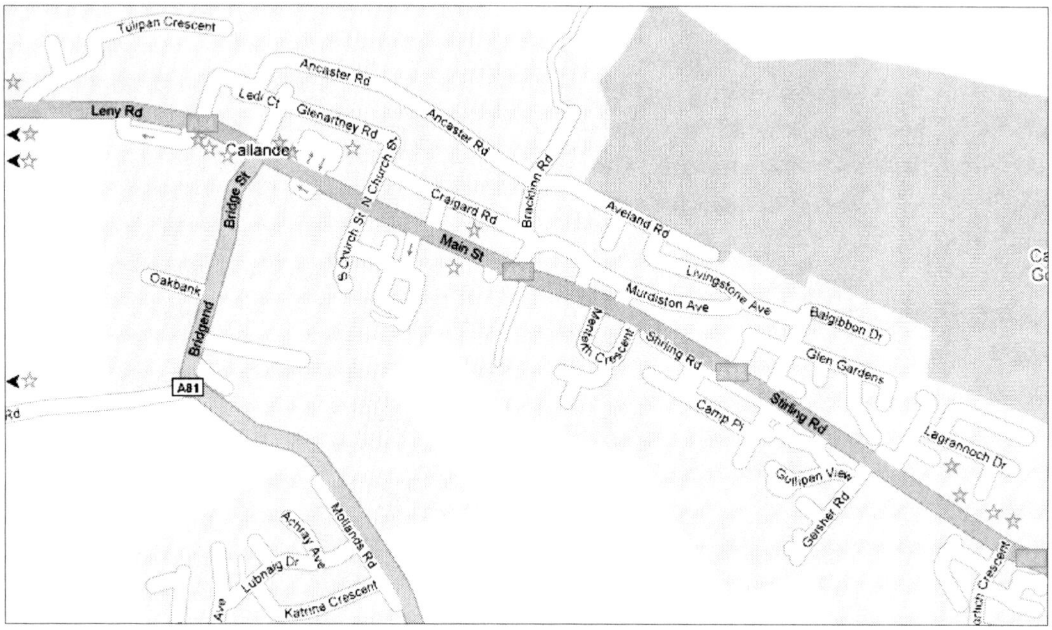

with basic instructions on how to use the system and 3-fold A4 leaflets containing more detailed descriptions for the use of the system and the information contained therein. Additionally, the designer helped create a logo for the system which consisted of the standard Europe-wide symbol for tourism information (the *"i"* letter), coupled with the Bluetooth logo (signifying the availability of Tourist Information via Bluetooth). This logo (Figure 9) was used on all promotional material and was additionally printed on stickers that were meant to go on business shop windows to show the availability of the system within the premises of a business.

Callander has two main tourist information points, located across from one another on the town's main square. The Tourist Information Centre (the former "Rob Roy Centre"), is operated by VisitScotland, and provides general tourist information on the area surrounding Callander. Given its central location and establishment inside an attractive former church building, it is generally the first port of call for visitors to the area. The second information point is the National Park Office, operated by the Loch Lomond & Trossachs National Park Authority. It provides information on the conservation area of the Loch Lomond & Trossachs National Park. This office is probably not as visible or attractive to tourists as the Rob Roy Centre although it is located on the main street, just off the square where the Rob Roy Centre is. We held several meetings with VisitScotland and the National Park Authority to allow the installation of an access point in these locations and although both organisations showed interest in the system, ultimately only the National Park Authority allowed us to proceed in time for the pilot launch.

Prior to the launch, members of our research group (MUCom) visited the participating businesses and installed the MiniGIST AP software on their computers, to ensure that installation for the pilot scheme went smoothly for all participants. During this process, it was discovered that the diversity in the age and specification of computing hardware available at local businesses posed significant problems in installing and operating the APs. We found that some businesses operated computers that were over 8 years old, running antiquated operating systems (e.g. Windows 98 or ME), making these incompatible with our system. Other computers had so little disk storage space available that the .NET framework required for the AP software to run could not be installed, or due to slow processor speeds and minimal RAM, this took up to 2 hours to install. Additionally, while some business computers were directly connected to the Internet (typically through ADSL), others

Figure 9. The MiniGIST logo as implemented on the mobile client (left) and the promotional material (posters, leaflets, window stickers) (middle). The window sticker is shown on a local business' window along with the running mobile client (right)

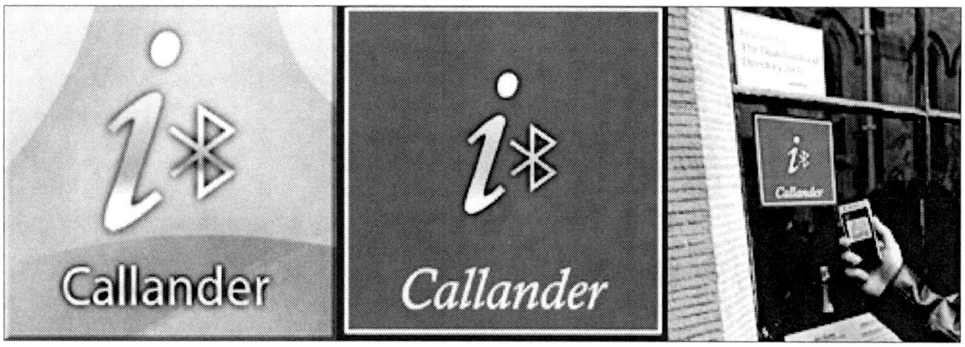

relied on connectivity through wireless routers, which, depending on the machine configuration, could take quite a while to establish and as such the AP software (configured to automatically run at start-up), would load and attempt to connect prior to the connection being available. While it was impossible to work around the problems of hardware and OS limitations described above, minor changes to the AP software were made so that it would keep attempting to connect every 30 seconds if a connection was not available, until it succeeded. Finally, some problems were encountered with the reach-ability of the AP over Bluetooth, as some businesses' computers were located in a back office that prevented the AP from covering the customer area. Some businesses were happy to re-locate their computer but for some businesses where this was not possible, we lent a couple of portable TabletPCs (Ubiquio 701) to act as dedicated APs for the pilot. Eventually, even though some businesses had to be turned down due to hardware incompatibilities, 16 businesses had an AP installed for the pilot launch.

The project was officially launched on the 31st of May 2008 by the Lord Provost of Stirling, the Chairman of Callander Enterprise, *KIT-OUT the Park*'s[1] Project Manager and the MUCom group (Figure 10). Following the launch, press releases were issued to local newspapers, university publications and websites, to raise awareness of the system. Additionally, the promotional material (leaflets, posters and window stickers), for which *KIT-OUT the Park* staff had undertaken the responsibility of printing, were given to Callander Enterprise for distribution amongst their members, so these could start to get displayed following the launch. The system was officially supported by KIT-OUT and the MUCom group during the pilot project period which was officially brought to a close on 15th December 2008.

Uptake and Evaluation of MiniGIST in Callander

As mentioned previously, the MiniGIST APs are able to report download and connection data back to the MiniGIST server. In examining this data, we found that during the evaluation period there were a total of 74 attempts to connect and download the application, by a total of 24 distinct devices. Out of these attempts, 10 were unsuccessful. In the first month of the operation of the system (June 08), we found 40 downloads, out of which six (15%) were unsuccessful. Out of these six attempts, four were made repeatedly by the same device in the space of three minutes, indicating that an incompatible device (e.g. Palm or Windows Mobile) was used. These statistics

Figure 10. MiniGIST promotional material & hardware used (left) and MiniGIST demonstrated working in local business (right)

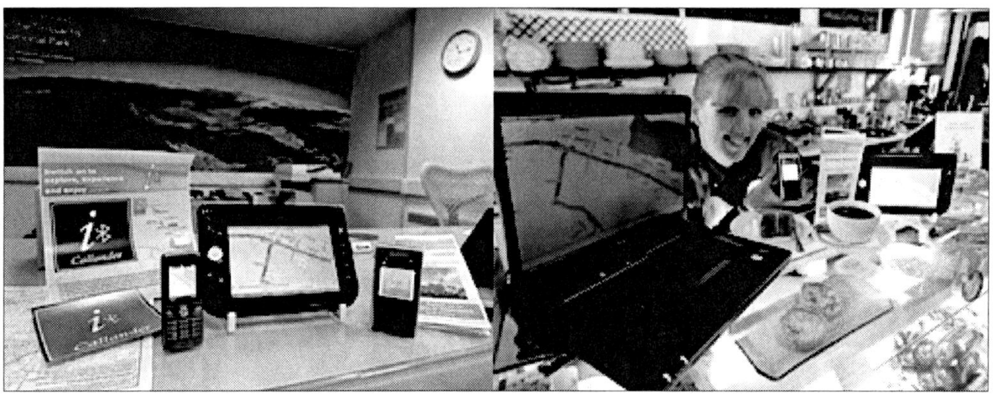

gave us confidence in the robustness of the system but we were disappointed on the seemingly low number of downloads.

In visiting the deployment area at the end of the first month, we were disappointed to discover that while most businesses had the leaflets on display, only two of the posters, which were meant to attract the attention and interest of visitors, were installed in town, and additionally these were in locations that were not easy to spot. Only two of the window stickers that were printed and distributed had actually gone up on business windows.

To potentially increase the visibility of the system, we agreed with Callander Enterprise to switch the access points to a "Push" mode and that more aggressive promotion of the system would be undertaken locally, ensuring that the promotional material was made more visible. In the following two months (July and August 08) and despite the agreed changes, uptake was actually worse (25 connection attempts, one failure in July and nine attempts in August with three consecutive failures from the same device). It was also discovered that despite promises, no additional work had been done to promote the system or enhance the visibility of the material.

In order to analyse the reasons of failure of uptake of the system, we interviewed local businesses as well as the chairman of Callander Enterprise as well as examining the logged updates of information that businesses made in the database. We found that only five out of the sixteen businesses of businesses actually used the system to update their data during the pilot season (Table 3), which shows a low level of interest in businesses for the system. The chairman of Callander Enterprise indicated that while promotional material had been distributed and clear instructions had been given to businesses to take a more proactive role in promoting the system, ultimately it was not possible for him to convince or oblige any of them towards this goal. Businesses themselves indicated that while they understood the potential of the system and its possible contribution in attracting more business, they were caught up in the daily running of their businesses and felt that active participation in the system was not a priority. Additionally, when queried whether they felt any additional business had ensued as a result of the introduction of the system, some businesses indicated that while they did encounter customers actively asking to find out more about the system, they could not be certain of any customers having appeared as a direct result of the system. We asked the chairman of Callander Enterprise whether the fact that participation in the scheme had no financial cost for the businesses influenced the low levels of interest from businesses. His opinion was that given the lack of any financial commitment (the system, support and hardware were all provided to businesses free of charge) and lack of visibility of the effectiveness of the system probably contributed to the low levels of engagement with the system, which was limited to the most enthusiastic ("champion") businesses. Finally, on the issue of relatively few downloads of the mobile client, he commented that given the demographics and age range of tourists visiting Callander (typically >35 year olds), familiarity with the technology could have played a role in the low uptake numbers.

As a final step of evaluation, we invited businesses to either fill in an on-line survey or to arrange a meeting with our research team, in order for us to guide them through the system and discuss the questions with them. The questions in the survey aimed to investigate the expectations of local businessmen who were not involved in the pilot phase in terms of business information systems and to gauge their perceived value of the system that we developed.

We received a total of five responses to our request, three were online survey responses and two were through face-to-face meetings. Sadly these numbers do not afford the results of this exercise statistical significance, but some of the findings are worth reporting as they provide valuable insight in the perception of the system. Out

Table 3. Number of businesses having actively updated their data at least once since the roll out of the system

Business Type	Number of Businesses	Businesses having updated data
Accommodation	3	2
Eating & Drinking	7	2
Shop	5	1
Attraction	1	0

of the five respondents, one classed themselves as being in the Accommodation sector, one in the Food & Drink, one in Retail and two respondents classed themselves as "Other". All businesses had a computer and internet connection for their use and all indicated that this was mostly used for business (managing their web presence, keeping in touch with clients and other businesses, managing other aspects of their business). Three respondents also mentioned that they did use their business computer for personal matters as well. Additionally, all businesses mentioned that they had their own websites as well as listings in other tourism-related sites. Two were in the Yellow Pages and three were also listed in local business catalogues or business groupings.

All respondents indicated that through the media that they advertise their services (web, leaflets, print etc), they offer information such as contact details and prices. Only three of them made a regular effort to update their information with special offers. However, when we asked them what category of information they would like more support with in order to provide better information, two mentioned that they were not happy with their current methods of providing contact details and costs, while four said they would want something to help them publish and advertise special offers more easily. One business said it was rather content with its current set-up: *"We are very small. It all works pretty well at the moment with our own web site and two web ads and I don't really need anything more as I'm getting as much business as I want already - but good luck with it anyway."*

In terms of ease of use of the system, all businesses either agreed or strongly agreed with the statements that registration and logging into the system was quick and easy, and all apart from one business felt that updating their details was easy. When asked whether they felt the system would do well to promote their business, one business strongly agreed, two agreed, one was unsure and one disagreed. These results are perhaps indicating a positive reflection on the value of MiniGIST. Even more encouragingly, four businesses agreed that they would use the system if it was free, a number which dropped to three when we asked if they would still use it if there was a small yearly fee attached (£20). Finally, we asked if they did use the system, how often they would update their details and special offers. One business responded that they were likely to do this daily, two businesses on a weekly basis, one business on a monthly basis and one on a yearly basis.

Deployment and Evaluation Overview

In summarising the results of our experience in demonstrating the MiniGIST system in the town of Callander, while pleased with the overall technical performance of the system, we were disappointed with the low uptake from visitors and lack of engagement on behalf of the local business community. We can conclude that first and foremost, for community-driven systems such as this to succeed, marketing and awareness promotion of the existence of the system is critical. Constant effort and participation of all parties involved in ensuring the system is visible to outsiders (visitors) is required.

The fact that we could not gain permission from VisitScotland to use the Tourist Information

Centre (TIC) in Callander as an access point was perhaps the most crucial point in the low visibility of the pilot scheme. This is generally the first port of call of visitors to Callander and although posters and information leaflets were available in the TIC, visitors could not access it from there.

Additionally, to make sure that continued support for the promotion of the system is provided by local businesses, it is important to ensure that a sense of ownership and stake into the system is cultivated, as well as clear indication of dividends arising from the participation in the system be provided. To this end, a mechanism to show tangible benefits and uptake feedback to the businesses should be implemented. This mechanism could take the form of agreed discounts or offers made available exclusively through the system (e.g. upon showing the system installed on their device, a customer might receive 10% off their bill). However, such mechanisms would require coordination and agreement through the local enterprise group.

In terms of technical improvements, we felt that while using existing business PCs as access points was a good way to reduce the roll-out costs for the system, in practice the benefits of this approach are outweighed by the significant problems in installation, maintenance and support posed by the diversity of computing hardware and operating systems available on these PCs. Based on our experiences in Callander, we feel that the use of dedicated AP hardware (miniaturised PC as shown in figure 8) could have double benefits. Firstly, it allows for a much more tightly controlled platform that is easier to operate, support and maintain; Secondly, given the hardware cost for this (~£200), it gives businesses that have to invest in its installation a sense of a "buy-in" to the system and should encourage more active participation so that a return on their investment could be achieved.

Reflections on the Principles of Pervasive Computing

Hansmann (2004) states four widely acknowledged basic principles that should drive the development of Pervasive Computing systems: Decentralisation, Diversification, Connectivity and Simplicity. The principle of Decentralisation advocates for the advantages of the distribution of tasks across multiple computing platforms in pervasive computing landscapes. We feel that in this respect, our system adheres to the principle, given its distributed nature and the facilitation of the sharing of the effort required to keep an up-to-date information repository of tourism business and services. Our system is designed in order to de-centralise the task of maintaining the repository (each business edits and maintains its own details without the need for central management) and additionally the task of dispersing the information to end users (tourists), through the distributed architecture of access points. The principle of Diversification argues that in Pervasive Computing, a multitude of devices of different types will co-exist, and though they may have overlapping functionality, each device would be designed to perform optimally in single tasks or for single user groups. In this respect, our method of employing diverse hardware types (servers, workstations, dedicated APs, mobile devices and multiple connectivity types) fulfils this criterion, making optimal use of different device types and exploiting overlapping functionality characteristics (e.g. a business PC acting as an AP) where necessary. The third principle of Connectivity discusses the need for standards in communication so that interconnected systems and devices can exchange information to help users accomplish tasks. Although we cannot claim to have made any breakthroughs in this area since the project did not revolve around improving connectivity hardware and protocols, we feel that this principle has been adhered to during our design and development of the project, where we have tried to build bridges between different connection types (Bluetooth, broadband) using industry communication standards, to allow devices that would have otherwise been disconnected from the rest of the world to become part of the pervasive computing landscape. The final principle of Simplicity advocates the need for intuitive and simple interfaces to pervasive computing systems. We feel that this has been demonstrated in the development of our system, with the emphasis on simplicity, learnability and ease of use paying dividends during the evaluation of the system, attracting positive subjective opinions from business and tourist users alike.

When considering the outcomes of the deployment of our system, we cannot ignore the fact that despite our adherence to well accepted guidelines, the integration of our system in the societal fabric of the tourism business community has been less than smooth. We encountered several issues with adoption and use of the system, perhaps reflecting a mindset of resistance to change, or adherence to traditional methods of work. Additionally, it seems that although in theory, business growth and development is an attractive prospect for many, perhaps "making do and getting by" with current income and business levels is sufficient in societal business and practice. Perhaps also, the prospect of task decentralisation and the affordance of control is not as desirable a proposition as the advocates of user empowerment believe. In attempting to define a design framework for pervasive systems, Kostakos and O'Neill (2004, p. 4) examined the notion of a successful "public space" and believed that they tend to share some common characteristics in affording expectations for uniformity and consistency of services. In this, they perceived that these spaces have a somewhat centralized structure when it comes to delivering such services. This has resulted in the development of notions and ideas such as a "station", a "centre", or a "provider". Kostakos and O'Neill (2004, p. 4) further argue that *"...not one of the above services actively relies on its users for its day to day operation. Users may enjoy the services without much work. It seems that we prefer the stability and consistency of a centralized service provider instead of a flexible decentralized system in which the user has increased responsibilities. This could be the case for pervasive systems as well"*. However, this thesis does not explain the success or popularity of participatory information spaces such as Wikipedia or Facebook, whose content and success is exclusively provided by their users.

In terms of pervasive systems, most research is done in carefully controlled lab environments, or limited field trials with careful monitoring. Despite the theory, it is unfortunate that we still do not seem to have conclusive evidence to support either argument for the integration of pervasive systems in society. Although our work seems to point more towards the analysis by Kostakos and O'Neill (2004), we did uncover some evidence from our post-experiment interviews that users can be encouraged to "buy into" a decentralised pervasive system, given the right rewards (or sight of progress towards a reward). Though our collective understanding of integration and acceptance issues in pervasive systems is (still) limited and we cannot generalise from just a handful of research projects, it seems that a fifth, hedonic principle, could be appropriate in the design of Pervasive Systems. We might thus name this fifth principle as "*Gratification*" and define it as the need for pervasive systems to be designed so as to keep their users and stakeholders in the system constantly gratified, by providing instant tangible or perceptible rewards that arise from active participation in the pervasive computing landscape.

SUMMARY OF CONCLUSION AND CONTRIBUTION

In summarising the results of our experience in demonstrating the MiniGIST system in the town of Callander, Scotland, while pleased with the overall technical performance of the system, we were disappointed with the low uptake from visitors and lack of engagement on behalf of the local business community. We can conclude that first and foremost, for community-driven systems such as this to succeed, marketing and awareness promotion of the existence of the system is critical. Constant effort and participation of all parties involved in ensuring the system is visible to outsiders (visitors) is required. The book chapter discussed the major barriers encountered in this respect and suggested how these can be overcome.

The contribution of the chapter is three-fold; first, we discuss the technical solution to a pervasive computing problem and show how introducing a multi-tiered architecture that caters for a diversity of computing devices can help non-expert users integrate with the pervasive landscape, to offer and receive services. Secondly, we discuss the societal, organisational and financial aspects that penetrate the pervasive computing landscape and suggest potential pitfalls and how these can be avoided. Thirdly, we examine the applicability of the pervasive computing principles of Diversification, Decentralisation, Connectivity and Simplicity in our system as defined by Hansmann (2004) and provide evidence in support of this theory for the design of future pervasive computing systems, as well as introduce the concept of reward-based design and the introduction of hedonic values in pervasive computing systems.

ACKNOWLEDGMENT

We would like to firstly thank the team at GCU's KIT-OUT the Park project (Derek Gallaher, Audrey Meikle and Abu-Zar Aziz) for its financial and business support and for making this pilot demonstration project possible. Additionally, Robert Wallace and Laura McIntyre for helping out in this project. We would also like to thank the local businesses in Callander that agreed to participate in this project and in particular, the Chairman of Callander Enterprise (Frank Park) whose vision and enthusiasm made the project possible. Finally, we would like to thank Stirling Council for its financial support in producing the promotional material for this project.

REFERENCES

Buick, I. (2003). Information technology in small Scottish hotels: Is it working? *International Journal of Contemporary Hospitality Management MCB UP Ltd.*, *15*(4), 243–247. doi:10.1108/09596110310475711

Cheverst, K., Coulton, P., Bamford, W., & Taylor, N. (2008). *Supporting (mobile) user experience at a rural village scarecrow festival: A formative study of a geolocated photo mashup utilising a situated display*. In Third Intl. Workshop on Mobile Interaction with the Real World (MIRW 2008), Amsterdam, Netherlands (pp. 27-38).

Cheverst, K., Davies, N., Mitchell, K., & Friday, A. (2000). Experiences of developing and deploying a context-aware tourist guide: The GUIDE project. In *Proceedings of the 6th annual international conference on Mobile computing and networking* (pp. 20-31). Boston, MA: ACM Press.

Deakins, D., Mochrie, R., & Galloway, L. (2004). Rural business use of Information and Communications Technologies (ICTs): A study of the relative impact of collective activity in rural Scotland. [John Wiley & Sons.]. *Journal of Strategic Change*, *13*(3), 139–150. doi:10.1002/jsc.683

Dearden, A., & Lo, C. M. (2004). Supporting user decisions in travel and tourism. In *People and Computers XVIII: Design for Life: Proceedings of HCI 2004* (pp.103-116). ACM Press.

Duffy, S. (2006). Information and Communication Technology (ICT) adoption amongst small rural accommodation providers in Ireland. In Hitz, M., Sigala, M., & Murphy, J. (Eds.), *Information and Communication Technologies in tourism* (p. 182). New York, NY: Springer-Verlag. doi:10.1007/3-211-32710-X_26

Dunlop, M. D., Ptasinski, P., Morrison, A., McCallum, S., Risbey, C., & Stewart, F. (2004). Design and development of Taeneb city guide - from paper maps and guidebooks to electronic guides. In A. Frew (Ed.), *Proceedings of Intl. Conference on Information & Communication Technologies in Tourism 2004* (pp. 58-64). New York, NY: Springer-Verlag.

Hansmann, U., Merk, L., Nicklous, M. S., & Stober, T. (2003). *Pervasive computing* (2nd ed.). Berlin/ Heidelberg, Germany & New York, NY: Springer.

Huggins, R., & Izushi, H. (2002). The digital divide and ICT learning in rural communities: Examples of good practice service delivery. *Routledge Journal of Local Economy, 17*(2), 111–122. doi:10.1080/02690940210129870

Jones, S., Jones, M., Marsden, G., Patel, D., & Cockburn, A. (2005). An evaluation of integrated zooming and scrolling on small screens. [IJMMS]. *International Journal of Man-Machine Studies, 63*(3), 271–303.

Kenteris, M., Gavalas, D., & Economou, D. (2009). An innovative mobile electronic tourist guide application. *Springer Personal and Ubiquitous Computing, 13*(2), 103–118. doi:10.1007/s00779-007-0191-y

Kostakos, V., & O'Neill, E. (2004). *Designing pervasive systems for society*. Paper presented at the Second International Conference on Pervasive Computing, Volume 2, First International Workshop on Sustainable Pervasive Computing. Vienna, Austria.

Parikh, T. S., & Lazowska, E. D. (2006). Designing an architecture for delivering mobile information services to the rural developing world. In *Proceedings of the 15th international Conference on World Wide Web, Edinburgh, Scotland,* (pp. 791-800). New York, NY: ACM Press.

Pease, W., Rowe, M., & Cooper, M. (2005). Regional tourist destinations - the role of information and communications technology (ICT) in collaboration amongst tourism providers. In G. Madder (Ed.), *Proceedings ITS Africa-Asia-Australasia Regional Conference - ICT Networks - Building Blocks for Economic Development.*

Vansteenwegen, P., & Van Oudheusden, D. (2006). Selection of tourist attractions and routing using personalised electronic guides. In *Proceedings of the International Conference on Information and Communication Technologies in Tourism 2006. Lausanne, Switzerland* (pp. 55-55). Vienna, Austria: Springer.

KEY TERMS AND DEFINITIONS

Pervasive Computing: A model of Human-Computer Interaction with Distributed Computing Systems in which Information processing does not only take place using dedicated desktop computers, has been integrated into everyday objects and activities.

Mobile Information Access: The process of Information Creation, Retrieval and Access, using mobile (pervasive) computing devices.

Hedonic computing: A discipline in Computer Science concerned as much with the "enjoyment" of use of computer systems as much as formalism in the design and development of such systems.

Gratification in Pervasive Computing: A design principle in pervasive systems that aims to keep their users and stakeholders in the system constantly gratified, by providing instant tangible or perceptible rewards that arise from active participation in the pervasive computing landscape.

Participatory Pervasive Systems: Pervasive Computer Systems in which users actively participate not only by requesting and retrieving information, but also by generating information "scraps" or meta-data that other users may retrieve through the same system.

ENDNOTE

1 Kit-Out (Knowledge, Innovation & Technology Out of University into Tourism) the Park is a project that aims to encourage the uptake of the latest technological developments by small and medium sized businesses within the Loch Lomond and National Park area.

Chapter 15
Pervasive Applications in the Aged Care Service

Ly-Fie Sugianto
Monash University, Australia

Stephen P. Smith
Monash University, Australia

Carla Wilkin
Monash University, Australia

Andrzej Ceglowski
Monash University, Australia

ABSTRACT

This chapter presents a case study about the adoption of a wireless handheld care management system at an aged care facility in Victoria, Australia. The research evaluated the motivation for adoption and usefulness of the system in collecting patient data. It employed a qualitative technique to gather insights from two perspectives: operations staff as end users and management as strategic decision makers. These findings indicate conflicting views in terms of the usefulness of the pervasive application by the operations staff and the significance of this IT investment by senior management. Based on the understanding that IT investment often cannot be measured solely in monetary terms, the authors propose the use of the Balanced Scorecard approach to systematically evaluate the performance of the pervasive application in aged care facilities as such.

INTRODUCTION

Wireless Technology has brought forward a new spectrum of business practices. It is the key driver for pervasive computing that significantly transforms the way people do business in virtually every sector. Pervasive computing is experiencing rapid growth in terms of the capabilities of hand-held devices, services and applications development, as well as standards and network implementations. Key characteristics brought forward by this technology include scalability, invisibility, integration and heterogeneity (Saha & Mukherjee, 2003).

DOI: 10.4018/978-1-60960-611-4.ch015

With the convergence of wireless and computing technologies, the Australian health care and aged care industries are moving towards the adoption and deployment of pervasive systems. To date, research into the design of pervasive care applications includes: ways to incorporate human values in the design; identification of the issues involved in capturing and satisfying multiple stakeholders' needs and requirements in the design; augmentation of health care applications into everyday mobile devices; and assurance about the systems' validity and usability through the use of a set of standard evaluation methods. As health care technologies are increasingly pervasive, we need sound evaluation strategies to assist with measuring performance. Research in this field indicates that evaluating ubiquitous systems can be difficult as evaluation approaches tend to focus on different aspects of the system, such as the users and usability aspect, the suitability aspect and the dependability aspect, to name a few. A variety of factors including scalability and context made it difficult to introduce a technical based evaluation framework. Besides, as this case study shows, a uni-dimensional (technical) evaluation can lead to differences in opinion between management and operation staff. Hence this chapter proposes the adoption of the Balanced Scorecard approach to evaluate performance of the pervasive application.

In exploring this issue, the chapter is organised as follows. The following section provides the context of the study, namely aged health care services in Victoria, Australia and presents an overview of the health care options, both public and private. The next section outlines the use of IT and pervasive systems in aged care services, highlighting the potential for productivity improvements raised by the deployment of this technology. This is followed by the reporting of a case study on the adoption of a wireless handheld system as part of an integrated health care management system at an aged care facility. Motivation for adopting the medication management system was concerned with the increase in incidences of medication related errors. In the subsequent section we propose the use of the Balanced Scorecard approach as a performance management tool for evaluating the performance of this system, as well as guiding future development in the use of pervasive systems. Finally we conclude the chapter.

CONTEXT OF THE STUDY

The context of this study is aged care in the state of Victoria, Australia. We limit our study to one state because, while health care is a federal responsibility in Australia, each state in the Commonwealth has their framework for administering health. With this limitation aside, the study may easily be extended to many other countries because the issues faced are similar in situations like ours where there is a mix of private and public options for aged care.

In the context of this study *residential aged care services* are public-health funded residential options for older Victorians who need care and can no longer stay in their own homes. Care may be high or low (as assessed by an Aged Care Assessment Service). Low care includes accommodation together with services such as laundry, meals, cleaning, and personal care services that help with daily living activities. High care additionally includes 24-hour personal and nursing care, and medical equipment. Services may specialize in low or high care, or offer both. The latter means that low care residents do not need to transfer to another facility when they are assessed as high care. This is referred to as 'ageing in place'.

Supported Residential Services (SRSs) differ from the above. SRSs are private businesses that provide accommodation and care for: the frail; aged; those that have a physical, psychiatric, intellectual, or acquired brain injury or other disability; or those with particular needs such as dementia. SRSs vary in the services they provide, people they accommodate and the fees they charge. Some specialize in particular types of care, but generally care includes assistance with showering, personal hygiene, toileting, dressing, meals and medication, as well as physical and emotional support. Furthermore, some SRSs also provide nursing or allied health services.

SRSs are required to employ a qualified personal care coordinator who coordinates care for all residents. The proprietor may also be the personal care coordinator if suitably qualified. There must be at least one staff member for every 30 residents, with extra staff required to provide adequate levels of care for residents. Moreover, sufficient number of staff is required to be on site overnight to respond to the residents' care needs and to ensure their safety. While SRSs do not receive direct government funding, residents can access some government-funded services and community services. For example, residents may be assisted to attend government-funded services or the service may visit the SRS. These services may include allied health, mental health, disability services, veterans' affairs and neighborhood houses. SRSs operate in the community in purpose-built facilities or in modified buildings. Whatever the type of building, SRS proprietors must provide a home-like environment.

In the course of conducting a study into trends in aged care provision, the Australian Productivity Commission invited comments from aged care providers and community groups on the likely future care preferences. These comments centred on the present demands of the "Baby Boomer" generation and their future requirements. The present demands are expectations for high care for their parents and these expectations may be extended to their own future preferences – in particular the demand for involvement in decision making processes (and have influence over decisions) and have a choice of service delivery that includes services that enable them to stay in their own home for as long as possible (Productivity Commission, 2008). These trends indicate that future services will need to encompass care in the home and it is foreseeable that electronic technologies will have an ever increasing role to play in the monitoring and management of home-based aged care services.

According to the Productivity Commission (2008) anecdotal evidence suggests that there may be potential for productivity improvements in the aged care sector by adopting advances in information technologies; increasing the use of assistive technologies; and restructuring operations. The necessity to leverage off the effectiveness of electronic technologies in the aged care sector is exacerbated by the increasing need for aged care services in an environment where populations are ageing; there is a shortage of suitably qualified staff; the proportion of high care patients is increasing; and polypharmacy (multiple prescribed medications) is occurring at an increasing rate (Hurley et al., 2009; Mundy et al., 2009).

USE OF INFORMATION TECHNOLOGY AND PERVASIVE APPLICATIONS IN AGED CARE SERVICES

The repetitive nature of many tasks in aged care provides impetus for applying IT to achieve efficiency improvements. Herein smart use of IT enables automation of such tasks as: rostering and shift management (with possible links to payroll systems); data administration (including the lodgment of reports to accreditation and governing agencies); the submission of claims and payments; and the ordering, monitoring and provision of medications (Opticon Australia, 2008; Stefanacci, 2008).

Eight years ago the utilization of IT within Australian aged care facilities was low. Although more than 95% of facilities had at least one computer, less than 4% of the facilities recorded IT use in care planning and management (Albert Research, 2002). This situation is reputed to have improved in recent years, but the penetration of IT into aged care applications is still slow. The typical obstacle when implementing IT in aged care facilities has been habit: people are often not comfortable with the idea of new IT solutions replacing the manual paper-based systems with which they are familiar. Even in situations where staff wish to implement IT, the feasibility of doing so is often constrained by fixed capital and policy settings (in public health). These factors limit the opportunities for restructuring work processes around electronic initiatives (Productivity Commission, 2008).

Health care practitioners have, for some years, been concerned about the high incidence of medication-related errors in the aged care sector in Australia (Runciman, Roughead et al., 2003; Lim, Chiu et al. 2010). Similar problems have been reported with medication management elsewhere in the world (Spinewine, Schmader et al. 2007). Much of the current thrust towards integrating IT into a pervasive computing environment within the aged care sector has been through electronic medication management because, of the 40,000 hospitalisations each year from aged care facilities, it is estimated that 30% are the result of adverse drug events (Dearne, 2009). This high incidence is not surprising given that aged-care patients depend on nursing staff for their medication needs, and typically receive between seven and eleven separate medications per day compared to around three per day for patients in the hospital sector (Bushardt, Massey et al. 2008). Studies that investigated the adverse incidents that occur in medical contexts concluded, however, that although some environmental factors make mistakes more likely, well designed procedures prevent most errors. Common mistakes include administering the wrong dose or drug, administering a drug late or not at all, and misidentifying the patient (DeLucia, Ott et al. 2009). Research into the underlying causes of these mistakes in aged care facilities indicates that poor communication between the patient, the nursing staff, and the physician is the most common problem, with more than 40 per cent of mistakes attributable to this (Hodgkinson, Koch et al. 2006). Performing tedious administrative work, such as documenting medication treatment, is also problematic because it is associated with burnout and with taking procedural shortcuts like bulk updating of records either before or after an event, both of which compromise data quality (Laschinger, Heather et al. 2006). Medication management systems have been shown to reduce error rates in clinical settings, partly because they automate a significant proportion of recording tasks (fewer clerical errors), but also because they improve adherence to standard procedures (Roughead, Semple et al. 2003).

Computerized Physician Order Entry (CPOE) is a key element in integrating IT into a pervasive computing environment. CPOE allows doctors and other authorized staff to enter orders electronically for medication and diagnostic tests. These systems are commonly implemented in order to (1) make best practice information (and warnings and alerts) available at the time the medication is being applied; (2) improve the linkage of records between actors so that more complete information (i.e. a complete medication record) is available to facilitate decision making; and (3) use of bar coding and related technology in order to minimize the mismatch of patients and medication (Black et al., 2003). Electronic medication systems are intended to remove the need for paperwork and associated transport or delivery systems, ideally through access to electronic patient records and associated care plans, provision of pertinent guidelines and automatic population of medication reports. Moreover, these systems allow drug prescriptions to be entered (and authorized) online and transmitted electronically to pharmacies. The electronic linkage between care plans, ordering of medications and administering is viewed as the lynchpin of efficient and effective medication management and is likely to lead to substantial savings in terms of efficiencies (and patient safety).

Numerous articles have outlined the relative merits of handheld technology within health care (Lo, 2009; Morris & Guilak, 2009; de Sa, 2007; San Pedro, et. al., 2005; Grasso, 2004; Przeworski & Newman, 2004; San Pedro et. al., 2004), but little work has been done on evaluating the impact of this technology on the users and the organisations involved. For example, one study that investigated this (Chau and Taylor, 2006) found that the wireless handheld clinical care management system used for data collection at an aged care facility could be viewed as beneficial to the end-users and facility as a whole.

Unfortunately electronic medication initiatives often fail because of a lack of executive leadership, absence of clinical champions, and the failure to involve end users (Black et al., 2003, Georgiou and Westbrook, 2006). Insufficient planning manifests in failures where manual processes are not reengineered prior to being converted to electronic ones and there is a general lack of attention given to the user interface. Furthermore, inadequate resources impact on implementations through the lack of terminals provided in facilities and insufficient time being spent with key clinicians, pharmacists and nurses during the specification and design stages (Black et al., 2003)

Many software experts argue that systems should reflect an explicit description of the environment in which they are to be used (Lauesen, 2003). This is critical for pervasive computing (Christensen and Bardram, 2002) because pervasive systems aim to integrate unobtrusively into work processes, permitting a more natural interaction with information and services (Estrin et al., 2002). There are a number of software providers in the aged care domain that aim to provide a level of support for pervasive computing. Software vendors operating in this sector in Australia include ERx Script Exchange (www.erx.com.au) and iCare (www.icare.com.au). Medical software vendors such as Fred, Amfac, Lots, Medical Director, Best Practice, Genie and Zedmed have committed to integrate their core desktop software packages and provide user support to facilitate ePrescribing and medication management.

iCare's solution for medication management links doctors, pharmacies and people who administer medications. The system provides an electronic record of the resident's drug history and current medications, and has the ability to record the administration of drugs at the point of administration. It consists of a mobile device that is used on the medication round. A photograph of the resident is displayed to aid identification and to combat administration of medication to the wrong person. Additional instructions may also be displayed, such as the necessity of patches, creams or eye-drops. The health care worker enters data indicating that medication has been administered and the system records the time and date this was done. Data is then automatically transmitted to a host computer, where it is stored and processed in a structured manner to comply with regulations governing the facility.

The system facilitates reporting because it provides medication charts and the necessary signing sheets. Tracking data can be produced for any period along with any comments, thereby allowing managers to review who administered what drugs, at what times and to whom. Moreover, communication with the pharmacy is electronic, the doctor's review schedule is automatically monitored, and record keeping protocols facilitate government subsidy claims.

Figure 1 shows the use of the pervasive application, iCare, and wireless handheld devices in an aged care facility. As shown in the Figure, the information system in the aged care facility is interconnected allowing carers to be equipped with wireless handheld devices when administering medication and monitoring the health of the residents. In the following section we depict the experiences of our chosen aged care facility in Australia that adopted iCare and deployed wireless handheld devices to run this application as part of their daily routine.

Figure 1. Overview of the Information System in the Aged Care Facility

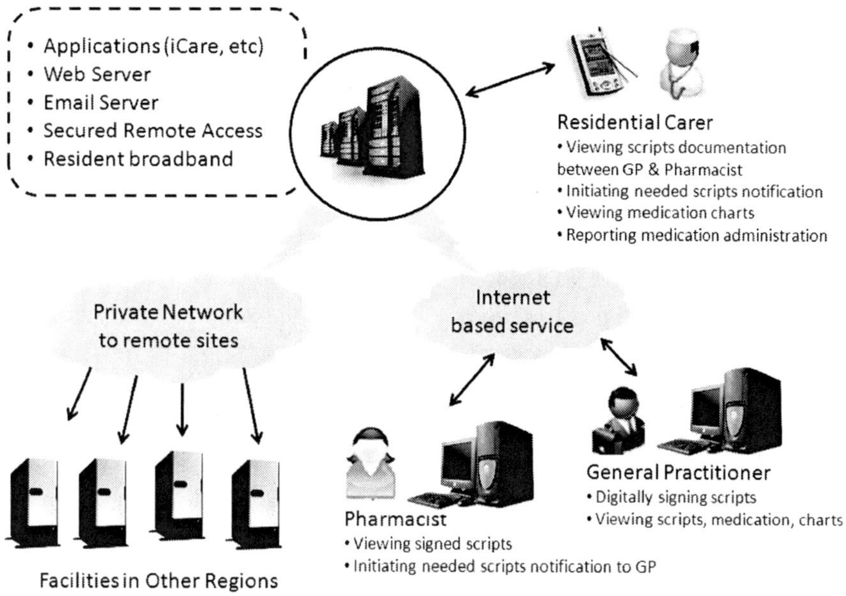

CASE STUDY ON THE ADOPTION OF PERVASIVE APPLICATIONS IN AN AUSTRALIAN AGED CARE FACILITY

Using a case study approach we studied a pervasive computing project in a real world setting (Yin 2003). The backdrop for this study was an aged care facility in the state of Victoria, Australia. The specific unit of analysis examined involved a project to implement a medication management system within an aged care facility, wherein our focus was on the theoretical construct *motivation for adoption*. The motivation was determined based on participant statements about the organisational problems that the system was seen to address. When gathering data we were given full access to key decision-makers closely associated with the project (the operations manager, the head of nursing, and the Chief Information Officer) who explained the specific issues that each was hoping to address through the implementation of the system and the outcomes.

CASE SITE

Elderville is a medium sized, church-based, non-profit enterprise that provides aged-care and community health services in the southern states of Australia. It has revenue of around $US 60M and employs approximately 700 staff. In the residential aged care division, Elderville operates seven facilities that look after around 850 people. Information processing is conducted using desktop computers, with many separate non-integrated applications used for budgeting, planning, and various operations management functions.

Operations Staff Perspective

Senior nursing staff accredited many of the most common medication and treatment errors present to sub-standard administrative practices. Consequently, they formed the view that an IT-based treatment management system would help improve the quality of care as well as assist with producing the regular reports about medication administration required by external bodies such as the Department of Aged Care.

Nursing Manager

The paper-based way of checking medication is so tedious and it is not possible to know really what is going on. Are medications given at the right time? I've seen occasions where an agency nurse finishes [the morning round] at 11:00 and then starts the lunch round in reverse order. A patient might get paracetamol at 11:00 and then get more at 12:30, but that's an overdose.

We have found the new system much simpler, and it lets us divide the work much more effectively. Previously it was hard to train staff how to fill in the records. Now they just have to follow instructions [from the handheld device].

Quality of Care and Efficiency

Staff are very focused on delivering a high quality of care, and believe that the computer-based system is significantly more advanced than the paper-based systems used in the aged care sector. Interestingly, from the perspective of nursing staff, their responsibility for patient care includes both direct interaction with the patient (medication and other treatment managed by nursing staff) and indirect interactions like those involving the doctor and pharmacist, both of who are administratively external to the aged care facility, but closely involved in patient welfare.

Business Manager

Doctors have access to the system. They can go into the system to check the patient records without needing to be here physically. If we need a script urgently, we can ring the doctor, the doctor has a look at the records, sends an electronic script straight to the pharmacy, and half an hour later we have the medication.

Implementation

The method used to implement the system is worth noting. Computer-based administrative innovations tend to diffuse slowly in medical settings, at least in part because of the sensitivity of the environment to system faults (Paré and Elam, 1998; Kaplan, 2001). Pervasive applications are even more difficult to implement in this setting because the scope of activities covered is larger than that for single-purpose systems, and so the potential impact of errors is consequently larger (Tooey and Mayo, 2003; Frisse, 2006).

Business Manager

We introduced the computer system slowly. They used the paper system with the computer system side-by-side so that they could see what was happening. They were also allowed to play with some demo units for a few months. We set up fake medication rounds and let them practice with each other using Tic Tacs. They seemed to infect each other with their enthusiasm.

Nursing Manager

Also, the software is really easy to learn. You don't need to know how to do everything. You just need to know how to follow the instructions. The registered nurses who had been working in aged care for 30 years or so were reluctant to use it. They stressed over it and said whoa, we can't turn this on. But they found they could and actually enjoyed it. Then we find that they are using email and wanting to use the more advanced features. The agency staff we have trained love it. It really cuts down on paperwork, and some of the reports we get are great. At the touch of a button we can get a report that tells us what medication a patient has been given in the past 24 hours and when it was given. That is really useful when we have to send a patient to hospital and safer.

Management Perspective

The senior manager interviewed in the case organisation (the CIO) highlighted the many conflicting demands of his role, explaining that from his perspective, a pervasive patient management system is only partly concerned with medication delivery and care from nursing staff.

CIO

Medication management is actually just a small part of the functionality when it comes to looking after patient needs. There are really five things you need to manage: patient information, client management, medication and medical treatment management, financial, and government funding, which depend on the type of care the patient is receiving. They are all related, so they are the activities that you want [a pervasive system] like this to handle. The biggest challenge is the lack of integration between our systems. The government has mandated [the] use of some systems, so we have to ensure that they integrate somehow with our existing information systems. We haven't done that well. In some cases we are entering data three times: one for government compliance, and twice because patient management and financial systems are not integrated.

He also expressed concern that the system did not maximise the return on investment and may even be a waste of resources because the quality improvements would not increase funding. His view was that he can afford to approve only a few projects per year, and is particularly looking for investments that will reduce recurrent expenditure so that he can free resources to invest in new and more efficient IT infrastructure. He also raised concerns about ensuring that business units had the capability to use a technology effectively before approving any project, and with managing the multitude of applications and technologies throughout the organisation.

CIO

The focus of all decisions has to be on the sustainability of the organisation. You set a budget each year and then walk around with a big stick to make sure that people stick to that. When deciding which project to run with, typically you line them up based on the Net Present Value (NPV), although some projects have to be quality driven. Certainly, the use of mobile devices can make a great business case. The ROI seems to be 200 to 300 per cent because it speeds things up dramatically. But I have a corporate view, and I have bigger fish to fry. My number one case is that I have fifty-million dollars of assets managed using paperwork circa 1975. That is a business case with an NPV of around four million dollars, so it is hard to approve something that will give a 10K, 20K, even a 100K return on a patient care system when I have a business case that has millions written all over it. A business case that generates an NPV of three million dollars lets us triple the amount of work we do in another area. If I allocate funding to the medication management system, yes I will get better care, but we already have one-hundred per cent compliance with government regulations. We have no compliance issues. Restricting funding will cause people grief, but improving other areas is more important than taking a bit of sweat off peoples' brows. We currently have two similar systems from different vendors. Ultimately we will roll out the same patient management system across our entire network. That's going to be a tough decision. I don't know which one I will choose.

Although quality of care is clearly important, the CIO's primary focus is on managing the IT budget effectively, and particularly on the extent to which a business case can be presented for every investment in technology

CIO

The evaluation we prepared a few months ago for the whole package proposed alternative business cases: get rid of it and go back to paper, or keep it. I put together an argument [to the board] that it would be retrograde to go back to paper, but I had to show how we could improve the amount of functionality we used. [The business manager] can see an operational view of our facility. He is a passionate, motivated guy, and I will assist him to the extent that I can. This system helps us to manage a crucial activity. The business case for this type of system is mainly time saved because so much time is spent in a paper system on documenting the care of patients. The more you can automate documentation tasks, the more attractive the business case becomes. There is a high error-rate around medication delivery, and this system helps us to minimise that rate. The target state for us is to have all records managed electronically rather than on paper, and to have systems that let you interact with the patient while updating information.

Discussion on Conflicting Perspectives

Pervasive IT applications create tension in this environment. Clinical staff are focused on improving the quality of care, while IT management are concerned with developing the organisation's administrative infrastructure, in particular freeing up resources to help fund future projects.

When viewed independently, both the CIO and the clinical staff are acting rationally and have the best interests of the organisation in mind. However, when viewed collectively these perspectives point to both short and long term potential problems. In the short term, conflict is likely as a result of the very different perspective that each group has on how to deliver value to the organisation, and indeed on fundamental concepts such as customer identity and organisational boundaries. To the clinical staff, the resident (or patient) is the customer, so organisational value is best delivered by maximising the quality and effectiveness of care. The CIO's "customers", however, are not residents, but the clinical and administrative staff requesting IT support. Organisational value, from this perspective, is maximized by selecting from the projects proposed by the customers the ones that maximise future resources (measured here via NPV calculations). From the CIO's perspective, quality of care is primarily an accreditation and revenue issue. The facility is currently meeting the minimum standards required for accreditation, so improving care will not increase revenue (possibly the reverse, in fact, if improving quality requires a significant investment in new technologies, training, and ongoing maintenance).

In the long term, these differing perspectives may become entrenched and limit the extent to which a truly strategic approach to IT planning is possible. For example, the CIO's stated project assessment criterion is NPV-based (although in practice he considers other factors as well). If all projects are currently assessed on that basis, over time it is likely that key projects will *only* be assessed in this manner. Using a single measure has the advantage that projects can be compared using a simple metric. However, some projects (or parts of projects) will not satisfy an ROI-based approval criterion process. For example, technical infrastructure and reporting projects that are mandated by external bodies will probably have a negative NPV, and the components of any pervasive IT application will similarly show a mixture of financial returns (e.g. projects that improve efficiency may show a positive return, while projects that build the information infrastructure may not). A simple financial metric is therefore ill-suited as the basis for developing a balanced portfolio of IT applications, particularly where that portfolio involves pervasive IT applications. Ideally, project value should instead be assessed using indicators of short-term and long-term value, and of external (customer-oriented) and internal (process-oriented) efficiency and effectiveness. Any new project can then be assessed on the basis of how it strengthens the portfolio of applications on these dimensions.

Having reported on the stakeholder experiences with the use of the pervasive system in our aged care service context, we now expand on the idea of multi-criteria value assessment by giving an example of how the (IS) Balanced Scorecard approach can assist with both assessing the value of individual projects and formulating a longer-term IT strategy.

MEASURING SYSTEM PERFORMANCE WITH THE BALANCED SCORECARD

Economic pressure, limited resources and government regulations present ongoing challenges for executives of health care organisations to balance such diverse issues as cost, quality, access and consumer choice (Shortell et al., 2000). Consequently many have looked for strategic management tools to differentiate themselves, whilst at the same time acquire operational improvements. We focus here on how one such tool, the Balanced Scorecard (BSC), can inform technology management. The BSC is a conceptual framework from Robert Kaplan and David Norton for describing a company's strategy and the business issues that must be addressed in order to achieve that strategy. It describes business issues and objectives from four perspectives: financial, customer, internal business process needs, and innovation. One important use of the BSC is as a measurement system because it provides a framework for organising and integrating performance measures according to the type of issue being assessed. It is, however, more than just a measurement tool. Kaplan and Norton (1996) claim that the technique is most powerful when used to define and communicate strategy, because it makes explicit both the strategy and what is required for a business to achieve that strategy.

The BSC has been proven to be appropriate in health care contexts such as regional public health (Impagliazzo et al., 2009); the Canadian health care sector (Chan, 2006); community health partnerships (Hageman et al., 1999); outpatient services (Curtright et al., 2000); and hospital contexts (Groene et al., 2009; Kershaw and Kershaw, 2001; Pink et al., 2001; Chow et al., 1998). Martinsons (1992) claims that it is also useful as a framework for formulating the information systems strategy of an organisation. However, in this latter application, the BSC requires some modification to account for unique aspects of technology management. In particular, the customer perspective in the BSC deals only with external customers. Information systems "customers," by contrast, can be both internal and external (depending on the project), so a perspective that focuses only on external customers is inadequate (Martinsons, 1992).

The modified version of the BSC, which we refer to as the IS Balanced Scorecard (IS-BSC), is shown in Figure 2 below. In that diagram, based on Martinsons (1992), four perspectives are evident: the financial perspective (which assesses business value through a financial lens), the technology user perspective (how well end user needs are met), the business process perspective (IT support for process needs), and the future readiness perspective (infrastructure requirements). The basic principle behind the IS-BSC is that a technology project should be described in terms of its impact on all four perspectives. All parties involved can then assess that project against specific performance criteria (measures) for key goals associated with each perspective. Projects that do not clearly meet the criteria for at least one perspective should be rejected on the basis that they do not help to achieve organisational objectives. It is not critical that a given project scores well on every perspective; however, the overall portfolio of projects should be balanced to ensure that key goals for each perspective can be met.

Figure 2. The Four Perspectives in the IS Balanced Scorecard (based on Martinsons, 1992)

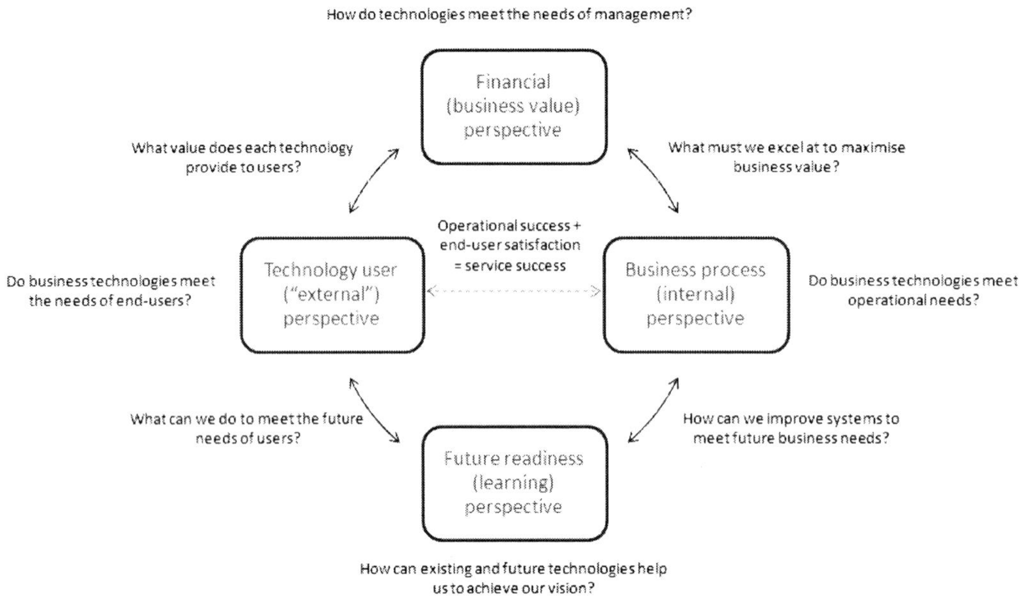

Figure 3 shows an illustrative set of goals that could be used to justify and assess a portable handheld device project like the one we described earlier. Each perspective suggests specific goals, and each goal is the basis for even more specific evaluative measures. For example, the technology supports the business value perspective (primarily concerned with financial control) by improving cost control and supply chain management, and supports the user orientation perspective (technology user requirements) by contributing to a variety of lower-level goals including *reliability of records*, quality of care, and medical safety. A variety of measures are shown to enable monitoring of progress towards each goal, and specific risks that need to be managed are identified. Taken as a whole, the goals described are particularly interesting, because they cover the full set of issues described by management and operations staff, but integrate all issues into a single coherent framework.

Like the BSC, the IS-BSC is also useful as a strategic evaluation tool. In this application of the tool, each goal should demonstrably contribute to the achievement of an overall business strategy. In Kaplan and Norton's formulation, learning and growth goals provide the basic infrastructure. This infrastructure supports the achievement of the internal perspective goals, and the internal perspective, in turn, supports the customer perspective. The customer perspective supports the achievement of the financial perspective goals, and achieving these financial perspective goals allows a business to meet higher-level strategic goals. By presenting multiple strategies side-by side, synergies between objectives become more apparent, and the contribution of individual project initiatives can be assessed more readily.

Figure 4 illustrates this approach by showing how a selection of goals from each perspective contributes to the achievement of two key business strategies: financial control and care effectiveness. Standardization and integration of systems provides the technology and information infrastructure for process improvement. The process improvements, in turn, allow the business to achieve four financial objectives (retire legacy systems, improve revenue systems, execute tasks

Figure 3. Proposed Balanced Scorecard to Evaluate the Use of the Wireless Handheld Device in the Aged Care Facility

Perspective	Goals	Measures	Risks
User Orientation Perspective	End-user acceptance	• Adoption rate • Staff attitude survey	• Fear of retribution for mistakes • Loss of device • Accountability
	Improved quality of care	• Accuracy in patient medication record • Clarity in patient medication record	
	Improved medical safety	• Reduction in medication errors	
	Non repudiation	• Number of validity disputes	
Business Value Perspective	Cost control	• IS expense per employee • Time savings • Workforce optimisation • Reduction in shrinkage	• Takes more time • Does not deliver efficiencies • Imposes overheads • Medication theft • Non delivery of medication
	Supply chain management	• Percentage of on-time delivery of medication • Accuracy in delivered medication	
Internal Process Perspective	Appropriate planning	• Percentage of resources devoted to planning for and reviewing of practices in preparation for IS	• Patient not given medication • Staff (full-time and agency) not familiar with the system • Staff (full-time and agency) unwilling to use the system • Theft of medication • Loss of devices • Damage to devices • System failure
	Efficient and effective implementation	• Percentage of resources devoted to implementation including infrastructure, fine-tuning and training	
	Cost control in system use	• Time and cost associated with training staff in system use • Time and costs associated with training agency staff in system use • Shrinkage in medication • Loss of devices • Damage to devices • Battery costs	
	Improved record keeping	• Failure rate of devices • Reduction in medication errors	
Future Readiness Perspective	Acceptance by staff	• Staff attitude survey	• Biases • Negative perceptions of technology • Negative perceptions of innovation
	Appropriate change management	• Staff attitude survey • Expertise of staff	
	IS champion	• Amount of IS training and development budget • Expertise with existing and emerging technologies • Turnover/retention of capable staff	
	Research into emerging technologies	• R&D budget for IS initiatives • Top management support via reporting opportunities	

more efficiently, and reduce the risk of claims for medical errors). Looked at this way, it is evident that the pervasive technology is an integral part of an over-arching technology management plan, and it is also clear which goals from each perspective must be achieved, and the relationships between these goals.

CONCLUSION

In this chapter we depict a case about the adoption and use of wireless handheld devices that form part of a health care management system in an aged care facility in Australia. Our findings indicate that the use of handheld devices to facilitate daily operations in the aged care facility have positive implications on compliance in the work place. It eliminates the paper based system, resolves the difficulty in training staff on how to fill paper based records, and anecdotally improves the quality of care as carers need to strictly follow the pre-programmed procedure in the devices for administering medication.

Other reported benefits from using electronic devices to communicate and disseminate work in aged care facilities include: a reduction in the time taken by staff to prepare and submit information; improvement in the quality of the data; reductions in the time taken to prepare monthly claims; faster access to up-to-date information; and an overall improvement in business processes and activities (Opticon Australia, 2008).

Challenges with implementing the system concern the selection of the implementation method. Further, according to the literature, pervasive applications in medical setting tend to diffuse slowly because of the sensitivity of the environment to

Figure 4. Example of how the IS Balanced Scorecard can align strategies (based on Kaplan and Norton, 1996, p. 152)

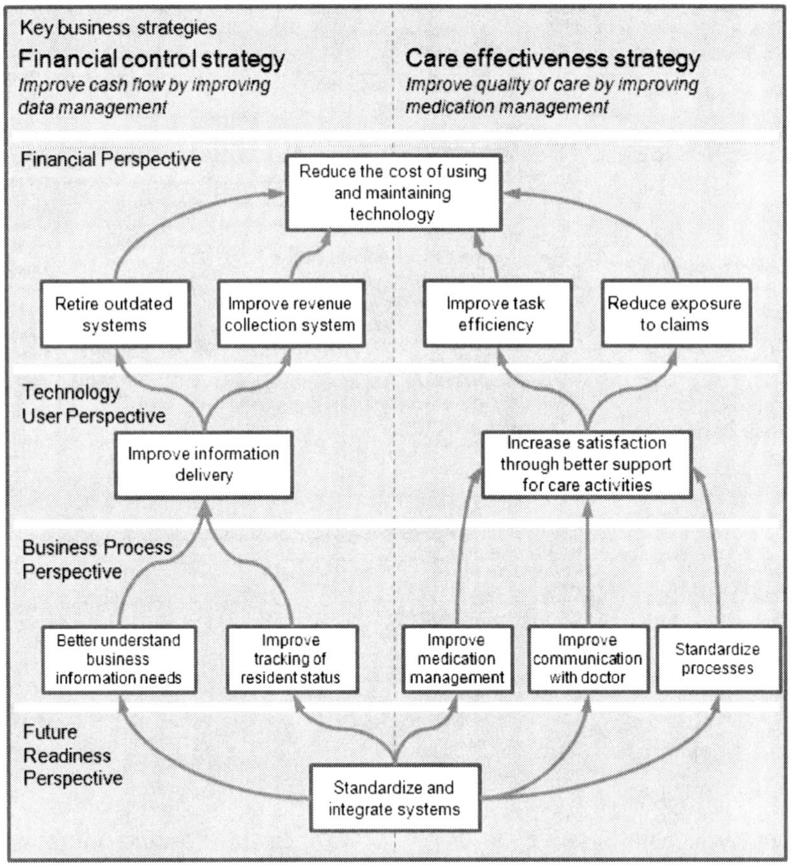

system faults. These two challenges relate closely to the scalability and the invisibility characteristics of pervasive systems. Herein a small glitch or error may propagate and have serious consequences in other parts of the system.

Like many other IT investments, a pervasive system requires some kind of evaluation strategy or performance management measures. Instead of using the traditional methods that focus primarily on financial measures, alternative methods that use multiple indicators can deal with the mismatch of measuring IT investment against productivity and profit. Here, quantitative analysis can be used to evaluate the technical component of the system, whereas qualitative methods can be used to evaluate how the system integrates with the business activities. In this chapter we proposed the use of the Balanced Scorecard approach (Kaplan and Norton, 1996) and its IS version (Martinsons, 1992; Martinsons, et al., 1999) for evaluating the pervasive applications deployed in our context. Embracing user orientation, business value, internal processes and future readiness, we submit that this enables strategic alignment and provides accountability for performance at all levels, both internal and external to the organisation. Internally, the strategic Balanced Scorecard indicates alignment of the scorecard with the organisation's core value adding activity. This provides a case for indicating that patient care might be weighted over the financial aspect. Externally, the Balanced

Scorecard promotes compliance with government regulations.

REFERENCES

Albert Research. (2002). *Results of research into the residential aged care industry's use of computers and the Internet for Commonwealth Department of Health and Ageing*. Canberra, Aged Care eConnect project within the E-Commerce Strategy Unit.

Allen Consulting Group. (2008). *Economic impacts of a national Individual Electronic Health Records system*.

Black, J., Dooley, M., Feekery, C., Graham, I., Harper, S., & Hart, G. … Weeks, G. (2003). *Electronic medication management.* Victorian Drug Usage Advisory Committee. Melbourne, Australia: Victorian Hospitals Electronic Prescribing and Decision Support Group.

Bushardt, R. L., Massey, E. B., Simpson, T. W., Ariail, J. C., & Simpson, K. N. (2008). Polypharmacy: Misleading, but manageable. *Clinical Interventions in Aging*, *3*(2), 383.

Chan, Y.-C. L. (2006). An analytic hierarchy framework for evaluating Balanced Scorecards of healthcare organizations. *Canadian Journal of Administrative Sciences*, *23*(2), 84–104.

Chau, S., & Turner, P. (2006). Utilisation of mobile handhld devices for care management at an Australian aged care facility. *Electronic Commerce Research and Applications*, 5305–5312.

Chow, C. W., Ganulin, D., Tekinka, O., Haddad, K., & Williamson, J. (1998). The Balanced Scorecard: A potent tool for energizing and focusing healthcare organization management. *Journal of Healthcare Management*, *43*(3), 263–280.

Christensen, H. B., & Bardram, J. (2002). Supporting human activities - exploring activity-centered computing. *Proceedings of the 4th International Conference on Ubiquitous Computing.* Göteborg, Sweden: Springer-Verlag.

Curtright, J. W., Stolp-Smith, S., & Edell, E. (2000). Strategic performance management: Development of a performance measurement system at the Mayo Clinic. *Journal of Healthcare Management*, *45*(1), 58–68.

De Lucia, P. R., Ott, T. E., & Palmieri, P. A. (2009). Performance in nursing. *Reviews of Human Factors and Ergonomics*, *5*(1), 1–40. doi:10.1518/155723409X448008

De Sa, M., Carrico, L., & Antunes, P. (2007). Ubiquitous psychotherapy. *IEEE Pervasive Computing / IEEE Computer Society [and] IEEE Communications Society*, *6*(1), 22–27.

Dearne, K. (2009, 19 August). Health rebate cuts could fund e-health: Roxon. *The Australian*.

Estrin, D., Culler, D., Pister, K., & Sukhatme, G. (2002). Connecting the physical world with pervasive networks. *IEEE Pervasive Computing / IEEE Computer Society [and] IEEE Communications Society*, *1*(1), 59–69. doi:10.1109/MPRV.2002.993145

Frisse, M. E. (2006). Comments on return on investment (ROI) as it applies to clinical systems. *Journal of the American Medical Informatics Association*, *13*(3), 365–367. doi:10.1197/jamia.M2072

Georgiou, A., & Westbrook, J. (2006). Computerized order entry systems and pathology services - a synthesis of the evidence. *The Clinical Biochemist. Reviews / Australian Association of Clinical Biochemists*, *27*(2), 79–87.

Grasso, M. A. (2004). Clinical applications of handheld computers. *Proceedings 17th IEEE Symposium on Computer-Based Medical Systems* (CBMS 04) (pp. 141–146). IEEE Press.

Groene, O., Brandt, E., Schmidt, W., & Moeller, J. (2009). The Balanced Scorecard of acute settings: Development process, definition of 20 strategic objectives and implementation. *International Journal for Quality in Health Care*, *21*(4), 259–271. doi:10.1093/intqhc/mzp024

Hageman, W. M., Harmata, R., Zuckerman, H., Weiner, B., Alexander, J., & Bogue, R. (1999). Collaborations that work: Strategies for building community health partnerships. *Health Forum Journal*, *42*(5), 46–48.

Hodgkinson, B., & Koch, S. (2006). Strategies to reduce medication errors with reference to older adults. *International Journal of Evidence-Based Healthcare*, *4*(1), 2–41. doi:10.1111/j.1479-6988.2006.00029.x

Holt, T. (2001). Developing an activity-based management system for the Army medical department. *Journal of Health Care Finance*, *27*(3), 41–46.

Hurley, E., Mcrae, I., Bigg, I., Stackhouse, L., Boxall, A.-M., & Broadhead, P. (2009). *The Australian healthcare system: The potential for efficiency gains - a review of the literature. Background paper prepared for the National Health and Hospitals Reform Commission*. Canberra: The National Health and Hospitals Reform Commission.

Impagliazzo, C., Ippolito, A., & Zoccoli, P. (2009). The Balanced Scorecard as a strategic management tool: Its application in the regional public health system in Campania. *The Health Care Manager*, *28*(1), 44–54.

Inamdar, N., & Kaplan, R. S. (2002). Applying the Balanced Scorecard in healthcare provider. *Journal of Healthcare Management*, *47*(3), 179–196.

Kaplan, B. (2001). Evaluating informatics applications—clinical decision support systems literature review. *International Journal of Medical Informatics*, *64*(1), 15–37. doi:10.1016/S1386-5056(01)00183-6

Kaplan, R. S., & Norton, D. P. (1996). *The Balanced Scorecard*. Boston, MA: Harvard Business School Press.

Kershaw, R., & Kershaw, S. (2001). Developing a Balanced Scorecard to implement strategy at St. Elsewhere hospital. *Management Accounting Quarterly*, *2*(2), 28–35.

Laschinger, S., Heather, K., & Leiter, M. P. (2006). The impact of nursing work environments on patient safety outcomes: The mediating role of burnout engagement. *The Journal of Nursing Administration*, *36*(5), 259–267. doi:10.1097/00005110-200605000-00019

Lauesen, S. (2003). Task descriptions as functional requirements. *IEEE Software*, *20*(2), 58–65. doi:10.1109/MS.2003.1184169

Lim, L. M., Chiu, L. H., Dohrmann, J., & Tan, K.-L. (2010). Registered nurses' medication management of the elderly in aged care facilities. *International Nursing Review*, *57*(1), 98–106. doi:10.1111/j.1466-7657.2009.00760.x

Lo, J.-L., Chi, P.-Y., Chu, H.-H., Wang, H.-Y., & Chou, S.-C. T. (2009). Pervasive computing in play-based occupational therapy for children. *IEEE Pervasive Computing / IEEE Computer Society [and] IEEE Communications Society*, *8*(3), 66–73. doi:10.1109/MPRV.2009.52

Martinsons, M., Davison, R., & Tse, D. (1999). The balanced scorecard: A foundation for the strategic management of information systems. *Decision Support Systems*, *25*(1), 71–88. doi:10.1016/S0167-9236(98)00086-4

Martinsons, M. G. (1992). *Strategic thinking about information management*. Keynote Address to the 11th Annual Conference of the International Association of Management Consultants, Toronto.

Morris, M., & Guilak, F. (2009). Mobile heart health: Project highlight. *IEEE Pervasive Computing / IEEE Computer Society [and] IEEE Communications Society*, *8*(2), 57–61. doi:10.1109/MPRV.2009.31

Mundy, G., Young, R., & Ramanathan, S. (2009). *Case for electronic medication management in aged care*. Aged Care Industry IT Council.

Opticon Australia. (2008). *Information Technology for aged care providers. Department of Health and Ageing*. Canberra: Department of Health and Ageing.

Paré, G., & Elam, J. J. (1998). Introducing information technology in the clinical setting: Lessons learned in a trauma center. *International Journal of Technology Assessment in Health Care*, *14*(2), 331–343. doi:10.1017/S0266462300012290

Pink, G., McKillop, I., Schraa, E., Preyra, C., Montgomery, C., & Baker, G. R. (2001). Creating a Balanced Scorecard for a hospital system. *Journal of Health Care Finance*, *27*(2), 1–20.

Productivity Commission. (2008). *Trends in aged care provision. Council of Australian Governments*. Canberra: Productivity Commission.

Przeworski, A., & Newman, M. G. (2004). Palmtop computer-assisted group therapy for social phobia. *Journal of Clinical Psychology*, *60*(2), 179–188. doi:10.1002/jclp.10246

Roughead, E. E., Semple, S. J., & Gilbert, A. L. (2003). Quality use of medicines in aged-care facilities in Australia. *Drugs & Aging*, *20*(9), 643–653. doi:10.2165/00002512-200320090-00002

Runciman, W. B., Roughead, E. E., Semple, S. J., & Adams, R. J. (2003). Adverse drug events and medication errors in Australia. *International Journal for Quality in Health Care*, *15*(Supplement I), i49–i59. doi:10.1093/intqhc/mzg085

Saha, D., & Mukherjee, A. (2003). Pervasive computing: A paradigm for the 21st century. *IEEE Computer*, *36*(3), 25–31.

San Pedro, J., Burstein, F., Cao, P., Churilov, L., Zaslavsky, A., & Wassertheil, J. (2004). *Mobile decision support for triage in emergency departments*. The 2004 IFIP International Conference on Decision Support Systems. Prato, Italy.

San Pedro, J., Burstein, F., Wassertheil, J., Arora, N., Churilov, L., & Zaslavsky, A. C. (2005). On development and evaluation of prototype mobile decision support for hospital triage. In R. H. Sprague (Ed.), *The 38th Hawaii International Conference on System Sciences,* IEEE Press.

Shortell, S., Gillies, R., Anderson, D., Erickson, K., & Mitchell, J. (2000). *Remaking healthcare in America*. San Francisco, CA: Jossey-Bass.

Spinewine, A., Schmader, K. E., Barber, N. C., & Hughes, K. L. (2007). Appropriate prescribing in elderly people: How well can it be measured and optimised? *Lancet*, *370*(9582), 173–184. doi:10.1016/S0140-6736(07)61091-5

Stefanacci, R. G. (2008). Electronic medication management systems in long-term care and beyond. *Assisted Living Consult*, *4*(2), 19–20.

Tooey, M., & Mayo, A. (2003). Handheld technologies in a clinical setting: State of the technology and resources. *American Association of Critical Care Nurses Advanced Critical Care*, *14*(3), 342.

Yin, R. K. (2003). *Case study research: Design and methods*. Thousand Oaks, CA: Sage Publications, Inc.

KEY TERMS AND DEFINITIONS

Baby Boomer: People born during the demographic birth boom between 1946 and 1964.

Net Present Value: Net present value (NPV) of a series of incoming and outgoing cash flows over time is the sum of the present values (PVs) of the individual cash flows. This is generally used in the determination of whether to invest in a project, where the initial outflow of capital is balanced against inflows over a period of time. The project will represent value if the net sum of outflows and inflows is positive.

Non-repudiation: In the aged care context, non-repudiation means people cannot dispute the validity of records. This is particularly important when investigating adverse events such as medication errors. Systemic problems are harder to detect and fix when the integrity of the data is questionable.

Productivity Commission: The Australian government's principal review and advisory body on microeconomic policy.

Residential Aged Care Services: Public-health funded residential options for older Victorians who need care and can no longer stay in their own homes. Also referred to as nursing homes.

Return On Investment: Return on investment is the ratio of benefits returned by the investment divided by the investment costs. For example, 5:1 ratio means $5 of benefits derived for every $1 of cost.

System Validity: System validity is the term used when a system is validated against the system requirements. It is to ensure that the system does what is required of it without errors.

System Usability: System usability is the term referring to the appropriateness, usefulness and ease of use of an Information System or computer software.

Compilation of References

Adusei, K., Kaymakya, I. K., & Erbas, F. (2004). *Location-based services: Advances and challenges*. IEEE Canadian Conference on Electrical and Computer Engineering- CCECE (pp. 1-7).

Ahamed, S. I., Vyas, A., & Zulkernine, M. (2004). Towards developing sensor networks monitoring as a middleware service. In *Proceedings of the 2004 International Conference on Parallel Processing Workshops - ICPPW'04* (pp. 465–471).

Ahn, J. G., & Sandhu, R. (2000). Role-based authorization constraints specification. [TISSEC]. *ACM Transactions on Information and System Security*, *3*(4), 207–226. doi:10.1145/382912.382913

AJAX public repository. (2010). *HTTP streaming protocol.* Retrieved June, 8, 2010, from http://ajaxpatterns.org/HTTP_Streaming

Akkaya, K., & Younis, M. (2005). A survey on routing protocols for wireless sensor networks. *Ad Hoc Networks*, *3*(3), 325–349. doi:10.1016/j.adhoc.2003.09.010

Akyildiz, I. F., Weilian, S., Sankarasubramaniam, Y., & Cayirci, E. (2002). A survey on sensor networks. *IEEE Communications Magazine*, *40*(8), 102–114. doi:10.1109/MCOM.2002.1024422

Akyildiz, I. F., Su, W., Sankarasubramaniam, Y., & Cayirci, E. (2001). Wireless sensor networks: A survey. *Elsevier Journal of Computer Networks*, *38*(4), 393–422. doi:10.1016/S1389-1286(01)00302-4

Alasti, H. (2009). *Level based sampling techniques for energy conservation in large scale wireless sensor networks*. Unpublished doctoral dissertation, University of North Carolina, Charlotte.

Albert Research. (2002). *Results of research into the residential aged care industry's use of computers and the Internet for Commonwealth Department of Health and Ageing*. Canberra, Aged Care eConnect project within the E-Commerce Strategy Unit.

Allen Consulting Group. (2008). *Economic impacts of a national Individual Electronic Health Records system*.

Alvarez, I., Bernard, S., & Deffuant, G. (2007). Keep the decision tree and estimate the class probabilities using its decision boundary. *Proceedings of the International Joint Conference on Artificial Intelligence*, (pp. 654-660).

Ambient Networks. (2010). *The Ambient Networks Project, EU framework programme 6 integrated project (FP6)*. Retrieved June 1, 2010, from http://www.ambient-networks.org/

ANA. (2010) *Autonomic Network Architecture, EU framework programme 6 integrated project (FP6)*. Retrieved June 1, 2010, from http://www.ana-project.org/

Anderson, E. W., Fornell, C., & Lehmann, D. R. (1994). Customer satisfaction, market share, and profitability. *Journal of Marketing*, *58*(3), 53–66. doi:10.2307/1252310

Anderson, E. W., Fornell, C., & Mazvancheryl, S. K. (2004). Customer satisfaction and shareholder value. *Journal of Marketing*, *68*(4), 172–185. doi:10.1509/jmkg.68.4.172.42723

Andersson, J., Lemos, R., Malek, S., & Weyns, D. (2009). Modeling dimensions of self-adaptive software systems. In Cheng, B. H. C., de Lemos, R., Giese, H., Inverardi, P., & Magee, J. (Eds.), *Software engineering for self-adaptive systems* (pp. 27–47). New York, NY & Berlin/Heidelberg, Germany: Springer. doi:10.1007/978-3-642-02161-9_2

Anliker, U., Ward, V., Lukowitcz, P., Tröster, G., Dolveck, F., & Baer, M. (2004). AMON: A wearable multiparameter medical monitoring and alert system. *IEEE Transactions on Information Technology in Biomedicine*, *8*(4), 415–427. doi:10.1109/TITB.2004.837888

Apache. (2008). *Apache Tomcat software*. Retrieved June 2008 from http://tomcat.apache.org/

Article 29 Working Party. (2008). *Opinion on data protection issues related to search engines*. Retrieved July 4, 2010, from http://ec.europa.eu/justice_home/fsj/privacy/index_en.htm

Asgari, H. (Ed.). (2008). *I3CON project deliverable D3.42-1, sensor network and middleware implementation and proof of concept*. Retrieved July 20, 2010 from http://ww.i3con.org/

Aura, T., Nagarajan, A., & Gurtov, A. (2005). *Analysis of the HIP Base Exchange protocol*. Paper presented at 10th Australian Conference on Information Security and Privacy (ACISP 2005). Brisbane, Australia.

AUTOCONF. (2010) *IETF WG MANET Autoconfiguration*. Retrieved June 1, 2010, from http://tools.ietf.org/wg/autoconf/

Avizienis, A., Laprie, J.-C., Randell, B., & Landwehr, C. (2004). Basic concepts and taxonomy of dependable and secure computing. *IEEE Transactions on Dependable and Secure Computing*, *1*(1), 11–33. doi:10.1109/TDSC.2004.2

Avizienis, A., Laprie, J.-C., & Randell, B. (2001). *Fundamental concepts of dependability*. Newcastle University Technical Report. Retrieved March 30, 2010, from http://www.cs.ncl.ac.uk/research/trs/papers/739.ps

Baccelli, E. (2008). *Address autoconfiguration for MANET: Terminology and problem statement. Internet-draft*. IETF WG AUTOCONF.

Bachar, W. (2005). *Address autoconfiguration in ad hoc networks. Internal Report, Departement Logiciels Reseaux, Institut National des Telecommunications*. Paris, France: INT.

Bahl, P., & Padmanabhan, V. N. (2000). *RADAR: An in-building RF-based user location and tracking system* (pp. 775–784). IEEE INFOCOM.

Bailey, J. E., & Pearsons, S. W. (1983). Development of a tool for measurement and analyzing computer user satisfaction. *Management Science*, *29*(5), 530–545. doi:10.1287/mnsc.29.5.530

Bakker, D., Gilster, D., & Gilster, R. (2002). *Bluetooth end to end*. New York, NY: John Wiley & Sons.

Ball, T., Bounimova, E., Cook, B., Levin, V., Lichtenberg, J., & McGarvey, C. ... Ustuner, A. (2006). Thorough static analysis of device drivers. In *Proceedings 1st ACM SIGOPS/EuroSys European Conference on Computer Systems* (pp. 73-85), ACM press.

Bao, L., & Intille, S. S. (2004). *Activity recognition from user-annotated acceleration data*. In 2nd International Conference, PERVASIVE '04.

Baratoff, G., Neubeck, A., & Regenbrecht, H. (2002). *Interactive multi-marker calibration for augmented reality applications*. International Symposium on Mixed and Augmented Reality – ISMAR (pp.107-116).

Barbour, R. S., & Kitzinger, J. (1999). *Developing focus group research: Politics, theory and practice*. London, UK: Sage Publications.

Barkhuus, L., & Dey, A. K. (2003). Location-based services for mobile telephony: A study of users' privacy concerns. *Proceedings of the International Conference on Human-Computer Interaction - INTERACT- IFIP.* (pp. 1-5). ACM Press.

Barnes, J., Rizos, C., Wang, J., Small, D., Voigt, G., & Gambale, N. (2003). High precision indoor and outdoor positioning using LocataNet. *Journal of Global Positioning Systems*, *2*(2), 73–82. doi:10.5081/jgps.2.2.73

Barnes, S. J. (2002). The mobile commerce value chain: Analysis and future developments. *International Journal of Information Management*, *22*(2), 91–108. doi:10.1016/S0268-4012(01)00047-0

Barnes, S. J., & Vidgen, R. (2001). An evaluation of cyber-bookshops: The WebQual method. *International Journal of Electronic Commerce*, *6*(1), 11–20.

Barnett, N., Hodges, S., & Wiltshire, M. J. (2000). M-commerce: An operator's manual. *The McKinsey Quarterly*, *3*, 163–173.

Bäumle, S., Balser, M., Knapp, A., Reif, W., & Thums, A. (2004). Interactive verification of UML state machines. In Lau, K.-K., & Banach, R. (Eds.), *Formal methods and software engineering* (pp. 434–448). Springer.

Beauche, S., & Poizat, P. (2008). Automated service composition with adaptive planning. In *Proceedings of the 6th International Conference on Service-Oriented Computing (ICSOC'08)*, (LNCS 5364), (pp. 530–537). Springer.

Behringer, R., Park, J., & Sundareswaran, V. (2002). *Model-based visual tracking for outdoor augmented reality applications*. International Symposium on Mixed and Augmented Reality - ISMAR (pp.277-278).

Bell, D. E., & Leonard, J. (1973). *Secure computer systems: Mathematical foundations*. MITRE Corporation. Retrieved March 30, 2010, from http://www.albany.edu/acc/courses/ia/classics/belllapadula1.pdf

Bellavista, P., Kupper, A., & Helal, S. (2008). Location-based services: Back to the future. *IEEE Pervasive Computing / IEEE Computer Society [and] IEEE Communications Society*, *7*(2), 85–89. doi:10.1109/MPRV.2008.34

Bellifemine, F. L., Caire, G., & Greenwood, D. (2007). JADE software agent development platform. Retrieved June 10, 2010, from http://jade.tilab.com/

Belsis, P., Vassis, D., Skourlas, C., & Pantziou, G. (2008). Secure dissemination of electronic healthcare records in distributed wireless environments. In S. Anderssen, et al. (Eds.), *Proceedings of 21st International Congress of the European Federation for Medical Informatics,* (pp. 661-666), IOS Press.

Ben Mokhtar, S., Georgantas, N., & Issarny, V. (2007). COCOA: Conversation-based service composition in pervasive computing environments with QoS support. *Journal of Systems and Software*, *80*(12), 1941–1955. doi:10.1016/j.jss.2007.03.002

Benbya, H., Passiante, G., & Belbaly, N. A. (2004). Corporate portal: A tool for knowledge management synchronization. *International Journal of Information Management*, *24*(3), 204–220. doi:10.1016/j.ijinfomgt.2003.12.012

Bernardos, C., Calderon, M., & Moustafa, H. (2008). *Ad-hoc IP autoconfiguration solution space analysis. Internet-draft*. IETF WG AUTOCONF.

Bertolino, A., Angelis, G., Frantzen, L., & Polini, A. (2009). The PLASTIC framework and tools for testing service-oriented applications. In *Proceedings of the International Summer School on Software Engineering (ISSSE 2006-2008)*, (LNCS 5413), (pp. 106–139). Springer.

Biba, K. J. (1977). *Integrity considerations for secure computer systems*. Mitre Corporation Report TR-3153. Bedford Massachusetts.

Binghao, L., James, C. S. R., & Dempster, A. G. (2006). Indoor positioning techniques based on wireless LAN. In *Proceedings of Auswireless Conference 2006.*

Bisio, I., Agneessens, A., Lavagetto, F., & Marchese, M. (2010). Design and implementation of smartphone applications for speaker count and gender recognition. In Giusto, D., Iera, A., Morabito, G., & Atzori, L. (Eds.), *The Internet of things*. New York, NY: Springer Science.

Black, J., Dooley, M., Feekery, C., Graham, I., Harper, S., & Hart, G. … Weeks, G. (2003). *Electronic medication management.* Victorian Drug Usage Advisory Committee. Melbourne, Australia: Victorian Hospitals Electronic Prescribing and Decision Support Group.

Booth, D., Haas, H., McCabe, F., Newcomer, E., Champion, M., Ferris, C., & Orchard, D. (2004). Web services srchitecture. *World Wide Web Consortium (W3C) organization standardization.* Retrieved February 11, 2004, from http://www.w3.org/TR/ws-arch/

Bose, A., & Foh, C. H. (2007). A practical path loss model for indoor Wi-Fi positioning enhancement. In *Proc. International Conference on Information, Communications & Signal Processing (ICICS).*

Bottaro, A., Gerodolle, A., & Lalanda, P. (2007). Pervasive service composition in the home network. In *Proceedings of the 21st International Conference on Advanced Information Networking and Applications (AINA'07)*, (pp. 596–603).

Botts, M., Percivall, G., Reed, C., & Davidsson, J. (2008). *OpenGIS ® sensor Web enablement: Overview and high level architecture. LNCS GeoSensor Networks book* (pp. 175–190). Berlin/Heidelberg, Germany: Springer.

Boukerche, A., Oliveira, H. A., Nakamura, E. F., & Loureiro, A. A. (2007). Localization systems for wireless sensor networks. *IEEE Wireless Communications – Special Issue on Wireless Sensor Networks, 14*(6), 6–12.

Bozzano, M., & Villafiorita, A. (2006). The FSAP/NuSMV-SA safety analysis platform. [STTT]. *Springer International Journal on Software Tools for Technology Transfer, 9*(1), 5–24. doi:10.1007/s10009-006-0001-2

Brazier, D. (2006). *The m-care project*. Alpha Bravo Charlie Ltd. Retrieved June 10, 2010, from http://www.m-care.co.uk/tech.html

Broll, G., Haarlander, M., Paolucci, M., Wagner, M., Rukzio, E., & Schmidt, A. (2008). Collect&Drop: A technique for multi-tag interaction with real world objects and information book series. In *Proceedings of the European Conference on Ambient Intelligence (AmI '08)*, (LNCS 5355), (pp. 175–191). Springer.

Brown, S. R. (1993). A primer on Q methodology. *Operant Subjectivity, 16*(3/4), 91–138.

Bruneton, E., Coupaye, T., Leclercq, M., Quéma, V., & Stefani, J. B. (2006). The FRACTAL component model and its support in Java: Experiences with auto-adaptive and reconfigurable systems. *Software, Practice & Experience, 1*(36), 1257–1284. doi:10.1002/spe.767

Buford, J., Kumar, R., & Perkins, G. (2006). Composition trust bindings in pervasive computing service composition. In *Proceedings of the 4th Annual IEEE International Conference on Pervasive Computing and Communications Workshops (PERCOMW '06)*, (pp. 261–266). Washington, DC: IEEE Computer Society.

Buick, I. (2003). Information technology in small Scottish hotels: Is it working? *International Journal of Contemporary Hospitality Management MCB UP Ltd., 15*(4), 243–247. doi:10.1108/09596110310475711

Bushardt, R. L., Massey, E. B., Simpson, T. W., Ariail, J. C., & Simpson, K. N. (2008). Polypharmacy: Misleading, but manageable. *Clinical Interventions in Aging, 3*(2), 383.

Byun, J. W., Lee, S. M., Lee, D. H., & Hong, D. (2006). Constant-round password-based group key generation for multi-layer ad-hoc networks. In *Proceedings Third International Conference on Security in Pervasive Computing* (pp. 3-17). Springer.

Castro, P., & Muntz, R. (2000). Managing context for smart spaces. *IEEE Personal Communications, 7*(5), 44–46. doi:10.1109/98.878537

Chakrabarti, A. (2007). *Grid computing security*. Springer.

Chakravorty, R. (2006). Mobicare: A programmable service architecture for mobile medical care. In *Proceedings of IEEE PerCom Workshops* (pp. 532-536), IEEE Press.

Chan, Y.-C. L. (2006). An analytic hierarchy framework for evaluating Balanced Scorecards of healthcare organizations. *Canadian Journal of Administrative Sciences, 23*(2), 84–104.

Chan, L., Chiang, J., Chen, Y., Ke, C., Hsu, J., & Chu, H. (2006). *Collaborative localization enhancing WiFi-based position estimation with neighborhood links in clusters*. International Conference Pervasive Computing - (Pervasive 06), (pp. 50–66).

Chantzara, M., Anagnostou, M., & Sykas, E. (2006). Designing a quality-aware discovery mechanism for acquiring context information. In *Proceedings of the 20th International Conference on Advanced Information Networking and Applications (AINA '06)*, (pp. 211–216). Washington, DC: IEEE Computer Society.

Charles, P., Donawa, C., Ebcioglu, K., Grothoff, C., Kielstra, A., & von Praun, C. … Sarkar, V. (2005). X10: An object-oriented approach to non-uniform clustered. In *Proceedings of the 20th Annual ACM SIGPLAN Conference on Object-Oriented Programming, Systems, Languages, and Applications (OOPSLA '05)* (pp. 519-538). San Diego, CA: Association for Computing Machinery.

Chau, S., & Turner, P. (2006). Utilisation of mobile handhld devices for care management at an Australian aged care facility. *Electronic Commerce Research and Applications*, 5305–5312.

Chen, M., Haehnel, D., Hightower, J., Sohn, T., LaMarca, A., & Smith, I. … Potter, F. (2006). Practical metropolitan-scale positioning for gsm phones. *Proceedings of 8th Ubicomp*, (pp.225–242).

Chen, Y., Romanovsky, A., Gorbenko, A., et al. (2009). Benchmarking dependability of a system biology application. In *Proceedings 14th IEEE International Conference on Engineering of Complex Computer Systems* (pp. 146-153). IEEE Computer Society.

Cheng, B. H. C., Lemos, R., Giese, H., Inverardi, P., & Magee, J. (2009). Software engineering for self-adaptive systems: A research roadmap. In Cheng, B. H. C., de Lemos, R., Giese, H., Inverardi, P., & Magee, J. (Eds.), *Software engineering for self-adaptive systems* (pp. 48–70). New York, NY & Berlin/Heidelberg, Germany: Springer. doi:10.1007/978-3-642-02161-9_1

Cheng, L., Lin, T., Zhang, Y., & Ye, Q. (2004). Monitoring wireless sensor networks by heterogeneous collaborative groupware. In *Proceedings of the ISA/IEEE Sensors for Industry Conference* (pp.130 – 134).

Cheshire, S., Aboba, B., & Guttman, E. (2005). *Dynamic configuration of IPv4 link-local addresses*. (IETF RFC 3927).

Cheverst, K., Coulton, P., Bamford, W., & Taylor, N. (2008). *Supporting (mobile) user experience at a rural village scarecrow festival: A formative study of a geolocated photo mashup utilising a situated display*. In Third Intl. Workshop on Mobile Interaction with the Real World (MIRW 2008), Amsterdam, Netherlands (pp. 27-38).

Cheverst, K., Davies, N., Mitchell, K., & Friday, A. (2000). Experiences of developing and deploying a context-aware tourist guide: The GUIDE project. In *Proceedings of the 6th annual international conference on Mobile computing and networking* (pp. 20-31). Boston, MA: ACM Press.

Chin, J., Callaghan, V., & Clarke, G. (2006). An end-user tool for customising personal spaces in ubiquitous computing environments. In *Proceedings of the 3rd International Conference on Ubiquitous Intelligence and Computing, (UIC'06)*, (pp. 1080–1089).

Cho, N., & Park, S. (2001). Development of electronic commerce user-consumer satisfaction index (ECUSI) for internet shopping. *Industrial Management & Data Systems, 101*(8), 400–405. doi:10.1108/EUM0000000006170

Chong, C.-Y., & Kumar, S. P. (2003). Sensor networks: Evolution, opportunities and challenges. *Proceedings of the IEEE, 91*(8), 1247–1256. doi:10.1109/JPROC.2003.814918

Choudhri, A., Kagal, A., Joshi, A., Finin, T., & Yesha, Y. (2003). *PatientService: Electronic patient record redaction and delivery in pervasive environments*, Paper presented at the Fifth International Workshop on Enterprise Networking and Computing in Healthcare Industry (Healthcom), Santa Monica.

Chow, C. W., Ganulin, D., Tekinka, O., Haddad, K., & Williamson, J. (1998). The Balanced Scorecard: A potent tool for energizing and focusing healthcare organization management. *Journal of Healthcare Management, 43*(3), 263–280.

Christensen, H. B., & Bardram, J. (2002). Supporting human activities - exploring activity-centered computing. *Proceedings of the 4th International Conference on Ubiquitous Computing.* Göteborg, Sweden: Springer-Verlag.

Chu, X., Kobialka, T., Durnota, B., & Buyya, R. (2006). Open sensor Web architecture: Core services. In *Proceedings of 4th International Conference on Intelligent Sensing and Information Processing - ICISIP* (pp. 98-103), IEEE Press.

Churchill, G. A. (1979). A paradigm for developing better measures of marketing constructs. *JMR, Journal of Marketing Research, 19*(4), 491–504. doi:10.2307/3151722

Churchill, G. A., & Surprenant, C. (1982). An investigation into the determinants of customer satisfaction. *JMR, Journal of Marketing Research, 19*(4), 491–504. doi:10.2307/3151722

Clarke, E. M., Grumberg, O., & Peled, D. A. (1999). *Model checking*. Cambridge, MA: MIT Press.

Clarke, I. III, & Flaherty, T. B. (2003). Mobile portals: The development of m-commerce gateways. In Mennecke, B. E., & Strader, T. J. (Eds.), *Mobile commerce: Technology, theory and applications* (pp. 185–201). Hershey, PA: IRM Press (an imprint of Idea Group Inc.). doi:10.4018/9781591400448.ch010

Clements, P., & Northrop, L. (2001). *Software product lines: Practices and patterns*. Boston, MA: Addison-Wesley Professional.

Constantiou, I. D., Damsgaard, J., & Knutsen, L. (2006). Exploring perceptions and use of mobile services: User differences in an advancing market. *International Journal of Mobile Communications, 4*(3), 231–247.

Coverity Inc. Website (2010). Retrieved March 30, 2010 from http://www.coverity.com/products/static-analysis.html

Craton, E., & Robin, D. (2002). *Information model: The key to integration*. Retrieved July 20, 2010 from http://www.automatedbuildings.com/

Crossbow. (2009). *Crossbow technology company: Product related information*. Retrieved July 20, 2010 from http://www.xbow.com/Products/wproductsoverview.aspx

Crossbow. (2010). *Crossbow Technology, Inc. official website*. Retrieved July 5, 2010 from http://www.xbow.com

CURL. (2010). *cURL and libcurl, tool to transfer data using URL syntax*. Retrieved July 20, 2010 from http://curl.haxx.se/

Curtright, J. W., Stolp-Smith, S., & Edell, E. (2000). Strategic performance management: Development of a performance measurement system at the Mayo Clinic. *Journal of Healthcare Management*, *45*(1), 58–68.

DAIDALOS. (2010). *Designing advanced network interfaces for the delivery and administration of location independent, optimized personal services, EU framework programme 6 integrated project (FP6)*. Retrieved June 1, 2010, from http://www.ist-daidalos.org/

Davidyuk, O., Selek, I., Duran, J. I., & Riekki, J. (2008b). Algorithms for composing pervasive applications. *International Journal of Software Engineering and Its Applications*, *2*(2), 71–94.

Davidyuk, O., Georgantas, N., Issarny, V., & Riekki, J. (2010). MEDUSA: A middleware for end-user composition of ubiquitous applications. In Mastrogiovanni, F., & Chong, N.-Y. (Eds.), *Handbook of research on ambient intelligence and smart environments: Trends and perspectives*. Hershey, PA: IGI Global.

Davidyuk, O., Sánchez, I., Duran, J. I., & Riekki, J. (2008a). Autonomic composition of ubiquitous multimedia applications in reaches. In *Proceedings of the 7th International ACM Conference on Mobile and Ubiquitous Multimedia (MUM'08)*, (pp. 105–108). ACM.

Davidyuk, O., Sánchez, I., Duran, J. I., & Riekki, J. (2010). *CADEAU application scenario*. Retrieved June 8, 2010, from http://www.youtube.com/watch?v=sRjCisrdr18

Davis, F. D. (1989). Perceived usefulness, perceived ease of use and user acceptance of information technology. *Management Information Systems Quarterly*, *13*(3), 319–339. doi:10.2307/249008

Davydov, M. M. (2001). *Corporate portals and e-business integration*. New York, NY: McGraw-Hill.

de Cheveignè, A., & Kawahar, H. (2002). A fundamental frequency estimator for speech and music. *The Journal of the Acoustical Society of America*, *111*(4). doi:10.1121/1.1458024

De Lucia, P. R., Ott, T. E., & Palmieri, P. A. (2009). Performance in nursing. *Reviews of Human Factors and Ergonomics*, *5*(1), 1–40. doi:10.1518/155723409X448008

de Oliveira, K. M., Villela, K., Rocha, A. R., & Travassos, G. H. (2006). Use of ontologies in software development environments. In Calero, C., Ruiz, F., & Piattini, M. (Eds.), *Ontologies for software engineering and software technology* (pp. 276–309). Springer-Verlag. doi:10.1007/3-540-34518-3_10

De Sa, M., Carrico, L., & Antunes, P. (2007). Ubiquitous psychotherapy. *IEEE Pervasive Computing / IEEE Computer Society [and] IEEE Communications Society*, *6*(1), 22–27.

Deakins, D., Mochrie, R., & Galloway, L. (2004). Rural business use of Information and Communications Technologies (ICTs): A study of the relative impact of collective activity in rural Scotland. [John Wiley & Sons.]. *Journal of Strategic Change*, *13*(3), 139–150. doi:10.1002/jsc.683

Dearden, A., & Lo, C. M. (2004). Supporting user decisions in travel and tourism. In *People and Computers XVIII: Design for Life: Proceedings of HCI 2004* (pp.103-116). ACM Press.

Dearle, A., Kirby, G., Morrison, R., McCarthy, A., Mullen, K., & Yang, Y. … Wilson, A. (2003). *Architectural support for global smart spaces*. (LNCS 2574). (pp. 153-164). Springer-Verlag.

Dearne, K. (2009, 19 August). Health rebate cuts could fund e-health: Roxon. *The Australian*.

Deering, S., & Hinden, R. (1998). *Internet protocol, version 6 (IPv6) specification*. (IETF RFC 2460).

DeLone, W. H., & McLean, E. R. (1992). Information Systems success: The quest for the dependent variable. *Information Systems Research*, *3*(1), 60–95. doi:10.1287/isre.3.1.60

DeLone, W. H., & McLean, E. R. (2003). The DeLone and McLean model of information systems success: A ten year update. *Journal of Management Information Systems*, *19*(4), 9–30.

Detlor, B. (2000). The corporate portal as information infrastructure: Towards a framework for portal design. *International Journal of Information Management, 20*(2), 91–101. doi:10.1016/S0268-4012(99)00058-4

Dey, A. K., & Abowd, G. D. (2000). Towards a better understanding of context and context awareness. In *The What, Who, Where, When, Why and How of Context-Awareness Workshop at the Conference on Human Factors in Computing Systems (CHI)*.

Dholakia, N., & Rask, M. (2002). *Configuring mobile commerce portals for customer retention*. Retrieved December 17, 2008 from http://ritim.cba.uri.edu/wp2002/pdf_format/M-Commerce-M-Portal-Strategies-Chapter-v04.pdf

Diffie, W., & Hellman, M. (1976). New directions in cryptography. *IEEE Transactions on Information Theory, 22*(6), 644–654. doi:10.1109/TIT.1976.1055638

Dix, A. J., & Runciman, C. (1985). Abstract models of interactive systems. In *Proceedings HCI '85: People and Computer: Designing the Interface* (pp. 13-22). Cambridge, UK: University Press.

Doets, P. J. O., Gisbert, M., & Lagendijk, R. L. (2006). On the comparison of audio fingerprints for extracting quality parameters of compressed audio. *Security, steganography, and watermarking of multimedia contents VII, Proceedings of the SPIE.*

Dogan, S. (2005). Peer-to-peer technology and the copyright crossroads. In Subramanian, R., & Goodman, B. D. (Eds.), *Peer to peer computing: The evolution of a disruptive technology* (pp. 166–194). Hershey, PA: IGI Global.

Dolev, D., & Yao, A. (1983). On the security of public key protocols. *IEEE Transactions on Information Theory, 29*(2), 198–208. doi:10.1109/TIT.1983.1056650

Doll, W. J., & Torkzadeh, G. (1988). The measurement of end-user computing satisfaction. *Management Information Systems Quarterly*, (June): 259–274. doi:10.2307/248851

Draves, R. (2003). *Default address selection for Internet protocol version 6 (IPv6)*. (IETF RFC 3484).

Droms, R. (1997). *Dynamic host configuration protocol*. (IETF RFC 2131).

Droms, R., Bound J., Volz, B., Lemon, T., Perkins, C., & Carney, M. (2003). *Dynamic host configuration protocol for IPv6 (DHCPv6)*. (IETF RFC 3315).

Duffy, S. (2006). Information and Communication Technology (ICT) adoption amongst small rural accommodation providers in Ireland. In Hitz, M., Sigala, M., & Murphy, J. (Eds.), *Information and Communication Technologies in tourism* (p. 182). New York, NY: Springer-Verlag. doi:10.1007/3-211-32710-X_26

Dunlop, M. D., Ptasinski, P., Morrison, A., McCallum, S., Risbey, C., & Stewart, F. (2004). Design and development of Taeneb city guide - from paper maps and guidebooks to electronic guides. In A. Frew (Ed.), *Proceedings of Intl. Conference on Information & Communication Technologies in Tourism 2004* (pp. 58-64). New York, NY: Springer-Verlag.

Eastlake, D. (1999). *RSA keys and SIGs in the Domain Name System (DNS)*. (IETF RFC 2536).

Eastlake, D. (2001). *RSA/SHA-1 SIGs and RSA KEYs in the Domain Name System (DNS)*. (IETF RFC 3110).

Eckerson, W. W. (1999). *Plumtree blossoms: New version fulfils enterprise portal requirements*. Boston, MA: Patricia Seybold Group.

Eclipse Foundation. (2010). *Graphical modeling framework*. Retrieved July 4, 2010, from http://www.eclipse.org/modeling/gmf/

Edwards, W. K., & Grinter, R. E. (2001). At home with ubiquitous computing: Seven challenges. In *Proceedings of the 3rd International conference on Ubiquitous Computing* (pp. 256-272). London, UK: Springer-Verlag.

Eggert, A., & Ulaga, W. (2002). Customer perceived value: Substitute for satisfaction in business markets? *Journal of Business and Industrial Marketing, 17*(2/3), 107–118. doi:10.1108/08858620210419754

Ehrlich, P. (2003). Guideline for XML/Web services for building control. In *Proceedings of BuilConn 2003*. Retrieved July 20, 2010 from http://www.builconn.com/

EKAHAU. (2010). *EKAHAU positioning engine 2.0*. Retrieved July 10, 2010 from http://www.ekahau.com/

El-Rabbany, A. (Ed.). (2006). *Introduction to GPS: The Global Positioning System* (2nd ed.). Artech House, Inc.

EMANICS. (2010) *European network of excellence for the management of Internet technologies and complex services, EU framework programme 6 integrated project (FP6)*. Retrieved June 1, 2010, from http://www.emanics.org/

Emerson, E. A. (1990). Temporal and modal logic. In J. Leeuwen (Ed.), *Handbook of theoretical computer science (vol. B): Formal models and semantics* (pp. 995-1072). Cambridge, MA: MIT Press.

EPRI report. (2008). *Substation-wide monitoring through applications of networked wireless sensor devices- phase-II: Scalability and sustainability studies*.

Erl, T. (2005). *Service-oriented architecture: Concepts, technology and design*. New York, NY: Prentice Hall PTR.

Escoffier, C., Bourcier, J., Lalanda, P., & Yu, J. Q. (2008). Towards a home application server. In *Proceedings the IEEE International Consumer Communications and Networking Conference* (pp. 321-325). Las Vegas, NV: IEEE Computer Society.

Escoffier, C., Hall, R. S., & Lalanda, P. (2007). iPOJO: An extensible service-oriented component framework. In *Proceedings of SCC'07: Proceedings of the IEEE International Conference on Services Computing, Application and Industry Track* (pp. 474-481). Salt Lake City, UT: IEEE Computer Society.

Estrin, D., Culler, D., Pister, K., & Sukhatme, G. (2002). Connecting the physical world with pervasive networks. *IEEE Pervasive Computing / IEEE Computer Society [and] IEEE Communications Society*, *1*(1), 59–69. doi:10.1109/MPRV.2002.993145

Fazio, M., Villari, M., & Puliafito, A. (2006). AIPAC: Automatic IP address configuration in mobile ad hoc networks. *Computer Communications*, *29*(8), 1189–1200. doi:10.1016/j.comcom.2005.07.006

Fazio, M., Villari, M., & Puliafito, A. (2004). Merging and partitioning in ad hoc networks. In *Proceedings of the 9th International Symposium on Computers and Communications (ISCC 2004)*, (pp. 164-169).

Fiala, M. (2010). Designing highly reliable fiducial markers. *IEEE Transactions on Pattern Analysis and Machine Intelligence*, *32*(7), 1317–1324. doi:10.1109/TPAMI.2009.146

Fiala, M. (2005). *ARTag, a fiducial marker system using digital techniques*. IEEE Conference on Computer Vision and Pattern Recognition - CVPR (pp.590-596).

Fielding, R. T. (2000). *Representational State Transfer (REST)*. Unpublished PhD thesis. Retrieved July 20, 2010 from http://www.ics.uci.edu/~fielding/pubs/dissertation/rest_arch_style.htm

Findlater, L., & McGrenere, J. (2008). Impact of screen size on performance, awareness, and user satisfaction with adaptive graphical user interfaces. *Proceeding of the Twenty-Sixth annual SIGCHI Conference on Human factors in computing systems* (pp. 1247-1256), Florence, Italy.

FIPA. (2005). *Foundation for Intelligent Physical Agents: FIPA specifications*. Retrieved June 10, 2010, from http://www.fipa.org/specifications/index.html

Fontana, R. J., Richley, E., & Barney, J. (2003). *Commercialization of an ultra wideband precision asset location system*. IEEE Conference on Ultra Wideband Systems and Technologies, (pp.369–373).

Forde, T. K., Doyle, L. E., & O'Mahony, D. (2005). Self-stabilizing network-layer auto-configuration for mobile ad hoc network nodes. In *Proceedings of the IEEE International Conference on Wireless and Mobile Computing, Networking and Communications, 3*, (pp. 178-185).

Fornell, C., Johnson, M. D., Anderson, E. W., Cha, J., & Byrant, B. E. (1996). The American customer satisfaction index: Nature, purpose, and findings. *Journal of Marketing*, *60*(4), 7–18. doi:10.2307/1251898

Forum, N. F. C. (2010a). *Near Field Communication (NFC) standard for short-range wireless communication technology*. Retrieved June 8, 2010, from http://www.nfc-forum.org

Forum, N. F. C. (2010b). *NFC data exchange format*. Retrieved June 8, 2010, from http://www.nfc-forum.org/specs/

Fox, J. (2000). A river of money will flow through the wireless Web in coming years. All the big players want is a piece of the action. *Fortune*, *142*(8), 140–146.

Franks, J., Hallam-Baker, P., Hostetler, J., Lawrence, S., Leach, P., Luotonene, A., & Stewart, L. (1999). *RFC 2617 - HTTP authentication: Basic and digest access authentication*. IETF Standards Track.

Freescale Semiconductor, Inc. (2008). *Mobile extreme convergence: A streamlined architecture to deliver mass-market converged mobile devices*. White Paper of Freescale Semiconductor, Rev. 5.

Frisse, M. E. (2006). Comments on return on investment (ROI) as it applies to clinical systems. *Journal of the American Medical Informatics Association, 13*(3), 365–367. doi:10.1197/jamia.M2072

Gamma, E., Hem, R., Jahnson, R., & Vissides, J. (1994). *Design patterns: Elements of reusable object-oriented software*. Boston, MA: Addison-Wesley Professional.

García Villalba, L. J., Sandoval, O,. Ana, L., Triviño Cabrera, A., & Barenco Abbas, C. J. (2009). Routing protocols in wireless sensor networks. *MDPI - Open Access Publishing Sensors, 9*(11), 8399-8421.

Garcia-Hernandez, C. F., Ibarguengoytia-Gonzales, P. H., Garcia-Hernandez, J., & Perez-Diaz, J. A. (2007). Wireless sensor networks and applications: A survey. *International Journal of Computer Science and Network Security, 7*(3), 264–273.

Gardner, W. A. (1990). *Introduction to random processes: With applications to signals and systems*. New York, NY: McGraw-Hill.

Garlan, D., Cheng, S. W., Huang, A. C., Schmerl, B., & Steenkiste, P. (2004). Rainbow: Architecture-based self-adaptation with reusable infrastructure. *IEEE Computer, 10*(37), 46–54.

Gelderman, M. (1998). The relation between user satisfaction, usage of information systems and performance. *Information & Management, 34*(1), 11–18. doi:10.1016/S0378-7206(98)00044-5

Georgiou, A., & Westbrook, J. (2006). Computerized order entry systems and pathology services - a synthesis of the evidence. *The Clinical Biochemist. Reviews / Australian Association of Clinical Biochemists, 27*(2), 79–87.

German Organic Computing Initiative Website. (2010). Retrieved March 30, 2010 from http://www.organic-computing.de/

Ghiani, G., Paternò, F., & Spano, L. D. (2009). Cicero Designer: An environment for end-user development of multi-device museum guides. In *Proceedings of the 2nd Int. Symposium on End-User Development (IS-EUD'09)*, (pp. 265–274).

Global Mobile Suppliers Association. (2002). *Survey of mobile portal services* Q4 2002. Retrieved February 13, 2009 from http://www.gsacom.com/downloads/MPSQ4_2002.php4

Glover, B., & Bhatt, H. (2006). *RFID essentials*. O'Reilly.

Golbeck, J., Bijan, P., & Hendler, J. (2003). Trust networks on the Semantic Web. In Klusch, M. (Eds.), *Cooperative information agents VII* (pp. 238–249). Heidelberg/ Berlin, Germany: Springer. doi:10.1007/978-3-540-45217-1_18

Grandy, H., Haneberg, D., Reif, W., & Stenzel, K. (2006). Developing provably secure m-commerce applications. In Muller, G. (Ed.), *Emerging trends in information and communication security (ETRICS)* (pp. 115–129). Heidelberg/ Berlin, Germany: Springer. doi:10.1007/11766155_9

Grasso, M. A. (2004). Clinical applications of handheld computers. *Proceedings 17th IEEE Symposium on Computer-Based Medical Systems* (CBMS 04) (pp. 141–146). IEEE Press.

Graumann, D., Hightower, J., Lara, W., & Borriello, G. (2003). *Real-world implementation of the location stack: The universal location framework*. IEEE Workshop on Mobile Computing Systems & Applications - WMCSA (pp.122-129)

Greitans, M. (2006). Processing of non-stationary signals using level-crossing sampling. In *Proceedings of International Conference on Signal Processing and Multimedia Applications*, (pp. 170-177).

Greitans, M., & Shavelis, R. (2007). Speech sampling by level-crossing and its reconstruction using spline-based filtering. In *Proceedings of EURASIP Conference on Speech and Image Processing, Multimedia Communications and Services* (pp. 292-295), Maribor, Slovenia.

Grejner-Brzezinska, D. (2004). Positioning and tracking approaches and technologies. In Karimi, H. A., & Hammad, A. (Eds.), *Telegeoinformatics: Location-based computing and services* (pp. 69–110). CRC Press.

Groene, O., Brandt, E., Schmidt, W., & Moeller, J. (2009). The Balanced Scorecard of acute settings: Development process, definition of 20 strategic objectives and implementation. *International Journal for Quality in Health Care, 21*(4), 259–271. doi:10.1093/intqhc/mzp024

Gross, T., & Marquardt, N. (2007). CollaborationBus: An editor for the easy configuration of ubiquitous computing environments. In *Proceedings of the Euromicro Conference on Parallel, Distributed, and Network-Based Processing*, (pp. 307–314). IEEE Computer Society.

Gu, Y., Lo, A., & Niemegeers, I. (2009). A survey of indoor positioning systems for wireless personal networks. *IEEE Communications Surveys & Tutorials, 11*(1).

Guan, K. M., & Singer, A. C. (2006). A level-crossing sampling scheme for non-bandlimited signals. In *Proceedings of International Conference on Acoustic, Speech and Signal processing*: *Vol. 3*, (pp. 381-83). Toulouse, France.

Guan, K. M., & Singer, A. C. (2007). Opportunistic sampling by level-crossing. In *Proceedings of IEEE international conference on acoustic, speech and signal processing (ICASSP'07)*: Vol 3, (pp. 1513-1516). Honolulu, Hawaii.

Guan, K. M., Kozat, S. S., & Singer, A. C. (2008). Adaptive reference levels in a level-crossing analog-to-digital converter. *EURASIP Journal of Advances in Signal Processing*.

Guinard, D., & Trifa, V. (2009). *Towards the Web of things: Web mashups for embedded devices*. Paper presented at Workshop on Mashups, Enterprise Mashups and Lightweight Composition on the Web (MEM 2009), Madrid, Spain.

Gutierrez, J. A., Callaway, E. H., & Barrett, R. L. (2004). *IEEE 802.15.4 low-rate wireless personal area networks: Enabling wireless sensor networks. Standard Information Network*. IEEE Press.

Gwon, Y., Jain, R., & Kawahara, T. (2004). *Robust indoor location estimation of stationary and mobile users* (pp. 1032–1043). IEEE INFOCOM.

Hageman, W. M., Harmata, R., Zuckerman, H., Weiner, B., Alexander, J., & Bogue, R. (1999). Collaborations that work: Strategies for building community health partnerships. *Health Forum Journal*, *42*(5), 46–48.

Haitsma, J., & Kalker, T. (2002). A highly robust audio fingerprinting system. In *Proceedings of the International Symposium on Music Information Retrieval, Paris, France*.

Hallsteinsen, S., Hinchey, M., Park, S., & Schmid, K. (2008). Dynamic software product lines. *IEEE Computer*, *4*(41), 93–95.

Hallsteinsen, S., Stav, E., Solberg, A., & Floch, J. (2006). Using product line techniques to build adaptive systems. In *Proceedings of the 10th International Software Product Line Conference (SPLC'06)* (pp. 141-150) Baltimore, MD: IEEE Computer Society.

Han, L., Ma, J., & Yu, K. (2008). *Research on context-aware mobile computing*. International Conference on Advanced Information Networking and Applications - AINAW (pp. 24-30).

Hansen, A., Cottle, S., Negrine, R., & Newbold, C. (1998). Media audiences: Focus group interviewing. In Hansen, A., Cottle, S., Negrine, R., & Newbold, C. (Eds.), *Mass communication research methods* (pp. 257–287). Basingstoke, UK: Macmillan Press.

Hansmann, U., Merk, L., Nicklous, M. S., & Stober, T. (2003). *Pervasive computing* (2nd ed.). Berlin/ Heidelberg, Germany & New York, NY: Springer.

Hardian, B., Indulska, J., & Henricksen, K. (2006). Balancing autonomy and user control in context-aware systems - a survey. In *Proceedings of the 3rd Workshop on Context Modeling and Reasoning (part of the 4th IEEE International Conference on Pervasive Computing and Communication)*. IEEE Computer Society.

Hardian, B., Indulska, J., & Henricksen, K. (2008). Exposing contextual information for balancing software autonomy and user control in context-aware systems. In *Proceedings of the Workshop on Context-Aware Pervasive Communities: Infrastructures, Services and Applications (CAPS'08)*, (pp. 253–260).

Hedges, A. (1985). Group interviewing. In Walker, R. (Ed.), *Applied qualitative research* (pp. 71–91). Aldershot, UK: Gower.

Hinden, R., & Deering, S. (2006). *IP version 6 addressing architecture*. (IETF RFC 4291).

Hinden, R., & Haberman, B. (2005). *Unique local IPv6 Unicast addresses*. (IETF RFC 4193).

Ho, C. F., & Wu, W. H. (1999). Antecedents of customer satisfaction on the Internet: An empirical study of online shopping. *Proceedings of the 32nd Hawaii International Conference on Systems Sciences* (HICSS-32), January 5-8, 1999, Maui, Hawaii. IEEE Computer Society, (pp. 1-9).

Hodgkinson, B., & Koch, S. (2006). Strategies to reduce medication errors with reference to older adults. *International Journal of Evidence-Based Healthcare*, *4*(1), 2–41. doi:10.1111/j.1479-6988.2006.00029.x

Holt, T. (2001). Developing an activity-based management system for the Army medical department. *Journal of Health Care Finance*, *27*(3), 41–46.

Horn, P. (2001). *Autonomic computing: IBM's perspective on the state of Information Technology.* Paper presented at AGENDA, Scottsdale, AZ. Retrieved from http://www.research.ibm.com/autonomic/

Howard, J. A. (1974). The structure of buyer behavior. In Farley, J. U., Howard, J. A., & Ring, L. W. (Eds.), *Consumer behavior: Theory and application* (pp. 9–32). Boston, MA: Allyn & Bacon.

Huang, A. S., & Rudolph, L. (2007). *Bluetooth essentials for programmers*. Cambridge, UK: Cambridge University Press. doi:10.1017/CBO9780511546976

Huggins, R., & Izushi, H. (2002). The digital divide and ICT learning in rural communities: Examples of good practice service delivery. *Routledge Journal of Local Economy*, *17*(2), 111–122. doi:10.1080/02690940210129870

Hughes, J., & Maler, E. (2004). *Technical overview of the OASIS security assertion markup language* (SAML) V2.0. Retrieved June 10, 2010, from http://xml.coverpages.org/SAML-TechOverviewV20-Draft7874.pdf

Hunter, D., Cagle, K., & Dix, C. (2007). *Beginning XML*. Wrox Press Inc.

Hurley, E., Mcrae, I., Bigg, I., Stackhouse, L., Boxall, A.-M., & Broadhead, P. (2009). *The Australian healthcare system: The potential for efficiency gains - a review of the literature. Background paper prepared for the National Health and Hospitals Reform Commission*. Canberra: The National Health and Hospitals Reform Commission.

IANA. (2002). *Special-use IPv4 addresses*. (IETF RFC 3330).

IANA. (2010). *Internet assigned number authority*. Retrieved June 1, 2010, from http://www.iana.org/

Impagliazzo, C., Ippolito, A., & Zoccoli, P. (2009). The Balanced Scorecard as a strategic management tool: Its application in the regional public health system in Campania. *The Health Care Manager*, *28*(1), 44–54.

Inamdar, N., & Kaplan, R. S. (2002). Applying the Balanced Scorecard in healthcare provider. *Journal of Healthcare Management*, *47*(3), 179–196.

International Electrotechnical Commission Website [IEC 191-02-03] (2003). Retrieved March 30, 2010 from http://dom2.iec.ch/iev/iev.nsf/display?openform&ievref=191-02-03

International Federation for Information Processing Working group 10.4 - [IFIP 10.4] (2003). Retrieved March 30, 2010 from http://www.dependability.org/wg10.4/

International Telecommunication Union. (2007). *Mobile cellular, subscribers per 100 people*. Retrieved January 10, 2009 from http://www.itu.int/ITU-/icteye/Indicators/Indicators.aspx#

Isabelle Theorem Prover. (2010). Retrieved March 30, 2010 from http://www.cl.cam.ac.uk/research/hvg/Isabelle/

ISHTAR Consortium (Ed.). (2001). *Implementing secure healthcare telematics applications in Europe – ISHTAR*. Amsterdam, The Netherlands: IOS Press.

Ittner, C. D., & Larcker, D. F. (1996). Measuring the impact of quality initiatives on firm financial performance. In Fedor, D. B., & Ghosh, S. (Eds.), *Advances in the management of organizational quality* (pp. 1–37). London, UK: JAI Press.

Ives, B., Olson, H., & Baroudi, J. J. (1983). The measurement of user information satisfaction. *Communications of the ACM*, *26*(10), 785–793. doi:10.1145/358413.358430

Ives, B., Olson, H., & Baroudi, J. J. (1984). User involvement and MIS success: A review of research. *Management Science*, *30*(5), 586–603. doi:10.1287/mnsc.30.5.586

Ivester, M., & Lim, A. (2006). Interactive and extensible framework for execution and monitoring of wireless sensor networks. In *Proceedings of 1st International Conference on Communication System Software and Middleware - Comsware 2006* (pp.1-10).

Iyer, A. N., Ofoegbu, U. O., Yantorno, R. E., & Smolenski, B. Y. (2006). Generic modeling applied to speaker count. In *Proceedings IEEE, International Symposium On Intelligent Signal Processing and Communication Systems, ISPACS'06.*

Jay, R., & Hamilton, A. (2003). *Data protection law and practice*. London, UK: Thomson Sweet & Maxwell.

Jea, D., Yap, I. S., & Srivastava, M. B. (2007). *Context-aware access to public shared devices.* Presented at the First International Workshop on Systems and Networking Support for Health Care and Assisted Living Environments.

Jeong, J., Park, J., Jeong, H., & Kim, D. (2006). *Ad hoc IP address autoconfiguration. Internet-draft*. IETF WG AUTOCONF.

Jin, G. Y., Lu, X. Y., & Park, M. S. (2006). *An indoor localization mechanism using active RFID tag*. IEEE International Conference on Sensor Networks, Ubiquitous, and Trustworthy Computing (pp.40-43).

Jones, S., Jones, M., Marsden, G., Patel, D., & Cockburn, A. (2005). An evaluation of integrated zooming and scrolling on small screens. [IJMMS]. *International Journal of Man-Machine Studies*, *63*(3), 271–303.

Jones, M., Buchanan, G., & Thimbleby, H. (2002). Sorting out searching on small screen devices. In Paterno, F. (Ed.), *Mobile HCI 2002, LNCS 2411* (pp. 81–94). Heidelberg/ Berlin, Germany: Springer-Verlag.

Junglas, I. A., & Spitzmüller, C. (2005). *A research model for studying privacy concerns pertaining to location-based services*. Hawaii International Conference on System Sciences - HICSS (pp. 180-190).

Kalasapur, S., Kumar, M., & Shirazi, B. (2007). Dynamic service composition in pervasive computing. *IEEE Transactions on Parallel and Distributed Systems*, *18*(7), 907–918. doi:10.1109/TPDS.2007.1039

Kalkusch, M., Lidy, T., Knapp, M., Reitmayr, G., Kaufmann, H., & Schmalstieg, D. (2002). *Structured visual markers for indoor pathfinding*. International Workshop on Augmented Reality Toolkit (pp.1-8).

Kalofonos, D., & Wisner, P. (2007). A framework for end-user programming of smart homes using mobile devices. In *Proceedings of the 4th IEEE Consumer Communications and Networking Conference (CCNC'07)*, (pp. 716–721). IEEE Computer Society.

Kant, L., McAuley, A., & Morera, R. Sethi, A. S., & Steiner, M. (2003). Fault localization and self-healing with dynamic domain configuration. In *Proceedings of the IEEE Military Communications Conference (MILCOM 2003), 2*, (pp. 977-981).

Kanter, T. G. (2002). HotTown, enabling context-aware and extensible mobile interactive spaces. *IEEE Wireless Communications*, *9*(5), 18–27. doi:10.1109/ MWC.2002.1043850

Kaplan, E. D. (Ed.). (1996). *Understanding GPS principles and applications*. Artech House, Inc.

Kaplan, B. (2001). Evaluating informatics applications—clinical decision support systems literature review. *International Journal of Medical Informatics*, *64*(1), 15–37. doi:10.1016/S1386-5056(01)00183-6

Kaplan, R. S., & Norton, D. P. (1996). *The Balanced Scorecard*. Boston, MA: Harvard Business School Press.

Kargl, F., Klenk, A., Schlott, S., & Weber, M. (2004). Advanced detection of selfish or malicious nodes in ad hoc networks. In *Proceedings of the 1st European Workshop on Security in Ad-hoc and Sensor Networks (ESAS)*, (pp. 152-165).

Karl, H., & Willig, A. (2007). *Protocols and architectures for wireless sensor networks. Wiley. Hansmann, U. (2003). Pervasive computing: The mobile world*. Springer.

Karlsruhe Interactive Verifier. (2010). Retrieved March 30, 2010 from http://www.informatik.uni-augsburg.de/lehrstuehle/swt/se/kiv/

Katasonov, A. (2010). Enabling non-programmers to develop smart environment applications. In *Proceedings IEEE Symposium on Computers and Communications (ISCC'10)* (pp. 1055-1060). IEEE.

Kato, H., & Billinghurst, M. (1999). *Marker tracking and HMD calibration for a video-based augmented reality conferencing system*. ACM International Workshop on Augmented Reality - IWAR (pp.85-94).

Kawsar, F., Nakajima, T., & Fujinami, K. (2008). Deploy spontaneously: Supporting end-users in building and enhancing a smart home. In *Proceedings of the 10th International Conference on Ubiquitous Computing (UbiComp'08)*, (pp. 282–291). New York, NY: ACM.

Kenteris, M., Gavalas, D., & Economou, D. (2009). An innovative mobile electronic tourist guide application. *Springer Personal and Ubiquitous Computing*, *13*(2), 103–118. doi:10.1007/s00779-007-0191-y

Kephart, J., & Chess, D. (2003). The vision of autonomic computing. *IEEE Computer*, *1*(36), 41–50.

Kershaw, R., & Kershaw, S. (2001). Developing a Balanced Scorecard to implement strategy at St. Elsewhere hospital. *Management Accounting Quarterly*, *2*(2), 28–35.

Kettinger, W. J., & Lee, C. C. (1994). Perceived service quality and user satisfaction with information services function. *Decision Sciences*, *25*(5), 737–766. doi:10.1111/j.1540-5915.1994.tb01868.x

Kim, J., & Jun, H. (2008). Vision-based location positioning using augmented reality for indoor navigation. *IEEE Transactions on Consumer Electronics*, *54*(3), 954–962. doi:10.1109/TCE.2008.4637573

Kim, J. B. (2003). A personal identity annotation overlay system using a wearable computer for augmented reality. *IEEE Transactions on Consumer Electronics*, *49*(4), 1457–1467. doi:10.1109/TCE.2003.1261254

King, J., Bose, R., Yang, H., Pickles, S., & Helal, A. (2006). Atlas: A service-oriented sensor platform, hardware and middleware to enable programmable pervasive services. In *Proceedings 2006 of 31st IEEE Conference on Local Computer Networks- LCN* (pp. 630-638). IEEE Press.

Kokolakis, S., & Kiountouzis, E. (2000). Achieving interoperability in a multi-security-policies environment. *Computers & Security*, *19*(3), 267–281. doi:10.1016/S0167-4048(00)88615-0

Kostakos, V., & O'Neill, E. (2004). *Designing pervasive systems for society*. Paper presented at the Second International Conference on Pervasive Computing, Volume 2, First International Workshop on Sustainable Pervasive Computing. Vienna, Austria.

Küpper, A., Treu, G., & Linnhoff-Popien, C. (2006). Trax: A device-centric middleware framework for location-based services. *IEEE Communications Magazine*, *44*(9), 114–120. doi:10.1109/MCOM.2006.1705987

Kushwaha, M., Amundson, I., Koutsoukos, X., Neema, S., & Sztipanovits, J. (2007). OASiS: A programming framework for service-oriented sensor networks. In *Proceedings of 2nd IEEE International Conference on Communication Systems Software and Middleware – COMSWARE* (pp. 7-12). IEEE Press.

Kwiatkowska, M. Z., Norman, G., & Parker, D. (2002). Probabilistic symbolic model checking with PRISM: A hybrid approach. In *Proceedings 8th International Conference on Tools and Algorithms for the Construction and Analysis of Systems*. ACM Press.

Ladd, A. M., Bekris, K. E., Rudys, A., Marceau, G., Kavraki, L. E., & Dan, S. (2002). *Robotics-based location sensing using wireless ethernet*. Eighth ACM Int. Conf. on Mobile Computing & Networking (MOBICOM) (pp. 227-238).

Landre, W., & Wesenberg, H. (2007). *REST versus SOAP as architectural style for Web services*. Paper presented at the 5th International Workshop on SOA & Web Services, OOPSLA, Montreal, Canada.

Lang, D. (2008). *Routing protocols for mobile ad hoc networks - classification, evaluation and challenges*. VDM Verlag Dr. Mueller E.K.

Lappeteläinen, A., Tuupola, J. M., Palin, A., & Eriksson, T. (2008). *Networked systems, services and information*. Paper presented at the 1st International Network on Terminal Architecture Conference (NoTA2008), Helsinki, Finland.

Laschinger, S., Heather, K., & Leiter, M. P. (2006). The impact of nursing work environments on patient safety outcomes: The mediating role of burnout engagement. *The Journal of Nursing Administration*, *36*(5), 259–267. doi:10.1097/00005110-200605000-00019

Lauesen, S. (2003). Task descriptions as functional requirements. *IEEE Software*, *20*(2), 58–65. doi:10.1109/MS.2003.1184169

Lawrence, J. D. (1995). *Software safety hazard analysis*. Publication of Livermore National Laboratory. Retrieved March 30, 2010 from www.osti.gov/bridge/servlets/purl/201805-VM21Vg/webviewable/

Lazar, I. (2000). The state of the Internet. *IT Professional*, *2*(1), 52. doi:10.1109/6294.819940

Lee, J., & Kang, K. C. (2006). A feature-oriented approach to developing dynamically reconfigurable products in product line engineering. In *Proceedings of the 10th International Software Product Line Conference (SPLC '06)* (pp. 131-140). Baltimore, MD: IEEE Computer Society.

Lee, Y., Mosley, A., Wang, P. T., & Broadway, J. (2006). *Audio fingerprinting from ELEC 301 projects*. Retrieved from http://cnx.org/content/m14231

Leijdekkers, P., Gay, V., & Lawrence, E. (2007). *Smart homecare system for health tele-monitoring*. In ICDS '07, First International Conference on the Digital Society.

Levis, P., & Gay, D. (2009). *TinyOS programming*. Edinburgh, UK: Cambridge University Press. doi:10.1017/CBO9780511626609

Lewis, M. (2000). Focus group interviews in qualitative research: A review of the literature. *Action Research E-Reports, 2*. Retrieved February 24, 2009 from http://www.fhs.usyd.edu.au/arow/arer/002.htm

Lim, L. M., Chiu, L. H., Dohrmann, J., & Tan, K.-L. (2010). Registered nurses' medication management of the elderly in aged care facilities. *International Nursing Review*, *57*(1), 98–106. doi:10.1111/j.1466-7657.2009.00760.x

Lin, C. K., Jea, D., Dabiri, F., Massey, T., Tan, R., Sarrafzadeh, M., et al. Montemagno, C. (2007). *The development of an in-vivo active pressure monitoring system*. Presented at the 4th International Workshop on Wearable and Implantable Body Sensor Networks.

Lindenberg, J., Pasman, W., Kranenborg, K., Stegeman, J., & Neerincx, M. A. (2006). Improving service matching and selection in ubiquitous computing environments: A user study. *Personal and Ubiquitous Computing*, *11*(1), 59–68. doi:10.1007/s00779-006-0066-7

Ling, C. X., & Yan, R. J. (2003). Decision tree with better ranking. In *Proceedings of the International Conference on Machine Learning (ICML2003)*.

Liotta, A., & Liotta, A. (2008). P2P systems in a regulated environment: Threats and opportunities for the operator. *BT Technology Journal*, *26*(1), 150–157.

Litherland, M. (2009). *HL & Comm*. Retrieved June 10, 2010, from http://nule.org/wp/?page_id=63

Liu, H., Darabi, H., Banerjee, P., & Liu, J. (2007). Survey of wireless indoor positioning techniques and systems. *IEEE Transactions on Systems, Man and Cybernetics. Part C, Applications and Reviews*, *37*(6), 1067–1080. doi:10.1109/TSMCC.2007.905750

Liu, Z., Gu, N., & Yang, G. (2007). A reliability evaluation framework on service oriented architecture. In *Proceedings of 2nd International Conference on Pervasive Computing and Applications - ICPCA 2007* (pp. 466-471).

Liuha, P., Lappeteläinen, A., & Soininen, J.-P. (2009). Smart objects for intelligent applications – first results made open. *ARTEMIS Magazine*, *5*, 27–29.

Livshits, B. (2006). *Improving software security with precise static and runtime analysis*. Unpublished doctoral dissertation, Stanford University, USA. Retrieved March 30, 2010 from http://research.microsoft.com/en-us/um/people/livshits/papers/pdf/thesis.pdf

Lo, J.-L., Chi, P.-Y., Chu, H.-H., Wang, H.-Y., & Chou, S.-C. T. (2009). Pervasive computing in play-based occupational therapy for children. *IEEE Pervasive Computing / IEEE Computer Society [and] IEEE Communications Society*, *8*(3), 66–73. doi:10.1109/MPRV.2009.52

Loke, S. (2006). *Context-aware pervasive systems*. Auerbach Publications. doi:10.1201/9781420013498

LongTail Video. (2010). *JW Flash video player for FLV*. Retrieved June, 8, 2010, from http://www.longtailvideo.com/players/jw-player-5-for-flash

Luk, M., Mezzour, G., Perring, A., & Gligor, V. (2007). MiniSec: A secure sensor network communication architecture. In *Proceedings of 6th International Conference on Information Processing in Sensor Networks - IPSN 2007* (pp. 1-10).

Machado, C., & Mendes, J. A. (2007). *Sensors, actuators and communicators when building a ubiquitous computing system*. IEEE International Symposium on Industrial Electronics - ISIE (pp.1530-1535).

Malatras, A., Asgari, A. H., & Baugé, T. (2008b). Web enabled wireless sensor networks for facilities management. *IEEE Systems Journal*, *2*(4), 500–512. doi:10.1109/JSYST.2008.2007815

Malatras, A., Asgari, A. H., Bauge, T., & Irons, M. (2008a). A service-oriented architecture for building services integration. *Emerald Journal of Facilities Management*, *6*(2), 132–151. doi:10.1108/14725960810872659

Malatras, A., Pavlou, G., Belsis, P., Gritzalis, S., Skourlas, C., & Chalaris, I. (2005a). Deploying pervasive secure knowledge management infrastructures. *International Journal of Pervasive Computing and Communications Troubador Publishing*, *1*(4), 265–276. doi:10.1108/17427370580000130

Malatras, A., Pavlou, G., Belsis, P., Gritzalis, S., Skourlas, C., & Chalaris, I. (2005b). Secure and distributed knowledge management in pervasive environments. In *Proceedings of IEEE International Conference on Pervasive Services, Santorini - Greece*, IEEE Press.

Malik, O. (2008). *Mobile subscribers forecast to top 5 billion-mark by 2011*. Retrieved January 10, 2009 from http://gigaom.com/2008/08/06/mobile-subscribers-forecast-to-top-5-billion-mark-by-2011/

MANET. (2010). *IETF WG mobile ad-hoc network*. Retrieved June 1, 2010, from http://tools.ietf.org/wg/manet/

Manousakis, K., Baras, J. S., McAuley, A., & Morera, R. (2005). Network and domain autoconfiguration: A unified approach for large dynamic networks. *IEEE Communications Magazine*, *43*(8), 78–85. doi:10.1109/MCOM.2005.1497557

Manousakis, K. (2005). *Network and domain autoconfiguration: A unified framework for large mobile ad hoc networks*. Doctoral Dissertation, University of Maryland, 2005. Retrieved from http://hdl.handle.net/1903/3103

Mantel, H., Sudbrock, H., & Krausser, T. (2006). Combining different proof techniques for verifying information flow security. In *Proceedings 16th International Symposium on Logic Based Program Synthesis and Transformation* (pp. 94-110). Heidelberg/ Berlin, Germany: Springer.

Marengo, M., Salis, N., & Valla, M. (2007). Context awareness: Servizi mobili su misura. *Telecom Italia S.p.A. Technical Newsletter, 16*(1).

Mark, J. W., & Todd, T. D. (1982). A nonuniform sampling approach to data compression. *IEEE Transactions on Communications*, *29*, 24–32. doi:10.1109/TCOM.1981.1094872

Markov Reward Model checker Website (2010). Retrieved March 30, 2010 from http://www.mrmc-tool.org/trac/

Martinsons, M., Davison, R., & Tse, D. (1999). The balanced scorecard: A foundation for the strategic management of information systems. *Decision Support Systems*, *25*(1), 71–88. doi:10.1016/S0167-9236(98)00086-4

Martinsons, M. G. (1992). *Strategic thinking about information management*. Keynote Address to the 11th Annual Conference of the International Association of Management Consultants, Toronto.

Marvasti, F. (Ed.). (2001). *Nonuniform sampling: Theory and practice*. New York, NY: Kluwer Academic.

Mase, K., & Adjih, C. (2006). *No overhead autoconfiguration OLSR. Internet-draft*. IETF WG MANET.

Masuoka, R., Parsia, B., & Labrou, Y. (2003). Task computing - the Semantic Web meets pervasive computing. In *Proceedings of the 2nd International Semantic Web Conference (ISWC'03),* (LNCS 2870), (pp. 866–880). Springer.

Mautz, R. (2009). Overview of current indoor positioning systems. *Geodesy and Cartography*, *35*(1), 18–22. doi:10.3846/1392-1541.2009.35.18-22

Mavrommati, I., & Darzentas, J. (2007). End user tools for ambient intelligence environments: An overview. In *Human-Computer Interaction, Part II (HCII 2007)*, (LNCS 4551), (pp. 864–872). Springer.

McAuley, A., Das, S., Madhani, S., Baba, S., & Shobatake, Y. (2001). *Dynamic registration and configuration protocol (DRCP). Internet-draft*. IETF WG Network.

McDermott, R. E., Mikulak, R. J., & Beauregard, M. R. (1996). *The basics of FMEA*. New York, NY: Taylor & Francis Productivity Press.

McDermott-Wells, P. (2005). What is Bluetooth? *IEEE Potentials*, *23*(5), 33–35. doi:10.1109/MP.2005.1368913

McKeown, B., & Thomas, D. (1971). *Q methodology*. London, UK: Sage Publications.

Merrill, W. (2010). Where is the return on investment in wireless sensor networks? *IEEE Wireless Communications*, *17*(1), 4–6. doi:10.1109/MWC.2010.5416341

Merz, S. (2001). Model checking: A tutorial overview. In Cassez, F. (Eds.), *Modeling and verification of parallel processes* (pp. 3–38). Heidelberg/ Berlin, Germany: Springer. doi:10.1007/3-540-45510-8_1

Messer, A., Kunjithapatham, A., Sheshagiri, M., Song, H., Kumar, P., Nguyen, P., & Yi, K. H. (2006). InterPlay: A middleware for seamless device integration and task orchestration in a networked home. In *Proceedings of the 4th Annual IEEE Conference on Pervasive Computing and Communications*, (pp. 296–307). IEEE Computer Society.

Mills, H. D. (1980). The management of software engineering, part I: Principles of software engineering. *IBM Systems Journal*, *19*, 414–420. doi:10.1147/sj.194.0414

Miluzzo, E., Lane, N., Fodor, K., Peterson, R., Lu, H., Musolesi, M., et al. Campbell, A. T. (2008). Sensing meets mobile social networks: The design, implementation and evaluation of the CenceMe application. In *Proceedings of the 6th ACM Conference on Embedded Network Sensor Systems* (pp. 337–350).

Miskovicz, M. (2006). Efficiency of level-crossing sampling for bandlimited Gaussian random process. In *Proceedings of IEEE International Workshop on Factory Communication Systems*, (pp. 137-142). ANIPLA-Torino.

Moler, C. B. (2004). *Numerical computing with MATLAB*. Retrieved from http://www.mathworks.com/moler/chapters.html

Moodley, D., & Simonis, I. (2006). *A new architecture for the sensor Web: The SWAP framework.* Paper presented at the 5th International Semantic Web Conference (ISWC'06), Athens, GA, USA.

Moore, N. (2006). *Optimistic Duplicate Address Detection (DAD) for IPv6*. (IETF RFC 4429).

Morera, R., McAuley, A., & Wong, L. (2003). Robust router reconfiguration in large dynamic networks. In *Proceedings of the IEEE Military Communications Conference (MILCOM 2003), 2*, (pp. 1343-1347).

Morgan, D. L. (1988). *Focus groups as qualitative research*. Newbury Park, CA: Sage.

Morgan, D. L. (1997). *Focus group as qualitative research* (2nd ed.). Thousand Oaks, CA: Sage Publications.

Morris, M., & Guilak, F. (2009). Mobile heart health: Project highlight. *IEEE Pervasive Computing / IEEE Computer Society [and] IEEE Communications Society*, *8*(2), 57–61. doi:10.1109/MPRV.2009.31

Moskowitz, R., & Nikander, P. (2006). *Host Identity Protocol (HIP) architecture*. (IETF RFC 4423).

Moskowitz, R., Nikander, P., Jokela, P., & Henderson, T. (2008). *Host identity protocol*. (IETF RFC 5201).

Muller-Veerse, F. (2000). *Mobile commerce report*. London, UK: Durlacher Research Ltd.

Mundy, G., Young, R., & Ramanathan, S. (2009). *Case for electronic medication management in aged care*. Aged Care Industry IT Council.

Murray, B., Baugé, T., Egan, R., Tan, C., & Yong, C. (2008). *Dynamic duty cycle control with path and zone management in wireless sensor networks.* Paper presented at the IEEE International Wireless Communications and Mobile Computing Conference, Crete, Greece.

Musolesi, M., Miluzzo, E., Lane, N. D., Eisenman, S. B., Choudhury, T., & Campbell, A. T. (2008). The second life of a sensor - integrating real-world experience in virtual worlds using mobile phones. In *Proceedings of HotEmNets '08, Charlottesville*.

Muylle, S., Moenaert, R., & Despontin, M. (2004). The conceptualization and empirical validation of website user satisfaction. *Information & Management*, *41*, 543–560. doi:10.1016/S0378-7206(03)00089-2

MySQL. (2009). *MySQL DB official homepage*. Retrieved July 20, 2010 from http://www.mysql.com/?bydis_dis_index=1

Nakazawa, J., Yura, J., & Tokuda, H. (2004). Galaxy: A service shaping approach for addressing the hidden service problem. In *Proceedings of the 2nd IEEE Workshop on Software Technologies for Future Embedded and Ubiquitous Systems*, (pp. 35–39).

Narten, T., Draves, R., & Krishnan, S. (2007). *Privacy extensions for stateless addresses autoconfiguration in IPv6*. (IETF RFC 4941).

Narten, T., Nordmark, E., Simpson, W., & Soliman, H. (2007). *Neighbor discovery for IPv6*. (IETF RFC 4861).

Nasipuri, A., Alasti, H., Puthran, P. H., Cox, R., Conrad, J. M., Van der Zel, L., et al. Graziano, J. (2010). *Vibration sensing for equipment's health monitoring in power substations using wireless sensor.* Presented at IEEE Southeastcon, Charlotte, NC.

Nasipuri, A., Cox, R., Alasti, H., Van der Zel, L., Rodriguez, B., McKosky, R., & Graziano, J. A. (2008). *Wireless sensor network for substation monitoring: design and deployment*. Demo presented at Sensys, Raleigh, NC.

Nesargi, S., & Prakash, R. (2002). MANETconf: Configuration of hosts in a mobile ad hoc network. In *Proceedings of the 21st Annual Joint Conference of the IEEE Computer and Communications Societies, 2*, (pp. 1059-1068).

Newman, M., & Ackerman, M. (2008). Pervasive help @ home: Connecting people who connect devices. In *Proceedings of the International Workshop on Pervasive Computing at Home (PC@Home)*, (pp. 28–36).

Newman, M., Elliott, A., & Smith, T. (2008). Providing an integrated user experience of networked media, devices, and services through end-user composition. In *Proceedings of the 6th International Conference on Pervasive Computing (Pervasive '08)*, (pp. 213–227).

Ngu, A. H. H., Carlson, M. P., Sheng, Q. Z., & Paik, H.-Y. (2010). Semantic-based mashup of composite applications. *IEEE Transactions on Services Computing, 3*(1), 2–15. doi:10.1109/TSC.2010.8

Nierstrasz, O., Denker, M., & Renggli, L. (2009). Model-centric, context-aware software adaptation. In Cheng, B. H. C., de Lemos, R., Giese, H., Inverardi, P., & Magee, J. (Eds.), *Software engineering for self-adaptive systems* (pp. 128–145). New York, NY & Berlin/Heidelberg, Germany: Springer. doi:10.1007/978-3-642-02161-9_7

Nitto, E. D., Ghezzi, C., Metzger, A., Papazoglou, M., & Pohl, K. (2008). A journey to highly dynamic, self-adaptive service-based applications. *Automated Software Engineering, 3*(15), 313–341. doi:10.1007/s10515-008-0032-x

Noy, N. F., & McGuinness, D. L. (2001). *Ontology development 101: A guide to creating your first ontology.* (Stanford Knowledge Systems Laboratory Technical Report KSL-01-05 and Stanford Medical Informatics Technical Report SMI-2001-0880). Stanford, CA: Stanford University.

Object Management Group. (2006). *Object constraint logic 2.0 formal specification*. Retrieved March 30, 2010 from http://www.omg.org/technology/documents/formal/ocl.htm

OGC. (2010). *Open Geospatial Consortium Inc., official homepage*. Retrieved July 20, 2010 from http://www.opengeospatial.org/

Olumofin, F. G. (2007). *A holistic method for assessing software product line architectures*. Saarbrücken, Germany: VDM Verlag.

OMG. (2009). *Unified Modeling Language* (UML), version 2.2, Retrieved July 4, 2010, from http://www.omg.org/cgi-bin/doc?formal/09-02-02.pdf

OMG. (2009b). *Ontology Definition Metamodel*, version 1.0, Retrieved July 4, 2010, from http://www.omg.org/spec/ODM/1.0/

Open, I. D. (2010). *OpenID standard*. Retrieved July 20, 2010 from http://en.wikipedia.org/wiki/OpenID

Opticon Australia. (2008). *Information Technology for aged care providers. Department of Health and Ageing*. Canberra: Department of Health and Ageing.

Oram, A. (2001). *Peer-to-peer: Harnessing the power of disruptive technologies*. O'Reilly Media.

Ortmeier, F., Reif, W., & Schellhorn, G. (2006). *Deductive cause-consequence analysis*. Paper presented at IFAC World Congress, Istanbul, Turkey.

Otto, J. R., Najdawi, M. K., & Caron, K. M. (2000). Web-user satisfaction: An exploratory study (industry trend or event). *Journal of End User Computing, 12*(4), 3. doi:10.4018/joeuc.2000100101

Pace, P., Aloi, G., & Palmacci, A. (2009). A multi-technology location-aware wireless system for interactive fruition of multimedia contents. *IEEE Transactions on Consumer Electronics, 55*(2), 342–350. doi:10.1109/TCE.2009.5174391

Paluska, J. M., Pham, H., Saif, U., Chau, G., Terman, C., & Ward, S. (2008). Structured decomposition of adaptive applications. In *Proceedings of the 6th Annual IEEE International Conference on Pervasive Computing and Communications (PerCom'08)*, (pp. 1–10). IEEE Computer Society.

Papazoglou, M. (2003). Service-oriented computing: Concept, characteristics and directions. In *Proceedings of the 4th International Conference on Web Information Systems Engineering (WISE'03)* (pp. 3-12). Roma, Italy: IEEE Computer Society.

Parasuraman, A., Zeithaml, V. A., & Berry, L. L. (1985). A conceptual model of service quality and its implications for future research. *Journal of Marketing*, *49*(3), 41–50. doi:10.2307/1251430

Parasuraman, A., Zeithaml, V. A., & Berry, L. L. (1988). SERVQUAL: A multi-item scale for measuring consumer perceptions of service quality. *Journal of Retailing*, *64*(1), 12–40.

Paré, G., & Elam, J. J. (1998). Introducing information technology in the clinical setting: Lessons learned in a trauma center. *International Journal of Technology Assessment in Health Care*, *14*(2), 331–343. doi:10.1017/S0266462300012290

Parikh, T. S., & Lazowska, E. D. (2006). Designing an architecture for delivering mobile information services to the rural developing world. In *Proceedings of the 15th international Conference on World Wide Web, Edinburgh, Scotland,* (pp. 791-800). New York, NY: ACM Press.

Parsons, D. (2007). Mobile portal technologies and business models. In Tatnall, A. (Ed.), *Encyclopedia of portal technologies and applications* (pp. 583–587). Hershey, PA: IGI Global. doi:10.4018/9781591409892.ch098

Patterson, P., & Spreng, R. (1997). Modeling the relationship between perceived value, satisfaction and repurchase intentions in a business-to-business service context: An empirical examination. *International Journal of Service Industry Management*, *8*(5), 414–434. doi:10.1108/09564239710189835

Pautasso, C., Zimmermann, O., & Leymann, F. (2008). RESTful Web services vs. big Web services: Making the right architectural decision. In *Proceedings of the ACM 17th International Conference on World Wide Web - WWW 2008*, Beijing, China.

Paymans, T. F., Lindenberg, J., & Neerincx, M. (2004). Usability trade-offs for adaptive user interfaces: Ease of use and learnability. In *Proceedings of 9th International Conference on Intelligent User Interfaces.* ACM Press.

Pease, W., Rowe, M., & Cooper, M. (2005). Regional tourist destinations - the role of information and communications technology (ICT) in collaboration amongst tourism providers. In G. Madder (Ed.), *Proceedings ITS Africa-Asia-Australasia Regional Conference - ICT Networks - Building Blocks for Economic Development.*

Peng, W., Ser, W., & Zhang, M. (2001). *Bark scale equalizer design using wrapped filter*. Singapore: Center for Signal Processing Nanyang Technological University.

Peng, J. (2008). *A survey of location based service for Galileo system*. International Symposium on Computer Science and Computational Technology – ISCSCT (pp. 737-741).

Perkins, C. E., Malinen, J. T., Wakikawa, R., Belding-Royer, E. M., & Sun, Y. (2001). *IP address autoconfiguration for ad hoc networks. Internet-draft*. IETF WG MANET.

Perrig, A., Szewczyk, R., Wen, V., Culler, D., & Tygar, J. D. (2001). Spins: Security protocols for sensor networks. *Wireless Networks*, *8*(5), 521–534. doi:10.1023/A:1016598314198

Perrig, J., Stankovic, A., & Wagner, D. (2004). Security in wireless sensor networks. *Communications of the ACM*, *47*(6), 53–57. doi:10.1145/990680.990707

Perttunen, M., Van Kleek, M., Lassila, O., & Riekki, J. (2009). *An implementation of auditory context recognition for mobile devices*. In Tenth International Conference on Mobile Data Management: Systems, Services and Middleware.

Pink, G., McKillop, I., Schraa, E., Preyra, C., Montgomery, C., & Baker, G. R. (2001). Creating a Balanced Scorecard for a hospital system. *Journal of Health Care Finance*, *27*(2), 1–20.

Pitt, L., Watson, R., & Kavan, C. (1995). Service quality: A measure of information systems effectiveness. *Management Information Systems Quarterly*, (June): 173–187. doi:10.2307/249687

Pkix. (2009). *IETF public-key infrastructure* (X.509) (pkix) *Working Group*. Retrieved July 20, 2010 from http://www.ietf.org/dyn/wg/charter/pkix-charter.html

Polastre, J., Hill, J., & Culler, D. (2004). Versatile low power media access for wireless sensor networks. In *Proceedings of the 2nd ACM SenSys Conference* (pp. 95–107), Baltimore, USA.

Powell, S., & Shim, J. P. (2009). *Wireless technology: Applications, management, and security (Lecture Notes in Electrical Engineering)*. Springer.

Powers, R. F., & Dickson, G. W. (1973). MIS project management: Myths, opinions, and reality. *California Management Review*, *15*(3), 147–156.

Preuveneers, D., & Berbers, Y. (2005). Automated context-driven composition of pervasive services to alleviate non-functional concerns. *International Journal of Computing and Information Sciences*, *3*(2), 19–28.

Prism Model Checker. (2010). Retrieved March 30, 2010 from http://www.prismmodelchecker.org/

Productivity Commission. (2008). *Trends in aged care provision. Council of Australian Governments*. Canberra: Productivity Commission.

Przeworski, A., & Newman, M. G. (2004). Palmtop computer-assisted group therapy for social phobia. *Journal of Clinical Psychology*, *60*(2), 179–188. doi:10.1002/jclp.10246

PVS Specification and Verification System (2010). Retrieved March 30, 2010 from http://pvs.csl.sri.com/

Qaisar, S. M., Fesquet, L., & Renaudin, M. (2009). An adaptive resolution computationally efficient short-time Fourier transforms. *EURASIP. Research Letters in Signal Processing*, 12.

Qaisar, S. M., Fesquet, L., & Renaudin, M. (2007). Adaptive rate filtering for a signal driven sampling scheme. In *Proceedings of IEEE International Conference on Acoustic, Speech and Signal processing*: *Vol. 3*, (pp. 1465-1468).

Quinlan, M. (2005). *Galileo - a European global satellite navigation system* (pp. 1–16). IEE Seminar on New Developments and Opportunities in Global Navigation Satellite Systems.

Ranganathan, A., & Campbell, R. H. (2004). Autonomic pervasive computing based on planning. In *Proceedings of the International Conference on Autonomic Computing*, (pp. 80–87). Los Alamitos, CA: IEEE Computer Society.

Ransdell, E. (2000). *Portals for the people*. Retrieved February 8, 2009 from http://www.fastcompany.com/magazine/34/ideazone.html

Rantapuska, O., & Lahteenmaki, M. (2008). Task-based user experience for home networks and smart spaces. In *Proceedings of the International Workshop on Pervasive Mobile Interaction Devices*, (pp. 188–191).

Rashid, O., Coulton, P., & Edwards, R. (2008). Providing location based information/advertising for existing mobile phone users. *Journal of Personal and Ubiquitous Computing*, *12*(1), 3–10. doi:10.1007/s00779-006-0121-4

Raymond, L. (1987). Validating and applying user satisfaction as a measure of MIS success in small organizations. *Information & Management*, *12*, 173–179. doi:10.1016/0378-7206(87)90040-1

Rehman, K., Stajano, F., & Coulouris, G. (2007). An architecture for interactive context-aware applications. *IEEE Pervasive Computing / IEEE Computer Society [and] IEEE Communications Society*, *6*(1), 73–80. doi:10.1109/MPRV.2007.5

Resnick, M., Maloney, J., Monroy-Hernandez, A., Rusk, N., Eastmond, E., & Brennan, K. (2009). Scratch: Programming for all. *Communications of the ACM*, *52*(11), 60–67. doi:10.1145/1592761.1592779

Rice, R. O. (1945). Mathematical analysis of random noise. *The Bell System Technical Journal*, *24*, 46–156.

Rich, C., Sidner, C., Lesh, N., Garland, A., Booth, S., & Chimani, M. (2006). DiamondHelp: A new interaction design for networked home appliances. *Personal and Ubiquitous Computing*, *10*(2-3), 187–190. doi:10.1007/s00779-005-0020-0

Riekki, J., Sánchez, I., & Pyykkonen, M. (2010). Remote control for pervasive services. *International Journal of Autonomous and Adaptive Communications Systems*, *3*(1), 39–58. doi:10.1504/IJAACS.2010.030311

Rigole, P., Clerckx, T., Berbers, Y., & Coninx, K. (2007). Task-driven automated component deployment for ambient intelligence environments. *Pervasive and Mobile Computing*, *3*(3), 276–299. doi:10.1016/j.pmcj.2007.01.001

Rigole, P., Vandervelpen, C., Luyten, K., Berbers, Y., Vandewoude, Y., & Coninx, K. (2005). A component-based infrastructure for pervasive user interaction. In *Proceedings of Software Techniques for Embedded and Pervasive Systems* (pp. 1–16). Springer.

Roos, T., Myllymaki, P., Tirri, H., Misikangas, P., & Sievanen, J. (2002). A probabilistic approach to WLAN user location estimation. *International Journal of Wireless Information Networks*, *9*(3), 155–164. doi:10.1023/A:1016003126882

Roscoe, A. W., Woodcock, J. C. P., & Wulf, L. (1994). Non-interference through determinism. In *Proceedings of the Third European Symposium on Research in Computer Security* (pp. 33-53). London, UK: Springer-Verlag.

Roughead, E. E., Semple, S. J., & Gilbert, A. L. (2003). Quality use of medicines in aged-care facilities in Australia. *Drugs & Aging*, *20*(9), 643–653. doi:10.2165/00002512-200320090-00002

Roussos, G., Marsh, A. J., & Maglavera, S. (2005). Enabling pervasive computing with smart phones. *IEEE Pervasive Computing / IEEE Computer Society [and] IEEE Communications Society*, *4*(2), 20–27. doi:10.1109/MPRV.2005.30

Rouvoy, R., Barone, P., Ding, Y., Eliassen, F., Hallsteinsen, S. O., Lorenzo, J., et al. Scholz, U. (2009). MUSIC: Middleware support for self-adaptation in ubiquitous and service-oriented environments. In *Software Engineering for Self-Adaptive Systems*, (pp. 164–182).

Roxin, A., Gaber, J., Wack, M., & Nait-Sidi-Moh, A. (2007). *Survey of wireless geolocation techniques* (pp. 1–9). IEEE Globecom Workshops.

Rubel, D. (2006). The heart of Eclipse. *ACM Queue; Tomorrow's Computing Today*, *4*(6), 36–44. doi:10.1145/1165754.1165767

Ruiz, F., & Hilera, J. R. (2006). Using ontologies in software engineering and technology. In Calero, C., Ruiz, F., & Piattini, M. (Eds.), *Ontologies for software engineering and software technology* (pp. 49–102). Springer-Verlag. doi:10.1007/3-540-34518-3_2

Runciman, W. B., Roughead, E. E., Semple, S. J., & Adams, R. J. (2003). Adverse drug events and medication errors in Australia. *International Journal for Quality in Health Care*, *15*(Supplement 1), i49–i59. doi:10.1093/intqhc/mzg085

Ryder, J., Longstaff, B., Reddy, S., & Estrin, D. (2009). *Ambulation: A tool for monitoring mobility patterns over time using mobile phones*. Technical Report UC Los Angeles: Center for Embedded Network Sensing.

Saha, D., & Mukherjee, A. (2003). Pervasive computing: A paradigm for the 21st century. *IEEE Computer*, *36*(3), 25–31.

San Pedro, J., Burstein, F., Cao, P., Churilov, L., Zaslavsky, A., & Wassertheil, J. (2004). *Mobile decision support for triage in emergency departments*. The 2004 IFIP International Conference on Decision Support Systems. Prato, Italy.

San Pedro, J., Burstein, F., Wassertheil, J., Arora, N., Churilov, L., & Zaslavsky, A. C. (2005). On development and evaluation of prototype mobile decision support for hospital triage. In R. H. Sprague (Ed.), *The 38th Hawaii International Conference on System Sciences*, IEEE Press.

Sánchez, I., Riekki, J., & Pyykkonen, M. (2009). Touch&Compose: Physical user interface for application composition in smart environments. In *Proceedings of the International Workshop on Near Field Communication*, (pp. 61–66). IEEE Computer Society.

Sandhu, R., Ferraiolo, D., & Kuhn, R. (2000). The NIST model for role-based access control: Towards a unified standard. In *Proceedings of the Fifth ACM Workshop on Role-Based Access Control (RBAC '00)* (pp. 47–63). ACM Press.

Sarkar, S. K. (2007). *Ad hoc mobile wireless networks: Principles, protocols and applications*. Auerbach Publications. doi:10.1201/9781420062229

Sayiner, N., Sorensen, H. V., & Viswanathan, T. R. (1996). A level-crossing sampling scheme for A/D conversion. *IEEE Transactions on Circuits and Systems*, *43*, 335–339. doi:10.1109/82.488288

Sayood, K. (2000). *Introduction to data compression*. San Francisco, CA: Morgan Kaufmann.

Sayrafiezadeh, M. (1994). The birthday problem revisited. *Mathematics Magazine*, *67*, 220–223. doi:10.2307/2690615

Schellhorn, G., Thums, A., & Reif, W. (2002). Formal fault tree semantics. In *Proceedings of 6th World Conference on Integrated Design & Process Technology*. ACM Press.

Schilit, B. N., Hilbert, D. M., & Trevor, J. (2002). Context-aware communication. *IEEE Wireless Communications*, *9*(5), 46–54. doi:10.1109/MWC.2002.1043853

Schmidt, D. C. (2006). Model-driven engineering. *IEEE Computer*, *39*(2), 25–31.

Schmidt, R. de O., Gomes, R., Sadok, D., Kelner, J., & Johnsson, M. (2009). An autonomous addressing mechanism as support for auto-configuration in dynamic networks. In *Proceedings of the Latin American Network Operations and Management Symposium (LANOMS 2009)*, (pp. 1-12).

Schmidt-Belz, B. (2005). User trust in adaptive systems. In *Proceedings of GI-Workshop on Lernen, Wissenstransfer, Adaptivität.* Retrieved March 30, 2010, from http://www.dfki.de/lwa2005/

Segars, A. H. (1997). Assessing the unidimensionality of measurement: A paradigm and illustration within the context of information system research. *International Journal of Management Science*, *25*(1), 107–121.

Serenko, A., & Bontis, N. (2004). A model of user adoption of mobile portals. *Quarterly Journal of Electronic Commerce*, *4*(1), 69–98.

Shilakes, C. C., & Tylman, J. (1998). *Enterprise information portals*. New York, NY: Merrill Lynch Inc.

Shortell, S., Gillies, R., Anderson, D., Erickson, K., & Mitchell, J. (2000). *Remaking healthcare in America*. San Francisco, CA: Jossey-Bass.

Siadat, S. H., & Selamat, A. (2008). *Location-based system for mobile devices using RFID*. Asia International Conference on Modeling & Simulation – AMS (pp. 291-296).

Siau, K., Lim, E. P., & Shen, Z. (2001). Mobile commerce: Promises, challenges, and research agenda. *Journal of Database Management*, *12*(3), 4–13. doi:10.4018/jdm.2001070101

Sicard, S., Boyer, F., & Palma, N. D. (2008). Using component for architecture-based management. In *Proceedings of International Conference on Software Engineering (ICSE'08)*, Leipzig, Germany: ACM-Association for Computing Machinery.

Sichitiu, M. (2004). *Cross-layer scheduling for power efficiency in wireless sensor networks.* Paper presented at IEEE INFOCOM, Hong Kong.

Simmons, R., & Koenig, S. (1995). *Probabilistic robot navigation in partially observable environments*. In The International Joint Conference on Artificial Intelligence (IJCAI'95) (pp. 1080-1087).

Simon, G., & Berger, M. O. (2002). Pose estimation for planar structures. *IEEE CG & A*, *22*(6), 46–53.

Singer, A. C., & Guan, K. M. (2007). Opportunistic sampling of bursty signals by level-crossing – an information theoretical approach. In *Proceeding of Conference on Information Science and Systems*, (pp. 701-707). Baltimore, MD.

Singh, Y., & Sood, M. (2009). Model driven architecture: A perspective. In *Proceedings IEEE International Advance Computing Conference* (pp. 1644–1652). IEEE.

Sintoris, C., Raptis, D., Stoica, A., & Avouris, N. (2007). Delivering multimedia content in enabled cultural spaces. In *Proceedings of the 3rd international Conference on Mobile Multimedia Communications (MobiMedia'07)*, (pp. 1–6). Brussels, Belgium: ICST.

Smith, M. A. (2004). Portals: Toward an application framework for interoperability. *Communications of the ACM*, *47*(10), 93–97. doi:10.1145/1022594.1022600

Smithson, J. (2000). Using and analyzing focus groups: Limitations and possibilities. *International Journal of Social Research Methodology*, *3*(2), 103–119. doi:10.1080/136455700405172

SOAP. (2008). *W3C SOAP 1.2 specification*. Retrieved July 20, 2010 from http://www.w3.org/TR/soap12-part1/

Sohn, D. (2008). *Privacy principles for digital watermarking*. Center for Democracy and Technology. Retrieved July 4, 2010, from http://www.cdt.org/copyright/20080529watermarking.pdf

Sommerville, I. (2000). *Software engineering* (6th ed.). Harlow, UK: Addison-Wesley.

Sommerville, I. (2007). *Software engineering* (8th ed.). New York, NY: Addison- Wesley Pubs.

Song, H. L. (1994). Automatic vehicle location in cellular communications systems. *IEEE Transactions on Vehicular Technology*, *43*(4), 902–908. doi:10.1109/25.330153

Sousa, J. P., Poladian, V., Garlan, D., Schmerl, B., & Shaw, M. (2006). Task-based adaptation for ubiquitous computing. *IEEE Transactions on Systems, Man and Cybernetics. Part C, Applications and Reviews*, *36*, 328–340. doi:10.1109/TSMCC.2006.871588

Sousa, J. P., Schmerl, B., Poladian, V., & Brodsky, A. (2008a). uDesign: End-user design applied to monitoring and control applications for smart spaces. In *Proceedings of the Working IEEE/IFIP Conference on Software Architecture*, (pp. 71–80). IEEE Computer Society.

Sousa, J. P., Schmerl, B., Steenkiste, P., & Garlan, D. (2008b). Activity-oriented computing, chap. XI. In *Advances in Ubiquitous Computing: Future Paradigms and Directions.* (pp. 280–315). Hershey, PA: IGI Publishing.

Soylu, A., & de Causmaecker, P. (2009). Merging model driven and ontology driven system development approaches: Pervasive computing perspective. In *Proceedings 24th International Symposium on Computer and Information Sciences* (pp. 730–735). IEEE.

Spinewine, A., Schmader, K. E., Barber, N. C., & Hughes, K. L. (2007). Appropriate prescribing in elderly people: How well can it be measured and optimised? *Lancet*, *370*(9582), 173–184. doi:10.1016/S0140-6736(07)61091-5

Spring. (2009). *Spring framework's security project*. Retrieved July 20, 2010 from http://static.springframework.org/spring-security/

Stal, M. (2002). Web services: Beyond component-based computing. *Communications of the ACM*, *45*(10), 71–76. doi:10.1145/570907.570934

Starner, T. E. (2002). Wearable computers: No longer science fiction. *IEEE Pervasive Computing / IEEE Computer Society [and] IEEE Communications Society*, *1*(1), 86–88. doi:10.1109/MPRV.2002.993148

Stefanacci, R. G. (2008). Electronic medication management systems in long-term care and beyond. *Assisted Living Consult*, *4*(2), 19–20.

Stephenson, W. (1953). *The study of behavior: q-technique and its methodology*. Chicago, IL: University Chicago Press.

Stewart, D. W., Shamdasani, P. N., & Rook, D. W. (2007). *Focus groups: Theory and practice* (2nd ed.). Thousand Oaks, CA: Sage Publications.

Storey, N. (1996). *Safety critical systems*. Boston, MA: Addison Wesley Longman Publishing.

Subramanian, R., & Goodman, B. D. (Eds.). (2005). *Peer to peer computing: The evolution of a disruptive technology*. Hershey, PA: IGI Global.

Subramanian, S. P., Sommer, J., Schmitt, S., & Rosenstiel, W. (2007). *SBIL: Scalable indoor localization and navigation service*. International Conference on Wireless Communication and Sensor Networks - WCSN (pp. 27-30).

Sun, Y., & Belding-Royer, M. E. (2003). *Dynamic address configuration in mobile ad hoc networks*. Technical Report, University of California at Santa Barbara. Rep. 2003-11.

Swami, Q. Z. A., Hong, Y.-W., & Tong, L. (Eds.). (2007). *Wireless sensor networks: Signal processing and communications. Chichester/ West Essex*. UK: John Wiley & Sons.

Ta, T., Othman, N. Y., Glitho, R. H., & Khendek, F. (2006). Using Web services for bridging end-user applications and wireless sensor networks. In *Proceedings of 11th IEEE Symposium on Computers and Communications - ISCC '06* (pp. 347-352), Sardina, Italy: IEEE Press.

Takemoto, M., Oh-ishi, T., Iwata, T., Yamato, Y., Tanaka, Y., & Shinno, K. ... Shimamoto, N. (2004). A service-composition and service-emergence framework for ubiquitous-computing environments. In *Proceedings of the 2004 Workshop on Applications and the Internet, part of SAINT'04*, (pp. 313–318).

Takeyasu, K. (2009). Mobile marketing. In Cater-Steel, A., & Al-Hakim, L. (Eds.), *Information system research methods, epistemology, and application* (pp. 328–341). Hershey, PA & New York, NY: Information Science Reference.

Tapia, E. M., Intille, S. S., Haskell, W., Larson, K., Wright, J., King, A., & Friedman, R. (2007). Real-time recognition of physical activities and their intensities using wireless accelerometers and a heart rate monitor. In *Proceedings of International Symposium on Wearable Computers, IEEE Press* (pp. 37-40).

Tatnall, A. (2005). Portals, portals everywhere. In Tatnall, A. (Ed.), *Web portals: The new gateways to Internet information and services* (pp. 1–14). Hershey, PA: Idea Group Publishing.

Thomas, B., Close, B., Donoghue, J., Squires, J., Bondi, P. D., Morris, M., & Piekarski, P. (2000). *ARQuake: An outdoor/indoor augmented reality first person application.* International Symposium on Wearable Computers - ISWC (pp.139-146).

Thomson, S., Narten, T., & Jinmei, T. (2007). *IPv6 stateless address autoconfiguration.* (IETF RFC 4862).

Tojib, D. R., & Sugianto, L. F. (2008). User satisfaction with business-to-employee (B2E) portals: Conceptualization and scale development. *European Journal of Information Systems, 17*(6), 649–667. doi:10.1057/ejis.2008.55

Tooey, M., & Mayo, A. (2003). Handheld technologies in a clinical setting: State of the technology and resources. *American Association of Critical Care Nurses Advanced Critical Care, 14*(3), 342.

Toth, N., & Pataki, B. (2008). Classification confidence weighted majority voting using decision tree classifiers. *International Journal of Intelligent Computing and Cybernetics, 1*(2), 169–192. doi:10.1108/17563780810874708

Trakadas, T. Z. P., Voliotis, S., & Manasis, C. (2004). Efficient routing in pan and sensor networks. *ACM SIGMOBILE Mobile Computing and Communications Review, 8*(1), 10–17. doi:10.1145/980159.980165

Troan, O., & Droms, R. (2003). *IPv6 prefix options for dynamic host configuration protocol (DHCP) version 6.* (IETF RFC 3633).

Tsalgatidou, A., Veijalainen, J., & Pitoura, E. (2000). *Challenges in mobile electronic commerce.* Retrieved September 29, 2008, from http://cgi.di.uoa.gr/~afrodite/IeC_Manchester.PDF

Turel, O., & Serenko, A. (2007). Mobile portals. In Tatnall, A. (Ed.), *Encyclopedia of portal technologies and applications* (pp. 587–593). Hershey, PA: IGI Global. doi:10.4018/9781591409892.ch099

Turkyilmaz, A., & Ozkan, C. (2007). Development of a customer satisfaction index model: An application to the Turkish mobile phone sector. *Industrial Management & Data Systems, 107*(5), 672–687. doi:10.1108/02635570710750426

Turon, M. (2005). MOTE-VIEW: A sensor network monitoring and management tool. In *Proceedings of the 2nd IEEE Workshop on Embedded Network Sensors - EmNets'05* (pp. 11-18). IEEE press.

Uden, L., & Salmenjoki, K. (2007). Evolution of portals. In Tatnall, A. (Ed.), *Encyclopedia of portal technologies and applications* (pp. 391–396). Hershey, PA: IGI Global. doi:10.4018/9781591409892.ch066

UPnP Plug and Play Forum. (2008). *UPnP device architecture,* version 1.1. Device Architecture Documents. Retrieved October 15, 2008, from http://upnp.org/specs/arch/UPnP-arch-DeviceArchitecture-v1.1.pdf

Ustaran, E. (2004). *Data exports in data protection handbook.* London, UK: The Law Society.

Vaidya, N. (2002). Weak duplicate address detection in mobile ad hoc networks. In *Proceedings of the 3rd ACM International Symposium on Mobile Ad Hoc Networking & Computing,* (pp. 206-216).

van Dam, T., & Langendoen, K. (2003). An adaptive energy-efficient MAC protocol for wireless sensor networks. In *Proceedings of the 1st ACM SenSys Conference* (171–180), Los Angeles, CA: ACM Press.

Van Mulken, S., Andre, E., & Muller, J. (1999). An empirical study on the trustworthiness of life-like interface agents. In *Proceedings of the HCI International '99 (the 8th International Conference on Human-Computer Interaction) on Human-Computer Interaction: Communication, Cooperation, and Application Design-Volume 2* (pp. 152-156). Hillsdale, NJ: Lawrence Earlbaum Ass.

Vanden Bossche, M., Ross, P., MacLarty, I., Van Nuffelen, B., & Pelov, N. (2007). Ontology driven software engineering for real life applications. In *Proceedings 3rd International Workshop on Semantic Web Enabled Software Engineering (SWESE 2007)*. Springer-Verlag.

Vansteenwegen, P., & Van Oudheusden, D. (2006). Selection of tourist attractions and routing using personalised electronic guides. In *Proceedings of the International Conference on Information and Communication Technologies in Tourism 2006. Lausanne, Switzerland* (pp. 55-55). Vienna, Austria: Springer.

Varshavsky, A., Chen, M. Y., De Lara, E., Froehlich, J., Haehnel, D., & Hightower, J. … Smith, I. (2006). *Are GSM phones the solution for localization?* IEEE Workshop on Mobile Computing Systems and Applications - WMCSA (pp.20-28).

Vassis, D., Belsis, P., Skourlas, C., & Gritzalis, S. (2009). End to end secure communication in ad-hoc assistive medical environments using secure paths. In G. Pantziou (Ed.), *Proceedings of the PSPAE 2009 1st Workshop on Privacy and Security in Pervasive e-Health and Assistive Environments, in conjunction with PETRA 2009 2nd International Conference on Pervasive Technologies related to Assistive Environments*. ACM Press.

Vassis, D., Belsis, P., Skourlas, C., & Pantziou, G. (2008). A pervasive architectural framework for providing remote medical Treatment. *Proceedings of 1st International Conference on Pervasive Technologies Related to Assistive Environments, ACM International Conference Proceeding Series; Vol. 282, article No. 23,* ACM Press.

Vastenburg, M., Keyson, D., & de Ridder, H. (2007). Measuring user experiences of prototypical autonomous products in a simulated home environment. [HCI]. *Human-Computer Interaction, 2*, 998–1007.

Vesley, W., Dugan, J., Fragola, J., Minarick, J., & Railsback, J. (2002). *Fault tree handbook with aerospace applications*. NASA Office of Safety and Mission Assurance. Retrieved March 30, 2010 from http://www.hq.nasa.gov/office/codeq/doctree/fthb.pdf

Vistein, M., Ortmeier, F., Reif, W., Huuck, R., & Fehnker, A. (2009). An abstract specification language for static program analysis. In *Proceedings of 4th International Workshop on System Software Verification*. Elsevier.

Vlachogiannis, E., Velasco, C. A., Gappa, H., Nordbrock, G., & Darzentas, J. S. (2007). Accessibility of Internet portals in ambient intelligent scenarios: Re-thinking their design and implementation. In *Universal access in human-computer interaction. Ambient interaction* (pp. 245–253). Heidelberg/ Berlin, Germany: Springer. doi:10.1007/978-3-540-73281-5_26

Volanschi, N. (2006). A portable compiler-integrated approach to permanent checking. In *Proceedings 21st IEEE/ACM International Conference on Automated Software Engineering*. IEEE Press. ADDITIONAL READING SECTION Anderson, R. J. (2008). *Security Engineering: A Guide to Building Dependable Distributed Systems*. Wiley Publishing. Clark, J.A., Paige, R.F., Polack, F.A.C., & Brooke, P.J. (Eds.) (2006). *Security in Pervasive Computing*. Heidelberg: Springer Berlin.

W3C. (2000). Extensible Markup Language (XML) 1.0 (2nd ed.). In T. Bray, J. Paoli, C. M. Sperberg-McQueen, & E. Maler (Eds.), *W3C recommendation*. Retrieved July 4, 2010, from http://www.w3.org/TR/REC-xml

W3C. (2004). OWL Web ontology language overview. In D. L. McGuinness, & F. Van Harmelen (Eds.), *W3C recommendation*. Retrieved July 4, 2010, from http://www.w3.org/TR/owl-features/

W3C. (2004b). Resource Description Framework (RDF): Concepts and abstract syntax. In G. Klyne, & J. J. Carroll (Eds.), *W3C recommendation*. Retrieved July 4, 2010, from http://www.w3.org/TR/rdf-concepts/

W3C. (2004c). RDF Vocabulary Description Language 1.0: RDF schema. In D. Brickley, & R. V. Guha (Eds.), *W3C recommendation*. Retrieved July 4, 2010, from http://www.w3.org/TR/rdf-schema/

W3C. (2006). *Ontology driven architectures and potential uses of the Semantic Web in systems and software engineering*. Retrieved July 4, 2010, from http://www.w3.org/2001/sw/BestPractices/SE/ODA/

Wang, C., Sohraby, K., Li, B., Daneshmand, M., & Hu, Y. (2006b). A survey of transport protocols for wireless sensor networks. *IEEE Network Magazine, 20*(3), 34–40. doi:10.1109/MNET.2006.1637930

Wang, O., Zhu, Y., & Cheng, L. (2006c). Reprogramming wireless sensor networks: Challenges and approaches. *IEEE Network, 20*(3), 48–55. doi:10.1109/MNET.2006.1637932

Wang, S., Xu, Z., Cao, J., & Zhang, J. (2007). A middleware for Web service-enabled integration and interoperation of intelligent building systems. *Automation in Construction, 16*(1), 112–121. doi:10.1016/j.autcon.2006.03.004

Wang, Y., Attebury, G., & Ramamurthy, B. (2006a). A survey of security issues in wireless sensor networks. *IEEE Communications Surveys & Tutorials, 8*(2), 2–23. doi:10.1109/COMST.2006.315852

Wang, Y. S., & Liao, Y. W. (2007). The conceptualization and measurement of m-commerce user satisfaction. *Computers in Human Behavior, 23*, 381–398. doi:10.1016/j.chb.2004.10.017

Wang, Y. S., Tang, T. I., & Tang, J. T. E. (2001). An instrument for measuring customer satisfaction toward websites that market digital products and services. *Journal of Electronic Commerce Research, 2*(3), 89–102.

Wang, Y., Jia, X., & Lee, H. K. (2003). An indoor wireless positioning system based on wireless local area network infrastructure. In *Proceedings 6th International Symposium on Satellite Navigation Technology*.

WARD. (2010). *The 4WARD Project, EU framework programme 7 integrated project (FP7)*. Retrieved June 1, 2010, from http://www.4ward-project.eu/

Watson, R. T., Pitt, L. F., Berthon, P. Z., & Inkham, G. M. (2002). U-commerce: Extending the universe of marketing. *Journal of the Academy of Marketing Science, 30*(4), 329–342. doi:10.1177/009207002236909

Weiser, M. (1991). The computer for the 21st century. *ACM SIGMOBILE Mobile Computing and Communications Review, 3*(3), 3–11. doi:10.1145/329124.329126

Weiser, M. (1991). The computer for the 21st century. *Scientific American*, (September): 94–104. doi:10.1038/scientificamerican0991-94

Weniger, K. (2005). PACMAN: Passive autoconfiguration for mobile ad hoc networks. *IEEE Journal on Selected Areas in Communications, 23*(3), 507–519. doi:10.1109/JSAC.2004.842539

Weniger, K., & Zitterbart, M. (2004). Address autoconfiguration in mobile ad hoc networks: Current approaches and future directions. *IEEE Network, 18*(4), 6–11. doi:10.1109/MNET.2004.1316754

Weniger, K. (2003). Passive duplicate address detection in mobile ad hoc networks. In *Proceedings of the IEEE Wireless Communications and Networking (WCNC 2003), 3*, (pp. 1504-1509).

Williams, A. (2002). *Requirements for automatic configuration of IP hosts. Internet-draft*. IETF WG Zeroconf.

Wireless Medicenter. (2006). Retrieved June 10, 2010, from http://www.wirelessmedicenter.com/mc/glance.cfm

Wong, J. K. W., Li, H., & Wang, S. W. (2005). Intelligent building research: A review. *Automation in Construction, 14*(1), 143–159. doi:10.1016/j.autcon.2004.06.001

Woo, K., & Fock, H. K. Y. (1999). Customer satisfaction in the Hong Kong mobile phone industry. *The Service Industries Journal, 19*(3), 162–174. doi:10.1080/02642069900000035

Wright, T., Liotta, A., & Hodgkinson, D. (2008). *E-privacy and copyright in online content distribution: A European overview*. World Data Protection Report. BNA International.

XACML. (2007). *XACML extensible access control markup language specification* 2.0. Organization for the Advancement of Structured Information Standards (OASIS). Retrieved June 10, 2010, from http://www.oasis-open.org

XMesh. (2008). *XMesh routing protocol for wireless sensor networks*. Crossbow Company. Retrieved July 20, 2010 from http://www.xbow.com/Technology/MeshNetworking.aspx

Yan, J., Guorong, L., Shenghua, L., & Lian, Z. (2009). *A review on localization and mapping algorithm based on extended Kalman filtering* (pp. 435–440). International Forum on Information Technology and Applications – IFITA.

Yan, L. (2008). *The Internet of things: From RFID to the next-generation pervasive networked systems*. Auerbach Publications.

Ye, W., Heidemann, J., & Estrin, D. (2004). Medium access control with coordinated, adaptive sleeping for wireless sensor networks. *IEEE/ACM Transactions on Networking*, *12*(3), 493–506. doi:10.1109/TNET.2004.828953

Ye, J. H. W., & Estrin, D. (2004). Medium access control with coordinated adaptive sleeping for wireless sensor networks. *IEEE/ACM Transactions on Networking*, *12*(3), 493–506. doi:10.1109/TNET.2004.828953

Yick, J., Mukherjee, B., & Ghosal, D. (2008). Wireless sensor networks survey. *Computer Networks*, *52*(12), 2292–2330. doi:10.1016/j.comnet.2008.04.002

Yin, R. K. (2003). *Case study research: Design and methods*. Thousand Oaks, CA: Sage Publications, Inc.

Yu, M., Kim, H., & Mah, P. (2007). NanoMon: An adaptable sensor network monitoring software. In *Proceedings of IEEE International Symposium on Consumer Electronics - ISCE 2007* (pp. 1 – 6).

Zafeiris, V., Doulkeridis, C., Belsis, P., & Chalaris, I. (2005). *Agent-mediated knowledge management in multiple autonomous domains.* Paper presented at Workshop on Agent Mediated Knowledge Management, Univ. of Utrecht Netherlands.

Zeeb, E., Bobek, A., Bonn, H., & Golatowski, F. (2007). Lessons learned from implementing the devices profile for Web services. In *Proceedings of Inaugural IEEE-IES Digital EcoSystems and Technologies Conference (IEEE-DEST'07)* (pp. 229-232). Cairns, Australia: IEEE Computer Society.

ZEROCONF. (2010) *IETF WG zero configuration.* Retrieved June 1, 2010, from http://tools.ietf.org/wg/zeroconf/

Zhang, J. J., Yuan, Y., & Archer, N. (2002). Driving forces for m-commerce success. *Journal of Internet Commerce*, *1*(3), 81–105. doi:10.1300/J179v01n03_08

Zhang, X., Fronz, S., & Navab, N. (2002). *Visual marker detection and decoding in AR systems: A comparative study.* International Symposium on Mixed and Augmented Reality –ISMAR (pp.97–106).

Zhao, F., & Guibas, L. (2004). *Wireless sensor networks: An information processing approach*. San Francisco, CA: Morgan Kaufmann.

Zhou, Y., Fang, Y., & Zhang, Y. (2008). Securing wireless sensor networks: A survey. *IEEE Communications Surveys & Tutorials*, *10*(3), 6–28. doi:10.1109/COMST.2008.4625802

Zhou, H., Ni, L., & Mutka, M. W. (2003). Prophet address allocation for large scale MANETs. In *Proceedings of the 22nd Annual Joint Conference of the IEEE Computer and Communications Societies, 2*, (pp. 1304-1311).

Zipf, G. K. (1949). *Human behavior and the principle of least effort*. Cambridge, MA: Addison-Wesley Press.

Zittrain, J. (2008). *The future of the Internet and how to stop it*. London, UK: Penguin.

About the Contributors

Apostolos Malatras received the Diploma in Computer Science from the University of Piraeus, Greece, the MSc degree in Information Systems from the Athens University of Economics and Business, Greece, and the PhD degree in networking from the University of Surrey, UK. He is currently a Lecturer and Post-doctoral Fellow with the Pervasive and Artificial Intelligence research group, University of Fribourg, Switzerland. Prior to this position, he was a Senior Research Engineer with Thales Research and Technology, Berkshire, UK. He is the author and co-author of more than 30 research papers. His research interests focus on pervasive computing and communications, context awareness, network management, mobile ad hoc networks, service oriented architectures, wireless sensor networks, and communications middleware.

* * *

Michel Adiba is now a consultant at the HADAS group of the LIG Lab. For more than thirty years, he was a professor at Grenoble University. He also had a postdoctoral fellowship at IBM Research Laboratory in San Jose (California). His research focusses on databases, their evolution concerning data models, languages, systems, and architectures. In the last ten years, he contributed on the design and construction of active, temporal, multimedia object servers. He is the author and co-author of several books, book chapters, and research papers published in national and international journals and conference proceedings. He currently works on event and continuous data processing.

Hadi Alasti received B.Sc., M.Sc and PhD all in Electrical Engineering with focus in communications and signal processing from the University of Tehran, Isfahan University of Technology, and the University of North Carolina at Charlotte, respectively. His research interests are wireless sensor network applications, wireless communications, and efficient signal processing algorithms. Before his PhD, for a few years he worked in power system communication industry and collaborated with consultant engineering companies. Dr. Alasti served as adjunct lecturer at the University of North Carolina at Charlotte, ITT Technical Institute, and Johnson C. Smith University in North Carolina. Dr. Alasti has published a number of research papers in the areas of wireless communications and wireless sensor networks. Dr. Alasti is a member of IEEE and Phi-Kappa-Phi.

Gianluca Aloi received the MS degree in computer engineering from University of Calabria, Italy in 1999 and the Ph.D. degree from the University of Calabria, Italy, in 2002. Currently, he is an Assistant Professor at the University of Calabria where, since 1999, he has worked with the telecommunications research group, and he is involved in several projects concerning wireless communications. Dr. Aloi's research interests include enhanced wireless and satellite systems, mobility, traffic and resource management, QoS support in heterogeneous communications networks, and interworking of wireless and wired networks.

Abolghasem (Hamid) Asgari received his B.Sc. from Dr. Beheshti University in Tehran, M.Sc. (Hons) from the University of Auckland, New Zealand both in Computer Science, and his Ph.D. in Electronic Engineering (ATM networks) from University of Wales, Swansea, UK in 1997. He was with Iran Telecom Research Center (ITRC) from 1986 to 1990. He joined Thales Research & Technology (UK) Ltd (formerly Racal Research) in 1996 where he was with the Security and Communication Systems specializing in the data communication systems/networks. He is currently a Chief Engineer and Project Manger leading teams in advanced R&D projects and has been involved in design and analysis of integrated services and network architectures. He has held technical, managerial, and advisory roles both at TRT-UK and in collaborative research programs by actively participating in a number of European Commission projects, notably FP6-NMP-I3CON (2006-10), FP6-IST ENTHRONE I&II (2003-08), FP5/FP6-IST-VISNET I&II (2005-09), FP5-IST-MESCAL (2002-05) and FP5-IST-TEQUILA (2000-02). His main research interests are in wired/wireless network QoS management and monitoring, network performance evaluation, traffic engineering, service management, and wireless sensor networking solutions combined with middleware technologies for the purpose of monitoring, controlling, and managing the enterprise environments. He has more than 50 publications in these subject areas. He also served as a Visiting Professor at CNRS LaBRI in University of Bordeaux 1, France. He is a Senior Member of IEEE.

Peter Barrie's academic career covers two decades, including teaching and research at University of Strathclyde, Institute of System Level Integration and Glasgow Caledonian University. He has lectured on a wide range of computer science topics and programming languages, with specialist interests in pervasive, real-time, and embedded computing. Research interests include parallel computer architectures and embedded/pervasive systems. Mr. Barrie has also gained extensive design, consultancy, and training experience in the areas of pervasive systems, industrial automation, real-time software, operating systems, and clinical software. He has also spent several years in industry, firstly as technical director of a company producing leading-edge clinical trials software systems and latterly as an embedded product designer. He is currently lecturing at Glasgow Caledonian University, with research interests in pervasive computing, embedded systems, and wireless sensor networks. He is a co-director of the Mobile and Ubiquitous Computing (MUCom) research group – www.mucom.mobi.

Petros Belsis is currently a member of faculty at the department of Marketing at TEI of Athens. He holds a Diploma in Physics from the University of Athens, Greece, a Diploma in Computer Science from the Computer Science Department of Technological Education Institute, Athens, Greece, a M.Sc. degree in Information Systems from the Athens University of Economics and Business, Greece, and a PhD in Information Systems Security from the Department of Information and Communication systems Engineering, at the University of the Aegean, Greece. He has published many journal and conference scientific articles, mainly in the areas of Information Systems security, policy based management in distributed environments, knowledge management, et cetera. His research interests focus on distributed knowledge management systems, policy based systems, and security in distributed environments.

Igor Bisio was born in Novi Ligure, Italy in 1978. He got his "Laurea" degree in Telecommunication Engineering at the University of Genoa, Italy in 2002 and his Ph.D. degree in "Information and Communication Sciences" at the University of Genoa in 2006. He is currently in a Research Fellow position, and he is member of the Telecommunication Research Group and, in particular, of the Digital Signal Processing (DSP) and Satellite Communications and Networking (SCNL) Laboratories research staffs at the University of Genoa. He is also a ComSoc IEEE Member since 2004 and IEEE Satellite and Space Communications Technical Committee Member since 2005. Since July 2008, he has been Secretary and Webmaster, and since 2010 he is the Vice Chair of the Technical Committee. He is author of more than 60 scientific papers including international journals, international conferences, and book chapters. He is recipient of several international awards. He has organized special issues of international journals and magazines and he is Technical Committee Co-Chair of many international conferences. His main research activities concern resource allocation and management for satellite communication systems, optimization algorithms and architectures for satellite sensor networks, advanced controls for interplanetary networks and for heterogeneous networks, signal processing over smartphones, context and location awareness, adaptive coding mechanisms, indoor localization, security, and e-health applications.

Johann Bourcier is currently Postdoc at the University of Grenoble. He was a Postdoc in the Imperial College London in the Distributed Software Engineering team. He received a MS degree and a PhD in Computer Science from the University of Grenoble, France. His main areas of interest are pervasive computing, and more specifically, smart buildings, service oriented computing, and autonomic computing. He has been active in these communities for 5 years. His current research involves study of autonomic model-driven approaches to improve efficiency and reliability of smart building.

Pierre Bourret is Research Engineer in the ADELE team at the University of Grenoble since 2008, and is a contributor of the Apache Felix iPOJO project. He's currently working on ambient intelligence in the home context, through the H-Omega project, heavily relying on OSGi and iPOJO. He's also involved in several European Project, such as Osami. He is one of the co-founders of OW2 Chameleon.

Andrzej Ceglowski is a senior lecturer and researcher from Monash University in Melbourne, Australia. Andrzej's research interests focus on patterns in work and organisational systems. He researches and has published on various healthcare issues, including hospital emergency department overcrowding, medical emergency response, pathology ordering patterns, aged care management, elective surgery queues, and health supply chains and strategy. Prior to joining academia, he had been CEO of a national energy association and marketing and operations manager at direct marketing companies such as Readers Digest. His diverse work history has seen him work as a manager of a top US restaurant, member of a Police SWAT team and judge on the US professional surfing circuit.

Christine Collet is member of Grenoble Informatics Laboratory, HADAS group, and a full Professor of Computer Science at the Grenoble Institute of Technology (Grenoble INP) in France since 1999. Her research domain concerns databases and their evolution in terms of data models, languages, and architectures. She contributes to research activities on: object and active databases, distributed and heterogeneous databases, query processing in opportunistic networks and service-based applications, reliable and adaptive service coordination, and mashing up reliable semantics services for clouds.

Oleg Davidyuk received his MSc degree in Information Technology from Lappeenranta University of Technology, Finland, in 2004. He is currently working towards his PhD degree in the MediaTeam Oulu Research Group at the University of Oulu, Finland. His research interests include application and service composition, user interaction design, middleware, and ubiquitous computing. Oleg's publications can be found at www.cse.oulu.fi/OlegDavidyuk.

Thierry Delot is associate professor (HDR) in computer science at the University of Valenciennes and member of the LAMIH laboratory (CNRS FRE 3304) since 2002. His interests are broadly in the fields of databases and distributed information systems. He is interested in pervasive information systems, data management/query processing in mobile environments, Vehicle-to-Vehicle communications, and location-based services. His recent research work concerns mobile P2P networks. He proposed VESPA (Vehicular Event Sharing with a mobile P2P Architecture), a system designed to share different types of events in inter-vehicle ad hoc networks.

Reinaldo Gomes received his MSc and PhD degrees from the Informatics Center, at Federal University of Pernambuco, in 2005 and 2010 respectively. Currently, he is a research assistant at the Networking and Telecommunication Research Group and professor at the Federal University of Campina Grande, Brazil. His main interests are in the areas of autoconfiguration of networks, policies-based management, wireless communications, sensor and vehicular networks, and routing algorithms.

Stefanos Gritzalis holds a BSc in Physics, an MSc in Electronic Automation, and a PhD in Information and Communications Security from the Dept. of Informatics and Telecommunications, University of Athens, Greece. Currently he is the Deputy Head of the Department of Information and Communication Systems Engineering, University of the Aegean, Greece and the Director of the Laboratory of Information and Communication Systems Security (Info-Sec-Lab). He has been involved in several national and EU funded R&D projects. His published scientific work includes 30 books or book chapters and more than 200 journal and international refereed conference and workshop papers. The focus of these publications is on information and communications security and privacy. His most highly cited papers have more than 800 citations (h-index=16). He has acted as Guest Editor in 20 journal special issues, and has led more than 30 international conferences and workshops as General Chair or Program Committee Chair. He has served on more than 200 Program Committees of international conferences and workshops. He is an Editor-in-Chief or Editor or Editorial Board member for 15 journals and a Reviewer for more than 40 journals. He has supervised 10 PhD dissertations. He was an elected Member of the Board (Secretary General, Treasurer) of the Greek Computer Society. His professional experience includes senior consulting and researcher positions in a number of private and public institutions. He is a Member of the ACM, the IEEE, and the IEEE Communications Society "Communications and Information Security Technical Committee."

Noha Ibrahim is associate professor at Grenoble Institute of Technology, France. She works in the HADAS group of the LIG Lab. Her research focusses on pervasive computing environments concerning: middleware, data management, and network layers. At the middleware level, research focusses on services composition in pervasive environments based on semantics, negotiation, and contracts. At the network level, she addresses services location in wireless networks. Her research also addresses query evaluation and optimization in pervasive environments.

Martin Johnsson graduated from the Royal Institute of Technology (KTH), in January 1986. He mainly took courses within telecom but also real-time computer systems. His master thesis work was performed at Ellemtel (Stockholm, Sweden), and which was about the evaluation and implementation of a number of different speech recognition algorithms.

Artem Katasonov received his BSc (1999) and Engineer (2000) degrees in Artificial Intelligence from Kharkov National University of Radio Electronics, Ukraine. Then, he received his MSc (2001) and PhD (2006) degrees from the University of Jyväskylä, Finland, with both theses related to mobile and ubiquitous software systems. After graduation, he acted as an Assistant Professor at the University of Jyväskylä teaching courses on Software Requirements, Semantic Web, and Agent-based systems. In 2009, he moved to VTT Technical Research Center of Finland, where he is currently working as a Researcher. His present research work is focused on ontology-driven software engineering, as well as other applications of semantic technologies.

Judith Kelner received her PhD degree from the Computer Science Laboratory at Kent University (UK) in 1993. She is an associate professor at the Federal University of Pernambuco. Her interests include work on multimedia communications, network QoS, network management, smart devices, and interfaces.

Andreas Komninos received his B.Sc (Honours) in Computer Science from Glasgow Caledonian University in 2001, and a Ph.D. in Mobile Computing from the University of Strathclyde, UK in 2005. His main research interests include pervasive computing, mobile HCI and mobile information access. He has worked as a researcher and part-time lecturer at the University of Strathclyde since 2001, and has been a lecturer in Mobile and Ubiquitous Computing at Glasgow Caledonian University since 2005, where he co-directs the Mobile and Ubiquitous Research Group (http://www.mucom.mobi). He is a Certified IT Professional of the British Computer Society and a Chartered Engineer.

Philippe Lalanda is a professor at the University Joseph Fourier where he teaches software engineering. His research interests include the integration of business and operational processes, software components and services, and software architectures. He received a PhD in Computer Science from Nancy University, France and worked afterwards in Barbara Hayes-Roth's team at Stanford University. He has been working several years as a R&D project leader at Thales (Paris) and Schneider Electric (Grenoble).

Fabio Lavagetto was born in Genoa, Italy, on August 6, 1962. He is currently Full Professor in Telecommunications by DIST, the Department of Communication, Computer and System Sciences, University of Genoa. Since 2008 he is Vice Rector of the University of Genoa with Deputy for Research and Technology Transfer. Since 2005 he is Vice President of ISICT, the Italian Institute of Studies in Information and Communications Technologies. Since 1995 he heads the Digital Signal Processing Lab of DIST, University of Genoa in charge of many national and international research projects. In the period 1995-2000, he coordinated the European ACTS project "VIDAS," concerned with the application of MPEG-4 technologies in multimedia telecommunication products. In the period 2000-2002, he coordinated the European IST project "Interface" oriented to the development of advanced multimodal interfaces. Since 2004, he is responsible of a joint research laboratory with Telecom Italia on mobile computing, specifically oriented to energy efficient signal processing solutions. In 1990, he was visiting researcher by the Visual Communication Lab, AT&T Bell Laboratories, Holmdel, NJ (USA). He serves as Associate Editor for IEEE Transactions on Circuits and Systems for Video Technologies and as Guest Editor or reviewer for other international journals. He was General Chair of a few International Scientific Conferences and is author of more than 100 scientific papers.

Alessandro Liotta is a legal consultant at Axiom Legal, an international law firm, specializing in the technology, telecommunications, and outsourcing sectors. He assists businesses in corporate and commercial projects involving complex technology issues and advises clients on ICT-related matters including data protection and data retention compliance, e-commerce, and export control. Prior to joining Axiom, he worked with another American firm and with British Telecom developing his expertise in the IT and Telecoms industry. He regularly publishes articles on the relationship between new ICT technologies and the applicable legislation, more recently focusing his research on data protection issues and ISPs' responsibility in the online content distribution.

Antonio Liotta holds the Chair of Communication Network Protocols at the Eindhoven University of Technology (The Netherlands) where he leads the Autonomic Networks team. Antonio is a Fellow of the U.K. Higher Education Academy and serves the Peer Review College of the U.K. Engineering and Physical Sciences Research Council. For many years now he has been a member of the Advisory Board of Editors of the Journal of Network and System Management (Springer) and of the International Journal of Network Management (Wiley). Antonio has over 100 publications to his credit in the areas of autonomic network management, telecommunication services, and peer-to-peer networks. After co-editing four books, he has authored "Networks for Pervasive Applications" (Springer), to appear in 2011.

Mario Marchese was born in Genoa, Italy in 1967. He got his "Laurea" degree cum laude in 1992, and his Ph.D. in 1996, at the University of Genoa, Italy. From 1999 to 2004, he was Head of Research in the Italian Consortium of Telecommunications. From February 2005 he has been Associate Professor at the University of Genoa, Department of Communication, Computer and Systems Science (DIST) where he is the founder and technically responsible for the Satellite Communications and Networking Laboratory (SCNL). He was the Chair of the IEEE ComSoc Satellite and Space Communications Technical Committee. He is author and co-author of more than 150 scientific works, including international magazines, international conferences and book chapters. He is the author of the book "Quality of Service over Heterogeneous Networks," John Wiley & Sons, Chichester, 2007. He is Associate Editor of the International Journal of Communication Systems (Wiley) and of the IEEE Wireless Communications Magazine. He has organized special issues of international journals and magazines (Wiley IJCS, IEEE WCM, IEEE JSAC, Elsevier Computers and Electrical Engineering Journal, IEEE Systems Journal), and he is Technical Committee Co-Chair of many international conferences including SPECTS, IEEE Globecom, IEEE ICC. His main research activity concerns are: satellite and radio networks, transport architectures for cable, satellite and wireless networks, Quality of Service over heterogeneous networks, and performance evaluation of telecommunication networks.

Brian McDonald has a B.Sc.(Hons) degree in Computer Science and Pg.D in Video Games Technology from Glasgow Caledonian University. He is currently a Lecturer at Glasgow Caledonian University teaching modules in Games Programming, Video Games Graphics and iPhone Game Development. He has worked in numerous projects in his time at Glasgow Caledonian, including a video game system for serious game applications such as education, health and advertising, and miniGIST mobile tourist information system. His main research area is video game graphics. Mr. McDonald is a member of the British Computer Society and the Independent Game Developers Association.

Frank Ortmeier is a professor of Computer Systems in Engineering at the Otto-von-Guericke Universität in Magdeburg. He did his PhD at the University of Augsburg on "Model-based safety analysis" in 2005. His main research interests are in the domain of software challenges for technical applications, ranging from analysis of safety critical applications to systems engineering of software intensive applications. In particular, systems with self-X capabilities and robotic applications are research topics. Frank Ortmeier is responsible for a number European student exchange programs, member of several international program committees, and an active member of the pre-standardization group EWICS. He is also responsible for guidance of students in "Ingenieurinformatik" at the Otto-von-Guericke Universität. He has been and is leading several research projects funded by the German Research Council and the Ministry of Research and Innovation.

Pasquale Pace received the M.S. degree in computer engineering and the Ph.D. in Information Engineering from University of Calabria, Italy in 2000 and 2005, respectively. From March 2005 to September 2005, he was visiting researcher at the Centre for Communication Systems Research (CCSR) at the University of Surrey - UK where he did research on multimedia satellite systems; then, from October 2005 to April 2006, he was a visiting researcher at the Broadband and Wireless Networking Laboratory at Georgia Tech, USA, where he started research on wireless mesh networks. In May 2006, he joined the D.E.I.S. Department, University of Calabria as Research Fellow. Dr. Pace's research interests include multimedia satellite systems, DVB-RCS-satellite architectures, mobility management, traffic & resource management, call admission control, integration of satellite systems and high altitude platforms in heterogeneous communications networks, transport protocols for wireless mesh networks, and multimedia contents delivery over wireless networks.

Marko Palviainen received his MSc (Tech.) from the Lappeenranta University of Technology in 1998 and the PhD degree in computer science from the Tampere University of Technology in 2007. Since 1999, he has worked as a research scientist at VTT, Technical Research Centre of Finland. His current areas of research interest include mobile applications and application development methods, ontology-driven software engineering, and evaluation methods of parallel applications.

Jean Marc Petit is Professor of Computer Science at the University of Lyon (INSA), France. Since 2008, he has led the database group at the LIRIS laboratory (UMR 5205 CNRS) and he is director of the Master by research program in Computer Sciences since 2007. His main research interest concerns data management, data mining, and pervasive computing. His research is applied to areas such as bio-informatics and Semantic Web. He participates and coordinates several projects on data mining, stream querying, and service based data querying and optimization.

Jukka Riekki is professor at the University of Oulu, in the Department of Electrical and Information Engineering. He leads together with his colleague the Intelligent Systems Group. His main research interests are in context-aware systems serving people in their everyday environment. Currently he studies in several projects physical user interfaces, context recognition, and service composition. In these projects he cooperates with research groups from China, Japan, and Sweden. He is a member of IEEE. Jukka's publications can be found at www.cse.oulu.fi/JukkaRiekki.

Djamel Sadok received his PhD degree from the Computer Science Laboratory at Kent University (UK) in 1990. Since then he worked at Open Systems Marketing as a systems engineer and as a Research Fellow at UCL from 1991 to 1993. During this, he was involved with the PODASAX and PASSWORD European Esprit projects. Currently he leads a research group at the Federal University of Pernambuco working with a number of cooperation projects with industrial and academic partners in the areas of network provisioning, P2P networks, wireless communications, protocol security, and voice over IP.

Iván Sánchez Milara studied Telecommunication Engineering at the Technical University of Madrid, Spain. He is planning to start his PhD studies during 2011 in the Intelligent Systems Group at the University of Oulu, Finland. His research interests are related to tangible user interfaces (NFC technology, in particular), interactive spaces, and mobile applications. Iván's publications can be found at www.cse.oulu.fi/IvanSanchez.

Ricardo Schmidt holds a BSc in Computer Science from the University of Passo Fundo and an MSc, degree also in Computer Science, from the Federal University of Pernambuco, Brazil. From 2008 to 2010, he worked as a graduate research assistant at the Networking and Telecommunication Research Group, at the Federal University of Pernambuco, in projects in the context of the Ambient Networks European project, which were coordinated by Ericsson Research and focused on autoconfiguration of networks, wireless communications, routing, and addressing protocols.

Daisy Seng is a PhD candidate and an assistant lecturer in the Department of Accounting and Finance, Faculty of Business and Economics, Monash University, Australia. She holds a BCom from University of Melbourne and MBusSys and GradCertHigherEd from Monash University. Her research interests pertain to mobile/electronic commerce, portal technologies, process modeling, and optimization techniques. She has a number of refereed international publications. She is a member of CPA Australia and also The Institute for Operations Research and Management Sciences, USA (INFORMS).

Christos Skourlas is a professor of Databases at the Computer Science Department of Technological Education Institute, Athens Greece. He holds BSc in Mathematics and PhD in Informatics from the University of Athens, Greece. His research interests focus on information retrieval, knowledge management, multilingual systems, disambiguation and natural language processing, and medical informatics.

Stephen P. Smith is a lecturer in the Department of Accounting and Finance at Monash University. He received his PhD from the University of Melbourne. His work has been published in prestigious journals including Information Systems Research, and he has presented his work at significant international conferences including the International Conference on Information Systems and the European Conference on Information Systems. His major research interest is investigating methods to enhance understanding of information through personalisation.

Ly-Fie Sugianto is an associate professor in the Department of Accounting and Finance, Faculty of Business and Economics, Monash University, Australia. She holds First Class Honours in Bachelor of Engineering and PhD in Electrical Engineering. Dr. Sugianto has received several grants to conduct research in electricity markets and Information Systems. She has been appointed as an expert of international standing by the Australian Research Council College of Experts for her work in the electricity market. Her research interests include optimization techniques, DSS, and adoption studies of RFID, B2C e-commerce, B2E portal, and m-commerce. She has published over 70 refereed research articles in these topics.

Genoveva Vargas Solar is senior researcher of the CNRS in France LIG-LAFMIA Labs, HADAS group. Her fundamental research concerns the specification and implementation of mechanisms for enabling optimized access to distributed data in dynamic environments. She addresses QoS based persistent data and streams services composition by integrating non-functional aspects like fault tolerance, transactions, and security. She addresses event composition and monitoring for building autonomic data management services. She uses AOP techniques, reflexive systems, and ASM for formally specifying these systems. Her research results are validated in grids, embedded systems, and clouds.

Carla Wilkin is an associate professor in the Department of Accounting and Finance, Faculty of Business and Economics, Monash University, Australia. She holds a BCom (Hons) and a PhD from Deakin University and a GradCertHigherEd from Monash University. Her research interests concern IT governance, business value, managing IT quality, and user interactions with technological interfaces. She has published in outlets including Communications of the ACM, IT & People, Electronic Commerce Research, International Journal of Accounting Information Systems, Electronic Journal of Information Systems Evaluation and International Journal of Business Information Systems, and is an Associate Editor of the International Journal on IT/Business Alignment and Governance.

Jianqi Yu obtained a Master degree in Computer sciences and a Ph. D. in June 2010 about dynamic software product lines for service-based application in software engineering from LIG laboratory, University of Grenoble, France. Her main areas of interest are service oriented computing, software product line, pervasive computing, and more specifically, smart buildings. She has been active in these communities for 4 years. Her current research involves study of dynamic software product line approaches to efficiently build and execute reliable smart home applications.

Index

D

E

F

G

N

O

P

Q

R

S

CPSIA information can be obtained at www.ICGtesting.com
261698BV00002B/97-158/P